GABRIEL MANTZ

THE COMPLETE
WORLD CUP

2007-2010

British Library Cataloguing in Publication Data
A catalogue record for this book is available from the British Library

ISBN: 978-1-86223-211-2

Copyright © 2010, SOCCER BOOKS LIMITED (01472 696226)
72 St. Peter's Avenue, Cleethorpes, N.E. Lincolnshire, DN35 8HU, England
Web site   www.soccer-books.co.uk
e-mail   info@soccer-books.co.uk

Printed in the UK by 4Edge Ltd.

Dear Readers

The 19th edition of the FIFA World Cup, the final tournament of which was held between 11th June and 11th July 2010 was the most important sporting event of the year 2010.

For the first time an African country hosted the finals of the world's premier football competition and South Africa organised a good tournament, without blemish or any real organisational problems while demonstrating the unique qualities of the African continent.

No fewer than 205 countries started the long road to qualification and even South Africa (normally an automatic qualifier as the host country) took part in the preliminary phase due to the fact that the African section was also used as a qualifying group for the Africa Cup of Nations, held in Angola in January 2010.

So, with hindsight, what memories of this tournament remain, other than the noisy drone of the vuvuzelas? Overall, it was a disappointing finals series in which few teams other than the eventual winners, Spain, excelled. South American teams performed well in the early stages with 4 countries reaching the quarter-finals (Argentina, Brazil, Chile and Uruguay) but then collapsed with only Uruguay scraping through to a semi-final place. African countries (including the hosts) fared badly, although Ghana reached the quarter-finals and were perhaps unfortunate to lose to Uruguay in a penalty shoot-out, but the Asian countries also fared badly after the first round.

Surprisingly, perhaps, Europe came through strongly in the later stages in the guise of Germany, Holland and Spain, despite the fact that other favourites England and France performed very poorly. To sum up the finals, Spain lived up to expectations as the best team in the world and were deserved victors, Germany played much better than forecast and Holland were the villains of the piece, resorting to a cynical, violent brand of football which earned them no friends.

The Author

FIFA COUNTRY CODES – AFRICA

Algeria	**ALG**	Libya	**LBY**
Angola	**ANG**	Madagascar	**MAD**
Benin	**BEN**	Malawi	**MWI**
Botswana	**BOT**	Mali	**MLI**
Burkina Faso	**BFA**	Mauritania	**MTN**
Burundi	**BDI**	Mauritius	**MRI**
Cameroon	**CMR**	Morocco	**MAR**
Cape Verde Islands	**CPV**	Mozambique	**MOZ**
Central African Republic	**CTA**	Namibia	**NAM**
Chad	**CHA**	Niger	**NIG**
Comoros Islands	**COM**	Nigeria	**NGA**
Congo	**CGO**	Rwanda	**RWA**
Congo DR	**COD**	São Tome e Principe	**STP**
Djibouti	**DJI**	Senegal	**SEN**
Egypt	**EGY**	Seychelles	**SEY**
Equatorial Guinea	**EQG**	Sierra Leone	**SLE**
Eritrea	**ERI**	Somalia	**SOM**
Ethiopia	**ETH**	South Africa	**RSA**
Gabon	**GAB**	Sudan	**SUD**
Gambia	**GAM**	Swaziland	**SWZ**
Ghana	**GHA**	Tanzania	**TAN**
Guinea	**GUI**	Togo	**TOG**
Guinea-Bissau	**GNB**	Tunisia	**TUN**
Ivory Coast	**CIV**	Uganda	**UGA**
Kenya	**KEN**	Zambia	**ZAM**
Lesotho	**LES**	Zimbabwe	**ZIM**
Liberia	**LBR**		

FIFA COUNTRY CODES – ASIA

Afghanistan	**AFG**	Maldives	**MDV**
Australia	**AUS**	Mongolia	**MGL**
Bahrain	**BHR**	Myanmar	**MYA**
Bangladesh	**BAN**	Nepal	**NEP**
Bhutan	**BHU**	Korea D.P.R.	**PRK**
Brunei	**BRU**	Oman	**OMA**
Cambodia	**CAM**	Pakistan	**PAK**
China P.R.	**CHN**	Palestine	**PAL**
Chinese Taipei	**TPE**	Philippines	**PHI**
Guam	**GUM**	Qatar	**QAT**
Hong Kong	**HKG**	Saudi Arabia	**KSA**
India	**IND**	Singapore	**SIN**
Indonesia	**IDN**	Korea Republic	**KOR**
Iran	**IRN**	Sri Lanka	**SRI**
Iraq	**IRQ**	Syria	**SYR**
Japan	**JPN**	Tajikistan	**TJK**
Jordan	**JOR**	Thailand	**THA**
Kuwait	**KUW**	Timor-Leste	**TLS**
Kyrgyzstan	**KGZ**	Turkmenistan	**TKM**
Laos	**LAO**	United Arab Emirates	**UAE**
Lebanon	**LIB**	Uzbekistan	**UZB**

Macau	MAC	Vietnam	VIE
Malaysia	MAS	Yemen	YEM

FIFA COUNTRY CODES – EUROPE

Albania	ALB	Latvia	LVA
Andorra	AND	Liechtenstein	LIE
Armenia	ARM	Lithuania	LTU
Austria	AUT	Luxembourg	LUX
Azerbaijan	AZE	Macedonia	MKD
Belarus	BLR	Malta	MLT
Belgium	BEL	Moldova	MDA
Bosnia-Herzegovina	BIH	Montenegro	MNE
Bulgaria	BUL	Northern Ireland	NIR
Croatia	CRO	Norway	NOR
Cyprus	CYP	Poland	POL
Czech Republic	CZE	Portugal	POR
Denmark	DEN	Republic of Ireland	IRL
England	ENG	Romania	ROU
Estonia	EST	Russia	RUS
Faroe Islands	FRO	San Marino	SMR
Finland	FIN	Scotland	SCO
France	FRA	Serbia	SRB
Georgia	GEO	Slovakia	SVK
Germany	GER	Slovenia	SVN
Greece	GRE	Spain	ESP
Holland	NED	Sweden	SWE
Hungary	HUN	Switzerland	SUI
Iceland	ISL	Turkey	TUR
Israel	ISR	Ukraine	UKR
Italy	ITA	Wales	WAL
Kazakhstan	KAZ		

FIFA COUNTRY CODES – NORTH & CENTRAL AMERICA

Anguilla	AIA	Haiti	HAI
Antigua & Barbuda	ATG	Honduras	HON
Aruba	ARU	Jamaica	JAM
Bahamas	BAH	Martinique	MTQ
Barbados	BRB	Mexico	MEX
Belize	BLZ	Montserrat	MSR
Bermuda	BER	Netherlands Antilles	ANT
British Virgin Islands	VGB	Nicaragua	NIC
Canada	CAN	Panama	PAN
Cayman Islands	CAY	Puerto Rico	PUR
Costa Rica	CRC	Saint Lucia	LCA
Cuba	CUB	Saint Kitts and Nevis	SKN
Dominica	DMA	Saint Martin	SMT
Dominican Republic	DOM	St. Vincent and the Grenadines	VIN
El Salvador	SLV	Sint Maarten	SXM
French Guiana	GYF	Suriname	SUR
Grenada	GRN	Trinidad & Tobago	TRI
Guadeloupe	GPE	Turks and Caicos Islands	TCA
Guatemala	GUA	United States of America	USA

| Guyana | **GUI** | US Virgin Islands | **VIR** |

FIFA COUNTRY CODES – SOUTH AMERICA

Argentina	**ARG**	Ecuador	**ECU**
Bolivia	**BOL**	Paraguay	**PAR**
Brazil	**BRA**	Peru	**PER**
Chile	**CHI**	Uruguay	**URU**
Colombia	**COL**	Venezuela	**VEN**

FIFA COUNTRY CODES – OCEANIA

American Samoa	**ASA**	Samoa	**SAM**
Cook Islands	**COK**	Solomon Islands	**SOL**
Fiji	**FIJ**	Tahiti	**TAH**
New Caledonia	**NCL**	Tonga	**TGA**
New Zealand	**NZL**	Vanuatu	**VAN**

NON-FIFA COUNTRY CODES

| Tuvalu | **TUV** |

SUMMARY

Editorial	3
Abbreviations, FIFA Country Codes	4
Summary	6
World Cup Preliminaries	8
Europe	9
Group 1	10
Group 2	19
Group 3	28
Group 4	37
Group 5	46
Group 6	55
Group 7	64
Group 8	73
Group 9	82
Play-Offs	88
South America	91
North & Central America	125
First Round	125
Second Round	132
Third Round (Group 1 to 3)	140
Fourth Round	152
Africa	163
First Round	163
Second Round (Group 1 to 12)	165
Third Round (Group A to E)	211
Asia	231
First Round	231
Second Round	241
Third Round (Group 1 to 5)	244
Fourth Round (Group 1 to 2)	264
Oceania	278
First Phase (2007 South pacific Games)	278
Second Phase (2008 OFC Nations Cup)	285
Intercontinental Play-Offs	289
The Final Tournament	291
Group A	292
Group B	294
Group C	296
Group D	298
Group E	300
Group F	302
Group G	304
Group H	306
Round of 16	309
Quarter-Finals	312
Semi-Finals	314
3rd Place Play-Off, Final	315
World Cup 2010 Final Ranking, Awards	316
Goalscorers	317
List of Referees	318
World Cup squads	319

WORLD CUP
PRELIMINARIES

A total of 205 teams entered the preliminaries competition, with South Africa, as the host, being qualified automatically for the World Cup Final Tournament. Overall, 848 matches were played, the first preliminary matches were played on 25 August 2007 and qualification concluded on 18 November 2009. Above a table with the Continental Confederations, the number of participating teams and the number of places allocated for the final tournament:

Confederation	Number of tems started	Number of places for the final tournament
UEFA (Europe)	53	13
CONMEBOL (South America)	10	4**
CONCACAF (North, Central American and Caribbean)	35	3**
CAF (Africa)	53	6
AFC (Asia)	43	4***
OCF (Oceania)	11*	0***
Intercontinental Play-Off** South America – North & Central America	-	1
Intercontinental Play-Off*** Asia - Oceania	-	1
TOTAL	205	32

*including Tuvalu, a not-FIFA member.
***best team of Oceania qualified to play an Intercontinental Play-off against the 5th best team from Asia.

EUROPE

The draw for the group stage took place in Durban (South Africa) on 25 November 2007. The UEFA Executive Committee decided on 27 September 2007 at its meeting in Istanbul that seeding for the qualifiers would be based on the most recent FIFA World Rankings, namely the November 2007 edition. Before drawing, the 53 European teams were seeded into 6 pots:

Pot A: Italy, Spain, Germany, Czech Republic, France, Portugal, Holland, Croatia, Greece.
Pot B: England, Romania, Scotland, Turkey, Bulgaria, Russia, Poland, Sweden, Israel.
Pot C: Norway, Ukraine, Serbia, Denmark, Northern Ireland, Republic of Ireland, Finland, Switzerland, Belgium.
Pot D: Slovakia, Bosnia-Herzegovina, Hungary, Moldova, Wales, Macedonia, Belarus, Lithuania, Cyprus.
Pot E: Georgia, Albania, Slovenia, Latvia, Iceland, Armenia, Austria, Kazakhstan, Azerbaijan.
Pot F: Liechtenstein, Estonia, Malta, Luxembourg, Montenegro, Andorra, Faroe Islands, San Marino.

The 53 teams were drawn into eight groups of six teams and one group of five teams. The nine group-winners qualified directly, while the eight best second-placed teams contested home and away play-off matches for the remaining four places. In determining the best eight second-placed teams, the results against teams finishing last in the six-team groups were not counted for consistency between the five- and six-team groups.

The 9 qualifying groups were as following:

GROUP 1
Portugal, Sweden, Denmark, Hungary, Albania, Malta.

GROUP 2
Greece, Israel, Switzerland, Moldova, Latvia, Luxembourg.

GROUP 3
Czech Republic, Poland, Northern Ireland, Slovakia, Slovenia, San Marino.

GROUP 4
Germany, Russia, Finland, Wales, Azerbaijan, Liechtenstein.

GROUP 5
Spain, Turkey, Belgium, Bosnia-Herzegovina, Armenia, Estonia.

GROUP 6
Croatia, England, Ukraine, Belarus, Kazakhstan, Andorra.

GROUP 7
France, Romania, Serbia, Lithuania, Austria, Faroe Islands.

GROUP 8
Italy, Bulgaria, Republic of Ireland, Cyprus, Georgia, Montenegro.

GROUP 9
Holland, Scotland, Norway, Macedonia, Iceland.

GROUP 1

06.09.2008	Tiranë	Albania - Sweden	0-0
06.09.2008	Budapest	Hungary - Denmark	0-0
06.09.2008	Ta'Qali	Malta - Portugal	0-4(0-1)
10.09.2008	Stockholm	Sweden - Hungary	2-1(0-0)
10.09.2008	Tiranë	Albania - Malta	3-0(1-0)
10.09.2008	Lisboa	Portugal - Denmark	2-3(1-0)
11.10.2008	Budapest	Hungary - Albania	2-0(0-0)
11.10.2008	København	Denmark - Malta	3-0(2-0)
11.10.2008	Stockholm	Sweden - Portugal	0-0
15.10.2008	Ta'Qali	Malta - Hungary	0-1(0-1)
15.10.2008	Braga	Portugal - Albania	0-0
11.02.2009	Ta'Qali	Malta - Albania	0-0
28.03.2009	Ta'Qali	Malta - Denmark	0-3(0-2)
28.03.2009	Tiranë	Albania - Hungary	0-1(0-1)
28.03.2009	Porto	Portugal - Sweden	0-0
01.04.2009	Budapest	Hungary - Malta	3-0(1-0)
01.04.2009	København	Denmark - Albania	3-0(2-0)
06.06.2009	Stockholm	Sweden - Denmark	0-1(0-1)
06.06.2009	Tiranë	Albania - Portugal	1-2(1-1)
10.06.2009	Göteborg	Sweden - Malta	4-0(1-0)
05.09.2009	København	Denmark - Portugal	1-1(1-0)
05.09.2009	Budapest	Hungary - Sweden	1-2(0-1)
09.09.2009	Ta'Qali	Malta - Sweden	0-1(0-0)
09.09.2009	Tiranë	Albania - Denmark	1-1(0-1)
09.09.2009	Budapest	Hungary - Portugal	0-1(0-1)
10.10.2009	København	Denmark - Sweden	1-0(0-0)
10.10.2009	Lisboa	Portugal - Hungary	3-0(1-0)
14.10.2009	København	Denmark - Hungary	0-1(0-1)
14.10.2009	Guimarães	Portugal - Malta	4-0(2-0)
14.10.2009	Stockholm	Sweden - Albania	4-1(3-0)

FINAL STANDINGS

1.	**DENMARK**	10	6	3	1	16	-	5	21
2.	**Portugal**	10	5	4	1	17	-	5	19
3.	Sweden	10	5	3	2	13	-	5	18
4.	Hungary	10	5	1	4	10	-	8	16
5.	Albania	10	1	4	5	6	-	13	7
6.	Malta	10	0	1	9	0	-	26	1

Denmark qualified for the Final Tournament; Portugal qualified for the Play-Offs.

06.09.2008, Stadiumi „Qemal Stafa", Tiranë; Attendance: 13,522
Referee: Alberto Undiano Mallenco (Spain)
ALBANIA - SWEDEN   **0-0**
ALB: Arjan Beqaj, Armend Dallku, Elvin Beqiri, Lorik Çana, Kristi Vangjeli, Debatik Curri, Altin Lala (Cap), Jahmir Hyka, Klodian Duro, Ervin Skela (82.Admir Teli), Hamdi Salihi (75.Besart Berisha). Trainer: Arend Haan (Holland).
SWE: Andreas Isaksson, Olof Mellberg, Daniel Majstorovic, Petter Hansson, Mikael Nilsson, Daniel Andersson, Kim Källström (84.Samuel Holmén), Tobias Linderoth (6.Sebastian Larsson), Oscar Wendt (77.Fredrik Stoor), Henrik Larsson (Cap), Zlatan Ibrahimovic. Trainer: Lars Lagerbäck.

10

06.09.2008, „Puskás Ferenc" Stadion, Budapest; Attendance: 19,000
Referee: Alain Hamer (Luxembourg)
HUNGARY - DENMARK   **0-0**
HUN: Gábor Babos, László Bodnár, Vilmos Vanczák, Roland Juhász, Zoltán Szélesi, Krisztián Vadócz, Pál Dárdai, Tamás Hajnal, Zoltán Gera (Cap), Szabolcs Huszti (90+1.Gergely Rudolf), Balázs Dzsudzsák (46.Sándor Torghelle). Trainer: Erwin Koeman (Holland).
DEN: Stephan Andersen, Martin Laursen, Daniel Agger, Lars Christian Jacobsen, Christopher Poulsen, Christian Bjørnshøj Poulsen, Daniel Jensen, Martin Vingaard Hansen (61.Jonas Borring), Dennis Rommedahl, Jon Dahl Tomasson (Cap) (66.Martin Retov), Nicklas Bendtner (87.Marc Nygaard). Trainer: Morten Olsen.
Cautions: Balázs Dzsudzsák, Sándor Torghelle, Zoltán Gera, Gábor Babos / Martin Laursen, Christopher Poulsen, Christian Bjørnshøj Poulsen.

06.09.2008, National Stadium, Ta'Qali; Attendance: 11,000
Referee: Kevin Blom (Holland)
MALTA - PORTUGAL   **0-4(0-1)**
MLT: Justin Haber, Shaun Pierre Bajada, Brian Said, Luke Dimech, Gilbert Agius (Cap) (80.Ryan Fenech), Roderick Briffa, Michael Mifsud, Ivan Woods (59.George Mallia), Terence Scerri (70.Etienne Barbara), Jamie McDonald Pace, Kevin Sammut. Trainer: Dušan Fitzel (Czech Republic).
POR: Joaquim Manuel Sampaio Silva, José Bosingwa da Silva, Ricardo Alberto Silveira de Carvalho, Képler Laveran Lima Ferreira „Pepe", Vitorino Gabriel Pacheco Antunes, Raúl José Trindade Meireles „Raul Meireles", Carlos Jorge Neto Martins (63.Nuno Ricardo Oliveira Ribeiro „Maniche"), Anderson Luís de Souza „Deco", Luís Carlos Almeida da Cunha „Nani", Simão Pedro Fonseca Sabrosa (Cap) (75.João Filipe Iria Santos Moutinho), Hugo Miguel Pereira de Almeida (67.Nuno Miguel Soares Pereira Ribeiro „Nuno Gomes"). Trainer: Carlos Manuel Brito Leal Queiroz.
Goals: 0-1 Brian Said (26 own goal), 0-2 Hugo Miguel Pereira de Almeida (61), 0-3 Simão Pedro Fonseca Sabrosa (72), 0-4 Luís Carlos Almeida da Cunha „Nani" (78).

10.09.2008, Råsundastadion, Stockholm; Attendance: 28,177
Referee: Florian Meyer (Germany)
SWEDEN - HUNGARY   **2-1(0-0)**
SWE: Andreas Isaksson, Olof Mellberg, Daniel Majstorovic, Petter Hansson, Mikael Nilsson, Sebastian Larsson, Kim Källström, Daniel Andersson, Samuel Holmén, Henrik Larsson (Cap), Zlatan Ibrahimovic (81.Markus Rosenberg). Trainer: Lars Lagerbäck.
HUN: Gábor Babos, Zoltán Szélesi, Vilmos Vanczák, Roland Juhász, Boldizsár Bodor (80.Balázs Dzsudzsák), Krisztián Vadócz, Pál Dárdai (70.Gergely Rudolf), Zoltán Gera (Cap), Tamás Hajnal, Szabolcs Huszti, Sándor Torghelle. Trainer: Erwin Koeman (Holland).
Goals: 1-0 Kim Källström (55), 2-0 Samuel Holmén (64), 2-1 Gergely Rudolf (90+3).
Cautions: Zlatan Ibrahimovic / Zoltán Gera, Tamás Hajnal.

10.09.2008, Stadiumi „Qemal Stafa", Tiranë; Attendance: 7,400
Referee: Robert Schoergenhofer (Austria)
ALBANIA - MALTA   **3-0(1-0)**
ALB: Arjan Beqaj, Armend Dallku, Ansi Agolli, Lorik Çana, Debatik Curri, Ervin Bulku (54.Elvin Beqiri), Altin Lala (Cap), Klodian Duro (86.Besart Berisha), Jahmir Hyka, Ervin Skela, Erjon Bogdani (73.Hamdi Salihi). Trainer: Arend Haan (Holland).
MLT: Justin Haber, Aaron Xuereb, Shaun Pierre Bajada, Luke Dimech, Gilbert Agius (Cap) (85.Terence Scerri), Etienne Barbara (46.Cleavon Frendo), Roderick Briffa, Michael Mifsud, Andrè Schembri, Jamie McDonald Pace, Kevin Sammut. Trainer: Dušan Fitzel (Czech Republic).
Goals: 1-0 Erjon Bogdani (45+1), 2-0 Klodian Duro (84), 3-0 Armend Dallku (90).
Cautions: Elvin Beqiri, Lorik Çana, Armend Dallku / Shaun Pierre Bajada.

10.09.2008, Estádio "José Alvalade", Lisboa; Attendance: 33,000
Referee: Howard Melton Webb (England)
PORTUGAL - DENMARK   **2-3(1-0)**
POR: Joaquim Manuel Sampaio Silva, José Bosingwa da Silva, Ricardo Alberto Silveira de Carvalho,
Képler Laveran Lima Ferreira "Pepe", Paulo Renato Rebocho Ferreira, Raúl José Trindade Meireles
"Raul Meireles", Nuno Ricardo Oliveira Ribeiro "Maniche", Anderson Luís de Souza "Deco", Luís
Carlos Almeida da Cunha "Nani" (87.João Filipe Iria Santos Moutinho), Simão Pedro Fonseca Sabrosa
(Cap) (72.Nuno Miguel Soares Pereira Ribeiro "Nuno Gomes"), Hugo Miguel Pereira de Almeida
(72.Daniel Miguel Alves Gomes "Danny"). Trainer: Carlos Manuel Brito Leal Queiroz.
DEN: Stephan Andersen, Lars Christian Jacobsen (46.Michael Silberbauer), Martin Laursen, Daniel
Agger, Leon Andreasen (87.Martin Bernburg), Daniel Jensen, Christian Bjørnshøj Poulsen, Peter
Løvenkrands (72.Jonas Borring), Jon Dahl Tomasson (Cap), Dennis Rommedahl, Nicklas Bendtner.
Trainer: Morten Olsen.
Goals: 1-0 Luís Carlos Almeida da Cunha "Nani" (42), 1-1 Nicklas Bendtner (83), 2-1 Anderson Luís
de Souza "Deco" (86), 2-2 Christian Bjørnshøj Poulsen (88), 2-3 Daniel Jensen (90+2).
Cautions: Luís Carlos Almeida da Cunha "Nani", Daniel Miguel Alves Gomes "Danny" / Jon Dahl
Tomasson.

11.10.2008, "Puskás Ferenc" Stadion, Budapest; Attendance: 18,000
Referee: Claudio Circhetta (Switzerland)
HUNGARY - ALBANIA   **2-0(0-0)**
HUN: Márton Fülöp, László Bodnár, Zoltán Szélesi, Vilmos Vanczák, Roland Juhász, Pál Dárdai,
Péter Halmosi, Szabolcs Huszti (86.Krisztián Vadócz), Tamás Hajnal (Cap) (61.Ákos Buzsáky), Balázs
Dzsudzsák, Sándor Torghelle (90+3.Gergely Rudolf). Trainer: Erwin Koeman (Holland).
ALB: Arjan Beqaj, Armend Dallku, Elvin Beqiri (74.Edmond Kapllani), Ansi Agolli, Debatik Curri,
Kristi Vangjeli (54.Jahmir Hyka; 83.Ervin Bulku), Lorik Çana, Altin Lala (Cap), Klodian Duro, Ervin
Skela, Erjon Bogdani. Trainer: Arend Haan (Holland).
Goals: 1-0 Sándor Torghelle (49), 2-0 Roland Juhász (82).
Cautions: Roland Juhász, László Bodnár / Armend Dallku, Ervin Skela, Ansi Agolli.

11.10.2008, Parken Stadion, København; Attendance: 33,124
Referee: Levan Paniashvili (Georgia)
DENMARK - MALTA   **3-0(2-0)**
DEN: Thomas Sørensen (Cap), Martin Laursen, Daniel Agger, Thomas Rasmussen, Kasper Bøgelund,
Christian Bjørnshøj Poulsen, Daniel Jensen (82.Thomas Kristensen), Thomas Kahlenberg (60.Michael
Krohn-Dehli), Morten Nordstrand, Dennis Rommedahl, Søren Larsen (76.Morten Rasmussen). Trainer:
Morten Olsen.
MLT: Justin Haber, Jonathan Caruana, Ian Azzopardi, Aaron Xuereb, Luke Dimech, Gilbert Agius
(80.Udochukwu Nwoko), Roderick Briffa, Jamie McDonald Pace, Ivan Woods, Andrè Schembri
(60.Etienne Barbara), Michael Mifsud (Cap) (87.Terence Scerri). Trainer: Dušan Fitzel (Czech
Republic).
Goals: 1-0 Søren Larsen (10), 2-0 Daniel Agger (29 penalty), 3-0 Søren Larsen (58).
Cautions: Gilbert Agius, Aaron Xuereb.

11.10.2008, Råsundastadion, Stockholm; Attendance: 33,241
Referee: Roberto Rosetti (Italy)
SWEDEN - PORTUGAL   **0-0**
SWE: Andreas Isaksson, Mikael Nilsson, Daniel Majstorovic, Petter Hansson, Behrang Safari,
Sebastian Larsson, Daniel Andersson, Kim Källström, Samuel Holmén, Zlatan Ibrahimovic (Cap),
Johan Elmander. Trainer: Lars Lagerbäck.
POR: Joaquim Manuel Sampaio Silva, José Bosingwa da Silva, Képler Laveran Lima Ferreira "Pepe",
Bruno Eduardo Regufe Alves, Fernando José da Silva Freitas Meira, Paulo Renato Rebocho Ferreira,
Raúl José Trindade Meireles "Raul Meireles", João Filipe Iria Santos Moutinho, Luís Carlos Almeida

12

da Cunha „Nani" (86.Daniel Miguel Alves Gomes „Danny"), Hugo Miguel Pereira de Almeida (65.Ricardo Andrade Quaresma Bernardo), Cristiano Ronaldo dos Santos Aveiro (Cap). Trainer: Carlos Manuel Brito Leal Queiroz.
Cautions: Zlatan Ibrahimovic / Ricardo Andrade Quaresma Bernardo.

15.10.2008, National Stadium, Ta'Qali; Attendance: 7,000
Referee: Jóhannes Valgeirsson (Iceland)
MALTA - HUNGARY   **0-1(0-1)**
MLT: Justin Haber, Jonathan Caruana (35.Roderick Briffa), Aaron Xuereb, Luke Dimech (Cap), Shaun Pierre Bajada, Etienne Barbara (78.Udochukwu Nwoko), Jamie McDonald Pace, Andrè Schembri, Ivan Woods, Michael Mifsud, Terence Scerri (63.Gilbert Agius). Trainer: Dušan Fitzel (Czech Republic).
HUN: Márton Fülöp, László Bodnár, Vilmos Vanczák, Roland Juhász, Boldizsár Bodor, Pál Dárdai (86.Balázs Tóth), Péter Halmosi, Zoltán Gera (Cap), Balázs Dzsudzsák (70.Ákos Buzsáky), Sándor Torghelle, Szabolcs Huszti. Trainer: Erwin Koeman (Holland).
Goal: 0-1 Sándor Torghelle (23).
Cautions: Luke Dimech, Jamie McDonald Pace / Pál Dárdai, Roland Juhász, Zoltán Gera, László Bodnár.

15.10.2008, Estádio AXA, Braga; Attendance: 29,500
Referee: Knut Kircher (Germany)
PORTUGAL - ALBANIA   **0-0**
POR: Joaquim Manuel Sampaio Silva, Bruno Eduardo Regufe Alves, Luís Miguel Brito Garcia Monteiro (75.Nuno Ricardo Oliveira Ribeiro „Maniche"), Képler Laveran Lima Ferreira „Pepe", Paulo Renato Rebocho Ferreira, Raúl José Trindade Meireles „Raul Meireles", João Filipe Iria Santos Moutinho (55.Ricardo Andrade Quaresma Bernardo), Manuel Henriques Tavares Fernandes, Daniel Miguel Alves Gomes „Danny" (55.Luís Carlos Almeida da Cunha „Nani"), Hugo Miguel Pereira de Almeida, Cristiano Ronaldo dos Santos Aveiro (Cap). Trainer: Carlos Manuel Brito Leal Queiroz.
ALB: Arjan Beqaj, Elvin Beqiri (24.Admir Teli), Debatik Curri, Kristi Vangjeli, Lorik Çana, Ervin Bulku, Ansi Agolli, Altin Lala (Cap), Klodian Duro (77.Besart Berisha), Ervin Skela, Erjon Bogdani (46.Endrit Vrapi). Trainer: Arend Haan (Holland).
Cautions: Hugo Miguel Pereira de Almeida / Admir Teli, Altin Lala.
Sent off: Admir Teli (42, yellow-red card).

11.02.2009, National Stadium, Ta'Qali; Attendance: 2,041
Referee: Alexandru Deaconu (Romania)
MALTA - ALBANIA   **0-0**
MLT: Justin Haber, Alex Muscat (82.Clayton Failla), Andrei Agius, Luke Dimech, Andrew Cohen, Andrè Schembri, Terence Scerri (70.Roderick Briffa), Kevin Sammut, Shaun Pierre Bajada, Gilbert Agius (Cap) (87.Ryan Fenech), Michael Mifsud. Trainer: Dušan Fitzel (Czech Republic).
ALB: Isli Hidi, Armend Dallku, Elvin Beqiri, Ansi Agolli (46.Kristi Vangjeli; 80.Andi Lila), Debatik Curri, Endrit Vrapi, Ervin Bulku, Gilman Lika, Klodian Duro, Ervin Skela (Cap), Erjon Bogdani (79.Besart Berisha). Trainer: Arend Haan (Holland).
Cautions: Ansi Agolli, Endrit Vrapi, Andi Lila.

28.03.2009, National Stadium, Ta'Qali; Attendance: 6,235
Referee: Tomasz Mikulski (Poland)
MALTA - DENMARK   **0-3(0-2)**
MLT: Justin Haber, Jonathan Caruana (69.Alex Muscat), Andrei Agius, Daniel Bogdanovic, Luke Dimech, Roderick Briffa (84.Etienne Barbara), Andrew Cohen, Andrè Schembri (72.Gilbert Agius), Shaun Pierre Bajada, Jamie McDonald Pace, Michael Mifsud (Cap). Trainer: Dušan Fitzel (Czech Republic).
DEN: Thomas Sørensen, Per Krøldrup, Daniel Agger, Michael Jakobsen, Lars Christian Jacobsen, Christian Bjørnshøj Poulsen, Daniel Jensen (63.Leon Andreasen), Søren Larsen (82.Morten

Nordstrand), Nicklas Bendtner (29.Jonas Borring), Martin Jørgensen (Cap), Dennis Rommedahl. Trainer: Morten Olsen.
Goals: 0-1 Søren Larsen (12), 0-2 Søren Larsen (23), 0-3 Morten Nordstrand (89).
Cautions: Luke Dimech, Michael Mifsud, Andrew Cohen, Jamie McDonald Pace / Thomas Sørensen.

28.03.2009, Stadiumi „Qemal Stafa", Tiranë; Attendance: 12,000
Referee: Björn Kuipers (Holland)
ALBANIA - HUNGARY   **0-1(0-1)**
ALB: Isli Hidi, Armend Dallku, Kristi Vangjeli, Lorik Çana, Debatik Curri, Altin Lala (Cap), Gilman Lika (70.Elis Bakaj), Klodian Duro, Ervin Skela, Besart Berisha, Hamdi Salihi. Trainer: Arend Haan (Holland).
HUN: Gábor Babos, Zoltán Szélesi, Tamás Vaskó, Vilmos Vanczák, Boldizsár Bodor, Pál Dárdai, Tamás Hajnal (Cap) (79.Krisztián Vadócz), Péter Halmosi (90+2.Zoltán Gera), Szabolcs Huszti, Sándor Torghelle (86.Tamás Priskin), Gergely Rudolf. Trainer: Erwin Koeman (Holland).
Goal: 0-1 Sándor Torghelle (38).
Cautions: Lorik Çana, Klodian Duro, Armend Dallku / Vilmos Vanczák, Pál Dárdai, Gábor Babos, Péter Halmosi.

28.03.2009, Estádio Dragão, Porto; Attendance: 40,200
Referee: Frank De Bleeckere (Belgium)
PORTUGAL - SWEDEN   **0-0**
POR: Eduardo dos Reis Carvalho, José Bosingwa da Silva (46.Rolando Jorge Pires da Fonseca), Ricardo Alberto Silveira de Carvalho, Képler Laveran Lima Ferreira „Pepe", Bruno Eduardo Regufe Alves, Raúl José Trindade Meireles „Raul Meireles", Tiago Cardoso Mendes (61.Anderson Luís de Souza „Deco"), Sérgio Paulo Barbosa Valente „Duda", Daniel Miguel Alves Gomes „Danny" (65.Hugo Miguel Pereira de Almeida), Cristiano Ronaldo dos Santos Aveiro (Cap), Simão Pedro Fonseca Sabrosa. Trainer: Carlos Manuel Brito Leal Queiroz.
SWE: Andreas Isaksson, Mikael Nilsson, Olof Mellberg, Daniel Majstorovic, Adam Johansson, Rasmus Elm, Anders Svensson (81.Sebastian Larsson), Kim Källström, Samuel Holmén (57.Christian Wilhelmsson), Johan Elmander (86.Marcus Berg), Henrik Larsson (Cap). Trainer: Lars Lagerbäck.

01.04.2009, „Puskás Ferenc" Stadion, Budapest; Attendance: 35,800
Referee: Stanislav Suhina (Russia)
HUNGARY - MALTA   **3-0(1-0)**
HUN: Márton Fülöp, László Bodnár, Zoltán Szélesi, Roland Juhász, Vilmos Vanczák, Boldizsár Bodor, Tamás Hajnal (Cap) (46.Zoltán Gera), Péter Halmosi (90+3.Balázs Tóth), Szabolcs Huszti, Balázs Dzsudzsák (79.Krisztián Vadócz), Sándor Torghelle. Trainer: Erwin Koeman (Holland).
MLT: Justin Haber, Alex Muscat, Andrei Agius, Daniel Bogdanovic (89.Etienne Barbara), Jonathan Caruana, Andrè Schembri (46.Terence Scerri), Roderick Briffa (85.Ryan Fenech), Andrew Cohen, Shaun Pierre Bajada, Gilbert Agius (Cap), Michael Mifsud. Trainer: Dušan Fitzel (Czech Republic).
Goals: 1-0 Tamás Hajnal (7), 2-0 Zoltán Gera (80), 3-0 Roland Juhász (90+4).
Cautions: László Bodnár, Roland Juhász / Michael Mifsud, Jonathan Caruana, Daniel Bogdanovic.

01.04.2009, Parken Stadion, København; Attendance: 24,320
Referee: Damir Skomina (Slovenia)
DENMARK - ALBANIA   **3-0(2-0)**
DEN: Thomas Sørensen, Daniel Agger, Michael Jakobsen, Lars Christian Jacobsen, Christian Bjørnshøj Poulsen, Daniel Jensen (34.Nicklas Bendtner), Leon Andreasen, Thomas Kahlenberg, Martin Jørgensen (Cap) (46.Jakob Poulsen), Søren Larsen, Dennis Rommedahl (71.Jonas Borring). Trainer: Morten Olsen.
ALB: Isli Hidi, Armend Dallku, Kristi Vangjeli, Ansi Agolli, Debatik Curri, Ervin Bulku (46.Hamdi Salihi), Gilman Lika, Dorian Bylykbashi (62.Elvin Beqiri), Klodian Duro, Ervin Skela, Besart Berisha (85.Migen Memelli). Trainer: Arend Haan (Holland).
Goals: 1-0 Leon Andreasen (31), 2-0 Søren Larsen (37), 3-0 Christian Bjørnshøj Poulsen (80).

14

Cautions: Søren Larsen, Michael Jakobsen / Armend Dallku, Kristi Vangjeli.

06.06.2009, Råsundastadion, Stockholm; Attendance: 33,619
Referee: Michael Anthony Riley (England)
SWEDEN - DENMARK   **0-1(0-1)**
SWE: Andreas Isaksson, Mikael Nilsson (80.Sebastian Larsson), Olof Mellberg, Daniel Majstorovic, Adam Johansson, Rasmus Elm, Daniel Andersson (68.Viktor Elm), Kim Källström, Christian Wilhelmsson (58.Johan Elmander), Zlatan Ibrahimovic, Henrik Larsson (Cap). Trainer: Lars Lagerbäck.
DEN: Thomas Sørensen, Simon Kjær, Daniel Agger, William Kvist Jørgensen, Lars Christian Jacobsen, Christian Bjørnshøj Poulsen (71.Thomas Augustinussen), Jakob Poulsen, Thomas Kahlenberg, Nicklas Bendtner (83.Martin Bernburg), Martin Jørgensen (Cap) (56.Jesper Grønkjær), Dennis Rommedahl. Trainer: Morten Olsen.
Goal: 0-1 Thomas Kahlenberg (22).
Cautions: Kim Källström / Dennis Rommedahl, Lars Christian Jacobsen, Thomas Sørensen.

06.06.2009, Stadiumi „Qemal Stafa", Tiranë; Attendance: 13,320
Referee: Florian Meyer (Germany)
ALBANIA - PORTUGAL   **1-2(1-1)**
ALB: Isli Hidi, Elvin Beqiri, Kristi Vangjeli, Ansi Agolli, Lorik Çana, Debatik Curri, Endrit Vrapi, Ervin Bulku, Klodian Duro (86.Besart Berisha), Ervin Skela (Cap) (90+3.Dorian Bylykbashi), Erjon Bogdani (64.Hamdi Salihi). Trainer: Josip Kuž e (Croatia).
POR: Eduardo dos Reis Carvalho, José Bosingwa da Silva, Ricardo Alberto Silveira de Carvalho (75.Luís Carlos Almeida da Cunha „Nani"), Képler Laveran Lima Ferreira „Pepe", Bruno Eduardo Regufe Alves, Raúl José Trindade Meireles „Raul Meireles", Sérgio Paulo Barbosa Valente „Duda", Luís Boa Morte Pereira (46.Simão Pedro Fonseca Sabrosa), Anderson Luís de Souza „Deco", Cristiano Ronaldo dos Santos Aveiro (Cap), Hugo Miguel Pereira de Almeida (69.Arnaldo Edi Lopes da Silva „Edinho"). Trainer: Carlos Manuel Brito Leal Queiroz.
Goals: 0-1 Hugo Miguel Pereira de Almeida (27), 1-1 Erjon Bogdani (29), 1-2 Bruno Eduardo Regufe Alves (90+2).
Cautions: Debatik Curri, Ansi Agolli, Isli Hidi / Raúl José Trindade Meireles „Raul Meireles", Képler Laveran Lima Ferreira „Pepe".

10.06.2009, Ullevi Stadion, Göteborg; Attendance: 25,271
Referee: Calum Murray (Scotland)
SWEDEN - MALTA   **4-0(1-0)**
SWE: Andreas Isaksson, Adam Johansson, Olof Mellberg, Daniel Majstorovic, Behrang Safari, Rasmus Elm (77.Sebastian Larsson), Anders Svensson, Kim Källström, Viktor Elm (80.Samuel Holmén), Zlatan Ibrahimovic (Cap), Marcus Berg (Tobias Hysén). Trainer: Lars Lagerbäck.
MLT: Andrew Hogg, Jonathan Caruana, Shaun Pierre Bajada, Andrei Agius (84.Emmanuel Muscat), John Hutchinson, Luke Dimech (Cap), Roderick Briffa, Daniel Bogdanovic, Alex Muscat (88.Kevin Sammut), Andrè Schembri (80.Ryan Fenech), Jamie McDonald Pace. Trainer: Dušan Fitzel (Czech Republic).
Goals: 1-0 Kim Källström (21), 2-0 Daniel Majstorovic (52), 3-0 Zlatan Ibrahimovic (56), 4-0 Marcus Berg (58).

05.09.2009, Parken Stadion, København; Attendance: 37,998
Referee: Massimo Busacca (Switzerland)
DENMARK - PORTUGAL   **1-1(1-0)**
DEN: Stephan Andersen, Simon Kjær, Anders Møller Christensen, Lars Christian Jacobsen, Christian Bjørnshøj Poulsen, Jakob Poulsen (89.Jesper Grønkjær), Michael Silberbauer (66.William Kvist Jørgensen), Dennis Rommedahl, Jon Dahl Tomasson (Cap), Martin Jørgensen (61.Hjalte Bo Nørregaard), Nicklas Bendtner. Trainer: Morten Olsen.
POR: Eduardo dos Reis Carvalho, José Bosingwa da Silva, Ricardo Alberto Silveira de Carvalho,

Képler Laveran Lima Ferreira „Pepe", Bruno Eduardo Regufe Alves, Raúl José Trindade Meireles „Raul Meireles" (80.Nuno Miguel Soares Pereira Ribeiro „Nuno Gomes"), Tiago Cardoso Mendes (46.Liédson da Silva Muniz), Sérgio Paulo Barbosa Valente „Duda", Anderson Luís de Souza „Deco", Simão Pedro Fonseca Sabrosa (70.Luís Carlos Almeida da Cunha „Nani"), Cristiano Ronaldo dos Santos Aveiro (Cap). Trainer: Carlos Manuel Brito Leal Queiroz.
Goals: 1-0 Nicklas Bendtner (42), 1-1 Liédson da Silva Muniz (86).
Cautions: Simon Kjær, Stephan Andersen / Liédson da Silva Muniz.

05.09.2009, „Puskás Ferenc" Stadion, Budapest; Attendance: 42,000
Referee: Nicola Rizzoli (Italy)
HUNGARY - SWEDEN   **1-2(0-1)**
HUN: Gábor Babos, Zoltán Szélesi, Gábor Gyepes, Roland Juhász (64.Krisztián Tímár), Péter Halmosi, Krisztián Vadócz, Pál Dárdai (46.Sándor Torghelle), Zoltán Gera (Cap), Tamás Hajnal (84.Ákos Buzsáky), Szabolcs Huszti, Balázs Dzsudzsák. Trainer: Erwin Koeman (Holland).
SWE: Andreas Isaksson, Mikael Nilsson, Olof Mellberg, Daniel Majstorovic, Behrang Safari, Rasmus Elm, Anders Svensson, Kim Källström, Samuel Holmén (85.Tobias Hysén), Johan Elmander (72.Marcus Berg), 10 Zlatan Ibrahimovic (Cap).Trainer: Lars Lagerbäck.
Goals: 0-1 Olof Mellberg (9), 1-1 Szabolcs Huszti (79 penalty), 1-2 Zlatan Ibrahimovic (90+3).
Cautions: Pál Dárdai, Zoltán Gera / Anders Svensson, Olof Mellberg.

09.09.2009, National Stadium, Ta'Qali; Attendance: 4,705
Referee: Adrian McCourt (Northern Ireland)
MALTA - SWEDEN   **0-1(0-0)**
MLT: Andrew Hogg, Emmanuel Muscat, Ian Azzopardi, Brian Said, Alex Muscat (62.Roderick Briffa), Andrew Cohen, Shaun Pierre Bajada (73.Clayton Failla), Kenneth Scicluna, Jamie McDonald Pace, Gilbert Agius (Cap), Michael Mifsud. Trainer: John Buttigieg.
SWE: Andreas Isaksson, Mikael Nilsson, Olof Mellberg, Daniel Majstorovic, Behrang Safari, Rasmus Elm, Anders Svensson (71.Marcus Berg), Kim Källström, Samuel Holmén (58.Tobias Hysén), Johan Elmander (83.Sebastian Larsson), Zlatan Ibrahimovic (Cap). Trainer: Lars Lagerbäck.
Goal: 0-1 Ian Azzopardi (82 own goal).
Cautions: Michael Mifsud / Behrang Safari.

09.09.2009, Stadiumi „Qemal Stafa", Tiranë; Attendance: 8,000
Referee: Cüneyt Çakir (Turkey)
ALBANIA - DENMARK   **1-1(0-1)**
ALB: Samir Ujkani, Elvin Beqiri (46.Jahmir Hyka), Armend Dallku, Ansi Agolli, Lorik Çana, Debatik Curri, Ervin Bulku, Klodian Duro, Ervin Skela (Cap) (82.Emiljano Vila), Erjon Bogdani (75.Gilman Lika), Hamdi Salihi. Trainer: Josip Kuž e (Croatia).
DEN: Thomas Sørensen, Simon Kjær, Anders Møller Christensen, Lars Christian Jacobsen, William Kvist Jørgensen, Christian Bjørnshøj Poulsen, Jakob Poulsen (53.Jesper Grønkjær), Dennis Rommedahl, Jon Dahl Tomasson (Cap) (74.Søren Larsen), Martin Jørgensen (69.Hjalte Bo Nørregaard), Nicklas Bendtner. Trainer: Morten Olsen.
Goals: 0-1 Nicklas Bendtner (40), 1-1 Erjon Bogdani (51).
Cautions: Ansi Agolli, Armend Dallku.

09.09.2009, „Puskás Ferenc" Stadion, Budapest; Attendance: 42,000
Referee: Stéphane Lannoy (France)
HUNGARY - PORTUGAL   **0-1(0-1)**
HUN: Gábor Babos, László Bodnár, Gábor Gyepes, Roland Juhász (Cap), Péter Halmosi, Balázs Tóth (83.Ákos Buzsáky), Pál Dárdai (65.Tamás Priskin), Krisztián Vadócz, Szabolcs Huszti (65.Tamás Hajnal), Sándor Torghelle, Balázs Dzsudzsák. Trainer: Erwin Koeman (Holland).
POR: Eduardo dos Reis Carvalho, José Bosingwa da Silva, Ricardo Alberto Silveira de Carvalho, Képler Laveran Lima Ferreira „Pepe", Bruno Eduardo Regufe Alves, Raúl José Trindade Meireles „Raul Meireles" (80.Nuno Miguel Soares Pereira Ribeiro „Nuno Gomes"), Tiago Cardoso Mendes

16

(90.Rolando Jorge Pires da Fonseca), Sérgio Paulo Barbosa Valente „Duda", Anderson Luís de Souza „Deco" (49.Simão Pedro Fonseca Sabrosa), Liédson da Silva Muniz (82.Luís Carlos Almeida da Cunha „Nani"), Cristiano Ronaldo dos Santos Aveiro (Cap). Trainer: Carlos Manuel Brito Leal Queiroz.
Goal: 0-1 Képler Laveran Lima Ferreira „Pepe" (9).
Cautions: Balázs Tóth, Péter Halmosi / Képler Laveran Lima Ferreira „Pepe", Sérgio Paulo Barbosa Valente „Duda".

10.10.2009, Parken Stadion, København; Attendance: 37,800
Referee: Manuel Enrique Mejuto González (Spain)
DENMARK - SWEDEN   **1-0(0-0)**
DEN: Thomas Sørensen, Lars Christian Jacobsen, Simon Kjær, Daniel Agger, Michael Jacobsen, Dennis Rommedahl, Christian Bjørnshøj Poulsen, Martin Jørgensen (46.Michael Silberbauer), Jakob Poulsen, Jon Dahl Tomasson (Cap), Nicklas Bendtner. Trainer: Morten Olsen.
SWE: Andreas Isaksson, Mikael Nilsson (89.Markus Rosenberg), Olof Mellberg, Daniel Majstorovic, Behrang Safari, Rasmus Elm (80.Marcus Berg), Anders Svensson, Kim Källström, Samuel Holmén (63.Sebastian Larsson), Zlatan Ibrahimovic, Henrik Larsson (Cap). Trainer: Lars Lagerbäck.
Goal: 1-0 Jakob Poulsen (79).

10.10.2009, Estádio da Luz, Lisboa; Attendance: 50,115
Referee: Alain Hamer (Luxembourg)
PORTUGAL - HUNGARY   **3-0(1-0)**
POR: Eduardo dos Reis Carvalho, José Bosingwa da Silva, Ricardo Alberto Silveira de Carvalho, Bruno Eduardo Regufe Alves, Raúl José Trindade Meireles „Raul Meireles", Pedro Miguel da Silva Mendes, Sérgio Paulo Barbosa Valente „Duda", Anderson Luís de Souza „Deco", Simão Pedro Fonseca Sabrosa (81.Miguel Luís Pinto Veloso), Liédson da Silva Muniz (83.Nuno Miguel Soares Pereira Ribeiro „Nuno Gomes"), Cristiano Ronaldo dos Santos Aveiro (Cap) (27.Luís Carlos Almeida da Cunha „Nani"). Trainer: Carlos Manuel Brito Leal Queiroz.
HUN: Gábor Babos, László Bodnár, Gábor Gyepes, Roland Juhász (Cap), Vilmos Vanczák, Krisztián Vadócz (56.Tamás Priskin), Balázs Tóth, Zoltán Gera (Cap), Szabolcs Huszti (67.Ákos Buzsáky), Balázs Dzsudzsák (82.József Varga), Sándor Torghelle. Trainer: Erwin Koeman (Holland).
Goals: 1-0 Simão Pedro Fonseca Sabrosa (18), 2-0 Liédson da Silva Muniz (74), 3-0 Simão Pedro Fonseca Sabrosa (79).

14.10.2009, Parken Stadion, København; Attendance: 36,966
Referee: Florian Meyer (Germany)
DENMARK - HUNGARY   **0-1(0-1)**
DEN: Thomas Sørensen, Daniel Agger, Anders Møller Christensen, Michael Jakobsen, Lars Christian Jacobsen, Christian Bjørnshøj Poulsen, Thomas Enevoldsen (46.Søren Larsen), Jakob Poulsen, Dennis Rommedahl (71.Michael Silberbauer), Nicklas Bendtner, Jon Dahl Tomasson (Cap) (62.Daniel Jensen). Trainer: Morten Olsen.
HUN: Gábor Babos, László Bodnár, Vilmos Vanczák, Roland Juhász (Cap), Péter Halmosi, Balázs Tóth, Ákos Buzsáky (77.Szabolcs Huszti), József Varga, Balázs Dzsudzsák (90.Tamás Priskin), Sándor Torghelle, Gergely Rudolf (87.Krisztián Vadócz). Trainer: Erwin Koeman (Holland).
Goal: 0-1 Ákos Buzsáky (35).
Cautions: Anders Møller Christensen, Daniel Jensen.

14.10.2009, Estádio „D. Afonso Henriques", Guimarães; Attendance: 29,350
Referee: Alan Kelly (Republic of Ireland)
PORTUGAL - MALTA   **4-0(2-0)**
POR: Eduardo dos Reis Carvalho, José Bosingwa da Silva, Ricardo Alberto Silveira de Carvalho, Képler Laveran Lima Ferreira „Pepe", Raúl José Trindade Meireles „Raul Meireles" (62.Nuno Assis Lopes de Almeida), Pedro Miguel da Silva Mendes, Miguel Luís Pinto Veloso, Anderson Luís de Souza „Deco", Simão Pedro Fonseca Sabrosa (Cap), Luís Carlos Almeida da Cunha „Nani" (73.João Filipe Iria Santos Moutinho), Liédson da Silva Muniz (62.Arnaldo Edi Lopes da Silva „Edinho").

17

Trainer: Carlos Manuel Brito Leal Queiroz.

MLT: Andrew Hogg, Emmanuel Muscat, Ian Azzopardi, Brian Said (Cap), John Hutchison, Shaun Pierre Bajada (73.Ryan Fenech), Roderick Briffa (88.Kevin Sammut), Andrew Cohen (23.Clayton Failla), Kenneth Scicluna, Jamie McDonald Pace, Michael Mifsud. Trainer: John Buttigieg.

Goals: 1-0 Luís Carlos Almeida da Cunha „Nani" (14), 2-0 Simão Pedro Fonseca Sabrosa (45), 3-0 Miguel Luís Pinto Veloso (52), 4-0 Arnaldo Edi Lopes da Silva „Edinho" (90).

Cautions: José Bosingwa da Silva, Képler Laveran Lima Ferreira „Pepe" / Kenneth Scicluna, Clayton Failla.

14.10.2009, Råsundastadion, Stockholm; Attendance: 25,342
Referee: Nikolai Ivanov (Russia)
SWEDEN - ALBANIA   **4-1(3-0)**
SWE: Andreas Isaksson, Mikael Nilsson, Olof Mellberg, Daniel Majstorovic, Behrang Safari, Sebastian Larsson, Anders Svensson, Kim Källström (21.Daniel Andersson), Rasmus Elm, Zlatan Ibrahimovic (Cap) (76.Markus Rosenberg), Johan Elmander (37.Marcus Berg). Trainer: Lars Lagerbäck.

ALB: Samir Ujkani, Armend Dallku, Lorik Çana, Debatik Curri, Altin Haxhi (22.Jahmir Hyka), Ervin Skela (Cap), Ervin Bulku, Elvin Beqiri, Klodian Duro, Hamdi Salihi (79.Edmond Kapllani). Trainer: Josip Kuž e (Croatia).

Goals: 1-0 Olof Mellberg (6), 2-0 Marcus Berg (40), 3-0 Olof Mellberg (42), 3-1 Hamdi Salihi (57), 4-1 Anders Svensson (86).

Cautions: Anders Svensson / Armend Dallku.

GROUP 2

06.09.2008	Tiraspol	Moldova - Latvia	1-2(0-2)
06.09.2008	Tel Aviv	Israel - Switzerland	2-2(0-1)
06.09.2008	Luxembourg	Luxembourg - Greece	0-3(0-2)
10.09.2008	Chişinău	Moldova - Israel	1-2(1-2)
10.09.2008	Riga	Latvia - Greece	0-2(0-1)
10.09.2008	Zürich	Switzerland - Luxembourg	1-2(1-1)
11.10.2008	St. Gallen	Switzerland - Latvia	2-1(0-0)
11.10.2008	Luxembourg	Luxembourg - Israel	1-3(1-1)
11.10.2008	Peiraiás	Greece - Moldova	3-0(2-0)
15.10.2008	Riga	Latvia - Israel	1-1(0-0)
15.10.2008	Luxembourg	Luxembourg - Moldova	0-0
15.10.2008	Peiraiás	Greece - Switzerland	1-2(0-1)
28.03.2009	Luxembourg	Luxembourg - Latvia	0-4(0-1)
28.03.2009	Chişinău	Moldova - Switzerland	0-2(0-1)
28.03.2009	Tel Aviv	Israel - Greece	1-1(0-1)
01.04.2009	Riga	Latvia - Luxembourg	2-0(1-0)
01.04.2009	Iraklion	Greece - Israel	2-1(1-0)
01.04.2009	Genève	Switzerland - Moldova	2-0(1-0)
05.09.2009	Chişinău	Moldova - Luxembourg	0-0
05.09.2009	Tel Aviv	Israel - Latvia	0-1(0-0)
05.09.2009	Basel	Switzerland - Greece	2-0(0-0)
09.09.2009	Tel Aviv	Israel - Luxembourg	7-0(4-0)
09.09.2009	Riga	Latvia - Switzerland	2-2(0-1)
09.09.2009	Chişinău	Moldova - Greece	1-1(0-1)
10.10.2009	Luxembourg	Luxembourg - Switzerland	0-3(0-3)
10.10.2009	Tel Aviv	Israel - Moldova	3-1(1-0)
10.10.2009	Athína	Greece - Latvia	5-2(1-2)
14.10.2009	Athína	Greece - Luxembourg	2-1(2-0)
14.10.2009	Riga	Latvia - Moldova	3-2(2-1)
14.10.2009	Basel	Switzerland - Israel	0-0

FINAL STANDINGS

1.	**SWITZERLAND**	10	6	3	1	18	-	8	21
2.	**Greece**	10	6	2	2	20	-	10	20
3.	Latvia	10	5	2	3	18	-	15	17
4.	Israel	10	4	4	2	20	-	10	16
5.	Luxembourg	10	1	2	7	4	-	25	5
6.	Moldova	10	0	3	7	6	-	18	3

Switzerland qualified for the Final Tournament; Greece qualified for the Play-Offs.

06.09.2008, Sheriff Stadium, Tiraspol; Attendance: 4,300
Referee: Mark Courtney (Northern Ireland)
MOLDOVA - LATVIA   **1-2(0-2)**
MDA: Nicolai Calancea, Serghei Laşcencov, Victor Golovatenco, Alexandru Epureanu, Radu Rebeja (Cap), Andrei Corneencov, Valeriu Andronic (61.Serghei Alekseev), Igor Picusciac, Viorel Frunză, Alexandr Suvorov (69.Igor Ţîgîrlaş), Vitalie Bordian. Trainer: Igor Dobrovolskiy (Russia)
LVA: Andris Vaņins, Igors N. Stepanovs, Vitālijs Astafjevs (Cap), Kaspars Gorkšs, Juris Laizāns, Oskars Kļava, Deniss Kačanovs (90+3.Dzintars Zirnis), Genādijs Soloņicins (83.Vladimirs Koļesničenko), Māris Verpakovskis (75.Andrejs Rubins), Andrejs Perepļotkins, Ģirts Karlsons. Trainer: Aleksandrs Starkovs.

19

Goals: 0-1 Ģirts Karlsons (8), 0-2 Vitālijs Astafjevs (22), 1-2 Serghei Alekseev (76).
Cautions: Serghei Laşcencov, Victor Golovatenco / Oskars Kļava, Juris Laizāns.

06.09.2008, National Stadium, Ramat-Gan, Tel Aviv; Attendance: 31,236
Referee: Martin Hansson (Sweden)
ISRAEL - SWITZERLAND   **2-2(0-1)**
ISR: David Awat, Shmuel Kozokin, Tal Ben Haim, Avi Strool, Yoav David Ziv, Baram Kayal (62.Moshe Ohayon), Tamir Cohen, Yossi Benayoun (Cap), Salim Toama, Omer Golan (60.Elyaniv Barda), Roberto Damián Colautti (46.Ben Sahar). Trainer: Dror Kashtan.
SUI: Diego Benaglio, Stephan Lichtsteiner, Stéphane Grichting, Johannes Djourou, Ludovic Magnin (Cap), Gökhan Inler, Benjamin Huggel, Valon Behrami (90.Christoph Spycher), Tranquillo Barnetta (71.Johan Vonlanthen), Hakan Yakin (74.Almen Abdi), Blaise Nkufo. Trainer: Ottmar Hitzfeld (Germany).
Goals: 0-1 Hakan Yakin (45), 0-2 Blaise Nkufo (56), 1-2 Yossi Benayoun (73), 2-2 Ben Sahar (90+2).
Cautions: Omer Golan, Tamir Cohen / Benjamin Huggel.

06.09.2008, Stade „Josy Barthel", Luxembourg; Attendance: 4,596
Referee: Anders Hermansen (Denmark)
LUXEMBOURG - GREECE   **0-3(0-2)**
LUX: Jonathan Joubert, Kim Kintziger, Eric Hoffmann, Ben Payal, René Peters, Claudio Lombardelli (69.Benoît Lang), Jeff Strasser (Cap), Alphonse Leweck (58.Daniel Alves Da Mota), Gilles Bettmer, Mario Mutsch, Joël Kitenge (80.Aurélien Joachim). Trainer: Guy Hellers.
GRE: Konstantinos Halkiás, Giórgos Seitarídis, Traïanós Dellas, Sotírios Kyrgiakos, Vasílis Torosídis, Angelos Basinás (Cap) (46.Dimítris Salpingídis), Giórgos Karagoúnis, Konstantinos Katsouránis, Theofánis Gékas (80.Nikolaos Leonidas Spiropoulos), Nikolaos Liberópoulos (66.Hrístos Patsatzoglou), Angelos Haristéas. Trainer: Otto Rehhagel (Germany).
Goals: 0-1 Vasílis Torosídis (36), 0-2 Theofánis Gékas (45+1), 0-3 Angelos Haristéas (77 penalty).
Cautions: Alphonse Leweck, Claudio Lombardelli, Joël Kitenge, Eric Hoffmann, Jeff Strasser, Benoît Lang / Konstantinos Katsouránis.

10.09.2008, Baza Zimbru, Chişinău; Attendance: 10,500
Referee: César Muñiz Fernández (Spain)
MOLDOVA - ISRAEL   **1-2(1-2)**
MDA: Stanislav Namaşco, Serghei Laşcencov, Victor Golovatenco, Alexandru Epureanu, Radu Rebeja (Cap), Andrei Corneencov (27.Alexei Savinov), Victor Comlionoc (76.Valeriu Andronic), Igor Picusciac, Alexandr Suvorov, Viorel Frunză (69.Serghei Alekseev), Vitalie Bordian. Trainer: Igor Dobrovolskiy (Russia).
ISR: David Awat, Shmuel Kozokin (38.Rahamin Saban), Tal Ben Haim, Dekel Keinan, Yoav David Ziv, Moshe Ohayon, Tamir Cohen (68.Baram Kayal), Yossi Benayoun (Cap), Salim Toama, Omer Golan, Ben Sahar (4.Maor Bar Buzaglo). Trainer: Dror Kashtan.
Goals: 1-0 Igor Picusceac (1), 1-1 Omer Golan (39), 1-2 Rahamin Saban (45).
Cautions: Alexandru Epureanu, Serghei Laşcencov / Tamir Cohen.
Sent off: Victor Golovatenco (64).

10.09.2008, Skonto Stadium, Riga; Attendance: 8,600
Referee: Tony Chapron (France)
LATVIA - GREECE   **0-2(0-1)**
LVA: Andris Vaņins, Igors N. Stepanovs, Vitālijs Astafjevs (Cap), Kaspars Gorkšs, Juris Laizāns, Oskars Kļava, Deniss Kačanovs, Genādijs Soloņicins (65.Andrejs Rubins), Māris Verpakovskis, Andrejs Perepļotkins (79.Aleksejs Višņakovs), Ģirts Karlsons (60.Kristaps Grebis). Trainer: Aleksandrs Starkovs.
GRE: Konstantinos Halkiás, Giórgos Seitarídis, Vasílis Torosídis, Sotírios Kyrgiakos, Traïanós Dellas, Avraam Papadópoulos, Konstantinos Katsouránis, Giórgos Samarás (88.Nikolaos Liberópoulos), Giórgos Karagoúnis (Cap) (61.Angelos Basinás), Angelos Haristéas, Theofánis Gékas (76.Dimítris

Salpingídis). Trainer: Otto Rehhagel (Germany).
Goals: 0-1 Theofánis Gékas (10), 0-2 Theofánis Gékas (49).
Cautions: Oskars Kļava.

10.09.2008, Letzigrund Stadion, Zürich; Attendance: 20,500
Referee: Dejan Filipović (Serbia)
SWITZERLAND - LUXEMBOURG   **1-2(0-1)**
SUI: Diego Benaglio, Alain Nef (73.Johan Vonlanthen), Johannes Djourou, Stéphane Grichting, Ludovic Magnin (Cap), Gökhan Inler, Tranquillo Barnetta, Hakan Yakin (65.Mauro Lustrinelli), Valentin Stocker, Alexander Frei (65.Almen Abdi), Blaise Nkufo. Trainer: Ottmar Hitzfeld (Germany).
LUX: Jonathan Joubert, Benoît Lang (44.Alphonse Leweck), Kim Kintziger, Eric Hoffmann, Ben Payal, René Peters, Claudio Lombardelli (76.Lars Christian Krogh Gerson), Jeff Strasser (Cap), Gilles Bettmer, Mario Mutsch, Joël Kitenge (66.Aurélien Joachim). Trainer: Guy Hellers.
Goals: 0-1 Jeff Strasser (27), 1-1 Blaise Nkufo (43), 1-2 Alphonse Leweck (87).
Cautions: Hakan Yakin, Mauro Lustrinelli, Johan Vonlanthen / Joël Kitenge, Eric Hoffmann, Kim Kintziger, Claudio Lombardelli, Jeff Strasser, Claude Reiter (on the bench).

11.10.2008, AFG Arena, St. Gallen; Attendance: 18,026
Referee: Lucilio Cardoso Cortez Batista (Portugal)
SWITZERLAND - LATVIA   **2-1(0-0)**
SUI: Diego Benaglio, Stephan Lichtsteiner, Stéphane Grichting, Johannes Djourou (46.Mario Eggimann), Christoph Spycher, Tranquillo Barnetta (84.Gelson Tavares Fernandes), Gökhan Inler, Benjamin Huggel, Valon Behrami, Alexander Frei (Cap) (78.Hakan Yakin), Blaise Nkufo. Trainer: Ottmar Hitzfeld (Germany).
LVA: Andris Vaņins, Kaspars Gorkšs, Deniss Ivanovs, Deniss Kačanovs, Igors Savčenkovs, Vitālijs Astafjevs (Cap), Aleksandrs Cauņa (60.Andrejs Rubins), Juris Laizāns, Genādijs Soloņicins (81.Aleksejs Višņakovs), Ģirts Karlsons, Andrejs Perepļotkins (70.Vladimirs Koļesničenko). Trainer: Aleksandrs Starkovs (60).
Goals: 1-0 Alexander Frei (63), 1-1 Deniss Ivanovs (71), 2-1 Blaise Nkufo (73).
Cautions: Stéphane Grichting / Juris Laizāns, Vitālijs Astafjevs.
Sent off: Juris Laizāns (69).

11.10.2008, Stade „Josy Barthel", Luxembourg; Attendance: 3,562
Referee: Igoe Egorov (Russia)
LUXEMBOURG - ISRAEL   **1-3(1-1)**
LUX: Jonathan Joubert, Kim Kintziger, Ben Payal, Claude Reiter, Jean Wagner, René Peters (Cap), Paul Bossi (67.Daniel Alves Da Mota), Gilles Bettmer, Alphonse Leweck, Stefano Bensi (46.Aurélien Joachim), Mario Mutsch. Trainer: Guy Hellers.
ISR: David Awat, Rahamin Saban, Tal Ben Haim, Dekel Keinan, Gal Alberman (90+3.Moshe Ohayon), Salim Toama (81.Ben Sahar), Baram Kayal, David Ben Dayan, Omer Golan, Elyaniv Barda, Yossi Benayoun (Cap) (87.Maor Bar Buzaglo). Trainer: Dror Kashtan.
Goals: 0-1 Yossi Benayoun (2 penalty), 1-1 René Peters (14), 1-2 Omer Golan (54), 1-3 Salim Toama (81).
Cautions: Jonathan Joubert, Mario Mutsch, Aurélien Joachim, René Peters / Salim Toama, Tal Ben Haim, Dekel Keinan, David Ben Dayan.

11.10.2008, Karaïskáki Stadio, Peiraiás; Attendance: 13,684
Referee: Espen Berntsen (Norway)
GREECE - MOLDOVA   **3-0(2-0)**
GRE: Konstantinos Halkiás, Giórgos Seitarídis, Traïanós Dellas, Sotírios Kyrgiakos, Avraam Papadópoulos, Angelos Basinás (Cap), Konstantinos Katsouránis (72.Hrístos Patsatzoglou), Vasílis Torosídis, Giórgos Samarás (70.Giánnis Amanatídis), Angelos Haristéas, Theofánis Gékas (46.Dimítris Salpingídis). Trainer: Otto Rehhagel (Germany).
MDA: Nicolai Calancea, Igor Armaș, Radu Rebeja (Cap), Alexei Savinov, Alexandru Epureanu,

Vitalie Bordian, Andrei Corneencov (79.Valeriu Andronic), Eugeniu Cebotaru, Igor Țîgîrlaș, Serghei Alekseev (46.Igor Picusciac), Igor Bugaiov (68.Aleksandr Suvorov). Trainer: Igor Dobrovolskiy (Russia).
Goals: 1-0 Angelos Haristéas (31), 2-0 Konstantinos Katsouránis (40), 3-0 Angelos Haristéas (51).
Cautions: Giórgos Samarás, Giórgos Seitarídis.

15.10.2008, Skonto Stadium, Riga; Attendance: 7,100
Referee: Vladimír Hriňák (Slovakia)
LATVIA - ISRAEL   **1-1(0-0)**
LVA: Andris Vaņins, Kaspars Gorkšs, Vitālijs Astafjevs (Cap), Genādijs Soloņicins (74.Aleksejs Višņakovs), Oskars Kļava, Deniss Ivanovs, Deniss Kačanovs, Andrejs Perepļotkins (61.Aleksandrs Cauņa), Vladimirs Koļesničenko, Andrejs Rubins, Ģirts Karlsons (61.Kristaps Grebis). Trainer: Aleksandrs Starkovs.
ISR: David Awat, Tal Ben Haim, Dekel Keinan, Salim Toama, Rahamin Saban, David Ben Dayan, Gal Alberman, Omer Golan (83.Ben Sahar), Yossi Benayoun (Cap), Elyaniv Barda (90+2.Maor Bar Buzaglo), Baram Kayal (67.Moshe Ohayon). Trainer: Dror Kashtan.
Goals: 0-1 Yossi Benayoun (50), 1-1 Vladimirs Koļesničenko (89).

15.10.2008, Stade „Josy Barthel", Luxembourg; Attendance: 2,157
Referee: Marcin Borski (Poland)
LUXEMBOURG - MOLDOVA   **0-0**
LUX: Jonathan Joubert, Kim Kintziger, Ben Payal (46.Lars Christian Krogh Gerson), Eric Hoffmann, René Peters, Jeff Strasser (Cap), Gilles Bettmer, Paul Bossi (46.Claudio Lombardelli), Alphonse Leweck (69.Aurélien Joachim), Mario Mutsch, Joël Kitenge. Trainer: Guy Hellers (36).
MDA: Nicolai Calancea, Serghei Lașcencov, Radu Rebeja (Cap), Alexandru Epureanu, Igor Armaș, Vitalie Bordian, Andrei Corneencov (73.Eugeniu Cebotaru), Aleksandr Suvorov, Igor Picusciac (65.Igor Țîgîrlaș), Viorel Frunză, Igor Bugaiov (54.Victor Bulat). Trainer: Igor Dobrovolskiy (Russia).
Cautions: Radu Rebeja, Igor Picusciac, Igor Armaș, Victor Bulat.

15.10.2008, Karaïskáki Stadio, Peiraiás; Attendance: 28,810
Referee: Luis Medina Cantalejo (Spain)
GREECE - SWITZERLAND   **1-2(0-1)**
GRE: Konstantinos Halkiás, Avraam Papadópoulos, Traïanós Dellas, Sotírios Kyrgiakos (30.Hrístos Patsatzoglou), Giórgos Seitarídis, Konstantinos Katsouránis, Angelos Basinás (Cap), Vasílis Torosídis, Angelos Haristéas, Theofánis Gékas (46.Nikolaos Liberópoulos), Giórgos Samarás (62.Giórgos Karagoúnis). Trainer: Otto Rehhagel (Germany).
SUI: Diego Benaglio, Stephan Lichtsteiner, Mario Eggimann, Stéphane Grichting, Christoph Spycher, Valon Behrami, Gökhan Inler, Benjamin Huggel, Tranquillo Barnetta (33.Gelson Tavares Fernandes), Alexander Frei (Cap) (75.Hakan Yakin), Blaise Nkufo (86.Eren Derdiyok). Trainer: Ottmar Hitzfeld (Germany).
Goals: 0-1 Alexander Frei (42 penalty), 1-1 Angelos Haristéas (68), 1-2 Blaise Nkufo (77).
Cautions: Avraam Papadópoulos, Konstantinos Katsouránis / Gelson Tavares Fernandes, Stephan Lichtsteiner.

28.03.2009, Stade „Josy Barthel", Luxembourg; Attendance: 2,516
Referee: Mark Whitby (Wales)
LUXEMBOURG - LATVIA   **0-4(0-1)**
LUX: Jonathan Joubert, Eric Hoffmann, Jacques Plein, Mathias Jänisch, Jeff Strasser (Cap), Mario Mutsch, Gilles Bettmer, Alphonse Leweck (66.Claudio Lombardelli), Ben Payal (46.Lars Christian Krogh Gerson), René Peters, Stefano Bensi (70.Joël Kitenge). Trainer: Guy Hellers.
LVA: Andris Vaņins, Oskars Kļava, Vitalijs Astafjevs (Cap), Kaspars Gorkšs, Vladimirs Koļesničenko, Aleksandrs Cauņa (77.Andrejs Rubins), Deniss Ivanovs, Deniss Kačanovs, Māris Verpakovskis (72.Andrejs Perepļotkins), Jurijs Žigajevs (66.Aleksejs Višņakovs), Ģirts Karlsons. Trainer: Aleksandrs Starkovs.

22

Goals: 0-1 Ģirts Karlsons (24), 0-2 Aleksandrs Cauņa (48), 0-3 Aleksejs Višņakovs (72), 0-4 Andrejs Perepļotkins (86).
Cautions: Stefano Bensi, Eric Hoffmann, Jeff Strasser / Jurijs Žigajevs.

28.03.2009, Baza Zimbru, Chişinău; Attendance: 10,500
Referee: George Douglas McDonald (Scotland)
MOLDOVA - SWITZERLAND   **0-2(0-1)**
MDA: Stanislav Namaşco, Serghei Laşcencov (Cap), Alexei Savinov, Igor Armaş (86.Vitalie Manaliu), Victor Golovatenco, Alexandru Epureanu, Alexandru Gâţcan, Artur Ioniţă (56.Eugeniu Cebotaru), Igor Bugaiov, Serghei Alekseev, Denis Calincov. Trainer: Igor Dobrovolskiy (Russia).
SUI: Diego Benaglio, Stephan Lichtsteiner, Philippe Senderos, Stéphane Grichting, Ludovic Magnin, Gökhan Inler, Benjamin Huggel, Marco Padalino (80.Gelson Tavares Fernandes), Tranquillo Barnetta (90.Johannes Djourou), Alexander Frei (Cap), Blaise Nkufo (80.Eren Derdiyok). Trainer: Ottmar Hitzfeld (Germany).
Goals: 0-1 Alexander Frei (32), 0-2 Gelson Tavares Fernandes (90+3).
Cautions: Igor Armaş, Alexandru Epureanu, Alexei Savinov.

28.03.2009, National Stadium, Ramat Gan, Tel Aviv; Attendance: 38,000
Referee: Roberto Rosetti (Italy)
ISRAEL - GREECE   **1-1(0-1)**
ISR: David Awat, Tal Ben Haim, Dekel Keinan, Rahamin Saban, David Ben Dayan, Gal Alberman, Tamir Cohen (84.Gil Vermouth), Yossi Benayoun (Cap) (77.Baram Kayal), Elyaniv Barda (59.Barak Itzhaki), Omer Golan, Ben Sahar. Trainer: Dror Kashtan.
GRE: Konstantinos Halkiás, Giórgos Seitarídis, Avraam Papadópoulos, Traïanós Dellas, Sotírios Kyrgiakos, Vasílis Torosídis, Angelos Basinás (Cap) (62.Giórgos Samarás), Alexandros Tziólis (87.Hrístos Patsatzoglou), Giórgos Karagoúnis, Angelos Haristéas, Theofánis Gékas. Trainer: Otto Rehhagel (Germany).
Goals: 0-1 Theofánis Gékas (41), 1-1 Omer Golan (55).
Cautions: Ben Sahar / Traïanós Dellas.

01.04.2009, Skonto Stadium, Riga; Attendance: 6,700
Referee: Fı rat Aydı nus (Turkey)
LATVIA - LUXEMBOURG   **2-0(1-0)**
LVA: Andris Vaņins, Oskars Kļava, Vitālijs Astafjevs (Cap), Kaspars Gorkšs, Deniss Ivanovs, Deniss Kačanovs, Vladimirs Kolesņičenko, Aleksandrs Cauņa, Jurijs Žigajevs (88.Genādijs Soloņicins; 69.Andrejs Rubins), Māris Verpakovskis, Ģirts Karlsons (20.Andrejs Perepļotkins). Trainer: Aleksandrs Starkovs.
LUX: Jonathan Joubert, Kim Kintziger, Eric Hoffmann (80.Stefano Bensi), Mathias Jänisch, Jeff Strasser (Cap), Mario Mutsch, Gilles Bettmer, Joël Kitenge, Claudio Lombardelli (60.Alphonse Leweck), Ben Payal (83.João Carlos Ferreira), René Peters. Trainer: Guy Hellers.
Goals: 1-0 Žigajevs Jurijs (44), 2-0 Māris Verpakovskis (75).
Cautions: Deniss Kačanovs / Mario Mutsch, Joël Kitenge.

01.04.2009, Pankritio Stadio, Iraklión; Attendance: 22,794
Referee: Olegário Manuel Bartolo Faustino Benquerença (Portugal)
GREECE - ISRAEL   **2-1(1-0)**
GRE: Konstantinos Halkiás, Giórgos Seitarídis, Avraam Papadópoulos, Sotírios Kyrgiakos, Evangélios Móras, Vasílis Torosídis, Konstantinos Katsouránis, Giórgos Karagoúnis (Cap) (70.Hrístos Patsatzoglou), Dimítris Salpingídis, Angelos Haristéas (84.Angelos Basinás), Theofánis Gékas (64.Giórgos Samarás). Trainer: Otto Rehhagel (Germany).
ISR: David Awat (Cap), Tal Ben Haim, Yoav David Ziv (40.Elyaniv Barda), Dekel Keinan, Rahamin Saban, David Ben Dayan, Gal Alberman, Baram Kayal, Omer Golan, Ben Sahar (46.Yossi Benayoun), Itay Menachem Shechter (74.Barak Itzhaki). Trainer: Dror Kashtan.
Goals: 1-0 Dimítris Salpingídis (32), 1-1 Elyaniv Barda (58), 2-1 Giórgos Samarás (66 penalty).

23

Cautions: Vasílis Torosídis, Konstantinos Katsouránis / Elyaniv Barda, Tal Ben Haim.

01.04.2009, Stade de Genève, Genève; Attendance: 20,100
Referee: Gianluca Rocchi (Italy)
SWITZERLAND - MOLDOVA   **2-0(1-0)**
SUI: Diego Benaglio, Stephan Lichtsteiner, Philippe Senderos, Stéphane Grichting, Ludovic Magnin, Gökhan Inler, Benjamin Huggel (71.Blerim Dzemaili), Marco Padalino (86.Almen Abdi), Tranquillo Barnetta, Alexander Frei (Cap), Blaise Nkufo (83.Eren Derdiyok). Trainer: Ottmar Hitzfeld (Germany).
MDA: Stanislav Namaşco, Alexei Savinov, Serghei Laşcencov (Cap), Victor Golovatenco, Alexandru Onica, Alexandru Gâţcan (57.Serghei Alekseev), Eugeniu Cebotaru, Victor Bulat, Vitalie Manaliu (79.Igor Ţîgîrlaş), Igor Bugaiov, Denis Calincov (67.Valeriu Andronic). Trainer: Igor Dobrovolskiy (Russia).
Goals: 1-0 Blaise Nkufo (20), 2-0 Alexander Frei (52).
Cautions: Stephan Lichtsteiner / Victor Bulat, Alexandru Gâţcan.

05.09.2009, Baza Zimbru, Chişinău; Attendance: 7,820
Referee: Gediminas Maž eika (Lithuania)
MOLDOVA - LUXEMBOURG   **0-0**
MDA: Stanislav Namaşco, Valeriu Catinsus, Victor Golovatenco, Igor Armaş, Serghei Laşcencov (Cap), Alexandru Onica, Alexandru Gâţcan, Victor Comlionoc (81.Valeriu Andronic), Denis Calincov, Igor Bugaiov (77.Alexandr Suvorov), Veaceslav Sofroni. Trainer: Igor Dobrovolskiy (Russia).
LUX: Jonathan Joubert, Guy Blaise, Eric Hoffmann, Mathias Jänisch (58.Dan Collette), Kim Kintziger, Jeff Strasser (Cap), Gilles Bettmer, Claudio Lombardelli (78.Alphonse Leweck), Ben Payal, René Peters, Sergio Pupovac (84.Daniel Alves Da Mota). Trainer: Guy Hellers.
Cautions: Alexandru Onica, Victor Golovatenco / Claudio Lombardelli, Guy Blaise, Jonathan Joubert, Jeff Strasser, Ben Payal.

05.09.2009, National Stadium, Ramat-Gan, Tel Aviv; Attendance: 20,000
Referee: Knut Kircher (Germany)
ISRAEL - LATVIA   **0-1(0-0)**
ISR: David Awat, Dekel Keinan, Avi Strool, Yuval Shpungin, David Ben Dayan, Gal Alberman (46.Tamir Cohen), Baram Kayal, Yossi Benayoun (Cap) (67.Aviram Baruchyan), Elyaniv Barda, Omer Golan (63.Ben Sahar), Yaniv Katan. Trainer: Dror Kashtan.
LVA: Andris Vaņins, Vitālijs Astafjevs (Cap), Oskars Kļava, Deniss Ivanovs, Deniss Kačanovs, Aleksandrs Cauņa (81.Jurijs Ž igajevs), Andrejs Rubins (81.Dzintars Zirnis), Ģirts Karlsons, Kaspars Gorkšs, Māris Verpakovskis (90+2.Andrejs Perepļotkins), Vladimirs Koļesničenko. Trainer: Aleksandrs Starkovs.
Goal: 0-1 Kaspars Gorkšs (59).
Cautions: Yuval Shpungin, Dekel Keinan / Māris Verpakovskis, Dzintars Zirnis.

05.09.2009, St. Jakob-Park Stadion, Basel; Attendance: 38,500
Referee: Frank De Bleeckere (Belgium)
SWITZERLAND - GREECE   **2-0(0-0)**
SUI: Diego Benaglio, Alain Nef (61.Eren Derdiyok), Steve Von Bergen, Stéphane Grichting, Ludovic Magnin, Gelson Tavares Fernandes (67.Hakan Yakin), Marco Padalino, Benjamin Huggel, Tranquillo Barnetta, Alexander Frei (Cap), Blaise Nkufo (81.Johan Vonlanthen). Trainer: Ottmar Hitzfeld (Germany).
GRE: Konstantinos Halkiás, Loukás Víntra, Evangélios Móras, Nikolaos Leonidas Spiropoulos, Sotírios Kyrgiakos, Konstantinos Katsouránis (Cap), Sokratís Papastathópoulos, Hrístos Patsatzoglou, Angelos Haristéas (73.Avraam Papadópoulos), Giánnis Amanatídis (81.Theofánis Gékas), Dimítris Salpingídis (46.Giórgos Samarás). Trainer: Otto Rehhagel (Germany).
Goals: 1-0 Stéphane Grichting (84), 2-0 Marco Padalino (87).
Cautions: Ludovic Magnin / Loukás Víntra, Sotírios Kyrgiakos, Nikolaos Leonidas Spiropoulos.
Sent off: Loukás Víntra (42).

09.09.2009, National Stadium, Ramat-Gan, Tel Aviv; Attendance: 7,038
Referee: Michael Svendsen (Denmark)
ISRAEL - LUXEMBOURG   **7-0(4-0)**
ISR: David Awat (46.Nir Davidovich), Tal Ben Haim, Avi Strool, Yoav David Ziv, David Ben Dayan, Aviram Baruchyan, Tamir Cohen, Baram Kayal, Yossi Benayoun (Cap), Elyaniv Barda (59.Ben Sahar), Omer Golan (67.Barak Itzhaki). Trainer: Dror Kashtan.
LUX: Marc Oberweis, Guy Blaise, Eric Hoffmann, Mathias Jänisch (51.Dan Collette), Kim Kintziger, Mario Mutsch, Gilles Bettmer, Claudio Lombardelli (62.Alphonse Leweck), Ben Payal (46.Joël Pedro), René Peters (Cap), Sergio Pupovac. Trainer: Guy Hellers.
Goals: 1-0 Elyaniv Barda (9), 2-0 Aviram Baruchyan (15), 3-0 Elyaniv Barda (21), 4-0 Elyaniv Barda (43), 5-0 Omer Golan (58), 6-0 Ben Sahar (62), 7-0 Ben Sahar (84).
Cautions: Omer Golan.

09.09.2009, Skonto Stadium, Riga; Attendance: 8,600
Referee: Pavel Kralovec (Czech Republic)
LATVIA - SWITZERLAND   **2-2(0-1)**
LVA: Andris Vaņins, Kaspars Gorkšs, Vitālijs Astafjevs (Cap), Vladimirs Koļesničenko (86.Maksims Rafaļskis), Oskars Kļava, Deniss Ivanovs, Deniss Kačanovs, Aleksandrs Cauņa (89.Dzintars Zirnis), Māris Verpakovskis, Andrejs Rubins, Ģirts Karlsons (85.Kristaps Grebis). Trainer: Aleksandrs Starkovs.
SUI: Diego Benaglio, Stephan Lichtsteiner, Steve Von Bergen, Stéphane Grichting, Christoph Spycher, Gelson Tavares Fernandes (79.Eren Derdiyok), Marco Padalino (76.Hakan Yakin), Benjamin Huggel, Tranquillo Barnetta (76.Johan Vonlanthen), Alexander Frei (Cap), Blaise Nkufo. Trainer: Ottmar Hitzfeld (Germany).
Goals: 0-1 Alexander Frei (43), 1-1 Aleksandrs Cauņa (62), 2-1 Vitālijs Astafjevs (75), 2-2 Eren Derdiyok (80).
Cautions: Deniss Ivanovs, Vitālijs Astafjevs, Vladimirs Koļesničenko / Stéphane Grichting.

09.09.2009, Baza Zimbru, Chişinău; Attendance: 9,870
Referee: Daniel Stålhammar (Sweden)
MOLDOVA - GREECE   **1-1(0-1)**
MDA: Stanislav Namaşco, Alexei Savinov (79.Valeriu Andronic), Serghei Laşcencov (Cap), Igor Armaş, Valeriu Catinsus, Victor Bulat, Serghei Namaşco (56.Victor Comlionoc), Alexandru Epureanu, Alexandru Găţcan, Denis Calincov, Igor Bugaiov (46.Veaceslav Sofroni). Trainer: Igor Dobrovolskiy (Russia).
GRE: Konstantinos Halkiás, Hrístos Patsatzoglou, Nikolaos Leonidas Spiropoulos, Evangélios Móras (58.Avraam Papadópoulos), Sotírios Kyrgiakos, Alexandros Tziólis, Konstantinos Katsouránis, Giórgos Karagoúnis (75.Giánnis Amanatídis), Angelos Haristéas (Cap), Giórgos Samarás, Theofánis Gékas. Trainer: Otto Rehhagel (Germany).
Goals: 0-1 Theofánis Gékas (33), 1-1 Valeriu Andronic (90).
Cautions: Alexandru Găţcan, Serghei Laşcencov / Alexandros Tziólis, Sotírios Kyrgiakos, Avraam Papadópoulos, Angelos Haristéas.

10.10.2009, Stade „Josy Barthel", Luxembourg; Attendance: 8,031
Referee: Eduardo Iturralde González (Spain)
LUXEMBOURG - SWITZERLAND   **0-3(0-3)**
LUX: Jonathan Joubert, Guy Blaise, Kim Kintziger, Tom Laterza (46.Alphonse Leweck), Jeff Strasser (Cap), Mario Mutsch, Gilles Bettmer, Joël Kitenge (59.Sergio Pupovac), Ben Payal, René Peters, Dan Collette (73.Mathias Jänisch). Trainer: Guy Hellers.
SUI: Diego Benaglio, Stephan Lichtsteiner, Steve Von Bergen, Philippe Senderos, Christoph Spycher, Gökhan Inler, Benjamin Huggel, Tranquillo Barnetta (82.Reto Ziegler), Johan Vonlanthen (65.Hakan Yakin), Alexander Frei (Cap) (65.Eren Derdiyok), Blaise Nkufo. Trainer: Ottmar Hitzfeld (Germany).
Goals: 0-1 Philippe Senderos (6), 0-2 Philippe Senderos (8), 0-3 Benjamin Huggel (22).

25

Cautions: Gilles Bettmer / Steve Von Bergen, Tranquillo Barnetta.

10.10.2009, National Stadium, Ramat-Gan, Tel Aviv; Attendance: 8,700
Referee: Kevin Blom (Holland)
ISRAEL - MOLDOVA   **3-1(1-0)**
ISR: David Awat, Tal Ben Haim, Avi Strool, Yoav David Ziv (29.Rahamin Saban), David Ben Dayan, Tamir Cohen, Gil Vermouth, Avihai Yadin, Yossi Benayoun (Cap), Elyaniv Barda (72.Roberto Damián Colautti), Ben Sahar (61.Itay Menachem Shechter). Trainer: Dror Kashtan.
MDA: Stanislav Namaşco, Alexei Savinov, Serghei Laşcencov, Victor Golovatenco, Alexandru Epureanu, Eugeniu Cebotaru (67.Valeriu Andronic), Valeriu Catinsus, Victor Bulat, Denis Calincov, Veaceslav Sofroni (79.Gheorghi Ovseannicov), Igor Bugaiov (74.Alexandr Suvorov). Trainer: Igor Dobrovolskiy (Russia).
Goals: 1-0 Elyaniv Barda (22), 2-0 David Ben Dayan (65), 3-0 Elyaniv Barda (70), 3-1 Denis Calincov (90+2).
Cautions: Tamir Cohen, David Ben Dayan, Ben Sahar / Victor Bulat, Igor Bugaiov.

10.10.2009, Olympiako „Spiros Louis" Stadio, Athína; Attendance: 18,981
Referee: Tom Henning Øvrebø (Norway)
GREECE - LATVIA   **5-2(1-2)**
GRE: Alexandros Tzórvas, Giórgos Seitarídis, Vasílis Torosídis, Evangélios Móras, Sokratís Papastathópoulos, Alexandros Tziólis (46.Hrístos Patsatzoglou), Konstantinos Katsouránis, Giórgos Karagoúnis (Cap) (89.Vasílis Pliátsikas), Dimítris Salpingídis (46.Giánnis Amanatídis), Giórgos Samarás, Theofánis Gékas. Trainer: Otto Rehhagel (Germany).
LVA: Andris Vaņins, Oskars Kļava, Kaspars Gorkšs (Cap), Vladimirs Koļesničenko, Juris Laizāns, Deniss Ivanovs, Deniss Kačanovs, Aleksandrs Cauņa, Māris Verpakovskis (84.Andrejs Perepļotkins), Andrejs Rubins (78.Genādijs Soloņicins), Ģirts Karlsons (71.Kristaps Grebis). Trainer: Aleksandrs Starkovs.
Goals: 1-0 Theofánis Gékas (4), 1-1 Māris Verpakovskis (12), 1-2 Māris Verpakovskis (40), 2-2 Theofánis Gékas (47 penalty), 3-2 Theofánis Gékas (57), 4-2 Giórgos Samarás (73), 5-2 Theofánis Gékas (90+1).
Cautions: Giórgos Samarás, Giórgos Seitarídis, Hrístos Patsatzoglou.

14.10.2009, Olympiako „Spiros Louis" Stadio, Athína; Attendance: 13,932
Referee: Darko Čeferin (Slovenia)
GREECE - LUXEMBOURG   **2-1(2-0)**
GRE: Mihális Sifákis, Sotírios Kyrgiakos (43.Evangélios Móras), Avraam Papadópoulos, Hrístos Patsatzoglou, Loukás Víntra (83.Sotírios Nínis), Nikolaos Leonidas Spiropoulos, Vasílis Torosídis, Giórgos Fotákis (46.Vasílis Pliátsikas), Giórgos Karagoúnis (Cap), Theofánis Gékas, Dimítris Salpingídis. Trainer: Otto Rehhagel (Germany).
LUX: Jonathan Joubert, Guy Blaise, Eric Hoffmann, Mathias Jänisch (46.Alphonse Leweck), (80.Massimo Martino), Mario Mutsch, Ben Payal, René Peters, Jeff Strasser (Cap), Gilles Bettmer, Joël Kitenge (73.Sergio Pupovac). Trainer: Guy Hellers.
Goals: 1-0 Vasílis Torosídis (30), 2-0 Theofánis Gékas (33), 2-1 Avraam Papadópoulos (90 own goal).
Cautions: Vasílis Pliátsikas / Ben Payal, Massimo Martino, Alphonse Leweck, Mario Mutsch.
Sent off: Ben Payal (58).

14.10.2009, Skonto Stadium, Riga; Attendance: 3,800
Referee: Jouni Hyytiä (Finland)
LATVIA - MOLDOVA   **3-2(2-1)**
LVA: Andris Vaņins, Oskars Kļava, Vitālijs Astafjevs (Cap), Kaspars Gorkšs, Vladimirs Koļesničenko (74.Juris Laizāns), Deniss Ivanovs, Deniss Kačanovs, Aleksandrs Cauņa, Māris Verpakovskis, Andrejs Rubins (63.Genādijs Soloņicins), Ģirts Karlsons (69.Kristaps Grebis). Trainer: Aleksandrs Starkovs.
MDA: Stanislav Namaşco, Alexei Savinov, Valeriu Catinsus, Victor Golovatenco, Serghei Laşcencov (Cap), Igor Armaş (81.Valeriu Andronic), Alexandru Epureanu, Serghei Namaşco, Denis Calincov,

26

Igor Bugaiov (70.Alexandr Suvorov), Gheorghi Ovseannicov (76.Veaceslav Sofroni). Trainer: Igor Dobrovolskiy (Russia).
Goals: 0-1 Gheorghe Ovseannicov (25), 1-1 Andrejs Rubins (32), 2-1 Andrejs Rubins (44), 3-1 Kristaps Grebis (76), 3-2 Veaceslav Sofroni (90).
Cautions: Ģirts Karlsons, Andrejs Rubins / Victor Golovatenco, Igor Armaş.
Sent off: Serghei Laşcencov (30).

14.10.2009, St. Jakob-Park, Basel; Attendance: 38,500
Referee: Alexandru Dan Tudor (Romania)
SWITZERLAND - ISRAEL 0-0
SUI: Marco Wölfli, Stephan Lichtsteiner, Philippe Senderos, Stéphane Grichting, Christoph Spycher (Cap), Gelson Tavares Fernandes, Marco Padalino, Gökhan Inler, Tranquillo Barnetta, Eren Derdiyok (69.Alexander Frei), Blaise Nkufo. Trainer: Ottmar Hitzfeld (Germany).
ISR: David Awat, Tal Ben Haim, Avi Strool, Rahamin Saban, Yoav David Ziv, Tamir Cohen, Baram Kayal, Avihai Yadin, Yossi Benayoun (Cap), Elyaniv Barda (85.Gil Vermouth), Roberto Damián Colautti (68.Itay Menachem Shechter). Trainer: Dror Kashtan.
Cautions: Marco Padalino, Gökhan Inler, Gelson Tavares Fernandes, Stephan Lichtsteiner / Avihai Yadin, Baram Kayal, Yoav David Ziv, Roberto Damián Colautti.
Sent off: Avihai Yadin (60).

GROUP 3

06.09.2008	Wrocław	Poland - Slovenia	1-1(1-1)
06.09.2008	Bratislava	Slovakia – Northern Ireland	2-1(0-0)
10.09.2008	Serravalle	San Marino - Poland	0-2(0-1)
10.09.2008	Belfast	Northern Ireland – Czech Republic	0-0
10.09.2008	Maribor	Slovenia - Slovakia	2-1(1-0)
11.10.2008	Chorzów	Poland – Czech Republic	2-1(1-0)
11.10.2008	Serravalle	San Marino - Slovakia	1-3(1-2)
11.10.2008	Maribor	Slovenia – Northern Ireland	2-0(0-0)
15.10.2008	Teplice	Czech Republic - Slovenia	1-0(0-0)
15.10.2008	Bratislava	Slovakia - Poland	2-1(0-0)
15.10.2008	Belfast	Northern Ireland – San Marino	4-0(2-0)
19.11.2008	Serravalle	San Marino – Czech Republic	0-3(0-0)
11.02.2009	Serravalle	San Marino – Northern Ireland	0-3(0-2)
28.03.2009	Belfast	Northern Ireland - Poland	3-2(1-1)
28.03.2009	Maribor	Slovenia – Czech Republic	0-0
01.04.2009	Praha	Czech Republic - Slovakia	1-2(1-1)
01.04.2009	Kielce	Poland – San Marino	10-0(4-0)
01.04.2009	Belfast	Northern Ireland - Slovenia	1-0(0-0)
06.06.2009	Bratislava	Slovakia – San Marino	7-0(5-0)
12.08.2009	Maribor	Slovenia – San Marino	5-0(2-0)
05.09.2009	Chorzów	Poland – Northern Ireland	1-1(0-1)
05.09.2009	Bratislava	Slovakia – Czech Republic	2-2(0-0)
09.09.2009	Uherské Hradiště	Czech Republic – San Marino	7-0(3-0)
09.09.2009	Belfast	Northern Ireland - Slovakia	0-2(0-1)
09.09.2009	Maribor	Slovenia - Poland	3-0(2-0)
10.10.2009	Praha	Czech Republic - Poland	2-0(0-0)
10.10.2009	Bratislava	Slovakia - Slovenia	0-2(0-0)
14.10.2009	Praha	Czech Republic – Northern Ireland	0-0
14.10.2009	Chorzów	Poland - Slovakia	0-1(0-0)
14.10.2009	Serravalle	San Marino - Slovenia	0-3(0-1)

FINAL STANDINGS

1.	SLOVAKIA	10	7	1	2	22	-	10	22
2.	Slovenia	10	6	2	2	18	-	4	20
3.	Czech Republic	10	4	4	2	17	-	6	16
4.	Northern Ireland	10	4	3	3	13	-	9	15
5.	Poland	10	3	2	5	19	-	14	11
6.	San Marino	10	0	0	10	1	-	47	0

Slovakia qualified for the Final Tournament; Slovenia qualified for the Play-Offs.

06.09.2008, Stadion Oporowska, Wrocław; Attendance7,300
Referee: Kristinn Jakobsson (Iceland)
POLAND - SLOVENIA **1-1(1-1)**
POL: Łukasz Fabiański, Marcin Wasilewski, Bartosz Bosacki (51.Mariusz Jop), Michał Żewłakow, Marcin Kowalczyk, Rafał Murawski (46.Tomasz Bandrowski), Mariusz Lewandowski, Jacek Krzynówek, Roger Guerreiro (73.Marek Saganowski), Jakub Błaszczykowski, Łukasz Piszczek. Trainer: Leo Beenhakker (Holland).
SVN: Samir Handanovič, Mišo Brečko, Marko Šuler, Boštjan Cesar, Branko Ilič, Mirnes Sead Šišič, Robert Koren (Cap), Zlatko Dedič (90+1.Darijan Matić), Andrej Komac (85.Anton Žlogar), Andraž Kirm (70.Valter Birsa), Milivoje Novakovič. Trainer: Matjaž Kek.

28

Goals: 1-0 Michał Żewł akow (17 penalty), 1-1 Zlatko Dedč (35).
Cautions: Marcin Kowalczyk, Marek Saganowski / Zlatko Dedič, Robert Koren, Andrej Komac, Mišo Brečko.

06.09.2008, Tehelné pole štadión, Bratislava; Attendance: 5,445
Referee: Nikolai Ivanov (Russia)
SLOVAKIA – NORTHERN IRELAND   **2-1(0-0)**
SVK: Štefan Senecký, Martin Škrteľ, Peter Pekarík, Martin Petráš, Ján Ďurica, Miroslav Karhan (Cap) (75.Radoslav Zabavník), Ján Kozák, Marek Sapara, Marek Hamšík, Martin Jakubko (59.Dušan Švento), Róbert Vittek (78.Marek Mintál). Trainer: Vladimír Weiss.
NIR: Maik Stefan Taylor, Christopher Patrick Baird (84.Dean Shiels), Jonathan Evans, Aaron William Hughes (Cap), Stephen James Craigan, George McCartney, Samuel Clingan, Steven Davis, Keith Robert Gillespie (53.Warren Feeney), David Jonathan Healy, Martin Andrew Paterson (66.Christopher Brunt). Manager: Nigel Worthington.
Goals: 1-0 Martin Škrteľ (46), 2-0 Marek Hamšik (70), 2-1 Ján Ďurica (81 own goal).
Cautions: Marek Hamšik / Keith Robert Gillespie, Jonathan Evans, Christopher Brunt.

10.09.2008, Stadio Olimpico, Serravalle; Attendance: 2,374
Referee: Christoforos Zográfos (Greece)
SAN MARINO - POLAND   **0-2(0-1)**
SMR: Aldo Simoncini (73.Federico Valentini), Carlo Valentini, Michele Marani, Nicola Albani, Davide Simoncini, Fabio Bollini (46.Damiano Vannucci), Matteo Bugli, Fabio Vitaioli, Maicol Berretti (80.Mauro Marani), Manuel Marani, Andy Selva (Cap). Trainer: Gian Paolo Mazza.
POL: Ł ukasz Fabiański, Grzegorz Wojtkowiak, Michał Żewł akow, Mariusz Jop, Marcin Kowalczyk (28.Jacek Krzynówek), Jakub Bł aszczykowski, MariuszLewandowski, Roger Guerreiro, Ł ukasz Piszczek (88.Rafał Murawski), Marek Saganowski, Euebiusz Smolarek (59.Robert Lewandowski). Trainer: Leo Beenhakker (Holland).
Goals: 0-1 Euzebiusz Smolarek (36), 1-1 Robert Lewandowski (67).
Cautions: Maicol Berretti, Davide Simoncini, Michele Marani, Mauro Marani.

10.09.2008, Windsor Park, Belfast; Attendance: 12,882
Referee: Ivan Bebek (Croatia)
NORTHERN IRELAND – CZECH REPUBLIC   **0-0**
NIR: Maik Stefan Taylor, Christopher Patrick Baird, Jonathan Evans, Aaron William Hughes (Cap), Stephen James Craigan, George McCartney, Samuel Clingan (46.Michael O'Connor), Christopher Brunt, Keith Robert Gillespie (83.Dean Shiels), Warren Feeney (72.Martin Andrew Paterson), David Jonathan Healy. Manager: Nigel Worthington.
CZE: Petr Čech, Zdeněk Grygera, Tomáš Ujfaluši (Cap), David Rozehnal, Marek Jankulovski, Radoslav Kováč, Libor Sionko (67.Zdeněk Pospěch), Jan Polák, Jaroslav Plašil, Radek Šírl, Milan Baroš (77.Mıroslav Slepička). Trainer: Petr Rada.
Cautions: Tomáš Ujfaluši, Radoslav Kováč.

10.09.2008, Stadion Ljudski vrt, Maribor; Attendance: 9,900
Referee: Svein Oddvar Moen (Norway)
SLOVENIA - SLOVAKIA   **2-1(1-0)**
SVN: Samir Handanovič, Mišo Brečko, Marko Šuler, Boštjan Cesar, Branko Ilič, Mirnes Sead Šišič (85.Anton Ž logar), Robert Koren (Cap), Zlatko Dedč (76.Zlatan Ljubijankič), Andrej Komac, Andraž Kirm (90.Darijan Matič), Milivoje Novakovič. Trainer: Matjaž Kek.
SVK: Štefan Senecký, Martin Škrteľ, Peter Pekarík, Martin Petráš, Ján Ďurica (78.Ján Kozák), Miroslav Karhan (Cap) (58.Martin Jakubko), Marek Sapara, Marek Hamšík, Zdeno Štrba, Filip Hološko (59.Dušan Švento), Róbert Vittek. Trainer: Vladimír Weiss.
Goals: 1-0 Milivoje Novakovič (22), 2-0 Milivoje Novakovič (82), 2-1 Martin Jakubko (83).
Cautions: Boštjan Cesar, Branko Ilič, Marko Šuler / Štefan Senecký, Ján Ďurica.

11.10.2008, Stadion Śląski, Chorzów; Attendance: 38,293
Referee: Wolfgang Stark (Germany)
POLAND – CZECH REPUBLIC   **2-1(1-0)**
POL: Artur Boruc, Jakub Wawrzyniak (43.Jacek Krzynówek), Marcin Wasilewski, Michał Żewł akow, Dariusz Dudka, Rafał Murawski (90+1.Tomasz Jodł owoję Jakub Bł aszczykowski, Mariusz Lewandowski, Euzebiusz Smolarek, Roger Guerreiro, Paweł Bróek (69.Robert Lewandowski). Trainer: Leo Beenhakker (Holland).
CZE: Petr Čech, Zdeněk Grygera (58.Libor Sionko), David Rozehnal, Tomáš Ujfaluši (Cap), Marek Jankulovski, Zdeněk Pospěch, Radoslav Kováč, Jaroslav Plašil, Radek Šírl, Miroslav Slepička (58.Václav Svěrkoš), Milan Baroš (81.Martin Fenin). Trainer: Petr Rada.
Goals: 1-0 Paweł Bróek (27), 2-0 Jakub Bł aszczykowski (53), 2-1 MartirFenin (87).
Cautions: Dariusz Dudka / Radoslav Kováč.

11.10.2008, Stadio Olimpico, Serravalle; Attendance: 1,037
Referee: Sascha Kever (Switzerland)
SAN MARINO - SLOVAKIA   **1-3(1-2)**
SMR: Aldo Simoncini, Carlo Valentini, Damiano Vannucci, Davide Simoncini (83.Matteo Vitaioli), Mauro Marani, Alessandro Della Valle, Maicol Berretti (71.Giovanni Bonini), Simone Bacciocchi (46.Nicola Albani), Michele Marani, Manuel Marani, Andy Selva (Cap). Trainer: Gian Paolo Mazza.
SVK: Ľuboš Kamenár, Martin Petráš, Matej Krajčík, Marek Čech, Roman Kratochvíl, Ján Kozák, Balázs Borbély (46.Miroslav Karhan), Stanislav Šesták (84.Peter Petráš), Róbert Vittek (Cap), Marek Mintál (81.Martin Jakubko), Erik Jendrišek. Trainer: Vladimír Weiss.
Goals: 0-1 Stanislav Šesták (33), 0-2 Ján Kozák (39), 1-2 Andy Selva (45), 1-3 Miroslav Karhan (50).
Cautions: Carlo Valentini, Maicol Berretti / Roman Kratochvíl, Peter Petráš.
Sent off: Roman Kratochvíl (73).

11.10.2008, Stadion Ljudski vrt, Maribor; Attendance: 12,385
Referee: Eduardo Ituralde González (Spain)
SLOVENIA – NORTHERN IRELAND   **2-0(0-0)**
SVN: Samir Handanovič, Mišo Brečko, Marko Šuler, Boštjan Cesar, Branko Ilič, Andrej Komac, Mirnes Sead Šišić (80.Valter Birsa), Robert Koren (Cap), Zlatko Dedič (68.Zlatan Ljubijankič), Andraž Kirm (89.Darijan Matić), Milivoje Novakovič. Trainer: Matjaž Kek.
NIR: Maik Stefan Taylor, Gareth McAuley, Aaron William Hughes (Cap), Jonathan Evans, George McCartney, Christopher Patrick Baird, Keith Robert Gillespie, Steven Davis, Grant Samuel McCann (72.Ryan McGivern), Kyle Ivanhoe Lafferty, David Jonathan Healy. Manager: Nigel Worthington.
Goals: 1-0 Milivoje Novakovič (83), 2-0 Zlatan Ljubijankič (84).
Cautions: Boštjan Cesar, Mirnes Sead Šišić, Andrej Komac, Andraž Kirm / Steven Davis, Kyle Ivanhoe Lafferty, Christopher Patrick Baird, George McCartney, Jonathan Evans.

15.10.2008, Na Stínadlech Stadion, Teplice; Attendance: 15,220
Referee: Martin Atkinson (England)
CZECH REPUBLIC - SLOVENIA   **1-0(0-0)**
CZE: Daniel Zitka, Zdeněk Pospěch, David Rozehnal, Tomáš Ujfaluši (Cap), Marek Jankulovski, Jan Rajnoch, Libor Sionko, David Jarolím (66.Radek Šírl), Jaroslav Plašil, Martin Fenin (81.Václav Svěrkoš), Milan Baroš (90+1.Jiří Kladrubský). Trainer: Petr Rada.
SVN: Samir Handanovič, Mišo Brečko (87.Aleš Mejač), Marko Šuler, Mitja Mörec, Branko Ilič, Mirnes Sead Šišić (65.Valter Birsa), Robert Koren (Cap), Aleksander Radosavljevič, Zlatko Dedič (79.Bojan Jokić), Andraž Kirm, Milivoje Novakovč. Trainer: Matjaž Kek.
Goal: 1-0 Libor Sionko (62).
Cautions: David Jarolím, Zdeněk Pospěch, Milan Baroš / Branko Ilič, Mišo Brečko, Marko Šuler.

15.10.2008, Tehelné pole štadión, Bratislava; Attendance: 17,650
Referee: Bertrand Layec (France)
SLOVAKIA - POLAND   **2-1(0-0)**
SVK: Štefan Senecký, Peter Pekarík, Martin Petráš, Ján Ďurica, Marek Čech, Radoslav Zabavník (83.Ján Kozák), Marek Sapara (73.Martin Jakubko), Stanislav Šesták, Marek Hamšík, Erik Jendrišek (80.Branislav Obž era), Róbert Vittek (Cap). Trainer Vladimír Weiss.
POL: Artur Boruc, Grzegorz Wojtkowiak, Dariusz Dudka, Michał Żewł akow (Cap), Marcin Wasilewski, Jakub Bł aszczykowski, Mariusz Lewandowski, Roger Guerreiro (89.Robert Lewandowski), Rafał Murawski (65.Ł ukasz Garguł a)aweł Brœk (84.Jacek Krzynówek), Euzebiusz Smolarek. Trainer: Leo Beenhakker (Holland).
Goals: 0-1 Euzebiusz Smolarek (70), 1-1 Stanislav Šesták (84), 2-1 Stanislav Šesták (86).
Cautions: Radoslav Zabavník, Branislav Obž era / Grzegorz Wojtkowiak.

15.10.2008, Windsor Park, Belfast; Attendance: 12,957
Referee: Petteri Kari (Finland)
NORTHERN IRELAND – SAN MARINO   **4-0(2-0)**
NIR: Maik Stefan Taylor, Gareth McAuley (61.Ryan McGivern), George McCartney, Aaron William Hughes (Cap), Christopher Patrick Baird, Michael O'Connor, Keith Robert Gillespie, Steven Davis, Grant Samuel McCann (73.Martin Andrew Paterson), David Jonathan Healy, Kyle Ivanhoe Lafferty (82.Warren Feeney). Manager: Nigel Worthington.
SMR: Federico Valentini, Carlo Valentini, Mauro Marani, Nicola Albani, Damiano Vannucci, Alessandro Della Valle, Simone Bacciocchi, Giovanni Bonini (77.Fabio Vitaioli), Michele Marani, Manuel Marani (86.Enrico Cibelli), Andy Selva (Cap) (46.Matteo Vitaioli). Trainer: Gian Paolo Mazza.
Goals: 1-0 David Jonathan Healy (31), 2-0 Grant Samuel McCann (43), 3-0 Kyle Ivanhoe Lafferty (56), 4-0 Steven Davis (75).
Cautions: Gareth McAuley, Ryan McGivern / Alessandro Della Valle, Carlo Valentini.
Sent off: Mauro Marani (63).

19.11.2008, Stadio Olimpico, Serravalle; Attendance: 1,318
Referee: Hannes Kaasik (Estonia)
SAN MARINO – CZECH REPUBLIC   **0-3(0-0)**
SMR: Aldo Simoncini, Michele Marani (81.Enrico Cibelli), Damiano Vannucci, Davide Simoncini, Alessandro Della Valle, Simone Bacciocchi, Maicol Berretti, Riccardo Muccioli (70.Matteo Andreini), Manuel Marani, Matteo Vitaioli (88.Danilo Ezequiel Rinaldi), Giovanni Bonini. Trainer: Gian Paolo Mazza.
CZE: Daniel Zitka, Zdeněk Pospěch, David Rozehnal, Tomáš Ujfaluši (Cap), Marek Jankulovski, Libor Sionko, Radoslav Kováč, Jan Polák (70.David Jarolím), Radek Šírl, Milan Baroš (81.Roman Bednář), Martin Fenin (66.Tomáš Necid). Trainer: Petr Rada.
Goals: 0-1 Radoslav Kováč (47), 0-2 Zdeněk Pospěch (53), 0-3 Tomáš Necid (83).
Cautions: Damiano Vannucci / Martin Fenin.

11.02.2009, Stadio Olimpico, Serravalle; Attendance: 1,942
Referee: Dragomir Stanković (Serbia)
SAN MARINO – NORTHERN IRELAND   **0-3(0-2)**
SMR: Federico Valentini, Carlo Valentini, Damiano Vannucci (Cap), Davide Simoncini, Alessandro Della Valle, Simone Bacciocchi (79.Fabio Vitaioli), Maicol Berretti, Riccardo Muccioli (67.Matteo Bugli), Manuel Marani, Matteo Vitaioli (86.Marco Casadei), Michele Marani. Trainer: Gian Paolo Mazza.
NIR: Maik Stefan Taylor, Gareth McAuley, George McCartney, Aaron William Hughes (Cap) (80.Patrick McCourt), Stephen James Craigan, Steven Davis, Damien Michael Johnson, Grant Samuel McCann, Martin Andrew Paterson (77.Warren Feeney), David Jonathan Healy, Kyle Ivanhoe Lafferty (55.Christopher Brunt). Manager: Nigel Worthington.
Goals: 1-0 Gareth McAuley (5), 2-0 Grant Samuel McCann (32), 3-0 Christopher Brunt (63).

Cautions: Riccardo Muccioli, Manuel Marani / Kyle Ivanhoe Lafferty, Steven Davis, George McCartney.
Sent off: Manuel Marani (69).

28.03.2009, Windsor Park, Belfast; Attendance: 13,357
Referee: Martin Hansson (Sweden)
NORTHERN IRELAND - POLAND   **3-2(1-1)**
NIR: Maik Stefan Taylor, Gareth McAuley, Jonathan Evans, Aaron William Hughes, Stephen James Craigan, Samuel Clingan, Damien Michael Johnson (Cap), Grant Samuel McCann, Christopher Brunt. Warren Feeney (84.Christopher Patrick Baird), David Jonathan Healy (90+2.Andrew Little). Manager: Nigel Worthington.
POL: Artur Boruc, Michał Żewł akow (65.Bartosz Bosacki), Jakub Wawrzyniak, Dariusz Dudka, Marcin Wasilewski, Jacek Krzynówek, Roger Guerreiro, Tomasz Bandrowski (60.Jakub Bł aszczykowski), Robert Lewandowski, Mariusz Lewandwski, Ireneusz Jeleń (71.Marek Saganowski). Trainer: Leo Beenhakker (Holland).
Goals: 1-0 Warren Feeney (10), 1-1 (27), 2-1 Jonathan Evans (47), 3-1 Michał Żewł akow (61 own goal), 3-2 (90+1).
Cautions: Christopher Brunt / Roger Guerreiro, Marcin Wasilewski, Jacek Krzynówek.

28.03.2009, Stadion Ljudski vrt, Maribor; Attendance: 15,200
Referee: Pedro Proença Oliveira Alves Garcia (Portugal)
SLOVENIA – CZECH REPUBLIC   **0-0**
SVN: Jasmin Handanovič, Suad Filekovič, Matej Mavrič, Boštjan Cesar, Mirnes Sead Šišić (86.Anton Ž logar), Andrej Komac (84.Aleš Mejač), Robert Koren (Cap), Bojan Jokić, Zlatko Dedič (67.Zlatan Ljubijankič), Andraž Kirm, Milivoje Novakovč. Trainer: Matjaž Kek.
CZE: Petr Čech, Zdeněk Grygera, Tomáš Ujfaluši (Cap), David Rozehnal, Marek Jankulovski, Libor Sionko, Jaroslav Plašil, Jan Polák, Radek Šírl (76.Michal Kadlec), Václav Svěrkoš (79.Tomáš Necid), Milan Baroš (90.Martin Fenin). Trainer: Petr Rada.
Cautions: Mirnes Sead Šišić / David Rozehnal, Tomáš Ujfaluši.

01.04.2009, AXA Arena, Praha; Attendance: 14,956
Referee: Alberto Undiano Mallenco (Spain)
CZECH REPUBLIC - SLOVAKIA   **1-2(1-1)**
CZE: Petr Čech (Cap), Zdeněk Grygera, Radoslav Kováč (72.Zdeněk Pospěch), David Rozehnal, Marek Jankulovski, Jan Polák, Libor Sionko (84.David Lafata), Jaroslav Plašil, David Jarolím, Tomáš Necid (79.Martin Fenin), Milan Baroš. Trainer: Petr Rada.
SVK: Ján Mucha, Martin Škrteľ, Ján Ďurica, Peter Pekarík, Radoslav Zabavník, Miroslav Karhan (Cap), Zdeno Štrba, Marek Hamšík (86.Marek Sapara), Filip Hološko, Stanislav Šesták (74.Miroslav Stoch), Erik Jendrišek (89.Róbert Vittek). Trainer: Vladimír Weiss.
Goals: 0-1 Stanislav Šesták (22), 1-1 Marek Jankulovski (30), 1-2 Erik Jendrišek (82).
Cautions: Martin Škrteľ, Zdeno Štrba, Stanislav Šesták.

01.04.2009, Arena Kielc, Kielce; Attendance: 15,200
Referee: Alexey Kulbakov (Belarus)
POLAND – SAN MARINO   **10-0(4-0)**
POL: Ł ukasz Fabiański, Jacek Krzynówek, Dariusz Dudka, Bartosz Bosacki, Marcin Wasilewski, Euzebiusz Smolarek, Ireneusz Jeleń (71.Jakub Bł aszczykowski), Roger Guerreiro, RafałBoguski (80.Marek Saganowski), Mariusz Lewandowski, Robert Lewandowski (65.Ł ukasz Sosin). Trainer: Leo Beenhakker (Holland).
SMR: Federico Valentini, Nicola Albani, Davide Simoncini, Alessandro Della Valle, Simone Bacciocchi (Cap), Matteo Bugli, Matteo Vitaioli (64.Maicol Berretti), Danilo Ezequiel Rinaldi, Matteo Andreini (82.Damiano Vannucci), Michele Marani, Giovanni Bonini (53.Andy Selva). Trainer: Gian Paolo Mazza.
Goals: 1-0 Rafał Boguski (1), 2-0 Euzebiusz Smolarek (1), 3-0 Rafał Boguski (27), 4-0 Robert

Lewandowski (43), 5-0 Ireneusz Jeleń (51), 6-0 Euzebiusz Smolarek (60), 7-0 Mariusz Lewandowski (63), 8-0 Euzebiusz Smolarek (72), 9-0 Euzebiusz Smolarek (81), 10-0 Marek Saganowski (88).
Cautions: Alessandro Della Valle, Simone Bacciocchi, Andy Selva.

01.04.2009, Windsor Park, Belfast; Attendance: 13,243
Referee: Alon Yefet (Israel)
NORTHERN IRELAND - SLOVENIA   **1-0(0-0)**
NIR: Maik Stefan Taylor, Gareth McAuley (15.Christopher Patrick Baird), Jonathan Evans, Aaron William Hughes (Cap), George McCartney (46.Ryan McGivern), Samuel Clingan, Steven Davis, Damien Michael Johnson, Grant Samuel McCann, Warren Feeney, David Jonathan Healy. Manager: Nigel Worthington.
SVN: Jasmin Handanovič, Mišo Brečko (84.Aleš Mejač), Suad Filekovič, Boštjan Cesar, Matej Mavrič, Andrej Komac, Robert Koren (Cap), Bojan Jokić, Zlatko Dedič (64.Zlatan Ljubijankič), Andraž Kirm (77.Nejc Pečnik), Milivoje Novakovič. Trainer: Matjaž Kek.
Goal: 1-0 Warren Feeney (73).
Cautions: George McCartney, Jonathan Evans, Warren Feeney, Christopher Patrick Baird / Zlatko Dedič, Suad Filekovič.

06.06.2009, Tehelné pole štadion, Bratislava; Attendance: 6,652
Referee: Jérôme Efong Nzolo (Belgium)
SLOVAKIA – SAN MARINO   **7-0(5-0)**
SVK: Ján Mucha, Ján Ďurica (46.Kornel Saláta), Peter Pekarík, Marek Čech, Ľuboš Hanzel, Miroslav Karhan (Cap), Ján Kozák, Marek Hamšík (46.Ján Novák), Martin Jakubko, Miroslav Stoch (62.Balázs Borbély), Róbert Vittek. Trainer: Vladimír Weiss.
SMR: Aldo Simoncini, Michele Marani (85.Giovanni Bonini), Damiano Vannucci, Davide Simoncini, Mauro Marani, Simone Bacciocchi, Fabio Vitaioli, Danilo Ezequiel Rinaldi (64.Nicola Ciacci), Maicol Berretti (78.Matteo Andreini), Matteo Bugli, Andy Selva. Trainer: Gian Paolo Mazza.
Goals: 1-0 Marek Čech (3), 2-0 Peter Pekarík (12), 3-0 Marek Čech (32), 4-0 Miroslav Stoch (35), 5-0 Ján Kozák (42), 6-0 Martin Jakubko (63), 7-0 Ľuboš Hanzel (68).
Cautions: Ľuboš Hanzel, Miroslav Stoch / Michele Marani, Matteo Andreini, Mauro Marani.

12.08.2009, Stadion Ljudski vrt, Maribor; Attendance: 4,400
Referee: Dimitar Meckarovski (Macedonia)
SLOVENIA – SAN MARINO   **5-0(2-0)**
SVN: Samir Handanovič, Mišo Brečko, Boštjan Cesar, Marko Šuler, Aleksander Radosavljevič (74.Armin Bačinović), Bojan Jokić, Robert Koren (Cap), Valter Birsa, Zlatan Ljubijankič, Nejc Pečnik (46.Andraž Kirm), Etien Velikonja (72.Milivoje Novakovič). Trainer: Matjaž Kek.
SMR: Aldo Simoncini, Davide Simoncini, Damiano Vannucci (Cap) (66.Nicola Albani), Simone Bacciocchi, Alessandro Della Valle, Fabio Vitaioli (59.Matteo Vitaioli), Nicola Ciacci, Matteo Bugli, Manuel Marani (80.Giovanni Bonini), Maicol Berretti, Matteo Andreini. Trainer: Gian Paolo Mazza.
Goals: 1-0 Robert Koren (19), 2-0 Aleksandar Radosavljevič (39), 3-0 Andraž Kirm (54), 4-0 Robert Koren (74), 5-0 Zlatan Ljubijankič (90+3).
Cautions: Davide Simoncini, Aldo Simoncini, Matteo Bugli.

05.09.2009, Stadion Śląski, Chorzów; Attendance: 38,914
Referee: Manuel Enrique Mejuto González (Spain)
POLAND – NORTHERN IRELAND   **1-1(0-1)**
POL: Artur Boruc, Michał Żewłakow, Dariusz Dudka, Paweł Golski, Jacek Krzynówek, Rafał Murawski (61.Robert Lewandowski), Jakub Błaszczykowski, Roger Guerreiro, Ludovic Obraniak (46.Euzebiusz Smolarek), Mariusz Lewandowski, Paweł Brożek. Trainer: Leo Beenhakker (Holland).
NIR: Maik Stefan Taylor, Gareth McAuley, Aaron William Hughes, Jonathan Evans, Stephen James Craigan, Samuel Clingan, Steven Davies, Damien Michael Johnson, Grant Samuel McCann, David Jonathan Healy, Kyle Ivanhoe Lafferty (54.Martin Andrew Paterson). Manager: Nigel Worthington.
Goals: 0-1 Kyle Ivanhoe Lafferty (38), 1-1 Mariusz Lewandowski (80).

33

Cautions: Paweł Golánski.

05.09.2009, Tehelné pole Stadion, Bratislava; Attendance: 23,800
Referee: Tom Henning Øvrebø (Norway)
SLOVAKIA – CZECH REPUBLIC   **2-2(0-0)**
SVK: Ján Mucha, Martin Škrteľ, Ján Ďurica, Peter Pekarík, Radoslav Zabavník, Zdeno Štrba, Vladimír Weiss (73.Marek Sapara), Marek Hamšík, Filip Hološko (87.Erik Jendrišek), Stanislav Šesták (82.Marek Čech), Róbert Vittek (Cap). Trainer: Vladimír Weiss.
CZE: Petr Čech (Cap), Zdeněk Grygera, Tomáš Sivok, Michal Kadlec, Marek Jankulovski, Tomáš Hübschman, Jiří Štajner (83.Václav Svěrkoš), David Jarolím (65.Tomáš Necid), Jaroslav Plašil, Daniel Pudil, Jan Koller (55.Milan Baroš). Trainer: Ivan Hašek.
Goals: 1-0 Stanislav Šesták (59), 1-1 Daniel Pudil (68), 2-1 Marek Hamšik (73 penalty), 2-2 Milan Baroš (83).
Cautions: Marek Hamšik / Zdeněk Grygera.
Sent off: Marek Hamšik (75).

09.09.2009, Městský fotbalový stadion, Uherské Hradiště; Attendance: 8,121
Referee: Arman Amirkhanyan (Armenia)
CZECH REPUBLIC – SAN MARINO   **7-0(3-0)**
CZE: Petr Čech (Cap), Zdeněk Grygera (77.Jiří Štajner), Roman Hubník, David Rozehnal, Michal Kadlec (46.Daniel Pudil), Tomáš Hübschman, Tomáš Rosický (56.David Jarolím), Jaroslav Plašil, Václav Svěrkoš, Tomáš Necid, Milan Baroš. Trainer: Ivan Hašek.
SMR: Aldo Simoncini, Damiano Vannucci, Simone Bacciocchi, Alessandro Della Valle, Fabio Vitaioli, Mauro Marani (65.Giovanni Bonini), Nicola Ciacci (75.Matteo Vitaioli), Matteo Bugli (89.Michele Cervellini), Maicol Berretti, Matteo Andreini, Andy Selva (Cap). Trainer: Gian Paolo Mazza.
Goals: 1-0 Milan Baroš (28), 2-0 Milan Baroš (44), 3-0 Milan Baroš (45+3 penalty), 4-0 Václav Svěrkoš (47), 5-0 Milan Baroš (66), 6-0 Tomáš Necid (86), 7-0 Václav Svěrkoš (90+4).
Cautions: Daniel Pudil / Alessandro Della Valle, Maicol Berretti, Fabio Vitaioli, Simone Bacciocchi, Mauro Marani, Damiano Vannucci.
Sent off: Simone Bacciocchi (83).

09.09.2009, Windsor Park, Belfast; Attendance: 13,019
Referee: Björn Kuipers (Holland)
NORTHERN IRELAND - SLOVAKIA   **0-2(0-1)**
NIR: Maik Stefan Taylor, Gareth McAuley, Aaron William Hughes (Cap), Jonathan Evans, Stephen James Craigan, Samuel Clingan (70.Christopher Patrick Baird), Steven Davies, Damien Michael Johnson, Grant Samuel McCann (70.Niall McGinn), David Jonathan Healy, Martin Andrew Paterson (76.Christopher Brunt). Manager: Nigel Worthington.
SVK: Ján Mucha, Martin Škrteľ, Ján Ďurica, Peter Pekarík, Radoslav Zabavník, Kamil Kopúnek, Zdeno Štrba, Vladimír Weiss (90+1.Marek Sapara), Stanislav Šesták (65.Filip Hološko), Miroslav Stoch (80.Erik Jendrišek), Róbert Vittek (Cap). Trainer: Vladimír Weiss.
Goals: 0-1 Stanislav Šesták (15), 0-2 Filip Hološko (67).
Cautions: Samuel Clingan, David Jonathan Healy / Stanislav Šesták.

09.09.2009, Stadion Ljudski vrt, Maribor; Attendance: 10,226
Referee: William Collum (Scotland)
SLOVENIA - POLAND   **3-0(2-0)**
SVN: Samir Handanovič, Mišo Brečko, Marko Šuler, Matej Mavrič, Bojan Jokić, Aleksander Radosavljevič (89.Nejc Pečnik), Robert Koren (Cap), Valter Birsa (71.Andrej Komac), Zlatko Dedič (58.Zlatan Ljubijankič), Andraž Kirm, Milivoje Novakovč. Trainer: Matjaž Kek.
POL: Artur Boruc, Michał Żewł akow, Dariusz Dudka, Bartosz Bosacki, Seweryn Gacarczyk (61.Euzebiusz Smolarek), Jacek Krzynówek, Jakub Bł szczykowski, Roger Guerreiro, Ludovic Obraniak (46.Wojciech Ł obodziński), Mariusz Lewandowski, Paweł Brȯek (61.Robert

34

Lewandowski). Trainer: Leo Beenhakker (Holland).
Goals: 1-0 Zlatko Dedič (13), 2-0 Milivoje Novakovič (44), 3-0 Valter Birsa (62).
Cautions: Zlatko Dedič, Mišo Brečko / Jakub Bł aszczykowski, Ludovic Obraniak.

10.10.2009, AXA Arena, Praha; Attendance: 14,010
Referee: Claus Bo Larsen (Denmark)
CZECH REPUBLIC - POLAND   **2-0(0-0)**
CZE: Petr Čech, Roman Hubník, Tomáš Hübschman, Zdeněk Pospěch, Marek Jankulovski, Tomáš Sivok, Jaroslav Plašil, Daniel Pudil (87.Jiří Štajner), Tomáš Rosický (78.David Jarolím), Milan Baroš, Michal Papadopulos (46.Tomáš Necid). Trainer: Ivan Hašek.
POL: Wojciech Kowalewski, Jakub Rzeźniczak, Arkadiusz Gł owacki, Piotr Polczak, Seweryn Gancarczyk, Jakub Bł aszczykowski (67.Sł awomir Peszk, Mariusz Lewandowski, Maciej Iwański, Ludovic Obraniak, Ireneusz Jeleń (63.Robert Lewandowski), Kamil Grosicki (81.Dawid Janczyk). Trainer: Stefan Majewski.
Goals: 1-0 Tomáš Necid (51), 2-0 Jaroslav Plašil (72).
Cautions: Marek Jankulovski, Tomáš Necid / Piotr Polczak, Maciej Iwański, Arkadiusz Gł owacki.

10.10.2009, Tehelné pole štadion, Bratislava; Attendance: 23,800
Referee: Wolfgang Stark (Germany)
SLOVAKIA - SLOVENIA   **0-2(0-0)**
SVK: Ján Mucha, Martin Škrteľ, Ján Ďurica, Peter Pekarík, Radoslav Zabavník, Zdeno Štrba (84.Ján Novák), Vladimír Weiss, Marek Hamšík, Martin Jakubko (46.Miroslav Karhan), Miroslav Stoch, Róbert Vittek (Cap) (80.Erik Jendrišek). Trainer: Vladimír Weiss.
SVN: Samir Handanovič, Mišo Brečko, Marko Šuler, Boštjan Cesar, Bojan Jokić, Aleksander Radosavljevič, Robert Koren (Cap), Valter Birsa (89.Dalibor Stevanović), Zlatko Dedič (78.Nejc Pečnik), Andraž Kirm, Milivoje Novakovč. Trainer: Matjaž Kek.
Goals: 0-1 Valter Birsa (56), 0-2 Nejc Pečnik (90+3).
Cautions: Miroslav Stoch, Ján Ďurica, Vladimír Weiss, Radoslav Zabavník, Martin Škrteľ / Robert Koren.

14.10.2009, AXA Arena, Praha; Attendance: 8,002
Referee: Laurent Duhamel (France)
CZECH REPUBLIC – NORTHERN IRELAND   **0-0**
CZE: Petr Čech, Zdeněk Pospěch, Tomáš Hübschman, Roman Hubník, Marek Jankulovski, David Jarolím (83.Michal Papadopulos), Tomáš Sivok, Tomáš Rosický (72.Jiří Štajner), Jaroslav Plašil, Tomáš Necid (59.Adam Hloušek), Milan Baroš. Trainer: Ivan Hašek.
NIR: Maik Stefan Taylor, Gareth McAuley, Aaron William Hughes (Cap), Ryan McGivern, Stephen James Craigan, Christopher Patrick Baird, Steven Davies, Damien Michael Johnson (83.Andrew Kirk), Grant Samuel McCann (80.Michael O'Connor), Niall McGinn, David Jonathan Healy (69.Warren Feeney). Manager: Nigel Worthington.
Cautions: Milan Baroš / Warren Feeney.

14.10.2009, Stadion Śląski, Chorzów; Attendance: 4,500
Referee: Jonas Eriksson (Sweden)
POLAND - SLOVAKIA   **0-1(0-1)**
POL: Jerzy Dudek, Jakub Rzeźniczak, Arkadiusz Gł owacki, Jarosł aw Bieniuk, Sewȩr Gancarczyk, Jakub Bł aszczykowski, Mariusz Lewandowski, Roger Gȩrreiro (60.Sł awomir Peszko), Ludovic Obraniak, Ireneusz Jeleń (68.Robert Lewandowski), Paweł Broek (86.Dawid Janczyk). Trainer: Stefan Majewski.
SVK: Ján Mucha, Martin Petráš, Kornel Saláta, Peter Pekarík, Kamil Kopúnek, Ján Kozák (85.Miroslav Karhan), Zdeno Štrba, Vladimír Weiss (65.Ján Novák), Marek Hamšík (Cap), Stanislav Šesták (74.Dušan Švento), Erik Jendrišek. Trainer: Vladimír Weiss.
Goal: 0-1 Seweryn Gancarczyk (3 own goal).
Cautions: Vladimír Weiss.

14.10.2009, Stadio Olimpico, Serravalle; Attendance: 1,745
Referee: Zsolt Szabó (Hungary)
SAN MARINO - SLOVENIA   **0-3(0-1)**
SMR: Aldo Simoncini, Carlo Valentini (77.Michele Cervellini), Davide Simoncini, Michele Marani, Fabio Vitaioli, Manuel Marani, Mauro Marani, Matteo Vitaioli, Nicola Albani, Maicol Berretti (45+1.Matteo Bugli), Andy Selva (Cap) (62.Danilo Ezequiel Rinaldi). Trainer: Gian Paolo Mazza.
SVN: Samir Handanovič, Mišo Brečko (85.Branko Ilič), Marko Šuler, Boštjan Cesar, Bojan Jokić, Aleksander Radosavljevič, Valter Birsa, Zlatko Dedič (51.Zlatan Ljubijankič), Dalibor Stevanovič (85.Rene Krhin), Andraž Kirm, Milivoje Novakovč (Cap). Trainer: Matjaž Kek.
Goals: 0-1 Milivoje Novakovič (24), 0-2 Dalibor Stevanovič (68), 0-3 Marko Šuler (81).
Cautions: Manuel Marani, Maicol Berretti, Matteo Bugli, Matteo Vitaioli, Nicola Albani / Dalibor Stevanovič.

GROUP 4

06.09.2008	Cardiff	Wales - Azerbaijan	1-0(0-0)
06.09.2008	Vaduz	Liechtenstein - Germany	0-6(0-1)
10.09.2008	Moskva	Russia - Wales	2-1(1-0)
10.09.2008	Baki	Azerbaijan - Liechtenstein	0-0
10.09.2008	Helsinki	Finland - Germany	3-3(2-2)
11.10.2008	Helsinki	Finland - Azerbaijan	1-0(0-0)
11.10.2008	Cardiff	Wales - Liechtenstein	2-0(1-0)
11.10.2008	Dortmund	Germany - Russia	2-1(2-0)
15.10.2008	Moskva	Russia - Finland	3-0(1-0)
15.10.2008	Mönchengladbach	Germany - Wales	1-0(0-0)
28.03.2009	Moskva	Russia - Azerbaijan	2-0(1-0)
28.03.2009	Cardiff	Wales - Finland	0-2(0-1)
28.03.2009	Leipzig	Germany - Liechtenstein	4-0(2-0)
01.04.2009	Vaduz	Liechtenstein - Russia	0-1(0-1)
01.04.2009	Cardiff	Wales - Germany	0-2(0-1)
06.06.2009	Baki	Azerbaijan - Wales	0-1(0-1)
06.06.2009	Helsinki	Finland - Liechtenstein	2-1(1-1)
10.06.2009	Helsinki	Finland - Russia	0-3(0-1)
12.08.2009	Baki	Azerbaijan - Germany	0-2(0-1)
05.09.2009	Länkäran	Azerbaijan - Finland	1-2(0-0)
05.09.2009	St. Petersburg	Russia - Liechtenstein	3-0(3-0)
09.09.2009	Vaduz	Liechtenstein - Finland	1-1(0-0)
09.09.2009	Hannover	Germany - Azerbaijan	4-0(1-0)
09.09.2009	Cardiff	Wales - Russia	1-3(0-1)
10.10.2009	Helsinki	Finland - Wales	2-1(1-1)
10.10.2009	Moskva	Russia - Germany	0-1(0-1)
10.10.2009	Vaduz	Liechtenstein - Azerbaijan	0-2(0-0)
14.10.2009	Baki	Azerbaijan - Russia	1-1(0-1)
14.10.2009	Hamburg	Germany – Finland	1-1(0-1)
14.10.2009	Vaduz	Liechtenstein - Wales	0-2(0-1)

FINAL STANDINGS

1.	**GERMANY**	10	8	2	0	26	-	5	26
2.	**Russia**	10	7	1	2	19	-	6	22
3.	Finland	10	5	3	2	14	-	14	18
4.	Wales	10	4	0	6	9	-	12	12
5.	Azerbaijan	10	1	2	7	4	-	14	5
6.	Liechtenstein	10	0	2	8	2	-	23	2

Germany qualified for the Final Tournament; Russia qualified for the Play-Offs.

06.09.2008, Millennium Stadium, Cardiff; Attendance: 17,106
Referee: Aleksandar Stavrev (Macedonia)
WALES - AZERBAIJAN   **1-0(0-0)**
WAL: Wayne Robert Hennessey, Christopher Ross Gunter, Ashley Errol Williams, Gareth Frank Bale, Craig Morgan, Carl Neil Fletcher, Simon Davies (Cap), Jason Koumas (88.Carl Phillip Robinson), Joseph Christopher Ledley, Robert Earnshaw (62.Chedwyn Michael Evans), David Alexander Edwards (72.Samuel Michael Vokes). Manager: John Benjamin Toshack.
AZE: Kamran Agayev, Rail Melikov, Rashad Ferhad Sadygov (Cap), Saša Yunisoğlu, Fabio Luis Ramin, Nodar Mamedov (77.Usim Nduka), Elmar Bakhshiyev, Samir Abbasov, Elvin Mamedov, Dzhavid Huseynov (46.Agil Nabiyev), Branimir Subašić. Trainer: Hans-Hubert Vogts (Germany).

37

Goal: 1-0 Samuel Michael Vokes (83).
Cautions: Gareth Frank Bale, Jason Koumas / Elmar Bakhshiyev, Fábio Luís Ramim, Rashad Ferhad Sadygov, Samir Abbasov, Kamran Agayev.
Sent off: Fábio Luís Ramim (68).

06.09.2008, Rheinpark Stadion, Vaduz; Attendance: 7,842
Referee: Duarte Nuno Pereira Gomes (Portugal)
LIECHTENSTEIN - GERMANY   **0-6(0-1)**
LIE: Peter Jehle, Fabio D'Elia, Martin Stocklasa, Andreas Gerster, Franz Burgmeier, Marco Ritzberger, Martin Büchel, Michele Polverino (64.Raphael Rohrer), Mathias Christen (74.Thomas Beck), Benjamin Fischer (87.Ronny Büchel), Mario Frick. Trainer: Hans-Petter Zaugg.
GER: Robert Enke, Clemens Fritz, Serdar Tasci, Heiko Westermann, Philipp Lahm, Bastian Schweinsteiger, Simon Rolfes (69.Marko Marin), Thomas Hitzlsperger, Piotr Trochowski, Miroslav Klose (Cap) (65.Mario Gómez), Lukas Podolski (76.Kevin Dennis Kurányi). Trainer: Joachim Löw.
Goals: 0-1 Lukas Podolski (21), 0-2 Lukas Podolski (48), 0-3 Simon Rolfes (65), 0-4 Bastian Schweinsteiger (66), 0-5 Thomas Hitzlsperger (76), 0-6 Heiko Westermann (87).
Cautions: Franz Burgmeier, Fabio D'Elia.

10.09.2008, Lokomotiv Stadium, Moskva; Attendance: 28,000
Referee: Damir Skomina (Slovenia)
RUSSIA - WALES   **2-1(1-0)**
RUS: Igor Akinfeyev, Aleksandr Anyukov, Denis Kolodin, Sergey Ignashevich, Yuriy Zhirkov, Konstantin Zyryanov, Dmitriy Torbinskiy (59.Ivan Saenko), Igor Semshov, Sergey Semak (Cap) (74.Pavel Pogrebnyak), Andrey Arshavin, Roman Pavlyuchenko (90+3.Vladimir Bystrov). Trainer: Guus Hiddink (Holland).
WAL: Wayne Robert Hennessey, Christopher Ross Gunter, Ashley Errol Williams, Gareth Frank Bale, Craig Morgan, Carl Neil Fletcher, Simon Davies (Cap), Carl Phillip Robinson (46.Samuel Ricketts), Joseph Christopher Ledley, David Alexander Edwards (77.Steven Evans), Samuel Michael Vokes (62.Chedwyn Michael Evans). Manager: John Benjamin Toshack.
Goals: 1-0 Roman Pavlyuchenko (22 penalty), 1-1 Joseph Christopher Ledley (67), 2-1 Pavel Pogrebnyak (81).
Cautions: Carl Phillip Robinson, Ashley Errol Williams, David Alexander Edwards, Samuel Ricketts.

10.09.2008, Tofik Bahramov" Stadium, Baku; Attendance: 25,000
Referee: Tsvetan Georgiev (Bulgaria)
AZERBAIJAN - LIECHTENSTEIN   **0-0**
AZE: Kamran Agayev, Rail Melikov, Rashad Ferhad Sadygov (Cap), Saša Yunisoğlu, Elmar Bakhshiyev, Makhmud Kurbanov (71.Zeynal Zeynalov), Aleksandr Chertoganov, Samir Abbasov, Branimir Subašić, Vagif Dzhavadov (46.Dzhavid Huseynov), Elvin Mamedov (65.Leandro Melino Gomes). Trainer: Hans-Hubert Vogts (Germany).
LIE: Peter Jehle, Marco Ritzberger (20.Yves Oehri), Fabio D'Elia, Martin Stocklasa, Andreas Gerster, Franz Burgmeier, Benjamin Fischer, Martin Büchel, Michele Polverino (46.Raphael Rohrer), Mathias Christen (68.Thomas Beck), Mario Frick. Trainer: Hans-Petter Zaugg.
Cautions: Elmar Bakhshiyev, Aleksandr Chertoganov / Michele Polverino, Martin Büchel.

10.09.2008, Olympiastadion, Helsinki; Attendance: 37,150
Referee: Viktor Kassai (Hungary)
FINLAND - GERMANY   **3-3(2-2)**
FIN: Jussi Jääskeläinen, Veli Lampi, Petri Pasanen, Sami Hyypiä (Cap), Toni Kallio, Roman Eremenko, Markus Heikkinen, Jonatan Johansson, Mika Väyrynen (75.Njezi Kuqi), Joonas Kolkka, Mikael Forssell (41.Daniel Sjölund). Trainer: Stuart Baxter (England).
GER: Robert Enke, Clemens Fritz (82.Andreas Hinkel), Serdar Tasci, Heiko Westermann, Philipp Lahm, Bastian Schweinsteiger, Simon Rolfes (82.Patrick Helmes), Thomas Hitzlsperger (69.Mario Gómez), Piotr Trochowski, Miroslav Klose (Cap), Lukas Podolski. Trainer: Joachim Löw.

Goals: 1-0 Jonatan Johansson (33), 1-1 Miroslav Klose (38), 2-1 Mika Väyrynen (43), 2-2 Miroslav Klose (45), 3-2 Daniel Sjölund (53), 3-3 Miroslav Klose (83).
Cautions: Toni Kallio.

11.10.2008, Olympiastadion, Helsinki; Attendance: 22,480
Referee: William Collum (Scotland)
FINLAND - AZERBAIJAN   **1-0(0-0)**
FIN: Jussi Jaaskelainen, Petri Pasanen, Toni Kallio, Sami Hyypiä (Cap), Hannu Tihinen, Mika Väyrynen, Roman Eremenko (79.Jari Litmanen), Teemu Tainio (90+2.Markus Heikkinen), Mikael Forssell, Paulus Roiha (62.Antti Pohja), Daniel Sjölund. Trainer: Stuart Baxter (England).
AZE: Kamran Agayev, Rail Melikov, Saša Yunisoğlu, Mahir Shukyurov, Aleksandr Chertoganov (79.Araz Abdullayev), Samir Abbasov, Branimir Subašić (73.Anatoli Ponomaryov), Rashad Ferhad Sadygov (Cap), Elvin Mamedov (59.Dzhavid Huseynov), Zeynal Zeynalov, Leandro Melino Gomes. Trainer: Hans-Hubert Vogts (Germany).
Goal: 1-0 Mikael Forssell (61 penalty).
Cautions: Mika Väyrynen, Toni Kallio / Branimir Subašić, Saša Yunisoğlu, Araz Abdullayev.

11.10.2008, Millennium Stadium, Cardiff; Attendance: 13,356
Referee: Thomas Vejlgaard (Denmark)
WALES - LIECHTENSTEIN   **2-0(1-0)**
WAL: Wayne Robert Hennessey, Christopher Ross Gunter, Gareth Frank Bale, Craig Morgan, Ashley Errol Williams, Simon Davies, Carl Neil Fletcher (56.Carl Phillip Robinson), Jason Koumas, David Alexander Edwards, Samuel Michael Vokes (51.Chedwyn Michael Evans), Craig Douglas Bellamy (Cap) (80.James Michael Collins). Manager: John Benjamin Toshack.
LIE: Peter Jehle, Marco Ritzberger (67.Mathias Christen), Fabio D'Elia, Andreas Gerster, Martin Stocklasa, Benjamin Fischer, Franz Burgmeier, Martin Büchel, Michele Polverino (80.Ronny Büchel), Thomas Beck, Mario Frick (Cap). Trainer: Hans-Petter Zaugg.
Goals: 1-0 David Alexander Edwards (42), 2-0 Mario Frick (80 own goal).
Cautions: Craig Douglas Bellamy / Martin Büchel, Franz Burgmeier, Michele Polverino, Fabio D'Elia.

11.10.2008, Signal-Iduna Park, Dortmund; Attendance: 65,607
Referee: Peter Fröjdfeldt (Sweden)
GERMANY - RUSSIA   **2-1(2-0)**
GER: René Adler, Arne Friedrich, Per Mertesacker, Heiko Westermann, Philipp Lahm, Piotr Trochowski (83.Torsten Frings), Michael Ballack (Cap), Thomas Hitzlsperger (90+3.Simon Rolfes), Bastian Schweinsteiger, Miroslav Klose (71.Mario Gómez), Lukas Podolski. Trainer: Joachim Löw.
RUS: Igor Akinfeyev, Aleksandr Anyukov, Sergey Ignashevich, Vasiliy Berezutskiy, Yuriy Zhirkov, Konstantin Zyryanov, Sergey Semak (Cap) (84.Dmitriy Sychev), Renat Yanbayev (46.Alan Dzagoev), Igor Denisov, Andrey Arshavin, Pavel Pogrebnyak. Trainer: Guus Hiddink (Holland).
Goals: 1-0 Lukas Podolski (9), 2-0 Michael Ballack (28), 2-1 Andrey Arshavin (51).
Cautions: Konstantin Zyryanov, Vasiliy Berezutskiy.

15.10.2008, Lokomotiv Stadium, Moskva; Attendance: 28,000
Referee: Kyros Vassaras (Greece)
RUSSIA - FINLAND   **3-0(1-0)**
RUS: Igor Akinfeyev, Aleksandr Anyukov, Sergey Ignashevich, Vasiliy Berezutskiy, Yuriy Zhirkov, Igor Denisov, Igor Semshov, Sergey Semak (Cap), Konstantin Zyryanov, Andrey Arshavin (90+2.Alan Dzagoev), Pavel Pogrebnyak (60.Ivan Saenko). Trainer: Guus Hiddink (Holland).
FIN: Jussi Jääskeläinen, Petri Pasanen, Veli Lampi, Sami Hyypiä (Cap), Hannu Tihinen, Joonas Kolkka, Markus Heikkinen, Roman Eremenko (66.Teemu Tainio), Mika Väyrynen (69.Paulus Roiha), Daniel Sjölund (85.Jari Litmanen), Mikael Forssell. Trainer: Stuart Baxter (England).
Goals: 1-0 Petri Pasanen (22 own goal), 2-0 Veli Lampi (65 own goal), 3-0 Andrey Arshavin (89).
Cautions: Aleksandr Anyukov / Joonas Kolkka.

15.10.2008, Borussia-Park, Mönchengladbach; Attendance: 44,500
Referee: Laurent Duhamel (France)
GERMANY - WALES   **1-0(0-0)**
GER: René Adler, Arne Friedrich (64.Clemens Fritz), Per Mertesacker, Heiko Westermann, Philipp Lahm, Bastian Schweinsteiger, Michael Ballack (Cap), Thomas Hitzlsperger, Piotr Trochowski, Miroslav Klose (46.Patrick Helmes), Lukas Podolski (82.Mario Gómez). Trainer: Joachim Löw.
WAL: Wayne Robert Hennessey, Christopher Ross Gunter (86.Samuel Ricketts), Gareth Frank Bale, Craig Morgan, Ashley Errol Williams, James Michael Collins, Simon Davies, Carl Neil Fletcher (77.Chedwyn Michael Evans), Jason Koumas, David Alexander Edwards (77.Carl Phillip Robinson), Craig Douglas Bellamy (Cap). Manager: John Benjamin Toshack.
Goal: 1-0 Piotr Trochowski (72).
Cautions: Samuel Ricketts.

28.03.2009, Luzhniki Stadium, Moskva; Attendance: 62,000
Referee: Serge Gumienny (Belgium)
RUSSIA - AZERBAIJAN   **2-0(1-0)**
RUS: Igor Akinfeyev, Aleksandr Anyukov, Sergey Ignashevich, Vasiliy Berezutskiy, Yuriy Zhirkov, Konstantin Zyryanov, Sergey Semak (55.Alan Dzagoev), Igor Denisov, Igor Semshov, Roman Pavlyuchenko (72.Pavel Pogrebnyak), Andrey Arshavin (Cap). Trainer: Guus Hiddink (Holland).
AZE: Farhad Veliyev, Rail Melikov, Saša Yunisoğlu, Rashad Ferhad Sadygov (Cap), Samir Abbasov, Mahir Shukyurov, Elmar Bakhshiyev, Fábio Luís Ramim (61.Leandro Melino Gomes), Jamshid Maharramov, Vugar Nadirov, Branimir Subašić (46.Vagif Dzhavadov). Trainer: Hans-Hubert Vogts (Germany).
Goals: 1-0 Roman Pavlyuchenko (32), 2-0 Konstantin Zyryanov (71).
Cautions: Igor Denisov / Saša Yunisoğlu, Vugar Nadirov, Rail Melikov, Samir Abbasov.

28.03.2009, Millennium Stadium, Cardiff; Attendance: 22,604
Referee: Eduardo Iturralde González (Spain)
WALES - FINLAND   **0-2(0-1)**
WAL: Wayne Robert Hennessey, Christopher Ross Gunter, Gareth Frank Bale, Lewin John Nyatanga, James Michael Collins, Carl Neil Fletcher (65.Carl Phillip Robinson), Simon Davies, David Alexander Edwards (56.Aaron James Ramsey), Joseph Christopher Ledley (71.Robert Earnshaw), Jason Koumas, Craig Douglas Bellamy (Cap). Manager: John Benjamin Toshack.
FIN: Jussi Jääskeläinen, Petri Pasanen, Sami Hyypiä (Cap), Hannu Tihinen, Toni Kallio, Alexei Eremenko jr. (78.Daniel Sjölund), Roman Eremenko, Jari Litmanen (90.Roni Porokara), Markus Heikkinen, Mikael Forssell (89.Shefki Kuqi), Jonatan Johansson. Trainer: Stuart Baxter (England).
Goals: 0-1 Jonatan Johansson (42), 0-2 Shefki Kuqi (90+1).
Cautions: Markus Heikkinen, Jussi Jääskeläinen.

28.03.2009, Zentralstadion, Leipzig; Attendance: 43,368
Referee: Ihor Ishchenko (Ukraine)
GERMANY - LIECHTENSTEIN   **4-0(2-0)**
GER: Robert Enke, Andreas Beck, Per Mertesacker, Serdar Tasci, Philipp Lahm, Bastian Schweinsteiger (88.Simon Rolfes), Michael Ballack (Cap), Thomas Hitzlsperger (78.Marko Marin), Marcell Jansen (64.Patrick Helmes), Mario Gómez, Lukas Podolski. Trainer: Joachim Löw.
LIE: Peter Jehle, Yves Oehri, Martin Stocklasa, Michael Stocklasa, Franz-Josef Vogt, Marco Ritzberger, Ronny Büchel, Andreas Gerster, Raphael Rohrer, Mario Frick (Cap), Thomas Beck (74.Roger Beck). Trainer: Hans-Petter Zaugg.
Goals: 1-0 Michael Ballack (4), 2-0 Marcell Jansen (9), 3-0 Bastian Schweinsteiger (48), 4-0 Lukas Podolski (50).
Cautions: Serdar Tasci / Raphael Rohrer, Thomas Beck, Mario Frick.

01.04.2009, Rheinpark Stadion, Vaduz; Attendance: 5,679
Referee: David McKeon (Republic of Ireland)
LIECHTENSTEIN - RUSSIA   **0-1(0-1)**
LIE: Peter Jehle, Yves Oehri (46.Raphael Rohrer), Martin Stocklasa, Michael Stocklasa, Franz-Josef Vogt (60.Fabio D'Elia), Marco Ritzberger, Martin Büchel (75.Thomas Beck), Andreas Gerster, Franz Burgmeier, Michele Polverino, Mario Frick (Cap). Trainer: Hans-Petter Zaugg.
RUS: Igor Akinfeyev, Aleksandr Anyukov, Sergey Ignashevich, Vasiliy Berezutskiy, Yuriy Zhirkov, Igor Denisov, Igor Semshov, Dmitriy Torbinskiy (66.Sergey Semak), Konstantin Zyryanov, Roman Pavlyuchenko (84.Pavel Pogrebnyak), Andrey Arshavin (Cap). Trainer: Guus Hiddink (Holland).
Goal: 0-1 Konstantin Zyryanov (38).
Cautions: Aleksandr Anyukov.

01.04.2009, Millennium Stadium, Cardiff; Attendance: 26,064
Referee: Terje Hauge (Norway)
WALES - GERMANY   **0-2(0-1)**
WAL: Wayne Robert Hennessey, Samuel Ricketts (53.Christopher Ross Gunter), Gareth Frank Bale, Lewin John Nyatanga (74.David Rhys George Best Cotterill), Ashley Errol Williams, James Michael Collins, Simon Davies (Cap), Joseph Christopher Ledley, Aaron James Ramsey, Robert Earnshaw, Samuel Michael Vokes (62.Chedwyn Michael Evans). Manager: John Benjamin Toshack.
GER: Robert Enke, Andreas Beck, Per Mertesacker, Serdar Tasci, Philipp Lahm, Bastian Schweinsteiger (86.Patrick Helmes), Simon Rolfes (79.Heiko Westermann), Michael Ballack (Cap), Thomas Hitzlsperger, Lukas Podolski (72.Piotr Trochowski), Mario Gómez. Trainer: Joachim Löw.
Goals: 0-1 Michael Ballack (11), 0-2 Ashley Errol Williams (48 own goal).
Cautions: Simon Rolfes.

06.06.2009, „Tofik Bahramov" Stadium, Baku; Attendance: 26,728
Referee: Markus Strombergsson (Sweden)
AZERBAIJAN - WALES   **0-1(0-1)**
AZE: Farhad Veliyev, Rail Melikov, Rashad Ferhad Sadygov (Cap), Vladimir Levin, Mahir Shukyurov, Elmar Bakhshiyev, Fábio Luís Ramim (46.Branimir Subašić), Agil Nabiyev (50.Dzhavid Huseynov), Zeynal Zeynalov, Daniel Akhtyamov (60.Vugar Nadirov), Vagif Dzhavadov. Trainer: Hans-Hubert Vogts (Germany).
WAL: Wayne Robert Hennessey, Christopher Ross Gunter, Neal James Eardley, Lewin John Nyatanga, Ashley Errol Williams, Craig Morgan, David Alexander Edwards, Joseph Christopher Ledley (Cap), Aaron James Ramsey, Simon Richard Church (83.Owain Tudur Jones), Robert Earnshaw (70.Samuel Michael Vokes). Manager: John Benjamin Toshack.
Goal: 0-1 David Alexander Edwards (42).
Cautions: Craig Morgan, Wayne Robert Hennessey, Aaron James Ramsey.

06.06.2009, Olympiastadion, Helsinki; Attendance: 20,319
Referee: Libor Kovarik (Czech Republic)
FINLAND - LIECHTENSTEIN   **2-1(1-1)**
FIN: Jussi Jääskeläinen, Petri Pasanen (46.Veli Lampi), Sami Hyypiä (Cap), Hannu Tihinen, Toni Kallio, Roman Eremenko, Teemu Tainio (67.Markus Heikkinen), Jari Litmanen (72.Shefki Kuqi), Alexei Eremenko jr., Mikael Forssell, Jonatan Johansson. Trainer: Stuart Baxter (England).
LIE: Peter Jehle, Marco Ritzberger, Martin Stocklasa, Michael Stocklasa, Franz-Josef Vogt (66.Raphael Rohrer), Benjamin Fischer, Ronny Büchel (76.Stefan Büchel), Martin Büchel (58.Mathias Christen), Franz Burgmeier, Michele Polverino, Mario Frick (Cap). Trainer: Hans-Petter Zaugg.
Goals: 0-1 Mario Frick (13), 1-1 Mikael Forssell (33), 2-1 Jonatan Johansson (71).
Cautions: Veli Lampi / Michele Polverino, Raphael Rohrer.

10.06.2009, Olympiastadion, Helsinki; Attendance: 37,028
Referee: Konrad Plautz (Austria)
FINLAND - RUSSIA   **0-3(0-1)**
FIN: Jussi Jääskeläinen, Petri Pasanen, Sami Hyypiä (Cap), Hannu Tihinen, Toni Kallio (54.Niklas Moisander), Roman Eremenko, Jari Litmanen (69.Teemu Tainio), Markus Heikkinen, Alexei Eremenko jr. (61.Joonas Kolkka), Mikael Forssell, Jonatan Johansson. Trainer: Stuart Baxter (England).
RUS: Igor Akinfeyev, Vasiliy Berezutskiy, Sergey Ignashevich, Denis Kolodin, Yuriy Zhirkov, Igor Denisov, Konstantin Zyryanov, Igor Semshov, Andrey Arshavin (Cap), Vladimir Bystrov (77.Sergey Semak), Aleksandr Kerzhakov (67.Roman Pavlyuchenko). Trainer: Guus Hiddink (Holland).
Goals: 0-1 Aleksandr Kerzhakov (27), 0-2 Aleksandr Kerzhakov (53), 0-3 Konstantin Zyryanov (71).
Cautions: Toni Kallio, Hannu Tihinen, Roman Eremenko.

12.08.2009, „Tofik Bahramov" Stadium, Baku; Attendance: 22,500
Referee: Alan Kelly (Republic of Ireland)
AZERBAIJAN - GERMANY   **0-2(0-1)**
AZE: Farhad Veliyev, Rail Melikov, Elnur Allahverdiev, Rashad Ferhad Sadygov (Cap), Samir Abbasov, Saša Yunisoğlu, Mahir Shukyurov, Aleksandr Chertoganov, Elvin Mamedov, Vagif Dzhavadov, Vugar Nadirov (74.Daniel Akhtyamov). Trainer: Hans-Hubert Vogts (Germany).
GER: Robert Enke, Philipp Lahm, Per Mertesacker, Serdar Tasci, Marcel Schäfer, Bastian Schweinsteiger, Michael Ballack (Cap), Thomas Hitzlsperger, Piotr Trochowski (77.Marcell Jansen), Miroslav Klose (75.Claudemir Jerónimo Barretto da Silva „Cacau"), Mario Gómez (84.Mesut Özil). Trainer: Joachim Löw.
Goals: 0-1 Bastian Schweinsteiger (11), 0-2 Miroslav Klose (53).
Cautions: Elnur Allahverdiev, Mahir Shukyurov, Rail Melikov, Aleksandr Chertoganov.

05.09.2009, City Stadium, Länkäran; Attendance: 12,000
Referee: Stelios Trifonos (Cyprus)
AZERBAIJAN - FINLAND   **1-2(0-0)**
AZE: Kamran Agayev, Rashad Ferhad Sadygov (Cap), Saša Yunisoğlu, Ruslan Abishov (46.Dzhavid Huseynov), Vladimir Levin, Elnur Allahverdiev, Mahir Shukyurov, Samir Abbasov, Elvin Mamedov (84.Rahid Amirquliev), Vagif Dzhavadov, Vugar Nadirov (72.Daniel Akhtyamov). Trainer: Hans-Hubert Vogts (Germany).
FIN: Jussi Jääskeläinen, Petri Pasanen, Hannu Tihinen (Cap), Niklas Moisander, Veli Lampi, Roman Eremenko, Teemu Tainio (46.Jari Litmanen), Markus Heikkinen, Jonatan Johansson, Alexei Eremenko jr., Shefki Kuqi (74.Daniel Sjölund; 84.Joonas Kolkka). Trainer: Stuart Baxter (England).
Goals: 1-0 Elvin Mamedov (49), 1-1 Hannu Tihinen (74), 1-2 Jonatan Johansson (85).
Cautions: Saša Yunisoğlu / Petri Pasanen.

05.09.2009, Petrovskiy Stadium, St. Petersburg; Attendance: 22,000
Referee: Augustus Constantin (Romania)
RUSSIA - LIECHTENSTEIN   **3-0(3-0)**
RUS: Igor Akinfeyev, Aleksandr Anyukov, Sergey Ignashevich, Vasiliy Berezutskiy (58.Aleksey Berezutskiy), Konstantin Zyryanov (46.Igor Semshov), Sergey Semak (Cap), Diniyar Bilyaletdinov, Vladimir Bystrov, Igor Denisov (69.Pavel Pogrebnyak), Aleksandr Kerzhakov, Roman Pavlyuchenko. Trainer: Guus Hiddink (Holland).
LIE: Peter Jehle, Marco Ritzberger, Yves Oehri, Michael Stocklasa, Martin Rechsteiner, Ronny Büchel, Thomas Beck (57.David Hasler), Franz Burgmeier, Franz-Josef Vogt (81.Stefan Büchel), Mathias Christen (72.Roger Beck), Mario Frick (Cap). Trainer: Hans-Petter Zaugg.
Goals: 1-0 Vasiliy Berezutskiy (17), 2-0 Roman Pavlyuchenko (40 penalty), 3-0 Roman Pavlyuchenko (45 penalty).
Cautions: Igor Denisov, Roman Pavlyuchenko / Franz Burgmeier, Franz-Josef Vogt.

09.09.2009, Rheinpark Stadion, Vaduz; Attendance: 3,132
Referee: Novo Panić (Bosnia-Herzegovina)
LIECHTENSTEIN - FINLAND   **1-1(0-0)**
LIE: Peter Jehle, Marco Ritzberger, Yves Oehri, Michael Stocklasa, Martin Rechsteiner, Franz Burgmeier, Raphael Rohrer (85.Roger Beck), Ronny Büchel, Martin Büchel *(sent off 76 on the bench!)* (65.Michele Polverino), David Hasler (80.Thomas Beck), Mario Frick (Cap). Trainer: Hans-Petter Zaugg.
FIN: Jussi Jääskeläinen, Petri Pasanen, Sami Hyypiä (Cap), Hannu Tihinen, Niklas Moisander, Roman Eremenko, Jari Litmanen (82.Shefki Kuqi), Markus Heikkinen, Jonatan Johansson, Alexei Eremenko jr., Berat Sadik (59.Joonas Kolkka). Trainer: Stuart Baxter (England).
Goals: 0-1 Jari Litmanen (74 penalty), 1-1 (75).
Cautions: Peter Jehle, David Hasler, Michele Polverino, Mario Frick / Markus Heikkinen.
Sent off: Martin Büchel (75, on the bench).

09.09.2009, AWD-Arena, Hannover; Attendance: 35,369
Referee: Anastasion Kakos (Greece)
GERMANY - AZERBAIJAN   **4-0(1-0)**
GER: René Adler, Philipp Lahm, Per Mertesacker, Heiko Westermann, Marcel Schäfer (46.Andreas Beck), Bastian Schweinsteiger (67.Piotr Trochowski), Michael Ballack (Cap), Thomas Hitzlsperger, Mesut Özil, Lukas Podolski, Mario Gómez (46.Miroslav Klose). Trainer: Joachim Löw.
AZE: Kamran Agayev, Rashad Ferhad Sadygov (Cap), Saša Yunisoğlu, Vladimir Levin, Elnur Allahverdiev, Samir Abbasov, Mahir Shukyurov, Aleksandr Chertoganov, Elvin Mamedov (66.Dzhavid Huseynov), Vagif Dzhavadov, Vugar Nadirov (57.Ernani Pereira). Trainer: Hans-Hubert Vogts (Germany).
Goals: 1-0 Michael Ballack (14 penalty), 2-0 Miroslav Klose (55), 3-0 Miroslav Klose (65), 4-0 Lukas Podolski (71).
Cautions: Samir Abbasov, Ernani Pereira.
Sent off: Samir Abbasov (50).

09.09.2009, Millennium Stadium, Cardiff; Attendance: 14,505
Referee: Manuel Jorge de Sousa (Portugal)
WALES - RUSSIA   **1-3(0-1)**
WAL: Wayne Robert Hennessey, Christopher Ross Gunter, Daniel Leon Gabbidon (74.Samuel Michael Vokes), Ashley Errol Williams, Samuel Ricketts, James Michael Collins, David Alexander Edwards, Joseph Christopher Ledley, Aaron James Ramsey, Brian Benjamin Stock, Craig Douglas Bellamy (Cap). Manager: John Benjamin Toshack.
RUS: Igor Akinfeyev, Aleksandr Anyukov, Sergey Ignashevich, Vasiliy Berezutskiy, Renat Yanbaev, Konstantin Zyryanov, Igor Semshov (70.Roman Pavlyuchenko), Sergey Semak, Andrei Arshavin (Cap), Vladimir Bystrov, Aleksandr Kerzhakov (84.Aleksey Rebko). Trainer: Guus Hiddink (Holland).
Goals: 0-1 Igor Semshov (36), 1-1 James Michael Collins (53), 1-2 Sergey Ignashevich (71), 1-3 Roman Pavlyuchenko (90+1).
Cautions: Samuel Ricketts / Aleksandr Anyukov.

10.10.2009, Olympiastadion, Helsinki; Attendance: 14,000
Referee: Milorad Mažić (Serbia)
FINLAND - WALES   **2-1(1-1)**
FIN: Jussi Jääskeläinen, Petri Pasanen, Sami Hyypiä (Cap), Hannu Tihinen, Niklas Moisander, Roman Eremenko, Jari Litmanen (90+2.Alexei Eremenko jr.), Tim Sparv, Jonatan Johansson (88.Shefki Kuqi), Roni Porokara, Joonas Kolkka (68.Kasper Hämäläinen). Trainer: Stuart Baxter (England).
WAL: Wayne Robert Hennessey, Christopher Ross Gunter, Gareth Frank Bale, Lewin John Nyatanga (83.Neal James Eardley), Ashley Errol Williams, James Michael Collins, David Owen Vaughan, David Alexander Edwards, Ashley Errol Williams, Craig Douglas Bellamy (Cap), Simon Richard Church (62.Samuel Michael Vokes). Manager: John Benjamin Toshack.
Goals: 1-0 Roni Porokara (5), 1-1 Craig Douglas Bellamy (17), 2-1 Niklas Moisander (77).

Cautions: Hannu Tihinen, Petri Pasanen / Craig Douglas Bellamy, Wayne Robert Hennessey.

10.10.2009, Luzhniki Stadium, Moskva; Attendance: 72,100
Referee: Massimo Busacca (Switzerland)
RUSSIA - GERMANY   **0-1(0-1)**
RUS: Igor Akinfeyev, Aleksandr Anyukov, Sergey Ignashevich, Vasiliy Berezutskiy, Yuriy Zhirkov, Konstantin Zyryanov, Igor Semshov (77.Pavel Pogrebnyak), Vladimir Bystrov, Igor Denisov (46.Dmitriy Torbinskiy), Andrey Arshavin (Cap), Aleksandr Kerzhakov (54.Roman Pavlyuchenko). Trainer: Guus Hiddink (Holland).
GER: René Adler, Jérôme Agyenim Boateng, Per Mertesacker, Heiko Westermann, Philipp Lahm, Bastian Schweinsteiger, Mesut Özil (72.Arne Friedrich), Michael Ballack (Cap), Simon Rolfes, Lukas Podolski (86.Piotr Trochowski), Miroslav Klose (89.Mario Gómez). Trainer: Joachim Löw.
Goal: 0-1 Miroslav Klose (35).
Cautions: Yuriy Zhirkov, Igor Semshov / Jérôme Agyenim Boateng,
Sent off: Jérôme Agyenim Boateng (69).

10.10.2009, Rheinpark Stadion, Vaduz; Attendance: 1,635
Referee: Pavle Radovanović (Montenegro)
LIECHTENSTEIN - AZERBAIJAN   **0-2(0-0)**
LIE: Peter Jehle, Marco Ritzberger (81.Mathias Christen), Fabio D'Elia, Yves Oehri, Martin Rechsteiner, Franz Burgmeier, Ronny Büchel (Cap), Wolfgang Kieber, Raphael Rohrer (58.Roger Beck), David Hasler, Stefan Büchel (68.Thomas Beck). Trainer: Hans-Petter Zaugg.
AZE: Kamran Agayev, Ruslan Abishov, Elnur Allahverdiev, Vladimir Levin, Maksim Medvedev (90+4.Rail Melikov), Mahir Shukyurov (Cap), Aleksandr Chertoganov, Elvin Mamedov, Daniel Akhtyamov, Vagif Dzhavadov (90+1.Dzhavid Huseynov), Vugar Nadirov (46.Rashad Ferhad Sadygov). Trainer: Hans-Hubert Vogts (Germany).
Goals: 0-1 Vagif Dzhavadov (55), 0-2 Elvin Mamedov (82).
Cautions: Thomas Beck, Wolfgang Kieber, Franz Burgmeier, Roger Beck, Martin Rechsteiner / Aleksandr Chertoganov, Daniel Akhtyamov, Vagif Dzhavadov, Elnur Allahverdiev.

14.10.2009, „Tofik Bahramov" Stadium, Baku; Attendance: 17,000
Referee: Howard Melton Webb (England)
AZERBAIJAN - RUSSIA   **1-1(0-1)**
AZE: Kamran Agayev, Rashad Ferhad Sadygov (46.Vugar Nadirov), Ruslan Abishov, Vladimir Levin, Maksim Medvedev (73.Dzhavid Huseynov), Rail Melikov, Samir Abbasov (Cap), Mahir Shukyurov, Aleksandr Chertoganov, Elvin Mamedov, Vagif Dzhavadov. Trainer: Hans-Hubert Vogts (Germany).
RUS: Igor Akinfeyev, Renat Yanbaev, Aleksey Berezutskiy, Sergey Ignashevich, Dmitriy Torbinskiy, Sergey Semak, Diniyar Bilyaletdinov, Vladimir Bystrov (64.Aleksandr Bukharov), Aleksey Rebko (64.Igor Denisov), Alan Dzagoev, Andrey Arshavin (Cap). Trainer: Guus Hiddink (Holland).
Goals: 0-1 Andrey Arshavin (13), 1-1 Vagif Dzhavadov (54).
Cautions: Mahir Shukyurov / Renat Yanbaev, Sergey Semak, Dmitriy Torbinskiy.

14.10.2009, HSH Nordbank-Arena, Hamburg; Attendance: 51,500
Referee: Howard Melton Webb (England)
GERMANY - FINLAND   **1-1(0-1)**
GER: René Adler, Andreas Beck, Arne Friedrich, Heiko Westermann, Philipp Lahm, Michael Ballack (Cap) (46.Mesut Özil), Thomas Hitzlsperger (46.Christian Gentner), Piotr Trochowski, Claudemir Jerónimo Barretto da Silva „Cacau", Mario Gómez (77.Miroslav Klose), Lukas Podolski. Trainer: Joachim Löw.
FIN: Jussi Jääskeläinen, Veli Lampi, Markus Heikkinen, Sami Hyypiä, Niklas Moisander, Kasper Hämäläinen (66.Joonas Kolkka), Tim Sparv, Roman Eremenko, Ronio Porokara (72.Shefki Kuqi), Jari Litmanen (87.Ari Nyman), Jonatan Johansson. Trainer: Stuart Baxter (England).
Goals: 0-1 Jonatan Johansson (11), 1-1 Lukas Podolski (90).
Cautions: Tim Sparv, Niklas Moisander.

14.10.2009, Rheinpark Stadion, Vaduz; Attendance: 1,858
Referee: Sten Kaldma (Estonia)
LIECHTENSTEIN - WALES   **0-2(0-1)**
LIE: Peter Jehle, Yves Oehri, Marco Ritzberger, Fabio D'Elia, Martin Rechsteiner, Lucas Eberle, Wolfgang Kieber, Ronny Büchel (70.Michele Polverino), Raphael Rohrer (36.Roger Beck), David Hasler (72.Mathias Christen), Mario Frick (Cap). Trainer: Hans-Petter Zaugg.
WAL: Glyn Oliver Myhill, Christopher Ross Gunter (88.Neal James Eardley), Gareth Frank Bale (84.Lewin John Nyatanga), Ashley Errol Williams, James Michael Collins (Cap), Craig Morgan, David Owen Vaughan, David Alexander Edwards (10.Andrew King), Aaron James Ramsey, Simon Richard Church, Jermaine Maurice Easter. Manager: John Benjamin Toshack.
Goals: 0-1 David Owen Vaughan (16), 0-2 Aaron James Ramsey (80).
Cautions: Ronny Büchel, Fabio D'Elia, Lucas Eberle / Craig Morgan.

GROUP 5

06.09.2008	Yerevan	Armenia - Turkey	0-2(0-0)
06.09.2008	Liège	Belgium - Estonia	3-2(1-0)
06.09.2008	Murcia	Spain – Bosnia-Herzegovina	1-0(0-0)
10.09.2008	Istanbul	Turkey - Belgium	1-1(0-1)
10.09.2008	Zenica	Bosnia-Herzegovina - Estonia	7-0(2-0)
10.09.2008	Albacete	Spain - Armenia	4-0(2-0)
11.10.2008	Istanbul	Turkey - Bosnia-Herzegovina	2-1(0-1)
11.10.2008	Bruxelles	Belgium - Armenia	2-0(2-0)
11.10.2008	Tallinn	Estonia - Spain	0-3(0-2)
15.10.2008	Zenica	Bosnia-Herzegovina - Armenia	4-1(2-0)
15.10.2008	Tallinn	Estonia - Turkey	0-0
15.10.2008	Bruxelles	Belgium - Spain	1-2(1-1)
28.03.2009	Yerevan	Armenia - Estonia	2-2(1-1)
28.03.2009	Genk	Belgium - Bosnia-Herzegovina	2-4(0-1)
28.03.2009	Madrid	Spain - Turkey	1-0(0-0)
01.04.2009	Tallinn	Estonia - Armenia	1-0(0-0)
01.04.2009	Istanbul	Turkey - Spain	1-2(1-0)
01.04.2009	Zenica	Bosnia-Herzegovina - Belgium	2-1(2-0)
05.09.2009	Yerevan	Armenia - Bosnia-Herzegovina	0-2(0-1)
05.09.2009	Kayseri	Turkey - Estonia	4-2(2-1)
05.09.2009	La Coruña	Spain - Belgium	5-0(1-0)
09.09.2009	Yerevan	Armenia - Belgium	2-1(1-0)
09.09.2009	Zenica	Bosnia-Herzegovina - Turkey	1-1(1-1)
09.09.2009	Mérida	Spain - Estonia	3-0(1-0)
10.10.2009	Yerevan	Armenia - Spain	1-2(0-1)
10.10.2009	Tallinn	Estonia - Bosnia-Herzegovina	0-2(0-1)
10.10.2009	Bruxelles	Belgium - Turkey	2-0(1-0)
14.10.2009	Zenica	Bosnia-Herzegovina - Spain	2-5(0-2)
14.10.2009	Bursa	Turkey - Armenia	2-0(2-0)
14.10.2009	Tallinn	Estonia - Belgium	2-0(1-0)

FINAL STANDINGS

1.	**SPAIN**	10	10	0	0	28	-	5	30
2.	**Bosnia-Herzegovina**	10	6	1	3	25	-	13	19
3.	Turkey	10	4	3	3	13	-	10	15
4.	Belgium	10	3	1	6	13	-	20	10
5.	Estonia	10	2	2	6	9	-	24	8
6.	Armenia	10	1	1	8	6	-	22	4

Spain qualified for the Final Tournament; Bosnia-Herzegovina qualified for the Play-Offs.

06.09.2008, Hrazdan Stadium, Yerevan; Attendance: 30,000
Referee: Tom Henning Øvrebø (Norway)
ARMENIA - TURKEY   **0-2(0-0)**
ARM: Roman Berezovski, Ararat Arakelyan, Sargis Hovsepyan (Cap), Robert Arzumanyan (35.Romik Khachatryan), Aleksander Tadevosyan, Artur Voskanyan, Artavazd Karamyan, Aghvan Mkrtchyan, Hamlet V. Mkhitaryan (66.Robert Zebelyan), Levon Pachajyan, Edgar Manucharyan (76.Arman Karamyan). Trainer: Jan Børge Poulsen (Denmark).
TUR: Volkan Demirel, Servet Çetin, Hakan Kadir Balta, Gökhan Zan, Gökhan Gönül, Mehmet Aurélio, Emre Belözoğlu (Cap), Arda Turan, Semih Şentürk (83.Gökhan Ünal), Mevlüt Erdinç (55.Colin Kazim-Richards), Tuncay Şanlı (66.Ayhan Akman). Trainer: Fatih Terim.

Goals: 0-1 Tuncay Şanlı (61), 02 Semih Şentürk (77).
Cautions: Hamlet V. Mkhitaryan / Gökhan Zan.

06.09.2008, Stade „Maurice Dufrasne", Liège; Attendance: 17,992
Referee: Michael Leslie Dean (England)
BELGIUM - ESTONIA   **3-2(1-0)**
BEL: Stijn Stijnen, Thomas Vermaelen (70.Jelle Van Damme), Vincent Jean Mpoy Kompany, Timmy Simons (Cap), Daniel Van Buyten, Axel Tomas Witsel, Jan Vertonghen, Steven Arnold Defour, Marouane Fellaini, Kevin Antonio Mirallas (76.Tom De Sutter), Wesley Sonck (90+2.Stein Huysegems). Trainer: René Vandereycken.
EST: Pavel Londak, Enar Jääger, Alo Bärengrub, Raio Piiroja (44.Andrei Stepanov), Dmitri Kruglov, Tarmo Kink (77.Sander Puri), Aleksandr Dmitrijev, Ragnar Klavan, Joel Lindpere, Sergei Zenjov (60.Martin Vunk), Andres Oper. Trainer: Tarmo Rüütli.
Goals: 1-0 Wesley Sonck (39), 1-1 Sergei Zenjov (57), 2-1 Steven Arnold Defour (75), 3-1 Wesley Sonck (81), 3-2 Andres Oper (90+2).
Cautions: Sander Puri.

06.09.2008, Estadio Nueva Condomina, Murcia; Attendance: 29,152
Referee: Craig Alexander Thomson (Scotland)
SPAIN – BOSNIA-HERZEGOVINA   **1-0(0-0)**
ESP: Iker Casillas Fernández (Cap), Sergio Ramos García, Carles Puyol Saforcada, Raúl Albiol Tortajada, Joan Capdevila Méndez, Marcos Antônio Senna da Silva, Andrés Iniesta Luján, Xavier Hernández Creus „Xavi", Francesc „Cesc" Fàbregas Soler (65.Xabier „Xabi" Alonso Olano), Diego Capel Trinidad (72.Santiago Cazorla González), David Villa Sánchez (85.Daniel Gonzalez Güiza). Trainer: Vicente Del Bosque González.
BIH: Kenan Hasagić, Dž emal Berberovć (65.Vedad Ibišević), Safet Nadarević, Admir Vladavić, Ivan Radeljić, Dario Damjanović (79.Senijad Ibričić), Sejad Salihović, Samir Muratović, Elvir Rahimić, Zvjezdan Misimović, Edin Dž eko (85.Miralem Pjanć). Trainer: Miroslav Blaž evć (Croatia).
Goal: 1-0 David Villa Sánchez (58).
Cautions: Carles Puyol Saforcada / Dž emal Berberovć, Dario Damjanović, Ivan Radeljić.

10.09.2008, Şükrü Saracoğlu Stadyumu, Istanbul; Attendance: 34,097
Referee: Stéphane Lannoy (France)
TURKEY - BELGIUM   **1-1(0-1)**
TUR: Volkan Demirel, Servet Çetin, Çağlar Birinci, Gökhan Zan, Gökhan Gönül, Emre Belözoğlu (Cap), Mehmet Topal (69.Mevlüt Erdinç), Arda Turan, Semih Şentürk, Colin Kazim-Richards (46.Mehmet Topuz), Tuncay Şanlı (14.Halil Altı ntop). Trainer: Fatih Terim.
BEL: Stijn Stijnen, Gill Swerts, Vincent Jean Mpoy Kompany, Timmy Simons (Cap), Thomas Vermaelen, Axel Tomas Witsel (76.Filip Daems), Jan Vertonghen, Steven Arnold Defour (46.Gaby Mudingayi), Marouane Fellaini, Moussa Dembélé, Wesley Sonck (85.Tom De Sutter). Trainer: René Vandereycken.
Goals: 0-1 Wesley Sonck (31), 1-1 Emre Belözoğlu (74 penalty).
Cautions: Mehmet Topal, Semih Şentürk / Gill Swerts, Gaby Mudingayi, Thomas Vermaelen, Stijn Stijnen.

10.09.2008, Bilino Polje Stadium, Zenica; Attendance: 14,000
Referee: Pavel Cristian Balaj (Romania)
BOSNIA-HERZEGOVINA - ESTONIA   **7-0(2-0)**
BIH: Kenan Hasagić, Dž emal Berberovć, Emir Spahić (Cap), Safet Nadarević, Samir Muratović (73.Senijad Ibričić), Dario Damjanović, Elvir Rahimić, Sejad Salihović, Zvjezdan Misimović (66.Miralem Pjanić), Edin Dž eko, Zlatan Muslimovć (71.Vedad Ibišević). Trainer: Miroslav Blaž evć (Croatia).
EST: Pavel Londak (70.Mihkel Aksalu), Enar Jääger, Alo Bärengrub, Taavi Rähn, Ragnar Klavan, Ats Purje, Aleksandr Dmitrijev (65.Kaimar Saag), Martin Vunk, Joel Lindpere (65.Dmitri Kruglov),

Konstantin Vassiljev, Andres Oper. Trainer: Tarmo Rüütli
Goals: 1-0 Zvjezdan Misimović (25), 2-0 Zvjezdan Misimović (30 penalty), 3-0 Zvjezdan Misimović (56), 4-0 Zlatan Muslimović (58), 5-0 Edin Dž eko (60), 6-0 Edin Dž eko (73), 7-Senijad Ibričić (88).
Cautions: Safet Nadarević / Ragnar Klavan.

10.09.2008, Estadio „Carlos Belmonte", Albacete; Attendance: 16,996
Referee: Tony Asumaa (Finland)
SPAIN - ARMENIA   **4-0(2-0)**
ESP: Iker Casillas Fernández (Cap), Sergio Ramos García, Carles Puyol Saforcada, Raúl Albiol Tortajada, Joan Capdevila Méndez, Marcos Antônio Senna da Silva, Andrés Iniesta Luján, Xavier Hernández Creus „Xavi" (74.Francesc „Cesc" Fàbregas Soler), Daniel Gonzalez Güiza (56.Xabier „Xabi" Alonso Olano), Santiago Cazorla González (65.Bojan Krkić Pérez), David Villa Sánchez. Trainer: Vicente Del Bosque González.
ARM: Roman Berezovski, Aghvan Mkrtchyan, Sargis Hovsepyan (Cap), Robert Arzumanyan, Aleksander Tadevosyan, Ararat Arakelyan, Artur Voskanyan, Karen Aleksanyan (79.Romik Khachatryan), Artavazd Karamyan (52.Arman Karamyan), Levon Pachajyan, Samvel Melkonyan (46.Edgar Manucharyan). Trainer: Jan Børge Poulsen (Denmark).
Goals: 1-0 Joan Capdevila Méndez (7), 2-0 David Villa Sánchez (16), 3-0 David Villa Sánchez (79), 4-0 Marcos Antônio Senna da Silva (83).
Cautions: Karen Aleksanyan, Levon Pachajyan, Romik Khachatryan.

11.10.2008, BJK İnönü Stadı , Istanbul; Attendance: 23,628
Referee: Viktor Kassai (Hungary)
TURKEY - BOSNIA-HERZEGOVINA   **2-1(0-1)**
TUR: Volkan Demirel, Servet Çetin (Cap), Hakan Kadir Balta, İbrahim Kaş, Sabrı Sarığlı, Arda Turan, Mehmet Aurélio, Colin Kazim-Richards, Ayhan Akman (63.Halil Altı ntop), Mevlüt Erdinç (79.Yusuf Şimşek), Batuhan Karadeniz (38.Nuri Şahin). Trainer: Fatih Terim.
BIH: Kenan Hasagić (74.Goran Brašnić, Dž emal Berberovč, Emir Spahić (Cap), Samir Muratović (80.Miralem Pjanić), Ivan Radeljić, Dario Damjanović, Elvir Rahimić, Sejad Salihović, Zvjezdan Misimović, Edin Dž eko, Senijad Ibrčić (63.Vedad Ibišević). Trainer: Miroslav Blaž evč (Croatia).
Goals: 0-1 Edin Dž eko (27), 1-1 Arda Turan (51), 2-1 Mevlüt Erdinç (66).
Cautions: Colin Kazim-Richards / Ivan Radeljić, Miralem Pjanić.

11.10.2008, Stade „Roi Baudouin", Bruxelles; Attendance: 20,949
Referee: Peter Rasmussen (Denmark)
BELGIUM - ARMENIA   **2-0(2-0)**
BEL: Stijn Stijnen, Guillaume Gillet, Vincent Jean Mpoy Kompany, Timmy Simons (Cap), Jelle Van Damme, Axel Tomas Witsel, Marouane Fellaini, Jan Vertonghen, Steven Arnold Defour (72.Stein Huysegems), Wesley Sonck (87.Tom De Sutter), Moussa Dembélé. Trainer: René Vandereycken.
ARM: Roman Berezovski, Sargis Hovsepyan (Cap), Robert Arzumanyan, Aleksander Tadevosyan, Aghvan Mkrtchyan, Karen Aleksanyan (64.Ara Hakobyan), Ararat Arakelyan, Levon Pachajyan, Artur Voskanyan, Arman Karamyan (85.Henrikh Mkhitaryan), Robert Zebelyan (80.Samvel Melkonyan). Trainer: Jan Børge Poulsen (Denmark).
Goals: 1-0 Wesley Sonck (22), 2-0 Marouane Fellaini (38).
Cautions: Aleksander Tadevosyan, Karen Aleksanyan.

11.10.2008, A Le Coq Arena, Tallinn; Attendance: 9,200
Referee: Jonas Eriksson (Sweden)
ESTONIA - SPAIN   **0-3(0-2)**
EST: Pavel Londak, Enar Jääger, Alo Bärengrub, Raio Piiroja (Cap), Dmitri Kruglov, Tarmo Kink (59.Sander Puri), Aleksandr Dmitrijev, Joel Lindpere (75.Ragnar Klavan), Martin Vunk, Konstantin Vassiljev, Vladimir Voskoboinikov (73.Kaimar Saag). Trainer: Tarmo Rüütli.
ESP: Iker Casillas Fernández (Cap), Sergio Ramos García (53.Andoni Iraola Sagarna), Juan Gutiérrez Moreno „Juanito", Carles Puyol Saforcada, Joan Capdevila Méndez, Andrés Iniesta Luján (79.Albert

Riera Ortega), Xavier Hernández Creus „Xavi", Xabier „Xabi" Alonso Olano, Santiago Cazorla González, David Villa Sánchez (70.Francesc „Cesc" Fàbregas Soler), Fernando José Torres Sanz. Trainer: Vicente Del Bosque González.
Goals: 0-1 Juan Gutiérrez Moreno „Juanito" (33), 0-2 David Villa Sánchez (38 penalty), 0-3 Carles Puyol Saforcada (69).
Cautions: Alo Bärengrub, Tarmo Kink, Raio Piiroja / Andoni Iraola Sagarna.

15.10.2008, Bilino Polje Stadium, Zenica; Attendance: 13,000
Referee: Asaf Kenan (Israel)
BOSNIA-HERZEGOVINA - ARMENIA   **4-1(2-0)**
BIH: Goran Brašnić, Dž emal Berberovč (61.Admir Vladavić), Emir Spahić (Cap) (68.Velibor Vasilić), Samir Muratović, Dario Damjanović, Elvir Rahimić, Adnan Mravac, Sejad Salihović, Zvjezdan Misimović, Edin Dž eko, Vedad Ibiševč (46.Zlatan Muslimović). Trainer: Miroslav Blaž evč (Croatia).
ARM: Roman Berezovski, Sargis Hovsepyan (Cap), Robert Arzumanyan, Aleksander Tadevosyan, Aghvan Mkrtchyan, Artur Yedigaryan (59.Vahagn Minasyan), Samvel Melkonyan (41.Ararat Arakelyan), Artur Voskanyan, Arman Karamyan, Levon Pachajyan, Robert Zebelyan (73.Ara Hakobyan). Trainer: Jan Børge Poulsen (Denmark).
Goals: 1-0 Emir Spahić (31), 2-0 Edin Dž eko (39), 3-0 Zlatan Muslimovč (56), 3-1 Vahagn Minasyan (85), 4-1 Zlatan Muslimović (89).
Cautions: Emir Spahić / Arman Karamyan.

15.10.2008, A Le Coq Arena, Tallinn; Attendance: 6,500
Referee: Robert Mał ek (Poland)
ESTONIA - TURKEY   **0-0**
EST: Pavel Londak, Tihhon Šišov, Alo Bärengrub, Raio Piiroja (Cap), Dmitri Kruglov, Martin Vunk (77.Sander Puri), Aleksandr Dmitrijev, Ragnar Klavan, Konstantin Vassiljev, Andres Oper, Vladimir Voskoboinikov (63.Sergei Zenjov). Trainer: Tarmo Rüütli.
TUR: Volkan Demirel, Servet Çetin (Cap), Hakan Kadir Balta, İbrahim Kaş, Sabrı Sarığbı, Arda Turan, Mehmet Aurélio, Colin Kazim-Richards (72.Uğur Boral), Halil Altı ntop, Ayhan Akman (60.Yusuf Şimşek), Nuri Şahin (35.Mevlüt Erdinç). Trainer: Fatih Terim.
Cautions: Arda Turan.

15.10.2008, Stade „Roi Baudouin", Bruxelles; Attendance: 45,888
Referee: Tom Henning Øvrebø (Norway)
BELGIUM - SPAIN   **1-2(1-1)**
BEL: Stijn Stijnen, Anthony Vanden Borre (88.Guillaume Gillet), Vincent Jean Mpoy Kompany, Timmy Simons (Cap), Daniel Van Buyten (46.Filip Daems), Thomas Vermaelen, Axel Tomas Witsel, Marouane Fellaini, Jan Vertonghen, Steven Arnold Defour (73.Jelle Van Damme), Wesley Sonck. Trainer: René Vandereycken.
ESP: Iker Casillas Fernández (Cap), Sergio Ramos García, Juan Gutiérrez Moreno „Juanito", Carles Puyol Saforcada, Joan Capdevila Méndez, Andrés Iniesta Luján (85.Daniel Gonzalez Güiza), Xavier Hernández Creus „Xavi", Marcos Antônio Senna da Silva, Santiago Cazorla González (64.Xabier „Xabi" Alonso Olano), David Villa Sánchez, Fernando José Torres Sanz (15.Francesc „Cesc" Fàbregas Soler). Trainer: Vicente Del Bosque González.
Goals: 1-0 Wesley Sonck (7), 1-1 Andrés Iniesta Luján (35), 1-2 David Villa Sánchez (88).
Cautions: Timmy Simons, Jan Vertonghen / Andrés Iniesta Luján, Carles Puyol Saforcada, Francesc „Cesc" Fàbregas Soler, David Villa Sánchez.

28.03.2009, "Vazgen Sargsyan" Hanrapetakan Stadium, Yerevan; Attendance: 3,000
Referee: Luc Wilmes (Luxembourg)
ARMENIA - ESTONIA   **2-2(1-1)**
ARM: Roman Berezovski, Sargis Hovsepyan (Cap), Robert Arzumanyan, Vahagn Minasyan, Aghvan Mkrtchyan, Levon Pachajyan (82.Artur Yedigaryan), Artur Voskanyan (46.Gevorg Ghazaryan), Ararat

Arakelyan, Artavazd Karamyan, Henrikh Mkhitaryan, Arman Karamyan (61.Edgar Manucharyan). Trainer: Jan Børge Poulsen (Denmark).

EST: Sergei Pareiko, Enar Jääger, Taavi Rähn, Raio Piiroja, Ragnar Klavan, Aleksandr Dmitrijev, Martin Vunk, Konstantin Vassiljev (87.Kaimar Saag), Tarmo Kink, Joel Lindpere (76.Sander Puri), Vladimir Voskoboinikov (63.Sergei Zenjov). Trainer: Tarmo Rüütli.
Goals: 1-0 Henrikh Mkhitaryan (33), 1-1 Konstantin Vassiljev (38), 1-2 Sergei Zenjov (67), 2-2 Gevorg Ghazaryan (87).

28.03.2009, Stade Fenix, Genk; Attendance: 20,041
Referee: Nikolay Ivanov (Russia)
BELGIUM - BOSNIA-HERZEGOVINA   **2-4(0-1)**
BEL: Stijn Stijnen, Gill Swerts, Timmy Simons (Cap), Thomas Vermaelen, Filip Daems (79.Tom De Sutter), Gaby Mudingayi, Marouane Fellaini, Steven Arnold Defour (59.Sébastien Pocognoli), Moussa Dembélé, Wesley Sonck, Igor Albert Rinck De Camargo (45+1.Eden Hazard). Trainer: René Vandereycken.
BIH: Nemanja Supić, Dž emal Berberović, Safet Nadarević, Emir Spahić (Cap) (60.Adnan Mravac), Samir Muratović, Sanel Jahić, Zlatan Muslimović (70.Zlatan Bajramović), Boris Pandž a, Zvjezdan Misimović, Edin Dž eko (89.Miralem Pjanić), Senijad Ibričić. Trainer: Miroslav Blaž ević (Croatia).
Goals: 0-1 Edin Dž eko (7), 1-1 Moussa Dembélé (65), 1-2Sanel Jahić (74), 1-3 Zlatan Bajramović (81), 1-4 Zvjezdan Misimović (86), 2-4 Wesley Sonck (89 penalty).
Cautions: Marouane Fellaini, Moussa Dembélé / Zvjezdan Misimović, Senijad Ibričić, Samir Muratović, Adnan Mravac.

28.03.2009, Estadio „Santiago Bernabéu", Madrid; Attendance: 73,820
Referee: Massimo Busacca (Switzerland)
SPAIN - TURKEY   **1-0(0-0)**
ESP: Iker Casillas Fernández (Cap), Sergio Ramos García, Raúl Albiol Tortajada, Gerard Piqué Bernabeu, Joan Capdevila Méndez, Xavier Hernández Creus „Xavi", Xabier „Xabi" Alonso Olano, Marcos Antônio Senna da Silva, Santiago Cazorla González (77.David Josué Jiménez Silva), David Villa Sánchez (63.Juan Manuel Mata García), Fernando José Torres Sanz (88.Fernando Llorente Torres). Trainer: Vicente Del Bosque González.
TUR: Volkan Demirel, Gökhan Gönül, Emre Aşı k, Hakan Kadir Balta, İbrahim Üzülmez, Emre Belözoğlu (84.Sabrı Sarıoğlu), Mehmet Aurélio, Tuncay Şanlı , Arda Turan (78.Gökhan Ünal), Nı hat Kahvecı (Cap), Semilİşentürk (57.Ayhan Akman). Trainer: Fatih Terim.
Goal: 1-0 Gerard Piqué Bernabeu (60).

01.04.2009, A Le Coq Arena, Tallinn; Attendance: 5,200
Referee: Cyril Zimmermann (Switzerland)
ESTONIA - ARMENIA   **1-0(0-0)**
EST: Sergei Pareiko, Enar Jääger, Taavi Rähn, Raio Piiroja, Ragnar Klavan, Sander Puri, Konstantin Vassiljev, Aleksandr Dmitrijev, Tarmo Kink (69.Joel Lindpere), Vladimir Voskoboinikov (87.Martin Vunk), Kristen Viikmäe (61.Sergei Zenjov). Trainer: Tarmo Rüütli.
ARM: Gevorg Kasparov, Sargis Hovsepyan (Cap), Robert Arzumanyan, Ararat Arakelyan, Vahagn Minasyan, Artur Yedigaryan (84.Arman Karamyan), Aghvan Mkrtchyan, Henrikh Mkhitaryan, Artavazd Karamyan (89.Gevorg Ghazaryan), Levon Pachajyan, Edgar Manucharyan. Trainer: Vardan Minasyan.
Goal: 1-0 Sander Puri (83).
Cautions: Sergei Pareiko / Aghvan Mkrtchyan.

01.04.2009, „Ali Sami Yen" Stadyumu, Istanbul; Attendance: 5,200
Referee: Michael Anthony Riley (England)
TURKEY - SPAIN   **1-2(1-0)**
TUR: Volkan Demirel, Gökhan Gönül, Emre Aşı k, Hakan Kadir Balta, İbrahim Üzülmez, Emre Belözoğlu, Mehmet Aurélio, Tuncay Şanlı (Cap), Arda Turan (88.Nuri Şahin), Nı hat Kahvecı

(77.Batuhan Karadeniz), Semih Şentürk (81.Sabrı Sarığbı). Trainer: Fatih Terim.
ESP: Iker Casillas Fernández (Cap), Sergio Ramos García, Carlos Marchena López, Joan Capdevila Méndez, Gerard Piqué Bernabeu, David Josué Jiménez Silva (73.Sergio Busquets Burgos), Xavier Hernández Creus „Xavi", Xabier „Xabi" Alonso Olano, Marcos Antônio Senna da Silva (66.Santiago Cazorla González), Albert Riera Ortega, Fernando José Torres Sanz (85.Daniel Gonzalez Güiza). Trainer: Vicente Del Bosque González.
Goals: 1-0 Semih Şentürk (26), 1-1 Xabier „Xabi" Alonso Olano (63 penalty), 1-2 Albert Riera Ortega (90+2).
Cautions: İbrahim Üzülmez, Emre Aşı k, Semih Şentürk, Emre Belözoğlu / Xavier Hernández Creus „Xavi", Sergio Ramos García.

01.04.2009, Bilino Polje Stadium, Zenica; Attendance: 13,800
Referee: Vladimír Hriňák (Slovakia)
BOSNIA-HERZEGOVINA - BELGIUM   **2-1(2-0)**
BIH: Nemanja Supić, Dž emal Berberović, Safet Nadarević, Samir Muratović (87.Zlatan Bajramović), Emir Spahić (Cap), Boris Pandž a, Elvir Rahimić, Sanel Jahić, Zvjezdan Misimović, Edin Dž eko (90.Marko Topić), Senijad Ibričić (77.Miralem Pjanić). Trainer: Miroslav Blaž ević (Croatia).
BEL: Stijn Stijnen, Gill Swerts, Timmy Simons (Cap), Vincent Jean Mpoy Kompany, Thomas Vermaelen, Gaby Mudingayi (58.Tom De Sutter), Marouane Fellaini, Moussa Dembélé, Axel Tomas Witsel, Kevin Antonio Mirallas (73.Eden Hazard), Wesley Sonck (90+1.Guillaume Gillet). Trainer: René Vandereycken.
Goals: 1-0 Edin Dž eko (12), 2-0 Edin Dž eko (15), 2-1 Gill Swerts (88).
Cautions: Zvjezdan Misimović, Sanel Jahić, Nemanja Supić / Gill Swerts.
Sent off: Axel Tomas Witsel (61).

05.09.2009, "Vazgen Sargsyan" Hanrapetakan Stadium, Yerevan; Attendance: 1,800
Referee: Frederikus Johannes "Eric" Braamhaar (Holland)
ARMENIA - BOSNIA-HERZEGOVINA   **0-2(0-1)**
ARM: Gevorg Kasparov, Sargis Hovsepyan (Cap), Robert Arzumanyan, Aleksander Tadevosyan, Aghvan Mkrtchyan, Artur Yedigaryan (75.Hirac Yagan), Ararat Arakelyan (66.Vahagn Minasyan), Arman Karamyan, Artavazd Karamyan, Henrikh Mkhitaryan, Eghya Yavruyan (46.Hovhannes Goharyan). Trainer: Vardan Minasyan.
BIH: Nemanja Supić, Safet Nadarević, Admir Vladavić, Emir Spahić (Cap), Samir Muratović (64.Miralem Pjanić), Elvir Rahimić, Sejad Salihović, Sanel Jahić, Senijad Ibričić (84.Zlatan Bajramović), Edin Dž eko, Vedad Ibišević (69.Zlatan Muslimović). Trainer: Miroslav Blaž ević (Croatia).
Goals: 0-1 Senijad Ibričić (6), 0-2 Zlatan Muslimović (74).
Cautions: Gevorg Kasparov, Artavazd Karamyan, Robert Arzumanyan, Henrikh Mkhitaryan / Zlatan Bajramović.

05.09.2009, Kayseri Kadir Has Şehir Stadyumu; Attendance: 28,659
Referee: Tommy Skjerven (Norway)
TURKEY - ESTONIA   **4-2(2-1)**
TUR: Volkan Demirel, Servet Çetin, Hakan Kadir Balta, Gökhan Gönül, Gökhan Zan (36.Önder Turacı), Hamit Altı ntop, Arda Turan, Emre Belöğbu (78.Ceyhun Gülselam), Colin Kazim-Richards (61.Halil Altı ntop), Tuncay Şanlı (Cap), Sercan Yı ldı rı m. Trainer: Fatih Terim.
EST: Sergei Pareiko, Enar Jääger, Raio Piiroja, Alo Bärengrub, Ragnar Klavan, Joel Lindpere, Konstantin Vassiljev, Aleksandr Dmitrijev (73.Martin Vunk), Dmitri Kruglov, Vladimir Voskoboinikov (54.Sergei Zenjov), Andres Oper (74.Tarmo Kink). Trainer: Tarmo Rüütli.
Goals: 0-1 Vladimir Voskoboinikov (7), 1-1 Tuncay Şanlı (29), 2-1 Sercan Yı ldı rı m (37), 2-2 Konstantin Vassiljev (52), 3-2 Arda Turan (62), 4-2 Tuncay Şanlı (72).
Cautions: Gökhan Gönül / Vladimir Voskoboinikov.

05.09.2009, Estadio Riazor, La Coruña; Attendance: 30,441
Referee: Bertrand Layec (France)
SPAIN - BELGIUM **5-0(1-0)**
ESP: Iker Casillas Fernández, Gerard Piqué Bernabeu, Carles Puyol Saforcada, Joan Capdevila Méndez, Álvaro Arbeloa Coca (83.Raúl Albiol Tortajada), Sergio Busquets Burgos, Xabier „Xabi" Alonso Olano, Xavier Hernández Creus „Xavi" (71.Francesc „Cesc" Fàbregas Soler), David Josué Jiménez Silva, David Villa Sánchez, Fernando José Torres Sanz (67.Albert Riera Ortega). Trainer: Vicente Del Bosque González.
Jean-François Gillet, Anthony Vanden Borre, Daniel Van Buyten, Thomas Vermaelen, Jan Vertonghen (30.Olivier Deschacht), Steven Arnold Defour, Marouane Fellaini, Timmy Simons (Cap), Moussa Dembélé, Eden Hazard (57.Kevin Antonio Mirallas), Wesley Sonck (70.Igor De Camargo). Trainer: Frank Vercauteren.
Goals: 1-0 David Josué Jiménez Silva (41), 2-0 David Villa Sánchez (49), 3-0 David Josué Jiménez Silva (41), 4-0 Gerard Piqué Bernabeu (52), 5-0 David Villa Sánchez (85).
Cautions: Sergio Busquets Burgos, Carles Puyol Saforcada / Thomas Vermaelen, Marouane Fellaini.

09.09.2009, "Vazgen Sargsyan" Hanrapetakan Stadium, Yerevan; Attendance: 2,300
Referee: Ljubomir Krstevski (Macedonia)
ARMENIA - BELGIUM **2-1(1-0)**
ARM: Gevorg Kasparov, Sargis Hovsepyan, Hrayr Mkoyan, Robert Arzumanyan, Aghvan Mkrtchyan, Artur Yedigaryan (89.Eduard Kakosyan), Ararat Arakelyan (14.Karlen Mkrtchyan), Artavazd Karamyan, Arman Karamyan, Henrikh Mkhitaryan, Hovhannes Goharyan (31.Eghya Yavruyan). Trainer: Vardan Minasyan.
BEL: Jean-François Gillet, Gill Swerts, Daniel Van Buyten, Timmy Simons (Cap), Olivier Deschacht, Steven Arnold Defour, Maarten Martens (53.Tom De Sutter), Igor De Camargo, Moussa Dembélé, Kevin Antonio Mirallas (72.Eden Hazard), Wesley Sonck (81.Roland Conde Lamah). Trainer: Frank Vercauteren.
Goals: 1-0 Hovhannes Goharyan (23), 2-0 Sargis Hovsepyan (50), 2-1 Daniel Van Buyten (90+2).
Cautions: Henrikh Mkhitaryan, Eghya Yavruyan / Wesley Sonck, Timmy Simons.

09.09.2009, Bilino Polje Stadium, Zenica; Attendance: 30,000
Referee: Olegário Manuel Bartolo Faustino Benquerença (Portugal)
BOSNIA-HERZEGOVINA - TURKEY **1-1(1-1)**
BIH: Nemanja Supić, Safet Nadarević, Emir Spahić (Cap), Samir Muratović (61.Miralem Pjanić), Elvir Rahimić, Sejad Salihović, Sanel Jahić, Senijad Ibričić (79.Admir Vladavić), Zvezdjan Misimović, Edin Dž eko, Vedad Ibiševč (68.Zlatan Muslimović). Trainer: Miroslav Blaž evč (Croatia).
TUR: Volkan Demirel, Servet Çetin, Hakan Kadir Balta, Gökhan Gönül, Önder Turacı (46.Ismail Köybaşı), Hamit Altı ntop (46.Sercan Yı ldı rı m), Ceyhun Gülselam, Emre Belözoğlu, Arda Turan, Tuncay Şanlı (Cap), Semih Şentürk. Trainer: Fatih Terim.
Goals: 0-1 Emre Belözoğlu (4), 1-1 Sejad Salihović (25).
Cautions: Elvir Rahimić, Miralem Pjanić, Nemanja Supić, Zvezdjan Misimović / Emre Belözoğlu, Arda Turan, Ceyhun Gülselam, Semih Şentürk.

09.09.2009, Estadio Romano, Mérida; Attendance: 14,362
Referee: Oleh Oriekhov (Ukraine)
SPAIN - ESTONIA **3-0(1-0)**
ESP: Iker Casillas Fernández (Cap), Raúl Albiol Tortajada, Gerard Piqué Bernabeu, Carlos Marchena López, Joan Capdevila Méndez, Xavier Hernández Creus „Xavi", Francesc „Cesc" Fàbregas Soler, Marcos Antônio Senna da Silva, David Josué Jiménez Silva (78.Juan Manuel Mata García), David Villa Sánchez (65.Santiago Cazorla González), Fernando José Torres Sanz (57.Daniel Gonzalez Güiza). Trainer: Vicente Del Bosque González.
EST: Sergei Pareiko, Tihhon Šišov (64.Enar Jääger), Taavi Rähn, Raio Piiroja, Ragnar Klavan, Dmitri Kruglov, Martin Vunk, Konstantin Vassiljev, Sergei Zenjov (46.Vladimir Voskoboinikov), Tarmo Kink

(71.Joel Lindpere), Andres Oper. Trainer: Tarmo Rüütli.
Goals: 1-0 Francesc „Cesc" Fàbregas Soler (32), 2-0 Santiago Cazorla González (81), 3-0 Juan Manuel Mata García (90+2).
Cautions: Raio Piiroja, Konstantin Vassiljev, Taavi Rähn.

10.10.2009, "Vazgen Sargsyan" Hanrapetakan Stadium, Yerevan; Attendance: 10,500
Referee: Jiří Jech (Czech Republic)
ARMENIA - SPAIN   **1-2(0-1)**
ARM: Roman Berezovski, Robert Arzumanyan, Sargis Hovsepyan (Cap), Hrayr Mkoyan, Artur Yedigaryan 974.Ararat Arakelyan), Aghvan Mkrtchyan, Karlen Mkrtchyan, Marcos Piñeiro Pizelli (66.Artak Dashyan), Artavazd Karamyan, Hovhannes Goharyan (60.Samvel Melkonyan), Arman Karamyan. Trainer: Vardan Minasyan.
ESP: José Manuel Reina Páez, Sergio Ramos García, Ignacio Monreal Eraso, Carlos Marchena López (46.Gerard Piqué Bernabeu), Carles Puyol Saforcada, Xavier Hernández Creus „Xavi" (Cap), Francesc „Cesc" Fàbregas Soler, Santiago Cazorla González, Juan Manuel Mata García (67.Andrés Iniesta Luján), Marcos Antônio Senna da Silva, Fernando José Torres Sanz (55.Álvaro Negredo Sánchez). Trainer: Vicente Del Bosque González.
Goals: 0-1 Francesc „Cesc" Fàbregas Soler (33), 1-1 Robert Arzumanyan (58), 1-2 Juan Manuel Mata García (64 penalty).
Cautions: Roman Berezovski, Sargis Hovsepyan / Carlos Marchena López, Carles Puyol Saforcada.

10.10.2009, A Le Coq Arena, Tallinn; Attendance: 6,450
Referee: Nicola Rizzoli (Italy)
ESTONIA - BOSNIA-HERZEGOVINA   **0-2(0-1)**
EST: Sergei Pareiko, Enar Jääger, Taavi Rähn, Alo Bärengrub, Ragnar Klavan, Sander Puri, Konstantin Vassiljev, Aleksandr Dmitrijev, Dmitri Kruglov, Tarmo Kink (73.Ats Purje), Vladimir Voskoboinikov (59.Kaimar Saag). Trainer: Tarmo Rüütli.
BIH: Kenan Hasagić (90+2.Asmir Begović), Safet Nadarević, Emir Spahić, Sanel Jahić, Elvir Rahimić, Sejad Salihović, Senijad Ibričić, Zvezdjan Misimović, Samir Muratović (85.Dž emal Berberović), Edin Dž eko, Vedad Ibišević. Trainer: Miroslav Blaž ević (Croatia).
Goals: 0-1 Edin Dž eko (30), 0-2 Vedad Ibišević (64).
Cautions: Aleksandr Dmitrijev / Senijad Ibričić.

10.10.2009, Stade „Roi Baudouin", Bruxelles; Attendance: 30,131
Referee: Matteo Simone Trefoloni (Italy)
BELGIUM - TURKEY   **2-0(1-0)**
BEL: Logan Bailly, Gill Swerts, Daniel Van Buyten, Nicolas Lombaerts, Thomas Vermaelen (Cap), Jan Vertonghen, Marouane Fellaini, Moussa Dembélé, Kevin Antonio Mirallas (74.Eden Hazard), Emile Lokonda Mpenza (89.Tom De Sutter), Roland Lamah (78.Gaby Mudingayi). Trainer: Dirk Nicolaas Advocaat (Holland).
TUR: Volkan Demirel, Servet Çetin, Hakan Kadir Balta, Gökhan Gönül, Önder Turacı , Hamit Altı ntop, Nurşahin, Tuncay Şanlı (Cap), Ceyhun Eşi (46.Semih Şentürk), Nı hat Kahvecı (71.Yusuf Şimşek), Ayhan Akman (61.Colin Kazim-Richards). Trainer: Fatih Terim.
Goals: 1-0 Emile Lokonda Mpenza (8), 2-0 Emile Lokonda Mpenza (84).
Cautions: Daniel Van Buyten, Nicolas Lombaerts, Emile Lokonda Mpenza / Semih Şentürk.

14.10.2009, Bilino Polje Stadium, Zenica; Attendance: 13,500
Referee: Konrad Plautz (Austria)
BOSNIA-HERZEGOVINA – SPAIN   **2-5(0-2)**
BIH: Nemanja Supić, Sanel Jahić, Emir Spahić, Safet Nadarević, Sejad Salihović (73.Mirko Hrgović), Elvir Rahimić (46.Zlatan Bajramović), Samir Muratović (67.Admir Vladavić), Miralem Pjanić, Zvezdjan Misimović, Vedad Ibišević, Edin Dž eko. Trainer:Miroslav Blaž ević (Croatia).
ESP: Iker Casillas Fernández (Cap), Gerard Piqué Bernabeu (77.Sergio Ramos García), Raúl Albiol Tortajada, Joan Capdevila Méndez, Andoni Iraola Sagarna, Sergio Busquets Burgos, Andrés Iniesta

Luján (67.Marcos Antônio Senna da Silva), David Josué Jiménez Silva (82.Juan Manuel Mata García), Xabier „Xabi" Alonso Olano, Albert Riera Ortega, Álvaro Negredo Sánchez. Trainer: Vicente Del Bosque González.
Goals: 0-1 Gerard Piqué Bernabeu (13), 0-2 David Josué Jiménez Silva (14), 0-3 Álvaro Negredo Sánchez (50), 0-4 Álvaro Negredo Sánchez (55), 0-5 Juan Manuel Mata García (81), 1-5 Edin Dž eko (90), 2-5 Zvjezdan Misimović (90+2).
Cautions: Andrés Iniesta Luján.

14.10.2009, „Atatürk" Stadium, Bursa; Attendance: 18,000
Referee: Martin Hansson (Sweden)
TURKEY - ARMENIA   **2-0(2-0)**
TUR: Volkan Demirel (90.Rüştü Reçber), Servet Çetin, Gökhan Gönül, İsmail Köybaşı , Hamit Altı ntop (83.Colin Kazim-Richards), Ceyhun Gülselam Emre Belözoğlu, Tuncay Şanlı (Cap) (46.İbrahim Kaş), Arda Turan, Halil Altı ntop, Ayhan Akman. TrainerFatih Terim.
ARM: Roman Berezovski, Karlen Mkrtchyan, Sargis Hovsepyan (Cap), Robert Arzumanyan, Hrayr Mkoyan, Ararat Arakelyan (58.Marcos Piñeiro Pizelli), Aghvan Mkrtchyan, Henrikh Mkhitaryan, Artavazd Karamyan, Arman Karamyan (77.Eduard Kakosyan), Hovhannes Goharyan (46.Samvel Melkonyan). Trainer: Vardan Minasyan.
Goals: 1-0 Halil Altı ntop (16), 2-0 Servet Çetin (28).
Cautions: Ceyhun Gülselam, Emre Belözoğlu / Hovhannes Goharyan, Ararat Arakelyan, Hrayr Mkoyan.
Sent off: Ceyhun Gülselam (33).

14.10.2009, A. Le Coq Arena, Tallinn; Attendance: 4,680
Referee: Nicolai Vollquartz (Denmark)
ESTONIA - BELGIUM   **2-0(1-0)**
EST: Sergei Pareiko, Enar Jääger, Taavi Rähn, Raio Piiroja (62.Igor Morozov), Dmitri Kruglov, Tarmo Kink (59.Sander Puri), Aleksandr Dmitrijev, Martin Vunk, Joel Lindpere, Konstantin Vassiljev, Kaimar Saag (72.Vladimir Voskoboinikov). Trainer: Tarmo Rüütli.
BEL: Logan Bailly, Gill Swerts (76.Tom De Sutter), Daniel Van Buyten (46.Tobias Albertine Maurits Alderweireld), Nicolas Lombaerts, Thomas Vermaelen (Cap), Jan Vertonghen, Gaby Mudingayi (46.Thomas Buffel), Moussa Dembélé, Kevin Antonio Mirallas, Emile Lokonda Mpenza, Roland Lamah. Trainer: Dirk Nicolaas Advocaat (Holland).
Goals: 1-0 Raio Piiroja (30), 2-0 Konstantin Vassiljev (67).
Cautions: Martin Vunk / Gill Swerts.

GROUP 6

20.08.2008	Almaty	Kazakhstan - Andorra		3-0(3-0)
06.09.2008	Lviv	Ukraine - Belarus		1-0(0-0)
06.09.2008	Barcelona (Spain)	Andorra - England		0-2(0-0)
06.09.2008	Zagreb	Croatia - Kazakhstan		3-0(2-0)
10.09.2008	Almaty	Kazakhstan - Ukraine		1-3(0-1)
10.09.2008	Andorra laVella	Andorra - Belarus		1-3(0-1)
10.09.2008	Zagreb	Croatia - England		1-4(0-1)
11.10.2008	London	England - Kazakhstan		5-1(0-0)
11.10.2008	Kharkiv	Ukraine - Croatia		0-0
15.10.2008	Zagreb	Croatia - Andorra		4-0(2-0)
15.10.2008	Minsk	Belarus - England		1-3(1-1)
01.04.2009	Almaty	Kazakhstan - Belarus		1-5(1-0)
01.04.2009	Andorra la Vella	Andorra - Croatia		0-2(0-2)
01.04.2009	London	England - Ukraine		2-1(1-0)
06.06.2009	Almaty	Kazakhstan - England		0-4(0-2)
06.06.2009	Grodno	Belarus - Andorra		5-1(2-0)
06.06.2009	Zagreb	Croatia - Ukraine		2-2(1-1)
10.06.2009	Kyiv	Ukraine - Kazakhstan		2-1(1-1)
10.06.2009	London	England - Andorra		6-0(3-0)
12.08.2009	Minsk	Belarus - Croatia		1-3(0-1)
05.09.2009	Kyiv	Ukraine - Andorra		5-0(2-0)
05.09.2009	Zagreb	Croatia - Belarus		1-0(1-0)
09.09.2009	Minsk	Belarus - Ukraine		0-0
09.09.2009	Andorra la Vella	Andorra - Kazakhstan		1-3(0-3)
09.09.2009	London	England - Croatia		5-1(2-0)
10.10.2009	Brest	Belarus - Kazakhstan		4-0(1-0)
10.10.2009	Dnipropetrovsk	Ukraine - England		1-0(1-0)
14.10.2009	Andorra la Vella	Andorra - Ukraine		0-6(0-1)
14.10.2009	Astana	Kazakhstan - Croatia		1-2(1-1)
14.10.2009	London	England - Belarus		3-0(1-0)

FINAL STANDINGS

1.	ENGLAND	10	9	0	1	34	-	6	27
2.	Ukraine	10	6	3	1	21	-	6	21
3.	Croatia	10	6	2	2	19	-	13	20
4.	Belarus	10	4	1	5	19	-	14	13
5.	Kazakhstan	10	2	0	8	11	-	29	6
6.	Andorra	10	0	0	10	3	-	39	0

England qualified for the Final Tournament; Ukraine qualified for the Play-Offs.

20.08.2008, Tsentralny Stadium, Almaty; Attendance: 7,700
Referee: Veaceslav Banari (Moldova)
KAZAKHSTAN - ANDORRA **3-0(3-0)**
KAZ: David Loria, Farkhadbek Irismetov, Aleksandr Kuchma, Samat Smakov, Sergey Skorykh (68.Andrey Karpovich), Ulugbek Asanbaev (79.Maksat Baizhanov), Ruslan Baltiev, Kairat Nurdauletov, Nurbol Zhumaskaliyev (Cap), Sergey Ostapenko, Roman Uzdenov (63.Dmitriy Byakov). Trainer: Arnoldus Dick Pijpers (Holland).
AND: Josep Antonio Gómes Moreira, Josep Manuel Ayala Díaz (15.Jordi Escura Aixas), Marc Bernaus Cano, Antonio Lima Solá, Ildefons Lima Solá, Xavier Andorrà Julià, Marc Vales González, Marc Pujol Pons (82.Álex Somoza Losada), Fernando José Silva García, Márcio Vieira de

55

Vasconcelos, Juan Carlos Toscano Beltrán (72.José Manuel García Luena „Txema"). Trainer: David Rodrigo.
Goals: 1-0 Sergey Ostapenko (14), 2-0 Sergey Ostapenko (30), 3-0 Roman Uzdenov (44).
Cautions: Marc Bernaus Cano, Josep Antonio Gómes Moreira, Ildefons Lima Solá, Xavier Andorrà Julià, Jordi Escura Aixas.

06.09.2008, Ukraina Stadium, Lviv; Attendance: 25,000
Referee: Nicola Rizzoli (Italy)
UKRAINE - BELARUS 1-0(0-0)
UKR: Andriy Pyatov, Grigoriy Yarmash, Andriy Rusol, Vyacheslav Shevchuk, Taras Mykhalyk, Anatoliy Tymoschuk (Cap), Serhiy Kravchenko, Maxym Kalynychenko (46.Oleksandr Aliev), Serhiy Nazarenko, Andriy Voronin (58.Yevhen Seleznev), Artem Milevskiy (46.Andriy Shevchenko). Trainer: Oleksiy Mykhailychenko.
BLR: Yuriy Zhevnov, Aleksandr Kulchiy, Yegor Filipenko, Dmitriy Verkhovtsov, Sergey Omelyanchuk, Vladimir Korytko (67.Andrey Chukley), Vitaliy Bulyga (72.Vyacheslav Hleb), Oleg Strakhanovich, Anton Putsilo (80.Aleksandr Pavlov), Aleksandr Hleb (Cap), Vitaliy Kutuzov. Trainer: Bernd Stange (Germany).
Goal: 1-0 Andriy Shevchenko (90+4).
Cautions: Anatoliy Tymoschuk / Vladimir Korytko, Vitaliy Kutuzov, Aleksandr Kulchiy.

06.09.2008, Estadio Olímpic „Lluís Companys", Barcelona (Spain); Attendance: 10,300
Referee: Cuneyt Çakir (Turkey)
ANDORRA - ENGLAND 0-2(0-0)
AND: Jesús Luis Alvarez de Eulate „Koldo", Josep Manuel Ayala Díaz, José Manuel García Luena „Txema", Antonio Lima Solá (90+1.Juli Fernández Ariza), Ildefons Lima Solá, Xavier Andorrà Julià, Manuel Jiménez Soria „Manolo", Óscar Sonejee Masand, Marc Pujol Pons (90.Marc Vales González), Fernando José Silva García (65.Juan Carlos Toscano Beltrán), Márcio Vieira de Vasconcelos. Trainer: David Rodrigo.
ENG: David Benjamin James, Glen McLeod Johnson, Joleon Patrick Lescott, John George Terry (Cap), Ashley Cole, Theo James Walcott, Frank James Lampard (79.David Joseph Robert Beckham), Gareth Robert Barry, Stewart Downing (46.Joseph John Cole), Wayne Mark Rooney, Jermain Colin Defoe (46.Emile William Ivanhoe Heskey). Manager: Fabio Capello (Italy).
Goals: 0-1 Joseph John Cole (49), 0-2 Joseph John Cole (55).
Cautions: Fernando José Silva García, Márcio Vieira de Vasconcelos, Antonio Lima Solá.

06.09.2008, Maksimir Stadion, Zagreb; Attendance: 17,424
Referee: Stefan Johannesson (Sweden)
CROATIA - KAZAKHSTAN 3-0(2-0)
CRO: Stipe Pletikosa, Vedran Ćorluka, Robert Kovač, Josip Šimunić, Danijel Pranjić, Niko Kovač (Cap), Luka Modrić (85.Nikola Pokrivač), Darijo Srna, Ivan Rakitić, Ivica Olić (88.Jerko Leko), Ivan Klasnić (64.Mladen Petrić). Trainer: Slaven Bilić.
KAZ: David Loria, Farkhadbek Irismetov, Aleksandr Kuchma, Samat Smakov, Maksim Zhalmagambetov, Sergey Skorykh (81.Andrey Karpovich), Maksat Baizhanov (57.Anton Chichulin), Ruslan Baltiev, Nurbol Zhumaskaliyev (Cap), Sergey Ostapenko, Dmitriy Byakov (84.Roman Uzdenov). Trainer: Arnoldus Dick Pijpers (Holland).
Goals: 1-0 Niko Kovač (13), 2-0 Luka Modrić (36), 3-0 Mladen Petrić (81).
Cautions: Robert Kovač / Farkhadbek Irismetov, Ruslan Baltiev.

10.09.2008, Tsentralny Stadium, Almaty; Attendance: 17,000
Referee: Dr. Felix Brych (Germany)
KAZAKHSTAN - UKRAINE 1-3(0-1)
KAZ: David Loria, Yegor Azovskiy, Aleksandr Kuchma, Samat Smakov, Farkhadbek Irismetov, Sergey Skorykh, Andrey Karpovich, Ulugbek Asanbaev (73.Maksat Baizhanov), Ruslan Baltiev (88.Roman Uzdenov), Nurbol Zhumaskaliyev (Cap), Sergey Ostapenko. Trainer: Arnoldus Dick

Pijpers (Holland).
UKR: Andriy Pyatov, Oleksandr Kucher, Grigoriy Yarmash, Taras Mykhalyk, Vyacheslav Shevchuk, Anatoliy Tymoschuk, Yevhen Seleznev (87.Volodymyr Homenyuk), Oleksandr Aliev, Serhiy Nazarenko (81.Serhiy Kravchenko), Yevhen Levchenko, Andriy Shevchenko (Cap) (88.Andriy Voronin). Trainer: Oleksiy Mykhailychenko.
Goals: 0-1 Serhiy Nazarenko (45), 0-2 Andriy Shevchenko (54), 1-2 Sergey Ostapenko (68), 1-3 Serhiy Nazarenko (80).
Cautions: Yegor Azovskiy, Farkhadbek Irismetov, Aleksandr Kuchma / Grigoriy Yarmash.

10.09.2008, Estadio Comunal de Aixovall, Andorra La Vella; Attendance: 1,100
Referee: Simon Lee Evans (Wales)
ANDORRA - BELARUS   **1-3(0-1)**
AND: Jesús Luis Alvarez de Eulate „Koldo", Josep Manuel Ayala Díaz, Jordi Escura Aixas, Antonio Lima Solá, Ildefons Lima Solá, Xavier Andorrà Julià, Manuel Jiménez Soria „Manolo", Óscar Sonejee Masand, Marc Pujol Pons (82.Juan Carlos Toscano Beltrán), Fernando José Silva García (86.Sergio Moreno Marín), Márcio Vieira de Vasconcelos (62.Marc Vales González). Trainer: David Rodrigo.
BLR: Sergey Veremko, Sergey Omelyanchuk, Vladimir Korytko, Aleksandr Kulchiy, Yegor Filipenko, Dmitriy Verkhovtsov, Oleg Strakhanovich (87.Pavel Sitko), Vitaliy Kutuzov, Aleksandr Pavlov (57.Vitaliy Rodionov), Vitaliy Bulyga (63.Vyacheslav Hleb), Aleksandr Hleb (Cap). Trainer: Bernd Stange (Germany).
Goals: 0-1 Dmitriy Verkhovtsov (37), 1-1 Marc Pujol Pons (67 penalty), 1-2 Vitaliy Rodionov (79), 1-3 Vyacheslav Hleb (90).
Cautions: Josep Manuel Ayala Díaz, Marc Pujol Pons, Antonio Lima Solá / Aleksandr Hleb, Dmitriy Verkhovtsov.

10.09.2008, Maksimir Stadion, Zagreb; Attendance: 35,218
Referee: Ľuboš Micheľ (Slovakia)
CROATIA - ENGLAND   **1-4(0-1)**
CRO: Stipe Pletikosa, Vedran Ćorluka, Robert Kovač, Josip Šimunić, Danijel Pranjić, Niko Kovač (Cap) (62.Nikola Pokrivač), Luka Modrić, Darijo Srna, Ivan Rakitić, Ivica Olić (71.Mario Mandžukić), Mladen Petrić (56.Dario Knežević). Trainer: Slaven Bilić.
ENG: David Benjamin James, Wesley Michael Brown, Rio Gavin Ferdinand, John George Terry (Cap) (89.Matthew James Upson), Ashley Cole, Theo James Walcott (84.David Joseph Robert Beckham), Frank James Lampard, Gareth Robert Barry, Joseph John Cole (55.Jermaine Anthony Jenas), Emile William Ivanhoe Heskey, Wayne Mark Rooney. Manager: Fabio Capello (Italy).
Goals: 0-1 Theo James Walcott (26), 0-2 Theo James Walcott (59), 0-3 Wayne Mark Rooney (63), 1-3 Mario Mandžukić (78), 1-4 Theo James Walcott (82).
Cautions: Josip Šimunić, Darijo Srna / Emile William Ivanhoe Heskey.
Sent off: Robert Kovač (52).

11.10.2008, The National Stadium, Wembley, London; Attendance: 89,107
Referee: Paul Allaerts (Belgium)
ENGLAND - KAZAKHSTAN   **5-1(0-0)**
ENG: David Benjamin James, Wesley Michael Brown, Rio Gavin Ferdinand (Cap), Matthew James Upson, Ashley Cole, Gareth Robert Barry (46.Shaun Cameron Wright-Phillips), Frank James Lampard, Steven George Gerrard, Theo James Walcott (79.David Joseph Robert Beckham), Emile William Ivanhoe Heskey, Wayne Mark Rooney (86.Jermain Colin Defoe). Manager: Fabio Capello (Italy).
KAZ: Aleksandr Mokin, Aleksandr Kuchma, Aleksandr Kirov (85.Talgat Sabalakov), Aleksandr Kislitsin, Tanat Nuserbayev, Ruslan Baltiyev (Cap), Yuriy Logvinenko, Sergey Ostapenko (76.Gleb Maltsev), Sergey Skorykh, Sabyrkhan Ibrayev, Zhambil Kukeev. Trainer: Bernd Storck (Germany).
Goals: 1-0 Rio Gavin Ferdinand (52), 2-0 Aleksandr Kuchma (64 own goal), 2-1 Zhambil Kukeev (68), 3-1 Wayne Mark Rooney (76), 4-1 Wayne Mark Rooney (86), 5-1 Jermain Colin Defoe (90).

11.10.2008, Metalist Stadium, Kharkiv; Attendance: 38,500
Referee: Frederikus Johannes "Eric" Braamhaar (Holland)
UKRAINE - CROATIA   **0-0**
UKR: Andriy Pyatov, Grigoriy Yarmash, Taras Mykhalyk, Dmytro Chyhrynskiy, Vyacheslav Shevchuk, Anatoliy Tymoschuk, Serhiy Nazarenko, Oleksandr Aliev, Yevhen Levchenko (84.Serhiy Kravchenko), Denis Golaido, Andriy Shevchenko (Cap). Trainer: Oleksiy Mykhailychenko.
CRO: Stipe Pletikosa, Vedran Ćorluka, Ivica Križ anac, Josip Šimunć, Danijel Pranjić, Darijo Srna, Ognjen Vukojević, Niko Kovač (Cap), Ivan Rakitić (84.Mario Mandž ukć), Luka Modrić, Ivica Olić. Trainer: Slaven Bilić.
Cautions: Serhiy Kravchenko / Niko Kovač, Darijo Srna.

15.10.2008, Maksimir Stadion, Zagreb; Attendance: 14,441
Referee: István Vad (Hungary)
CROATIA - ANDORRA   **4-0(2-0)**
CRO: Stipe Pletikosa, Vedran Ćorluka, Josip Šimunić, Ivica Križ anac (78.Dario Knež ević), Danijel Pranjić, Ivan Rakitić, Ognjen Vukojević (61.Jerko Leko), Luka Modrić, Ivica Olić (68.Mario Mandž ukć), Mladen Petrić, Ivan Klasnić. Trainer: Slaven Bilić.
AND: Jesús Luis Alvarez de Eulate „Koldo", Josep Manuel Ayala Díaz, Jordi Escura Aixas (81.José Manuel García Luena „Txema"), Ildefons Lima Solá, Víctor Rodríguez, Xavier Andorrà Julià, Manuel Jiménez Soria „Manolo" (87.Álex Somoza Losada), Marc Vales González, Marc Pujol Pons, Fernando José Silva García (90.Juan Carlos Toscano Beltrán), Márcio Vieira de Vasconcelos. Trainer: David Rodrigo.
Goals: 1-0 Ivan Rakitić (16), 2-0 Ivica Olić (32), 3-0 Luka Modrić (75), 4-0 Ivan Rakitić (87 penalty).
Cautions: Josip Šimunić / Víctor Rodríguez, Josep Manuel Ayala Díaz, Ildefons Lima Solá.

15.10.2008, Dinamo Stadium, Minsk; Attendance: 29,600
Referee: Terje Hauge (Norway)
BELARUS - ENGLAND   **1-3(1-1)**
BLR: Yuriy Zhevnov, Sergey Omelyanchuk, Dmitriy Molosh, Yegor Filipenko, Dmitriy Verkhovtsov, Aleksandr Kulchiy (Cap), Igor Stasevich (90.Vyacheslav Hleb), Anton Putsilo (67.Vitaliy Rodionov), Pavel Sitko, Vitaliy Kutuzov (77.Oleg Strakhanovich), Vitaliy Bulyga. Trainer: Bernd Stange (Germany).
ENG: David Benjamin James, Wesley Michael Brown, Rio Gavin Ferdinand (Cap), Matthew James Upson, Wayne Michael Bridge, Gareth Robert Barry, Steven George Gerrard, Theo James Walcott (68.Shaun Cameron Wright-Phillips), Frank James Lampard, Emile William Ivanhoe Heskey (70.Peter James Crouch), Wayne Mark Rooney (88.David Joseph Robert Beckham). Manager: Fabio Capello (Italy).
Goals: 0-1 Steven George Gerrard (11), 1-1 Pavel Sitko (28), 1-2 Wayne Mark Rooney (50), 1-3 Wayne Mark Rooney (75).
Cautions: Anton Putsilo / David Benjamin James.

01.04.2009, Tsentralny Stadium, Almaty; Attendance: 19,000
Referee: Jiří Jech (Czech Republic)
KAZAKHSTAN - BELARUS   **1-5(1-0)**
KAZ: David Loria, Rinat Abdulin, Aleksandr Kislitsin, Farkhadbek Irismetov, Yuriy Logvinenko, Andrey Karpovich (65.Sabyrkhan Ibrayev), Ruslan Baltiev (Cap) (81.Azat Nurgaliev), Zhambil Kukeev, Samat Smakov, Sergey Ostapenko, Tanat Nuserbayev. Trainer: Bernd Storck (Germany).
BLR: Yuriy Zhevnov, Aleksandr Kulchiy (70.Nikolay Kashevskiy), Aleksandr Yurevich, Maxym Bordachev, Igor Shitov, Sergey Sosnovskiy, Timofei Kalachev, Igor Stasevich (80.Leonid Kovel), Aleksandr Hleb, Vitaliy Kutuzov (86.Gennadiy Bliznyuk), Vitaliy Rodionov. Trainer: Bernd Stange (Germany).
Goals: 1-0 Rinat Abdulin (10), 1-1 Aleksandr Hleb (48), 1-2 Timofei Kalachev (54), 1-3 Igor Stasevich (57), 1-4 Timofei Kalachev (64), 1-5 Vitaliy Rodionov (88).

Cautions: Zhambil Kukeev / Aleksandr Kulchiy.

01.04.2009, Estadio Comunal de Aixovall, Andorra La Vella; Attendance: 1,100
Referee: Leontios Trattou (Cyprus)
ANDORRA - CROATIA   **0-2(0-2)**
AND: Jesús Luis Alvarez de Eulate „Koldo", Jordi Escura Aixas (90+2.Víctor Rodríguez), Antonio Lima Solá, Marc Bernaus Cano, Xavier Andorrà Julià, Óscar Sonejee Masand, Marc Vales González, Marc Pujol Pons, Márcio Vieira de Vasconcelos, Fernando José Silva García (79.Víctor Hugo Moreira), Manuel Jiménez Soria „Manolo" (88.Sergio Moreno Marín). Trainer: David Rodrigo.
CRO: Stipe Pletikosa, Vedran Ćorluka, Hrvoje Vejić, Ivica Križ anac, Hrvoje Čale (69.Ognjen Vukojević), Ivan Jurić (64.Nikola Pokrivač), Darijo Srna (Cap), Niko Kranjčar, Ivan Rakitić, Eduardo Alves da Silva, Ivan Klasnić (78.Nikola Kalinić). Trainer: Slaven Bilić.
Goals: 0-1 Ivan Klasnić (15), 0-2 Eduardo Alves da Silva (35).
Cautions: Antonio Lima Solá,)), Manuel Jiménez Soria „Manolo" / Eduardo Alves da Silva.

01.04.2009, The National Stadium, Wembley, London; Attendance: 87,548
Referee: Claus Bo Larsen (Denmark)
ENGLAND - UKRAINE   **2-1(1-0)**
ENG: David Benjamin James, Glen McLeod Johnson, Rio Gavin Ferdinand (88.Philip Nikodem Jagielka), John George Terry (Cap), Ashley Cole, Aaron Justin Lennon (58.David Joseph Robert Beckham), Frank James Lampard, Gareth Robert Barry, Steven George Gerrard, Peter James Crouch (79.Shaun Cameron Wright-Phillips), Wayne Mark Rooney. Manager: Fabio Capello (Italy).
UKR: Andriy Pyatov, Grigoriy Yarmash, Taras Mykhalyk, Dmytro Chyhrynskiy, Oleksandr Aliev, Vyacheslav Shevchuk, Anatoliy Tymoschuk (Cap), Serhiy Valyayev (62.Serhiy Nazarenko), Valentyn Slyusar (88.Maxym Kalynychenko), Artem Milevskiy, Andriy Voronin (56.Andriy Shevchenko). Trainer: Oleksiy Mykhailychenko.
Goals: 1-0 Peter James Crouch (29), 1-1 Andriy Shevchenko (74), 2-1 John George Terry (85).
Cautions: Gareth Robert Barry, Glen McLeod Johnson, David Joseph Robert Beckham / Taras Mykhalyk.

06.06.2009, Tsentralnyi Stadium, Almaty; Attendance: 23,281
Referee: Kristinn Jakobsson (Iceland)
KAZAKHSTAN - ENGLAND   **0-4(0-2)**
KAZ: Aleksandr Mokin, Aleksandr Kirov, Rinat Abdulin, Aleksandr Kislitsin, Sergey Skorykh, Evgeniy Averchenko (72.Vyacheslav Erbes), Andrey Karpovich (Cap), Zhambil Kukeev, Yuriy Logvinenko, Tanat Nuserbayev, Sergey Ostapenko (27.Sabyrkhan Ibrayev). Trainer: Bernd Storck (Germany).
Robert Paul Green, Glen McLeod Johnson (75.David Joseph Robert Beckham), Matthew James Upson, John George Terry (Cap), Ashley Cole, Gareth Robert Barry, Frank James Lampard, Theo James Walcott (46.Shaun Cameron Wright-Phillips), Steven George Gerrard, Emile William Ivanhoe Heskey (80.Jermain Colin Defoe), Wayne Mark Rooney. Manager: Fabio Capello (Italy).
Goals: 0-1 Gareth Robert Berry (40), 0-2 Emile William Ivanhoe Heskey (45+1), 0-3 Wayne Mark Rooney (72), 0-4 Frank James Lampard (77 penalty).
Cautions: Tanat Nuserbayev, Rinat Abdulin / Gareth Robert Barry.

06.06.2009, Neman Stadium, Grodno; Attendance: 8,500
Referee: Robert Kranjc (Slovenia)
BELARUS - ANDORRA   **5-1(2-0)**
BLR: Yuriy Zhevnov, Igor Shitov (66.Filip Rudzik), Aleksandr Yurevich, Sergey Sosnovskiy, Dmitriy Verkhovtsov, Igor Stasevich, Aleksandr Hleb, Nikolay Kashevskiy (66.Leonid Kovel), Timofei Kalachev, Sergey Kornilenko (79.Vitaliy Rodionov), Gennadiy Bliznyuk. Trainer: Bernd Stange (Germany).
AND: Jesús Luis Alvarez de Eulate „Koldo", Josep Manuel Ayala Díaz, Jordi Escura Aixas, Antonio Lima Solá (89.Juli Fernández Ariza), Ildefons Lima Solá, Xavier Andorrà Julià (80.Víctor Rodríguez),

Óscar Sonejee Masand, Marc Vales González, Víctor Hugo Moreira (76.Manuel Jiménez Soria „Manolo"), Sergio Moreno Marín, Fernando José Silva García. Trainer: David Rodrigo.
Goals: 1-0 Gennadiy Bliznyuk (2), 2-0 Timofei Kalachev (44), 3-0 Sergey Kornilenko (50), 4-0 Sergey Kornilenko (65), 5-0 Gennadiy Bliznyuk (76), 5-1 Ildefons Lima Solá (90+3).
Cautions: Jesús Luis Alvarez de Eulate „Koldo", Óscar Sonejee Masand, Ildefons Lima Solá.

06.06.2009, Maksimir Stadion, Zagreb; Attendance: 32,073
Referee: Terje Hauge (Norway)
CROATIA - UKRAINE   **2-2(1-1)**
CRO: Vedran Runje, Vedran Ćorluka, Robert Kovač (Cap), Josip Šimunić, Danijel Pranjić, Ivan Jurić (46.Ognjen Vukojević), Darijo Srna, Luka Modrić, Ivan Rakitić (46.Jerko Leko), Mladen Petrić, Ivica Olić (60.Mario Mandž uké). Trainer: Slaven Bilić.
UKR: Andriy Pyatov, Dmytro Chyhrynskiy, Oleksandr Kucher, Vitaliy Mandzyuk, Vyacheslav Shevchuk, Anatoliy Tymoschuk (87.Andriy Rusol), Oleksiy Gay, Serhiy Nazarenko (76.Maxym Kalynychenko), Ruslan Rotan, Artem Milevskiy, Andriy Shevchenko (Cap) (24.Yevhen Seleznev). Trainer: Oleksiy Mykhailychenko.
Goals: 1-0 Mladen Petrić (2), 1-1 Andriy Shevchenko (13), 1-2 Oleksiy Gay (54), 2-2 Luka Modrić (68).
Cautions: Darijo Srna, Jerko Leko / Yevhen Seleznev, Serhiy Nazarenko, Vitaliy Mandzyuk, Oleksandr Kucher.

10.06.2009, „Valeriy Lobanovskiy" Stadium, Kyiv; Attendance: 11,500
Referee: Bruno Miguel Duarte Paixão (Portugal)
UKRAINE - KAZAKHSTAN   **2-1(1-1)**
UKR: Stanislav Bohush, Dmytro Chyhrynskiy, Vitaliy Mandzyuk, Andriy Rusol, Vyacheslav Shevchuk, Anatoliy Tymoschuk (Cap), Oleksiy Gay, Serhiy Nazarenko, Ruslan Rotan (81.Maxym Kalynychenko), Artem Milevskiy, Andriy Voronin (68.Yevhen Seleznev). Trainer: Oleksiy Mykhailychenko.
KAZ: Aleksandr Mokin, Aleksandr Kirov (69.Farkhadbek Irismetov), Rinat Abdulin, Aleksandr Kislitsin, Yuriy Logvinenko, Andrey Karpovich (Cap), Tanat Nuserbayev (62.Andrey Travin), Sergey Skorykh, Sergey Khizhnichenko, Zhambil Kukeev, Vyacheslav Erbes (73.Evgeniy Averchenko). Trainer: Bernd Storck (Germany).
Goals: 0-1 Tanat Nuserbayev (19), 1-1 Serhiy Nazarenko (32), 2-1 Serhiy Nazarenko (47).
Cautions: Serhiy Nazarenko, Artem Milevskiy / Tanat Nuserbayev, Andrey Travin.

10.06.2009, The National Stadium, Wembley, London; Attendance: 57,897
Referee: Bas Nijhuis (Holland)
ENGLAND - ANDORRA   **6-0(3-0)**
ENG: Robert Paul Green, Glen McLeod Johnson, Joleon Patrick Lescott, John George Terry (Cap), Ashley Cole (64.Wayne Michael Bridge), Theo James Walcott, David Joseph Robert Beckham, Frank James Lampard, Steven George Gerrard (46.Ashley Simon Young), Wayne Mark Rooney (46.Jermain Colin Defoe), Peter James Crouch. Manager: Fabio Capello (Italy).
AND: Jesús Luis Alvarez de Eulate „Koldo" (89.Josep Antonio Gómes Moreira), Josep Manuel Ayala Díaz, José Manuel García Luena „Txema", Antonio Lima Solá (47.Marc Vales González), Ildefons Lima Solá, Xavier Andorrà Julià, Manuel Jiménez Soria „Manolo", Óscar Sonejee Masand, Márcio Vieira de Vasconcelos, Sergio Moreno Marín, Fernando José Silva García (79.Juli Fernández Ariza). Trainer: David Rodrigo.
Goals: 1-0 Wayne Mark Rooney (4), 2-0 Frank James Lampard (29), 3-0 Wayne Mark Rooney (39), 4-0 Jermain Colin Defoe (73), 5-0 Jermain Colin Defoe (75), 6-0 Peter James Crouch (80).
Cautions: Xavier Andorrà Julià, Jesús Luis Alvarez de Eulate „Koldo", Ildefons Lima Solá.

12.08.2009, Dinamo Stadium, Minsk; Attendance: 21,651
Referee: Felix Brych (Germany)
BELARUS - CROATIA   **1-3(0-1)**

BLR: Yuriy Zhevnov, Nikolay Kashevskiy (54.Leonid Kovel), Sergey Sosnovskiy, Sergey Omelyanchuk, Dmitriy Verkhovtsov, Aleksandr Yurevich, Timofei Kalachev, Aleksandr Kulchiy, Aleksandr Hleb, Sergey Kornilenko (70.Vitaliy Rodionov), Vitaliy Kutuzov (85.Gennadiy Bliznyuk). Trainer: Bernd Stange (Germany).
CRO: Vedran Runje, Vedran Ćorluka, Ivica Križ anac (46.Ivan Rakitć), Josip Šimunić, Danijel Pranjić, Darijo Srna (Cap), Luka Modrić, Ognjen Vukojević, Niko Kranjčar (66.Mario Mandž ukć), Eduardo Alves da Silva (88.Ivan Jurić), Ivica Olić. Trainer: Slaven Bilić.
Goals: 0-1 Ivica Olić (22), 0-2 Eduardo Alves da Silva (69), 0-3 Ivica Olić (85), 1-3 Dmitriy Verkhovtsov (81).
Cautions: Sergey Sosnovskiy, Vitaliy Kutuzov / Mario Mandž ikić.

05.09.2009, „Valeriy Lobanovskiy" Stadium, Kyiv; Attendance: 14,870
Referee: Andrejs Sipailo (Latvia)
UKRAINE - ANDORRA   **5-0(2-0)**
UKR: Andriy Pyatov, Oleksandr Kucher, Dmytro Chyhrynskiy, Vitaliy Mandzyuk, Anatoliy Tymoschuk, Oleh Gusev (71.Oleksiy Gay), Vasyl Kobin, Andriy Yarmolenko, Artem Milevskiy, Andriy Shevchenko (Cap) (81.Volodymyr Homenyuk), Andriy Voronin (66.Yevhen Seleznev). Trainer: Oleksiy Mykhailychenko.
AND: Josep Antonio Gómes Moreira, Josep Manuel Ayala Díaz, Cristian Martínez, Marc Pujol Pons, Óscar Sonejee Masand, Marc Vales González, Sergio Moreno Marín (82.Genís García Iscla), Márcio Vieira de Vasconcelos (76.Jordi Escura Aixas), Juan Carlos Toscano Beltrán (84.Víctor Hugo Moreira), Manuel Jiménez Soria „Manolo", Fernando José Silva García (79.Juli Fernández Ariza). Trainer: David Rodrigo.
Goals: 1-0 Andriy Yarmolenko (18), 2-0 Artem Milevskiy (45+2), 3-0 Andriy Shevchenko (72 penalty), 4-0 Artem Milevskiy (90+2 penalty), 5-0 Yevhen Seleznev (90+4 penalty).
Cautions: Andriy Voronin / Marc Pujol Pons, Marc Vales González, Josep Manuel Ayala Díaz.

05.09.2009, Maksimir Stadion, Zagreb; Attendance: 25,628
Referee: Konrad Plautz (Austria)
CROATIA - BELARUS   **1-0(1-0)**
CRO: Vedran Runje, Vedran Ćorluka, Ivica Križ anac, Josip Šimunć, Danijel Pranjić, Darijo Srna (Cap), Ognjen Vukojević, Niko Kranjčar, Ivan Rakitić (65.Mario Mandž ukć), Eduardo Alves da Silva (81.Ivan Jurić), Ivica Olić (73.Mladen Petrić). Trainer: Slaven Bilić.
BLR: Yuriy Zhevnov, Maxym Bordachev (55.Igor Stasevich), Sergey Sosnovskiy, Dmitriy Verkhovtsov, Sergey Omelyanchuk, Igor Shitov, Aleksandr Yurevich, Aleksandr Kulchiy, Vyacheslav Hleb (63.Sergey Kryvets), Timofei Kalachev, Sergey Kornilenko (77.Leonid Kovel). Trainer: Bernd Stange (Germany).
Goal: 1-0 Ivan Rakitić (24).
Cautions: Vedran Ćorluka, Ivica Križ anac / Maxym Bordachev, Sergey Kornilenko, Vyacheslav Hleb, Dmitriy Verkhovtsov, Timofei Kalachev, Leonid Kovel.
Sent off: Vedran Ćorluka (78).

09.09.2009, Dinamo Stadium, Minsk; Attendance: 21,727
Referee: Viktor Kassai (Hungary)
BELARUS - UKRAINE   **0-0**
BLR: Yuriy Zhevnov, Pavel Plaskonny (57.Dmitriy Lentsevich), Sergey Sosnovskiy, Sergey Omelyanchuk, Igor Shitov, Aleksandr Yurevich, Aleksandr Kulchiy, Aleksandr Hleb, Sergey Kornilenko (76.Leonid Kovel), Timofei Kalachev, Vitaliy Kutuzov (86.Vyacheslav Hleb). Trainer: Bernd Stange (Germany).
UKR: Andriy Pyatov, Oleksandr Kucher, Dmytro Chyhrynskiy, Vitaliy Mandzyuk, Anatoliy Tymoschuk, Oleksiy Gay, Oleh Gusev (61.Serhiy Nazarenko), Vasyl Kobin, Andriy Yarmolenko, Artem Milevskiy, Andriy Shevchenko (Cap) (89.Andriy Voronin). Trainer: Oleksiy Mykhailychenko.
Cautions: Igor Shitov, Sergey Omelyanchuk / Vitaliy Mandzyuk, Andriy Shevchenko.

09.09.2009, Estadio Comunal de Aixovall, Andorra La Vella; Attendance: 510
Referee: Albert Toussaint (Luxembourg)

ANDORRA - KAZAKHSTAN 1-3(0-3)

AND: Josep Antonio Gómes Moreira, Josep Manuel Ayala Díaz, Cristian Martínez, Marc Bernaus Cano, Ildefons Lima Solá, Óscar Sonejee Masand, Marc Vales González (46.Jordi Escura Aixas), Manuel Jiménez Soria „Manolo" (55.Juan Carlos Toscano Beltrán), Sergio Moreno Marín, Fernando José Silva García, Márcio Vieira de Vasconcelos (87.Gabriel Riera Lancha). Trainer: David Rodrigo.

KAZ: Aleksandr Mokin, Aleksandr Kirov, Rinat Abdulin, Aleksandr Kislitsin, Yuriy Logvinenko, Andrey Karpovich, Evgeniy Averchenko, Ruslan Baltiev (Cap), Zhambil Kukeev (87.Azat Nurgaliev), Andrey Finonchenko (77.Sergey Skorykh), Sergey Khizhnichenko (90+2.Vyacheslav Erbes). Trainer: Bernd Storck (Germany).

Goals: 0-1 Sergey Khizhnichenko (14), 0-2 Ruslan Baltiev (29), 0-3 Sergey Khizhnichenko (35), 1-3 Óscar Sonejee Masand (70).

Cautions: Márcio Vieira de Vasconcelos, Óscar Sonejee Masand, Sergio Moreno Marín / Sergey Khizhnichenko, Andrey Karpovich.

09.09.2009, The National Stadium, Wembley, London; Attendance: 87,319
Referee: Alberto Undiano Mallenco (Spain)

ENGLAND - CROATIA 5-1(2-0)

ENG: Robert Paul Green, Glen McLeod Johnson, Matthew James Upson, John George Terry (Cap), Ashley Cole, Aaron Justin Lennon (46.David Joseph Robert Beckham), Gareth Robert Barry, Frank James Lampard, Steven George Gerrard (80.James Philip Milner), Wayne Mark Rooney, Emile William Ivanhoe Heskey (59.Jermain Colin Defoe). Manager: Fabio Capello (Italy).

CRO: Vedran Runje, Ivica Križ anac, Josip Šimunč, Nikola Pokrivač (46.Ivan Rakitić), Danijel Pranjić, Darijo Srna (Cap), Ognjen Vukojević, Niko Kranjčar, Mario Mandž ukč, Eduardo Alves da Silva (73.Ivan Klasnić), Ivica Olić (46.Mladen Petrić). Trainer: Slaven Bilić.

Goals: 1-0 Frank James Lampard (7 penalty), 2-0 Steven George Gerrard (18), 3-0 Frank James Lampard (59), 4-0 Steven George Gerrard (67), 4-1 Eduardo Alves da Silva (71), 5-1 Wayne Mark Rooney (77).

Cautions: John George Terry / Josip Šimunić

10.10.2009, Dinamo Stadium, Brest; Attendance: 10,000
Referee: Saïd Ennjimi (France)

BELARUS - KAZAKHSTAN 4-0(1-0)

BLR: Yuriy Zhevnov, Igor Shitov, Sergey Sosnovskiy, Aleksandr Yurevich, Dmitriy Verkhovtsov, Maxym Bordachev (83.Sergey Kryvets), Aleksandr Kulchiy (90.Vitaliy Rodionov), Sergey Omelyanchuk, Timofei Kalachev, Sergey Kornilenko, Vitaliy Kutuzov (73.Leonid Kovel). Trainer: Bernd Stange (Germany).

KAZ: Aleksandr Mokin, Aleksandr Kirov, Rinat Abdulin, Aleksandr Kislitsin, Sergey Skorykh (79.Vyacheslav Erbes), Evgeniy Averchenko, Ruslan Baltiev (Cap) (61.Tanat Nuserbayev), Andrey Karpovich, Zhambil Kukeev, Yuriy Logvinenko, Sergey Khizhnichenko. Trainer: Bernd Storck (Germany).

Goals: 1-0 Maxym Bardachov (23), 2-0 Timofei Kalachev (69), 3-0 Leonid Kovel (86), 4-0 Timofei Kalachev (90+3).

Cautions: Andrey Karpovich.

10.10.2009, Dnipro Arena, Dnipropetrovsk; Attendance: 31,000
Referee: Damir Skomina (Slovenia)

UKRAINE - ENGLAND 1-0(1-0)

UKR: Andriy Pyatov, Oleksandr Kucher, Yevhen Khacheridi, Anatoliy Tymoschuk, Oleksiy Gay, Vasyl Kobin, Serhiy Nazarenko (67.Andriy Yarmolenko), Yaroslav Rakytskiy, Ruslan Rotan, Artem Milevskiy, Andriy Shevchenko (Cap) (90+2.Oleh Gusev). Trainer: Oleksiy Mykhailychenko.

ENG: Robert Paul Green, Glen McLeod Johnson, Rio Gavin Ferdinand, John George Terry (Cap), Ashley Cole, Aaron Justin Lennon (12.David Benjamin James), Michael Carrick, Frank James

Lampard, Steven George Gerrard (46.James Philip Milner), Wayne Mark Rooney, Emile William Ivanhoe Heskey (72.Carlton Michael Cole Okirie). Manager: Fabio Capello (Italy).
Goals: 1-0 Serhiy Nazarenko (29).
Cautions: Vasyl Kobin, Yevhen Khacheridi, Anatoliy Tymoschuk, Ruslan Rotan, Andriy Pyatov.
Sent off: Robert Paul Green (12).

14.10.2009, Estadio Comunal de Aixovall, Andorra La Vella; Attendance: 820
Referee: Craig Alexander Thomson (Scotland)
ANDORRA - UKRAINE   **0-6(0-1)**
AND: Josep Antonio Gómes Moreira, Josep Manuel Ayala Díaz, Cristian Martínez, David Maneiro, Ildefons Lima Solá, Marc Pujol Pons, Xavier Andorrà Julià (89.Genís García Iscla), Manuel Jiménez Soria „Manolo" (74.Sergio Moreno Marín), Marc Vales González, Julián Sánchez Soto (79.Gabriel Riera Lancha), Fernando José Silva García. Trainer: David Rodrigo.
UKR: Andriy Pyatov, Oleksandr Kucher, Yevhen Khacheridi, Taras Mykhalyk, Vasyl Kobin, Oleh Gusev, Serhiy Nazarenko (74.Oleksiy Gay), Yaroslav Rakytskiy, Andriy Yarmolenko, Artem Milevskiy (76.Yevhen Seleznev), Andriy Shevchenko (Cap) (74.Oleksandr Aliyev). Trainer: Oleksiy Mykhailychenko.
Goals: 0-1 Andriy Shevchenko (22), 0-2 Oleh Gusev (62), 0-3 Ildefons Lima Solà (70 own goal), 0-4 Yaroslav Rakytskiy (80), 0-5 Yevhen Seleznev (81), 0-6 Andriy Yarmolenko (83).
Cautions: Julián Sánchez Soto, Manuel Jiménez Soria „Manolo", Marc Pujol Pons, Ildefons Lima Solá.

14.10.2009, Astana Arena, Astana; Attendance: 10,250
Referee: Claudio Circhetta (Switzerland)
KAZAKHSTAN - CROATIA   **1-2(1-1)**
KAZ: Aleksandr Mokin, Aleksandr Kirov, Rinat Abdulin, Aleksandr Kislitsin, Yuriy Logvinenko, Evgeniy Averchenko, Vyacheslav Erbes (89.Ruslan Baltiev), Sergey Skorykh (Cap), Azat Nurgaliev (55.Zhambil Kukeev), Tanat Nuserbayev (78.Denis Malinin), Sergey Khizhnichenko. Trainer: Bernd Storck (Germany).
CRO: Vedran Runje, Vedran Ćorluka, Darijo Srna (90+4.Nikola Pokrivač), Dejan Lovren, Danijel Pranjić, Robert Kovač (Cap), Ivan Rakitić, Ognjen Vukojević, Niko Kranjčar, Mario Mandžukić (63.Mate Bilić), Ivan Klasnić (76.Nikica Jelavić). Trainer: Slaven Bilić.
Goals: 0-1 Ognjen Vukojević (10), 1-1 Sergey Khizhnichenko (26), 1-2 Niko Kranjčar (90+3).
Cautions: Azat Nurgaliev, Tanat Nuserbayev, Ruslan Baltiev / Niko Kranjčar, Ognjen Vukojević, Darijo Srna, Nikica Jelavić.

14.10.2009, The National Stadium, Wembley, London; Attendance: 76,897
Referee: Lucilio Cardoso Cortez Batista (Portugal)
ENGLAND - BELARUS   **3-0(1-0)**
ENG: Benjamin Anthony Foster, Glen McLeod Johnson, Rio Gavin Ferdinand, John George Terry (Cap), Wayne Michael Bridge (78.James Philip Milner), Aaron Justin Lennon (58.David Joseph Robert Beckham), Frank James Lampard, Gareth Robert Barry, Shaun Cameron Wright-Phillips, Peter James Crouch, Gabriel Imuetinyan Agbonlahor (66.Carlton Michael Cole Okirie). Manager: Fabio Capello (Italy).
BLR: Yuriy Zhevnov, Aleksandr Yurevich, Igor Shitov, Dmitriy Verkhovtsov, Sergey Sosnovskiy, Aleksandr Kulchiy (Cap), Timofei Kalachev, Maxym Bordachev (84.Nikolay Kashevskiy) , Sergey Omelyanchuk, Sergey Kornilenko (76.Leonid Kovel), Vitaliy Kutuzov (46.Vitaliy Rodionov). Trainer: Bernd Stange (Germany).
Goals: 1-0 Peter James Crouch (4), 2-0 Shaun Cameron Wright-Phillips (60), 3-0 Peter James Crouch (76).
Cautions: Sergey Kornilenko.

63

06.09.2008	Cluj-Napoca	Romania - Lithuania	0-3(0-1)
06.09.2008	Beograd	Serbia – Faroe Islands	2-0(1-0)
06.09.2008	Wien	Austria - France	3-1(2-0)
10.09.2008	Tórshavn	Faroe Islands - Romania	0-1(0-0)
10.09.2008	Marijampole	Lithuania - Austria	2-0(0-0)
10.09.2008	Paris	France - Serbia	2-1(0-0)
11.10.2008	Tórshavn	Faroe Islands - Austria	1-1(0-0)
11.10.2008	Beograd	Serbia - Lithuania	3-0(2-0)
11.10.2008	Constanța	Romania - France	2-2(2-1)
15.10.2008	Kaunas	Lithuania – Faroe Islands	1-0(1-0)
15.10.2008	Wien	Austria - Serbia	1-3(0-3)
28.03.2009	Constanța	Romania - Serbia	2-3(0-2)
28.03.2009	Kaunas	Lithuania - France	0-1(0-0)
01.04.2009	Klagenfurt	Austria - Romania	2-1(2-1)
01.04.2009	Paris	France - Lithuania	1-0(0-0)
06.06.2009	Marijampole	Lithuania - Romania	0-1(0-1)
06.06.2009	Beograd	Serbia - Austria	1-0(1-0)
10.06.2009	Tórshavn	Faroe Islands - Serbia	0-2(0-1)
12.08.2009	Tórshavn	Faroe Islands - France	0-1(0-1)
05.09.2009	Graz	Austria – Faroe Islands	3-1(2-0)
05.09.2009	Paris	France - Romania	1-1(0-0)
09.09.2009	Toftir	Faroe Islands - Lithuania	2-1(2-1)
09.09.2009	Bucureşti	Romania - Austria	1-1(0-0)
09.09.2009	Beograd	Serbia - France	1-1(1-1)
10.10.2009	Innsbruck	Austria - Lithuania	2-1(1-0)
10.10.2009	Beograd	Serbia - Romania	5-0(1-0)
10.10.2009	Guingamp	France – Faroe Islands	5-0(2-0)
14.10.2009	Marijampole	Lithuania - Serbia	2-1(1-0)
14.10.2009	Piatra Neamţ	Romania – Faroe Islands	3-1(1-0)
14.10.2009	Paris	France - Austria	3-1(2-0)

FINAL STANDINGS

1.	**Serbia**	10	7	1	2	22	-	8		22
2.	*France*	10	6	3	1	18	-	9		21
3.	Austria	10	4	2	4	14	-	15		14
4.	Lithuania	10	4	0	6	10	-	11		12
5.	Romania	10	3	3	4	12	-	18		12
6.	Faroe Islands	10	1	1	8	5	-	20		4

Serbia qualified for the Final Tournament; France qualified for the Play-Offs.

06.09.2008, Stadionul „Dr. Constantin Rădulescu", Cluj-Napoca; Attendance: 15,000
Referee: Alan Kelly (Republic of Ireland)
ROMANIA - LITHUANIA   **0-3(0-1)**
ROU: Bogdan Ionuţ Lobonţ, Ionuţ Cristian Săpunaru, Sebastian Gabriel Tamaş, Dorin Nicolae Goian, Ştefan Daniel Radu (46.Marius Constantin Niculae), Cosmin Marius Contra (Cap), Mirel Matei Rădoi (72.Costin Lazăr), Constantin Nicolae Dică, Răzvan Vasile Cociş, Ciprian Andrei Marica (53.Florin Daniel Bratu), Daniel George Niculae. Trainer: Victor Piţurcă.
LTU: Ž ydūnas Karčemarskas, Arūnas Klimavičius, Ignas Dedura, Irmantas Zelmikas, Marius Stankevičius, Deividas Šemberas, Audrius Kšanavičius (62.Mindaugas Kalonas), Linas Pilibaitis (74.Mantas Savėnas), Saulius Mikoliūnas (80.Edgaras Česnauskis), Deividas Česnauskis, Tomas

Danilevičius (Cap). Trainer: José Júlio de Carvalho Peyroteo Martins Couceiro (Portugal).
Goals: 0-1 Marius Stankevičius (31), 0-2 Saulius Mikoliūnas (69), 0-3 Mindaugas Kalonas (86).
Cautions: Dorin Nicolae Goian, Marius Constantin Niculae / Deividas Česnauskis, Saulius Mikoliūnas, Irmantas Zelmikas, Mindaugas Kalonas.

06.09.2008, Stadion Crvena zvezda, Beograd; Attendance: 9,615
Referee: Alexey Nikolayev (Russia)
SERBIA – FAROE ISLANDS   **2-0(1-0)**
SRB: Vladimir Dišljenković, Antonio Rukavina, Ivica Dragutinović, Nemanja Vidić, Ivan Obradović, Dejan Stanković (Cap), Nenad Milijaš (61.Saša Ilić), Miloš Krasić, Zoran Tošić (75.Boško Janković), Marko Pantelić (56.Danko Lazović), Nikola Žigić. Trainer: Radomir Antić.
FRO: Jákup Mikkelsen (Cap), Egil á Bø, Jónas Þór Næs, Atli Danielsen, Jón Rói Jacobsen, Mikkjal Thomassen, Jóhan Troest Davidsen, Jákup á Borg, Christian Høgni Jacobsen, Símun Samuelsen (69.Bogi Løkin), Andrew av Fløtum.Trainer: Jógvan Martin Olsen.
Goals: 1-0 Jón Rói Jacobsen (30 own goal), 2-0 Nikola Žigić (88).
Cautions: Nikola Žigić / Jónas Þór Næs, Bogi Løkin.
Sent off: Jónas Þór Næs (83).

06.09.2008, „Ernst Happel" Stadium, Wien; Attendance: 48,000
Referee: Claus Bo Larsen (Denmark)
AUSTRIA - FRANCE   **3-1(2-0)**
AUT: Alexander Manninger, György Garics, Sebastian Prödl, Martin Stranzl, Emanuel Pogatetz, René Aufhauser, Paul Scharner, Martin Harnik (90.Joachim Standfest), Andreas Ivanschitz (Cap) (81.Christoph Leitgeb), Christian Fuchs, Marc Janko (88.Stefan Maierhofer). Trainer: Karel Brückner (Czech Republic).
FRA: Stève Mandanda, Bakary Sagna (71.Yoann Miguel Gourcuff), William Éric Gallas, Philippe Mexès, Patrice Evra, Lassana Diarra, Jérémy Toulalan, Samir Nasri (79.Nicolas Sébastien Anelka), Sidney Govou, Karim Benzema, Thierry Henry (Cap). Trainer: Raymond Domenech.
Goals: 1-0 Marc Janko (8), 2-0 René Aufhauser (41), 2-1 Sidney Govou (61), 3-1 Andreas Ivanschitz (72 penalty).
Cautions: Marc Janko, René Aufhauser.

10.09.2008, Tórsvøllur Stadion, Tórshavn; Attendance: 805
Referee: Marijo Strahonja (Croatia)
FAROE ISLANDS - ROMANIA   **0-1(0-0)**
FRO: Jákup Mikkelsen (Cap), Pætur Dam Jacobsen (80.Bogi Løkin), Egil á Bø, Jón Rói Jacobsen, Jóhan Troest Davidsen, Jákup á Borg (90.Bartal Eliasen), Atli Danielsen, Mikkjal Thomassen, Christian Høgni Jacobsen, Símun Samuelsen, Andrew av Fløtum (76.Andreas Lava Olsen). Trainer: Jógvan Martin Olsen.
ROU: Bogdan Ionuţ Lobonţ, Cosmin Marius Contra (Cap), Dorin Nicolae Goian, Mirel Matei Rădoi (17.Sorin Ghionea), Mihai Mircea Neşu, Paul Constantin Codrea, Răzvan Vasile Cociş, Costin Lazăr, Marian Aliuţă (68.Cosmin Iosif Moţi), Florin Constantin Costea, Marius Constantin Niculae (89.Florin Daniel Bratu). Trainer: Victor Piţurcă.
Goal: 0-1 Răzvan Vasile Cociş (59).
Cautions: Mikkjal Thomassen, Christian Høgni Jacobsen, Jóhan Troest Davidsen / Florin Constantin Costea.
Sent off: Sorin Ghionea (50).

10.09.2008, Sūduva stadionas, Marijampolė; Attendance: 4,500
Referee: Paolo Tagliavento (Italy)
LITHUANIA - AUSTRIA   **2-0(0-0)**
LTU: Žydūnas Karčemarskas, Arūnas Klimavičius, Ignas Dedura, Irmantas Zelmikas, Marius Stankevičius, Deividas Šemberas, Linas Pilibaitis (80.Edgaras Česnauskis), Saulius Mikoliūnas, Deividas Česnauskis (65.Mindaugas Kalonas), Audrius Kšanavičius (74.Marius Žaliūkas), Tomas

65

Danilevičius (Cap). Trainer: José Júlio de Carvalho Peyroteo Martins Couceiro (Portugal).
AUT: Alexander Manninger, György Garics, Sebastian Prödl, Martin Stranzl, Emanuel Pogatetz, René Aufhauser (55.Jürgen Säumel), Paul Scharner (66.Erwin Hoffer), Martin Harnik, Andreas Ivanschitz (Cap), Christian Fuchs, Stefan Maierhofer. Trainer: Karel Brückner (Czech Republic).
Goals: 1-0 Tomas Danilevičius (52), 2-0 Tomas Danilevičius (58).
Cautions: Linas Pilibaitis / René Aufhauser, Christian Fuchs, Martin Stranzl, Martin Harnik.

10.09.2008, Stade de France, Saint-Denis, Paris; Attendance: 53,027
Referee: Olegario Manuel Bartolo Faustino Benquerença (Portugal)
FRANCE - SERBIA   **2-1(0-0)**
FRA: Stève Mandanda, Bakary Sagna, William Éric Gallas, Éric Abidal, Gaël Clichy, Lassana Diarra, Jérémy Toulalan, Sidney Govou (82.Alou Diarra), Yoann Miguel Gourcuff (90+2.Mathieu Flamini), Karim Benzema (46.Nicolas Sébastien Anelka), Thierry Henry (Cap). Trainer: Raymond Domenech.
SRB: Vladimir Stojković, Branislav Ivanović, Mladen Krstajić, Nemanja Vidić, Boško Janković, Dejan Stanković (Cap) (4.Gojko Kačar), Zdravko Kuzmanović, Ivan Ergić (56.Nikola Žigić), Zoran Tošić, Miralem Sulejmani (69.Miloš Krasić), Marko Pantelić. Trainer: Radomir Antić.
Goals: 1-0 Thierry Henry (53), 2-0 Nicolas Sébastien Anelka (63), 2-1 Branislav Ivanović (75).
Cautions: Branislav Ivanović.

11.10.2008, Tórsvøllur Stadion, Tórshavn; Attendance: 1,890
Referee: Darko Čeferin (Slovenia)
FAROE ISLANDS - AUSTRIA   **1-1(0-0)**
FRO: Jákup Mikkelsen (Cap), Jónas Þór Næs, Jóhan Troest Davidsen, Egil á Bø, Atli Danielsen, Jón Rói Jacobsen, Christian Høgni Jacobsen, Mikkjal Thomassen (37.Fróði Benjaminsen), Jákup á Borg (32.Bogi Løkin; 74.Andrew av Fløtum), Arnbjørn Theodor Hansen, Christian Lamhauge Holst. Trainer: Jógvan Martin Olsen.
AUT: Alexander Manninger, György Garics (67.Roman Kienast), Sebastian Prödl, Martin Stranzl, Emanuel Pogatetz, Martin Harnik (25.Andreas Hölzl), Paul Scharner, Andreas Ivanschitz (Cap), Christian Fuchs, Erwin Hoffer, Marc Janko (80.Marko Arnautovic). Trainer: Karel Brückner (Czech Republic).
Goals: 1-0 Bogi Løkin (47), 1-1 Martin Stranzl (49).
Cautions: Jákup á Borg, Christian Lamhauge Holst.

11.10.2008, Crvena zvezda Stadium, Beograd; Attendance: 22,000
Referee: Manuel Enrique Mejuto González (Spain)
SERBIA - LITHUANIA   **3-0(2-0)**
SRB: Vladimir Stojković, Branislav Ivanović, Ivica Dragutinović (25.Mladen Krstajić), Nemanja Vidić, Ivan Obradović, Dejan Stanković (Cap), Nenad Milijaš, Miloš Krasić (72.Boško Janković), Milan Jovanović, Marko Pantelić (56.Zdravko Kuzmanović), Nikola Žigić. Trainer: Radomir Antić.
LTU: Žydūnas Karčemarskas, Arūnas Klimavičius, Deividas Šemberas, Ignas Dedura, Marius Stankevičius, Tadas Papečkys (46.Edgaras Jankauskas), Saulius Mikoliūnas (46.Mindaugas Kalonas), Audrius Kšanavičius, Irmantas Zelmikas, Linas Pilibaitis (79.Andrius Skerla), Tomas Danilevičius (Cap). Trainer: José Júlio de Carvalho Peyroteo Martins Couceiro (Portugal).
Goals: 1-0 Branislav Ivanović (6), 2-0 Miloš Krasić (34), 3-0 Nikola Žigić (82).
Cautions: Dejan Stanković, Nemanja Vidić.
Sent off: Arūnas Klimavičius (74).

11.10.2008, Stadionul Farul, Constanța; Attendance: 12,800
Referee: Frank De Bleeckere (Belgium)
ROMANIA - FRANCE   **2-2(2-1)**
ROU: Bogdan Ionuț Lobonț, George Cristian Ogăraru, Sebastian Gabriel Tamaș, Dorin Nicolae Goian, Răzvan Dincă Raț, Gabriel Mureșan, Cristian Eugen Chivu (Cap), Florentin Petre (75.Gheorghe Bucur), Răzvan Vasile Cociș, Adrian Mutu (75.Florin Constantin Costea), Ciprian Andrei Marica. Trainer: Victor Pițurcă.

FRA: Stève Mandanda, Bakary Sagna, Jean-Alain Boumsong, Éric Abidal, Patrice Evra, Jérémy Toulalan, Alou Diarra, Franck Ribéry (90+1.Jimmy Briand), Yoann Miguel Gourcuff, Florent Malouda (37.Karim Benzema), Thierry Henry (Cap). Trainer: Raymond Domenech.
Goals: 1-0 Florentin Petre (6), 2-0 Dorin Nicolae Goian (17), 2-1 Franck Ribéry (36), 2-2 Yoann Miguel Gourcuff (68).
Cautions: Dorin Nicolae Goian / Jean-Alain Boumsong, Jérémy Toulalan.

15.10.2008, „Darius ir Girėnas" stadionas, Kaunas; Attendance: 5,000
Referee: Costas Kapitanis (Cyprus)
LITHUANIA – FAROE ISLANDS   **1-0(1-0)**
LTU: Žydrūnas Karčemarskas, Vidas Alunderis, Andrius Skerla, Ignas Dedura, Saulius Mikoliūnas, Deividas Šemberas, Linas Pilibaitis (90+1.Marius Žaliūkas), Audrius Kšanavičius (58.Mindaugas Kalonas), Marius Stankevičius, Andrius Velička (69.Robertas Poškus), Tomas Danilevičius (Cap). Trainer: José Júlio de Carvalho Peyroteo Martins Couceiro (Portugal).
FRO: Jákup Mikkelsen (Cap), Jónas Þór Næs, Jóhan Troest Davidsen, Atli Danielsen, Jón Rói Jacobsen, Fróði Benjaminsen (87.Rógvi Jacobsen), Christian Høgni Jacobsen, Símun Samuelsen (81.Ingi Højsted), Christian Lamhauge Holst, Egil á Bø, Bogi Løkin (85.Arnbjørn Theodor Hansen). Trainer: Jógvan Martin Olsen.
Goal: 1-0 Tomas Danilevičius (22).
Cautions: Linas Pilibaitis / Símun Samuelsen.

15.10.2008, „Ernst Happel" Stadium, Wien; Attendance: 47,998
Referee: Michael Anthony Riley (England)
AUSTRIA - SERBIA   **1-3(0-3)**
AUT: Alexander Manninger, György Garics, Sebastian Prödl, Martin Stranzl (18.Ronald Gercaliu), Emanuel Pogatetz, René Aufhauser (60.Jürgen Säumel), Paul Scharner, Erwin Hoffer (46.Marko Arnautovic), Andreas Ivanschitz (Cap), Christian Fuchs, Marc Janko. Trainer: Karel Brückner (Czech Republic).
SRB: Vladimir Stojković, Branislav Ivanović, Aleksandar Luković, Nemanja Vidić, Ivan Obradović, Dejan Stanković (76.Boško Janković), Nenad Milijaš (53.Zdravko Kuzmanović), Miloš Krasić, Milan Jovanović, Marko Pantelić (63.Zoran Tošić), Nikola Žigić. Trainer: Radomir Antić.
Goals: 0-1 Miloš Krasić (14), 0-2 Milan Jovanović (18), 0-3 Ivan Obradović (24), 1-3 Marc Janko (80).
Cautions: Andreas Ivanschitz / Ivan Obradović, Boško Janković.

28.03.2009, Stadionul Farul, Constanţa; Attendance: 15,000
Referee: Matteo Simone Trefoloni (Italy)
ROMANIA - SERBIA   **2-3(0-2)**
ROU: Bogdan Ionuţ Lobonţ, Cosmin Marius Contra, Sebastian Gabriel Tamaş, Dorel Stoica, Răzvan Dincă Raţ, Mirel Matei Rădoi, Răzvan Vasile Cociş (75.Marius Constantin Niculae), Paul Constantin Codrea (46.Cristian Tănase), Florin Constantin Costea (63.Gheorghe Bucur), Adrian Mutu (Cap), Ciprian Andrei Marica. Trainer: Victor Piţurcă.
SRB: Vladimir Stojković, Branislav Ivanović, Nemanja Vidić, Ivica Dragutinović, Ivan Obradović, Dejan Stanković, Nenad Milijaš, Miloš Krasić, Milan Jovanović (60.Boško Janković), Marko Pantelić (66.Neven Subotić), Nikola Žigić. Trainer: Radomir Antić.
Goals: 0-1 Milan Jovanović (18), 0-2 Dorel Stoica (44 own goal), 1-2 Ciprian Andrei Marica (50), 1-3 Branislav Ivanović (59), 2-3 Dorel Stoica (74).
Cautions: Adrian Mutu, Mirel Matei Rădoi, Florin Constantin Costea, Sebastian Gabriel Tamaş / Nikola Žigić, Neven Subotić.

28.03.2009, „Darius ir Girėnas" stadionas, Kaunas; Attendance: 8,700
Referee: Frederikus Johannes „Eric" Braamhaar (Holland)
LITHUANIA - FRANCE   **0-1(0-0)**
LTU: Žydrūnas Karčemarskas, Arūnas Klimavičius, Ignas Dedura, Andrius Skerla, Deividas Česnauskis, Edgaras Česnauskis (86.Saulius Mikoliūnas), Deividas Šemberas, Mindaugas Panka

(81.Robertas Poškus), Mantas Savėnas (66.Kęstutis Ivaškevičius), Darvydas Šernas, Tomas Danilevičius (Cap). Trainer: José Júlio de Carvalho Peyroteo Martins Couceiro (Portugal).
FRA: Stève Mandanda, Bakary Sagna, William Éric Gallas, Sébastien Squillaci, Patrice Evra, Peguy Luyindula (64.Karim Benzema), Lassana Diarra, Yoann Miguel Gourcuff (78.Samir Nasri), Jérémy Toulalan, Franck Ribéry, Thierry Henry (Cap). Trainer: Raymond Domenech.
Goal: 0-1 Franck Ribéry (68).
Cautions: Kęstutis Ivaškevičius / Jérémy Toulalan.

01.04.2009, Hypo-Arena, Klagenfurt; Attendance: 23,000
Referee: Craig Alexander Thomson (Scotland)
AUSTRIA - ROMANIA   **2-1(2-1)**
AUT: Michael Gspurning, Franz Schiemer, Sebastian Prödl, Emanuel Pogatetz (Cap), Manuel Ortlechner, Yasin Pehlivan, Paul Scharner, Marko Arnautovic (69.Ümit Korkmaz), Daniel Beichler (78.Andreas Hölzl), Erwin Hoffer (54.Rubin Rafael Okotie), Stefan Maierhofer. Trainer: Dietmar Constantini.
ROU: Bogdan Ionuț Lobonț, Cosmin Marius Contra (Cap), Sebastian Gabriel Tamaş, Dorin Nicolae Goian, Răzvan Dincă Raț, Mirel Matei Rădoi (46.Dorel Stoica), Răzvan Vasile Cociş, Cristian Tănase, Bănel Nicoliță (84.Maximilian Johannes Ştefan Nicu), Gheorghe Bucur (68.Marius Constantin Niculae), Ciprian Andrei Marica. Trainer: Victor Pițurcă.
Goals: 0-1 Cristian Tănase (24), 1-1 Erwin Hoffer (25), 2-1 Erwin Hoffer (44).
Cautions: Sebastian Prödl, Emanuel Pogatetz, Paul Scharner / Ciprian Andrei Marica.

01.04.2009, Stade de France, Saint-Denis, Paris; Attendance: 79,543
Referee: Howard Melton Webb (England)
FRANCE - LITHUANIA   **1-0(0-0)**
FRA: Stève Mandanda, Bakary Sagna, William Éric Gallas, Sébastien Squillaci, Patrice Evra, Alou Diarra, Lassana Diarra, Yoann Miguel Gourcuff (57.Karim Benzema), Peguy Luyindula (51.André-Pierre Gignac), Franck Ribéry, Thierry Henry (Cap). Trainer: Raymond Domenech.
LTU: Žydrūnas Karčemarskas, Arūnas Klimavičius, Andrius Skerla, Marius Žalūkas, Vidas Alunderis, Saulius Mikoliūnas (65.Edgaras Česnauskis), Linas Pilibaitis (82.Andrius Velička), Mindaugas Kalonas (59.Mantas Savėnas), Deividas Šemberas, Darvydas Šernas, Tomas Danilevičius (Çap). Trainer: José Júlio de Carvalho Peyroteo Martins Couceiro (Portugal).
Goal: 1-0 Franck Ribéry (75).
Cautions: Yoann Miguel Gourcuff, William Éric Gallas / Darvydas Šernas, Vidas Alunderis, Tomas Danilevičius.

06.06.2009, Sūduva stadionas, Marijampolė; Attendance: 5,850
Referee: Jonas Eriksson (Sweden)
LITHUNIA - ROMANIA   **0-1(0-1)**
LTU: Žydrūnas Karčemarskas, Arūnas Klimavičius (84.Povilas Lukšys), Marius Žalūkas, Andrius Skerla, Marius Stankevičius, Edgaras Česnauskis, Linas Pilibaitis (81.Ignas Dedura), Deividas Šemberas, Mindaugas Kalonas (64.Saulius Mikoliūnas), Darvydas Šernas, Tomas Danilevičius (Cap). Trainer: José Júlio de Carvalho Peyroteo Martins Couceiro (Portugal).
ROU: Dănuț Dumitru Coman, Ionuț Cristian Săpunaru, Mirel Matei Rădoi, Cristian Eugen Chivu (Cap), Răzvan Dincă Raț, Ion Bogdan Mara (73.Mihai Roman), Tiberiu Ghioane (90+2.Costin Lazăr), Iulian Cătălin Apostol, Cristian Tănase, Ionel Daniel Dănciulescu, Ciprian Andrei Marica (85.Marius Constantin Niculae), Răzvan Lucescu.
Goal: 0-1 Ciprian Andrei Marica (39).
Cautions: Linas Pilibaitis, Edgaras Česnauskis, Arūnas Klimavičius / Ionel Daniel Dănciulescu, Iulian Cătălin Apostol.

06.06.2009, Crvena zvezda Stadium, Beograd; Attendance: 50,000
Referee: Pieter Vink (Holland)
SERBIA - AUSTRIA   **1-0(1-0)**
SRB: Vladimir Stojković, Branislav Ivanović, Nemanja Vidić (46.Antonio Rukavina), Neven Subotić, Ivica Dragutinović, Miloš Krasić, Nenad Milijaš, Dejan Stanković, Milan Jovanović (82.Gojko Kačar), Marko Pantelić, Danko Lazović (56.Boško Janković). Trainer: Radomir Antić.
AUT: Michael Gspurning, Franz Schiemer, Martin Stranzl, Aleksandar Dragovic, Manuel Ortlechner, Andreas Hölzl (66.Stefan Lexa), Paul Scharner (Cap), Yasin Pehlivan, Jakob Jantscher, Erwin Hoffer (56.Marc Janko), Stefan Maierhofer (55.Rubin Rafael Okotie). Trainer: Dietmar Constantini.
Goal: 1-0 Nenad Milijaš (7 penalty).
Cautions: Antonio Rukavina, Boško Janković, Dejan Stanković / Michael Gspurning, Stefan Maierhofer, Franz Schiemer, Paul Scharner, Stefan Lexa

10.06.2009, Tórsvøllur Stadion, Tórshavn; Attendance: 2,896
Referee: Meir Levi (Israel)
FAROE ISLANDS - SERBIA   **0-2(0-1)**
FRO: Jákup Mikkelsen (Cap), Johan Troest Davidsen, Atli Gregersen, Egil á Bø, Atli Danielsen, Fróði Benjaminsen, Bogi Løkin, Jónas Tór Næs, Súni Olsen (77.Jann Ingi Petersen), Símun Samuelsen (69.Christian Høgni Jacobsen), Christian Lamhauge Holst (87.Andrew av Fløtum). Trainer: Brian Kerr (Republic of Ireland).
SRB: Vladimir Stojković, Branislav Ivanović, Neven Subotić, Aleksandar Luković, Aleksandar Kolarov, Miloš Krasić (83.Gojko Kačar), Zdravko Kuzmanović, Nenad Milijaš, Milan Jovanović (77.Miralem Sulejmani), Marko Pantelić (66.Danko Lazović), Nikola Žigić. Trainer: Radomir Antić.
Goals: 0-1 Milan Jovanović (44), 0-2 Neven Subotić (69).
Cautions: Atli Danielsen / Nenad Milijaš.

12.08.2009, Tórsvøllur Stadion, Tórshavn; Attendance: 2,974
Referee: Mihail Koukoulakis (Greece)
FAROE ISLANDS - FRANCE   **0-1(0-1)**
FRO: Jákup Mikkelsen (Cap), Johan Troest Davidsen, Atli Gregersen, Egil á Bø, Jónas Tór Næs, Atli Danielsen (42.Jann Ingi Petersen), Fróði Benjaminsen, Súni Olsen (85.Jákup á Borg), Símun Samuelsen, Christian Lamhauge Holst (28.Jóan Símun Edmundsson), Bogi Løkin. Trainer: Brian Kerr (Republic of Ireland).
FRA: Hugo Lloris, Bakary Sagna, William Éric Gallas (Cap), Julien Escudé, Patrice Evra, Lassana Diarra, Jérémy Toulalan, Yoann Miguel Gourcuff, Florent Malouda (65.Franck Ribéry), Nicolas Sébastien Anelka, André-Pierre Gignac. Trainer: Raymond Domenech.
Goal: 0-1 André-Pierre Gignac (41).
Cautions: Atli Gregersen, Fróði Benjaminsen, Jónas Tór Næs.

05.09.2009, UPC-Arena, Graz; Attendance: 12,300
Referee: Marco Borg (Malta)
AUSTRIA – FAROE ISLANDS   **3-1(2-0)**
AUT: Helge Payer, Jürgen Patocka (46.Manuel Ortlechner), Christian Fuchs, Franz Schiemer, Aleksandar Dragovic, Andreas Hölzl, Daniel Beichler (80.Roman Wallner), Yasin Pehlivan, Jakob Jantscher, Marc Janko (Cap), Stefan Maierhofer (61.Erwin Hoffer). Trainer: Dietmar Constantini.
FRO: Jákup Mikkelsen (Cap), Atli Gregersen, Einar T. Hansen, Egil á Bø, Atli Danielsen, Fróði Benjaminsen (80.Jann Ingi Petersen), Jónas Tór Næs, Bogi Løkin, Súni Olsen (67.Levi Hansen), Símun Samuelsen, Christian Lamhauge Holst (71.Andreas Lava Olsen). Trainer: Brian Kerr (Republic of Ireland).
Goals: 1-0 Stefan Maierhofer (1), 2-0 Marc Janko (16), 3-0 Marc Janko (59 penalty), 3-1 Andreas Lava Olsen (82).
Cautions: Marc Janko, Roman Wallner / Atli Danielsen, Fróði Benjaminsen, Einar T. Hansen, Bogi Løkin.

05.09.2009, Stade de France, Saint-Denis, Paris; Attendance: 78,209
Referee: Ivan Bebek (Croatia)
FRANCE - ROMANIA   **1-1(0-0)**
FRA: Hugo Lloris, Bakary Sagna, William Éric Gallas, Julien Escudé, Patrice Evra, Lassana Diarra, Jérémy Toulalan, Yoann Miguel Gourcuff (73.Karim Benzema), Nicolas Sébastien Anelka, André-Pierre Gignac, Thierry Henry (Cap) (57.Franck Ribéry). Trainer: Raymond Domenech.
ROU: Dănuţ Dumitru Coman, Vasile Maftei, Mirel Matei Rădoi, Cristian Eugen Chivu (Cap), Răzvan Dincă Raţ, Ion Bogdan Mara (61.Mihai Roman), Tiberiu Ghioane, Iulian Cătălin Apostol, Maximilian Johannes Ştefan Nicu (77.Gheorghe Bucur), Romeo Constantin Surdu (86.Paul Constantin Codrea), Ciprian Andrei Marica. Trainer: Răzvan Lucescu.
Goals: 1-0 Thierry Henry (48), 1-1 Julien Escudé (55 own goal).
Cautions: Bakary Sagna / Iulian Cătălin Apostol.

09.09.2009, Svangaskarð Stadion, Toftir; Attendance: 1,942
Referee: István Vad (Hungary)
FAROE ISLANDS - LITHUANIA   **2-1(2-1)**
FRO: Jákup Mikkelsen (Cap), Johan Troest Davidsen, Bartal Eliasen, Atli Gregersen, Einar T. Hansen, Jákup á Borg (89.Brian Olsen), Christian Lamhauge Holst, Súni Olsen, Jann Ingi Petersen, Símun Samuelsen, Arnbjørn Theodor Hansen (69.Andreas Lava Olsen). Trainer: Brian Kerr (Republic of Ireland).
LTU: Žydrūnas Karčemarskas, Arūnas Klimavičius (60.Saulius Mikoliūnas), Andrius Skerla, Ignas Dedura, Marius Stankevičius, Edgaras Česnauskis, Kęstutis Ivaškevičius (82.Mindaugas Kalonas), Deividas Šemberas, Linas Pilibaitis (60.Valdas Trakys), Darvydas Šernas, Tomas Danilevičius (Cap). Trainer: José Júlio de Carvalho Peyroteo Martins Couceiro (Portugal).
Goals: 1-0 Súni Olsen (13), 1-1 Tomas Danilevičius (22 penalty), 2-1 Arnbjørn Theodor Hansen (34).
Cautions: Christian Lamhauge Holst, Jákup á Borg, Einar T. Hansen, Símun Samuelsen, Jákup Mikkelsen / Arūnas Klimavičius, Saulius Mikoliūnas, Kęstutis Ivaškevičius.

09.09.2009, Stadionul Steaua, Bucureşti; Attendance: 7,505
Referee: Martin Atkinson (England)
ROMANIA - AUSTRIA   **1-1(0-0)**
ROU: Dănuţ Dumitru Coman, Ionuţ Cristian Săpunaru, Mirel Matei Rădoi, Cristian Eugen Chivu (Cap), Răzvan Dincă Raţ, Mihai Roman, Paul Constantin Codrea (71.Costin Lazăr), Tiberiu Ghioane, Adrian Cristea (86.Romeo Constantin Surdu), Gheorghe Bucur, Ciprian Andrei Marica (78.Ionuţ Costinel Mazilu). Trainer: Răzvan Lucescu.
AUT: Helge Payer, Franz Schiemer, Aleksandar Dragovic, Paul Scharner (Cap), Christian Fuchs, Andreas Hölzl, Yasin Pehlivan, Julian Baumgartlinger, Jakob Jantscher (62.Christopher Trimmel), Daniel Beichler (73.Roman Wallner), Erwin Hoffer (46.Stefan Maierhofer). Trainer: Dietmar Constantini.
Goals: 1-0 Gheorghe Bucur (54), 1-1 Franz Schiemer (83).
Cautions: Cristian Eugen Chivu, Gheorghe Bucur / Paul Scharner, Christian Fuchs, Yasin Pehlivan.

09.09.2009, Stadion Crvena zvezda, Beograd; Attendance: 49,456
Referee: Roberto Rosetti (Italy)
SERBIA - FRANCE   **1-1(1-1)**
SRB: Vladimir Stojković, Branislav Ivanović, Ivan Obradović, Aleksandar Luković, Nemanja Vidić, Nenad Milijaš (71.Zdravko Kuzmanović), Dejan Stanković (Cap), Gojko Kačar (46.Miloš Ninković), Miloš Krasić, Milan Jovanović (74.Danko Lazović), Nikola Žigić. Trainer: Radomir Antić.
FRA: Hugo Lloris (*sent off 9*), Bakary Sagna, William Éric Gallas, Éric Abidal, Patrice Evra, Lassana Diarra, Jérémy Toulalan, Yoann Miguel Gourcuff (85.Alou Diarra), Nicolas Sébastien Anelka, André-Pierre Gignac (12.Stève Mandanda), Thierry Henry (Cap) (77.Franck Ribéry). Trainer: Raymond Domenech.
Goals: 1-0 Nenad Milijaš (12 penalty), 1-1 Thierry Henry (36).

Cautions: Dejan Stanković, Milan Jovanović, Nikola Žigić, Zdravko Kuzmanović / Patrice Evra, Éric Abidal, Lassana Diarra.
Sent off: Hugo Lloris (9), Danko Lazović (89).

10.10.2009, Tivoli Neu Stadion, Innsbruck; Attendance: 14,200
Referee: Serge Gumienny (Belgium)
AUSTRIA - LITHUANIA   **2-1(1-0)**
AUT: Helge Payer, Franz Schiemer, Paul Scharner (Cap), Aleksandar Dragovic, Andreas Ulmer, Veli Kavlak, Thomas Prager (57.Julian Baumgartlinger), Yasin Pehlivan, Daniel Beichler (57.Christopher Drazan), Roman Wallner, Marc Janko (73.Stefan Maierhofer). Trainer: Dietmar Constantini.
LTU: Žydrūnas Karčemarskas, Vidas Alunderis (82.Vytautas Lukša), Tadas Kijanskas, Ignas Dedura, Marius Stankevičius, Edgaras Česnauskis, Tomas Ražanauskas (46.Mindaugas Kalonas) Deividas Šemberas, Mindaugas Panka (89.Valdas Trakys), Darvydas Šernas, Tomas Danilevičius (Cap). Trainer: José Júlio de Carvalho Peyroteo Martins Couceiro (Portugal).
Goals: 1-0 Marc Janko (16), 1-1 Marius Stankevičius (66), 2-1 Roman Wallner (80 penalty).
Cautions: Franz Schiemer, Veli Kavlak, Christopher Drazan / Edgaras Česnauskis, Tomas Danilevičius, Ignas Dedura, Vidas Alunderis, Deividas Šemberas.

10.10.2009, Stadion Crvena zvezda, Beograd; Attendance: 39,839
Referee: Costas Kapitanis (Cyprus)
SERBIA - ROMANIA   **5-0(1-0)**
SRB: Vladimir Stojković, Branislav Ivanović, Aleksandar Luković (46.Ivica Dragutinović), Nemanja Vidić (73.Neven Subotić), Aleksandar Kolarov, Nenad Milijaš (64.Zdravko Kuzmanović), Dejan Stanković (Cap), Miloš Krasić, Milan Jovanović, Marko Pantelić, Nikola Žigić. Trainer: Radomir Antić.
ROU: Dănuţ Dumitru Coman, Vasile Maftei, Mirel Matei Rădoi, Cristian Eugen Chivu (Cap), Răzvan Dincă Raţ, Tiberiu Ghioane (59.Gheorghe Bucur), Dacian Şerban Varga, Iulian Cătălin Apostol, Adrian Cristea, Adrian Mutu (75.Andrei Cristea), Ciprian Andrei Marica (60.Dorin Nicolae Goian). Trainer: Răzvan Lucescu.
Goals: 1-0 Nikola Žigić (37), 2-0 Marko Pantelić (50), 3-0 Zdravko Kuzmanović (78), 4-0 Milan Jovanović (87), 5-0 Milan Jovanović (90+3).
Cautions: Aleksandar Luković, Zdravko Kuzmanović, Dejan Stanković / Andrei Cristea, Răzvan Dincă Raţ, Dacian Şerban Varga, Adrian Mutu.
Sent off: Cristian Eugen Chivu (85).

10.10.2009, Stade de Roudourou, Guingamp; Attendance: 16,000
Referee: Robert Małek (Poland)
FRANCE – FAROE ISLANDS   **5-0(2-0)**
FRA: Stève Mandanda, Bakary Sagna, William Éric Gallas, Éric Abidal, Patrice Evra, Lassana Diarra, Jérémy Toulalan (62.Moussa Sissoko), Sidney Govou (62.Florent Malouda), Nicolas Sébastien Anelka, André-Pierre Gignac (73.Karim Benzema), Thierry Henry (Cap). Trainer: Raymond Domenech.
FRO: Jákup Mikkelsen, Atli Gregersen, Atli Danielsen, Egil á Bø, Johan Troest Davidsen, Súni Olsen (90.Brian Olsen), Fróði Benjaminsen, Bogi Løkin, Jann Ingi Petersen (64.Jónas Tór Næs), Rógvi Jacobsen (80.Andreas Lava Olsen), Christian Høgni Jacobsen. Trainer: Brian Kerr (Republic of Ireland).
Goals: 1-0 André-Pierre Gignac (34), 2-0 André-Pierre Gignac (38), 3-0 William Éric Gallas (52), 4-0 Nicolas Sébastien Anelka (86), 5-0 Karim Benzema (88).
Cautions: Lassana Diarra.

14.10.2009, Sūduva stadionas, Marijampolė; Attendance: 2,000
Referee: Anton Guenov (Bulgaria)
LITHUANIA - SERBIA **2-1(1-0)**
LTU: Žydrūnas Karčemarskas, Arūnas Klimavičius, Tadas Kijanskas, Ignas Dedura, Marius Stankevičius, Mindaugas Kalonas (82.Tomas Ražanauskas), Mindaugas Panka, Saulius Mikoliūnas (67.Vytautas Lukša), Kęstutis Ivaškevičius, Darvydas Šernas (89.Valdas Trakys), Linas Pilibaitis. Trainer: José Júlio de Carvalho Peyroteo Martins Couceiro (Portugal).
SRB: Vladimir Dišljenković, Branislav Ivanović, Ivan Obradović (60.Aleksandar Luković), Neven Subotić, Ivica Dragutinović, Gojko Kačar, Radosav Petrović, Miloš Krasić (46.Zoran Tošić), Milan Jovanović, Marko Pantelić (75.Miloš Ninković), Nikola Žigić. Trainer: Radomir Antić.
Goals: 1-0 Mindaugas Kalonas (20 penalty), 1-1 Zoran Tošić (60), 2-1 Marius Stankevičius (68 penalty).
Cautions: Neven Subotić, Ivan Obradović, Zoran Tošić, Ivica Dragutinović.

14.10.2009, Stadionul Ceahlăul, Piatra Neamţ; Attendance: 10,500
Referee: Alexander Gvardis (Russia)
ROMANIA – FAROE ISLANDS **3-1(1-0)**
ROU: Costel Fane Pantilimon, Cristian Călin Panin, Dorin Nicolae Goian (26.George Daniel Galamaz), Mirel Matei Rădoi (Cap), Răzvan Dincă Raţ, Ion Bogdan Mara, Iulian Cătălin Apostol, Nicolae Grigore, Dacian Şerban Varga, Gheorghe Bucur (76.Andrei Cristea), Ciprian Andrei Marica (82.Ionuţ Costinel Mazilu). Trainer: Răzvan Lucescu.
FRO: Jákup Mikkelsen, Atli Gregersen, Egil á Bø, Atli Danielsen, Fróði Benjaminsen (81.Christian Høgni Jacobsen), Jákup á Borg, Rógvi Jacobsen (73.Arnbjørn Theodor Hansen), Jónas Tór Næs, Súni Olsen, Christian Lamhauge Holst (70.Bogi Løkin), Símun Samuelsen. Trainer: Brian Kerr (Republic of Ireland).
Goals: 1-0 Iulian Cătălin Apostol (16), 2-0 Gheorghe Bucur (65), 2-1 Egil á Bø (83), 3-1 Ionuţ Costinel Mazilu (87).
Cautions: Cristian Călin Panin, Nicolae Grigore / Egil á Bø, Jákup á Borg, Símun Samuelsen, Atli Gregersen.

14.10.2009, Stade de France, Saint-Denis, Paris; Attendance: 78,099
Referee: Pedro Proença Oliveira Alves Garcia (Portugal)
FRANCE - AUSTRIA **3-1(2-0)**
FRA: Hugo Lloris, Gaël Clichy, Julien Escudé, Sébastien Squillaci, Rod Fanni, Moussa Sissoko, Alou Diarra, Florent Malouda, Sidney Govou, Karim Benzema (79.Bafetimbi Gomis), Thierry Henry (Cap) (51.André-Pierre Gignac). Trainer: Raymond Domenech.
AUT: Helge Payer (46.Christian Gratzei), Jürgen Patocka, Paul Scharner (Cap), Aleksandar Dragovic, Christian Fuchs (80.David Alaba), Veli Kavlak, Julian Baumgartlinger, Yasin Pehlivan, Jakob Jantscher, Stefan Maierhofer (46.Erwin Hoffer), Marc Janko. Trainer: Dietmar Constantini.
Goals: 1-0 Karim Benzema (18), 2-0 Thierry Henry (26 penalty), 2-1 Marc Janko (49), 3-1 André-Pierre Gignac (66).
Cautions: Christian Fuchs, Veli Kavlak.

06.09.2008	Mainz (Germany)	Georgia – Republic of Ireland	1-2(0-1)
06.09.2008	Podgorica	Montenegro - Bulgaria	2-2(0-1)
06.09.2008	Lárnaka	Cyprus - Italy	1-2(1-1)
10.09.2008	Podgorica	Montenegro - Republic of Ireland	0-0
10.09.2008	Udine	Italy - Georgia	2-0(1-0)
11.10.2008	Tbilisi	Georgia - Cyprus	1-1(0-0)
11.10.2008	Sofia	Bulgaria - Italy	0-0
15.10.2008	Tbilisi	Georgia - Bulgaria	0-0
15.10.2008	Dublin	Republic of Ireland - Cyprus	1-0(1-0)
15.10.2008	Lecce	Italy - Montenegro	2-1(2-1)
11.02.2009	Dublin	Republic of Ireland - Georgia	2-1(0-1)
28.03.2009	Lárnaka	Cyprus - Georgia	2-1(1-0)
28.03.2009	Podgorica	Montenegro - Italy	0-2(0-1)
28.03.2009	Dublin	Republic of Ireland - Bulgaria	1-1(1-0)
01.04.2009	Sofia	Bulgaria - Cyprus	2-0(1-0)
01.04.2009	Tbilisi	Georgia - Montenegro	0-0
01.04.2009	Bari	Italy - Republic of Ireland	1-1(1-0)
06.06.2009	Sofia	Bulgaria - Republic of Ireland	1-1(1-1)
06.06.2009	Lárnaka	Cyprus - Montenegro	2-2(2-0)
05.09.2009	Sofia	Bulgaria - Montenegro	4-1(1-1)
05.09.2009	Tbilisi	Georgia - Italy	0-2(0-0)
05.09.2009	Nicosia	Cyprus - Republic of Ireland	1-2(1-1)
09.09.2009	Podgorica	Montenegro- Cyprus	1-1(0-0)
09.09.2009	Torino	Italy - Bulgaria	2-0(2-0)
10.10.2009	Lárnaka	Cyprus - Bulgaria	4-1(2-1)
10.10.2009	Podgorica	Montenegro - Georgia	2-1(1-1)
10.10.2009	Dublin	Republic of Ireland - Italy	2-2(1-1)
14.10.2009	Sofia	Bulgaria - Georgia	6-2(6-1)
14.10.2009	Parma	Italy - Cyprus	3-2(0-1)
14.10.2009	Dublin	Republic of Ireland - Montenegro	0-0

FINAL STANDINGS

1. **ITALY**	10	7	3	0	18	-	7	24
2. **Republic of Ireland**	10	4	6	0	12	-	8	18
3. Bulgaria	10	3	5	2	17	-	13	14
4. Cyprus	10	2	3	5	14	-	16	9
5. Montenegro	10	1	6	3	9	-	14	9
6. Georgia	10	0	3	7	7	-	19	3

Italy qualified for the Final Tournament; Republic of Ireland qualified for the Play-Offs.

06.09.2008, Stadion am Bruchweg, Mainz (Germany); Attendance: 4,500
Referee: Zsolt Szabó (Hungary)
GEORGIA – REPUBLIC OF IRELAND   **1-2(0-1)**
GEO: Giorgi Loria, Ucha Lobjanidze, Zurab Khizanishvili (83.Malkhaz Asatiani), Kakhaber Kaladze (Cap), Giorgi Shashiashvili, Zurab Menteshashvili, Levan Kenia, David Odikadze, Levan Kobiashvili, Aleksandre Iashvili (77.Levan Mchedlidze), Rati Aleksidze (61.David Siradze). Trainer: Héctor Raúl Cúper (Argentina).
IRL: Seamus John Given, Stephen John Finnan (80.Paul David McShane), John Francis O'Shea, Richard Patrick Dunne, Kevin Daniel Kilbane, Aiden McGeady (86.Andrew Declan Keogh), Steven John Reid, Glenn Whelan, Stephen Patrick Hunt, Robert David Keane (Cap), Kevin Edward Doyle (77.William

Peter Miller). Trainer: Giovanni Trapattoni (Italy).
Goals: 0-1 Kevin Edward Doyle (13), 0-2 Glenn Whelan (70), 1-2 Levan Kenia (90+2).
Cautions: Zurab Khizanishvili, Rati Aleksidze.

06.09.2008, Gradski Stadium, Podgorica; Attendance: 9,000
Referee: Oleh Oriekhov (Ukraine)
MONTENEGRO - BULGARIA   **2-2(0-1)**
MNE: Vukasin Poleksić, Savo Pavićević, Radoslav Batak, Jovan Tanasijević, Vladimir Bož ović, Branko Bošković (83.Igor Burzanović), Milorad Peković, Dragan Bogavac (53.Simon Vukčević), Nikola Drinčić, Stevan Jovetić, Mirko Vučinić (Cap) (86.Radomir Đalović). Trainer: Zoran Filipović.
BUL: Dimitar Ivankov, Zhivko Milanov (48.Igor Tomašic), Aleksandar Blagov Tunchev, Valentin Iliev, Stanislav Angelov, Stanislav Genchev (66.Blagoi Georgiev), Stilian Petrov, Zdravko Lazarov, Ivelin Popov (40.Chavdar Yankov), Velizar Dimitrov, Dimitar Berbatov (Cap). Trainer: Plamen Markov.
Goals: 0-1 Stilian Petrov (11), 1-1 Mirko Vučinić (62), 2-1 Stevan Jovetić (82 penalty), 2-2 Blagoi Georgiev (90+2).
Cautions: Stevan Jovetić, Savo Pavićević, Mirko Vučinić, Milorad Peković / Velizar Dimitrov, Stanislav Angelov, Blagoi Georgiev.
Sent off: Stanislav Angelov (81).

06.09.2008, „Andónis Papadópoulos", Lárnaka; Attendance: 8,000
Referee: Pieter Vink (Holland)
CYPRUS - ITALY   **1-2(1-1)**
CYP: Antonis Georgallides, Elias Charalambous, Paraskevas Christou, Chrysostomos Michail (72.Yiasoumakis Yiasoumi), Constantinos Charalambides, Alexandros Garpozis, Constantinos Makrides, Marios Nicolaou, Yiannakis Okkas (Cap) (74.Kyriakos Pavlou), Michalis Konstantinou (64.Demetris Christofi), Efstathios Panayotis Aloneftis. Trainer: Angelos Anastasiadis (Greece).
ITA: Gianluigi Buffon, Gianluca Zambrotta, Alessandro Gamberini (4.Andrea Barzagli), Fabio Cannavaro (Cap), Fabio Grosso (18.Marco Cassetti), Daniele De Rossi, Andrea Pirlo, Mauro Camoranesi, Antonio Di Natale, Alberto Gilardino, Luca Toni (46.Gennaro Gattuso). Trainer: Marcello Lippi.
Goals: 0-1 Antonio Di Natale (8), 1-1 Efstathios Panayotis Aloneftis (29), 1-2 Antonio Di Natale (90+2).
Cautions: Alexandros Garpozis, Marios Nicolaou, Constantinos Charalambides, Constantinos Makrides / Luca Toni, Marco Cassetti, Mauro Camoranesi.

10.09.2008, Gradski Stadium, Podgorica; Attendance: 12,000
Referee: Sten Kaldma (Estonia)
MONTENEGRO - REPUBLIC OF IRELAND   **0-0**
MNE: Vukasin Poleksić, Elsad Zverotić, Savo Pavićević, Milan Jovanović, Radoslav Batak, Jovan Tanasijević, Vladimir Bož ović (54.Simon Vukčević), Milorad Peković, Nikola Drinčić, Stevan Jovetić, Mirko Vučinić (Cap). Trainer: Zoran Filipović.
IRL: Seamus John Given, Stephen John Finnan, John Francis O'Shea, Richard Patrick Dunne, Kevin Daniel Kilbane, Aiden McGeady, Steven John Reid, Glenn Whelan, Stephen Patrick Hunt, Robert David Keane (Cap), Kevin Edward Doyle. Trainer: Giovanni Trapattoni (Italy).
Cautions: Milorad Peković.

10.09.2008, Stadio Friuli, Udine; Attendance: 27,164
Referee: Thomas Einwaller (Austria)
ITALY - GEORGIA   **2-0(1-0)**
ITA: Gianluigi Buffon, Gianluca Zambrotta, Nicola Legrottaglie, Fabio Cannavaro (Cap), Andrea Dossena, Daniele De Rossi, Andrea Pirlo (46.Angelo Palombo), Alberto Aquilani, Mauro Camoranesi, Antonio Di Natale (56.Alessandro Del Piero), Luca Toni (70.Vincenzo Iaquinta). Trainer: Marcello Lippi.
GEO: Giorgi Loria, Ucha Lobjanidze, Lasha Salukvadze, Kakhaber Kaladze (Cap), Zaal Eliava (46.David Kvirkvelia), Levan Kenia, Levan Khmaladze, Zurab Menteshashvili (68.David Odikadze),

Levan Kobiashvili, Aleksandre Iashvili, Levan Mchedlidze (55.David Siradze). Trainer: Héctor Raúl Cúper (Argentina).
Goals: 1-0 Daniele De Rossi (17), 2-0 Daniele De Rossi (89).
Cautions: Andrea Pirlo, Alberto Aquilani / Levan Kenia.

11.10.2008, "Boris Paichadze" Stadium, Tbilisi; Attendance: 40,000
Referee: Radek Matejek (Czech Republic)
GEORGIA - CYPRUS   **1-1(0-0)**
GEO: Giorgi Lomaia, Ucha Lobjanidze, Lasha Salukvadze, Zurab Khizanishvili, Giorgi Shashiashvili, Zurab Menteshashvili, Levan Kobiashvili (Cap), Luka Razmadze, Levan Kenia (65.Beka Gotsiridze), Aleksandre Iashvili, Levan Mchedlidze (76.Rati Aleksidze). Trainer: Héctor Raúl Cúper (Argentina).
CYP: Antonis Georgallides, Elias Charalambous, Andreas Konstantinou, Chrysostomos Michail (37.Marios Nicolaou), Constantinos Charalambides, Marios Elia (83.Lambros Lambrou), Alexandros Garpozis, Constantinos Makrides, Yiannakis Okkas (Cap), Michalis Konstantinou, Efstathios Panayotis Aloneftis (90+3.Georgios Panayi). Trainer: Angelos Anastasiadis (Greece).
Goals: 0-1 Michalis Konstantinou (66), 1-1 Levan Kobiashvili (73).
Cautions: Lasha Salukvadze, Levan Mchedlidze, Zurab Khizanishvili, Rati Aleksidze / Constantinos Charalambides, Andreas Konstantinou.

11.10.2008, „Vasil Levski" National Stadium, Sofia; Attendance: 45,000
Referee: Stephane Lannoy (France)
BULGARIA - ITALY   **0-0**
BUL: Dimitar Ivankov, Zhivko Milanov, Aleksandar Blagov Tunchev, Valentin Iliev, Lúcio Wagner (37.Ivan Ivanov), Stilian Petrov, Chavdar Yankov, Blagoi Georgiev, Velizar Dimitrov, Martin Petrov (90.Ivelin Popov), Dimitar Berbatov (Cap). Trainer: Plamen Markov.
ITA: Marco Amelia, Gianluca Zambrotta, Fabio Cannavaro, Giorgio Chiellini, Andrea Dossena, Gennaro Gattuso, Daniele De Rossi, Riccardo Montolivo (68.Simone Perrotta), Simone Pepe, Alberto Gilardino (73.Luca Toni), Antonio Di Natale (68.Giuseppe Rossi). Trainer: Marcello Lippi.
Cautions: Giorgio Chiellini, Daniele De Rossi, Luca Toni.

15.10.2008, „Boris Paichadze" Stadium, Tbilisi; Attendance: 35,250
Referee: Bjorn Kuipers (Holland)
GEORGIA - BULGARIA   **0-0**
GEO: Giorgi Lomaia, Ucha Lobjanidze, Lasha Salukvadze, Aleksandre Kvakhadze, Giorgi Shashiashvili, Zurab Mentesahshvili, Levan Kobiashvili (Cap), Luka Razmadze, Beka Gotsiridze (84.David Odikadze), Aleksandre Iashvili (71.Giorgi Merebashvili), Levan Mchedlidze (32.David Siradze). Trainer: Héctor Raúl Cúper (Argentina).
BUL: Georgi Petkov, Zhivko Milanov, Aleksandar Blagov Tunchev, Valentin Iliev, Ivan Ivanov, Stilian Petrov, Chavdar Yankov (56.Stanislav Angelov), Blagoi Georgiev, Velizar Dimitrov (73.Dimitar Rangelov), Martin Petrov (29.Ivelin Popov), Dimitar Berbatov (Cap). Trainer: Plamen Markov.
Cautions: Luka Razmadze, Giorgi Shashiashvili / Stilian Petrov, Aleksandar Blagov Tunchev.

15.10.2008, Croke Park, Dublin; Attendance: 55,833
Referee: Alexandru Dan Tudor (Romania)
REPUBLIC OF IRELAND - CYPRUS   **1-0(1-0)**
IRL: Seamus John Given, John Francis O'Shea, Richard Patrick Dunne, Paul David McShane, Kevin Daniel Kilbane, Darron Thomas Daniel Gibson, Glenn Whelan, Aiden McGeady, Damien Anthony Duff, Robert David Keane (Cap), Kevin Edward Doyle (90+2.Caleb Colman Folan). Trainer: Giovanni Trapattoni (Italy).
CYP: Antonis Georgallides, Elias Charalambous, Marios Elia, Lambros Lambrou (46.Andreas Papathanasiou), Demetris Christofi, Andreas Konstantinou, Alexandros Garpozis, Christos Marangos (52.Georgios Panayi), Constantinos Makrides, Yiannakis Okkas (Cap), Michalis Konstantinou (79.Yiasoumakis Yiasoumi). Trainer: Angelos Anastasiadis (Greece).
Goal: 1-0 Robert David Keane (5).

Cautions: Aiden McGeady, Seamus John Given / Marios Elia, Andreas Konstantinou.

15.10.2008, Stadio Via Del Mare, Lecce; Attendance: 20,162
Referee: Pedro Proença Oliveira Alves Garcia (Portugal)
ITALY - MONTENEGRO 2-1(2-1)
ITA: Marco Amelia, Gianluca Zambrotta, Fabio Cannavaro, Giorgio Chiellini, Andrea Dossena (58.Daniele Bonera), Gennaro Gattuso, Daniele De Rossi, Simone Pepe, Alberto Aquilani (65.Simone Perrotta), Antonio Di Natale (75.Fabio Quagliarella), Alberto Gilardino. Trainer: Marcello Lippi.
MNE: Vukasin Poleksić, Savo Pavićević, Milan Jovanović, Radoslav Batak, Jovan Tanasijević, Nikola Drinčić, Elsad Zverotić (88.Mitar Novaković), Branko Bošković (80.Vladimir Bož ové), Simon Vukčević, Stevan Jovetić, Mirko Vučinić (Cap) (90.Dejan Damjanović). Trainer: Zoran Filipović.
Goals: 1-0 Alberto Aquilani (8), 1-1 Mirko Vučinić (19), 2-1 Alberto Aquilani (29).
Cautions: Gennaro Gattuso, Marco Amelia / Mirko Vučinić, Milan Jovanović, Jovan Tanasijević.

11.02.2009, Croke Park, Dublin; Attendance: 45,000
Referee: Jouni Hyytia (Finland)
REPUBLIC OF IRELAND - GEORGIA 2-1(0-1)
IRL: Seamus John Given, Stephen Michael Kelly, Richard Patrick Dunne, John Francis O'Shea, Kevin Daniel Kilbane, Aiden McGeady, Glenn Whelan, Keith Joseph Andrews, Damien Anthony Duff (80.Stephen Patrick Hunt), Kevin Edward Doyle, Robert David Keane. Trainer: Giovanni Trapattoni (Italy).
GEO: Giorgi Lomaia, Ucha Lobjanidze, Zurab Khizanishvili, Kakhaber Kaladze (Cap), David Kvirkvelia, Levan Kobiashvili, Zurab Menteshashvili (70.Levan Khmaladze), Luka Razmadze, Beka Gotsiridze (68.Giorgi Merebashvili), David Siradze (77.Rati Aleksidze), Aleksandre Iashvili. Trainer: Héctor Raúl Cúper (Argentina).
Goals: 0-1 Aleksandre Iashvili (1), 1-1 Robert David Keane (73 penalty), 2-1 Robert David Keane (78).
Cautions: Keith Joseph Andrews / Zurab Menteshashvili, Ucha Lobjanidze, David Kvirkvelia, Levan Kobiashvili, Zurab Khizanishvili.

28.03.2009, „Andónis Papadópoulos" Stadium, Lárnaka; Attendance: 3,000
Referee: Freddy Fautrel (France)
CYPRUS - GEORGIA 2-1(1-0)
CYP: Antonis Georgallides, Paraskevas Christou, Elias Charalambous (90.Yiasoumakis Yiasoumi), Chrysostomos Michail, Marios Elia, Marinos Satsias (82.Andreas Avraam), Nektarios Alexandrou, Efstathios Panayotis Aloneftis (69.Georgios Panayi), Demetris Christofi, Alexandros Garpozis, Michalis Konstantinou. Trainer: Angelos Anastasiadis (Greece).
GEO: Giorgi Lomaia, Ucha Lobjanidze, Zurab Khizanishvili, Aleksandre Kvakhadze, Giorgi Shashiashvili, Luka Razmadze, David Odikadze, Levan Kobiashvili (Cap), Beka Gotsiridze, Aleksandre Iashvili, Levan Mchedlidze (28.David Siradze). Trainer: Héctor Raúl Cúper (Argentina).
Goals: 1-0 Michalis Konstantinou (33), 2-0 Demetris Christofi (56), 2-1 Levan Kobiashvili (71 penalty).
Cautions: Marinos Satsias, Elias Charalambous / Ucha Lobjanidze, Beka Gotsiridze, Aleksandre Iashvili, Zurab Khizanishvili, Giorgi Shashiashvili.

28.03.2009, Gradski Stadium, Podgorica; Attendance: 10,500
Referee: Martin Atkinson (England)
MONTENEGRO - ITALY 0-2(0-1)
MNE: Vukasin Poleksić, Marko Baša, Radoslav Batak, Savo Pavićević, Vladimir Bož ové, Branko Bošković (Cap), Nikola Drinčić, Milorad Peković (79.Nikola Vujović), Simon Vukčević (88.Elsad Zverotić), Stevan Jovetić, Radomir Đalović (71.Fatos Bećiraj). Trainer: Zoran Filipović.
ITA: Gianluigi Buffon, Gianluca Zambrotta, Fabio Cannavaro, Giorgio Chiellini, Fabio Grosso, Angelo Palombo, Daniele De Rossi, Fabio Quagliarella, Andrea Pirlo (81.Matteo Brighi), Antonio Di Natale (9.Simone Pepe), Vincenzo Iaquinta (59.Giampaolo Pazzini). Trainer: Marcello Lippi.
Goals: 0-1 Andrea Pirlo (11 penalty), 0-2 Giampaolo Pazzini (73).
Cautions: Radoslav Batak, Milorad Peković, Savo Pavićević / Angelo Palombo, Fabio Cannavaro.

28.03.2009, Croke Park, Dublin; Attendance: 59,000
Referee: Ivan Bebek (Croatia)
REPUBLIC OF IRELAND - BULGARIA 1-1(1-0)
IRL: Seamus John Given, Paul David McShane, John Francis O'Shea, Richard Patrick Dunne, Kevin Daniel Kilbane, Aiden McGeady (90.Andrew Declan Keogh), Glenn Whelan, Keith Joseph Andrews, Stephen Patrick Hunt, Robert David Keane, Kevin Edward Doyle. Trainer: Giovanni Trapattoni (Italy).
BUL: Dimitar Ivankov, Zhivko Milanov (24.Radostin Kishishev), Stanislav Manolev, Ilian Stoianov, Igor Tomašic, Stanislav Angelov, Stilian Petrov (Cap), Blagoi Georgiev (66.Dimitar Makriev), Dimitar Telkiyski, Ivelin Popov (46.Velizar Dimitrov), Dimitar Rangelov. Trainer: Stanimir Stoilov.
Goals: 1-0 Richard Patrick Dunne (1), 1-1 Kevin Daniel Kilbane (74 own goal).
Cautions: Zhivko Milanov, Stanislav Manolev, Radostin Kishishev.

01.04.2009, „Vasil Levski" National Stadium, Sofia; Attendance:
Referee: Martin Ingvarsson (Sweden)
BULGARIA - CYPRUS 2-0(1-0)
BUL: Dimitar Ivankov, Radostin Kishishev, Stanislav Manolev, Ilian Stoianov, Igor Tomašic, Stanislav Angelov, Stilian Petrov (Cap), Blagoi Georgiev, Dimitar Telkiyski (62.Velizar Dimitrov), Ivelin Popov (74.Yordan Todorov), Dimitar Rangelov (89.Dimitar Makriev). Trainer: Stanimir Stoilov.
CYP: Antonis Georgallides, Paraskevas Christou, Elias Charalambous, Chrysostomos Michail (76.Christos Marangos), Marios Elia, Marinos Satsias, Nektarios Alexandrou (65.Andreas Avraam), Efstathios Panayotis Aloneftis, Demetris Christofi (59.Yiasoumakis Yiasoumi), Alexandros Garpozis, Michalis Konstantinou. Trainer: Angelos Anastasiadis (Greece).
Goals: 1-0 Ivelin Popov (8), 2-0 Dimitar Makriev (90+4).
Cautions: Ilian Stoianov, Stanislav Manolev, Yordan Todorov / Michalis Konstantinou, Paraskevas Christou.

01.04.2009, „Boris Paichadze" Stadium, Tbilisi; Attendance: 16,000
Referee: David Malcolm (Northern Ireland)
GEORGIA - MONTENEGRO 0-0
GEO: Giorgi Lomaia, Lasha Salukvadze, Guram Kashia, Aleksandre Kvakhadze, David Kvirkvelia, David Odikadze (65.Irakli Klimiashvili), Levan Khmaladze, Levan Kobiashvili (Cap), Aleksandre Iashvili, Beka Gotsiridze (77.David Siradze), Giorgi Merebashvili. Trainer: Héctor Raúl Cúper (Argentina).
MNE: Vukasin Poleksić, Marko Baša, Radoslav Batak, Luka Pejović, Jovan Tanasijević, Elsad Zverotić (86.Nikola Vujović), Branko Bošković (Cap), Nikola Drinčić, Milorad Peković, Stevan Jovetić, Radomir Đalović (68.Fatos Bećiraj). Trainer: Zoran Filipović.
Cautions: Aleksandre Iashvili / Elsad Zverotić, Stevan Jovetić, Milorad Peković.

01.04.2009, Stadio "San Nicola", Bari; Attendance: 48,000
Referee: Wolfgang Stark (Germany)
ITALY - REPUBLIC OF IRELAND 1-1(1-0)
ITA: Gianluigi Buffon, Gianluca Zambrotta, Fabio Cannavaro, Giorgio Chiellini, Fabio Grosso, Daniele De Rossi, Matteo Brighi, Andrea Pirlo (46.Angelo Palombo), Simone Pepe (54.Andrea Dossena), Giampaolo Pazzini, Vincenzo Iaquinta (90.Fabio Quagliarella). Trainer: Marcello Lippi.
IRL: Seamus John Given, Paul David McShane, John Francis O'Shea, Richard Patrick Dunne, Kevin Daniel Kilbane, Andrew Declan Keogh (22.Caleb Colman Folan), Glenn Whelan, Keith Joseph Andrews (54.Darron Thomas Daniel Gibson), Stephen Patrick Hunt, Robert David Keane, Kevin Edward Doyle (63.Noel Hunt). Trainer: Giovanni Trapattoni (Italy).
Goals: 1-0 Vincenzo Iaquinta (10), 1-1 Robert David Keane (88).
Cautions: Fabio Grosso, Vincenzo Iaquinta, Daniele De Rossi / Paul David McShane.
Sent off: Giampaolo Pazzini (3).

06.06.2009, Vasil Levski" National Stadium, Sofia; Attendance: 40,000
Referee: Claus Bo Larson (Denmark)
BULGARIA - REPUBLIC OF IRELAND   **1-1(1-1)**
BUL: Dimitar Ivankov, Zhivko Milanov, Ilian Stoianov, Igor Tomašic, Stanislav Angelov, Radostin Kishishev, Stilian Petrov (Cap), Martin Petrov (61.Blagoi Georgiev), Dimitar Telkiyski (82.Velizar Dimitrov), Dimitar Berbatov, Valeri Bojinov (59.Dimitar Makriev). Trainer: Stanimir Stoilov.
IRL: Seamus John Given, John Francis O'Shea (81.Stephen Michael Kelly), Sean Patrick St. Ledger-Hall, Richard Patrick Dunne, Kevin Daniel Kilbane, Damien Anthony Duff, Glenn Whelan, Keith Joseph Andrews, Stephen Patrick Hunt (70.Aiden McGeady), Caleb Colman Folan, Robert David Keane (74.Leon Julian Best). Trainer: Giovanni Trapattoni (Italy).
Goals: 0-1 Richard Patrick Dunne (24), 1-1 Dimitar Telkiyski (29).
Cautions: Zhivko Milanov, Dimitar Telkiyski / Glenn Whelan.

06.06.2009, „Andónis Papadópoulos" Stadium, Lárnaka; Attendance: 4,500
Referee: Carlos Velasco Carballo (Spain)
CYPRUS - MONTENEGRO   **2-2(2-0)**
CYP: Antonis Georgallides (46.Michalis Morphis), Paraskevas Christou, Marios Elia, Elias Charalambous, Constantinos Makrides, Chrysostomos Michail, Marios Nicolaou (78.Constantinos Charalambides), Efstathios Panayotis Aloneftis, Alexandros Garpozis (69.Marinos Satsias), Michalis Konstantinou, Yiannakis Okkas (Cap). Trainer: Angelos Anastasiadis (Greece).
MNE: Vukasin Poleksić, Miodrag Dž udovč, Radoslav Batak, Savo Pavićević, Jovan Tanasijević, Luka Pejović (86.Ivan Fatić), Nikola Drinčić (47.Dejan Damjanović), Mladen Kašćelan, Mitar Novaković (19.Elsad Zverotić), Mirko Vučinić (Cap), Goran Vujović. Trainer: Zoran Filipović.
Goals: 1-0 Michalis Konstantinou (14), 2-0 Chrysostomos Michail (45 penalty), 2-1 Dejan Damjanović (65), 2-2 Dejan Damjanović (77).
Cautions: Michalis Konstantinou, Yiannakis Okkas, Efstathios Panayotis Aloneftis, Constantinos Makrides / Savo Pavićević, Mladen Kašćelan, Miodrag Dž udovč, Vukasin Poleksić, Elsad Zverotić.

05.09.2009, „Vasil Levski" National Stadium, Sofia; Attendance: 7,543
Referee: Tony Asumaa (Finland)
BULGARIA - MONTENEGRO   **4-1(1-1)**
BUL: Dimitar Ivankov, Kiril Kotev (46.Dimitar Telkiyski), Stanislav Manolev, Ilian Stoianov, Stanislav Angelov, Radostin Kishishev, Stilian Petrov, Chavdar Yankov, Martin Petrov (75.Blagoi Georgiev), Dimitar Berbatov (Cap), Dimitar Rangelov (83.Valeri Domovchiyski). Trainer: Stanimir Stoilov.
MNE: Vukašin Poleksić (Cap), Miodrag Dž udovč, Savo Pavićević, Marko Baša (73.Ivan Fatić), Luka Pejović, Milorad Peković (59.Mirko Vučinić), Simon Vukčević, Nikola Drinčić, Vladimir Bož ovč (55.Branko Bošković), Stevan Jovetić, Dejan Damjanović. Trainer: Zoran Filipović.
Goals: 0-1 Stevan Jovetić (8), 1-1 Radostin Kishishev (45), 2-1 Dimitar Telkiyski (49), 3-1 Dimitar Berbatov (85 penalty), 4-1 Valeri Domovchiyski (90).
Cautions: Kiril Kotev, Martin Petrov, Dimitar Telkiyski / Vladimir Bož ovč, Dejan Damjanović, Milorad Peković, Miodrag Dž udovč, Ivan Fatić.

05.09.2009, „Boris Paichadze" Stadium, Tbilisi; Attendance: 32,000
Referee: Marcin Borski (Poland)
GEORGIA - ITALY   **0-2(0-0)**
GEO: Giorgi Lomaia, Ucha Lobjanidze, Zurab Menteshashvili, Kakhaber Kaladze (Cap), Amiran Sanaia, Levan Kobiashvili, Luka Razmadze (73.Levan Tskitishvili), Levan Khmaladze, Levan Kenia, Vladimir Dvalishvili, Jano Ananidze (59.Mate Vatsadze). Trainer: Héctor Raúl Cúper (Argentina).
ITA: Gianluigi Buffon, Gianluca Zambrotta, Fabio Cannavaro, Giorgio Chiellini, Domenico Criscito, Marco Marchionni (58.Gaetano D'Agostino), Andrea Pirlo, Angelo Palombo, Mauro Camoranesi (70.Davide Santon), Vincenzo Iaquinta, Giuseppe Rossi (58.Fabio Quagliarella). Trainer: Marcello Lippi.
Goals: 0-1 Kakhaber Kaladze (56 own goal), 0-2 Kakhaber Kaladze (66 own goal).
Cautions: Levan Khmaladze, Levan Kobiashvili / Domenico Criscito.

05.09.2009, Neo GSP Stadium, Nicosia; Attendance: 5,191
Referee: Thomas Einwaller (Austria)
CYPRUS - REPUBLIC OF IRELAND   **1-2(1-1)**
CYP: Sofronis Avgousti, Paraskevas Christou, Marios Elia, Elias Charalambous, Constantinos Charalambides, Chrysostomos Michail (71.Nektarios Alexandrou), Marios Nicolaou, Marinos Satsias (90.Christos Marangos), Efstathios Panayotis Aloneftis, Andreas Avraam, Yiannakis Okkas (Cap) (90+1.Demetris Christofi). Trainer: Angelos Anastasiadis (Greece).
IRL: Seamus John Given, John Francis O'Shea, Richard Patrick Dunne, Sean Patrick St. Ledger-Hall, Kevin Daniel Kilbane, Stephen Patrick Hunt (67.Aiden McGeady), Keith Joseph Andrews, Glenn Whelan, Damien Anthony Duff; Robert David Keane, Kevin Edward Doyle (75.Caleb Colman Folan). Trainer: Giovanni Trapattoni (Italy).
Goals: 0-1 Kevin Edward Doyle (5), 1-1 Marios Elia (30), 1-2 Robert David Keane (83).
Cautions: Marios Elia, Andreas Avraam / Caleb Colman Folan.

09.09.2009, Gradski Stadium, Podgorica; Attendance: 4,000
Referee: Carlo Bertolini (Switzerland)
MONTENEGRO - CYPRUS   **1-1(0-0)**
MNE: Vukašin Poleksić, Savo Pavićević, Marko Baša, Ivan Fatić, Luka Pejović, Nikola Drinčić, Milorad Peković (70.Dejan Damjanović), Branko Bošković (61.Mladen Kašćelan), Simon Vukčević, Stevan Jovetić, Mirko Vučinić (Cap). Trainer: Zoran Filipović.
CYP: Sofronis Avgousti, Paraskevas Christou, Elias Charalambous, Constantinos Makrides, Chrysostomos Michail, Marios Nicolaou (83.Christos Marangos), Marinos Satsias, Nektarios Alexandrou (46.Efstathios Panayotis Aloneftis), Andreas Avraam, Michalis Konstantinou, Yiannakis Okkas (Cap) (90+1.Georgios Efrem). Trainer: Angelos Anastasiadis (Greece).
Goals: 1-0 Mirko Vučinić (56 penalty), 1-1 Yiannakis Okkas (64).
Cautions: Milorad Peković, Savo Pavićević, Stevan Jovetić / Michalis Konstantinou, Elias Charalambous, Yiannakis Okkas.

09.09.2009, Stadio Olimpico, Torino; Attendance: 20,760
Referee: Florian Meyer (Germany)
ITALY - BULGARIA   **2-0(2-0)**
ITA: Gianluigi Buffon, Gianluca Zambrotta, Fabio Cannavaro, Giorgio Chiellini, Fabio Grosso, Mauro Camoranesi, Daniele De Rossi, Claudio Marchisio (73.Simone Pepe), Andrea Pirlo, Alberto Gilardino (58.Giuseppe Rossi), Vincenzo Iaquinta (84.Gaetano D'Agostino). Trainer: Marcello Lippi.
BUL: Dimitar Ivankov, Radostin Kishishev, Stanislav Manolev, Ilian Stoianov, Stanislav Angelov, Stilian Petrov, Chavdar Yankov (73.Valeri Domovchiyski), Martin Petrov (57.Blagoi Georgiev), Georgi Sarmov, Dimitar Berbatov (Cap), Dimitar Rangelov (57.Valeri Bojinov). Trainer: Stanimir Stoilov.
Goals: 1-0 Fabio Grosso (11), 2-0 Vincenzo Iaquinta (40).
Cautions: Fabio Cannavaro / Chavdar Yankov.

10.10.2009, „Andónis Papadópoulos" Stadium, Lárnaka; Attendance: 3,700
Referee: Paul Allaerts (Belgium)
CYPRUS - BULGARIA   **4-1(2-1)**
CYP: Sofronis Avgousti, Paraskevas Christou, Marios Elia (75.Marios Nicolaou), Constantinos Charalambides, Chrysostomos Michail, Constantinos Makrides, Marinos Satsias, Efstathios Panayotis Aloneftis (86.Georgios Efrem), Andreas Avraam, Siniša Dobrašinović, Michalis Konstantinou (89.Andreas Papathanasiou). Trainer: Angelos Anastasiadis (Greece).
BUL: Dimitar Ivankov (68.Nikolai Mihailov), Ivan Ivanov, Veselin Minev, Plamen Nikolov, Kostadin Stoyanov, Stanislav Angelov, Stilian Petrov (68.Kosta Yanev), Blagoi Georgiev, Martin Petrov, Dimitar Berbatov, Valeri Bojinov (62.Valeri Domovchiyski).Trainer: Stanimir Stoilov.
Goals: 1-0 Constantinos Charalambides (11), 2-0 Constantinos Charalambides (20), 2-1 Dimitar Berbatov (44), 3-1 Michalis Konstantinou (58), 4-1 Efstathios Panayotis Aloneftis (78).
Cautions: Constantinos Charalambides / Stilian Petrov, Kosta Yanev.

10.10.2009, Gradski Stadium, Podgorica; Attendance: 5,420
Referee: Selçuk Dereli (Turkey)
MONTENEGRO - GEORGIA   **2-1(1-1)**
MNE: Vukašin Poleksić, Radoslav Batak, Marko Baša, Luka Pejović (46.Milan Jovanović), Elsad
Zverotić, Nikola Drinčić, Mitar Novaković (71.Mladen Kašćelan), Branko Bošković (Cap), Simon
Vukčević, Stevan Jovetić, Dejan Damjanović (61.Andrija Delibašić). Trainer: Zoran Filipović.
GEO: Giorgi Lomaia, Ucha Lobjanidze, Zurab Khizanishvili, Kakhaber Kaladze, Levan Khmaladze,
Luka Razmadze, Amiran Sanaia (79.Giorgi Popkhadze), Giorgi Merebashvili (76.David Odikadze),
Vladimir Dvalishvili, Nikoloz Gelashvili (67.Jaba Lipartia), Aleksandre Iashvili. Trainer: Héctor Raúl
Cúper (Argentina).
Goals: 1-0 Radoslav Batak (13), 1-1 Vladimir Dvalishvili (45), 2-1 Andrija Delibašić (78).
Cautions: Stevan Jovetić, Mitar Novaković, Andrija Delibašić, Nikola Drinčić, Mladen Bož ové (on the
bench) / Ucha Lobjanidze, Giorgi Merebashvili, Kakhaber Kaladze, Giorgi Lomaia, Vladimir Dvalishvili.

10.10.2009, Croke Park, Dublin; Attendance: 70,670
Referee: Terje Hauge (Norway)
REPUBLIC OF IRELAND - ITALY   **2-2(1-1)**
IRL: Seamus John Given, John Francis O'Shea, Richard Patrick Dunne, Sean Patrick St. Ledger-Hall,
Kevin Daniel Kilbane, Liam Lawrence, Glenn Whelan (76.Martin Charles Rowlands), Keith Joseph
Andrews, Aiden McGeady (78.Stephen Patrick Hunt), Kevin Edward Doyle (67.Leon Julian Best),
Robert David Keane. Trainer: Giovanni Trapattoni (Italy).
ITA: Gianluigi Buffon, Gianluca Zambrotta, Giorgio Chiellini, Nicola Legrottaglie, Fabio Grosso
(76.Salvatore Bocchetti), Daniele De Rossi, Angelo Palombo (89.Simone Pepe), Andrea Pirlo, Mauro
Camoranesi, Antonio Di Natale (76.Alberto Gilardino), Vincenzo Iaquinta. Trainer: Marcello Lippi.
Goals: 1-0 Glenn Whelan (8), 1-1 Mauro Camoranesi (26), 2-1 Sean Patrick St. Ledger-Hall (87), 2-2
Alberto Gilardino (90).
Cautions: Glenn Whelan, Leon Julian Best / Daniele De Rossi.

14.10.2009, „Vasil Levski" National Stadium, Sofia; Attendance: 700
Referee: Kristinn Jakobsson (Iceland)
BULGARIA - GEORGIA   **6-2(6-1)**
BUL: Nikolai Mihailov, Ivan Ivanov, Veselin Minev, Plamen Nikolov, Kostadin Stoyanov (46.Ivan
Bandalovski), Stanislav Angelov (78.Valeri Bojinov), Blagoi Georgiev, Martin Petrov, Kosta Yanev,
Dimitar Berbatov, Dimitar Rangelov (64.Ivan Stoyanov). Trainer: Stanimir Stoilov.
GEO: Giorgi Lomaia (29.Zurab Mamaladze), Ucha Lobjanidze, Zurab Khizanishvili, Kakhaber Kaladze,
Levan Khmaladze, Levan Kobiashvili, Luka Razmadze, Amiran Sanaia (78.Giorgi Merebashvili), Levan
Kenia (88.David Odikadze), Vladimir Dvalishvili, Aleksandre Iashvili. Trainer: Héctor Raúl Cúper
(Argentina).
Goals: 1-0 Dimitar Berbatov (6), 2-0 Martin Petrov (14), 3-0 Dimitar Berbatov (23), 4-0 Stanislav
Angelov (31), 4-1 Vladimir Dvalishvili (34), 5-1 Dimitar Berbatov (35), 6-1 Martin Petrov (44), 6-2
Levan Kobiashvili (51 penalty).
Cautions: Ivan Bandalovski / Levan Kenia, Levan Khmaladze.
Sent off: Levan Khmaladze (58).

14.10.2009, Stadio "Ennio Tardini", Parma; Attendance: 15,009
Referee: Alon Yefet (Israel)
ITALY - CYPRUS   **3-2(0-1)**
ITA: Federico Marchetti, Salvatore Bocchetti, Fabio Cannavaro, Alessandro Gamberini, Davide Santon,
Gaetano D'Agostino (66.Daniele De Rossi), Gennaro Gattuso, Simone Pepe (46.Antonio Di Natale),
Fabio Quagliarella, Giuseppe Rossi (46.Mauro Camoranesi), Alberto Gilardino. Trainer: Marcello Lippi.
CYP: Sofronis Avgousti, Elias Charalambous, Paraskevas Christou (30.Marinos Satsias), Marios Elia,
Chrysostomos Michail, Constantinos Charalambides, Constantinos Makrides, Yiannakis Okkas
(85.Nektarios Alexandrou), Efstathios Panayotis Aloneftis (74.Michalis Konstantinou), Andreas Avraam,

Siniša Dobrašinović. Trainer: Angelos Anastasiadis (Greece).
Goals: 0-1 Constantinos Makrides (12), 0-2 Chrysostomos Michail (48), 2-1 Alberto Gilardino (78), 2-2 Alberto Gilardino (81), 3-2 Alberto Gilardino (90+2).
Cautions: Gennaro Gattuso / Marinos Satsias, Marios Elia.

14.10.2009, Croke Park, Dublin; Attendance: 36,442
Referee: Vladimír Hriňák (Slovakia)
REPUBLIC OF IRELAND - MONTENEGRO 0-0
IRL: Seamus John Given, Paul David McShane, Richard Patrick Dunne, Sean Patrick St. Ledger-Hall, Kevin Daniel Kilbane, Damien Anthony Duff, Martin Charles Rowlands (39.John Francis O'Shea), William Peter Miller, Stephen Patrick Hunt (88.Andrew Declan Keogh), Robert David Keane, Noel Hunt (67.Leon Julian Best). Trainer: Giovanni Trapattoni (Italy).
MNE: Vukašin Poleksić, Radoslav Batak (31.Miodrag Dž udović), Marko Baša, Milan Jovanović, Elsad Zverotić, Nikola Drinčić, Milorad Peković, Mitar Novaković, Branko Bošković (Cap) (81.Mladen Kašćelan), Simon Vukčević, Andrija Delibašić (69.Dejan Damjanović). Trainer: Zoran Filipović.
Cautions: Martin Charles Rowlands / Milorad Peković, Milan Jovanović.

GROUP 9

06.09.2008	Skopje	Macedonia - Scotland	1-0(1-0)
06.09.2008	Oslo	Norway - Iceland	2-2(1-1)
10.09.2008	Reykjavík	Iceland - Scotland	1-2(0-1)
10.09.2008	Skopje	Macedonia - Holland	1-2(0-1)
11.10.2008	Glasgow	Scotland - Norway	0-0
11.10.2008	Rotterdam	Holland - Iceland	2-0(1-0)
15.10.2008	Oslo	Norway - Holland	0-1(0-0)
15.10.2008	Reykjavík	Iceland - Macedonia	1-0(1-0)
28.03.2009	Amsterdam	Holland - Scotland	3-0(2-0)
01.04.2009	Amsterdam	Holland - Macedonia	4-0(2-0)
01.04.2009	Glasgow	Scotland - Iceland	2-1(1-0)
06.06.2009	Skopje	Macedonia - Norway	0-0
06.06.2009	Reykjavík	Iceland - Holland	1-2(0-2)
10.06.2009	Skopje	Macedonia - Iceland	2-0(1-0)
10.06.2009	Rotterdam	Holland - Norway	2-0(1-0)
12.08.2009	Oslo	Norway - Scotland	4-0(2-0)
05.09.2009	Glasgow	Scotland - Macedonia	2-0(0-0)
05.09.2009	Reykjavík	Iceland - Norway	1-1(1-1)
09.09.2009	Oslo	Norway - Macedonia	2-1(2-0)
09.09.2009	Glasgow	Scotland - Holland	0-1(0-0)

FINAL STANDINGS

1.	**HOLLAND**	8	8	0	0	17	-	2	24
2.	Norway	8	2	4	2	9	-	7	10
3.	Scotland	8	3	1	4	6	-	11	10
4.	Macedonia	8	2	1	5	5	-	11	7
5.	Iceland	8	1	2	5	7	-	13	5

Holland qualified for the Final Tournament.

06.09.2008, Gradski Stadium, Skopje; Attendance: 9,000
Referee: Pavel Královec (Czech Republic)
MACEDONIA - SCOTLAND   **1-0(1-0)**
MKD: Petar Miloševski, Nikolče Noveski, Goce Sedloski (Cap), Igor Mitreski, Vlade Lazarevski, Robert Petrov (79.Boban Grnčarov), Vlatko Grozdanovski, Veliče Šumulikoski, Goran Maznov, Goran Pandev (83.Darko Tasevski), Ilčo Naumoski (69.Vančo Trajanov). Trainer: Srečko Katanec (Slovenia).
SCO: Craig Sinclair Gordon, Graham Alexander, Gary Andrew Naysmith, Stephen McManus (Cap), Gary Robert Caldwell, Paul James Hartley (65.Kristian Arron Commons), Darren Barr Fletcher, Scott Brown, Kenneth Miller (80.Kris Boyd), James McFadden, Barry Robson (76.Shaun Richard Maloney). Manager: George Elder Burley.
Goal: 1-0 Ilčo Naumoski (5).
Cautions: Ilčo Naumoski, Veliče Šumulikoski, Goran Pandev / James McFadden.

06.09.2008, Ullevaal Stadion, Oslo; Attendance: 17,254
Referee: Alon Yefet (Israel)
NORWAY - ICELAND   **2-2(1-1)**
NOR: Rune Almenning Jarstein, Tom Høgli, Tore Reginiussen, Brede Paulsen Hangeland (Cap), John Arne Riise, Per Ciljan Skjelbred (70.Christian Grindheim), Martin Andresen, Fredrik Winsnes, John Alieu Carew (65.Morten Gamst Pedersen), Steffen Iversen, Thorstein Helstad. Trainer: Åge Hareide.
ISL: Kjartan Sturluson, Grétar Rafn Steinsson, Kristján Örn Sigurðsson, Birkir Már Sævarsson, Bjarni Ólafur Eiríksson, Aron Einar Gunnarsson (68.Pálmi Rafn Pálmason), Stefán Gíslason, Hermann

82

Hreiðarsson (Cap), Emil Hallfreðsson (74.Guðmundur Steinarsson), Eiður Smári Guðjohnsen, Heiðar Helguson (85.Veigar Páll Gunnarsson). Trainer: Ólafur Davíð Jóhanesson.
Goals: 1-0 Steffen Iversen (36 penalty), 1-1 Heiðar Helguson (39), 2-1 Steffen Iversen (50), 2-2 Eiður Smári Guðjohnsen (69).
Cautions: Grétar Rafn Steinsson, Stefán Gíslason, Hermann Hreiðarsson.

10.09.2008, Laugardalsvöllur Stadium, Reykjavík; Attendance: 9,764
Referee: Serge Gumienny (Belgium)
ICELAND - SCOTLAND **1-2(0-1)**
ISL: Kjartan Sturluson, Bjarni Ólafur Eiríksson (46.Indriði Sigurðsson), Hermann Hreiðarsson (Cap), Kristján Örn Sigurðsson, Grétar Rafn Steinsson, Birkir Már Sævarsson (78.Veigar Páll Gunnarsson), Stefán Gíslason, Aron Einar Gunnarsson (64.Pálmi Rafn Pálmason), Emil Hallfreðsson, Eiður Smári Guðjohnsen, Heiðar Helguson. Trainer: Ólafur Davíð Jóhanesson.
SCO: Craig Sinclair Gordon, Kirk Broadfoot, Gary Andrew Naysmith, Stephen McManus (Cap), Gary Robert Caldwell, Scott Brown, Darren Barr Fletcher, Shaun Richard Maloney (78.Graham Alexander), James McFadden (80.Paul James Hartley), Kristian Arron Commons (62.Kenneth Miller), Barry Robson. Manager: George Elder Burley.
Goals: 0-1 Kirk Broadfoot (18), 0-2 James McFadden (59), 1-2 Eiður Smári Guðjohnsen (77 penalty).
Cautions: Indriði Sigurðsson, Pálmi Rafn Pálmason / Kirk Broadfoot, Barry Robson, Craig Sinclair Gordon.
Sent off: Stephen McManus (76).

10.09.2008, Gradski Stadium, Skopje; Attendance: 12,000
Referee: Grzegorz Gilewski (Poland)
MACEDONIA - HOLLAND **1-2(0-0)**
MKD: Petar Miloševski, Nikolče Noveski, Goce Sedloski (Cap), Igor Mitreski, Vlade Lazarevski (58.Robert Petrov), Vlatko Grozdanovski, Veliče Šumulikoski, Vančo Trajanov (83.Stevica Ristić), Goran Maznov (61.Darko Tasevski), Goran Pandev, Ilčo Naumoski. Trainer: Srečko Katanec (Slovenia).
NED: Maarten Stekelenburg, John Gijsbert Alan Heitinga, André Antonius Maria Ooijer (28.Khalid Boulahrouz), Joris Mathijsen, Giovanni Christiaan van Bronckhorst (Cap), Mark Peter Gertruda Andreas van Bommel, Nigel de Jong, Rafael Ferdinand Van der Vaart, Robin van Persie (70.Dirk Kuijt), Arjen Robben (82.Ibrahim Afellay), Klaas-Jan Huntelaar. Trainer: Lambertus van Marwijk.
Goals: 0-1 John Gijsbert Alan Heitinga (46), 0-2 Rafael Ferdinand Van der Vaart (59), 1-2 Goran Pandev (77 penalty).
Cautions: Ilčo Naumoski, Vlatko Grozdanovski, Stevica Ristić / Robin van Persie, Rafael Ferdinand Van der Vaart, Maarten Stekelenburg.

11.10.2008, Hampden Park, Glasgow; Attendance: 51,300
Referee: Massimo Busacca (Switzerland)
SCOTLAND - NORWAY **0-0**
SCO: Craig Sinclair Gordon, Kirk Broadfoot, Gary Andrew Naysmith, David Gillespie Weir, Gary Robert Caldwell, Scott Brown, Darren Barr Fletcher (Cap), James Clark Morrison (56.Steven Kenneth Fletcher), James McFadden (56.Christopher Robert Iwelumo), Barry Robson, Shaun Richard Maloney. Manager: Manager: George Elder Burley
NOR: Jon Knudsen, Jon Inge Høiland, Kjetil Wæhler, Brede Paulsen Hangeland (Cap), John Arne Riise, Bjørn Helge Riise (56.Daniel Omoya Braaten), Christian Grindheim, Fredrik Winsnes, Fredrik Strømstad (77.Morten Gamst Pedersen), John Alieu Carew, Steffen Iversen. Trainer: Åge Hareide.
Cautions: Jon Inge Høiland, Steffen Iversen.

11.10.2008, Feyenoord Stadion, Rotterdam; Attendance: 37,500
Referee: Matteo Trefoloni (Italy)
HOLLAND - ICELAND   **2-0(1-0)**
NED: Edwin van der Sar, Dirk Marcellis, André Antonius Maria Ooijer, Joris Mathijsen, Giovanni Christiaan van Bronckhorst (Cap), Mark Peter Gertruda Andreas van Bommel, Rafael Ferdinand Van der Vaart (81.Wesley Benjamin Sneijder), Nigel de Jong (14.Demy Patrick René de Zeeuw), Dirk Kuijt, Ryan Guno Babel (68.Ibrahim Afellay), Klaas-Jan Huntelaar. Trainer: Lambertus van Marwijk
ISL: Gunnleifur Vignir Gunnleifsson, Ragnar Sigurðsson (51.Theodór Elmar Bjarnason), Indriði Sigurðsson, Hermann Hreiðarsson (Cap), Birkir Már Sævarsson, Brynjar Björn Gunnarsson (73.Aron Einar Gunnarsson), Stefán Gíslason, Kristján Örn Sigurðsson, Eiður Smári Guðjohnsen, Veigar Páll Gunnarsson (87.Arnór Smárason), Emil Hallfreðsson. Trainer: Ólafur Davíð Jóhanesson.
Goals: 1-0 Joris Mathijsen (15), 2-0 Klaas-Jan Huntelaar (65).

15.10.2008, Ullevaal Stadion, Oslo; Attendance: 23,840
Referee: Konrad Plautz (Austria)
NORWAY - HOLLAND   **0-1(0-0)**
NOR: Jon Knudsen, Jon Inge Høiland, Brede Paulsen Hangeland (Cap), Kjetil Wæhler, John Arne Riise, Morten Gamst Pedersen (78.Tarik El Younoussi), Henning Hauger (85.Thorstein Helstad), Christian Grindheim, Fredrik Winsnes, Steffen Iversen, John Alieu Carew. Trainer: Åge Hareide.
NED: Edwin van der Sar, Dirk Marcellis, André Antonius Maria Ooijer, Joris Mathijsen, Giovanni Christiaan van Bronckhorst (Cap), Dirk Kuijt, Mark Peter Gertruda Andreas van Bommel, Rafael Ferdinand Van der Vaart (76.Wesley Benjamin Sneijder), Demy Patrick René de Zeeuw, Ryan Guno Babel (26.Ibrahim Afellay), Klaas-Jan Huntelaar (57.Robin van Persie). Trainer: Lambertus van Marwijk.
Goal: 0-1 Mark Peter Gertruda Andreas van Bommel (64).
Cautions: Brede Paulsen Hangeland, Henning Hauger.

15.10.2008, Laugardalsvöllur Stadium, Reykjavík; Attendance: 5,527
Referee: Selçuk Dereli (Turkey)
ICELAND - MACEDONIA   **1-0(1-0)**
ISL: Gunnleifur Vignir Gunnleifsson, Birkir Már Sævarsson, Hermann Hreiðarsson (Cap), Indriði Sigurðsson, Grétar Rafn Steinsson, Brynjar Björn Gunnarsson (26.Aron Einar Gunnarsson), Stefán Gíslason, Kristján Örn Sigurðsson, Eiður Smári Guðjohnsen (80.Theodór Elmar Bjarnason), Veigar Páll Gunnarsson (65.Pálmi Rafn Pálmason), Emil Hallfreðsson. Trainer: Ólafur Davíð Jóhanesson.
MKD: Petar Miloševski, Nikolče Noveski, Robert Petrov (52.Vančo Trajanov), Goce Sedloski (Cap), Igor Mitreski, Darko Tasevski (78.Stevica Ristić), Vlade Lazarevski, Vlatko Grozdanovski, Velice Šumulikoski, Goran Maznov (60.Aco Stojkov), Goran Pandev. Trainer: Srečko Katanec (Slovenia).
Goal: 1-0 Veigar Páll Gunnarsson (16).
Cautions: Stefán Gíslason, Kristján Örn Sigurðsson, Aron Einar Gunnarsson, Gunnleifur Vignir Gunnleifsson.

28.03.2009, ArenA, Amsterdam; Attendance: 49,500
Referee: Laurent Duhamel (France)
HOLLAND - SCOTLAND   **3-0(2-0)**
NED: Maarten Stekelenburg, Gregory Kurtley van der Wiel, André Antonius Maria Ooijer, Joris Mathijsen, Giovanni Christiaan van Bronckhorst (Cap), Mark Peter Gertruda Andreas van Bommel, Nigel de Jong (80.Stefanus Johannes Schaars), Robin van Persie (65.Wesley Benjamin Sneijder), Dirk Kuijt, Klaas-Jan Huntelaar (80.Ibrahim Afellay), Arjen Robben. Trainer: Lambertus van Marwijk.
SCO: Allan James McGregor, Graham Alexander (73.Alan Hutton), Christophe Michael Berra, Gary Robert Caldwell, Gary Andrew Naysmith, Scott Brown, Barry Ferguson (Cap), Darren Barr Fletcher, Gary Stewart Teale (85.James Clark Morrison), Ross McCormack, Kenneth Miller (71.Steven Kenneth Fletcher). Manager: George Elder Burley.
Goals: 1-0 Klaas-Jan Huntelaar (30), 2-0 Robin van Persie (45+1), 3-0 Dirk Kuijt (77 penalty).

Cautions: Nigel de Jong, Klaas-Jan Huntelaar.

01.04.2009, ArenA, Amsterdam; Attendance: 47,750
Referee: Peter Rasmussen (Denmark)
HOLLAND - MACEDONIA   **4-0(3-0)**
NED: Maarten Stekelenburg, Gregory Kurtley van der Wiel, André Antonius Maria Ooijer, Joris Mathijsen, Giovanni Christiaan van Bronckhorst (Cap), Mark Peter Gertruda Andreas van Bommel, Nigel de Jong, Wesley Benjamin Sneijder (77.Rafael Ferdinand Van der Vaart), Dirk Kuijt (81.Ibrahim Afellay), Klaas-Jan Huntelaar, Arjen Robben (46.Ryan Guno Babel). Trainer: Lambertus van Marwijk.
MKD: Tomislav Pačovski, Nikolče Noveski, Goce Sedloski (Cap), Igor Mitreski, Goran Popov, Darko Tasevski (46.Goran Maznov), Vlatko Grozdanovski (57.Vlade Lazarevski), Velice Šumulikoski, Vančo Trajanov (63.Artim Polož ani), Goran Pandev, Ilčo Naumoski. Trainer: Srečko Katanec (Slovenia).
Goals: 1-0 Dirk Kuijt (16), 2-0 Klaas-Jan Huntelaar (25), 3-0 Dirk Kuijt (41), 4-0 Rafael Ferdinand Van der Vaart (88).
Cautions: Artim Polož ani.

01.04.2009, Hampden Park, Glasgow; Attendance: 42,259
Referee: Thomas Einwaller (Austria)
SCOTLAND - ICELAND   **2-1(1-0)**
SCO: Craig Sinclair Gordon, Alan Hutton, Gary Robert Caldwell, Stephen McManus (Cap), Gary Andrew Naysmith, Ross McCormack, Darren Barr Fletcher, Scott Brown, James Clark Morrison (90+1.Gavin Paul Rae), Kenneth Miller, Steven Kenneth Fletcher (78.Gary Stewart Teale). Manager: George Elder Burley.
ISL: Gunnleifur Vignir Gunnleifsson, Bjarni Ólafur Eiríksson, Hermann Hreiðarsson (Cap), Kristján Örn Sigurðsson, Indriði Sigurðsson (80.Ármann Smári Björnsson), Grétar Rafn Steinsson, Helgi Valur Daníelsson, Pálmi Rafn Pálmason, Aron Einar Gunnarsson (70.Eggert Gunnþór Jónsson), Eiður Smári Guðjohnsen, Arnór Smárason. Trainer: Ólafur Davíð Jóhanesson.
Goals: 1-0 Ross McCormack (39), 1-1 Indriði Sigurðsson (54), 2-1 Steven Kenneth Fletcher (65).
Cautions: Arnór Smárason.

06.06.2009, „Philip II" Arena, Skopje; Attendance: 10,000
Referee: Paolo Tagliavento (Italy)
MACEDONIA - NORWAY   **0-0**
MKD: Jane Nikolovski, Filip Despotovski, Goce Sedloski (Cap), Igor Mitreski, Goran Popov, Slavčo Georgievski, Velice Šumulikoski (64.Goran Maznov), Boban Grnčarov, Aco Stojkov (81.Vlatko Grozdanovski), Goran Pandev, Ilčo Naumoski (75.Stevica Ristić). Trainer: Mirsad Jonuz.
NOR: Jon Knudsen, Jon Inge Høiland, Kjetil Wæhler, Brede Paulsen Hangeland (Cap), John Arne Riise, Daniel Omoya Braaten (57.Erik Huseklepp), Per Ciljan Skjelbred (46.Bjørn Helge Riise), Fredrik Winsnes, Christan Grindheim (73.Henning Hauger), Morten Gamst Pedersen, John Alieu Carew. Trainer: Egil Roger Olsen.
Cautions: Brede Paulsen Hangeland, Bjørn Helge Riise.

06.06.2009, Laugardalsvöllur Stadium, Reykjavík; Attendance: 9,635
Referee: Michael Leslie Dean (England)
ICELAND - HOLLAND   **1-2(0-2)**
ISL: Gunnleifur Vignir Gunnleifsson, Bjarni Ólafur Eiríksson (76.Arnór Smárason), Birkir Már Sævarsson, Hermann Hreiðarsson (Cap), Kristján Örn Sigurðsson, Indriði Sigurðsson, Grétar Rafn Steinsson, Helgi Valur Daníelsson (46.Brynjar Björn Gunnarsson), Stefán Gíslason (68.Aron Einar Gunnarsson), Pálmi Rafn Pálmason, Eiður Smári Guðjohnsen. Trainer: Ólafur Davíð Jóhanesson.
NED: Maarten Stekelenburg, John Gijsbert Alan Heitinga, André Antonius Maria Ooijer, Joris Mathijsen, Giovanni Christiaan van Bronckhorst (Cap), Mark Peter Gertruda Andreas van Bommel, Nigel de Jong (80.David Mendes da Silva Gonçalves), Rafael Ferdinand Van der Vaart (76.Ryan Guno Babel), Robin van Persie, Dirk Kuijt (67.Klaas-Jan Huntelaar), Arjen Robben. Trainer: Lambertus van Marwijk.

Goals: 0-1 Nigel de Jong (8), 0-2 Mark Peter Gertruda Andreas van Bommel (15), 1-2 Kristján Örn Sigurðsson (87).

Cautions: Stefán Gíslason, Indriði Sigurðsson, Aron Einar Gunnarsson, Hermann Hreiðarsson / Nigel de Jong.

10.06.2009, „Philip II" Arena, Skopje; Attendance: 7,000
Referee: Saïd Ennjimi (France)
MACEDONIA - ICELAND 2-0(1-0)
MKD: Jane Nikolovski (72.Tomislav Pačovski), Filip Despotovski, Goce Sedloski (Cap), Igor Mitreski, Goran Popov, Slavčo Georgievski, Velice Šumulikoski (77.Vlatko Grozdanovski), Vlade Lazarevski, Aco Stojkov (64.Filip Ivanovski), Goran Pandev, Ilčo Naumoski. Trainer: Mirsad Jonuz.
ISL: Gunnleifur Vignir Gunnleifsson, Bjarni Ólafur Eiríksson, Sölvi Geir Ottesen Jónsson, Kristján Örn Sigurðsson, Grétar Rafn Steinsson (Cap), Stefán Gíslason, Brynjar Björn Gunnarsson, Eggert Gunnþór Jónsson (62.Birkir Már Sævarsson), Pálmi Rafn Pálmason (74.Jóhann Berg Guðmundsson), Arnór Smárason, Emil Hallfreðsson. Trainer: Ólafur Davíð Jóhanesson.
Goals: 1-0 Aco Stojkov (9), 2-0 Filip Ivanovski (85).
Cautions: Ilčo Naumoski, Filip Despotovski / Pálmi Rafn Pálmason.

10.06.2009, Feyenoord Stadion, Rotterdam; Attendance: 45,000
Referee: Yuri Baskakov (Russia)
HOLLAND - NORWAY 2-0(1-0)
NED: Maarten Stekelenburg, John Gijsbert Alan Heitinga, André Antonius Maria Ooijer, Joris Mathijsen, Giovanni Christiaan van Bronckhorst (Cap) (46.Edson René Braafheid), Mark Peter Gertruda Andreas van Bommel, Stefanus Johannes Schaars, Rafael Ferdinand Van der Vaart, Robin van Persie (83.Klaas-Jan Huntelaar), Dirk Kuijt, Arjen Robben (78.Ryan Guno Babel). Trainer: Lambertus van Marwijk.
NOR: Jon Knudsen, Jon Inge Høiland, Kjetil Wæhler, Morten Fevang, John Arne Riise, Bjørn Helge Riise (42.Daniel Omoya Braaten), Fredrik Winsnes (79.Alexander Banor Tettey), Henning Hauger, Christian Grindheim (67.Per Ciljan Skjelbred), Morten Gamst Pedersen, John Alieu Carew (Cap). Trainer: Egil Roger Ols.
Goals: 1-0 André Antonius Maria Ooijer (33), 2-0 Arjen Robben (51).
Cautions: Christian Grindheim, Morten Gamst Pedersen.

12.08.2009, Ullevaal Stadion, Oslo; Attendance: 24,493
Referee: Alain Hamer (Luxembourg)
NORWAY - SCOTLAND 4-0(2-0)
NOR: Jon Knudsen, Tom Høgli, Kjetil Wæhler, Brede Paulsen Hangeland (Cap), John Arne Riise, Bjørn Helge Riise (84.Per Ciljan Skjelbreid), Christian Grindheim, Magne Hoseth, Morten Gamst Pedersen, John Alieu Carew (84.Thorstein Helstad), Erik Huseklepp (76.Steffen Iversen). Trainer: Egil Roger Olsen.
SCO: David Marshall, Graham Alexander, Gary Robert Caldwell, Steven Caldwell (48.James McFadden), Callum Ian Davidson, Alan Hutton, Scott Brown, Darren Barr Fletcher (Cap), Kristian Arron Commons, Ross McCormack (37.Christophe Michael Berra; 79.Steven Gordon Whittaker), Kenneth Miller. Manager: George Elder Burley.
Goals: 1-0 John Arne Riise (36), 2-0 Morten Gamst Pedersen (45), 3-0 Erik Huseklepp (60), 4-0 Morten Gamst Pedersen (90).
Cautions: John Alieu Carew, Magne Hoseth, John Arne Riise / Gary Robert Caldwell, Steven Caldwell.
Sent off: Gary Robert Caldwell (34).

05.09.2009, Hampden Park, Glasgow; Attendance: 50,214
Referee: Wolfgang Stark (Germany)
SCOTLAND - MACEDONIA 2-0(0-0)
SCO: Craig Sinclair Gordon, Graham Alexander, Stephen McManus, David Gillespie Weir (14.Steven

Gordon Whittaker), Callum Ian Davidson, Alan Hutton, Scott Brown (73.Paul James Hartley), Darren Barr Fletcher (Cap), James McFadden, Steven Kenneth Fletcher (68.Shaun Richard Maloney), Kenneth Miller. Manager: George Elder Burley.
MKD: Jane Nikolovski, Filip Despotovski, Nikolče Noveski, Goce Sedloski (Cap), Igor Mitreski, Goran Popov, Slavčo Georgievski (69.Vlatko Grozdanovski), Velice Šumulikoski, Aco Stojkov (78.Besart Ibraimi), Goran Pandev, Ilčo Naumoski (65.Darko Tasevski). Trainer: Mirsad Jonuz.
Goals: 1-0 Scott Brown (56), 2-0 James McFadden (80).
Cautions: Scott Brown, James McFadden / Igor Mitreski, Filip Despotovski.

05.09.2009, Laugardalsvöllur Stadium, Reykjavík; Attendance: 7,321
Referee: Alexandru Dan Tudor (Romania)
ICELAND - NORWAY   **1-1(1-1)**
ISL: Gunnleifur Vignir Gunnleifsson, Sölvi Geir Ottesen Jónsson (90.Ragnar Sigurðsson), Indriði Sigurðsson, Grétar Rafn Steinsson, Brynjar Björn Gunnarsson (Cap), Kristján Örn Sigurðsson, Aron Einar Gunnarsson (80.Stefán Gíslason), Rúrik Gíslason, Eiður Smári Guðjohnsen, Heiðar Helguson, Emil Hallfreðsson (88.Veigar Páll Gunnarsson). Trainer: Ólafur Davíð Jóhanesson.
NOR: Jon Knudsen, Tom Høgli, Kjetil Wæhler, Brede Paulsen Hangeland (Cap), John Arne Riise, Morten Moldskred (87.Thorstein Helstad), Magne Hoseth (46.Simen Brenne), Christian Grindheim, Morten Gamst Pedersen, Erik Huseklepp (79.Bjørn Helge Riise), John Alieu Carew. Trainer: Egil Roger Olsen.
Goals: 0-1 (11), 1-1 Eiður Smári Guðjohnsen (29).
Cautions: Emil Hallfreðsson, Indriði Sigurðsson, Heiðar Helguson / Kjetil Wæhler.

09.09.2009, Ullevaal Stadion, Oslo; Attendance: 14,766
Referee: Bruno Miguel Duarte Paixão (Portugal)
NORWAY - MACEDONIA   **2-1(2-0)**
NOR: Jon Knudsen, Jon Inge Høiland, Kjetil Wæhler, Brede Paulsen Hangeland (Cap), John Arne Riise, Bjørn Helge Riise, Henning Hauger, Christian Grindheim (71.Fredrik Winsnes), Morten Gamst Pedersen, John Alieu Carew (84.Daniel Omoya Braaten), Thorstein Helstad (76.Morten Moldskred). Trainer: Egil Roger Olsen.
MKD: Tomislav Pačovski, Goce Sedloski (Cap), Igor Mitreski, Goran Popov, Slavčo Georgievski, Darko Tasevski (65.Armend Alimi), Boban Grnčarov, Velice Šumulikoski, Aco Stojkov (60.Besart Ibraimi), Goran Pandev, Ilčo Naumoski (75.Filip Ivanovski). Trainer: Mirsad Jonuz.
Goals: 1-0 Thorstein Helstad (2), 2-0 John Arne Riise (25), 2-1 Boban Grnčarov (79).
Cautions: Igor Mitreski, Goran Popov.

09.09.2009, Hampden Park, Glasgow; Attendance: 51,230
Referee: Claus Bo Larsen (Denmark)
SCOTLAND - HOLLAND   **0-1(0-0)**
SCO: David Marshall, Alan Hutton, Stephen McManus, David Gillespie Weir, Steven Gordon Whittaker, Scott Brown, Paul James Hartley (66.Kristian Arron Commons), Darren Barr Fletcher (Cap), Shaun Richard Maloney (81.Garry Lawrence O'Connor), , Kenneth Miller. Manager: George Elder Burley.
NED: Michel Vorm, Gregory Kurtley van der Wiel, André Antonius Maria Ooijer, Joris Mathijsen, Giovanni Christiaan van Bronckhorst (Cap), Demy Patrick René de Zeeuw, Nigel de Jong, Wesley Benjamin Sneijder (77.Rafael Ferdinand Van der Vaart), Robin van Persie (85.Klaas-Jan Huntelaar), Dirk Kuijt, Arjen Robben (73.Eljero George Rinaldo Elia). Trainer: Lambertus van Marwijk.
Goal: 0-1 Eljero George Rinaldo Elia (82).
Cautions: Steven John Naismith, Paul James Hartley, Darren Barr Fletcher / Robin van Persie, Dirk Kuijt, Arjen Robben

PLAY-OFFS

RANKING OF SECOND-PLACED TEAMS
(matches against the sixth-placed team in each group are not included).

1.	Russia	8	5	1	2	15	-	6	16
2.	Greece	8	5	1	2	16	-	9	16
3.	Ukraine	8	4	3	1	10	-	6	15
4.	France	8	4	3	1	12	-	9	15
5.	Slovenia	8	4	2	2	10	-	4	14
6.	Bosnia-Herzegovina	8	4	1	3	19	-	12	13
7.	Portugal	8	3	4	1	9	-	5	13
8.	Republic of Ireland	8	2	6	0	8	-	6	12
9.	Norway	8	2	4	2	9	-	7	10

For the draw for the ties, helded in Zürich on 19 October 2009, the eight teams were seeded according to the FIFA World Rankings released on 16 October 2009 (shown in parentheses):

Pot A: France (9), Portugal (10), Russia (12), Greece (16).
Pot B: Ukraine (22), Republic of Ireland (34), Bosnia-Herzegovina (42), Slovenia (49).

14.11.2009	Dublin	Republic of Ireland - France	0-1(0-0)
14.11.2009	Lisboa	Portugal - Bosnia-Herzegovina	1-0(1-0)
14.11.2009	Athína	Greece - Ukraine	0-0
14.11.2009	Moskva	Russia - Slovenia	2-1(1-0)
18.11.2009	Paris	**France** - Republic of Ireland	1-1(0-1,0-1,1-1)
18.11.2009	Zenica	Bosnia-Herzegovina - **Portugal**	0-1(0-0)
18.11.2009	Donetsk	Ukraine - **Greece**	0-1(0-1)
18.11.2009	Maribor	**Slovenia** - Russia	1-0(1-0)

France, Portugal, Greece and Slovenia qualified for the World Cup Final Tournament 2010.

FIRST LEGS

14.11.2009, Croke Park, Dublin; Attendance: 74,103
Referee: Felix Brych (Germany)
REPUBLIC OF IRELAND - FRANCE   **0-1(0-0)**
IRL: Seamus John Given, John Francis O'Shea, Sean Patrick St. Ledger-Hall, Richard Patrick Dunne, Kevin Daniel Kilbane, Keith Joseph Andrews, Glenn Whelan, Liam Lawrence (81.Stephen Patrick Hunt), Damien Anthony Duff (76.Aiden McGeady), Kevin Edward Doyle (71.Leon Julian Best), Robert David Keane (Cap). Trainer: Giovanni Trapattoni (Italy).
FRA: Hugo Lloris, Bakary Sagna, William Éric Gallas, Éric Abidal, Patrice Evra, Lassana Diarra, Yoann Miguel Gourcuff, Alou Diarra, Thierry Henry (Cap), Nicolas Sébastien Anelka, André-Pierre Gignac (90+1.Florent Malouda). Trainer: Raymond Domenech.
Goal: 0-1 Nicolas Sébastien Anelka (72).

14.11.2009, Estádio da Luz, Lisboa; Attendance: 60,588
Referee: Martin Atkinson (England)
PORTUGAL – BOSNIA-HERZEGOVINA   **1-0(1-0)**
POR: Eduardo dos Reis Carvalho, Paulo Renato Rebocho Ferreira, Ricardo Alberto Silveira de Carvalho, Bruno Eduardo Regufe Alves, Sérgio Paulo Barbosa Valente „Duda", Képler Laveran Lima Ferreira „Pepe", Raúl José Trindade Meireles „Raul Meireles", Anderson Luís de Souza „Deco" (84.Tiago Cardoso Mendes), Luís Carlos Almeida da Cunha „Nani" (69.Fábio Alexandre da Silva

Coentrão), Simão Pedro Fonseca Sabrosa (88.Hugo Miguel Pereira de Almeida), Liédson da Silva Muniz. Trainer: Carlos Manuel Brito Leal Queiroz.
BIH: Kenan Hasagić, Sanel Jahić, Emir Spahić, Safet Nadarević, Sejad Salihović, Elvir Rahimić, Samir Muratović (87.Miralem Pjanić), Vedad Ibišević, Zvezdjan Misimović (81.Zlatan Muslimović), Senijad Ibričić, Edin Dž eko. Trainer:Miroslav Blaž evč (Croatia).
Goal: 1-0 Bruno Eduardo Regufe Alves (31).
Cautions: Anderson Luís de Souza „Deco" / Vedad Ibišević, Samir Muratović, Elvir Rahimić, Emir Spahić.

14.11.2009, Olympiako „Spiros Louis" Stadio, Athína; Attendance: 39,045
Referee: Laurent Duhamel (France)
GREECE - UKRAINE   **0-0**
GRE: Alexandros Tzórvas, Sotírios Kyrgiakos, Evangélios Móras, Sokratís Papastathópoulos, Loukás Víntra, Nikolaos Leonidas Spiropoulos, Konstantinos Katsouránis, Giórgos Karagoúnis (Cap), Theofánis Gékas (65.Angelos Haristéas), Dimítris Salpingídis (71.Konstantinos Mitroglou), Giórgos Samarás. Trainer: Otto Rehhagel (Germany).
UKR: Andriy Pyatov, Olexandr Kucher, Yevhen Khacheridi, Anatoliy Tymoschuk, Oleh Gusev (53.Oleksandr Aliyev), Vasyl Kobin, Taras Mykhalyk, Yaroslav Rakytskiy, Ruslan Rotan (46.Andriy Yarmolenko), Artem Milevskiy, Andriy Shevchenko (Cap). Trainer: Oleksiy Mykhailychenko.
Cautions: Sokratís Papastathópoulos.

14.11.2009, Luzhniki Stadium, Moskva; Attendance: 71,600
Referee: Claus Bo Larsen (Denmark)
RUSSIA - SLOVENIA   **2-1(1-0)**
RUS: Igor Akinfeyev, Aleksandr Anyukov, Sergey Ignashevich, Vasiliy Berezutskiy, Yuriy Zhirkov, Konstantin Zyryanov, Sergey Semak (61.Vladimir Bystrov), Igor Denisov, Diniyar Bilyaletdinov, Roman Pavlyuchenko (80.Dmitriy Sychev), Andrey Arshavin (Cap). Trainer: Guus Hiddink (Holland).
SVN: Samir Handanovič, Mišo Brečko, Marko Šuler, Boštjan Cesar, Bojan Jokić, Robert Koren (Cap), Aleksander Radosavljevič, Andraž Kirm (82.Nejc Pčnik), Valter Birsa (77.Dalibor Stevanović), Zlatko Dedič (67.Elvedin Dž inč), Milivoje Novakovič. Trainer: Matjaž Kek.
Goals: 1-0 Diniyar Bilyaletdinov (40), 2-0 Diniyar Bilyaletdinov (52), 2-1 Nejc Pečnik (88).
Cautions: Andrey Arshavin, Dmitriy Sychev.

SECOND LEGS

18.11.2009, Stade de France, Saint-Denis, Paris; Attendance: 79,145
Referee: Martin Hansson (Sweden)
FRANCE – REPUBLIC OF IRELAND   **1-1(0-1,0-1)**
FRA: Hugo Lloris, Bakary Sagna, William Éric Gallas, Julien Escudé (9.Sébastien Squillaci), Patrice Evra, Alou Diarra, Lassana Diarra, Yoann Miguel Gourcuff (87.Florent Malouda), Nicolas Sébastien Anelka, Thierry Henry (Cap), André-Pierre Gignac (57.Sidney Govou). Trainer: Raymond Domenech.
IRL: Seamus John Given, John Francis O'Shea (67.Paul David McShane), Sean Patrick St. Ledger-Hall, Richard Patrick Dunne, Kevin Daniel Kilbane, Keith Joseph Andrews, Glenn Whelan (63.Darron Thomas Daniel Gibson), Liam Lawrence (107.Aiden McGeady), Damien Anthony Duff, Robert David Keane (Cap), Kevin Edward Doyle. Trainer: Giovanni Trapattoni (Italy).
Goals: 0-1 Robert David Keane (32), 1-1 William Éric Gallas (103).
Cautions: Sébastien Squillaci, Florent Malouda, Sidney Govou / Kevin Daniel Kilbane, Paul David McShane, Damien Anthony Duff.

18.11.2009, Stadion Bilino Polje, Zenica; Attendance: 13,000
Referee: Roberto Rosetti (Italy)
BOSNIA-HERZEGOVINA - PORTUGAL   **0-1(0-1)**
BIH: Kenan Hasagić, Safet Nadarević, Sanel Jahić, Boris Pandž a, Sejad Salihovč, Zlatan Bajramović (83.Dž emal Berberovč), Miralem Pjanić, Senijad Ibričić, Haris Medunjanin (46.Zlatan Muslimović),

Vedad Ibišević, Edin Dž eko. Trainer:Miroslav Blaž evć (Croatia).
POR: Eduardo dos Reis Carvalho, Sérgio Paulo Barbosa Valente „Duda", Ricardo Alberto Silveira de Carvalho, Bruno Eduardo Regufe Alves, Paulo Renato Rebocho Ferreira, Képler Laveran Lima Ferreira „Pepe", Raúl José Trindade Meireles „Raul Meireles", Simão Pedro Fonseca Sabrosa (80.Anderson Luís de Souza „Deco"), Tiago Cardoso Mendes, Luís Carlos Almeida da Cunha „Nani" (73.Arnaldo Edi Lopes da Silva „Edinho"), Liédson da Silva Muniz (90+1.Miguel Luís Pinto Veloso). Trainer: Carlos Manuel Brito Leal Queiroz.
Goal: 0-1 Raúl José Trindade Meireles „Raul Meireles" (56).
Cautions: Sanel Jahić, Safet Nadarević, Edin Dž eko, Dž emal Berberovći / Simão Pedro Fonseca Sabrosa.
Sent off: Sejad Salihović (77).

18.11.2009, Donbass Arena, Donetsk; Attendance: 31,643
Referee: Olegário Manuel Bartolo Faustino Benquerença (Portugal)
UKRAINE - GREECE   **0-1(0-1)**
UKR: Andriy Pyatov, Olexandr Kucher, Yevhen Khacheridi, Vasyl Kobin, Oleksandr Aliyev (57.Yevhen Seleznev), Anatoliy Tymoschuk, Taras Mykhalyk (66.Oleksiy Gay), Yaroslav Rakytskiy, Andriy Yarmolenko (69.Oleh Gusev), Artem Milevskiy, Andriy Shevchenko (Cap). Trainer: Oleksiy Mykhailychenko.
GRE: Alexandros Tzórvas, Sokratís Papastathópoulos (29.Vasílis Pliátsikas), Evangélios Móras, Sotírios Kyrgiakos, Loukás Víntra, Nikolaos Leonidas Spiropoulos, Konstantinos Katsouránis, Giórgos Karagoúnis (Cap), Dimítris Salpingídis, Angelos Haristéas (71.Alexandros Tzíolis), Giórgos Samarás (63.Theofánis Gékas). Trainer: Otto Rehhagel (Germany).
Goal: 0-1 Dimítris Salpingídis (31).
Cautions: Andriy Yarmolenko / Konstantinos Katsouránis, Loukás Víntra, Sotírios Kyrgiakos.

18.11.2009, Stadion Ljudski vrt, Maribor; Attendance: 12,510
Referee: Terje Hauge (Norway)
SLOVENIA - RUSSIA   **1-0(1-0)**
SVN: Samir Handanovič, Mišo Brečko, Marko Suler, Boštjan Cesar, Bojan Jokić, Aleksander Radosavljevič, Valter Birsa (78.Nejc Pečnik), Robert Koren (Cap), Andraž Kirm, Zlatko Dedč (90+4.Dalibor Stevanović)., Milivoje Novakovič. Trainer: Matjaž Kek.
RUS: Igor Akinfeyev, Aleksandr Anyukov, Vasiliy Berezutskiy, Sergey Ignashevich, Renat Yanbaev (46.Sergey Semak), Igor Denisov, Diniyar Bilyaletdinov (77.Pavel Pogrebnyak), Konstantin Zyryanov, Andrey Arshavin (Cap), Yuriy Zhirkov, Roman Pavlyuchenko (46.Aleksandr Kerzhakov). Trainer: Guus Hiddink (Holland).
Goal: 1-0 Zlatko Dedič (44).
Cautions: Valter Birsa, Samir Handanovič, Robert Koren / Yuriy Zhirkov, Diniyar Bilyaletdinov, Igor Denisov.
Sent off: Aleksandr Kerzhakov (66), Yuriy Zhirkov (90+2).

SOUTH AMERICA

10 national teams of South America competed to reach the Final Tournament. Identical to used format for the previous three World Cup qualifying tournaments, all national teams played a home and away match against each other competing team. The top-4 national teams qualify automatically for the Final Tournament. The 5th placed South American team will play against the 4th placed team from the CONCACAF Qualifiers.

13.10.2007	Montevideo	Uruguay - Bolivia	5-0(2-0)
13.10.2007	Buenos Aires	Argentina - Chile	2-0(2-0)
13.10.2007	Quito	Ecuador - Venezuela	0-1(0-0)
13.10.2007	Lima	Peru - Paraguay	0-0
14.10.2007	Bogotá	Colombia - Brazil	0-0
16.10.2007	Maracaibo	Venezuela - Argentina	0-2(0-2)
17.10.2007	La Paz	Bolivia - Colombia	0-0
17.10.2007	Santiago	Chile - Peru	2-0(1-0)
17.10.2007	Asunción	Paraguay - Uruguay	1-0(1-0)
17.10.2007	Rio de Janeiro	Brazil - Ecuador	5-0(1-0)
17.11.2007	Buenos Aires	Argentina - Bolivia	3-0(1-0)
17.11.2007	Bogotá	Colombia - Venezuela	1-0(0-0)
17.11.2007	Asunción	Paraguay - Ecuador	5-1(2-0)
18.11.2007	Montevideo	Uruguay - Chile	2-2(1-0)
18.11.2007	Lima	Peru - Brazil	1-1(0-1)
20.11.2007	San Cristóbal	Venezuela - Bolivia	5-3(2-2)
20.11.2007	Bogotá	Colombia - Argentina	2-1(0-1)
21.11.2007	Quito	Ecuador - Peru	5-1(3-0)
21.11.2007	São Paulo	Brazil - Uruguay	2-1(1-1)
21.11.2007	Santiago	Chile - Paraguay	0-3(0-2)
14.06.2008	Montevideo	Uruguay - Venezuela	1-1(1-0)
14.06.2008	Lima	Peru - Colombia	1-1(1-1)
15.06.2008	Asunción	Paraguay - Brazil	2-0(1-0)
15.06.2008	Buenos Aires	Argentina - Ecuador	1-1(0-0)
15.06.2008	La Paz	Bolivia - Chile	0-2(0-1)
17.06.2008	Montevideo	Uruguay - Peru	6-0(2-0)
18.06.2008	La Paz	Bolivia - Paraguay	4-2(2-0)
18.06.2008	Quito	Ecuador - Colombia	0-0
18.06.2008	Belo Horizonte	Brazil - Argentina	0-0
19.06.2008	Puerto la Cruz	Venezuela - Chile	2-3(0-0)
06.09.2008	Buenos Aires	Argentina - Paraguay	1-1(0-1)
06.09.2008	Quito	Ecuador - Bolivia	3-1(1-1)
06.09.2008	Bogotá	Colombia - Uruguay	0-1(0-1)
06.09.2008	Lima	Peru - Venezuela	1-0(1-0)
07.09.2008	Santiago	Chile - Brazil	0-3(0-2)
09.09.2008	Asunción	Paraguay - Venezuela	2-0(2-0)
10.09.2008	Montevideo	Uruguay - Ecuador	0-0
10.09.2008	Santiago	Chile - Colombia	4-0(2-0)
10.09.2008	Rio de Janeiro	Brazil - Bolivia	0-0
10.09.2008	Lima	Peru - Argentina	1-1(0-0)
11.10.2008	La Paz	Bolivia - Peru	3-0(2-0)
11.10.2008	Buenos Aires	Argentina - Uruguay	2-1(2-1)
11.10.2008	Bogotá	Colombia - Paraguay	0-1(0-1)
12.10.2008	San Cristóbal	Venezuela - Brazil	0-4(0-3)

12.10.2008	Quito	Ecuador - Chile	1-0(0-0)
14.10.2008	La Paz	Bolivia - Uruguay	2-2(2-0)
15.10.2008	Asunción	Paraguay - Peru	1-0(0-0)
15.10.2008	Santiago	Chile - Argentina	1-0(1-0)
15.10.2008	Rio de Janeiro	Brazil - Colombia	0-0
15.10.2008	Puerto la Cruz	Venezuela - Ecuador	3-1(0-1)
28.03.2009	Montevideo	Uruguay - Paraguay	2-0(1-0)
28.03.2009	Buenos Aires	Argentina - Venezuela	4-0(1-0)
28.03.2009	Bogotá	Colombia - Bolivia	2-0(1-0)
29.03.2009	Quito	Ecuador - Brazil	1-1(0-0)
29.03.2009	Lima	Peru - Chile	1-3(1-2)
31.03.2009	Puerto Ordaz	Venezuela - Colombia	2-0(0-0)
01.04.2009	La Paz	Bolivia - Argentina	6-1(3-1)
01.04.2009	Quito	Ecuador - Paraguay	1-1(0-0)
01.04.2009	Santiago	Chile - Uruguay	0-0
01.04.2009	Porto Alegre	Brazil - Peru	3-0(2-0)
06.06.2009	Montevideo	Uruguay - Brazil	0-4(0-2)
06.06.2009	La Paz	Bolivia - Venezuela	0-1(0-1)
06.06.2009	Buenos Aires	Argentina - Colombia	1-0(0-0)
06.06.2009	Asunción	Paraguay - Chile	0-2(0-1)
07.06.2009	Lima	Peru - Ecuador	1-2(0-1)
10.06.2009	Quito	Ecuador - Argentina	2-0(0-0)
10.06.2009	Medellín	Colombia - Peru	1-0(1-0)
10.06.2009	Recife	Brazil - Paraguay	2-1(1-1)
10.06.2009	Santiago	Chile - Bolivia	4-0(1-0)
10.06.2009	Puerto Ordaz	Venezuela - Uruguay	2-2(1-0)
05.09.2009	Medellín	Colombia - Ecuador	2-0(0-0)
05.09.2009	Lima	Peru - Uruguay	1-0(0-0)
05.09.2009	Asunción	Paraguay - Bolivia	1-0(1-0)
05.09.2009	Rosario	Argentina - Brazil	1-3(0-2)
05.09.2009	Santiago	Chile - Venezuela	2-2(1-2)
09.09.2009	La Paz	Bolivia - Ecuador	1-3(0-1)
09.09.2009	Montevideo	Uruguay - Colombia	3-1(1-0)
09.09.2009	Asunción	Paraguay - Argentina	1-0(1-0)
09.09.2009	Salvador	Brazil - Chile	4-2(2-1)
09.09.2009	Puerto la Cruz	Venezuela - Peru	3-1(1-1)
10.10.2009	Buenos Aires	Argentina - Peru	2-1(0-0)
10.10.2009	Medellín	Colombia - Chile	2-4(1-2)
10.10.2009	Quito	Ecuador - Uruguay	1-2(0-0)
10.10.2009	Puerto Ordaz	Venezuela - Paraguay	1-2(0-0)
11.10.2009	La Paz	Bolivia - Brazil	2-1(2-0)
14.10.2009	Lima	Peru - Bolivia	1-0(0-0)
14.10.2009	Campo Grande	Brazil - Venezuela	0-0
14.10.2009	Santiago	Chile - Ecuador	1-0(0-0)
14.10.2009	Montevideo	Uruguay - Argentina	0-1(0-0)
14.10.2009	Asunción	Paraguay - Colombia	0-2(0-0)

FINAL STANDINGS

1.	**BRAZIL**	18	9	7	2	33	-	11	34
2.	**CHILE**	18	10	3	5	32	-	22	33
3.	**PARAGUAY**	18	10	3	5	24	-	16	33
4.	**ARGENTINA**	18	8	4	6	23	-	20	28
5.	Uruguay	18	6	6	6	28	-	20	24
6.	Ecuador	18	6	5	7	22	-	26	23
7.	Colombia	18	6	5	7	14	-	18	23
8.	Venezuela	18	6	4	8	23	-	29	22
9.	Bolivia	18	4	3	11	22	-	36	15
10.	Peru	18	3	4	11	11	-	34	13

Brazil, Chile, Paraguay and Argentina qualified for the World Cup Final Tournament 2010. Uruguay qualified for the Intercontinental Play-Offs against the 4th placed team from North & Central America.

Intercontinental Play-Offs

14.11.2009	San José	Costa Rica - Uruguay	0-1(0-1)
18.11.2009	Montevideo	Uruguay – Costa Rica	1-1(0-0)

Uruguay qualified for the World Cup Final Tournament 2010.

13.10.2007, Estadio Centenario, Montevideo; Attendance: 25,200
Referee: Rubén Selmán Albornoz (Chile)
URUGUAY - BOLIVIA   **5-0(2-0)**
URU: Héctor Fabián Carini Hernández, Victorio Maximiliano Pereira Páez, Andrés Scotti Ponce de León, Diego Roberto Godín Leal, Jorge Ciro Fucile Perdomo, Diego Fernando Pérez Aguado, Pablo Gabriel García Pérez (Cap), Cristian Gabriel Rodríguez Barrotti, Luis Alberto Suárez Díaz (65.Vicente Martín Sánchez Bragunde), Washington Sebastián Abreu Gallo (73.Carlos Heber Bueno Suárez), Diego Martín Forlán Corazo (66.Mario Ignacio Regueiro Pintos). Trainer: Óscar Wáshington Tabárez Silva.
BOL: Sergio Daniel Galarza Soliz, Miguel Ángel Hoyos Guzmán (75.Nicolás Suárez Vaca), Ronald Raldés Balcázar (Cap), Santos Amador Quispe, Lorgio Álvarez Roca, Sacha Silvestro Lima Saucedo, Hermán Solíz Salvatierra (46.Diego Aroldo Cabrera Flores), Ronald Lázaro García Justiniano, Joselito Vaca Velasco, Jaime Moreno Morales (59.Jaime Cardozo), Marcelo Moreno Martins. Trainer: Erwin Sánchez Frerking.
Goals: 1-0 Luis Alberto Suárez Díaz (4), 2-0 Diego Martín Forlán Corazo (38), 3-0 Washington Sebastián Abreu Gallo (48), 4-0 Vicente Martín Sánchez Bragunde (67), 5-0 Carlos Heber Bueno Suárez (83).
Cautions: Victorio Maximiliano Pereira Páez / Ronald Lázaro García Justiniano,
Sent off: Ronald Lázaro García Justiniano (42), Ronald Raldés Balcázar, Santos Amador Quispe.

13.10.2007, Estadio Monumental „Antonio Vespucio Liberti", Buenos Aires; Attendance: 55,000
Referee: Martín Vázquez Broquetas (Uruguay)
ARGENTINA - CHILE   **2-0(2-0)**
ARG: Roberto Carlos Abbondanzieri, Javier Adelmar Zanetti (Cap), Martín Gastón Demichelis, Gabriel Alejandro Milito, Gabriel Iván Heinze, Javier Alejandro Mascherano, Esteban Matías Cambiasso, Maximiliano Rubén Rodríguez (68.Fernando Rubén Gago), Juan Román Riquelme, Lionel Andrés Messi (84.Javier Pedro Saviola), Carlos Alberto Tévez (74.Sergio Leonel Agüero del Castillo). Trainer: Alfio Oscar Basile.
CHI: Claudio Andrés Bravo Muñoz, Cristián Andrés Álvarez Valenzuela, Waldo Alonso Ponce Carrizo, Miguel Augusto Riffo Garay, Gonzalo Antonio Fierro Caniullán (37.Hugo Patricio Droguett Diocares), Manuel Rolando Iturra Urrutia (63.Claudio Andrés Maldonado Rivera), Arturo Erasmo

Vidal Pardo, Eduardo Javier Rubio Köstner (46.José Marcelo Salas Melinao), Matías Ariel Fernández Fernández, Mark Dennis González Hoffman, Humberto Andrés Suazo Pontivo. Trainer: Marcelo Alberto Bielsa Caldera (Argentina).
Goals: 1-0 Juan Román Riquelme (27), 2-0 Juan Román Riquelme (45).
Cautions: Maximiliano Rubén Rodríguez / Gonzalo Antonio Fierro Caniullán, Arturo Erasmo Vidal Pardo, Manuel Rolando Iturra Urrutia, Miguel Augusto Riffo Garay, Cristián Andrés Álvarez Valenzuela, Claudio Andrés Bravo Muñoz.
Sent off: Cristián Andrés Álvarez Valenzuela (54).

13.10.2007, Estadio Olimpico „Atahualpa", Quito; Attendance: 37,000
Referee: René Ortubé Betancourt (Bolivia)
ECUADOR - VENEZUELA   **0-1(0-0)**
ECU: Daniel Jimmy Viteri Vinces, Ulises Hernán de la Cruz Bernardo, Iván Jacinto Hurtado Angulo, Giovanny Patricio Espinoza Pabón, Óscar Dalmiro Bagüi Angulo (76.Mario David Quiroz Villón), Luis Antonio Valencia Mosquera (71.Félix Alexander Borja Valencia), Segundo Alejandro Castillo Nazareno, Édison Vicente Méndez Méndez, Christian Rolando Lara Anangonó (46.Walter Orlando Ayoví Corozo), Christian Rogelio Benítez Betancourt, Carlos Vicente Tenorio Medina. Trainer: Luis Fernando Suárez (Colombia).
VEN: Renny Vicente Vega Hernández, Luis José Vallenilla Pacheco, José Manuel Rey Cortegoso, Alejandro Enrique Cíchero Konarek, Enrique Andrés Rouga Rossi, Miguel Ángel Mea Vitali (79.Leonel Vielma Gerardo Peña), Luis Enrique Vera Martineau, Ricardo David Páez Gómez (77.Héctor Augusto Gonzalez Guzmán), Jorge Alberto Rojas Méndez, Juan Fernando Arango Sáenz (65.Alejandro Abraham Guerra Morales), Giancarlo Gregorio Maldonado Marrero. Trainer: Richard Alfred Mayela Páez Monzón.
Goal: 0-1 José Manuel Rey Cortegoso (67).
Cautions: Iván Jacinto Hurtado Angulo / Alejandro Enrique Cíchero Konarek, Luis Enrique Vera Martineau.

13.10.2007, Estadio Monumental, Lima; Attendance: 50,000
Referee: Carlos Eugênio Simon (Brazil)
PERU - PARAGUAY   **0-0**
PER: Leao Butrón Gotuzzo, John Christian Galliquio Castro (74.Flavio Francisco Maestri Andrade), Alberto Junior Rodríguez Valdelomar, Wilmer Santiago Acasiete Ariadela, Wálter Ricardo Vílchez Soto, Paolo Giancarlo De La Haza Urquiza, Henry Edson Quinteros Sánchez (86.Juan José Jayo Legario), Nolberto Albino Solano Todco, Juan Manuel Vargas Risco (84.William Medardo Chiroque Tavara), Claudio Miguel Pizarro Bossio, Jefferson Agustín Farfán Guadalupe. Trainer: José Guillermo del Solar Alvarez-Calderón.
PAR: Justo Wilmar Villar Viveros, Denis Ramón Caniza Acuña, Julio César Cáceres López, Paulo César da Silva Barrios, Claudio Marcelo Morel Rodríguez, Enrique Daniel Vera Torres, Édgar Osvaldo Barreto Cáceres (86.Jorge Orlando Brítez Larramendi), Víctor Javier Cáceres Centurión, Cristian Miguel Riveros Núñez, Salvador Cabañas Ortega (76.Jorge Daniel Achucarro), Nelson Antonio Haedo Valdéz (67.Óscar René Cardozo Marín). Trainer: Gerardo Daniel Martino (Argentina).
Cautions: Alberto Junior Rodríguez Valdelomar / Enrique Daniel Vera Torres, Justo Wilmar Villar Viveros, Claudio Marcelo Morel Rodríguez.

14.10.2007, Estadio „Nemesio Camacho" El Campín, Bogotá; Attendance:
Referee: Carlos Arencio Amarilla Demarqui (Paraguay)
COLOMBIA - BRAZIL   **0-0**
COL: Agustín Julio Castro, Juan Camilo Zúñiga Mosquera, Walter José Moreno, Aquivaldo Mosquera Romaña, Juan Estiven Vélez Upegui, José Antonio Amaya Pardo, Carlos Alberto Sánchez Moreno, David Arturo Ferreira Rico (56.Aldo Leão Ramírez), Jaime Alberto Castrillón Vásquez (56.Freddy Indurley Grisales), Radamel Falcao García Zárate (82.Édixon Perea Valencia), Wason Libardo Rentería Cuesta. Trainer: Jorge Luis Pinto Afanador.
BRA: Júlio César Soares de Espíndola, Maicon Douglas Sisenando, Lucimar Ferreira da Silva „Lúcio"

94

(Cap), Juan Silveira dos Santos, Gilberto da Silva Melo, Carlos Luciano da Silva "Mineiro", Gilberto Aparecido da Silva, Ricardo Izecson dos Santos Leite „Kaká" (84.Afonso Alves Martins Jr.), Ronaldo de Assis Moreira „Ronaldinho", Róbson de Souza „Robinho" (62.Júlio César Baptista), Vágner Silveira de Souza "Vágner "Love"" (70.Josué Anunciado de Oliveira). Trainer: Carlos Caetano Bledorn Verri "Dunga".

Cautions: Wason Libardo Rentería Cuesta, Édixon Perea Valencia / Lucimar Ferreira da Silva „Lúcio", Ricardo Izecson dos Santos Leite „Kaká", Júlio César Soares de Espíndola, Gilberto Aparecido da Silva.

16.10.2007, Estadio "José Encarnación "Pachencho" Romero", Maracaibo; Attendance: 35,000
Referee: Carlos Eugênio Simon (Brazil)
VENEZUELA - ARGENTINA   **0-2(0-2)**
VEN: Renny Vicente Vega Hernández, Luis José Vallenilla Pacheco (46.Roberto José Rosales Altuve), José Manuel Rey Cortegoso, Alejandro Enrique Cíchero Konarek, Enrique Andrés Rouga Rossi, Miguel Ángel Mea Vitali, Jorge Alberto Rojas Méndez (67.Daniel Enrique Arismendi Marchán), Ricardo David Páez Gómez, Luis Manuel Seijas Gunther (54.Alejandro Abraham Guerra Morales), Juan Fernando Arango Sáenz, Giancarlo Gregorio Maldonado Marrero. Trainer: Richard Alfred Mayela Páez Monzón.
ARG: Roberto Carlos Abbondanzieri, Hugo Benjamín Ibarra (64.Fernando Rubén Gago), Martín Gastón Demichelis, Gabriel Alejandro Milito, Nicolás Andrés Burdisso (74.Daniel Alberto Díaz), Javier Adelmar Zanetti (Cap), Javier Alejandro Mascherano, Esteban Matías Cambiasso, Juan Román Riquelme, Lionel Andrés Messi, Carlos Alberto Tévez (81.Germán Gustavo Denis). Trainer: Alfio Oscar Basile.
Goals: 0-1 Gabriel Alejandro Milito (16), 0-2 Lionel Andrés Messi (43).
Cautions: Alejandro Enrique Cíchero Konarek, Giancarlo Gregorio Maldonado Marrero, Roberto José Rosales Altuve / Hugo Benjamín Ibarra, Fernando Rubén Gago.

17.10.2007, Estadio "Hernándo Siles Zuazo", La Paz; Attendance: 19,469
Referee: Mauricio Reinoso Fabara (Ecuador)
BOLIVIA - COLOMBIA   **0-0**
BOL: Sergio Daniel Galarza Soliz, Luis Gatty Ribeiro Roca, Ronald Raldés Balcázar (Cap), Santos Amador Quispe, Ricardo Verdúguez, Gualberto Mojica Olmos, Leonel Alfredo Reyes Saravia, Jhasmani Campos Dávalos (46.Joselito Vaca Velasco), Limberg Gutiérrez Mariscal, Augusto Andaveris Iriondo (55.Diego Aroldo Cabrera Flores), Juan Carlos Arce Justiniano (72.Ronald Gutiérrez Flores). Trainer: Erwin Sánchez Frerking.
COL: Agustín Julio Castro, Gerardo Enrique Vallejos, Walter José Moreno, Aquivaldo Mosquera Romaña, Javier Eduardo Arizala Caicedo, José Yulián Anchico Patiño (85.Jorge Eliecer Banguero), José Antonio Amaya Pardo, Carlos Alberto Sánchez Moreno, David Arturo Ferreira Rico (55.Aldo Leão Ramírez), Carmelo Enrique Valencia Chaverra (63.Jaime Alberto Castrillón Vásquez), Wason Libardo Rentería Cuesta. Trainer: Jorge Luis Pinto Afanador.
Cautions: Sergio Daniel Galarza Soliz, Leonel Alfredo Reyes Saravia / Aquivaldo Mosquera Romaña, Javier Eduardo Arizala Caicedo, José Yulián Anchico Patiño, Agustín Julio Castro.
Sent off: Leonel Alfredo Reyes Saravia (69).

17.10.2007, Estadio Nacional „Julio Martínez Prádanos", Santiago; Attendance: 60,000
Referee: Óscar Julián Ruiz Acosta (Colombia)
CHILE - PERU   **2-0(1-0)**
CHI: Claudio Andrés Bravo Muñoz, Waldo Alonso Ponce Carrizo, Miguel Augusto Riffo Garay, Arturo Erasmo Vidal Pardo, Gonzalo Antonio Fierro Caniullán (89.Ismael Ignacio Fuentes Castro), Manuel Rolando Iturra Urrutia, Hugo Patricio Droguett Diocares, Matías Ariel Fernández Fernández, Humberto Andrés Suazo Pontivo (84.Eduardo Javier Rubio Köstner), José Marcelo Salas Melinao (88.Luis Antonio Jiménez Garcés), Mark Dennis González Hoffman. Trainer: Marcelo Alberto Bielsa Caldera (Argentina).
PER: Leao Butrón Gotuzzo, John Christian Galliquio Castro, Alberto Junior Rodríguez Valdelomar,

Wilmer Santiago Acasiete Ariadela, Wálter Ricardo Vílchez Soto (73.Paulo Rinaldo Cruzado Durand), Paolo Giancarlo De La Haza Urquiza (46.Henry Edson Quinteros Sánchez), Juan José Jayo Legario, Nolberto Albino Solano Todco, Juan Manuel Vargas Risco, Claudio Miguel Pizarro Bossio, Jefferson Agustín Farfán Guadalupe. Trainer: José Guillermo del Solar Alvarez-Calderón.
Goals: 1-0 Humberto Andrés Suazo Pontivo (11), 2-0 Matías Ariel Fernández Fernández (51).
Cautions: Hugo Patricio Droguett Diocares, Matías Ariel Fernández Fernández, Manuel Rolando Iturra Urrutia / Wálter Ricardo Vílchez Soto, Paolo Giancarlo De La Haza Urquiza, Juan Manuel Vargas Risco, Nolberto Albino Solano Todco, John Christian Galliquio Castro.

17.10.2007, Estadio Defensores del Chaco, Asunción; Attendance: 25,000
Referee: Héctor Walter Baldassi (Argentina)
PARAGUAY - URUGUAY   **1-0(1-0)**
PAR: Justo Wilmar Villar Viveros, Denis Ramón Caniza Acuña, Julio César Cáceres López, Paulo César da Silva Barrios, Claudio Marcelo Morel Rodríguez, Enrique Daniel Vera Torres, Édgar Osvaldo Barreto Cáceres (86.Jonathan Santana Ghere), Víctor Javier Cáceres Centurión, Cristian Miguel Riveros Núñez, Nelson Antonio Haedo Valdéz (65.Óscar René Cardozo Marín), Salvador Cabañas Ortega (78.Jorge Daniel Achucarro). Trainer: Gerardo Daniel Martino (Argentina).
URU: Héctor Fabián Carini Hernández, Diego Alfredo Moreno Lugano (Cap), Andrés Scotti Ponce de León, Diego Roberto Godín Leal, Victorio Maximiliano Pereira Páez, Diego Fernando Pérez Aguado (68.Álvaro Rafael González Luengo), Pablo Gabriel García Pérez, Jorge Ciro Fucile Perdomo, Cristian Gabriel Rodríguez Barrotti (79.Carlos Heber Bueno Suárez), Luis Alberto Suárez Díaz (62.Vicente Martín Sánchez Bragunde), Diego Martín Forlán Corazo. Trainer: Óscar Wáshington Tabárez Silva.
Goal: 1-0 Nelson Antonio Haedo Valdéz (14).
Cautions: Cristian Miguel Riveros Núñez, Nelson Antonio Haedo Valdéz, Óscar René Cardozo Marín / Pablo Gabriel García Pérez, Diego Fernando Pérez Aguado.

17.10.2007, Estádio „Jornalista Mário Filho" (Maracanã), Rio de Janeiro; Attendance: 76,657
Referee: Jorge Larrionda Pietrafiesa (Uruguay)
BRAZIL - ECUADOR   **5-0(1-0)**
BRA: Júlio César Soares de Espíndola, Maicon Douglas Sisenando, Lucimar Ferreira da Silva „Lúcio" (Cap), Juan Silveira dos Santos, Gilberto da Silva Melo, Carlos Luciano da Silva "Mineiro", Gilberto Aparecido da Silva, Ricardo Izecson dos Santos Leite „Kaká" (89.Diego Ribas da Cunha), Ronaldo de Assis Moreira „Ronaldinho", Róbson de Souza „Robinho", Vágner Silveira de Souza "Vágner "Love"" (76.Elano Ralph Blumer). Trainer: Carlos Caetano Bledorn Verri "Dunga".
ECU: Daniel Jimmy Viteri Vinces, Ulises Hernán de la Cruz Bernardo, Iván Jacinto Hurtado Angulo, Giovanny Patricio Espinoza Pabón, Óscar Dalmiro Bagüi Angulo, Mario David Quiroz Villón (46.Carlos Vicente Tenorio Medina), Segundo Alejandro Castillo Nazareno, Patricio Javier Urrutia Espinoza, Édison Vicente Méndez Méndez, Walter Orlando Ayoví Corozo (76.Joffre David Guerrón Méndez), Christian Rogelio Benítez Betancourt (82.Christian Rolando Lara Anangonó). Trainer: Luis Fernando Suárez (Colombia).
Goals: 1-0 Vágner Silveira de Souza "Vágner "Love"" (19), 2-0 Ronaldo de Assis Moreira „Ronaldinho" (72), 3-0 Ricardo Izecson dos Santos Leite „Kaká" (77), 4-0 Elano Ralph Blumer (83), 5-0 Ricardo Izecson dos Santos Leite „Kaká" (85).
Cautions: Óscar Dalmiro Bagüi Angulo, Iván Jacinto Hurtado Angulo.

17.11.2007, Estadio Monumental „Antonio Vespucio Liberti", Buenos Aires; Attendance: 43,308
Referee: Víctor Hugo Rivera (Peru)
ARGENTINA - BOLIVIA   **3-0(1-0)**
ARG: Roberto Carlos Abbondanzieri, Javier Adelmar Zanetti (Cap), Martín Gastón Demichelis, Gabriel Alejandro Milito, Hugo Benjamín Ibarra, Javier Alejandro Mascherano, Esteban Matías Cambiasso (69.Fernando Rubén Gago), Juan Román Riquelme, Lionel Andrés Messi, Sergio Leonel Agüero del Castillo (75.Maximiliano Rubén Rodríguez), Carlos Alberto Tévez (83.Germán Gustavo Denis). Trainer: Alfio Oscar Basile.
BOL: Carlos Erwin Arias Eguez, Miguel Ángel Hoyos Guzmán, Ronald Raldés Balcázar (Cap),

96

Limberg Méndez Rocha, Luis Alberto Gutiérrez Herrera, Ronald Lázaro García Justiniano, Nicolás Suárez Vaca, Limberg Gutiérrez Mariscal (61.Juan Carlos Arce Justiniano), Joselito Vaca Velasco, Jaime Moreno Morales (60.Ronald Gutiérrez Flores), Diego Aroldo Cabrera Flores (79.Marcelo Moreno Martins). Trainer: Erwin Sánchez Frerking.
Goals: 1-0 Sergio Leonel Agüero del Castillo (41), 2-0 Juan Román Riquelme (57), 3-0 Juan Román Riquelme (74).
Cautions: Luis Alberto Gutiérrez Herrera, Ronald Gutiérrez Flores, Limberg Méndez Rocha.

17.11.2007, Estadio "Nemesio Camacho" El Campin; Attendance: 28,273
Referee: Rubén Marcos Selmán (Chile)
COLOMBIA - VENEZUELA   **1-0(0-0)**
COL: Agustín Julio Castro, Rubén Darío Bustos Torres, Walter José Moreno, Aquivaldo Mosquera Romaña, Juan Estiven Vélez Upegui, José Antonio Vélez Pardo, Carlos Alberto Sánchez Moreno (70.Freddy Indurley Grisales), Aldo Leão Ramírez (46.Macnelly Torres Berrio), Jaime Alberto Castrillón Vásquez, Wason Libardo Rentería Cuesta, Radamel Falcao García Zárate (50.Malher Tressor Moreno Baldrich). Trainer: Jorge Luis Pinto Afanador.
VEN: José Leonardo Morales Lares, Luis José Vallenilla Pacheco, José Manuel Rey Cortegoso, Leonel Vielma Gerardo Peña, Enrique Andrés Rouga Rossi, Miguel Ángel Mea Vitali, Jorge Alberto Rojas Méndez, Ricardo David Páez Gómez (66.César Eduardo González Amais), Juan Fernando Arango Sáenz, Nicolás Ladislao Fedor Flores (77.Gabriel Alejandro Cichero Konarek), Giancarlo Gregorio Maldonado Marrero (55.Alejandro Abraham Guerra Morales). Trainer: Richard Alfred Mayela Páez Monzón.
Goal: 1-0 Rubén Darío Bustos Torres (82).
Cautions: José Antonio Amaya Pardo, Juan Estiven Vélez Upegui / Luis José Vallenilla Pacheco, Alejandro Abraham Guerra Morales, Enrique Andrés Rouga Rossi.

17.11.2007, Estadio Defensores del Chaco, Asunción; Attendance: 30,000
Referee: Héber Lopes (Brazil)
PARAGUAY - ECUADOR   **5-1(2-0)**
PAR: Justo Wilmar Villar Viveros, Enrique Daniel Vera Torres, Julio César Cáceres López, Paulo César da Silva Barrios, Claudio Marcelo Morel Rodríguez (78.Darío Anastacio Verón Maldonado), Édgar Osvaldo Barreto Cáceres, Víctor Javier Cáceres Centurión, Cristian Miguel Riveros Núñez, Roque Luis Santa Cruz Cantero (75.Néstor Ayala Villagra), Salvador Cabañas Ortega, Nelson Antonio Haedo Valdéz (60.Carlos Bonet Cáceres). Trainer: Gerardo Daniel Martino (Argentina).
ECU: Marcelo Ramón Elizaga Ferrero, John Jairo Montaño Victoria, Giovanny Patricio Espinoza Pabón, Jorge Daniel Guagua Tamayo, Óscar Dalmiro Bagüi Angulo, Patricio Javier Urrutia Espinoza (46.Jairo Rolando Campos León), Segundo Alejandro Castillo Nazareno, Édison Vicente Méndez Méndez, Walter Orlando Ayoví Corozo, Christian Rogelio Benítez Betancourt (77.Felipe Salvador Caicedo Corozo), Ebelio Agustín Ordóñez Martínez (64.Jaime Iván Kaviedes Llorenty). Trainer: Luis Fernando Suárez (Colombia).
Goals: 1-0 Nelson Antonio Haedo Valdéz (9), 2-0 Cristian Miguel Riveros Núñez (26), 3-0 Roque Luis Santa Cruz Cantero (50), 3-1 Jaime Iván Kaviedes Llorenty (80), 4-1 Néstor Ayala Villagra (82), 5-1 Cristian Miguel Riveros Núñez (88).
Cautions: Édison Vicente Méndez Méndez.

18.11.2007, Estadio Centenario, Montevideo; Attendance: 43,000
Referee: Sergio Pezzotta (Argentina)
URUGUAY - CHILE   **2-2(1-0)**
URU: Héctor Fabián Carini Hernández, Andrés Scotti Ponce de León (61.Victorio Maximiliano Pereira Páez), Diego Alfredo Moreno Lugano (Cap), Diego Roberto Godín Leal, Jorge Ciro Fucile Perdomo, Diego Fernando Pérez Aguado (46.Egidio Raúl Arévalo Ríos), Wálter Alejandro Gargano Guevara, Cristian Gabriel Rodríguez Barrotti, Luis Alberto Suárez Díaz, Washington Sebastián Abreu Gallo, Vicente Martín Sánchez Bragunde (64.Ignacio María González Gatti). Trainer: Óscar Wáshington Tabárez Silva.

CHI: Claudio Andrés Bravo Muñoz, Cristián Andrés Álvarez Valenzuela (60.Ismael Ignacio Fuentes Castro), Miguel Augusto Riffo Garay, Waldo Alonso Ponce Carrizo, Gonzalo Alejandro Jara Reyes, Arturo Erasmo Vidal Pardo, Hugo Patricio Droguett Diocares, Humberto Andrés Suazo Pontivo (72.Rodolfo Antonio Moya Spuler), Matías Ariel Fernández Fernández, Eduardo Javier Rubio Köstner (46.Carlos Andrés Villanueva Roland), José Marcelo Salas Melinao. Trainer: Marcelo Alberto Bielsa Caldera (Argentina).
Goals: 1-0 Luis Alberto Suárez Díaz (42), 1-1 José Marcelo Salas Melinao (59), 1-2 José Marcelo Salas Melinao (69 penalty), 2-2 Washington Sebastián Abreu Gallo (81).
Cautions: Cristian Gabriel Rodríguez Barrotti, Andrés Scotti Ponce de León, Wálter Alejandro Gargano Guevara, Diego Alfredo Moreno Lugano / Humberto Andrés Suazo Pontivo, Eduardo Javier Rubio Köstner, Waldo Alonso Ponce Carrizo, Arturo Erasmo Vidal Pardo.

18.11.2007, Estadio Monumental, Lima; Attendance: 45,847
Referee: Carlos Manuel Torres (Paraguay)
PERU - BRAZIL   **1-1(0-1)**
PER: Diego Alonso Penny Valdez,   Guillermo Sandro Salas Suárez, Wilmer Santiago Acasiete Ariadela, Alberto Junior Rodríguez Valdelomar, Juan Manuel Vargas Risco, Juan José Jayo Legario (62.Andrés Augusto Mendoza Azevedo), Carlos Augusto Lobatón Espejo (65.Paolo Giancarlo De La Haza Urquiza), Nolberto Albino Solano Todco, Jefferson Agustín Farfán Guadalupe, Claudio Miguel Pizarro Bossio, José Paolo Guerrero Gonzales (46.Roberto Carlos Palacios Mestas). Trainer: José Guillermo del Solar Alvarez-Calderón.
BRA: Júlio César Soares de Espíndola, Maicon Douglas Sisenando, Lucimar Ferreira da Silva „Lúcio" (Cap), Juan Silveira dos Santos, Gilberto da Silva Melo, Carlos Luciano da Silva „Mineiro", Gilberto Aparecido da Silva, Ricardo Izecson dos Santos Leite „Kaká", Ronaldo de Assis Moreira „Ronaldinho", Róbson de Souza „Robinho" (74.Elano Ralph Blumer), Vágner Silveira de Souza "Vágner "Love"" (68.Luís Fabiano Clemente). Trainer: Carlos Caetano Bledorn Verri "Dunga".
Goals: 0-1 Ricardo Izecson dos Santos Leite „Kaká" (40), 1-1 Juan Manuel Vargas Risco (72).
Cautions: Nolberto Albino Solano Todco, Juan Manuel Vargas Risco, Paolo Giancarlo De La Haza Urquiza, Andrés Augusto Mendoza Azevedo / Lucimar Ferreira da Silva „Lúcio".

20.11.2007, Estadio Polideportivo de Pueblo Nuevo, San Cristóbal; Attendance: 24,000
Referee: Sálvio Spínola Fagundes Filho (Brazil)
VENEZUELA - BOLIVIA   **5-3(2-2)**
VEN: José Leonardo Morales Lares,   Roberto José Rosales Altuve, José Manuel Rey Cortegoso, Alejandro Enrique Cíchero Konarek, Jorge Alberto Rojas Méndez, Luis Enrique Vera Martineau (59.Miguel Ángel Mea Vitali), Ricardo David Páez Gómez (74.Alejandro Abraham Guerra Morales), Juan Fernando Arango Sáenz, Luis Manuel Seijas Gunther (64.Edder Alfonso Pérez Consuegra), Daniel Enrique Arismendi Marchán, Giancarlo Gregorio Maldonado Marrero. Trainer: Richard Alfred Mayela Páez Monzón.
BOL: Carlos Erwin Arias Eguez, Luis Gatty Ribeiro Roca, Ronald Raldés Balcázar (Cap), Limberg Méndez Rocha, Luis Alberto Gutiérrez Herrera, Ronald Lázaro García Justiniano, Alejandro Jesús Gómez, Gualberto Mojica Olmos (70.Limberg Gutiérrez Mariscal), Joselito Vaca Velasco (46.Sacha Silvestro Lima Saucedo), Juan Carlos Arce Justiniano, Marcelo Moreno Martins (82.Jaime Moreno Morales). Trainer: Erwin Sánchez Frerking.
Goals: 0-1 Marcelo Moreno Martins (19), 1-1 Daniel Enrique Arismendi Marchán (20), 1-2 Juan Carlos Arce Justiniano (27), 2-2 Daniel Enrique Arismendi Marchán (40), 2-3 Marcelo Moreno Martins (78), 3-3 Alejandro Abraham Guerra Morales (82), 4-3 Giancarlo Gregorio Maldonado Marrero (89), 5-3 Giancarlo Gregorio Maldonado Marrero (90+1).
Cautions: Joselito Vaca Velasco.

20.11.2007, Estadio „Nemesio Camacho El Campín", Bogotá; Attendance: 41,700
Referee: Jorge Luis Larrionda Pietrafesa (Uruguay)
COLOMBIA - ARGENTINA **2-1(0-1)**
COL: Agustín Julio Castro, Rubén Darío Bustos Torres, Walter José Moreno, Aquivaldo Mosquera Romaña, Juan Estiven Vélez Upegui, José Antonio Amaya Pardo, Carlos Alberto Sánchez Moreno, David Arturo Ferreira Rico (46.Macnelly Torres Berrio), Malher Tressor Moreno Baldrich (73.Dayro Mauricio Moreno Galindo), Jaime Alberto Castrillón Vásquez (46.Freddy Indurley Grisales), Wason Libardo Rentería Cuesta. Trainer: Jorge Luis Pinto Afanador.
ARG: Roberto Carlos Abbondanzieri, Javier Adelmar Zanetti (Cap), Martín Gastón Demichelis, Gabriel Alejandro Milito, Hugo Benjamín Ibarra, Javier Alejandro Mascherano, Esteban Matías Cambiasso (75.Maximiliano Rubén Rodríguez), Juan Román Riquelme, Fernando Rubén Gago, Lionel Andrés Messi, Carlos Alberto Tévez (*sent off 25*). Trainer: Alfio Oscar Basile.
Goals: 0-1 Lionel Andrés Messi (36), 1-1 Rubén Darío Bustos Torres (62), 2-1 Dayro Mauricio Moreno Galindo (82).
Cautions: Jaime Alberto Castrillón Vásquez, Aquivaldo Mosquera Romaña, José Antonio Amaya Pardo, Rubén Darío Bustos Torres, Wason Libardo Rentería Cuesta, Dayro Mauricio Moreno Galindo / Martín Gastón Demichelis, Juan Román Riquelme, Gabriel Alejandro Milito.
Sent off: Carlos Alberto Tévez (25).

21.11.2007, Estadio Olimpico „Atahualpa", Quito; Attendance: 35,000
Referee: Carlos Chandía Alarcón (Chile)
ECUADOR - PERU **5-1(3-0)**
ECU: Marcelo Ramón Elizaga Ferrero (67.Edwin Alberto Villafuerte Posligua), Omar Andrés de Jesús Borja, Iván Jacinto Hurtado Angulo, Vicente Paúl Ambrosi Zambrano, Mario David Quiroz Villón, Segundo Alejandro Castillo Nazareno, Édison Vicente Méndez Méndez, Walter Orlando Ayoví Corozo, Christian Rogelio Benítez Betancourt (85.Jefferson Antonio Montero Vite), Jaime Iván Kaviedes Llorenty (69.Patricio Javier Urrutia Espinoza). Trainer: Luis Fernando Suárez (Colombia).
PER: Diego Alonso Penny Valdez, Guillermo Sandro Salas Suárez, Wilmer Santiago Acasiete Ariadela, Wálter Ricardo Vílchez Soto (9.Carlos Javier Solís Alvarado), Mario Augusto Gómez Urbina, Juan Carlos Bazalar Cruzado (58.Jefferson Agustín Farfán Guadalupe), Carlos Augusto Lobatón Espejo, Julio César García Mesones, Roberto Carlos Palacios Mestas, Miguel Ángel Mostto Fernández-Prada, Claudio Miguel Pizarro Bossio (58.Andrés Augusto Mendoza Azevedo). Trainer: José Guillermo del Solar Alvarez-Calderón.
Goals: 1-0 Walter Orlando Ayoví Corozo (10), 2-0 Jaime Iván Kaviedes Llorenty (24), 3-0 Édison Vicente Méndez Méndez (44), 4-0 Walter Orlando Ayoví Corozo (48), 5-0 Édison Vicente Méndez Méndez (62), 5-1 Andrés Augusto Mendoza Azevedo (86).
Cautions: Christian Rogelio Benítez Betancourt / Carlos Javier Solís Alvarado, Carlos Augusto Lobatón Espejo, Mario Augusto Gómez Urbina, Jefferson Agustín Farfán Guadalupe.

21.11.2007, Estádio „Cicero Pompeu de Toledo" (Morumbi), São Paulo; Attendance: 65,379
Referee: Héctor Walter Baldassi (Argentina)
BRAZIL - URUGUAY **2-1(1-1)**
BRA: Júlio César Soares de Espíndola, Maicon Douglas Sisenando (86.Daniel Alves da Silva „Dani Alves"(13/1)), Alex Rodrigo Dias da Costa, Juan Silveira dos Santos, Gilberto da Silva Melo, Gilberto Aparecido da Silva (Cap), Carlos Luciano da Silva "Mineiro", Ronaldo de Assis Moreira „Ronaldinho" (60.Josué Anunciado de Oliveira), Ricardo Izecson dos Santos Leite „Kaká", Róbson de Souza „Robinho" (74.Vágner Silveira de Souza "Vágner "Love"")), Luís Fabiano Clemente. Trainer: Carlos Caetano Bledorn Verri "Dunga".
URU: Héctor Fabián Carini Hernández, Victorio Maximiliano Pereira Páez, Diego Alfredo Moreno Lugano (Cap), Diego Roberto Godín Leal, Jorge Ciro Fucile Perdomo, Álvaro Rafael González Luengo, Wálter Alejandro Gargano Guevara, Ignacio María González Gatti (82.Carlos Heber Bueno Suárez), Cristian Gabriel Rodríguez Barrotti, Luis Alberto Suárez Díaz (71.Vicente Martín Sánchez Bragunde), Washington Sebastián Abreu Gallo. Trainer: Óscar Wáshington Tabárez Silva.

Goals: 0-1 Washington Sebastián Abreu Gallo (9), 1-1 Luís Fabiano Clemente (45), 2-1 Luís Fabiano Clemente (65).
Cautions: Luis Alberto Suárez Díaz, Jorge Ciro Fucile Perdomo, Álvaro Rafael González Luengo, Cristian Gabriel Rodríguez Barrotti.

21.11.2007, Estadio Nacional „Julio Martínez Prádanos", Santiago; Attendance: 60,000
Referee: Óscar Julián Ruiz Acosta (Colombia)
CHILE - PARAGUAY 0-3(0-2)
CHI: Claudio Andrés Bravo Muñoz, Cristián Andrés Álvarez Valenzuela, Waldo Alonso Ponce Carrizo, Miguel Augusto Riffo Garay, Manuel Rolando Iturra Urrutia (46.Luis Antonio Jiménez Garcés), Claudio Andrés Maldonado Rivera, Hugo Patricio Droguett Diocares, Matías Ariel Fernández Fernández, Humberto Andrés Suazo Pontivo, José Marcelo Salas Melinao, Eduardo Javier Rubio Köstner (Carlos Andrés Villanueva Roland). Trainer: Marcelo Alberto Bielsa Caldera (Argentina).
PAR: Justo Wilmar Villar Viveros, Carlos Bonet Cáceres, Julio César Cáceres López, Paulo César da Silva Barrios, Claudio Marcelo Morel Rodríguez, Enrique Daniel Vera Torres, Víctor Javier Cáceres Centurión, Jonathan Santana Ghere, Cristian Miguel Riveros Núñez (79.Édgar Osvaldo Barreto Cáceres), Salvador Cabañas Ortega (63.Roque Luis Santa Cruz Cantero), Nelson Antonio Haedo Valdéz (67.Jorge Daniel Achucarro). Trainer: Gerardo Daniel Martino (Argentina).
Goals: 0-1 Salvador Cabañas Ortega (23), 0-2 Paulo César da Silva Barrios (45+2), 0-3 Paulo César da Silva Barrios (57).
Cautions: Luis Antonio Jiménez Garcés / Cristian Miguel Riveros Núñez, Víctor Javier Cáceres Centurión, Jorge Daniel Achucarro, Claudio Marcelo Morel Rodríguez.

14.06.2008, Estadio Centenario, Montevideo; Attendance: 41,831
Referee: Alfredo Intriago (Ecuador)
URUGUAY - VENEZUELA 1-1(1-0)
URU: Héctor Fabián Carini Hernández, Victorio Maximiliano Pereira Páez (76.Bruno Ramón Silva Barone), Diego Alfredo Moreno Lugano (Cap), Diego Roberto Godín Leal, José Martín Cáceres Silva, Diego Fernando Pérez Aguado, Wálter Alejandro Gargano Guevara, Ignacio María González Gatti, Diego Martín Forlán Corazo (65.Carlos Heber Bueno Suárez), Washington Sebastián Abreu Gallo, Luis Alberto Suárez Díaz (65.Vicente Martín Sánchez Bragunde). Trainer: Óscar Wáshington Tabárez Silva.
VEN: Renny Vicente Vega Hernández, Gerzon Armando Chacón Varela, Leonel Vielma Gerardo Peña, José Manuel Rey Cortegoso, Jonay Miguel Hernández Santos, Miguel Ángel Mea Vitali, Tomás Eduardo Rincón Hernández, Ronald Alejandro Vargas Aranguren (73.Alexander Rondón Heredia), Jorge Alberto Rojas Méndez (79.Luis Manuel Seijas Gunther), Juan Fernando Arango Sáenz, Giancarlo Gregorio Maldonado Marrero (87.Pedro Luis Boada Noya). Trainer: César Alejandro Farías.
Goals: 1-0 Diego Alfredo Moreno Lugano (12), 1-1 Ronald Alejandro Vargas Aranguren (56).

14.06.2008, Estadio Monumental, Lima; Attendance: 25,000
Referee: Carlos Manuel Torres (Paraguay)
PERU - COLOMBIA 1-1(1-1)
PER: Leao Butrón Gotuzzo, Amilton Jair Prado Barron, Alberto Junior Rodríguez Valdelomar, Wálter Ricardo Vílchez Soto, Juan Manuel Vargas Risco, Donny Renzo Neyra Ferrada (76.Hernán Rengifo Trigoso), Rainer Torres Salas, Nolberto Albino Solano Todco, Emilio Martín Hidalgo Conde (60.Juan Elías Cominges Mayorga), Juan Carlos Mariño Márquez, José Paolo Guerrero Gonzales. Trainer: José Guillermo del Solar Alvarez-Calderón.
COL: Agustín Julio Castro, Rubén Darío Bustos Torres, Walter José Moreno, Cristián Eduardo Zapata Valencia, Juan Juan Estiven Vélez Upegui (72.Juan Camilo Zúñiga Mosquera), Carlos Alberto Sánchez Moreno, Fabián Andrés Vargas Rivera (60.Freddy Indurley Grisales), Macnelly Torres Berrio (86.Pedro Paulo Portocarrero Angulo), Freddy Alejandro Guarín Vásquez, Édixon Perea Valencia, Hugo Rodallega Martínez. Trainer: Jorge Luis Pinto Afanador.
Goals: 0-1 Hugo Rodallega Martínez (8), 1-1 Juan Carlos Mariño Márquez (40).
Cautions: Nolberto Albino Solano Todco, Wálter Ricardo Vílchez Soto, Hernán Rengifo Trigoso / Róbinson Zapata Montaño (on the bench), Carlos Alberto Sánchez Moreno.

15.06.2008, Estadio Defensores del Chaco, Asunción; Attendance: 36,011
Referee: Jorge Luis Larrionda Pietrafesa (Uruguay)
PARAGUAY - BRAZIL   **2-0(1-0)**
PAR: Justo Wilmar Villar Viveros, Darío Anastacio Verón Maldonado, Julio César Cáceres López, Paulo César da Silva Barrios, Denis Ramón Caniza Acuña, Édgar Osvaldo Barreto Cáceres, Enrique Daniel Vera Torres, Jonathan Santana Ghere, Nelson Antonio Haedo Valdéz (52.Víctor Javier Cáceres Centurión), Roque Luis Santa Cruz Cantero (81.Óscar René Cardozo Marín), Salvador Cabañas Ortega (74.Aureliano Torres Román). Trainer: Gerardo Daniel Martino (Argentina).
BRA: Júlio César Soares de Espíndola, Maicon Douglas Sisenando, Lucimar Ferreira da Silva „Lúcio", Juan Silveira dos Santos, Gilberto da Silva Melo, Josué Anunciado de Oliveira (46.Ânderson Luís de Abreu Oliveira "Ânderson II"), Carlos Luciano da Silva "Mineiro" (60.Adriano Leite Ribeiro), Gilberto Aparecido da Silva, Diego Ribas da Cunha (69.Júlio César Baptista), Luís Fabiano Clemente, Róbson de Souza „Robinho". Trainer: Carlos Caetano Bledorn Verri „Dunga".
Goals: 1-0 Roque Luis Santa Cruz Cantero (25), 2-0 Salvador Cabañas Ortega (48).
Cautions: Darío Anastacio Verón Maldonado, Julio César Cáceres López / Juan Silveira dos Santos.
Sent off: Darío Anastacio Verón Maldonado (47).

15.06.2008, Estadio Monumental „Antonio Vespucio Liberti", Buenos Aires; Attendance: 41,167
Referee: René Ortubé Betancourt (Bolivia)
ARGENTINA - ECUADOR   **1-1(0-0)**
ARG: Roberto Carlos Abbondanzieri, Nicolás Andrés Burdisso, Martín Gastón Demichelis, Gabriel Iván Heinze, Javier Adelmar Zanetti, Javier Alejandro Mascherano (63.Julio Ricardo Cruz), Juan Sebastián Verón (89.Rodrigo Sebastián Palacio), Maximiliano Rubén Rodríguez (46.Fernando Rubén Gago), Juan Román Riquelme, Sergio Leonel Agüero del Castillo, Lionel Andrés Messi. Trainer: Alfio Oscar Basile.
ECU: José Francisco Cevallos Villavicencio, Omar Andrés de Jesús Borja, Iván Jacinto Hurtado Angulo, Giovanny Patricio Espinoza Pabón, Isaac Bryan Mina Arboleda, Segundo Alejandro Castillo Nazareno, Patricio Javier Urrutia Espinoza, Luis Antonio Valencia Mosquera, Joffre David Guerrón Méndez (90+2.Ulises Hernán de la Cruz Bernardo), Walter Orlando Ayoví Corozo (85.Luis Alberto Bolaños León), Carlos Vicente Tenorio Medina (88.Christian Rogelio Benítez Betancourt). Trainer: Sixto Rafael Vizuete Toapanta.
Goals: 0-1 Patricio Javier Urrutia Espinoza (69), 1-1 Rodrigo Sebastián Palacio (89).
Cautions: Martín Gastón Demichelis / Luis Antonio Valencia Mosquera, Isaac Bryan Mina Arboleda, José Francisco Cevallos Villavicencio.

15.06.2008, Estadio "Hernándo Siles Zuazo", La Paz; Attendance: 27,722
Referee: Victor Hugo Rivera (Peru)
BOLIVIA - CHILE   **0-2(0-1)**
BOL: Sergio Daniel Galarza Soliz, Miguel Ángel Hoyos Guzmán (78.Mauricio Saucedo Guardia), Ronald Raldés Balcázar, Luis Alberto Gutiérrez Herrera, Abdón Reyes Cardozo, Leonel Alfredo Reyes Saravia, Lorgio Álvarez Roca (46.Luis Gatty Ribeiro Roca), Jhasmani Campos Dávalos (65.Joaquín Botero Vaca), Limberg Gutiérrez Mariscal, Juan Carlos Arce Justiniano, Marcelo Moreno Martins. Trainer: Erwin Sánchez Freking.
CHI: Claudio Andrés Bravo Muñoz, Gary Alexis Medel Soto, Ismael Ignacio Fuentes Castro, Gonzalo Alejandro Jara Reyes, José Pedro Fuenzalida Gana (46.Marco Andrés Estrada Quinteros), Carlos Emilio Carmona Tello, Roberto Andrés Cereceda Guajardo, Pedro Andrés Morales Flores (55.Carlos Andrés Villanueva Roland), Alexis Alejandro Sánchez Sánchez, Humberto Andrés Suazo Pontivo, Jean André Emanuel Beausejour Coliqueo (58.Mark Dennis González Hoffman). Trainer: Marcelo Alberto Bielsa Caldera (Argentina).
Goals: 0-1 Gary Alexis Medel Soto (28), 0-2 Gary Alexis Medel Soto (76).
Cautions: Limberg Gutiérrez Mariscal / Roberto Andrés Cereceda Guajardo, Carlos Andrés Villanueva Roland.

17.06.2008, Estadio Centenario, Montevideo; Attendance: 20,016
Referee: Pablo Antonio Pozo Quinteros (Chile)
URUGUAY - PERU   **6-0(2-0)**
URU: Juan Guillermo Castillo Iriart, Bruno Ramón Silva Barone, Diego Alfredo Moreno Lugano (Cap), Diego Roberto Godín Leal, José Martín Cáceres Silva, Diego Fernando Pérez Aguado (70.Sebastián Eguren Ledesma), Wálter Alejandro Gargano Guevara, Ignacio María González Gatti (73.Luis Alberto Suárez Díaz), Cristian Gabriel Rodríguez Barrotti, Diego Martín Forlán Corazo, Carlos Heber Bueno Suárez (79.Washington Sebastián Abreu Gallo). Trainer: Óscar Wáshington Tabárez Silva.
PER: Leao Butrón Gotuzzo, Amilton Jair Prado Barron, Alberto Junior Rodríguez Valdelomar, Miguel Ángel Villalta Hurtado, Juan Manuel Vargas Risco (46.Hernán Rengifo Trigoso), Nolberto Albino Solano Todco, Rainer Torres Salas, Miguel Ángel Cevasco Abad, Emilio Martín Hidalgo Conde (67.Guillermo Sandro Salas Suárez), Juan Carlos Mariño Márquez (71.Paulo Rinaldo Cruzado Durand), José Paolo Guerrero Gonzales. Trainer: José Guillermo del Solar Alvarez-Calderón.
Goals: 1-0 Diego Martín Forlán Corazo (8), 2-0 Diego Martín Forlán Corazo (38 penalty), 3-0 Diego Martín Forlán Corazo (57), 4-0 Carlos Heber Bueno Suárez (61), 5-0 Carlos Heber Bueno Suárez (69), 6-0 Washington Sebastián Abreu Gallo (90).
Cautions: Diego Roberto Godín Leal / Juan Carlos Mariño Márquez, José Paolo Guerrero Gonzales, Miguel Ángel Villalta Hurtado, Miguel Ángel Cevasco Abad.
Sent off: José Paolo Guerrero Gonzales (37).

18.06.2008, Estadio "Hernándo Siles Zuazo", La Paz; Attendance: 8,561
Referee: Leonardo Gaciba da Silva (Brazil)
BOLIVIA - PARAGUAY   **4-2(2-0)**
BOL: Carlos Erwin Arias Eguez, Leonel Alfredo Reyes Saravia, Ronald Raldés Balcázar, Luis Alberto Gutiérrez Herrera, Abdón Reyes Cardozo (67.Ronald Taylor Rivero Khun), Luis Gatty Ribeiro Roca, Ronald Lázaro García Justiniano (46.Ronald Gutiérrez Flores), Marcelo Eduardo Torrico, Joselito Vaca Velasco, Marcelo Moreno Martins, Joaquín Botero Vaca (73.Mauricio Saucedo Guardia). Trainer: Erwin Sánchez Freking.
PAR: Aldo Antonio Bobadilla Ávalos, Carlos Bonet Cáceres, Julio César Cáceres López, Paulo César da Silva Barrios, Claudio Marcelo Morel Rodríguez, Enrique Daniel Vera Torres (46.Pablo Daniel Zeballos Ocampos), Édgar Osvaldo Barreto Cáceres, Víctor Javier Cáceres Centurión, Cristian Miguel Riveros Núñez, Salvador Cabañas Ortega (62.Roque Luis Santa Cruz Cantero), Óscar René Cardozo Marín (62.Nelson Antonio Haedo Valdéz). Trainer: Gerardo Daniel Martino (Argentina).
Goals: 1-0 Joaquín Botero Vaca (23), 2-0 Ronald Lázaro García Justiniano (25), 2-1 Roque Luis Santa Cruz Cantero (66), 3-1 Joaquín Botero Vaca (70), 4-1 Marcelo Moreno Martins (76), 4-2 Nelson Antonio Haedo Valdéz (82).
Cautions: Ronald Gutiérrez Flores / Víctor Javier Cáceres Centurión.

18.06.2008, Estadio Olimpico "Atahualpa", Quito; Attendance: 33,588
Referee: Héctor Walter Baldassi (Argentina)
ECUADOR - COLOMBIA   **0-0**
ECU: José Francisco Cevallos Villavicencio, Omar Andrés de Jesús Borja, Iván Jacinto Hurtado Angulo, Giovanny Patricio Espinoza Pabón, Vicente Paúl Ambrosi Zambrano, Segundo Alejandro Castillo Nazareno, Patricio Javier Urrutia Espinoza (46.Joffre David Guerrón Méndez), Luis Antonio Valencia Mosquera, Walter Orlando Ayoví Corozo (72.Luis Alberto Bolaños León), Carlos Vicente Tenorio Medina (81.Felipe Salvador Caicedo Corozo), Christian Rogelio Benítez Betancourt. Trainer: Sixto Rafael Vizuete Toapanta.
COL: Agustín Julio Castro, Walter José Moreno, Freddy Alejandro Guarín Vásquez, Juan Camilo Zúñiga Mosquera, José Antonio Amaya Pardo, Elvis Javier González Herrera, Juan Carlos Escobar (54.Dayro Mauricio Moreno Galindo), Macnelly Torres Berrio (63.Giovanni Hernández Soto), Aquivaldo Mosquera Romaña, Elkin Soto Jaramillo (80.Carlos Alberto Sánchez Moreno), Hugo Rodallega Martínez. Trainer: Jorge Luis Pinto Afanador.
Cautions: Luis Antonio Valencia Mosquera, Carlos Vicente Tenorio Medina / Walter José Moreno,

José Antonio Amaya Pardo, Freddy Alejandro Guarín Vásquez.

18.06.2008, Estádio „Governador Magalhães Pinto", Belo Horizonte; Attendance: 65,000
Referee: Óscar Julián Ruiz Acosta (Colombia)
BRAZIL - ARGENTINA   **0-0**
BRA: Júlio César Soares de Espíndola, Maicon Douglas Sisenando, Lucimar Ferreira da Silva „Lúcio", Juan Silveira dos Santos, Gilberto da Silva Melo, Ânderson Luís de Abreu Oliveira "Ânderson II" (34.Diego Ribas da Cunha; 79.Daniel Alves da Silva „Dani Alves"), Carlos Luciano da Silva "Mineiro", Gilberto Aparecido da Silva, Júlio César Baptista, Adriano Leite Ribeiro (70.Luís Fabiano Clemente), Róbson de Souza „Robinho". Trainer: Carlos Caetano Bledorn Verri „Dunga".
ARG: Roberto Carlos Abbondanzieri, Javier Adelmar Zanetti, Nicolás Andrés Burdisso, Fabricio Coloccini, Gabriel Iván Heinze, Javier Alejandro Mascherano, Fernando Rubén Gago, Jonás Manuel Gutiérrez, Juan Román Riquelme (84.Sebastián Alejandro Battaglia), Lionel Andrés Messi (90+2.Rodrigo Sebastián Palacio), Julio Ricardo Cruz (67.Sergio Leonel Agüero del Castillo). Trainer: Alfio Oscar Basile.
Cautions: Juan Silveira dos Santos, Adriano Leite Ribeiro / Julio Ricardo Cruz, Fernando Rubén Gago, Javier Alejandro Mascherano, Jonás Manuel Gutiérrez.

19.06.2008, Estadio Olímpico "Luis Ramos", Puerto la Cruz; Attendance: 38,000
Referee: Roberto Carlos Silvera (Uruguay)
VENEZUELA - CHILE   **2-3(0-0)**
VEN: Renny Vicente Vega Hernández, Gerzon Armando Chacón Varela, Leonel Vielma Gerardo Peña, José Manuel Rey Cortegoso, Jonay Miguel Hernández Santos, Miguel Ángel Mea Vitali (80.Luis Manuel Seijas Gunther), Ronald Alejandro Vargas Aranguren (59.Tomás Eduardo Rincón Hernández), Jorge Alberto Rojas Méndez, Juan Fernando Arango Sáenz, Alexander Rondón Heredia (55.Daniel Enrique Arismendi Marchán), Giancarlo Gregorio Maldonado Marrero. Trainer: César Alejandro Farías.
CHI: Claudio Andrés Bravo Muñoz, Gonzalo Alejandro Jara Reyes, Ismael Ignacio Fuentes Castro, Marco Andrés Estrada Quinteros, Gary Alexis Medel Soto, Carlos Emilio Carmona Tello, Roberto Andrés Cereceda Guajardo (76.Waldo Alonso Ponce Carrizo), Pedro Andrés Morales Flores (60.Daúd Jared Gazale Álvarez), Alexis Alejandro Sánchez Sánchez, Humberto Andrés Suazo Pontivo, Jean André Emanuel Beausejour Coliqueo (59.Mark Dennis González Hoffman). Trainer: Marcelo Alberto Bielsa Caldera (Argentina).
Goals: 1-0 Giancarlo Gregorio Maldonado Marrero (59), 1-1 Humberto Andrés Suazo Pontivo (65 penalty), 1-2 Gonzalo Alejandro Jara Reyes (72), 2-2 Juan Fernando Arango Sáenz (80), 2-3 Humberto Andrés Suazo Pontivo (90+2).
Cautions: Jonay Miguel Hernández Santos, Renny Vicente Vega Hernández / Carlos Emilio Carmona Tello, Gonzalo Alejandro Jara Reyes.

06.09.2008, Estadio Monumental „Antonio Vespucio Liberti", Buenos Aires; Attendance: 46,250
Referee: Carlos Eugênio Simon (Brazil)
ARGENTINA – PARAGUAY   **1-1(0-1)**
ARG: Roberto Carlos Abbondanzieri (14.Juan Pablo Carrizo), Fabricio Coloccini, Martín Gastón Demichelis, Gabriel Iván Heinze (46.Daniel Alberto Díaz), Javier Adelmar Zanetti, Javier Alejandro Mascherano, Esteban Matías Cambiasso, Ángel Fabián di María (46.Sergio Leonel Agüero del Castillo), Juan Román Riquelme, Lionel Andrés Messi, Carlos Alberto Tévez. Trainer: Alfio Oscar Basile.
PAR: Justo Wilmar Villar Viveros, Darío Anastacio Verón Maldonado, Julio César Cáceres López, Claudio Marcelo Morel Rodríguez (46.Aureliano Torres Román), Paulo César da Silva Barrios, Édgar Osvaldo Barreto Cáceres, Cristian Miguel Riveros Núñez, Jonathan Santana Ghere, Enrique Daniel Vera Torres, Óscar René Cardozo Marín (71.Dante Rafael López Fariña), Nelson Antonio Haedo Valdéz. Trainer: Gerardo Daniel Martino (Argentina).
Goals: 0-1 Gabriel Iván Heinze (13 own goal), 1-1 Sergio Leonel Agüero del Castillo (60).
Cautions: Julio César Cáceres López, Édgar Osvaldo Barreto Cáceres, Jonathan Santana Ghere,

Enrique Daniel Vera Torres / Carlos Alberto Tévez, Javier Alejandro Mascherano.
Sent off: Carlos Alberto Tévez (30).

06.09.2008, Estadio Olímpico "Atahualpa", Quito; Attendance: 28,000
Referee: Pablo Antonio Pozo Quinteros (Chile)
ECUADOR - BOLIVIA   **3-1(1-1)**
ECU: José Francisco Cevallos Villavicencio, Néicer Reasco Yano (28.Omar Andrés de Jesús Borja), Iván Jacinto Hurtado Angulo, Giovanny Patricio Espinoza Pabón, Walter Orlando Ayoví Corozo, Segundo Alejandro Castillo Nazareno, Joffre David Guerrón Méndez, Édison Vicente Méndez Méndez, Luis Alberto Bolaños León (75.Patricio Javier Urrutia Espinoza), Christian Rogelio Benítez Betancourt, Felipe Salvador Caicedo Corozo (76.Pablo David Palacios Herreria). Trainer: Sixto Rafael Vizuete Toapanta.
BOL: Carlos Erwin Arias Eguez, Miguel Ángel Hoyos Guzmán, Ronald Raldés Balcázar, Ronald Taylor Rivero Khun, Ignacio Awad García Justiniano, Jesús Alejandro Gómez Lanza, Ronald Lázaro García Justiniano, Jaime Robles Céspedes, Pablo Daniel Escobar Olivetti (67.Darwin Peña Arce), Joselito Vaca Velasco (88.Mauricio Saucedo Guardia), Joaquín Botero Vaca (64.Marcelo Moreno Martins). Trainer: Erwin Sánchez Freking.
Goals: 1-0 Felipe Salvador Caicedo Corozo (21), 1-1 Joaquín Botero Vaca (40), 2-1 Édison Vicente Méndez Méndez (51 penalty), 3-1 Christian Rogelio Benítez Betancourt (72).
Cautions: Felipe Salvador Caicedo Corozo, Segundo Alejandro Castillo Nazareno, Walter Orlando Ayoví Corozo / Jesús Alejandro Gómez Lanza, Jaime Robles Céspedes.
Sent off: Jesús Alejandro Gómez Lanza (18).

06.09.2008, Estadio "Nemesio Camacho" El Campín, Bogotá; Attendance: 35,024
Referee: Leonardo Gaciba da Silva (Brazil)
COLOMBIA - URUGUAY   **0-1(0-1)**
COL: Agustín Julio Castro, Juan Camilo Zúñiga Mosquera, Luis Amaranto Perea Mosquera, Aquivaldo Mosquera Romaña, Juan Estiven Vélez Upegui, Carlos Alberto Sánchez Moreno, Freddy Alejandro Guarín Vásquez, Fabián Andrés Vargas Rivera (46.Macnelly Torres Berrio), Giovanni Hernández Soto (63.Malher Tressor Moreno Baldrich), Radamel Falcao García Zárate (60.Dayro Mauricio Moreno Galindo), Hugo Rodallega Martínez. Trainer: Jorge Luis Pinto Afanador.
URU: Juan Guillermo Castillo Iriart, Bruno Ramón Silva Barone (80.Álvaro Rafael González Luengo), Diego Alfredo Moreno Lugano (Cap), Diego Roberto Godín Leal, Jorge Ciro Fucile Perdomo, Victorio Maximiliano Pereira Páez, Wálter Alejandro Gargano Guevara, Sebastián Eguren Ledesma (90.Andrés Scotti Ponce de León), Cristian Gabriel Rodríguez Barrotti, Diego Martín Forlán Corazo, Luis Alberto Suárez Díaz (68.Vicente Martín Sánchez Bragunde). Trainer: Óscar Wáshington Tabárez Silva.
Goal: 0-1 Sebastián Eguren Ledesma (15).
Cautions: Jorge Ciro Fucile Perdomo, Juan Guillermo Castillo Iriart, Cristian Gabriel Rodríguez Barrotti.

06.09.2008, Estadio Monumental, Lima; Attendance: 15,000
Referee: Óscar Maldonado (Bolivia)
PERU - VENEZUELA   **1-0(1-0)**
PER: Leao Butrón Gotuzzo, Amilton Jair Prado Barron, Alberto Junior Rodríguez Valdelomar, Carlos Augusto Zambrano Ochandarte, Juan Manuel Vargas Risco, Paolo Giancarlo De La Haza Urquiza, Daniel Chávez Castillo (90+1.Juan Carlos La Rosa Llontop), Nolberto Albino Solano Todco (62.Henry Edson Quinteros Sánchez), Rainer Torres Salas, Piero Fernando Alva Niezen, Johan Javier Fano Espinoza (80.Hernán Rengifo Trigoso). Trainer: José Guillermo del Solar Alvarez-Calderón.
VEN: Renny Vicente Vega Hernández, Gerzon Armando Chacón Varela, José Manuel Rey Cortegoso, Pedro Luis Boada Noya, Jonay Miguel Hernández Santos, Miguel Ángel Mea Vitali (71.Leonel Vielma Gerardo Peña), Tomás Eduardo Rincón Hernández, Jorge Alberto Rojas Méndez (55.Alejandro Enrique Moreno Riera), Ronald Alejandro Vargas Aranguren (66.Alejandro Abraham Guerra Morales), Juan Fernando Arango Sáenz, Giancarlo Gregorio Maldonado Marrero. Trainer: César Alejandro Farías.
Goal: 1-0 Piero Fernando Alva Niezen (39).

104

Cautions: Alberto Junior Rodríguez Valdelomar / Miguel Ángel Mea Vitali, Tomás Eduardo Rincón Hernández.

07.09.2008, Estadio Nacional. Santiago; Attendance: 60,239
Referee: Carlos Manuel Torres (Paraguay)
CHILE - BRAZIL   **0-3(0-2)**
CHI: Claudio Andrés Bravo Muñoz, Gary Alexis Medel Soto, Gonzalo Alejandro Jara Reyes, Marco Andrés Estrada Quinteros, Carlos Emilio Carmona Tello, Arturo Erasmo Vidal Pardo (46.Jean André Emanuel Beausejour Coliqueo), Hugo Patricio Droguett Diocares (34.Jorge Luis Valdivia Toro), Matías Ariel Fernández Fernández, Alexis Alejandro Sánchez Sánchez, Humberto Andrés Suazo Pontivo, Mark Dennis González Hoffman (46.Roberto Andrés Cereceda Guajardo). Trainer: Marcelo Alberto Bielsa Caldera (Argentina).
BRA: Júlio César Soares de Espíndola, Maicon Douglas Sisenando, Lucimar Ferreira da Silva „Lúcio", Ânderson Luís da Silva „Luisão", Kléber de Carvalho Corrêa, Josué Anunciado de Oliveira, Gilberto Aparecido da Silva, Diego Ribas da Cunha (78.Elano Ralph Blumer), Róbson de Souza „Robinho", Ronaldo de Assis Moreira „Ronaldinho" (54.Júan Maldonado Jaimez Junior), Luís Fabiano Clemente (86.João Alves de Assis Silva „Jô"). Trainer: Carlos Caetano Bledorn Verri „Dunga".
Goals: 0-1 Luís Fabiano Clemente (21), 0-2 Róbson de Souza „Robinho" (44), 0-3 Luís Fabiano Clemente (83).
Cautions: Marco Andrés Estrada Quinteros, Jean André Emanuel Beausejour Coliqueo, Alexis Alejandro Sánchez Sánchez, Carlos Emilio Carmona Tello / Diego Ribas da Cunha, Kléber de Carvalho Corrêa, Luís Fabiano Clemente, Ânderson Luís da Silva „Luisão", Gilberto Aparecido da Silva.
Sent off: Kléber de Carvalho Corrêa (47), Jorge Luis Valdivia Toro (62).

09.09.2008, Estadio Defensores del Chaco, Asunción; Attendance: 25,909
Referee: Héctor Walter Baldassi (Argentina)
PARAGUAY - VENEZUELA   **2-0(2-0)**
PAR: Justo Wilmar Villar Viveros, Carlos Bonet Cáceres, Julio César Manzur Caffarena, Paulo César da Silva Barrios, Claudio Marcelo Morel Rodríguez, Édgar Osvaldo Barreto Cáceres (79.Aureliano Torres Román), Víctor Javier Cáceres Centurión, Jonathan Santana Ghere (73.Denis Ramón Caniza Acuña), Cristian Miguel Riveros Núñez, Roque Luis Santa Cruz Cantero, Nelson Antonio Haedo Valdéz (63.Dante Rafael López Fariña). Trainer: Gerardo Daniel Martino (Argentina).
VEN: Renny Vicente Vega Hernández, Gerzon Armando Chacón Varela (35.Franklin José Lucena Peña), José Manuel Rey Cortegoso, Pedro Luis Boada Noya, Jonay Miguel Hernández Santos (55.Juan José Fuenmayor Núñez), Alejandro Abraham Guerra Morales, Tomás Eduardo Rincón Hernández, Miguel Ángel Mea Vitali, Juan Fernando Arango Sáenz, Alejandro Enrique Moreno Riera, Giancarlo Gregorio Maldonado Marrero (71.José Antonio Torrealba Acevedo). Trainer: César Alejandro Farías.
Goals: 1-0 Cristian Miguel Riveros Núñez (28), 2-0 Nelson Antonio Haedo Valdéz (45).
Cautions: Jonathan Santana Ghere, Julio César Manzur Caffarena, Claudio Marcelo Morel Rodríguez / Tomás Eduardo Rincón Hernández, Juan Fernando Arango Sáenz.

10.09.2008, Estadio Centenario, Montevideo; Attendance: 43,392
Referee: Óscar Julián Ruiz Acosta (Colombia)
URUGUAY - ECUADOR   **0-0**
URU: Juan Guillermo Castillo Iriart, Bruno Ramón Silva Barone, Diego Alfredo Moreno Lugano (Cap), Diego Roberto Godín Leal, José Martín Cáceres Silva, Sebastián Eguren Ledesma, Wálter Alejandro Gargano Guevara (46.Victorio Maximiliano Pereira Páez), Cristian Gabriel Rodríguez Barrotti, Ignacio María González Gatti (61.Luis Alberto Suárez Díaz), Diego Martín Forlán Corazo, Carlos Heber Bueno Suárez (70.Washington Sebastián Abreu Gallo). Trainer: Óscar Wáshington Tabárez Silva.
ECU: José Francisco Cevallos Villavicencio, Omar Andrés de Jesús Borja, Iván Jacinto Hurtado Angulo, Giovanny Patricio Espinoza Pabón, Isaac Bryan Mina Arboleda, Segundo Alejandro Castillo Nazareno, Luis Antonio Valencia Mosquera, Édison Vicente Méndez Méndez, Walter Orlando Ayoví

Corozo, Joffre David Guerrón Méndez (82.José Luis Cortéz Arroyo), Felipe Salvador Caicedo Corozo (79.Félix Alexander Borja Valencia). Trainer: Sixto Rafael Vizuete Toapanta.
Cautions: Sebastián Eguren Ledesma / Édison Vicente Méndez Méndez, Luis Antonio Valencia Mosquera, Isaac Bryan Mina Arboleda, José Francisco Cevallos Villavicencio.

10.09.2008, Estadio Nacional „Julio Martínez Prádanos", Santiago; Attendance: 47,459
Referee: Jorge Luis Larrionda Pietrafesa (Uruguay)
CHILE - COLOMBIA   **4-0(2-0)**
CHI: Claudio Andrés Bravo Muñoz, Gary Alexis Medel Soto, Gonzalo Alejandro Jara Reyes, Ismael Ignacio Fuentes Castro, Arturo Erasmo Vidal Pardo, Marco Andrés Estrada Quinteros, Roberto Andrés Cereceda Guajardo (78.Pablo Andrés Contreras Fica), Matías Ariel Fernández Fernández, Alexis Alejandro Sánchez Sánchez (81.Gonzalo Antonio Fierro Caniullán), Humberto Andrés Suazo Pontivo (85.Pedro Andrés Morales Flores), Mark Dennis González Hoffman. Trainer: Marcelo Alberto Bielsa Caldera (Argentina).
COL: Agustín Julio Castro, Luis Amaranto Perea Mosquera, Pedro Paulo Portocarrero Angulo, Aquivaldo Mosquera Romaña, Pablo Stifer Armero, José Yulián Anchico Patiño (54.Juan Camilo Zúñiga Mosquera), Carlos Alberto Sánchez Moreno, José Antonio Amaya Pardo, Giovanni Hernández Soto (46.Dayro Mauricio Moreno Galindo), Malher Tressor Moreno Baldrich, Hugo Rodallega Martínez (75.Milton Fabián Rodríguez Suárez). Trainer: Jorge Luis Pinto Afanador.
Goals: 1-0 Gonzalo Alejandro Jara Reyes (26), 2-0 Humberto Andrés Suazo Pontivo (38), 3-0 Ismael Ignacio Fuentes Castro (48), 4-0 Matías Ariel Fernández Fernández (71).
Cautions: Ismael Ignacio Fuentes Castro / Carlos Alberto Sánchez Moreno, Pablo Stifer Armero.

10.09.2008, Estádio Olímpico „João Havelange", Rio de Janeiro; Attendance: 31,422
Referee: Alfredo Intriago (Ecuador)
BRAZIL - BOLIVIA   **0-0**
BRA: Júlio César Soares de Espíndola, Maicon Douglas Sisenando, Lucimar Ferreira da Silva „Lúcio", Ânderson Luís da Silva „Luisão", Júan Maldonado Jaimez Junior, Lucas Pezzini Leiva (60.Júlio César Baptista), Josué Anunciado de Oliveira, Diego Ribas da Cunha (76.Elano Ralph Blumer), Róbson de Souza „Robinho", Ronaldo de Assis Moreira „Ronaldinho" (76.Nilmar Honorato da Silva), Luís Fabiano Clemente. Trainer: Carlos Caetano Bledorn Verri „Dunga".
BOL: Carlos Erwin Arias Eguez, Miguel Ángel Hoyos Guzmán, Ronald Raldés Balcázar, Ronald Taylor Rivero Khun, Ignacio Awad García Justiniano, Wálter Alberto Flores Condarco, Ronald Lázaro García Justiniano, Jaime Robles Céspedes, Joselito Vaca Velasco (89.Diego Aroldo Cabrera Flores), Jaime Moreno Morales (56.Luis Alberto Gutiérrez Herrera), Marcelo Moreno Martins (78.Pablo Daniel Escobar Olivetti). Trainer: Erwin Sánchez Freking.
Cautions: Josué Anunciado de Oliveira, Júan Maldonado Jaimez Junior, Diego Ribas da Cunha, Ânderson Luís da Silva „Luisão" / Jaime Moreno Morales, Miguel Ángel Hoyos Guzmán.
Sent off: Ignacio Awad García Justiniano (53).

10.09.2008, Estadio Monumental, Lima; Attendance: 40,000
Referee: Carlos Arecio Amarilla Demarqui (Paraguay)
PERU - ARGENTINA   **1-1(0-0)**
PER: Leao Butrón Gotuzzo, Amilton Jair Prado Barron, Carlos Augusto Zambrano Ochandarte, Wálter Ricardo Vílchez Soto, Juan Manuel Vargas Risco, Rainer Torres Salas, Paolo Giancarlo De La Haza Urquiza, Nolberto Albino Solano Todco, Daniel Chávez Castillo (75.Hernán Rengifo Trigoso), Piero Fernando Alva Niezen (66.Guillermo Sandro Salas Suárez), Johan Javier Fano Espinoza. Trainer: José Guillermo del Solar Alvarez-Calderón.
ARG: Juan Pablo Carrizo, Fabricio Coloccini, Daniel Alberto Díaz, Martín Gastón Demichelis, Javier Adelmar Zanetti, Esteban Matías Cambiasso (87.Pablo Javier Zabaleta Girod), Fernando Rubén Gago, Juan Román Riquelme, Jonás Manuel Gutiérrez (16.Sebastián Alejandro Battaglia), Lionel Andrés Messi, Sergio Leonel Agüero del Castillo (63.Germán Gustavo Denis). Trainer: Alfio Oscar Basile.
Goals: 0-1 Esteban Matías Cambiasso (82), 1-1 Johan Javier Fano Espinoza (90+3).
Cautions: Paolo Giancarlo De La Haza Urquiza, Nolberto Albino Solano Todco, Carlos Augusto

Zambrano Ochandarte, Rainer Torres Salas, Wálter Ricardo Vílchez Soto / Daniel Alberto Díaz, Martín Gastón Demichelis, Fernando Rubén Gago, Sebastián Alejandro Battaglia.

11.10.2008, Estadio "Hernándo Siles Zuazo", La Paz; Attendance: 23,147
Referee: José Hernando Buitrago Arango (Colombia)
BOLIVIA - PERU   **3-0(2-0)**
BOL: Carlos Erwin Arias Eguez, Christian Israel Vargas Claros, Ronald Raldés Balcázar (83.Luis Alberto Gutiérrez Herrera), Ronald Taylor Rivero Khun, Abdón Reyes Cardozo, Wálter Alberto Flores Condarco, Ronald Lázaro García Justiniano, Joselito Vaca Velasco (81.Marcelo Eduardo Torrico), Jaime Robles Céspedes, Joaquín Botero Vaca, Marcelo Moreno Martins (64.Pablo Daniel Escobar Olivetti). Trainer: Erwin Sánchez Freking.
PER: Leao Butrón Gotuzzo, Amilton Jair Prado Barron, Carlos Augusto Zambrano Ochandarte, Wálter Ricardo Vílchez Soto, Juan Manuel Vargas Risco, Rainer Torres Salas, Paolo Giancarlo De La Haza Urquiza, Juan Carlos Mariño Márquez, Daniel Chávez Castillo (46.Roberto Carlos Guizasola La Rosa), Johan Javier Fano Espinoza (Hernán Rengifo Trigoso), Piero Fernando Alva Niezen (62.Wilmer Alexander Aguirre Vásquez). Trainer: José Guillermo del Solar Alvarez-Calderón.
Goals: 1-0 Joaquín Botero Vaca (3), 2-0 Joaquín Botero Vaca (16), 3-0 Ronald Lázaro García Justiniano (81).
Cautions: Christian Israel Vargas Claros, Marcelo Moreno Martins, Joaquín Botero Vaca / Juan Manuel Vargas Risco, Johan Javier Fano Espinoza, Carlos Augusto Zambrano Ochandarte.

11.10.2008, Estadio Monumental „Antonio Vespucio Liberti", Buenos Aires; Attendance: 42,421
Referee: Carlos Manuel Torres (Paraguay)
ARGENTINA - URUGUAY   **2-1(2-1)**
ARG: Juan Pablo Carrizo, Javier Adelmar Zanetti, Martín Gastón Demichelis, Nicolás Andrés Burdisso, Gabriel Iván Heinze, Javier Alejandro Mascherano, Esteban Matías Cambiasso, Juan Román Riquelme (72.Cristian Raúl Ledesma), Sergio Leonel Agüero del Castillo (71.Diego Alberto Milito), Lionel Andrés Messi (88.Daniel Alberto Díaz), Carlos Alberto Tévez. Trainer: Alfio Oscar Basile.
URU: Juan Guillermo Castillo Iriart, Jorge Ciro Fucile Perdomo (24.Edinson Roberto Cavani Gómez), Diego Alfredo Moreno Lugano (Cap), Diego Roberto Godín Leal, José Martín Cáceres Silva, Victorio Maximiliano Pereira Páez, Sebastián Eguren Ledesma, Diego Fernando Pérez Aguado, Cristian Gabriel Rodríguez Barrotti (74.Carlos Heber Bueno Suárez), Luis Alberto Suárez Díaz, Washington Sebastián Abreu Gallo (74.Ernesto Javier Chevantón Espinosa). Trainer: Óscar Wáshington Tabárez Silva.
Goals: 1-0 Lionel Andrés Messi (6), 2-0 Sergio Leonel Agüero del Castillo (13), 2-1 Diego Alfredo Moreno Lugano (40).
Cautions: Juan Román Riquelme, Carlos Alberto Tévez, Gabriel Iván Heinze, Javier Alejandro Mascherano, Lionel Andrés Messi / Sebastián Eguren Ledesma, Diego Roberto Godín Leal, Luis Alberto Suárez Díaz, Carlos Heber Bueno Suárez, Diego Fernando Pérez Aguado.

11.10.2008, Estadio "Nemesio Camacho" El Campín, Bogotá; Attendance: 26,000
Referee: Pablo Alejandro Lunati (Argentina)
COLOMBIA - PARAGUAY   **0-1(0-1)**
COL: Agustín Julio Castro, Juan Camilo Zúñiga Mosquera, Mario Alberto Yepes Díaz, Luis Amaranto Perea Mosquera, Pablo Stifer Armero, Gerardo Alberto Bedoya de Galindo, Freddy Alejandro Guarín Vásquez (72.Gustavo Adrián Ramos Vásquez), Fabián Andrés Vargas Rivera, Giovanni Hernández Soto (54.David Arturo Ferreira Rico), Wason Libardo Rentería Cuesta, Fredy Henkyer Montero Muñoz (54.Carlos Darwin Quintero Villalba). Trainer: Eduardo Lara Lozano.
PAR: Justo Wilmar Villar Viveros, Darío Anastacio Verón Maldonado, Julio César Cáceres López, Paulo César da Silva Barrios, Víctor Javier Cáceres Centurión, Édgar Osvaldo Barreto Cáceres (83.Carlos Bonet Cáceres), Enrique Daniel Vera Torres, Cristian Miguel Riveros Núñez, Aureliano Torres Román, Salvador Cabañas Ortega (85.Óscar René Cardozo Marín), Nelson Antonio Haedo Valdéz (75.Ariel Gregorio Bogado Llanos). Trainer: Gerardo Daniel Martino (Argentina).
Goal: 0-1 Salvador Cabañas Ortega (9).
Cautions: Gerardo Alberto Bedoya de Galindo / Darío Anastacio Verón Maldonado, Salvador Cabañas

Ortega.

12.10.2008, Estadio Polideportivo de Pueblo Nuevo, San Cristóbal; Attendance: 38,000
Referee: Victor Hugo Rivera (Peru)
VENEZUELA - BRAZIL   **0-4(0-3)**
VEN: Renny Vicente Vega Hernández, Gerzon Armando Chacón Varela, José Manuel Rey Cortegoso, Pedro Luis Boada Noya, Jorge Alberto Rojas Méndez, Miguel Ángel Mea Vitali (70.Franklin José Lucena Peña), Leonel Vielma Gerardo Peña, Alejandro Abraham Guerra Morales (61.Alejandro Enrique Moreno Riera), Ronald Alejandro Vargas Aranguren (55.Luis Manuel Seijas Gunther), Juan Fernando Arango Sáenz, Giancarlo Gregorio Maldonado Marrero. Trainer: César Alejandro Farías.
BRA: Júlio César Soares de Espíndola, Maicon Douglas Sisenando, Lucimar Ferreira da Silva „Lúcio", Juan Silveira dos Santos (46.Thiago Emiliano da Silva), Kléber de Carvalho Corrêa, Gilberto Aparecido da Silva, Josué Anunciado de Oliveira (78.Alessandro Amantín Faiolhe Mancini), Elano Ralph Blumer, Ricardo Izecson dos Santos Leite „Kaká" (71.Alexandre Raphael Meschini), Adriano Leite Ribeiro, Róbson de Souza „Robinho". Trainer: Carlos Caetano Bledorn Verri „Dunga".
Goals: 0-1 Ricardo Izecson dos Santos Leite „Kaká" (6), 0-2 Róbson de Souza „Robinho" (9), 0-3 Adriano Leite Ribeiro (19), 0-4 Róbson de Souza „Robinho" (66).
Cautions: Jorge Alberto Rojas Méndez / Adriano Leite Ribeiro.

12.10.2008, Estadio Olimpico "Atahualpa", Quito; Attendance: 33,079
Referee: Martín Vázquez Broquetas (Uruguay)
ECUADOR - CHILE   **1-0(0-0)**
ECU: Marcelo Ramón Elizaga Ferrero, Omar Andrés de Jesús Borja, Iván Jacinto Hurtado Angulo, Giovanny Patricio Espinoza Pabón, Vicente Paúl Ambrosi Zambrano (46.Luis Alberto Bolaños León), Segundo Alejandro Castillo Nazareno (43.Patricio Javier Urrutia Espinoza), Walter Orlando Ayoví Corozo, Joffre David Guerrón Méndez, Luis Antonio Valencia Mosquera, Christian Rogelio Benítez Betancourt, Felipe Salvador Caicedo Corozo (85.Fernando Roberto Hidalgo Maldonado). Trainer: Sixto Rafael Vizuete Toapanta.
CHI: Claudio Andrés Bravo Muñoz, Gary Alexis Medel Soto, Gonzalo Alejandro Jara Reyes, Ismael Ignacio Fuentes Castro, Arturo Erasmo Vidal Pardo, Carlos Emilio Carmona Tello, Roberto Andrés Cereceda Guajardo (53.Marco Andrés Estrada Quinteros), Matías Ariel Fernández Fernández (23.Pablo Andrés Contreras Fica), Mark Dennis González Hoffman, Alexis Alejandro Sánchez Sánchez, Humberto Andrés Suazo Pontivo (58.Pedro Andrés Morales Flores). Trainer: Marcelo Alberto Bielsa Caldera (Argentina).
Goal: 1-0 Christian Rogelio Benítez Betancourt (70).
Cautions: Iván Jacinto Hurtado Angulo, Giovanny Patricio Espinoza Pabón, Christian Rogelio Benítez Betancourt, Marcelo Ramón Elizaga Ferrero / Gonzalo Alejandro Jara Reyes, Roberto Andrés Cereceda Guajardo, Alexis Alejandro Sánchez Sánchez.
Sent off: Ismael Ignacio Fuentes Castro (20), Luis Antonio Valencia Mosquera (75), Gonzalo Alejandro Jara Reyes (82).

14.10.2008, Estadio "Hernándo Siles Zuazo", La Paz; Attendance: 21,075
Referee: Héctor Walter Baldassi (Argentina)
BOLIVIA - URUGUAY   **2-2(2-0)**
BOL: Carlos Erwin Arias Eguez, Christian Israel Vargas Claros, Ronald Raldés Balcázar, Ronald Taylor Rivero Khun, Abdón Reyes Cardozo, Wálter Alberto Flores Condarco, Ronald Lázaro García Justiniano, Joselito Vaca Velasco (64.Marcelo Eduardo Torrico), Jaime Robles Céspedes, Joaquín Botero Vaca (71.Pablo Daniel Escobar Olivetti), Marcelo Moreno Martins (88.Enrique Parada Salvatierra). Trainer: Erwin Sánchez Freking.
URU: Juan Guillermo Castillo Iriart, Bruno Ramón Silva Barone, Diego Alfredo Moreno Lugano (Cap), Andrés Scotti Ponce de León, José Martín Cáceres Silva, Álvaro Rafael González Luengo (55.Victorio Maximiliano Pereira Páez), Hugo Diego Arismendi Ciapparetta, Wálter Alejandro Gargano Guevara, Cristian Gabriel Rodríguez Barrotti (71.Washington Sebastián Abreu Gallo), Vicente Martín Sánchez Bragunde, Carlos Heber Bueno Suárez. Trainer: Óscar Wáshington Tabárez

Silva.

Goals: 1-0 Marcelo Moreno Martins (15), 2-0 Marcelo Moreno Martins (41), 2-1 Carlos Heber Bueno Suárez (64), 2-2 Washington Sebastián Abreu Gallo (88).

Cautions: Christian Israel Vargas Claros / Andrés Scotti Ponce de León, Bruno Ramón Silva Barone, Hugo Diego Arismendi Ciapparetta.

15.10.2008, Estadio Defensores del Chaco, Asunción; Attendance: 25,587
Referee: Sálvio Spínola Fagundes Filho (Brazil)
PARAGUAY - PERU   **1-0(0-0)**
PAR: Justo Wilmar Villar Viveros, Carlos Bonet Cáceres, Julio César Cáceres López, Paulo César da Silva Barrios, Claudio Marcelo Morel Rodríguez, Édgar Osvaldo Barreto Cáceres (46.Osvaldo David Martínez Arce), Jonathan Santana Ghere (66.Óscar René Cardozo Marín), Víctor Javier Cáceres Centurión, Cristian Miguel Riveros Núñez, Nelson Antonio Haedo Valdéz (66.Edgar Benítez Santander), Salvador Cabañas Ortega. Trainer: Gerardo Daniel Martino (Argentina).
PER: Leao Butrón Gotuzzo, Amilton Jair Prado Barron, Orlando Contreras Collantes, Wálter Ricardo Vílchez Soto, Juan Manuel Vargas Risco, Nolberto Albino Solano Todco, Paolo Giancarlo De La Haza Urquiza (85.Henry Edson Quinteros Sánchez), Rainer Torres Salas, Juan Carlos Mariño Márquez (70.Piero Fernando Alva Niezen), Johan Javier Fano Espinoza (84.Daniel Chávez Castillo), Hernán Rengifo Trigoso. Trainer: José Guillermo del Solar Alvarez-Calderón.
Goal: 1-0 Edgar Benítez Santander (81).
Cautions: Jonathan Santana Ghere, Paulo César da Silva Barrios / Nolberto Albino Solano Todco, Wálter Ricardo Vílchez Soto, Orlando Contreras Collantes, Leao Butrón Gotuzzo, Amilton Jair Prado Barron.

15.10.2008, Estadio Nacional „Julio Martínez Prádanos", Santiago; Attendance: 65,000
Referee: Óscar Julián Ruiz Acosta (Colombia)
CHILE - ARGENTINA   **1-0(1-0)**
CHI: Claudio Andrés Bravo Muñoz, Gary Alexis Medel Soto, Marco Andrés Estrada Quinteros, Waldo Alonso Ponce Carrizo (87.Arturo Erasmo Vidal Pardo), Pablo Andrés Contreras Fica, Carlos Emilio Carmona Tello, Matías Ariel Fernández Fernández, Mark Dennis González Hoffman (20.Hugo Patricio Droguett Diocares), Jean André Emanuel Beausejour Coliqueo, Fabián Ariel Orellana Valenzuela (85.Hans Alexis Martínez Cabrera), Humberto Andrés Suazo Pontivo. Trainer: Marcelo Alberto Bielsa Caldera (Argentina).
ARG: Juan Pablo Carrizo, Javier Adelmar Zanetti, Nicolás Andrés Burdisso (20.Daniel Alberto Díaz), Martín Gastón Demichelis, Gabriel Iván Heinze, Javier Alejandro Mascherano, Esteban Matías Cambiasso (83.José Gustavo Sand), Cristian Raúl Ledesma, Lionel Andrés Messi, Diego Alberto Milito (46.Gonzalo Rubén Bergessio), Sergio Leonel Agüero del Castillo. Trainer: Alfio Oscar Basile.
Goal: 1-0 Fabián Ariel Orellana Valenzuela (35).
Cautions: Pablo Andrés Contreras Fica, Fabián Ariel Orellana Valenzuela, Gary Alexis Medel Soto / Javier Adelmar Zanetti, Martín Gastón Demichelis.

15.10.2008, Estádio „Jornalista Mário Filho" (Maracanã), Rio de Janeiro; Attendance: 54,910
Referee: Rubén Marcos Selmán (Chile)
BRAZIL - COLOMBIA   **0-0**
BRA: Júlio César Soares de Espíndola, Maicon Douglas Sisenando, Lucimar Ferreira da Silva „Lúcio", Juan Silveira dos Santos (66.Thiago Emiliano da Silva), Kléber de Carvalho Corrêa, Gilberto Aparecido da Silva, Josué Anunciado de Oliveira, Elano Ralph Blumer (57.Alessandro Amantín Faiolhe Mancini), Ricardo Izecson dos Santos Leite „Kaká", Adriano Leite Ribeiro, Róbson de Souza „Robinho" (63.Alexandre Rodrigues da Silva "Alexandre Pato"), João Alves de Assis Silva „Jô". Trainer: Carlos Caetano Bledorn Verri „Dunga".
COL: Agustín Julio Castro, Juan Camilo Zúñiga Mosquera, Luis Amaranto Perea Mosquera, Mario Alberto Yepes Díaz, Pablo Stifer Armero, Freddy Alejandro Guarín Vásquez, Gerardo Alberto Bedoya de Galindo (66.Abel Enrique Aguilar Tapias), Fabián Andrés Vargas Rivera, Carlos Darwin Quintero Villalba (70.Dayro Mauricio Moreno Galindo), Juan Carlos Toja Vega, Wason Libardo Rentería Cuesta

(75.Gustavo Adrián Ramos Vásquez). Trainer: Eduardo Lara Lozano.
Cautions: Gerardo Alberto Bedoya de Galindo, Fabián Andrés Vargas Rivera, Wason Libardo Rentería Cuesta.

15.10.2008, Estadio "General José Antonio Anzoategui", Puerto La Cruz; Attendance: 10,581
Referee: Enrique Marcos Osses Zencovich (Chile)
VENEZUELA - ECUADOR   **3-1(0-1)**
VEN: Renny Vicente Vega Hernández, Roberto José Rosales Altuve, Gabriel Alejandro Cichero Konarek, José Manuel Rey Cortegoso, Juan José Fuenmayor Núñez, Franklin José Lucena Peña, Tomás Eduardo Rincón Hernández, Alejandro Enrique Moreno Riera (79.Pedro Luis Boada Noya), César Eduardo González Amais (70.Jorge Alberto Rojas Méndez), Juan Fernando Arango Sáenz, Giancarlo Gregorio Maldonado Marrero (74.Daniel Enrique Arismendi Marchán). Trainer: César Alejandro Farías.
ECU: José Francisco Cevallos Villavicencio, Isaac Bryan Mina Arboleda, Iván Jacinto Hurtado Angulo (36.Carlos Ernesto Castro Cadena), Giovanny Patricio Espinoza Pabón, Omar Andrés de Jesús Borja, José Luis Cortéz Arroyo, Édison Vicente Méndez Méndez, Patricio Javier Urrutia Espinoza, Walter Orlando Ayoví Corozo (60.Luis Alberto Bolaños León), Joffre David Guerrón Méndez (65.Félix Alexander Borja Valencia), Felipe Salvador Caicedo Corozo. Trainer: Sixto Rafael Vizuete Toapanta.
Goals: 0-1 Isaac Bryan Mina Arboleda (12), 1-1 Giancarlo Gregorio Maldonado Marrero (48), 2-1 Alejandro Enrique Moreno Riera (56), 3-1 Juan Fernando Arango Sáenz (67).
Cautions: Gabriel Alejandro Cichero Konarek / José Francisco Cevallos Villavicencio, Félix Alexander Borja Valencia.

28.03.2009, Estadio Centenario, Montevideo; Attendance: 45,000
Referee: Carlos Eugênio Simon (Brazil)
URUGUAY - PARAGUAY   **2-0(1-0)**
URU: Mario Sebastián Viera Galaín, Diego Roberto Godín Leal (81.Bruno Ramón Silva Barone), Diego Alfredo Lugano Moreno, José Martín Cáceres Silva, Victorio Maximiliano Pereira Páez, Álvaro Daniel Pereira Barragán, Sebastián Eguren Ledesma, Diego Fernando Pérez Aguado, Cristian Gabriel Rodríguez Barotti (72.Jorge Andrés Martínez Barrios), Diego Martín Forlán Corazo (79.Washington Sebastián Abreu Gallo), Luis Alberto Suárez Díaz. Trainer: Óscar Wáshington Tabárez Silva.
PAR: Justo Wilmar Villar Viveros, Julio César Cáceres López, Paulo César da Silva Barrios, Darío Anastacio Verón Maldonado, Aureliano Torres Román (58.Miguel Ángel Samudio), Édgar Osvaldo Barreto Cáceres, Cristian Miguel Riveros Núñez, Enrique Daniel Vera Torres (69.Óscar René Cardozo Marín), Marcelo Alejandro Estigarribia Balmori (46.Sergio Daniel Aquino), Salvador Cabañas Ortega, Nelson Antonio Haedo Valdéz. Trainer: Gerardo Daniel Martino (Argentina).
Goals: 1-0 Diego Martín Forlán Corazo (28), 2-0 Diego Alfredo Lugano Moreno (57).
Cautions: Álvaro Daniel Pereira Barragán / Marcelo Alejandro Estigarribia Balmori, Julio César Cáceres López, Édgar Osvaldo Barreto Cáceres.

28.03.2009, Estadio Monumental „Antonio Vespucio Liberti", Buenos Aires; Attendance: 46,085
Referee: Victor Hugo Rivera (Peru)
ARGENTINA - VENEZUELA   **4-0(1-0)**
ARG: Juan Pablo Carrizo, Javier Adelmar Zanetti, Marcos Alberto Angeleri, Gabriel Iván Heinze, Maximiliano Rubén Rodríguez (74.Ángel Fabián di María), Javier Alejandro Mascherano, Fernando Rubén Gago, Jonás Manuel Gutiérrez, Lionel Andrés Messi, Sergio Leonel Agüero del Castillo (78.Diego Alberto Milito), Carlos Alberto Tévez (70.Juan Sebastián Verón). Trainer: Diego Armando Maradona.
VEN: Renny Vicente Vega Hernández, Gabriel Alejandro Cichero Konarek, Jorge Alberto Rojas Méndez (83.Rafael Eduardo Acosta Cammarota), José Manuel Velázquez Rodríguez, Juan José Fuenmayor Núñez, Roberto José Rosales Altuve (50.Alejandro Enrique Moreno Riera), Gerzon Armando Chacón Varela, Tomás Eduardo Rincón Hernández, César Eduardo González Amais, Juan Fernando Arango Sáenz, Giancarlo Gregorio Maldonado Marrero (78.Francisco Javier Flores Sequera).

Trainer: César Alejandro Farías.
Goals: 1-0 Lionel Andrés Messi (26), 2-0 Carlos Alberto Tévez (47), 3-0 Maximiliano Rubén Rodríguez (51), 4-0 Sergio Leonel Agüero del Castillo (73).
Cautions: Marcos Alberto Angeleri, Jonás Manuel Gutiérrez / Gabriel Alejandro Cichero Konarek, Jorge Alberto Rojas Méndez, Tomás Eduardo Rincón Hernández.

28.03.2009, Estadio „Nemesio Camacho" El Campín, Bogotá; Attendance: 22,044
Referee: Alfredo Intriago (Ecuador)
COLOMBIA - BOLIVIA   **2-0(1-0)**
COL: David Ospina Ramírez, Mario Alberto Yepes Díaz, Cristián Eduardo Zapata Valencia, Pablo Stifer Armero, Juan Camilo Zúñiga Mosquera, Vladimir Marín Ríos, Abel Enrique Aguilar Tapias, Fabián Andrés Vargas Rivera, Macnelly Torres Berrio (70.Stalin Motta Vaquiro), Radamel Falcao García Zárate (70.Wason Libardo Rentería Cuesta), Carlos Darwin Quintero Villalba (79.Hugo Rodallega Martínez). Trainer: Eduardo Lara Lozano.
BOL: Carlos Erwin Arias Eguez, Luis Alberto Gutiérrez Herrera, Juan Manuel Peña Montaño, Ronald Taylor Rivero Khun, Miguel Ángel Hoyos Guzmán, Wálter Alberto Flores Condarco, Ronald Lázaro García Justiniano, Jaime Robles Céspedes (46.Didí Torrico Camacho), Joselito Vaca Velasco (77.Julio César Hurtado), Pablo Daniel Escobar Olivetti, Diego Aroldo Cabrera Flores (67.José Alfredo Castillo Parada). Trainer: Erwin Sánchez Freking.
Goals: 1-0 Macnelly Torres Berrio (26), 2-0 Wason Libardo Rentería Cuesta (88).
Cautions: Fabián Andrés Vargas Rivera, Pablo Stifer Armero, Wason Libardo Rentería Cuesta / Pablo Daniel Escobar Olivetti, Wálter Alberto Flores Condarco, Didí Torrico Camacho, Luis Alberto Gutiérrez Herrera, Joselito Vaca Velasco.
Sent off: José Alfredo Castillo Parada (90).

29.03.2009, Estadio Olímpico „Atahualpa", Quito; Attendance: 40,000
Referee: Carlos Chandía Alarcón (Chile)
ECUADOR - BRAZIL   **1-1(0-0)**
ECU: José Francisco Cevallos Villavicencio, Giovanny Patricio Espinoza Pabón, Iván Jacinto Hurtado Angulo, Néicer Reasco Yano, Segundo Alejandro Castillo Nazareno, Walter Orlando Ayoví Corozo, Luis Antonio Valencia Mosquera, Édison Vicente Méndez Méndez, Felipe Salvador Caicedo Corozo (90+2.Pablo David Palacios Herreria), Christian Rogelio Benítez Betancourt, Joffre David Guerrón Méndez (75.Christian Fernando Noboa Tello). Trainer: Sixto Rafael Vizuete Toapanta.
BRA: Júlio César Soares de Espíndola, Maicon Douglas Sisenando (24.Daniel Alves da Silva „Dani Alves"), Ânderson Luís da Silva „Luisão", Lucimar Ferreira da Silva „Lúcio", Marcelo Vieira da Silva Júnior, Felipe Melo de Carvalho, Gilberto Aparecido da Silva, Elano Ralph Blumer (61.Josué Anunciado de Oliveira), Ronaldo de Assis Moreira „Ronaldinho" (71.Júlio César Baptista), Róbson de Souza „Robinho", Luís Fabiano Clemente. Trainer: Carlos Caetano Bledorn Verri „Dunga".
Goals: 0-1 Júlio César Baptista (72), 1-1 Christian Fernando Noboa Tello (89).
Cautions: Walter Orlando Ayoví Corozo / Elano Ralph Blumer, Gilberto Aparecido da Silva, Marcelo Vieira da Silva Júnior, Daniel Alves da Silva „Dani Alves".

29.03.2009, Estadio Monumental, Lima; Attendance: 48,700
Referee: Carlos Arecio Amarilla Demarqui (Paraguay)
PERU - CHILE   **1-3(1-2)**
PER: Leao Butrón Gotuzzo, Alberto Junior Rodríguez Valdelomar, Ámilton Jair Prado Barrón, Carlos Augusto Zambrano Ochandarte, Juan Manuel Vargas Risco, Nolberto Albino Solano Todco (78.Alexander Gustavo Sánchez Reyes), Luis Alberto Ramírez Lucay, Rainer Torres Salas, Miguel Ángel Torres Quintana (46.Paolo Giancarlo De La Haza Urquiza), Daniel Chávez Castillo (59.Piero Fernando Alva Niezen), Johan Javier Fano Espinoza. Trainer: José Guillermo del Solar Alvarez-Calderón.
CHI: Claudio Andrés Bravo Muñoz, Gonzalo Alejandro Jara Reyes, Waldo Alonso Ponce Carrizo, Roberto Andrés Cereceda Guajardo, Mauricio Aníbal Isla Isla (63.Pablo Andrés Contreras Fica), Carlos Emilio Carmona Tello (75.Marco Andrés Estrada Quinteros), Matías Ariel Fernández Fernández

(72.Rodrigo Álvaro Tello Valenzuela), Mark Dennis González Hoffman, Alexis Alejandro Sánchez Sánchez, Humberto Andrés Suazo Pontivo, Jean André Emanuel Beausejour Coliqueo. Trainer: Marcelo Alberto Bielsa Caldera (Argentina).

Goals: 0-1 Alexis Alejandro Sánchez Sánchez (2), 0-2 Humberto Andrés Suazo Pontivo (32 penalty), 1-2 Johan Javier Fano Espinoza (34), 1-3 Matías Ariel Fernández Fernández (70).

Cautions: Carlos Augusto Zambrano Ochandarte, Luis Alberto Ramírez Lucay, Juan Manuel Vargas Risco, Paolo Giancarlo De La Haza Urquiza / Alexis Alejandro Sánchez Sánchez, Carlos Emilio Carmona Tello, Marco Andrés Estrada Quinteros

Sent off: Juan Manuel Vargas Risco (52).

31.03.2009, Estadio Polideportivo Cachamay, Puerto Ordaz; Attendance: 35,000
Referee: Pablo Antonio Pozo Quinteros (Chile)
VENEZUELA - COLOMBIA   2-0(0-0)
VEN: Renny Vicente Vega Hernández, Franklin José Lucena Peña, Carlos Eduardo Salazar, José Manuel Velázquez Rodríguez, Juan José Fuenmayor Núñez, Roberto José Rosales Altuve, Tomás Eduardo Rincón Hernández, César Eduardo González Amais (65.Louis Ángelo Peña), Juan Fernando Arango Sáenz (85.Rafael Eduardo Acosta Cammarota), Giancarlo Gregorio Maldonado Marrero (74.Nicolás Ladislao Fedor Flores), Alejandro Enrique Moreno Riera. Trainer: César Alejandro Farías.
COL: David Ospina Ramírez, Mario Alberto Yepes Díaz, Cristián Eduardo Zapata Valencia, Gerardo Alberto Bedoya de Galindo, Luis Alberto Nuñez (46.Josimar Mosquera Angulo), Juan Camilo Zúñiga Mosquera, Vladimir Marín Ríos, Abel Enrique Aguilar Tapias, Macnelly Torres Berrio (74.Hugo Rodallega Martínez), Radamel Falcao García Zárate, Carlos Darwin Quintero Villalba (57.Cristian Camilo Marrugo Rodríguez). Trainer: Eduardo Lara Lozano.
Goals: 1-0 Nicolás Ladislao Fedor Flores (78), 2-0 Juan Fernando Arango Sáenz (82).
Cautions: Juan José Fuenmayor Núñez, César Eduardo González Amais, Rafael Eduardo Acosta Cammarota / Gerardo Alberto Bedoya de Galindo, Cristian Camilo Marrugo Rodríguez.
Sent off: Abel Enrique Aguilar Tapias (28).

01.04.2009, Estadio „Hernando Siles Zuazo", La Paz; Attendance: 30,487
Referee: Martín Vázquez Broquetas (Uruguay)
BOLIVIA - ARGENTINA   6-1(3-1)
BOL: Carlos Erwin Arias Eguez, Luis Gatty Ribeiro Roca, Juan Manuel Peña Montaño, Ronald Taylor Rivero Khun, Ronald Lázaro García Justiniano (79.Wálter Alberto Flores Condarco), Abdón Reyes Cardozo (55.Ignacio Awad García Justiniano), Leonel Alfredo Reyes Saravia, Didí Torrico Camacho, Álex Rodrigo da Rosa Dornelles (69.Mauricio Saucedo Guardia), Joaquín Botero Vaca, Marcelo Moreno Martins. Trainer: Erwin Sánchez Freking.
ARG: Juan Pablo Carrizo, Javier Adelmar Zanetti, Martín Gastón Demichelis, Gabriel Iván Heinze, Emiliano Ramiro Papa, Luis Oscar González (68.Marcos Alberto Angeleri), Fernando Rubén Gago, Javier Alejandro Mascherano, Maximiliano Rubén Rodríguez (56.Ángel Fabián di María), Carlos Alberto Tévez (74.Daniel Gastón Montenegro), Lionel Andrés Messi. Trainer: Diego Armando Maradona.
Goals: 1-0 Marcelo Moreno Martins (12), 1-1 Luis Oscar González (24), 2-1 Joaquín Botero Vaca (34 penalty), 3-1 Álex Rodrigo da Rosa Dornelles (45), 4-1 Joaquín Botero Vaca (55), 5-1 Joaquín Botero Vaca (66), 6-1 Didí Torrico Camacho (87).
Cautions: Leonel Alfredo Reyes Saravia, Álex Rodrigo da Rosa Dornelles, Didí Torrico Camacho, Luis Gatty Ribeiro Roca / Emiliano Ramiro Papa,
Sent off: Ángel Fabián di María (64).

01.04.2009, Estadio Olimpico „Atahualpa", Quito; Attendance: 36,853
Referee: Wilmar Roldán Pérez (Colombia)
ECUADOR - PARAGUAY   **1-1(0-0)**
ECU: José Francisco Cevallos Villavicencio, Giovanny Patricio Espinoza Pabón, Iván Jacinto Hurtado Angulo, Vicente Paúl Ambrosi Zambrano, Néicer Reasco Yano, Segundo Alejandro Castillo Nazareno, Luis Antonio Valencia Mosquera (85.Patricio Javier Urrutia Espinoza), Édison Vicente Méndez Méndez, Felipe Salvador Caicedo Corozo (46.Walter Richard Calderón Carcelén), Christian Rogelio Benítez Betancourt, Joffre David Guerrón Méndez (61.Christian Fernando Noboa Tello). Trainer: Sixto Rafael Vizuete Toapanta.
PAR: Justo Wilmar Villar Viveros, Julio César Manzur Caffarena, Paulo César da Silva Barrios, Darío Anastacio Verón Maldonado, Denis Ramón Caniza Acuña, Sergio Daniel Aquino (70.Osvaldo David Martínez Arce), Víctor Javier Cáceres Centurión, Cristian Miguel Riveros Núñez, Enrique Daniel Vera Torres (74.Carlos Bonet Cáceres), Salvador Cabañas Ortega, Nelson Antonio Haedo Valdéz (69.Edgar Benítez Santander). Trainer: Gerardo Daniel Martino (Argentina).
Goals: 1-0 Christian Fernando Noboa Tello (63), 1-1 Edgar Benítez Santander (90+2).
Cautions: Joffre David Guerrón Méndez, Giovanny Patricio Espinoza Pabón, Felipe Salvador Caicedo Corozo, Iván Jacinto Hurtado Angulo, Luis Antonio Valencia Mosquera, Édison Vicente Méndez Méndez / Darío Anastacio Verón Maldonado, Salvador Cabañas Ortega, Edgar Benítez Santander.
Sent off: Paulo César da Silva Barrios (85).

01.04.2009, Estadio Nacional „Julio Martínez Prádanos", Santiago; Attendance: 55,000
Referee: Héctor Walter Baldassi (Argentina)
CHILE - URUGUAY   **0-0**
CHI: Claudio Andrés Bravo Muñoz, Pablo Andrés Contreras Fica, Gonzalo Alejandro Jara Reyes, Waldo Alonso Ponce Carrizo, Mauricio Aníbal Isla Isla, Carlos Emilio Carmona Tello, Matías Ariel Fernández Fernández (60.Fabián Ariel Orellana Valenzuela), Mark Dennis González Hoffman, Alexis Alejandro Sánchez Sánchez, Humberto Andrés Suazo Pontivo, Jean André Emanuel Beausejour Coliqueo (38.Manuel Rolando Iturra Urrutia; 46.Roberto Andrés Cereceda Guajardo). Trainer: Marcelo Alberto Bielsa Caldera (Argentina).
URU: Mario Sebastián Viera Galaín, Diego Roberto Godín Leal, Diego Alfredo Lugano Moreno (Cap), José Martín Cáceres Silva, Victorino Maximiliano Pereira Páez, Álvaro Daniel Pereira Barragán (70.Washington Sebastián Abreu Gallo), Sebastián Eguren Ledesma, Diego Fernando Pérez Aguado (40.Álvaro Fernández), Cristian Gabriel Rodríguez Barotti (85.Edinson Roberto Cavani Gómez), Diego Martín Forlán Corazo, Luis Alberto Suárez Díaz. Trainer: Óscar Wáshington Tabárez Silva.
Cautions: Mauricio Aníbal Isla Isla / Diego Fernando Pérez Aguado, Diego Alfredo Lugano Moreno, Sebastián Eguren Ledesma, Diego Martín Forlán Corazo, José Martín Cáceres Silva, Cristian Gabriel Rodríguez Barotti.
Sent off: Mauricio Aníbal Isla Isla (33).

01.04.2009, Estádio „José Pinheiro Borda", Porto Alegre; Attendance: 55,000
Referee: Sergio Fabián Pezzotta (Argentina)
BRAZIL - PERU   **3-0(2-0)**
BRA: Júlio César Soares de Espíndola, Daniel Alves da Silva „Dani Alves", Ânderson Luís da Silva „Luisão" (12.João Miranda de Souza Filho), Lucimar Ferreira da Silva „Lúcio", Kléber de Carvalho Corrêa, Felipe Melo de Carvalho, Gilberto Aparecido da Silva, Elano Ralph Blumer (77.Ronaldo de Assis Moreira „Ronaldinho"), Ricardo Izecson dos Santos Leite „Kaká", Róbson de Souza „Robinho" (70.Alexandre Rodrigues da Silva „Alexandre Pato"), Luís Fabiano Clemente. Trainer: Carlos Caetano Bledorn Verri „Dunga".
PER: Leao Butrón Gotuzzo, Alberto Junior Rodríguez Valdelomar, Ámilton Jair Prado Barrón, Walter Ricardo Vílchez Soto, Carlos Augusto Zambrano Ochandarte, Nolberto Albino Solano Todco (70.José Carlos Fernández Piedra), Pedro Alejandro García de la Cruz (63.Alexander Gustavo Sánchez Reyes), Juan Carlos La Rosa Llontop, Luis Alberto Ramírez Lucay (80.Piero Fernando Alva Niezen), Rainer Torres Salas, Johan Javier Fano Espinoza. Trainer: José Guillermo del Solar Alvarez-Calderón.

113

Goals: 1-0 Luís Fabiano Clemente (18 penalty), 2-0 Luís Fabiano Clemente (27), 3-0 Felipe Melo de Carvalho (64).
Cautions: Nolberto Albino Solano Todco, Leao Butrón Gotuzzo.

06.06.2009, Estadio Centenario, Montevideo; Attendance: 52,000
Referee: Saúl Esteban Laverni (Argentina)
URUGUAY - BRAZIL   **0-4(0-2)**
URU: Mario Sebastián Viera Galaín, Diego Roberto Godín Leal, Carlos Adrián Valdez Suárez, José Martín Cáceres Silva, Victorio Maximiliano Pereira Páez, Álvaro Daniel Pereira Barragán (66.Álvaro Fernández), Sebastián Eguren Ledesma, Diego Fernando Pérez Aguado (46.Washington Sebastián Abreu Gallo), Jorge Andrés Martínez Barrios, Diego Martín Forlán Corazo (Cap), Luis Alberto Suárez Díaz (74.Edinson Roberto Cavani Gómez). Trainer: Óscar Wáshington Tabárez Silva.
BRA: Júlio César Soares de Espíndola, Daniel Alves da Silva „Dani Alves", Juan Silveira dos Santos, Lucimar Ferreira da Silva „Lúcio", Kléber de Carvalho Corrêa, Felipe Melo de Carvalho, Gilberto Aparecido da Silva, Elano Ralph Blumer (66.Ramires Santos do Nascimento), Ricardo Izecson dos Santos Leite „Kaká" (85.Josué Anunciado de Oliveira), Róbson de Souza „Robinho" (85.Júlio César Baptista), Luís Fabiano Clemente. Trainer: Carlos Caetano Bledorn Verri „Dunga".
Goals: 0-1 Daniel Alves da Silva „Dani Alves" (12), 0-2 Juan Silveira dos Santos (36), 0-3 Luís Fabiano Clemente (52), 0-4 Ricardo Izecson dos Santos Leite „Kaká" (75 penalty).
Cautions: Carlos Adrián Valdez Suárez, Sebastián Eguren Ledesma / Luís Fabiano Clemente,
Sent off: Luís Fabiano Clemente (65), Victorio Maximiliano Pereira Páez (86).

06.06.2009, Estadio „Hernán Siles Zuazo", La Paz; Attendance: 23,427
Referee: Carlos Vera (Ecuador)
BOLIVIA - VENEZUELA   **0-1(0-1)**
BOL: Carlos Erwin Arias Eguez, Ronald Raldes Balcázar, Ronald Taylor Rivero Khun, Miguel Ángel Hoyos Guzmán, Abdón Reyes Cardozo, Ronald Lázaro García Justiniano (77.Gilbert Álvarez), Leonel Alfredo Reyes Saravia, Joselito Vaca Velasco (63.Pablo Daniel Escobar Olivetti), Álex Rodrigo da Rosa Dornelles, Diego Aroldo Cabrera Flores (46.César Gerardo Yacerotte), Marcelo Moreno Martins. Trainer: Erwin Sánchez Freking.
VEN: Rafael Enrique Romo Pérez, Pedro Luis Boada Noya, José Manuel Velázquez Rodríguez, Grenddy Adrián Perozo, José Yégüez (63.Carlos Eduardo Salazar), Louis Ángelo Peña (55.Pedro Alfonso Fernández Camacho), Francisco Javier Flores Sequera, Giácomo Di Giorgi, Luis Manuel Seijas Gunther, Giancarlo Gregorio Maldonado Marrero, Juan Enrique García Rivas (69.Alexander Rondón Heredia). Trainer: César Alejandro Farías.
Goal: 0-1 Ronald Taylor Rivero Khun (33 own goal).
Cautions: Leonel Alfredo Reyes Saravia, César Gerardo Yacerotte, Ronald Taylor Rivero Khun, Marcelo Moreno Martins / Juan Enrique García Rivas, Luis Manuel Seijas Gunther, Giácomo Di Giorgi, Rafael Enrique Romo Pérez, Pedro Luis Boada Noya, Alexander Rondón Heredia, Grenddy Adrián Perozo.
Sent off: Marcelo Moreno Martins (80), Leonel Alfredo Reyes Saravia (90+2).

06.06.2009, Estadio Monumental „Antonio Vespucio Liberti", Buenos Aires; Attendance: 55,000
Referee: René Ortubé Betancourt (Bolivia)
ARGENTINA - COLOMBIA   **1-0(1-0)**
ARG: Mariano Gonzalo Andújar, Martín Gastón Demichelis, Daniel Alberto Díaz, Gabriel Iván Heinze, Fernando Rubén Gago (46.Javier Adelmar Zanetti), Javier Alejandro Mascherano, Jonás Manuel Gutiérrez, Juan Sebastián Verón, Lionel Andrés Messi, Sergio Leonel Agüero del Castillo (40.Diego Alberto Milito), Carlos Alberto Tévez (83.Nicolás Andrés Burdisso). Trainer: Diego Armando Maradona.
COL: David Ospina Ramírez, Luis Amaranto Perea Mosquera, Mario Alberto Yepes Díaz, Cristián Eduardo Zapata Valencia, Pablo Stifer Armero (82.Carlos Darwin Quintero Villalba), Vladimir Marín Ríos (65.Gustavo Adrián Ramos Vásquez), Juan Camilo Zúñiga Mosquera, Freddy Alejandro Guarín Vásquez, Fabián Andrés Vargas Rivera, Radamel Falcao García Zárate (73.Hugo Rodalega Martínez),

Wason Libardo Rentería Cuesta. Trainer: Eduardo Lara Lozano.
Goal: 1-0 Daniel Alberto Díaz (55).
Cautions: Javier Alejandro Mascherano, Martín Gastón Demichelis / Luis Amaranto Perea Mosquera, Vladimir Marín Ríos, Pablo Stifer Armero, Fabián Andrés Vargas Rivera.

06.06.2009, Estadio Defensores del Chaco, Asunción; Attendance: 34,000
Referee: Sergio Fabián Pezzotta (Argentina)
PARAGUAY - CHILE   **0-2(0-1)**
PAR: Justo Wilmar Villar Viveros, Julio César Cáceres López, Marcos Antonio Cáceres, Julio César Manzur Caffarena, Denis Ramón Caniza Acuña, Édgar Osvaldo Barreto Cáceres (49.Osvaldo David Martínez Arce), Víctor Javier Cáceres Centurión, Cristian Miguel Riveros Núñez, Enrique Daniel Vera Torres (59.Eduardo Fabián Ledesma Trinidad), Óscar René Cardozo Marín (61.Edgar Benítez Santander), Nelson Antonio Haedo Valdéz. Trainer: Gerardo Daniel Martino (Argentina).
CHI: Claudio Andrés Bravo Muñoz, Gonzalo Alejandro Jara Reyes, Waldo Alonso Ponce Carrizo, Gary Alexis Medel Soto, Carlos Emilio Carmona Tello, Marco Andrés Estrada Quinteros, Matías Ariel Fernández Fernández, Mark Dennis González Hoffman (46.Rodrigo Javier Millar Carvajal), Alexis Alejandro Sánchez Sánchez (88.Fabián Ariel Orellana Valenzuela), Humberto Andrés Suazo Pontivo (72.Héctor Raúl Mancilla), Jean André Emanuel Beausejour Coliqueo. Trainer: Marcelo Alberto Bielsa Caldera (Argentina).
Goals: 0-1 Matías Ariel Fernández Fernández (13), 0-2 Humberto Andrés Suazo Pontivo (50).
Cautions: Marcos Antonio Cáceres, Julio César Manzur Caffarena, Óscar René Cardozo Marín, Nelson Antonio Haedo Valdéz / Marco Andrés Estrada Quinteros, Carlos Emilio Carmona Tello.

07.06.2009, Estadio Monumental, Lima; Attendance: 17,050
Referee: Carlos Manuel Torres (Paraguay)
PERU - ECUADOR   **1-2(0-1)**
PER: Raúl Omar Fernández Valverde, Alberto Junior Rodríguez Valdelomar, Ámilton Jair Prado Barrón (62.Alexander Gustavo Sánchez Reyes), Walter Ricardo Vílchez Soto, Carlos Augusto Zambrano Ochandarte, Juan Manuel Vargas Risco, Paolo Giancarlo De La Haza Urquiza, Luis Alberto Ramírez Lucay (46.Roberto Merino Ramírez), Rainer Torres Salas (79.Josepmir Aaron Ballon Villacorta), José Paolo Guerrero Gonzales, Johan Javier Fano Espinoza. Trainer: José Guillermo del Solar Alvarez-Calderón.
ECU: Marcelo Ramón Elizaga Ferrero, Julio Marcelo Fleitas Silveira, Jorge Daniel Guagua Tamayo, Néicer Reasco Yano, Segundo Alejandro Castillo Nazareno, Walter Orlando Ayoví Corozo, Christian Fernando Noboa Tello, Édison Vicente Méndez Méndez, Jefferson Antonio Montero Vite (83.Isaac Bryan Mina Arboleda), Pablo David Palacios Herreria (60.Joffre David Guerrón Méndez), Carlos Vicente Tenorio Medina (87.Fernando Roberto Hidalgo Maldonado). Trainer: Sixto Rafael Vizuete Toapanta.
Goals: 0-1 Jefferson Antonio Montero Vite (38), 1-1 Juan Manuel Vargas Risco (52), 1-2 Carlos Vicente Tenorio Medina (59).
Cautions: Ámilton Jair Prado Barrón / Julio Marcelo Fleitas Silveira, Néicer Reasco Yano, Pablo David Palacios Herreria, Isaac Bryan Mina Arboleda.

10.06.2009, Estadio Olímpico Atahualpa, Quito; Attendance: 36,359
Referee: Carlos Chandía Alarcón (Chile)
ECUADOR - ARGENTINA   **2-0(0-0)**
ECU: Marcelo Ramón Elizaga Ferrero, Giovanny Patricio Espinoza Pabón, Iván Jacinto Hurtado Angulo, Néicer Reasco Yano, Segundo Alejandro Castillo Nazareno, Walter Orlando Ayoví Corozo, Christian Fernando Noboa Tello (46.Pablo David Palacios Herreria), Édison Vicente Méndez Méndez, Luis Antonio Valencia Mosquera, Felipe Salvador Caicedo Corozo (79.Joffre David Guerrón Méndez), Carlos Vicente Tenorio Medina (13.Jefferson Antonio Montero Vite). Trainer: Sixto Rafael Vizuete Toapanta.
ARG: Mariano Gonzalo Andújar, Javier Adelmar Zanetti, Martín Gastón Demichelis, Nicolás Hernán Otamendi, Gabriel Iván Heinze (83.Diego Alberto Milito), Maximiliano Rubén Rodríguez, Sebastián

Alejandro Battaglia, Fernando Rubén Gago (75.Juan Sebastián Verón), Jonás Manuel Gutiérrez, Lionel Andrés Messi, Carlos Alberto Tévez (67.Gonzalo Rubén Bergessio). Trainer: Diego Armando Maradona.
Goals: 1-0 Walter Orlando Ayoví Corozo (72), Pablo David Palacios Herreria (83).
Cautions: Christian Fernando Noboa Tello, Marcelo Ramón Elizaga Ferrero, Luis Antonio Valencia Mosquera / Jonás Manuel Gutiérrez.

10.06.2009, Estadio „Atanasio Girardot", Medellín; Attendance: 32,300
Referee: Carlos Eugênio Simon (Brazil)
COLOMBIA - PERU   **1-0(1-0)**
COL: David Ospina Ramírez, Luis Amaranto Perea Mosquera, Mario Alberto Yepes Díaz, Cristián Eduardo Zapata Valencia, Juan Camilo Zúñiga Mosquera, Vladimir Marín Ríos,Freddy Alejandro Guarín Vásquez, Fabián Andrés Vargas Rivera (54.Abel Enrique Aguilar Tapias), Macnelly Torres Berrío (67.Juan Pablo Pino Puello), Radamel Falcao García Zárate, Wason Libardo Rentería Cuesta (46.Hugo Rodallega Martínez). Trainer: Eduardo Lara Lozano.
PER: Leao Butrón Gotuzzo, Alberto Junior Rodríguez Valdelomar, Walter Ricardo Vílchez Soto, Carlos Augusto Zambrano Ochandarte, Juan Manuel Vargas Risco (21.Luis Enrique Trujillo Ortiz), Paolo Giancarlo De La Haza Urquiza, Josepmir Aaron Ballon Villacorta (81.Alexander Gustavo Sánchez Reyes), Juan Carlos La Rosa Llontop, Luis Alberto Ramírez Lucay, Johan Javier Fano Espinoza, José Paolo Guerrero Gonzales (87.Hernán Rengifo Trigoso). Trainer: José Guillermo del Solar Alvarez-Calderón.
Goal: 1-0 Radamel Falcao García Zárate (25).
Cautions: Hugo Rodallega Martínez / José Paolo Guerrero Gonzales, Johan Javier Fano Espinoza, Luis Enrique Trujillo Ortiz, Juan Carlos La Rosa Llontop.

10.06.2009, Estádio „José do Rego Maciel", Recife; Attendance: 56,682
Referee: Óscar Julián Ruiz Acosta (Colombia)
BRAZIL - PARAGUAY   **2-1(1-1)**
BRA: Júlio César Soares de Espíndola, Daniel Alves da Silva „Dani Alves", Juan Silveira dos Santos, Lucimar Ferreira da Silva „Lúcio", Kléber de Carvalho Corrêa, Felipe Melo de Carvalho, Gilberto Aparecido da Silva, Elano Ralph Blumer (60.Ramires Santos do Nascimento), Ricardo Izecson dos Santos Leite „Kaká", Róbson de Souza „Robinho" (85.José Kléberson Pereira), Nilmar Honorato da Silva (74.Alexandre Rodrigues da Silva „Alexandre Pato"). Trainer: Carlos Caetano Bledorn Verri „Dunga".
PAR: Justo Wilmar Villar Viveros, Julio César Cáceres López, Paulo César da Silva Barrios, Darío Anastacio Verón Maldonado, Denis Ramón Caniza Acuña, Carlos Bonet Cáceres (70.Edgar Benítez Santander), Víctor Javier Cáceres Centurión, Eduardo Fabián Ledesma Trinidad (61.Sergio Daniel Aquino), Cristian Miguel Riveros Núñez, Osvaldo David Martínez Arce (77.Dante Rafael López Fariña), Salvador Cabañas Ortega. Trainer: Gerardo Daniel Martino (Argentina).
Goals: 0-1 Salvador Cabañas Ortega (25), 1-1 Róbson de Souza „Robinho" (40), 2-1 Nilmar Honorato da Silva (49).
Cautions: Felipe Melo de Carvalho, Lucimar Ferreira da Silva „Lúcio", Ramires Santos do Nascimento / Víctor Javier Cáceres Centurión, Julio César Cáceres López.

10.06.2009, Estadio Nacional „Julio Martínez Prádanos", Santiago; Attendance: 60,124
Referee: Roberto Carlos Silvera (Uruguay)
CHILE - BOLIVIA   **4-0(1-0)**
CHI: Claudio Andrés Bravo Muñoz, Gonzalo Alejandro Jara Reyes, Waldo Alonso Ponce Carrizo, Gary Alexis Medel Soto, Marco Andrés Estrada Quinteros, Rodrigo Javier Millar Carvajal (84.Mauricio Aníbal Isla Isla), Matías Ariel Fernández Fernández (68.Jorge Luis Valdivia Toro), Mark Dennis González Hoffman, Alexis Alejandro Sánchez Sánchez, Humberto Andrés Suazo Pontivo (84.Héctor Raúl Mancilla), Jean André Emanuel Beausejour Coliqueo. Trainer: Marcelo Alberto Bielsa Caldera (Argentina).
BOL: Carlos Erwin Arias Eguez, Juan Manuel Peña Montaño, Ronald Raldes Balcázar, Ronald Taylor

116

Rivero Khun, Christian Israel Vargas Claros, Ignacio Awad García Justiniano, Ronald Lázaro García Justiniano, Didí Torrico Camacho (57.Abdón Reyes Cardozo), Jaime Robles Céspedes (84.Joselito Vaca Velasco), Álex Rodrigo da Rosa Dornelles (46.César Gerardo Yacerotte), Pablo Daniel Escobar Olivetti. Trainer: Erwin Sánchez Freking.
Goals: 1-0 Jean André Emanuel Beausejour Coliqueo (43), 2-0 Marco Andrés Estrada Quinteros (74), 3-0 Alexis Alejandro Sánchez Sánchez (78), 4-0 Alexis Alejandro Sánchez Sánchez (88).
Cautions: Waldo Alonso Ponce Carrizo / Ronald Lázaro García Justiniano, Christian Israel Vargas Claros, Ronald Taylor Rivero Khun, Ignacio Awad García Justiniano.
Sent off: Ignacio Awad García Justiniano (72).

10.06.2009, Estadio Polideportivo Cachamay, Puerto Ordaz; Attendance: 37,000
Referee: Sálvio Spínola Fagundes Filho (Brazil)
VENEZUELA - URUGUAY   **2-2(1-0)**
VEN: Renny Vicente Vega Hernández, Gerzon Armando Chacón Varela (57.José Manuel Velázquez Rodríguez), José Manuel Rey Cortegoso, Carlos Eduardo Salazar, Juan José Fuenmayor Núñez, Franklin José Lucena Peña, Tomás Eduardo Rincón Hernández, César Eduardo González Amais (70.Louis Ángelo Peña), Juan Fernando Arango Sáenz, Giancarlo Gregorio Maldonado Marrero (62.Nicolás Ladislao Fedor Flores), Alejandro Enrique Moreno Riera. Trainer: César Alejandro Farías.
URU: Juan Guillermo Castillo Iriart, Diego Roberto Godín Leal, Diego Alfredo Lugano Moreno (Cap), José Martín Cáceres Silva (80.Edinson Roberto Cavani Gómez), Jorge Ciro Fucile Perdomo, Álvaro Daniel Pereira Barragán, Miguel Ángel Amado Alanis, Diego Fernando Pérez Aguado, Álvaro Fernández (46.Cristian Gabriel Rodríguez Barotti), Diego Martín Forlán Corazo, Luis Alberto Suárez Díaz (65.Washington Sebastián Abreu Gallo). Trainer: Óscar Wáshington Tabárez Silva.
Goals: 1-0 Giancarlo Gregorio Maldonado Marrero (9), 1-1 Luis Alberto Suárez Díaz (63), 1-2 Diego Martín Forlán Corazo (72), 2-2 José Manuel Rey Cortegoso (74).
Cautions: Louis Ángelo Peña / José Martín Cáceres Silva, Diego Alfredo Lugano Moreno, Edinson Roberto Cavani Gómez, Diego Fernando Pérez Aguado, Diego Martín Forlán Corazo.

05.09.2009, Estadio „Atanasio Girardot", Medellín; Attendance: 42,000
Referee: Sergio Fabián Pezzotta (Argentina)
COLOMBIA - ECUADOR   **2-0(0-0)**
COL: Agustín Julio Castro, Iván Ramiro Córdoba Sepúlveda, Luis Amaranto Perea Mosquera, Mario Alberto Yepes Díaz, Pablo Stifer Armero, Juan Camilo Zúñiga Mosquera (65.Jackson Arley Martínez Valencia), Freddy Alejandro Guarín Vásquez, Giovanni Andrés Moreno Cardona, Fabián Andrés Vargas Rivera (43.Jhon Eduis Viáfara Mina), Radamel Falcao García Zárate (53.Giovanni Hernández Soto), Teófilo Antonio Gutiérrez Rocancio. Trainer: Eduardo Lara Lozano.
ECU: José Francisco Cevallos Villavicencio, Giovanny Patricio Espinoza Pabón, Iván Jacinto Hurtado Angulo, Néicer Reasco Yano, Segundo Alejandro Castillo Nazareno, Walter Orlando Ayoví Corozo, Christian Fernando Noboa Tello, Édison Vicente Méndez Méndez (90.Jefferson Antonio Montero Vite), Luis Antonio Valencia Mosquera, Christian Rogelio Benítez Betancourt, Carlos Vicente Tenorio Medina (23.Pablo David Palacios Herreria). Trainer: Sixto Rafael Vizuete Toapanta.
Goals: 1-0 Jackson Arley Martínez Valencia (82), Teófilo Antonio Gutiérrez Rocancio (90+4).
Cautions: Mario Alberto Yepes Díaz / Néicer Reasco Yano, Pablo David Palacios Herreria, Giovanny Patricio Espinoza Pabón.
Sent off: Pablo David Palacios Herreria (49).

05.09.2009, Estadio Monumental, Lima; Attendance: 15,000
Referee: Carlos Chandía Alarcón (Chile)
PERU - URUGUAY   **1-0(0-0)**
PER: Leao Butrón Gotuzzo, Alberto Junior Rodríguez Valdelomar, Walter Ricardo Vílchez Soto, Carlos Augusto Zambrano Ochandarte, Juan Manuel Vargas Risco, Nolberto Albino Solano Todco (78.Rainer Torres Salas), Josepmir Aaron Ballon Villacorta, Paolo Giancarlo De La Haza Urquiza (46.Ámilton Jair Prado Barrón), Roberto Carlos Palacios Mestas, Daniel Chávez Castillo (59.Irven Beybe Ávila Acero), Hernán Rengifo Trigoso. Trainer: José Guillermo del Solar Alvarez-Calderón.

URU: Juan Guillermo Castillo Iriart, Diego Roberto Godín Leal, Diego Alfredo Lugano Moreno, Jorge Ciro Fucile Perdomo, Álvaro Daniel Pereira Barragán, Sebastián Eguren Ledesma (60.Álvaro Fernández), Walter Alejandro Gargano Guevara, Cristian Gabriel Rodríguez Barotti, Jorge Andrés Martínez Barrios (80.Jorge Marcelo Rodríguez Núñez), Washington Sebastián Abreu Gallo, Luis Alberto Suárez Díaz. Trainer: Óscar Wáshington Tabárez Silva.
Goal: 1-0 Hernán Rengifo Trigoso (86).
Cautions: Carlos Augusto Zambrano Ochandarte, Irven Beybe Ávila Acero, Juan Manuel Vargas Risco / Diego Alfredo Lugano Moreno, Cristian Gabriel Rodríguez Barotti.
Sent off: Diego Roberto Godín Leal (59).

05.09.2009, Estadio Defensores del Chaco, Asunción; Attendance: 25,094
Referee: Victor Hugo Carrillo (Peru)
PARAGUAY - BOLIVIA   **1-0(1-0)**
PAR: Justo Wilmar Villar Viveros, Paulo César da Silva Barrios, Claudio Marcelo Morel Rodríguez, Darío Anastacio Verón Maldonado, Carlos Bonet Cáceres, Eduardo Fabián Ledesma Trinidad (69.Édgar Osvaldo Barreto Cáceres), Cristian Miguel Riveros Núñez, Jonathan Santana Ghere, Osvaldo David Martínez Arce, Salvador Cabañas Ortega (88.Óscar René Cardozo Marín), Nelson Antonio Haedo Valdéz (75.Edgar Benítez Santander). Trainer: Gerardo Daniel Martino (Argentina).
BOL: Hugo Suárez Vaca, Luis Alberto Gutiérrez Herrera, Marvin Orlando Bejarano Jiménez, Luis Palacios, Edemir Rodríguez Mercado, Enrique Parada Salvatierra, Wálter Alberto Flores Condarco (53.Danner Pachi Pachi Bozo), Ronald Lázaro García Justiniano (83.Joselito Vaca Velasco), Jesús Alejandro Gómez Lanza, Pablo Daniel Escobar Olivetti (75.Diego Aroldo Cabrera Flores), Marcelo Moreno Martins. Trainer: Erwin Sánchez Freking.
Goal: 1-0 Salvador Cabañas Ortega (45+1 penalty).

05.09.2009, Estadio Gigante de Arroyito, Rosario; Attendance: 37,000
Referee: Óscar Julián Ruiz Acosta (Colombia)
ARGENTINA - BRAZIL   **1-3(0-2)**
ARG: Mariano Gonzalo Andújar, Javier Adelmar Zanetti, Sebastián Enrique Domínguez, Nicolás Hernán Otamendi, Gabriel Iván Heinze, Maximiliano Rubén Rodríguez (46.Sergio Leonel Agüero del Castillo), Javier Alejandro Mascherano, Juan Sebastián Verón, Jesús Alberto Dátolo, Lionel Andrés Messi, Carlos Alberto Tévez (68.Diego Alberto Milito). Trainer: Diego Armando Maradona.
BRA: Júlio César Soares de Espíndola, Maicon Douglas Sisenando, Ânderson Luís da Silva „Luisão", Lucimar Ferreira da Silva „Lúcio", André Clarindo dos Santos, Felipe Melo de Carvalho, Gilberto Aparecido da Silva, Elano Ralph Blumer (68.Daniel Alves da Silva „Dani Alves"), Ricardo Izecson dos Santos Leite „Kaká", Róbson de Souza „Robinho" (68.Ramires Santos do Nascimento), Luís Fabiano Clemente (77.Adriano Leite Ribeiro). Trainer: Carlos Caetano Bledorn Verri „Dunga".
Goals: 0-1 Ânderson Luís da Silva „Luisão" (23), 0-2 Luís Fabiano Clemente (30), 1-2 Jesús Alberto Dátolo (65), 1-3 Luís Fabiano Clemente (68).
Cautions: Javier Alejandro Mascherano, Juan Sebastián Verón / Lucimar Ferreira da Silva „Lúcio", Ricardo Izecson dos Santos Leite „Kaká", Ânderson Luís da Silva „Luisão", Luís Fabiano Clemente, Ramires Santos do Nascimento.

05.09.2009, Estadio Monumental „David Arellano", Santiago; Attendance: 44,000
Referee: René Ortubé Betancourt (Bolivia)
CHILE - VENEZUELA   **2-2(1-2)**
CHI: Claudio Andrés Bravo Muñoz, Gonzalo Alejandro Jara Reyes, Gary Alexis Medel Soto, Roberto Andrés Cereceda Guajardo (46.Rodrigo Javier Millar Carvajal), Mauricio Aníbal Isla Isla, Arturo Erasmo Vidal Pardo, Carlos Emilio Carmona Tello (46.Fabián Ariel Orellana Valenzuela), Matías Ariel Fernández Fernández, Alexis Alejandro Sánchez Sánchez, Humberto Andrés Suazo Pontivo (62.Jorge Luis Valdivia Toro), Jean André Emanuel Beausejour Coliqueo. Trainer: Marcelo Alberto Bielsa Caldera (Argentina).
VEN: Renny Vicente Vega Hernández, Gerzon Armando Chacón Varela (67.Pedro Luis Boada Noya), Oswaldo Augusto Vizcarrondo Araujo, José Manuel Rey Cortegoso, José Luis Granados Asprilla,

Franklin José Lucena Peña, Tomás Eduardo Rincón Hernández, Giácomo Di Giorgi (75.Ronald Alejandro Vargas Aranguren), Luis Manuel Seijas Gunther (64.Alejandro Enrique Moreno Riera), Juan Fernando Arango Sáenz, Giancarlo Gregorio Maldonado Marrero. Trainer: César Alejandro Farías.
Goals: 1-0 Arturo Erasmo Vidal Pardo (11), 1-1 Giancarlo Gregorio Maldonado Marrero (34), 1-2 José Manuel Rey Cortegoso (45+1), 2-2 Rodrigo Javier Millar Carvajal (53).
Cautions: Carlos Emilio Carmona Tello, Jorge Luis Valdivia Toro / Oswaldo Augusto Vizcarrondo Araujo, José Manuel Rey Cortegoso, Franklin José Lucena Peña, Tomás Eduardo Rincón Hernández, Giancarlo Gregorio Maldonado Marrero.

09.09.2009, Estadio „Hernán Siles Zuazo", La Paz; Attendance: 10,200
Referee: Héctor Walter Baldassi (Argentina)
BOLIVIA - ECUADOR   **1-3(0-1)**
BOL: Hugo Suárez Vaca, Marvin Orlando Bejarano Jiménez, Luis Gatty Ribeiro Roca, Ronald Taylor Rivero Khun, Edemir Rodríguez Mercado, Danner Pachi Pachi Bozo, Wálter Alberto Flores Condarco (46.Abdón Reyes Cardozo), Ronald Lázaro García Justiniano (64.Helmut Enrique Gutiérrez), Limberg Gutiérrez Mariscal, Diego Aroldo Cabrera Flores (51.César Gerardo Yacerotte), Marcelo Moreno Martins. Trainer: Erwin Sánchez Freking.
ECU: Marcelo Ramón Elizaga Ferrero, Giovanny Patricio Espinoza Pabón (61.Jorge Daniel Guagua Tamayo), Julio Marcelo Fleitas Silveira, Iván Jacinto Hurtado Angulo, Segundo Alejandro Castillo Nazareno, Walter Orlando Ayoví Corozo, Christian Fernando Noboa Tello, Édison Vicente Méndez Méndez, Luis Antonio Valencia Mosquera (80.Fernando Roberto Hidalgo Maldonado), Jefferson Antonio Montero Vite (75.Vicente Paúl Ambrosi Zambrano), Christian Rogelio Benítez Betancourt. Trainer: Sixto Rafael Vizuete Toapanta.
Goals: 0-1 Édison Vicente Méndez Méndez (4), 0-2 Luis Antonio Valencia Mosquera (46), 0-3 Christian Rogelio Benítez Betancourt (66), 1-3 César Gerardo Yacerotte (85).
Cautions: Wálter Alberto Flores Condarco, Ronald Taylor Rivero Khun.

09.09.2009, Estadio Centenario, Montevideo; Attendance: 30,000
Referee: Carlos Manuel Torres (Paraguay)
URUGUAY - COLOMBIA   **3-1(1-0)**
URU: Juan Guillermo Castillo Iriart, Carlos Adrián Valdez Suárez, Bruno Ramón Silva Barone, José Martín Cáceres Silva, Álvaro Daniel Pereira Barragán, Walter Alejandro Gargano Guevara, Diego Fernando Pérez Aguado, Cristian Gabriel Rodríguez Barotti (81.Sebastián Eguren Ledesma), Edinson Roberto Cavani Gómez (35.Andrés Scotti Ponce de León), Diego Martín Forlán Corazo, Luis Alberto Suárez Díaz (90+1.Washington Sebastián Abreu Gallo). Trainer: Óscar Wáshington Tabárez Silva.
COL: Agustín Julio Castro, Iván Ramiro Córdoba Sepúlveda, Luis Amaranto Perea Mosquera, Mario Alberto Yepes Díaz, Pablo Stifer Armero, Abel Enrique Aguilar Tapias, Freddy Alejandro Guarín Vásquez, Giovanni Andrés Moreno Cardona (60.Giovanni Hernández Soto), Jhon Eduis Viáfara Mina (60.Jackson Arley Martínez Valencia), Teófilo Antonio Gutiérrez Rocancio, Gustavo Adrián Ramos Vásquez (81.Dorlan Mauricio Pabón Ríos). Trainer: Eduardo Lara Lozano.
Goals: 1-0 Luis Alberto Suárez Díaz (7), 1-1 Jackson Arley Martínez Valencia (63), 2-1 Andrés Scotti Ponce de León (77), 3-1 Sebastián Eguren Ledesma (87).
Cautions: José Martín Cáceres Silva, Diego Fernando Pérez Aguado, Bruno Ramón Silva Barone.
Sent off: Carlos Adrián Valdez Suárez (30), Teófilo Antonio Gutiérrez Rocancio (46).

09.09.2009, Estadio Defensores del Chaco, Asunción; Attendance: 38,000
Referee: Sálvio Spínola Fagundes Filho (Brazil)
PARAGUAY - ARGENTINA   **1-0(1-0)**
PAR: Justo Wilmar Villar Viveros, Julio César Cáceres López, Paulo César da Silva Barrios, Darío Anastacio Verón Maldonado, Aureliano Torres Román, Édgar Osvaldo Barreto Cáceres (82.Víctor Javier Cáceres Centurión), Cristian Miguel Riveros Núñez, Jonathan Santana Ghere (67.Eduardo Fabián Ledesma Trinidad), Enrique Daniel Vera Torres, Salvador Cabañas Ortega, Nelson Antonio Haedo Valdéz (80.Edgar Benítez Santander). Trainer: Gerardo Daniel Martino (Argentina).
ARG: Sergio Germán Romero, Javier Adelmar Zanetti, Sebastián Enrique Domínguez (80.Rolando

Carlos Schiavi), Gabriel Iván Heinze, Emiliano Ramiro Papa, Juan Sebastián Verón, Javier Alejandro Mascherano, Fernando Rubén Gago, Jesús Alberto Dátolo (46.Ezequiel Iván Lavezzi), Lionel Andrés Messi, Sergio Leonel Agüero del Castillo (59.Martín Palermo). Trainer: Diego Armando Maradona.
Goal: 1-0 Nelson Antonio Haedo Valdéz (27).
Cautions: Enrique Daniel Vera Torres, Julio César Cáceres López, Jonathan Santana Ghere, Aureliano Torres Román / Juan Sebastián Verón.
Sent off: Juan Sebastián Verón (53).

09.09.2009, Estádio Metropolitano „Roberto Santos", Salvador; Attendance: 30,000
Referee: Jorge Luis Larrionda Pietrafesa (Uruguay)
BRAZIL - CHILE   **4-2(2-1)**
BRA: Júlio César Soares de Espíndola, Maicon Douglas Sisenando, Ânderson Luís da Silva „Luisão", João Miranda de Souza Filho, André Clarindo dos Santos (70.Elano Ralph Blumer), Daniel Alves da Silva „Dani Alves", Felipe Melo de Carvalho, Gilberto Aparecido da Silva, Júlio César Baptista (68.Sandro Ranieri Guimarães Cordeiro), Adriano Leite Ribeiro (68.Diego Tardelli Martins), Nilmar Honorato da Silva. Trainer: Carlos Caetano Bledorn Verri „Dunga".
CHI: Claudio Andrés Bravo Muñoz, Gonzalo Alejandro Jara Reyes, Waldo Alonso Ponce Carrizo, Gary Alexis Medel Soto, Arturo Erasmo Vidal Pardo (46.Roberto Andrés Cereceda Guajardo), Carlos Emilio Carmona Tello, Rodrigo Javier Millar Carvajal (68.Mauricio Aníbal Isla Isla), Matías Ariel Fernández Fernández (68.Jorge Luis Valdivia Toro), Alexis Alejandro Sánchez Sánchez, Humberto Andrés Suazo Pontivo, Jean André Emanuel Beausejour Coliqueo. Trainer: Marcelo Alberto Bielsa Caldera (Argentina).
Goals: 1-0 Nilmar Honorato da Silva (31), 2-0 Júlio César Baptista (40), 2-1 Humberto Andrés Suazo Pontivo (45+1 penalty), 2-2 Humberto Andrés Suazo Pontivo (52), 3-2 Nilmar Honorato da Silva (74), 4-2 Nilmar Honorato da Silva (76).
Cautions: Gonzalo Alejandro Jara Reyes, Alexis Alejandro Sánchez Sánchez.
Sent off: Felipe Melo de Carvalho (50), Alexis Alejandro Sánchez Sánchez (77).

09.09.2009, Estadio Olímpico „Luis Ramos", Puerto la Cruz; Attendance: 31,703
Referee: Carlos Vera (Ecuador)
VENEZUELA - PERU   **3-1(1-1)**
VEN: Renny Vicente Vega Hernández, Pedro Luis Boada Noya, Oswaldo Augusto Vizcarrondo Araujo, José Manuel Rey Cortegoso, Juan José Fuenmayor Núñez, Franklin José Lucena Peña, Luis Manuel Seijas Gunther, Ronald Alejandro Vargas Aranguren, Juan Fernando Arango Sáenz (81.Giácomo Di Giorgi), Nicolás Ladislao Fedor Flores (83.Yonathan Alexander del Valle Rodríguez), Alejandro Enrique Moreno Riera (77.Alexander Rondón Heredia). Trainer: César Alejandro Farías.
PER: Leao Butrón Gotuzzo, Alberto Junior Rodríguez Valdelomar, Christian Guillermo Martín Ramos Garagay, Ámilton Jair Prado Barrón, Walter Ricardo Vílchez Soto, Nolberto Albino Solano Todco (68.Joel Melchor Sánchez Alegría), Josepmir Aaron Ballon Villacorta, Rainer Torres Salas (67.Henry Edson Quinteros Sánchez), Roberto Carlos Palacios Mestas, José Paolo Guerrero Gonzales (15.Hernán Rengifo Trigoso), Johan Javier Fano Espinoza. Trainer: José Guillermo del Solar Alvarez-Calderón.
Goals: 1-0 Nicolás Ladislao Fedor Flores (33), 1-1 Juan José Fuenmayor Núñez (41 own goal), 2-1 Nicolás Ladislao Fedor Flores (52), 3-1 Ronald Alejandro Vargas Aranguren (65).
Cautions: José Manuel Rey Cortegoso, Nicolás Ladislao Fedor Flores / Nolberto Albino Solano Todco, Johan Javier Fano Espinoza, Josepmir Aaron Ballon Villacorta.

10.10.2009, Estadio Monumental „Antonio Vespucio Liberti", Buenos Aires; Attendance: 38,019
Referee: René Ortubé Betancourt (Bolivia)
ARGENTINA - PERU   **2-1(0-0)**
ARG: Sergio Germán Romero, Jonás Manuel Gutiérrez, Rolando Carlos Schiavi, Gabriel Iván Heinze, Emiliano Adrian Insúa Zapata, Enzo Nicolás Pérez (46.Martín Palermo), Javier Alejandro Mascherano, Ángel Fabián di María, Pablo César Aimar Giordano (75.Federico Insúa), Lionel Andrés Messi, Gonzalo Gerardo Higuaín (67.Martín Gastón Demichelis). Trainer: Diego Armando Maradona.
PER: Leao Butrón Gotuzzo, Alberto Junior Rodríguez Valdelomar, Ámilton Jair Prado Barrón, Walter

Ricardo Vílchez Soto, Carlos Augusto Zambrano Ochandarte, Juan Manuel Vargas Risco, Nolberto Albino Solano Todco (65.Roberto Carlos Palacios Mestas), Josepmir Aaron Ballon Villacorta, Luis Alberto Ramírez Lucay (90.Juan Carlos La Rosa Llontop), Rainer Torres Salas, Johan Javier Fano Espinoza (71.Hernán Rengifo Trigoso). Trainer: José Guillermo del Solar Alvarez-Calderón.
Goals: 1-0 Gonzalo Gerardo Higuaín (48), 1-1 Hernán Rengifo Trigoso (89), 2-1 Martín Palermo (90+2).
Cautions: Martín Palermo / Carlos Augusto Zambrano Ochandarte.

10.10.2009, Estadio „Atanasio Girardot", Medellín; Attendance: 18,000
Referee: Victor Hugo Rivera (Peru)
COLOMBIA - CHILE   **2-4(1-2)**
COL: David Ospina Ramírez, Cristián Eduardo Zapata Valencia, Mario Alberto Yepes Díaz, Pablo Stifer Armero, Juan Camilo Zúñiga Mosquera, Freddy Alejandro Guarín Vásquez (56.Cristian Camilo Marrugo Rodríguez), Abel Enrique Aguilar Tapias, Dorlan Mauricio Pabón Ríos (62.Hugo Rodallega Martínez), Giovanni Hernández Soto (56.Giovanni Andrés Moreno Cardona), Radamel Falcao García Zárate, Jackson Arley Martínez Valencia. Trainer: Eduardo Lara Lozano.
CHI: Claudio Andrés Bravo Muñoz, Waldo Alonso Ponce Carrizo, Gary Alexis Medel Soto, Arturo Erasmo Vidal Pardo, Carlos Emilio Carmona Tello, Rodrigo Javier Millar Carvajal, Matías Ariel Fernández Fernández (31.Jorge Luis Valdivia Toro), Mark Dennis González Hoffman (63.Gonzalo Antonio Fierro Caniullán), Fabián Ariel Orellana Valenzuela, Humberto Andrés Suazo Pontivo, Jean André Emanuel Beausejour Coliqueo (46.Ismael Ignacio Fuentes Castro). Trainer: Marcelo Alberto Bielsa Caldera (Argentina).
Goals: 1-0 Jackson Arley Martínez Valencia (14), 1-1 Waldo Alonso Ponce Carrizo (34), 1-2 Humberto Andrés Suazo Pontivo (35), 2-2 Giovanni Andrés Moreno Cardona (53), 2-3 Jorge Luis Valdivia Toro (71), 2-4 Fabián Ariel Orellana Valenzuela (78).
Cautions: Mario Alberto Yepes Díaz, Abel Enrique Aguilar Tapias, Juan Camilo Zúñiga Mosquera / Matías Ariel Fernández Fernández, Mark Dennis González Hoffman, Carlos Emilio Carmona Tello, Arturo Erasmo Vidal Pardo.
Sent off:), Fabián Ariel Orellana Valenzuela (90+2).

10.10.2009, Estadio Olimpico „Atahualpa", Quito; Attendance: 42,700
Referee: Sálvio Spínola Fagundes Filho (Brazil)
ECUADOR - URUGUAY   **1-2(0-0)**
ECU: Marcelo Ramón Elizaga Ferrero, Giovanny Patricio Espinoza Pabón (79.Jorge Daniel Guagua Tamayo), Iván Jacinto Hurtado Angulo, Néicer Reasco Yano, Segundo Alejandro Castillo Nazareno, Walter Orlando Ayoví Corozo, Christian Fernando Noboa Tello (58.Jefferson Antonio Montero Vite), Édison Vicente Méndez Méndez, Luis Antonio Valencia Mosquera, Felipe Salvador Caicedo Corozo (66.Edmundo Salomón Zura de Jesús), Christian Rogelio Benítez Betancourt. Trainer: Sixto Rafael Vizuete Toapanta.
URU: Néstor Fernando Muslera Micol, Diego Alfredo Lugano Moreno (Cap), José Martín Cáceres Silva, Victorio Maximiliano Pereira Páez, Álvaro Daniel Pereira Barragán, Andrés Scotti Ponce de León, Walter Alejandro Gargano Guevara, Diego Fernando Pérez Aguado (73.Sebastián Eguren Ledesma), Jorge Marcelo Rodríguez Núñez (59.Jorge Ciro Fucile Perdomo), Diego Martín Forlán Corazo, Luis Alberto Suárez Díaz (85.Edinson Roberto Cavani Gómez). Trainer: Óscar Wáshington Tabárez Silva.
Goals: 1-0 Luis Antonio Valencia Mosquera (68), 1-1 Luis Alberto Suárez Díaz (69), 1-2 Diego Martín Forlán Corazo (90+3 penalty).
Cautions: Christian Fernando Noboa Tello, Luis Antonio Valencia Mosquera, Walter Orlando Ayoví Corozo, Marcelo Ramón Elizaga Ferrero / Diego Alfredo Lugano Moreno, Andrés Scotti Ponce de León.

10.10.2009, Estadio Polideportivo Cachamay, Puerto Ordaz; Attendance: 41,680
Referee: Carlos Chandía Alarcón (Chile)
VENEZUELA - PARAGUAY   **1-2(0-0)**
VEN: Renny Vicente Vega Hernández, Pedro Luis Boada Noya, Franklin José Lucena Peña, Oswaldo Augusto Vizcarrondo Araujo, Juan José Fuenmayor Núñez, Tomás Eduardo Rincón Hernández, Luis Manuel Seijas Gunther (67.Roberto José Rosales Altuve), César Eduardo González Amais (82.Alexander Rondón Heredia), Juan Fernando Arango Sáenz, Giancarlo Gregorio Maldonado Marrero (65.Alejandro Enrique Moreno Riera), Nicolás Ladislao Fedor Flores. Trainer: César Alejandro Farías.
PAR: Justo Wilmar Villar Viveros, Antolín Alcaraz Viveros, Paulo César da Silva Barrios, Darío Anastacio Verón Maldonado, Denis Ramón Caniza Acuña, Néstor Ezequiel Ortigoza, Cristian Miguel Riveros Núñez, Enrique Daniel Vera Torres, Osvaldo David Martínez Arce (57.Eduardo Fabián Ledesma Trinidad), Salvador Cabañas Ortega (68.Óscar René Cardozo Marín), Nelson Antonio Haedo Valdéz (73.Edgar Benítez Santander). Trainer: Gerardo Daniel Martino (Argentina).
Goals: 0-1 Salvador Cabañas Ortega (56), 0-2 Óscar René Cardozo Marín (80), 1-2 Alexander Rondón Heredia (85).
Cautions: Pedro Luis Boada Noya / Darío Anastacio Verón Maldonado.

11.10.2009, Estadio „Hernán Siles Zuazo", La Paz; Attendance: 16,557
Referee: Pablo Antonio Pozo Quinteros (Chile)
BOLIVIA - BRAZIL   **2-1(2-0)**
BOL: Carlos Erwin Arias Eguez, Ronald Raldes Balcázar, Ronald Taylor Rivero Khun, Wilder Zabala Perrogón, Ignacio Awad García Justiniano, Helmut Enrique Gutiérrez, Edgar Rolando Olivares Burgoa, Leonel Alfredo Reyes Saravia, Abdón Reyes Cardozo (74.Joselito Vaca Velasco), Juan Carlos Arce Justiniano (79.Danner Pachi Pachi Bozo), Marcelo Moreno Martins (81.Ricardo Pedriel Suárez). Trainer: Erwin Sánchez Freking.
BRA: Júlio César Soares de Espíndola, Maicon Douglas Sisenando, Ânderson Luís da Silva „Luisão", João Miranda de Souza Filho, André Clarindo dos Santos (67.Elano Ralph Blumer), Daniel Alves da Silva „Dani Alves", Josué Anunciado de Oliveira, Ramires Santos do Nascimento, Diego Souza (46.Alexandre Raphael Meschini „Alex Meschini"), Adriano Leite Ribeiro (46.Diego Tardelli Martins), Nilmar Honorato da Silva. Trainer: Carlos Caetano Bledorn Verri „Dunga".
Goals: 1-0 Edgar Rolando Olivares Burgoa (10), 2-0 Marcelo Moreno Martins (32), 2-1 Nilmar Honorato da Silva (70).
Cautions: Wilder Zabala Perrogón, Helmut Enrique Gutiérrez, Ronald Raldes Balcázar / Ramires Santos do Nascimento, André Clarindo dos Santos, Josué Anunciado de Oliveira, Daniel Alves da Silva „Dani Alves".

14.10.2009, Estadio „Alejandro Villanueva", Lima; Attendance: 4,373
Referee: Juan Soto (Venezuela)
PERU - BOLIVIA   **1-0(0-0)**
PER: Leao Butrón Gotuzzo, Alberto Junior Rodríguez Valdelomar, Ámilton Jair Prado Barrón (87.Marcio André Valverde Zamora), Walter Ricardo Vílchez Soto, Carlos Augusto Zambrano Ochandarte, Juan Manuel Vargas Risco, Nolberto Albino Solano Todco (69.Henry Edson Quinteros Sánchez), Josepmir Aaron Ballon Villacorta, Luis Alberto Ramírez Lucay (61.Roberto Carlos Palacios Mestas), Johan Javier Fano Espinoza, Hernán Rengifo Trigoso. Trainer: José Guillermo del Solar Alvarez-Calderón.
BOL: Carlos Erwin Arias Eguez, Ronald Taylor Rivero Khun, Edemir Rodríguez Mercado, Wilder Zabala Perrogón, Ignacio Awad García Justiniano, Jesús Alejandro Gómez Lanza (81.José Luis Chávez Sánchez), Edgar Rolando Olivares Burgoa (77.Pablo Daniel Escobar Olivetti), Leonel Alfredo Reyes Saravia, Rosauro Rivero Céspedes, Joselito Vaca Velasco (81.Ricardo Pedriel Suárez), Marcelo Moreno Martins. Trainer: Erwin Sánchez Freking.
Goal: 1-0 Johan Javier Fano Espinoza (54).
Cautions: Carlos Augusto Zambrano Ochandarte / Rosauro Rivero Céspedes, Wilder Zabala Perrogón,

Ignacio Awad García Justiniano, Ronald Taylor Rivero Khun.
Sent off: Rosauro Rivero Céspedes (39), Johan Javier Fano Espinoza (55).

14.10.2009, Estádio Morenão (Universitário Pedro Pedrossian), Campo Grande; Attendance: 23,746
Referee: Victor Hugo Carrillo (Peru)
BRAZIL - VENEZUELA   0-0
BRA: Júlio César Soares de Espíndola, Maicon Douglas Sisenando, Ânderson Luís da Silva „Luisão", João Miranda de Souza Filho, Filipe (75.Alexandre Raphael Meschini „Alex Meschini"), Gilberto Aparecido da Silva, Lucas Pezzini Leiva, Ramires Santos do Nascimento (77.Elano Ralph Blumer), Ricardo Izecson dos Santos Leite „Kaká", Luís Fabiano Clemente (81.Diego Tardelli Martins), Nilmar Honorato da Silva. Trainer: Carlos Caetano Bledorn Verri „Dunga".
VEN: Renny Vicente Vega Hernández, Gerzon Armando Chacón Varela, José Manuel Rey Cortegoso, Oswaldo Augusto Vizcarrondo Araujo, José Luis Granados Asprilla, Giácomo Di Giorgi, Franklin José Lucena Peña, Tomás Eduardo Rincón Hernández (68.Luis Manuel Seijas Gunther), Juan Fernando Arango Sáenz (83.Nicolás Ladislao Fedor Flores), Giancarlo Gregorio Maldonado Marrero, Alejandro Enrique Moreno Riera (74.Alexander Rondón Heredia). Trainer: César Alejandro Farías.
Cautions: Luís Fabiano Clemente, Ânderson Luís da Silva „Luisão" / Gerzon Armando Chacón Varela, Oswaldo Augusto Vizcarrondo Araujo, Giácomo Di Giorgi, José Luis Granados Asprilla, Tomás Eduardo Rincón Hernández.
Sent off: João Miranda de Souza Filho (56).

14.10.2009, Estadio Monumental „David Arellano", Santiago; Attendance: 47,000
Referee: Carlos Arecio Amarilla Demarqui (Paraguay)
CHILE - ECUADOR   1-0(0-0)
CHI: Claudio Andrés Bravo Muñoz, Waldo Alonso Ponce Carrizo, Gary Alexis Medel Soto, Roberto Andrés Cereceda Guajardo (76.Ismael Ignacio Fuentes Castro), Arturo Erasmo Vidal Pardo (67.Gonzalo Alejandro Jara Reyes), Manuel Rolando Iturra Urrutia, Rodrigo Javier Millar Carvajal, Jorge Luis Valdivia Toro, Alexis Alejandro Sánchez Sánchez, Humberto Andrés Suazo Pontivo, Jean André Emanuel Beausejour Coliqueo (31.Esteban Efraín Paredes Quintanilla). Trainer: Marcelo Alberto Bielsa Caldera (Argentina).
ECU: Marcelo Ramón Elizaga Ferrero, Néicer Reasco Yano, Iván Jacinto Hurtado Angulo, Jorge Daniel Guagua Tamayo, Walter Orlando Ayoví Corozo, Segundo Alejandro Castillo Nazareno, Édison Vicente Méndez Méndez (76.Edmundo Salomón Zura de Jesús), Fernando Roberto Hidalgo Maldonado, Christian Rolando Lara Anangonó (57.Joao Robin Rojas Mendoza), Christian Rogelio Benítez Betancourt, Jefferson Antonio Montero Vite. Trainer: Sixto Rafael Vizuete Toapanta.
Goal: 1-0 Humberto Andrés Suazo Pontivo (53).
Cautions: Gary Alexis Medel Soto, Humberto Andrés Suazo Pontivo, Roberto Andrés Cereceda Guajardo / Segundo Alejandro Castillo Nazareno, Jorge Daniel Guagua Tamayo, Fernando Roberto Hidalgo Maldonado.
Sent off: Segundo Alejandro Castillo Nazareno (84).

14.10.2009, Estadio Centenario, Montevideo; Attendance: 60,000
Referee: Carlos Arecio Amarilla Demarqui (Paraguay)
URUGUAY - ARGENTINA   0-1(0-0)
URU: Néstor Fernando Muslera Micol, Diego Alfredo Lugano Moreno (Cap), José Martín Cáceres Silva, Victorio Maximiliano Pereira Páez, Álvaro Daniel Pereira Barragán, Andrés Scotti Ponce de León, Walter Alejandro Gargano Guevara (71.Cristian Gabriel Rodríguez Barotti), Diego Fernando Pérez Aguado, Jorge Marcelo Rodríguez Núñez (59.Edinson Roberto Cavani Gómez), Diego Martín Forlán Corazo, Luis Alberto Suárez Díaz (77.Washington Sebastián Abreu Gallo). Trainer: Óscar Wáshington Tabárez Silva.
ARG: Sergio Germán Romero, Nicolás Hernán Otamendi, Martín Gastón Demichelis, Rolando Carlos Schiavi, Gabriel Iván Heinze, Jonás Manuel Gutiérrez, Javier Alejandro Mascherano, Juan Sebastián Verón, Ángel Fabián di María (75.Luciano Fabián Monzón), Lionel Andrés Messi (85.Carlos Alberto Tévez), Gonzalo Gerardo Higuaín (79.Mario Ariel Bolatti). Trainer: Diego Armando Maradona.

Goal: 0-1 Mario Ariel Bolatti (84).
Cautions: Victorio Maximiliano Pereira Páez, Diego Fernando Pérez Aguado, José Martín Cáceres Silva, Andrés Scotti Ponce de León / Gabriel Iván Heinze, Nicolás Hernán Otamendi, Sergio Germán Romero, Luciano Fabián Monzón.
Sent off: José Martín Cáceres Silva (83), Cristian Gabriel Rodríguez Barotti (90+3).

14.10.2009, Estadio Defensores del Chaco, Asunción; Attendance: 17,503
Referee: Paulo Cesar De Oliveira (Brazil)
PARAGUAY - COLOMBIA   **0-2(0-0)**
PAR: Justo Wilmar Villar Viveros, Julio César Cáceres López, Paulo César da Silva Barrios, Elvis Israel Marecos (65.Óscar René Cardozo Marín), Darío Anastacio Verón Maldonado, Carlos Bonet Cáceres, Cristian Miguel Riveros Núñez, Jonathan Santana Ghere, Jorge Daniel Achucarro (56.Osvaldo David Martínez Arce), Salvador Cabañas Ortega, Nelson Antonio Haedo Valdéz (76.Edgar Benítez Santander). Trainer: Gerardo Daniel Martino (Argentina).
COL: David Ospina Ramírez, Iván Ramiro Córdoba Sepúlveda, Cristián Eduardo Zapata Valencia, Pablo Stifer Armero, Abel Enrique Aguilar Tapias, Vladimir Marín Ríos, José Yulián Anchico Patiño, Freddy Alejandro Guarín Vásquez, Radamel Falcao García Zárate (54.Hugo Rodallega Martínez), Jackson Arley Martínez Valencia (77.Teófilo Antonio Gutiérrez Rocancio), Gustavo Adrián Ramos Vásquez (80.Jhersson Enrique Córdoba Ospina). Trainer: Eduardo Lara Lozano.
Goals: 0-1 Gustavo Adrián Ramos Vásquez (61), 0-2 Hugo Rodallega Martínez (80).
Cautions: Cristian Miguel Riveros Núñez, Osvaldo David Martínez Arce / Iván Ramiro Córdoba Sepúlveda, Abel Enrique Aguilar Tapias, Pablo Stifer Armero.

NORTH, CENTRAL AMERICA AND CARIBBEAN

35 national teams entered the CONCACAF qualification stage for the 2010 FIFA World Cup. Three teams could qualify directly for the final tournament, a fourth team had the possibility to qualify too after playing an Intercontinental Play-off against a South American team.
The 35 national teams were divided into six groups (pots) according to FIFA World Rankings 2007:

Pot A (CONCACAF Places 1-3):
Mexico, United States, Costa Rica (top seeds for each 3rd Round Group)

Pot B (CONCACAF Places 4-6):
Honduras, Panama, Trinidad & Tobago (second seeds for each 3rd Round Group)

Pot C (CONCACAF Places 7-12):
Jamaica, Cuba, Haiti, Guatemala, Canada, Guyana

Pot D (CONCACAF Place 13):
Saint Vincent and The Grenadines

Pot E (CONCACAF Places 14-24):
Barbados, Suriname, Bermuda, Antigua & Barbuda, Saint Kitts and Nevis, Dominican Republic, El Salvador, Bahamas, Nicaragua, Grenada, Saint Lucia

Pot F (CONCACAF Places 25-35):
Turks and Caicos Islands, Netherlands Antilles, British Virgin Islands, Dominica, Cayman Islands, Puerto Rico, Anguilla, Belize, US Virgin Islands, Montserrat, Aruba

FIRST ROUND

Group 1A
| 06.02.2008 | Roseau | Dominica - Barbados | 1-1(1-1) |
| 26.03.2008 | Bridgetown | **Barbados** - Dominica | 1-0(0-0) |

Group 1B
| 06.02.2008 | Providenciales | Turks and Caicos Islands – Saint Lucia | 2-1(1-0) |
| 26.03.2008 | Vieux Fort | **Saint Lucia** - Turks and Caicos Islands | 2-0(1-0) |

Group 1C
| 03.02.2008 | Hamilton | Bermuda – Cayman Islands | 1-1(1-0) |
| 30.03.2008 | George Town | Cayman Islands - **Bermuda** | 1-3(0-2) |

Group 1D
| 06.02.2008 | Oranjestad | Aruba – Antigua and Barbuda | 0-3(0-3) |
| 26.03.2008 | Saint John's | **Antigua and Barbuda** - Aruba | 1-0(0-0) |

Group 2A
| 06.02.2008 | Guatemala City | Belize – Saint Kitts and Nevis | 3-1(2-1) |
| 26.03.2008 | Basseterre | Saint Kitts and Nevis – **Belize** | 1-1(0-1) |

Group 2B
| 26.03.2008 | Nassau | Bahamas – British Virgin Islands | 1-1(0-0) |
| 30.03.2008 | Nassau | British Virgin Islands - **Bahamas** | 2-2(0-1) |

Group 2C
| 26.03.2008 | Bayamón | **Puerto Rico** – Dominican Republic | 1-0(0-0,0-0) |

Group 3A

26.03.2008	St. George's	**Grenada** – US Virgin Islands	10-0(5-0)
Group 3B			
26.03.2008	Macoya (TRI)	Montserrat - **Suriname**	1-7(0-2)
Group 3C			
06.02.2008	San Salvador	El Salvador - Anguilla	12-0(4-0)
30.03.2008	Washington (USA)	Anguilla – **El Salvador**	0-4(0-4)
Group 3D			
06.02.2008	Diriamba	Nicaragua – Netherlands Antilles	0-1(0-1)
26.03.2008	Willemstad	**Netherlands Antilles** - Nicaragua	2-0(1-0)

All winners qualified for the Second Round.

Group 1A
06.02.2008, Windsor Park, Roseau; Attendance: 4,200
Referee: Walter Quesada Cordero (Costa Rica)
DOMINICA - BARBADOS   **1-1(1-1)**
DMA: Glenson Prince, Colin Bernard (85.Macaza White), Shern Dailey, Wayne Phillip, Paul Victor (60.Prince Austrie), Delbert Dailey, Ryan Edgar, Joel Etienne-Clarke, Daniel Francis (75.Lennard Remy), Sham John, Richard Pacquette. Trainer: Christopher Erickson.
BRB: Alvin Rouse, Dyson James, Jonathan Straker, Rondelle Vaughan (70.Riviere Williams), Bryan Neblett, Romell Brathwaite, Rashida Williams, Elvis Defreitas, Jonathan Nurse (59.Dwayne McClean), Norman Forde, Neil Harvey (67.John Parris). Trainer: Eyre Sealy.
Goals: 1-0 Richard Pacquette (21), 1-1 Rashida Williams (43).
Cautions: Wayne Phillip / Romell Brathwaite.

26.03.2008, Kensington Oval, Bridgetown; Attendance: 4,150
Referee: Carlos Alberto Batres González (Guatemala)
BARBADOS - DOMINICA   **1-0(0-0)**
BRB: Alvin Rouse, Dyson James, Bryan Neblett, Romell Brathwaite, Riviere Williams (69.Romelle Burgess), Jonathan Forte, Jonathan Nurse (64.Dwayne Stanford), Norman Forde (Cap) (85.John Parris), Rashida Williams, Elvis Defreitas, Emmerson Boyce. Trainer: Eyre Sealy.
DMA: Glenson Prince, Colin Bernard (Cap), Shern Dailey, Daniel Francis (89.Jerome Thomas), Delbert Dailey, Ryan Edgar (59.Euclid Bertrand), Joel Etienne-Clarke (71.Leo George), Jefferson Louis, Paul Victor, Macaza White, Richard Pacquette. Trainer: Christopher Erickson.
Goal: 1-0 Dwayne Stanford (80).
Cautions: Rashida Williams, Norman Forde / Macaza White, Richard Pacquette, Shern Dailey.
Sent off: Rashida Williams (59), Colin Bernard (59).

Group 1B
06.02.2008, National Stadium, Providenciales; Attendance: 2,200
Referee: Alfredo Whittaker (Cayman Islands)
TURKS AND CAICOS ISLANDS – SAINT LUCIA   **2-1(1-0)**
TCA: Ian Jones, Chris Bruno, Lee Coulton, Christopher Gannon, Charles Cook, Duan Glinton, Stephen Savage, Lenford Singh (46.Phillip Shearer), Billy Forbes, Gavin Glinton (Cap) (82.Ajah Johnson), David Lowery (90.Lagneau Brumvert). Trainer: Matthew Green (Bahamas).
LCA: Randy Poleon, Hezron Justin, Vernus Abbott, Levi Gilbert (72.Chad St. Croix), Shervon Jack, Everton Lambert (55.Nyhime Gilbert), Mogabi Polius, Germal Valcin (Cap), Angus William, Zaccheus Polius, Troy Prospere (62.Justin St. Clair). Trainer: Terrence Caroo.
Goals: 1-0 David Lowery (31), 2-0 Gavin Clinton (74), 2-1 Nyhime Gilbert (90+2).
Cautions: Charles Cook / Germal Valcin.

26.03.2008, Vieux Fort National Stadium, Vieux Fort; Attendance: 1,200
Referee: Mark Forde (Barbados)
SAINT LUCIA – TURKS AND CAICOS ISLANDS   **2-0(1-0)**
LCA: Danny Michael, Sheldon Emmanuel, John Perry Joseph, Vernus Abbott, Everton Lambert (67.Sheldon Mark), Zacchaeus Polius (56.Chad St. Croix), Germal Valcin (Cap), Titus Elva (89.Jack Shervon), Fabian Joseph, Kenwin McPhee, Mogabi Polius. Trainer: Terrence Caroo.
TCA: Ian Jones, Anay Bryne (73.Stephen Savage), Lee Coulton, Christopher Gannon, Ian Brown, Charles Cook, Duan Glinton (61.Lenford Singh), David Lowery, Billy Forbes, Phillip Shearer, Gavin Glinton (Cap). Trainer: Matthew Green (Bahamas).
Goals: 1-0 Kenwin McPhee (28), 2-0 Titus Elva (85).
Cautions: Lee Coulton.

Group 1C
03.02.2008, Bermuda National Stadium, Hamilton; Attendance: 2,000
Referee: Mauricio Navarro (Canada)
BERMUDA – CAYMAN ISLANDS   **1-1(1-0)**
BER: Timmy Figuerido, Antonio Lowe (85.Darius Cox), Kevin Richards, Omar Shakir, Wayne Keishan Bean, Jason Davis, Devaun Samuel DeGraff (78.Reginald Thompson-Lambe), Kwame Steede, Tyrell Burgess, Domico Coddington, John Barry Nusum (70.Stephen Astwood). Trainer: Keith Tucker.
CAY: Tuda Murphy, Thomas Elliot, Junior Fisher (90.Garth Anderson), Ian Lindo, Donald Solomon, Martin Waud, Christopher Douglas, Jedd Ebanks, Carson Fagan (83.Erickson Brown), Marshall Forbes (70.Aldene Forbes), Allean Grant. Trainer: Carl Brown (Jamaica).
Goals: 1-0 Tyrell Burgess (18), 1-1 Allean Grant (87).
Cautions: Stephen Astwood / Jedd Ebanks, Junior Fisher, Martin Waud.

30.03.2008, „Truman Bodden" Stadium, George Town; Attendance: 3,200
Referee: Jair Marrufo (United States)
CAYMAN ISLANDS - BERMUDA   **1-3(0-2)**
CAY: Tuda Murphy, Thomas Elliot (Cap), Alfredo Challenger, Junior Fisher, René Carter, Martin Waud, Jedd Ebanks (38.Marshall Forbes), Calvin Jefford, Carson Fagan (46.Dion Brandon), Oneil Taylor, Allean Grant (82.Erickson Brown). Trainer: Carl Brown (Jamaica).
BER: Timmy Figuerido, Darius Cox, Kevin Richards, Omar Shakir, Wayne Keishan Bean, Marquel Waldron, Khano Smith, Tyrrel Burgess (66.Damon Ming), Devaun Samuel DeGraff (64.Reginald Thompson-Lambe), Kwame Steede (Cap), John Barry Nusum (87.Seion Darrell). Trainer: Keith Tucker.
Goals: 0-1 Devaun Samuel DeGraff (18), 0-2 Devaun Samuel DeGraff (25), 0-3 Kwame Steede (52), 1-3 Marshall Forbes (63 penalty).
Cautions: Tuda Murphy, Allean Grant, Marshall Forbes, Junior Fisher, Oneil Taylor / Omar Shakir.

Group 1D
06.02.2008, Trinidad Stadium, Oranjestad; Attendance: 250
Referee: Roberto Delgado (Cuba)
ARUBA – ANTIGUA AND BARBUDA   **0-3(0-3)**
ARU: Antonio Giel, Theric Ruiz, Henry Tromp, Raymond Tromp, Regilio Kartoredjo, Rodney Gregory Lake, Sylvester Schwengle, Lionel Tromp (46.Rigmar Lodowica), Maurice Escalona (Cap), Edmond Eckmeyer (84.Raymondt Pimienta), Dario Sierra (46.Harmannus Ridderbos). Trainer: Marcelo Muñoz.
ATG: Janiel Simon, George Dublin (Cap), Damien Farrell, Dave Carr, Karanja Mack, Neil Schyan Jeffers (81.Teran Williams), Christian Ranjae, Lennox Julian (67.Verton Harris), Troy Simon, Peter Byers (83.Jamie Thomas), Gayson Gregory. Trainer: Rowan Benjamin.
Goals: 0-1 George Dublin (23), 0-2 Gason Gregory (27), 0-3 Dario Sierra (40 own goal).
Cautions: Sylvester Schwengle, Henry Tromp / Christian Ranjae.

26.03.2008, Antigua Recreation Ground, Saint John's; Attendance: 1,000
Referee: Courtney Campbell (Jamaica)
ANTIGUA AND BARBUDA - ARUBA   **1-0(0-0)**
ATG: Janiel Simon, Dave Carr, Karanja Mack, Damien Farrell, Troy Simon, Kerry Skepple (78.Teran Williams), Tyio Simon, Verton Harris (48.Garfield Gonsalves), Neil Schyan Jeffers, Randolph Burton (84.Okeem Challenger), George Dublin (Cap). Trainer: Derrick Edwards.
ARU: Jeffery Werleman, Theric Ruiz, Raymond Tromp, Regilio Kartoredjo, Sylvester Schwengle (54.Luis Rasmyn), Maurice Escalona (Cap), Jonathan Oduber, Andy Figaroa, Jelano Cruden, Jean Ras (59.Ezra Bosnie), Raymbert Bikker (46.Dario Sierra). Trainer: Marco Rasmyn.
Goal: 1-0 Okeem Challenger (86).
Cautions: Tyio Simon, Damien Farrell / Theric Ruiz, Andy Figaroa, Jeffery Werleman.
Sent off: George Dublin (45), Neil Schyan Jeffers (47), Damien Farrell (90+3).

Group 2A
06.02.2008, Estadio „Mateo Flores", Guatemala City (Guatemala); Attendance: 500
Referee: Howard Stennett (Jamaica)
BELIZE – SAINT KITTS AND NEVIS   **3-1(3-1)**
BLZ: Shane Orio (Cap), Tervor Lennen, Elroy Smith, Ryan Simpson, Albert Thurton, David Trapp (41.Harrison Tasher), Bernard Linarez (76.Ian Gaynair), Víctor Morales, Harrison Dwith Rochez, Deon McCalauy, Dennis Serano (58.Jeromy James). Trainer: Palmiro Salas (Guatemala).
SKN: Kayian Benjamin, Joel Jeffers, Patrice Liburd, Keithroy Richards (Cap), Rovan Wigley, Gerard Williams, Irandy Byron (54.Aiden Nurse), Orlando Mitchum (78.Kyle Collins), Jevon Francis, Atiba Harris, Aaron Moses (63.Kervin Benjamin). Trainer: Leonard Taylor (United States).
Goals: 1-0 Deon McCalauy (7), 1-1 Gerard Williams (13), 2-1 Harrison Roches (22), 3-1 Deon McCalauy (41).
Cautions: Bernard Linarez, Albert Thurton / Atiba Harris, Kervin Benjamin.

26.03.2008, Warner Park, Basseterre; Attendance: 2,000
Referee: Neal Brizan (Trinidad & Tobago)
SAINT KITTS AND NEVIS - BELIZE   **1-1(0-1)**
SKN: Kayian Benjamin, Thrizen Leader, Javin Matthew, John Queeley (60.Jevon Francis), Keithroy Richards (Cap), Irandy Byron (75.Errol O'Loughlin), George Isaac, Orlando Mitchum, Gerard Williams, Ian Lake, Alister Warner (54.Stephen Clarke). Trainer: Leonard Taylor (United States).
BLZ: Shane Orio, Tervor Lennen, Elroy Smith, Ryan Simpson, Albert Thurton, David Trapp (57.Lester Serano; 90.Ian Gaynair), Bernard Linarez, Víctor Morales, Deon McCauley, Daniel Jiménez (63.Jeromy James), Dennis Serano. Trainer: Palmiro Salas (Guatemala).
Goals: 0-1 Elroy Smith (39), 1-1 Orlando Mitchum (84).
Cautions: Ian Lake / Bernard Linarez.

Group 2B
26.03.2008, „Thomas Robinson" Stadium, Nassau; Attendance: 450
Referee: Roberto Moreno (Panama)
BAHAMAS – BRITISH VIRGIN ISLANDS   **1-1(0-0)**
BAH: Dwayne Whylly, Vincent Vanderpool-Wallace (46.Shermod Thompson), Kamal Degregory, Happy Hall (Cap), Connor Sheehan, Lesly St. Fleur, Demont Mitchell, Cameron Hepple, Dana Veth, Michael Bethel, Daron Beneby. Trainer: Neider dos Santos (Brazil).
VGB: Desire Butler, James Venton, Elvis Williams (55.Manford Pipe), Raymond Cummings (73.Jevon Demming), Andy Davis, Anadale Williams (Cap), Roger Alexander, Nole Isaac, Ranelie Cain, Rohan Lennon, Nano Ottley. Trainer: Mitchell Patrick.
Goals: 1-0 Lesly St. Fleur (47), 1-1 Rohan Lennon (68).
Cautions: Roger Alexander, Anadale Williams.

30.03.2008, „Thomas Robinson" Stadium, Nassau (Bahamas)*; Attendance: 940
Referee: Felix Mercedes Suazo (Dominican Republic)
BRITISH VIRGIN ISLANDS - BAHAMAS   **2-2(1-1)**
VGB: Desire Butler, Manford Pipe (46.Fitzroy Daley), James Venton, Raymond Cummings (65.Raul Ettienne), Andy Davis, Nole Issac, Ranelie Cain, Roger Alexander, Anadale Williams (Cap), Rohan Lennon (23.Lyndon Remy), Nano Ottley. Trainer: Mitchell Patrick.
BAH: Dwayne Whylly, Kamal Degregory, Happy Hall (87.Vincent Vanderpool-Wallace), Connor Sheehan, Lesly St. Fleur, Shemond Thompson, Demont Mitchell, Cameron Hepple, Dana Veth, Michael Bethel, Daron Beneby. Trainer: Neider dos Santos (Brazil).
Goals: 0-1 Michael Bethel (41), 0-2 Demont Mitchell (57), 1-2 Anadale Williams (78), 2-2 Anadale Williams (90 penalty).
Cautions: Ranelie Cain, Manford Pipe, Desire Butler, Anadale Williams, Nole Issac / Dana Veth, Shemond Thompson, Dwayne Whylly.
The British Virgin Islands elected to play their home leg in the Bahamas

Group 2C
26.03.2008, Estadio „Juan Ramón Loubriel", Bayamón; Attendance: 8,000
Referee: Mauricio Morales (Mexico)
PUERTO RICO – DOMINCAN REPUBLIC   **1-0(0-0,0-0)**
PUR: Terence Boss, Christopher Gores, Richard Martinez, Marco Vélez, Alexis Rivera Curet (65.Carlos Astondona), Noah Delgado, Raphel Ortiz, Andrés Cabrero (114.Kevin Muller), Petter Villegas (98.Eloy Matos), Gadiel Figueroa, Christopher Megaloudis. Trainer: Colin John Clarke (Northern Ireland).
DOM: Miguel Lloyd, Eduardo Acevedo, Yan Carlos Berroa, Ernesto Jiménez, Wally Contreras (67.Pablo Morillo; 104.José Díaz), Johan Lora, Jhoan Sánchez, Jonathan Faña, Solangel Miliano, Yohan Viola Sánchez (53.Darly Batista), Kelvin Rodríguez. Trainer: Juan Emilio Mojica.
Goal: 1-0 Petter Villegas (96 penalty).
Cautions: Alexis Rivera Curet, Marco Vélez, Terence Boss / Johan Lora, Ernesto Jiménez.
This tie was played as a one leg tie in Puerto Rico, as the Dominican Republic failed to meet FIFA's new stadium standards and was unable to secure a home venue.

Group 3A
26.03.2008, Grenada National Stadium, St. George's; Attendance: 3,000
Referee: Otis James (Guyana)
GRENADA – US VIRGIN ISLANDS   **10-0(5-0)**
GRN: Desmond Noel, Franklyn Baptiste, Cassim Langaigne, Marc Marshall, Patrick Modeste, Anthony Modeste (77.Kwan Baptiste), Shalrie Joseph (64.Dwayne Leo), Shane Rennie, Bryon Bubb, Ricky Charles, Jason Roberts (75.Denis Rennie). Trainer: Norris Wilson.
VIR: Terrence Jones, Raymond Chetiram (71.Joseph Limburner), Carmelo Rodríguez, Dwayne Thomas, Rocky Smith, Joshua Monty, Dereck Villafana, MacDonald Taylor (87.Kalid Gaillard), Dwight Ferguson, Ayinde Augustus, Cory Bishop (57.Christopher González). Trainer: Carlton Freeman.
Goals: 1-0 Jason Roberts (3), 2-0 Jason Roberts (8), 3-0 Ricky Charles (9), 4-0 Shane Rennie (22), 5-0 Ricky Charles (43), 6-0 Cassim Langaigne (57), 7-0 Ricky Charles (65), 8-0 Bryon Bubb (82), 9-0 Ricky Charles (87), 10-0 Dwight Ferguson (89 own goal).
Cautions: Rocky Smith, Ayinde Augustus.
This tie was played as a one leg tie in Grenada, as the U.S. Virgin Islands failed to meet FIFA's new stadium standards and was unable to secure a home venue.

Group 3B
26.03.2008, „Marvin Lee" Stadium, Macoya (Trinidad & Tobago); Attendance: 100
Referee: Joel Antonio Aguilar Chicas (El Salvador)
MONTSERRAT - SURINAME   **1-7(0-2)**
MSR: Jermaine Sweeney, Alex Daley (46.Synclair Adamson), Ellary White, Elton Williams, Alexander Bramble, Joseph Clifford, Kenny Dyer (Cap), Vladimir Farrell, Dorian Harper (46.Rowan Taylor), Andrew Julius, Michael Bramble (70.Leon Maede). Trainer: Cecil Lake.
SUR: Harold Blokland, Foline Abauna, Marlon Felter (Cap) (84.Raydell Schurman), Derrick Garden, Ferdinand Jap A Joe, Vangellino Sastromedjo, Jerome Strijder (61.Germaine Sergio Van Dijk), Geovanni Tiendari (78.Kenzo Huur), Cleon Wondel, Wensley Christoph, Melvin Valies. Trainer: Kenneth Jaliens.
Goals: 0-1 Wensley Christoph (36), 0-2 Cleon Wondel (44), 1-2 Vladimir Farrell (48), 1-3 Wensley Christoph (55), 1-4 Melvin Valies (64), 1-5 Kenzo Huur (80), 1-6 Raydell Schurman (86), 1-7 Raydell Schurman (88).

Group 3C
06.02.2008, Estadio Cuscatlán, San Salvador; Attendance: 15,000
Referee: Javier Rogelio Jáuregui Delgado (Netherlands Antilles)
EL SALVADOR - ANGUILLA   **12-0(4-0)**
SLV: Juan José Gómez, Marvin René González Leiva, Luis Miguel Hernández Campos, Alfredo Alberto Pacheco (Cap), Manuel Alejandro Salazar Rivas, Óscar Armando Jiménez Campos, Shawn Hasani Martin Henríquez, William Osael Romero Castillo (59.William Jeovanny Torres Alegría), Eliseo Antonio Quintanilla Ortíz (63.Ramón Alfredo Sánchez Paredes), Ronald Osvaldo Cerritos Flores, Rudis Alberto Rivera Corrales (84.Emerson David Umaña Corleto). Trainer: Jaime Alberto Rodríguez Jiménez.
AIA: Davy Godwin, Emmerson Brooks-Meade, Girdon Connor, Brian Connor (Cap), James Williams-Richardson, Kieran Kentish (70.Romare Kelsick), Romell Gumbs (47.Jaiden Abbott), Roy Gumbs, Jermaine Gumbs, Leon Jeffers (63.Andre Griffith), Roberto Paris. Trainer: Kerthney Carty.
Goals: 1-0 Shawn Hasani Martin Henríquez (5), 2-0 Shawn Hasani Martin Henríquez (18), 3-0 Rudis Alberto Rivera Corrales (31), 4-0 Rudis Alberto Rivera Corrales (33), 5-0 Ronald Osvaldo Cerritos Flores (47), 6-0 Rudis Alberto Rivera Corrales (54), 7-0 Rudis Alberto Rivera Corrales (65), 8-0 Rudis Alberto Rivera Corrales (68), 9-0 Eliseo Antonio Quintanilla Ortíz (70), 10-0 Ronald Osvaldo Cerritos Flores (77), 11-0 Ronald Osvaldo Cerritos Flores (84), 12-0 Emerson David Umaña Corleto (80).
Cautions: William Osael Romero Castillo, Eliseo Antonio Quintanilla Ortíz / Roy Gumbs.

30.03.2008, „Robert F. Kennedy" Memorial Stadium, Washington (United States); Attendance: 22,670
Referee: Valman Bedeau (Grenada)
ANGUILLA – EL SALVADOR   **0-4(0-4)**
AIA: Godwin Davy, Girdon Connor, Brian Connor (Cap), James Williams-Richardson, Romell Gumbs (79.Jaiden Abbott), Jermaine Gumbs, Ian Edwards, Kevin Hawley, Leon Jeffers, Robert Paris (72.Romare Kelsick), Walwyn Benjamin (67.Emmerson Brooks-Meade). Trainer: Colin Johnson.
SLV: Miguel Ángel Montes Moreno, Luis Alonso Anaya Merino, Alexander Escobar Rosales, Ramón Ulises Flores Aguirre, Carlos Romeo Monteagudo Alfaro, Manuel Alejandro Salazar Rivas, Óscar Armando Jiménez Campos (46.Dennis Jonathan Alas Morales), Ramón Alfredo Sánchez Paredes (52.Salvador Arturo Coreas Pérez), Ronald Osvaldo Cerritos Flores, William Jeovanny Torres Alegría, Rudis Alberto Rivera Corrales (67.Emerson David Umaña Corleto). Trainer: Carlos de los Cobos Martínez (Mexico).
Goals: 0-1 Ronald Osvaldo Cerritos Flores (8), 0-2 Rudis Alberto Rivera Corrales (15), 0-3 Carlos Romeo Monteagudo Alfaro (23), 0-4 William Jeovanny Torres Alegría (35).
Cautions: Girdon Connor / Salvador Arturo Coreas Pérez.

Group 3D
06.02.2008, Estadio „Cacique Diriangén", Diriamba; Attendance: 7,000
Referee: Walter López Castellanos (Guatemala)
NICARAGUA – HOLLAND ANTILLES   **0-1(0-1)**
NCA: Denis Jesús Espinoza Camacho (Cap), Silvio Ernesto Avilés Ramos, Mario Gastón, David Sebastián Solórzano Sánchez, Franklin Ulises López González (76.Armando José Collado Lanuza), Eustace Alertan Martín López, Miguel Ángel Masis (46.Samuel Israel Wilson Rostrán), Quelser Martín Rizo, Mílton David Martínez Delgadillo, Wilber Alejandro Sánchez Ramírez (76.Milton Busto), Ricardo Antonio Vega. Trainer: Mauricio Cruz.
ANT: Lournohelo Farrell, Rijanchelo Cyntie, Tyronne Loran, Jason Winklaar Djuric (46.Dyron Daal), Angelo Zimmerman, Revy Rosalia (86.Leon Kantelberg), Anton Jongsma, Giovanni Franken, Robin Nelisse (Cap), Shelton Martis, Orlando Smeekes (90.Benjamin Martha), Trainer: Leen Looyen (NED).
Goal: 0-1 Anton Jongsma (15).
Cautions: Quelser Martín Rizo / Jason Winklaar Djuric, Dyron Daal, Rijanchelo Cyntie, Shelton Martis, Anton Jongsma.

26.03.2008, Stadion „Ergilio Hato", Willemstad; Attendance: 9,000
Referee: Enrico Wijngaarde (Suriname)
HOLLAND ANTILLES - NICARAGUA   **2-0(1-0)**
ANT: Wencho Farrell, Angelo Cijntje, Tryonne Loran (Cap), Angelo Martha, Djuric Winklaar, Angelo Zimmerman, Giovanni Franken, Sendley Bito, Anton Jongsma, Dyron Daal (84.Reyv Rosalia), Orlando Smeeks (89.Benjamin Martha). Trainer: Leen Looyen (NED).
NCA: Denis Jesús Espinoza Camacho, Silvio Ernesto Avilés Ramos, Marvin Antonio Molina Benavídez (46.Quesler Martín Rizo), Armando José Collado Lanuza, David Sebastián Solórzano Sánchez, Franklin Ulises López González (46.Wilber Alejandro Sánchez Ramírez), Carlos Rigoberto Alonso Gómez, Mílton David Martínez Delgadillo (85.Jaime Ruiz), Emilio Palacios, Samuel Israel Wilson Rostrán, Eustace Alertan Martín López. Trainer: Mauricio Cruz.
Goals: 1-0 Tyronne Loran (42), 2-0 Angelo Zimmerman (81 penalty).
Cautions: Angelo Martha / Franklin Ulises López González, Armando José Collado Lanuza, Eustace Alertan Martín López, Denis Jesús Espinoza Camacho.
Sent off: Eustace Alertan Martín López (60).

SECOND ROUND

Group 1A
| 15.06.2008 | Carson | United States - Barbados | 8-0(3-0) |
| 22.06.2008 | Bridgetown | Barbados - **United States** | 0-1(0-1) |

Group 1B
| 15.06.2008 | Guatemala City | Guatemala – Saint Lucia | 6-0(3-0) |
| 22.06.2008 | Los Angeles (USA) | Saint Lucia - **Guatemala** | 1-3(1-2) |

Group 1C
| 15.06.2008 | Macoya | Trinidad & Tobago - Bermuda | 1-2(1-2) |
| 22.06.2008 | Hamilton | Bermuda – **Trinidad & Tobago** | 0-2(0-1) |

Group 1D
| 17.06.2008 | Saint John's | Antigua and Barbuda - Cuba | 3-4(2-2) |
| 22.06.2008 | Havana | **Cuba** - Antigua and Barbuda | 4-0(2-0) |

Group 2A
| 15.06.2008 | Houston (USA) | Belize – Mexico | 0-2(0-0) |
| 22.06.2008 | Monterrey | **Mexico** – Belize | 7-0(3-0) |

Group 2B
| 15.06.2008 | Kingston | Jamaica - Bahamas | 7-0(3-0) |
| 21.06.2008 | Daniel Town (JAM) | Bahamas - **Jamaica** | 0-6(0-5) |

Group 2C
| 04.06.2008 | San Pedro Sula | Honduras – Puerto Rico | 4-0(1-0) |
| 14.06.2008 | Bayamón | Puerto Rico - **Honduras** | 2-2(2-1) |

Group 2D
| 15.06.2008 | Kingstown | Saint Vincent and the Grenadines - Canada | 0-3(0-2) |
| 20.06.2008 | Montreal | Canada - Saint Vincent and the Grenadines | 4-1(2-0) |

Group 3A
| 14.06.2008 | St. George's | Grenada – Costa Rica | 2-2(2-1) |
| 21.06.2008 | San José | Costa Rica - Grenada | 3-0(2-0) |

Group 3B
| 14.06.2008 | Paramaribo | Suriname - Guyana | 1-0(0-0) |
| 22.06.2008 | Georgetown | Guyana - **Suriname** | 1-2(0-2) |

Group 3C
| 15.06.2008 | Ciudad de Panamá | Panama - El Salvador | 1-0(1-0) |
| 22.06.2008 | San Salvador | **El Salvador** - Panama | 3-1(0-1) |

Group 3D
| 15.06.2008 | Port-au-Prince | Haiti – Netherlands Antilles | 0-0 |
| 22.06.2008 | Willemstad | Netherlands Antilles - **Haiti** | 0-1(0-0) |

All winners qualified for the Third Round.

Group 1A
15.06.2008, The Home Depot Center, Carson; Attendance: 11,476
Referee: Marco Antonio Rodríguez Moreno (Mexico)
UNITED STATES - BARBADOS   **8-0(3-0)**
USA: Bradley Edwin Guzan, Steven Cherundolo, Carlos Manuel Bocanegra (Cap), Oguchialu Chijioke Onyewu, Heath Gregory Pearce, Michael Sheehan Bradley, Pablo Mastroeni (26.Fredua Koranteng Adu), DaMarcus Lamont Beasley, Clinton Drew Dempsey (71.Edward James Lewis), Landon Timothy Donovan (80.Edward Abraham Johnson), Brian Ching. Trainer: Robert Bradley.
BRB: Alvin Rouse, Dyson James, Daryl Ferguson, Greg Belle, Bryan Neblett, Paul Ifill, Jonathan Forte (68.Riviere Williams), Mark McCammon, Norman Forde (Cap) (71.Malcolm Marshall), Jonathan Nurse (75.John Parris), Romelle Burgess. Trainer: Eyre Sealy.
Goals: 1-0 Clinton Drew Dempsey (1), 2-0 Michael Sheehan Bradley (12), 3-0 Brian Ching (20), 4-0 Landon Timothy Donovan (58), 5-0 Clinton Drew Dempsey (62), 6-0 Edward Abraham Johnson (82),

7-0 Daryl Ferguson (85 own goal), 8-0 Brian Ching (88).
Cautions: Oguchialu Chijioke Onyewu / Norman Forde, Bryan Neblett, Malcolm Marshall.

22.06.2008, Kensington Oval, Bridgetown; Attendance: 2,000
Referee: Roberto Moreno (Panama)
BARBADOS – UNITED STATES   **0-1(0-1)**
BRB: Alvin Rouse, Bryan Neblett, Jonathan Straker, Paul Ifill (Cap), Mark McCammon, Jonathan Nurse (80.Malcolm Marshall), Riviere Williams (67.Rondelle Vaughan), Ramuel Miller, Emmerson Boyce, Barry Skeete, John Parris. Trainer: Eyre Sealy.
USA: Bradley Edwin Guzan, Danny Califf, Jay Michael DeMerit, Drew Moor, Edward James Lewis (Cap), Heath Gregory Pearce, Michael Sheehan Bradley, Sacha Kljestan, DaMarcus Lamont Beasley (78.John Thorrington), Daniel Szetela (66.Christopher Rolfe), Fredua Koranteng Adu (85.Chad Barrett). Trainer: Robert Bradley.
Goal: 0-1 Edward James Lewis (21).

Group 1B
15.06.2008, Estadio „Mateo Flores", Guatemala City; Attendance: 24,600
Referee: Benito Armando Archundia Téllez (Mexico)
GUATEMALA – SAINT LUCIA   **6-0(3-0)**
GUA: Ricardo Alberto Trigueño Foster, Gustavo Adolfo Cabrera Marroquín, Yony Wilson Flores Monroy, Carlos Eduardo Gallardo Nájera, ČCristian Jafeth Noriega Santizo, José Manuel Contreras y Contreras (64.Gonzalo Antonio Romero Paz), Freddy Alexander García Carrera (75.Abner Isai Trigueros Álvarez), Guillermo Ramírez Ortega, Mario Rafael Rodríguez Rodríguez, Fredy Williams Thompson León (74.Dwight Anthony Pezzarossi García), Carlos Humberto Ruiz Gutiérez (Cap). Trainer: Ramón Enrique Maradiaga Chávez (Honduras).
LCA: Danny Mitchel (61.Giovanni Deterville), Sheldon Emmanuel, Gilroy Mitchell, Vernus Abbott, John Perry Joseph, Germal Valcin (Cap), Everton Lambert, Barnett Bledman (56.Phillip Tisson), Angus William (50.Cleveland Emmanuel), Mogabi Polius, Kenwen McPhee. Trainer: Terrence Caroo.
Goals: 1-0 Mario Rafael Rodríguez Rodríguez (5), 2-0 Carlos Humberto Ruiz Gutiérez (36), 3-0 Carlos Humberto Ruiz Gutiérez (40), 4-0 Carlos Humberto Ruiz Gutiérez (58), 5-0 Abner Isai Trigueros Álvarez (90+1), 6-0 Carlos Humberto Ruiz Gutiérez (90+3).
Cautions: John Perry Joseph, Gilroy Mitchell.
Sent off: John Perry Joseph (78).

22.06.2008, Memorial Coliseum, Los Angeles (United States); Attendance: 12,000
Referee: Enrico Wijngaarde (Suriname)
SAINT LUCIA – GUATEMALA   **1-3(1-2)**
LCA: Danny Mitchel, Sheldon Emmanuel, Vernus Abbott, Gilroy Mitchell, Fabian Joseph, Germal Valcin (Cap), Barnett Bledman (56.Phillip Tisson), 88.Angus William), Tory Prospere (38.Chad St. Croix), Cleveland Emmanuel, Mogabi Polius, Kenwen McPhee. Trainer: Terrence Caroo.
GUA: Luis Pedro Molina Bruni, Carlos Mauricio Castrillo Alonzo, Yony Wilson Flores Monroy (46.WilsonClemente Lalin Salvatierra), Luis Ricardo Rodríguez Jérez, Jaime Darío Vides Ruano, Rigoberto Gómez Laínez (61.Carlos Rafael Castillo Rosales), Guillermo Ramírez Ortega, Mario Rafael Rodríguez Rodríguez, Gonzalo Antonio Romero Paz (73.Jean Jonathan Márquez Orellana), Carlos Humberto Ruiz Gutiérez (Cap), Abner Isai Trigueros Álvarez. Trainer: Ramón Enrique Maradiaga Chávez (Honduras).
Goals: 0-1 Gonzalo Antonio Romero Paz (24), 0-2 Gonzalo Antonio Romero Paz (43), 1-2 Kenwin McPhee (45), 1-3 Abner Isai Trigueros Álvarez (86).
Cautions: Barnett Bledman, Kenwin McPhee, Sheldon Emmanuel.

Group 1C

15.06.2008, „Marvin Lee" Stadium, Macoya; Attendance: 4,585
Referee: Walter Quesada Cordero (Costa Rica)
TRINIDAD & TOBAGO - BERMUDA   **1-2(1-2)**
TRI: Clayton Ince, Makan Hislop, Dennis Lawrence, Kareem Smith, Osei Telesford (75.Stephan David), Carlos Edwards, Keon Daniel, Khaleem Hyland (46.Ancil Farrier), Aurtis Whitley (Cap), Jason Scotland, Stern John. Trainer: Francisco Maturana (Colombia).
BER: Timothy Figuriedo, Kofi Dill, Antonio Lowe, Kevin Richards, Omar Shakir (Cap), Meshak Wade, Damon Ming (71.Reginald Thompson-Lambe), Wayne Keishan Bean (81.Kristofer Frick), Kwame Steede, Khano Smith, John Barry Nusum (73.Ralph Bean). Trainer: Kenneth Thompson.
Goals: 0-1 John Barry Nusum (7), 1-1 Stern John (22), 1-2 John Barry Nusum (38).

22.06.2008, Bermuda National Stadium, Hamilton; Attendance: 5,000
Referee: Carlos Alberto Batres González (Guatemala)
BERMUDA – TRINIDAD & TOBAGO   **0-2(0-1)**
BER: Timothy Figuriedo, Kofi Dill, Antonio Lowe, Kevin Richards, Omar Shakir (Cap), Meshak Wade, Wayne Keishan Bean, Khano Smith (78.Domico Coddington), Damon Ming, Kwame Steede (65.Jemeiko Jennings), John Barry Nusum (51.Stephen Astwood). Trainer: Kenneth Thompson.
TRI: Jan-Michael Williams, Makan Hislop, Dennis Lawrence, Michael Edwards (64.Kern Cupid), Osei Telesford, Carlos Edwards, Khaleem Hyland, Aurtis Whitley (Cap), Darryl Roberts (89.Stephan David), Jerol Forbes (46.Stern John), Keon Daniel. Trainer: Francisco Maturana (Colombia).
Goals: 0-1 Darryl Roberts (9), 0-2 Stern John (66).
Cautions: Kofi Dill, Omar Shakir, Damon Ming / Makan Hislop, Aurtis Whitley.

Group 1D

17.06.2008, „Sir Vivian Richards" Stadium, St. John's; Attendance: 4,500
Referee: Roberto Moreno (Panama)
ANTIGUA AND BARBUDA - CUBA   **3-4(2-2)**
ATG: Melvin James, Dave Carr (46.Tyio Simon), Marc Joseph, Garfield Gonsalves, Justine Cochrane, Gayson Gregory, Teran Williams, Kerry Skepple (62.Randolph Burton), Brian Samuel, Lennox Julian (76.Troy Mellanson), Peter Byers. Trainer: Derrick Edwards.
CUB: Dany Quintero, Jorge Luis Clavelo, Jaime Colomé, Yoel Colomé, Reysandri Fernández Cervantes, Yénier Márquez, Silvio Pedro Miñoso, Kanier Dranguet, Pedro Faife (88.Lázaro Alfonso), Jensy Muñoz (46.Leonel Duarte), Roberto Linares (77.Reinier Alcantara). Trainer: Reinhold Franz (Germany).
Goals: 1-0 Teran Williams (9), 1-1 Jaime Colomé (10), 2-1 Kerry Skepple (13), 2-2 Roberto Linares (22), 2-3 Jaime Colomé (74), 3-3 Tyio Simon (80), 3-4 Leonel Duarte (85)
Cautions: Kerry Skepple, Garfield Gonsalves / Jaime Colomé, Dany Quintero.

22.06.2008, Estadio „Pedro Marrero", La Habana; Attendance: 2,000
Referee: Walter Quesada Cordero (Costa Rica)
CUBA – ANTIGUA AND BARBUDA   **4-0(2-0)**
CUB: Dany Quintero, Jorge Luis Clavelo, Jaime Colomé, Yoel Colomé, Reysandri Fernández Cervantes, Yénier Márquez, Kanier Dranguet, Yusvanys Caballeros, Alain Cervantes (69.Lázaro Alfonso), Roberto Linares (56.Reinier Alcantara), Leonel Duarte (64.Jensy Muñoz). Trainer: Reinhold Franz (Germany).
ATG: Molvin James, Marc Joseph, Garfield Gonsalves, Justine Cochrane, Gayson Gregory, Teran Williams (46.Dave Carr), Kerry Skepple (64.Troy Mellanson), Brian Samuel, Lennox Julian (29.Troy Simon), Tyio Simon, Peter Byers. Trainer: Derrick Edwards.
Goals: 1-0 Roberto Linares (9), 2-0 Roberto Linares (45+2), 3-0 Roberto Linares (53), 4-0 Jeniel Márquez (69).
Cautions: Yusvanys Caballeros, Yénier Márquez / Peter Byers.

Group 2A

15.06.2008, Reliant Stadium, Houston (United States); Attendance: 50,137
Referee: Javier Santillán (Netherlands Antilles)
BELIZE - MEXICO   **0-2(0-0)**
BLZ: Shane Orio (Cap), Ian Gaynair (53.Ryan Simpson), Elroy Smith, Tervor Lennen, David Trapp, Harrison Tasher, Lester Serano, Deris Benavides (87.Daniel Jiménez), Víctor Morales, Harrison Dwith Rochez, Deon McCaulay (80.Jeromy James). Trainer: Ian Mork.
MEX: Oswaldo Javier Sánchez Ibarra (Cap), Aarón Galindo Rubio, José Jonny Magallón Oliva, Carlos Arnoldo Salcido Flores, Ricardo Osorio Mendoza, José Andrés Guardado Hernández, Gerardo Torrado Díez de Bonilla (46.Gonzalo Pineda Reyes), Fernando Enrique Arce Ruiz, Antônio Naelson Matías „Zinha" (62.César Osvaldo Villaluz Martínez), Luis Ernesto Pérez Gómez, Carlos Alberto Vela Garrido (77.Jared Francisco Borgetti Echavarría). Trainer: José de Jesús Ramírez Ruvalcaba.
Goals: 0-1 Carlos Alberto Vela Garrido (67), 0-2 Jared Francisco Borgetti Echavarría (90 penalty).
Cautions: Elroy Smith, Shane Orio / José Andrés Guardado Hernández, Carlos Arnoldo Salcido Flores.

22.06.2008, Estadio Universitario, Monterrey; Attendance: 42,000
Referee: Silviu Petrescu (Canada)
MEXICO - BELIZE   **7-0(3-0)**
MEX: Oswaldo Javier Sánchez Ibarra (Cap), Aarón Galindo Rubio, José Jonny Magallón Oliva, Óscar Adrián Rojas Castillón, Carlos Arnoldo Salcido Flores, José Andrés Guardado Hernández (48.Ricardo Osorio Mendoza), Gonzalo Pineda Reyes (65.Antônio Naelson Matías „Zinha"), Fernando Enrique Arce Ruiz (52.Jared Francisco Borgetti Echavarría), César Osvaldo Villaluz Martínez, Luis Ernesto Pérez Gómez, Carlos Alberto Vela Garrido. Trainer: José de Jesús Ramírez Ruvalcaba.
BLZ: Shane Orio (Cap), Tervor Lennen, Ian Gaynair, Elroy Smith (46.Albert Thurton), Harrison Tasher, Bernard Linarez, Lester Serano, Daniel Jiménez, Harrison Dwith Rochez (52.Jeromy James), Ryan Simpson (76.Dennis Serano), Deon McCaulay. Trainer: Ian Mork.
Goals: 1-0 Carlos Alberto Vela Garrido (8), 2-0 José Andrés Guardado Hernández (33), 3-0 Fernando Enrique Arce Ruiz (45+1), 4-0 Fernando Enrique Arce Ruiz (47), 5-0 Jared Francisco Borgetti Echavarría (62), 6-0 Tervor Lennen (90+2), 7-0 Jared Francisco Borgetti Echavarría (90+4).
Cautions: Ryan Simpson, Ian Gaynair, Lester Serano.

Group 2B

15.06.2008, Independence Park, Kingston; Attendance: 20,000
Referee: Mauricio Navarro (Canada)
JAMAICA - BAHAMAS   **7-0(3-0)**
JAM: Donovan Ricketts, Ian Goodison, Evan Taylor (76.Omar Daley), Ricardo Gardner, Tyrone Marshall, Demar Phillips, Rodolph Austin, Jermaine Taylor (64.O'Brian Woodbine), Marlon King (69.Deon Burton), Luton Shelton, Andrew Williams. Trainer: René Rodrigues Simões (Brazil).
BAH: Dwayne Whylly, Daron Beneby, Michael Bethel, Gavin Christie (84.Damani Horton), Happy Hall, Cameron Hepple, Nesley Jean, Connor Sheehan (60.Demont Mitchell), Lesly St. Fleur, Vincent Vanderpool-Wallace (46.Dwayne Forbes), Kyle Williams. Trainer: Neider dos Santos (Brazil).
Goals: 1-0 Ricardo Gardner (17), 2-0 Demar Phillips (23), 3-0 Marlon King (34), 4-0 Luton Shelton (51), 5-0 Luton Shelton (66), 6-0 Ian Goodison (75), 7-0 Omar Daley (89).
Cautions: Demar Phillips, Omar Daley / Nesley Jean, Dwayne Forbes.

21.06.2008, Greenfield Stadium, Daniel Town (Jamaica)*; Attendance: 10,500
Referee: Benito Armando Archundia Téllez (Mexico)
BAHAMAS - JAMAICA   **0-6(0-5)**
BAH: Dwayne Whylly, Happy Hall (Cap), Connor Sheenan (46.Michael Bethel), Lesley St. Fleur, Shemord Thompson, Demont Mitchell, Cameron Hepple (90+2.Denair Mitchell), Daron Beneby, Kyle Williams, Gavin Christie, Nesly Jean. Trainer: Neider dos Santos (Brazil).
JAM: Donovan Ricketts, Ian Goodison, Jermaine Taylor (46.Richard Langley), Ricardo Gardner (Cap) (46.O'Brian Woodbine), Tyrone Marshall, Demar Phillips, Rudolph Austin, Evan Taylor, Deon Burton, Andrew Williams (59.Omar Daley), Luton Shelton. Trainer: René Rodrigues Simões (Brazil).

Goals: 0-1 Deon Burton (29), 0-2 Luton Shelton (35), 0-3 Luton Shelton (37 penalty), 0-4 Tyrone Marshall (39), 0-5 Luton Shelton (42), 0-6 Deon Burton (55).
The Bahamas elected to play their home leg in Jamaica.

Group 2C
15.06.2008, Estadio Olimpico Metropolitano, San Pedro Sula; Attendance: 20,000
Referee: Courtney Campbell (Jamaica)
HONDURAS – PUERTO RICO   **4-0(1-0)**
HON: Noel Eduardo Valladares Bonilla, Víctor Salvador Bernárdez Blanco, Osman Danilo Chávez Guity (79.Mario Iván Guerrero Ramírez), Maynor Alexis Figueroa Róchez, Sergio Giovany Mendoza Escobar, Wilson Roberto Palacios Suazo, Amado Guevara (Cap) (88.Hendry Thomas), Danilo Elvis Turcios Funes, Julio César de León, Carlos Yaír Costly Molina (68.Walter Julián Martínez Ramos), Óscar David Suazo Velázquez. Trainer: Reinaldo Rueda Rivera (Colombia).
PUR: Terence Boss, Christopher Gores, Steven Ehricks, Marco Vélez (Cap), Alexis Rivera Curet, Noah Delgado, Scott Horta, Andrés Cabrero (87.Josh Villalobos), Petter Villegas (71.Carlos Astondona), Gadiel Figueroa, Christopher Megaloudis (80.Michael Caro). Trainer: Colin John Clarke (Northern Ireland).
Goals: 1-0 Julio César de León (25), 2-0 Wilson Roberto Palacios Suazo (51), 3-0 Óscar David Suazo Velázquez (52), 4-0 Óscar David Suazo Velázquez (90+2).
Cautions: Julio César de León / Alexis Rivera Curet, Marco Vélez, Noah Delgado.
Sent off: Marco Vélez (84).

22.06.2008, Estadio „Juan Ramón Loubriel", Bayamón; Attendance: 5,000
Referee: Walter López Castellanos (Guatemala)
PUERTO RICO - HONDURAS   **2-2(2-1)**
PUR: Terence Boss, Christopher Gores, Steven Ehricks, Richard Martinez, Noah Delgado, Scott Horta (58.Michael Caro), Raphel Ortiz (Cap), Gadiel Figueroa (69.Joshua Villalobos), Petter Villegas (77.Isaac Nieves), Andrés Cabrero, Christopher Megaloudis. Trainer: Colin John Clarke (Northern Ireland).
HON: Noel Eduardo Valladares Bonilla, Mario Roberto Beata Reyes, Víctor Salvador Bernárdez Blanco, Maynor Alexis Figueroa Róchez (71.Mario Iván Guerrero Ramírez), Sergio Giovany Mendoza Escobar, Wilson Roberto Palacios Suazo, Amado Guevara (Cap), Danilo Elvis Turcios Funes, Julio César De León (80.Miguel Angel Castillo Flores), Carlos Yaír Costly Molina (64.Walter Julián Martínez Ramos), Óscar David Suazo Velázquez. Trainer: Reinaldo Rueda Rivera (Colombia).
Goals: 0-1 Óscar David Suazo Velázquez (22), 1-1 Christopher Megaloudis (31), 2-1 Petter Villegas (40), 2-2 Wilson Roberto Palacios Suazo (52).
Cautions: Petter Villegas, Christopher Megaloudis / Danilo Elvis Turcios Funes.

Group 2D
15.06.2008, Arnos Vale Stadium, Kingstown; Attendance: 5,000
Referee: Carlos Alberto Batres González (Guatemala)
SAINT VINCENT AND GRENADINES - CANADA   **0-3(0-2)**
VIN: Melvin Andrews (46.Winslow McDowall), Wesley Charles, Richard Hayde, Cornelius Huggins, Roy Richards (36.Troy Jeffers), George Emerald, Darren Francis, Kendall Velox, Randolph Williams, Marlon James (Cap), Sean Glynn (63.Shandel Samuel). Trainer: Stewart Hall (England).
CAN: Patrick Stewart Onstad, Richard Cory Hastings, Michael Klukowski, Paul Andrew Stalteri (Cap), Adrian Serioux, Julien Bobby De Guzmán (72.Patrice Bernier), Issey Morgan Nakjima-Farran, Atiba Hutchinson, Dwayne Anthony De Rosario, Tomasz Radziński (85.James Gerald Brennan), Robert Douglas Friend (3.Ali Ngon Gerba). Trainer: Dale William Dink Mitchell.
Goals: 0-1 Issey Morgan Nakjima-Farran (29), 0-2 Ali Ngon Gerba (38), 0-3 Ali Ngon Gerba (89).
Cautions: Darren Francis, Richard Hayde, Troy Jeffers.

20.06.2008, Saputo Stadium, Montreal; Attendance: 11,502
Referee: Joel Antonio Aguilar Chicas (El Salvador)
CANADA – SAINT VINCENT AND GRENADINES   **4-1(2-0)**
CAN: Patrick Stewart Onstad, Adrian Cann, Adrian Serioux, Paul Andrew Stalteri (Cap), Michael Klukowski (46.James Gerald Brennan), Julien Bobby De Guzmán (67.Patrice Bernier), Atiba Hutchinson, Issey Morgan Nakjima-Farran (82.Marcel De Jong), Dwayne Anthony De Rosario, Tomasz Radziński, Ali Ngon Gerba. Trainer: Dale William Dink Mitchell.
VIN: Winslow McDowall, Wesley Charles, Darren Hamlet (58.Richard Hayde), Cornelius Huggins, Roy Richards, George Emerald, Darren Francis, Cornelius Stewart (79.Randolph Williams), Kendal Velox, Marlon James, Shandell Samuel (63.Alwyn Guy). Trainer: Stewart Hall (England).
Goals: 1-0 Dwayne Anthony De Rosario (29), 2-0 Ali Ngon Gerba (38), 3-0 Dwayne Anthony De Rosario (50), 4-0 Ali Ngon Gerba (63), 4-1 Marlon James (75).
Cautions: Julien Bobby De Guzmán, Tomasz Radziński / Roy Richards, Cornelius Stewart.

Group 3A
14.06.2008, Grenada National Stadium, St. George's; Attendance: 10,000
Referee: Neal Brizan (Trinidad & Tobago)
GRENADA – COSTA RICA   **2-2(2-1)**
GRN: Andre Charles, Jason James, Marc Marshall, Cassim Langaigne, Patrick Modeste (63.Dwayne Leo), Anthony Modeste (Cap), Shalrie Joseph, Ricky Charles, Shane Rennie (72.Kwan Baptiste), Byron Bubb (87.Denis Rennie), Jason Roberts. Trainer: Norris Wilson.
CRC: Ricardo González Fonseca, Gabriel Badilla Segura, Víctor Cordero Flores (Cap), Ricardo Harris Archival, Gonzalo Segares González (55.Rolando Fonseca Jiménez), Júnior Enrique Díaz Campbell, Armando Alonso Rodríguez (63.Alejandro Alpizar Delgado), José Luis López Ramírez, Randall Azofeifa Corrales, Bryan Ruiz González (70.Christian Bolaños Navarro), Víctor Núñez Rodríguez. Trainer: Hernán Evaristo Medford Bryan.
Goals: 1-0 Patrick Modeste (18), 2-0 Jason Roberts (27), 2-1 Armando Alonso Rodríguez (39), 2-2 Víctor Núñez Rodríguez (76).
Cautions: Shane Rennie, Shalrie Joseph / José Luis López Ramírez, Christian Bolaños Navarro, Víctor Núñez Rodríguez, Gabriel Badilla Segura, Ricardo González Fonseca.
Sent off: Ricky Charles (49).

21.06.2008, Estadio „Ricardo Saprissa", San José; Attendance: 16,000
Referee: Jair Marrufo (United States)
COSTA RICA - GRENADA   **3-0(2-0)**
CRC: Ricardo González Fonseca, Gabriel Badilla Segura, Víctor Cordero Flores (Cap), Ricardo Harris Archival, Gonzalo Segares González, Celso Borges Mora (48.Randall Azofeifa Corrales), José Luis López Ramírez, Andrés Núñez Vargas, Álvaro Alberto Saborío Chacón (66.Alejandro Alpizar Delgado), Víctor Núñez Rodríguez, Bryan Ruiz González (59.Armando Alonso Rodríguez). Trainer: Hernán Evaristo Medford Bryan.
GRN: Andre Charles, Jason James (46.Shane Rennie), Marc Marshall, Cassim Langaigne, Patrick Modeste, Anthony Modeste (Cap), Sharlie Joseph, Byron Bubb, Ian Perrotte (80.Stephen Peters), Lyndon Antonie (56.Denis Rennie), Jason Roberts. Trainer: Norris Wilson.
Goals: 1-0 Álvaro Alberto Saborío Chacón (17), 2-0 Bryan Ruiz González (32), 3-0 Randall Azofeifa Corrales (89).
Cautions: Bryan Ruiz González, Víctor Núñez Rodríguez, Gonzalo Segares González / Anthony Modeste, Ian Perrotte, Patrick Modeste.

Group 3B
15.06.2008, „André Kamperveen" Stadion, Paramaribo; Attendance: 3,000
Referee: José René Guerrero (Nicaragua)
SURINAME - GUYANA   **1-0(0-0)**
SUR: Ronny Aloema, Marlon Felter (Cap), Derrik Garden, Ferdinand Jap A Joe, Emilio Limon (86.Hesron Jeroe), Rinaldo Lupson, Clifton Sandvliet, Vangellino Sastromedjo, Romano Sordam (90.Germaine Sergio Van Dijk), Melvin Valies (65.Geovanni Tiendari), Wensley Christoph. Trainer: Kenneth Jaliens.
GUY: Richard Reynolds, Howard Lowe, Walter Moore, Charles Pollard (Cap), Carey Harris, Dwain Jacobs (62.Nigel Codrington), Collie Hercules (62.Anthony Abrams), Kayode McKinnon, Shawn Beveney, Quacy Johnson (78.Konata Mannings), Gregory Richardson. Trainer: Jamaal Shabazz (Trinidad & Tobago).
Goal: 1-0 Clifton Sandvliet (52).
Cautions: Clifton Sandvliet, Rinaldo Lupson / Anthony Abrams.
Sent off: Rinaldo Lupson (85).

22.06.2008, Providence Stadium, Georgetown; Attendance: 12,000
Referee: Courtney Campbell (Jamaica)
GUYANA - SURINAME   **1-2(0-2)**
GUY: Richard Reynolds, Howard Lowe, Walter Moore, Charles Pollard, Carey Harris (72.Dwight Peters), Nigel Codrington, Anthony Abrams (63.Collie Hercules), Shawn Bishop (79.Howard Newton), Kayode McKinnon, Shawn Beveney, Gregory Richardson. Trainer: Jamaal Shabazz (Trinidad & Tobago).
SUR: Ronny Aloema, Marlon Felter, Derrick Garden, Ferdinand Jap A Joe, Hesron Jeroe, Emilio Limon (84.Kenzo Huur), Clifton Sandvliet, Vangellino Sastromedjo (76.Jerome Strijder), Romano Sordam (86.Claudio Pinas), Germaine Sergio Van Dijk, Wensley Christoph. Trainer: Kenneth Jaliens.
Goals: 0-1 Germaine Sergio Van Dijk (11), 0-2 Clifton Sandvliet (37), 1-2 Nigel Codrington (85).
Cautions: Howard Lowe / Vangellino Sastromedjo, Derrick Garden, Romano Sordam.

Group 3C
15.06.2008, Estadio Nacional de Panamá, Ciudad de Panamá; Attendance: 22,150
Referee: Enrico Wijngaarde (Suriname)
PANAMA – EL SALVADOR   **1-0(1-0)**
PAN: Jaime Manuel Penedo Cano, Adolfo Machado, Luis Moreno, Carlos Rubén Rivera Moulton, Luis Alfonso Henríquez Ledezma (55.Román Aureliano Torres Morcillo), Rolando Emilio Escobar Batista (55.Edwin Enrique Aguilar Samaniego), Juan Pérez, José Luis Garcés Rivera, Blas Antonio Miguel Pérez Ortega (Cap), Gabriel Enrique Gómez Giron, Luis Carlos Tejada Hansell (67.Juan Ramón Solís). Trainer: Alexandre Borges Guimarães (Costa Rica).
SLV: Miguel Ángel Montes Moreno, Luis Alonso Anaya Merino, Marvin René González Leiva, Alfredo Alberto Pacheco (Cap), Manuel Alejandro Salazar Rivas, Christian Giovanni Castillo Martínez (46.Eliseo Antonio Quintanilla Ortíz), Óscar Armando Jiménez Campos, Shawn Hasani Martin Henríquez, Ramón Alfredo Sánchez Paredes, Salvador Arturo Coreas Pérez (67.Williams Enrique Reyes Rodríguez), Rudis Alberto Rivera Corrales (83.José Manuel Martínez). Trainer: Carlos de los Cobos Martínez (Mexico).
Goal: 1-0 Luis Tejada (21).
Cautions: Juan Pérez, Juan Ramón Solís / Alfredo Alberto Pacheco, Christian Giovanni Castillo Martínez, Manuel Alejandro Salazar Rivas,
Sent off: Juan Pérez (60), Manuel Alejandro Salazar Rivas (90).

22.06.2008, Estadio Cuscatlán, San Salvador; Attendance: 27,420
Referee: Marco Antonio Rodríguez Moreno (Mexico)
EL SALVADOR - PANAMA **3-1(0-1)**
SLV: Juan José Gómez, Luis Alonso Anaya Merino, Marvin René González Leiva, Alfredo Alberto Pacheco (Cap), Alexander Escobar Rosales, Óscar Armando Jiménez Campos (54.Christian Giovanni Castillo Martínez), Shawn Hasani Martin Henríquez (34.José Manuel Martínez), Ramón Alfredo Sánchez Paredes, Williams Enrique Reyes Rodríguez (72.Emerson David Umaña Corleto), Eliseo Antonio Quintanilla Ortíz, Rudis Alberto Rivera Corrales. Trainer: Carlos de los Cobos Martínez (Mexico).
PAN: Jaime Manuel Penedo Cano, Adolfo Machado, Luis Moreno, Carlos Rubén Rivera Moulton, Luis Alfonso Henríquez Ledezma, Román Aureliano Torres Morcillo, José Luis Garcés Rivera (63.Luis Carlos Tejada Hansell; 83.José Anthony Torres), Rolando Emilio Escobar Batista (58.Eric Vásquez), Blas Antonio Miguel Pérez Ortega (Cap), Gabriel Enrique Gómez Giron, Juan Ramón Solís. Trainer: Alexandre Borges Guimarães (Costa Rica).
Goals: 0-1 José Luis Garcés Rivera (14), 1-1 Eliseo Antonio Quintanilla Ortíz (70), 2-1 Eliseo Antonio Quintanilla Ortíz (81 penalty), 3-1 Luis Alonso Anaya Merino (88).
Cautions: Shawn Hasani Martin Henríquez, Alexander Escobar Rosales, Luis Alonso Anaya Merino / Carlos Rubén Rivera Moulton, Rolando Emilio Escobar Batista, Luis Alfonso Henríquez Ledezma.
Sent off: Carlos Rubén Rivera Moulton (80), Adolfo Machado (89).

Group 3D
15.06.2008, Stade „Sylvio Cator", Port-au-Prince; Attendance: 6,000
Referee: Joel Antonio Aguilar Chicas (El Salvador)
HAITI – HOLLAND ANTILLES **0-0**
HAI: Gabard Fenelon, Frantz Bertin, Meshack Jérôme, Lesly Fellinga (83.Ednerson Raymond), Pierre Mercier, Jean-Sony Alcenat, Brunel Fucien, Peterson Joseph, Jean Michel Alexandre Boucicaut (57.Fabrice Noël), Mones Chéry (Cap), Leonel Saint-Preux (69.Fritzon Jean-Baptiste). Trainer: Wagneau Eloi.
ANT: Wencho Farrell, Angelo Cijntje, Tyronne Loran (Cap), Angelo Martha, Djuric Winklaar, Sendley Bito, Giovanni Franken, Angelo Zimmerman, Anton Jongsma, Richmar Siberie (77.Dyron Daal), Orlando Smeekes (66.Revy Rosalia). Trainer: Leen Looyen (NED).
Cautions: Jean-Sony Alcenat / Giovanni Franken, Angelo Cijntje, Anton Jongsma.

22.06.2008, Stadion Ergilio Hato, Willemstad; Attendance: 9,000
Referee: Neal Brizan (Trinidad & Tobago)
HOLLAND ANTILLES - HAITI **0-1(0-0)**
ANT: Wencho Farrell, Angelo Martha, Tyronne Loran, Djuric Winklaar, Sendley Bito, Angelo Zimmerman, Giovanni Franken, Shelton Martis (41.Eugene Martha), Dyron Daal (80.Richmar Siberie), Robin Nelisse (Cap), Orlando Smeekes. Trainer: Leen Looyen (NED).
HAI: Gabard Fenelon, Judelin Aveska, Frantz Bertin, Pierre-Richard Bruny, Mones Chéry, Frantz Gilles, Jean-François Lescinel (60.Brunel Fucien), Jean-Sony Alcenat (84.Alain Vubert), Peter Germain, Éliphène Cadet (67.Leonel Saint-Preux), Fabrice Noël. Trainer: Wagneau Eloi.
Goal: 0-1 Eugene Martha (78 own goal).
Cautions: Dyron Daal / Judelin Aveska, Gabard Fenelon.

THIRD ROUND

GROUP 1

20.08.2008	Havana	Cuba – Trinidad & Tobago	1-3(0-1)
20.08.2008	Guatemala City	Guatemala – United States	0-1(0-0)
06.09.2008	Port of Spain	Trinidad & Tobago - Guatemala	1-1(0-0)
06.09.2008	Havana	Cuba – United States	0-1(0-1)
10.09.2008	Bridgeview	United States - Trinidad & Tobago	3-0(2-0)
10.09.2008	Guatemala City	Guatemala - Cuba	4-1(1-1)
11.10.2008	Washington DC	United States - Cuba	6-1(2-1)
11.10.2008	Guatemala City	Guatemala - Trinidad & Tobago	0-0
15.10.2008	Havana	Cuba - Guatemala	2-1(1-0)
15.10.2008	Port of Spain	Trinidad & Tobago – United States	2-1(0-0)
19.11.2008	Port of Spain	Trinidad & Tobago - Cuba	3-0(0-0)
19.11.2008	Commerce City	United States - Guatemala	2-0(0-0)

FINAL STANDINGS

1.	**United States**	6	5	0	1	14	-	3	15
2.	**Trinidad & Tobago**	6	3	2	1	9	-	6	11
3.	Guatemala	6	1	2	3	6	-	7	5
4.	Cuba	6	1	0	5	5	-	18	3

United States and Trinidad & Tobago qualified for the Fourth Round.

20.08.2008, Estadio „Pedro Marrero", La Habana; Attendance: 4,000
Referee: Benito Armando Archundia Téllez (Mexico)
CUBA – TRINIDAD & TOBAGO   **1-3(0-1)**
CUB: Dany Quintero, Jorge Luis Clavelo, Jaime Colomé, Reysandri Fernández Cervantes, Carlos Francisco, Silvio Miñoso, Yénier Márquez, Luis Villegas (59.Alain Cervantes), Heviel Cordovez (57.Leonel Duarte), Roberto Linares, Jensy Muñoz (81.Pedro Faife). Trainer: Reinhold Franz (Germany).
TRI: Marvin Phillip, Makan Hislop, Avery John, Dennis Lawrence, Clyde Leon, Cyd Gray, Christopher Birchall (39.Khaleem Hyland), Keon Daniel, Densill Theobald (67.Darryl Roberts), Anthony Wolfe, Cornell Glen (73.Osei Telesford). Trainer: Francisco Maturana (Colombia).
Goals: 0-1 Keon Daniel (22), 0-2 Keon Daniel (61), 0-3 Cornell Glen (69), 1-3 Jeniel Márquez (88).
Cautions: Reysandri Fernández Cervantes / Makan Hislop, Avery John, Dennis Lawrence.
Sent off: Khaleem Hyland (71).

20.08.2008, Estadio Nacional „Mateo Flores", Guatemala City; Attendance: 26,000
Referee: Enrico Wijngaarde (Suriname)
GUATEMALA – UNITED STATES   **0-1(0-0)**
GUA: Ricardo Alberto Trigueño Foster, Gustavo Adolfo Cabrera Marroquín, Yony Wilson Flores Monroy, Luis Ricardo Rodríguez Jérez, José Manuel Contreras y Contreras (75.Marco Pablo Pappa Ponce), Carlos Eduardo Gallardo Nájera, Freddy Alexander García Carrera (67.Carlos Mauricio Castrillo Alonzo), Guillermo Ramírez Ortega, Mario Rafael Rodríguez Rodríguez, Carlos Humberto Ruiz Gutiérez (Cap), Fredy Williams Thompson León (66.Jean Jonathan Márquez Orellana). Trainer: Ramón Enrique Maradiaga Chávez (Honduras).
USA: Tim Howard, Steven Cherundolo, Oguchialu Chijioke Onyewu, Carlos Manuel Bocanegra (Cap), Heath Gregory Pearce, Pablo Mastroeni (78.Maurice Edu), Edward James Lewis (66.DaMarcus Lamont Beasley), Michael Sheehan Bradley, Clinton Drew Dempsey (66.Francis Daniel Hejduk), Landon Timothy Donovan, Brian Ching. Trainer: Robert Bradley.
Goals: 0-1 Carlos Manuel Bocanegra (70).
Cautions: Guillermo Ramírez Ortega, José Manuel Contreras y Contreras / Steven Cherundolo, Clinton

Drew Dempsey, Pablo Mastroeni, Tim Howard.
Sent off: Steven Cherundolo (60), Gustavo Adolfo Cabrera Marroquín (63).

06.09.2008, „Hasely Crawford" Stadium, Port of Spain; Attendance: 9,500
Referee: Roberto Moreno (Panama)
TRINIDAD & TOBAGO - GUATEMALA   **1-1(0-0)**
TRI: Marvin Phillip, Keyeno Thomas, Avery John, Dennis Lawrence, Clyde Leon, Cyd Gray, Carlos Edwards (46.Anthony Wolfe), Keon Daniel, Densill Theobald (46.André Toussaint), Cornell Glen (88.Kerry Baptiste), Dwight Eversley Yorke. Trainer: Francisco Maturana (Colombia).
GUA: Ricardo Alberto Trigueño Foster (66.Luis Pedro Molina Bruni), Carlos Mauricio Castrillo Alonzo (90.Fredy Williams Thompson León), Yony Wilson Flores Monroy, Carlos Eduardo Gallardo Nájera, Luis Ricardo Rodríguez Jérez, José Manuel Contreras y Contreras (76.Marco Pablo Pappa Ponce), Freddy Alexander García Carrera, Guillermo Ramírez Ortega, Mario Rafael Rodríguez Rodríguez, Carlos Humberto Ruiz Gutiérez, Jean Jonathan Márquez Orellana. Trainer: Ramón Enrique Maradiaga Chávez (Honduras).
Goals: 1-0 Keon Daniel (84), 1-1 Carlos Eduardo Gallardo Nájera (90+2).
Cautions: Avery John, Cornell Glen, Anthony Wolfe / Freddy Alexander García Carrera.

06.09.2008, Estadio „Pedro Marrero", La Habana; Attendance: 12,000
Referee: Joel Antonio Aguilar Chicas (El Salvador)
CUBA – UNITED STATES   **0-1(0-1)**
CUB: Odelín Molina, Jorge Luis Clavelo, Jaime Colomé (52.Pedro Faife), Reysandri Fernández Cervantes, Carlos Francisco, Silvio Miñoso, Yénier Márquez, Luis Villegas, Heviel Cordovez, Roberto Linares (67.Leonel Duarte), Jensy Muñoz (46.Alain Cervantes). Trainer: Reinhold Franz (Germany).
USA: Tim Howard, Francis Daniel Hejduk, Carlos Manuel Bocanegra (Cap), Oguchialu Chijioke Onyewu, Heath Gregory Pearce, Michael Sheehan Bradley, Maurice Edu, DaMarcus Lamont Beasley, Clinton Drew Dempsey (75.Sacha Kljestan), Landon Timothy Donovan, Brian Ching. Trainer: Robert Bradley.
Goal: 0-1 Clinton Drew Dempsey (39).
Cautions: Luis Villegas, Jorge Luis Clavelo / Michael Sheehan Bradley, Francis Daniel Hejduk.

10.09.2008, Toyota Park, Bridgeview; Attendance: 11,452
Referee: Courtney Campbell (Jamaica)
UNITED STATES - TRINIDAD & TOBAGO   **3-0(2-0)**
USA: Tim Howard, Steven Cherundolo, Carlos Manuel Bocanegra (Cap), Oguchialu Chijioke Onyewu, Heath Gregory Pearce, Sacha Kljestan, Michael Sheehan Bradley (67.Ricardo Anthony Clark), DaMarcus Lamont Beasley, Clinton Drew Dempsey (78.Edward James Lewis), Landon Timothy Donovan, Brian Ching (67.Edward Abraham Johnson). Trainer: Robert Bradley.
TRI: Marvin Phillip, Aklie Edwards, Makan Hislop, Clyde Leon, Osei Telesford, Keyeno Thomas, Cyd Gray, Carlos Edwards, Keon Daniel, Densill Theobald (46.Anthony Wolfe), Cornell Glen. Trainer: Francisco Maturana (Colombia).
Goals: 1-0 Michael Sheehan Bradley (10), 2-0 Clinton Drew Dempsey (18), 3-0 Brian Ching (57).
Cautions: Steven Cherundolo / Aklie Edwards, Clyde Leon.

10.09.2008, Estadio Nacional „Mateo Flores", Guatemala City; Attendance: 19,750
Referee: Marco Antonio Rodríguez Moreno (Mexico)
GUATEMALA - CUBA   **4-1(1-1)**
GUA: Ricardo Alberto Trigueño Foster, Yony Wilson Flores Monroy, Carlos Eduardo Gallardo Nájera, Mario Rafael Rodríguez Rodríguez, Freddy Alexander García Carrera, Guillermo Ramírez Ortega (Cap), Fredy Williams Thompson León (46.Carlos Mauricio Castrillo Alonzo), Marco Pablo Pappa Ponce, Luis Ricardo Rodríguez Jérez, Carlos Humberto Ruiz Gutiérez (81.José Manuel Contreras y Contreras), Jean Jonathan Márquez Orellana. Trainer: Ramón Enrique Maradiaga Chávez (Honduras).
CUB: Odelín Molina, Jorge Luis Clavelo, Reysandri Fernández Cervantes, Carlos Francisco, Alain

Cervantes (73.Luis Villegas), Silvio Miñoso, Yénier Márquez, Alianni Montaya, Roberto Linares, Leonel Duarte (76.Heviel Cordovez), Pedro Faife (63.Jensy Muñoz). Trainer: Reinhold Franz (Germany).

Goals: 0-1 Roberto Linares (25), 1-1 Carlos Humberto Ruiz Gutiérez (38), 2-1 Carlos Humberto Ruiz Gutiérez (55), 3-1 Mario Rafael Rodríguez Rodríguez (85), 4-1 José Manuel Contreras y Contreras (90+1).

Cautions: Carlos Mauricio Castrillo Alonzo / Alain Cervantes.

Sent off: Roberto Linares (56).

11.10.2008, „Robert F. Kennedy" Memorial Stadium, Washington; Attendance: 20,249
Referee: Roberto Moreno (Panama)

UNITED STATES - CUBA   **6-1(2-1)**

USA: Tim Howard, Steven Cherundolo, Carlos Manuel Bocanegra (Cap), Oguchialu Chijioke Onyewu, Heath Gregory Pearce (68.José Francisco Torres Mezzell), Michael Sheehan Bradley, Sacha Kljestan (76.Fredua Koranteng Adu), DaMarcus Lamont Beasley, Clinton Drew Dempsey, Landon Timothy Donovan, Brian Ching (68.Josmer Volmy Altidore). Trainer: Robert Bradley.

CUB: Odelín Molina, Jorge Luis Clavelo, Yoel Colomé, Jaime Colomé (71.Alianni Montaya), Reysandri Fernández Cervantes, Luis Villegas (46.Carlos Francisco), Silvio Miñoso, Yénier Márquez, Alain Cervantes, Leonel Duarte, Jensy Muñoz (80.Mario Ruiz). Trainer: Reinhold Franz (Germany).

Goals: 1-0 DaMarcus Lamont Beasley (10), 2-0 DaMarcus Lamont Beasley (30), 2-1 Jensy Muñoz (31), 3-1 Landon Timothy Donovan (48), 4-1 (63), 5-1 (87), 6-1 (89).

Cautions: Michael Sheehan Bradley / Yoel Colomé, Reysandri Fernández Cervantes.

Sent off: Yoel Colomé (41).

11.10.2008, Estadio Nacional „Mateo Flores", Guatemala City; Attendance: 29,000
Referee: Silviu Petrescu (Canada)

GUATEMALA - TRINIDAD & TOBAGO   **0-0**

GUA: Ricardo Alberto Trigueño Foster, Yony Wilson Flores Monroy, Carlos Eduardo Gallardo Nájera, Luis Ricardo Rodríguez Jérez, Gustavo Adolfo Cabrera Marroquín (61.Abner Isai Trigueros Álvarez), Mario Rafael Rodríguez Rodríguez, Freddy Alexander García Carrera (46.José Manuel Contreras y Contreras), Guillermo Ramírez Ortega, Marco Pablo Pappa Ponce, Carlos Humberto Ruiz Gutiérez, Jean Jonathan Márquez Orellana (61.Gonzalo Antonio Romero Paz). Trainer: Ramón Enrique Maradiaga Chávez (Honduras).

TRI: Clayton Ince, Avery John, Keyeno Thomas, Dennis Lawrence, Cyd Gray, Christopher Birchall, Russell Nigel Latapy (46.Clyde Leon), Carlos Edwards, Jason Scotland (70.Keon Daniel), Anthony Wolfe (46.Cornell Glen), Dwight Eversley Yorke. Trainer: Francisco Maturana (Colombia).

Cautions: Guillermo Ramírez Ortega, Carlos Eduardo Gallardo Nájera / Anthony Wolfe, Cyd Gray, Christopher Birchall, Clayton Ince.

Sent off: Cyd Gray (40).

15.10.2008, Estadio „Pedro Marrero", La Habana; Attendance: 6,000
Referee: Courtney Campbell (Jamaica)

CUBA - GUATEMALA   **2-1(1-0)**

CUB: Odelín Molina, Jorge Luis Clavelo (Cap), Jaime Colomé (90.Alianni Montaya), Lázaro Alfonso (74.Carlos Francisco), Alain Cervantes, Silvio Miñoso, Kanier Dranguet, Yénier Márquez, Roberto Linares, Leonel Duarte, Jensy Muñoz (77.Luis Villegas). Trainer: Raúl González.

GUA: Ricardo Alberto Trigueño Foster, Yony Wilson Flores Monroy, Carlos Eduardo Gallardo Nájera, Gustavo Adolfo Cabrera Marroquín (71.Abner Isai Trigueros Álvarez), Cristian Jafeth Noriega Santizo, José Manuel Contreras y Contreras (46.Marvin Tomás Ávila Sánchez), Marco Pablo Pappa Ponce, Luis Ricardo Rodríguez Jérez, Fredy Williams Thompson León, Gonzalo Antonio Romero Paz (60.Jean Jonathan Márquez Orellana), Carlos Humberto Ruiz Gutiérez (Cap). Trainer: Ramón Enrique Maradiaga Chávez (Honduras).

Goals: 1-0 Jaime Colomé (45 penalty), 1-1 Marco Pablo Pappa Ponce (80), 2-1 Alianni Montaya (90).

Cautions: Silvio Miñoso, Alain Cervantes, Jaime Colomé, Jorge Luis Clavelo, Lázaro Alfonso /

Cristian Jafeth Noriega Santizo, Luis Ricardo Rodríguez Jérez, Gustavo Adolfo Cabrera Marroquín.

15.10.2008, „Hasely Crawford" Stadium, Port of Spain; Attendance: 19,000
Referee: Walter Quesada Cordero (Costa Rica)
TRINIDAD & TOBAGO – UNITED STATES   **2-1(0-0)**
TRI: Clayton Ince, Aklie Edwards, Dennis Lawrence, Keyeno Thomas (40.Makan Hislop), Carlos Edwards, Christopher Birchall, Keon Daniel, Russell Nigel Latapy (76.Khaleem Hyland), Silvio Spann, Jason Scotland (66.Stern John), Dwight Eversley Yorke (Cap). Trainer: Francisco Maturana (Colombia).
USA: Bradley Edwin Guzan, Francis Daniel Hejduk, Michael Orozco, Heath Gregory Pearce (87.Christopher Rolfe), José Francisco Torres Mezzell (83.Daniel Szetela), DaMarcus Lamont Beasley (Cap), Sacha Kljestan, Maurice Edu, Danny Califf, Fredua Koranteng Adu (69.Charlie Davies), Josmer Volmy Altidore. Trainer: Robert Bradley.
Goals: 1-0 Russell Nigel Latapy (60), 1-1 Charlie Davies (74), 2-1 Dwight Eversley Yorke (79).
Cautions: Josmer Volmy Altidore.

19.11.2008, „Hasely Crawford" Stadium, Port of Spain; Attendance: 18,000
Referee: Enrico Wijngaarde (Suriname)
TRINIDAD & TOBAGO - CUBA   **3-0(0-0)**
TRI: Clayton Ince, Aklie Edwards, Dennis Lawrence, Keyeno Thomas, Carlos Edwards, Christopher Birchall (80.Khaleem Hyland), Cyd Gray, Kenwyne Jones (78.Jason Scotland), Keon Daniel, Russell Nigel Latapy (74.Stern John), Dwight Eversley Yorke (Cap). Trainer: Francisco Maturana (Colombia).
CUB: Danis Quintero, Luis Villegas, Yoel Colomé (84.Juan Carlos Martínez), Yénier Márquez, Reysandri Fernández Cervantes, Lázaro Alfonso, Silvio Miñoso, Kanier Dranguet, Alianni Urguelles, Mario Ruiz (75.Heviel Cordovez), Roberto Linares (80.Jensee Muñoz). Trainer: Raúl González.
Goals: 1-0 Kenwyne Jones (67), 2-0 Dwight Eversley Yorke (69), 3-0 Keon Daniel (89).

19.11.2008, Dick's Sporting Goods Park, Commerce City; Attendance: 9,303
Referee: Benito Armando Archundia Téllez (Mexico)
UNITED STATES - GUATEMALA   **2-0(0-0)**
USA: Bradley Edwin Guzan, Clarence Goodson, Michael Parkhurst, Jonathan Bornstein, Pablo Mastroeni (Cap), John Thorrington, Ricardo Anthony Clark, Sacha Kljestan, Fredua Koranteng Adu (83.Davy Arnaud), Josmer Volmy Altidore (75.Brian Ching), Kenny Cooper (76.Conor Casey). Trainer: Robert Bradley.
GUA: Ricardo Antonio Jérez Figueroa, Carlos Mauricio Castrillo Alonzo, Yony Wilson Flores Monroy, Cristian Jafeth Noriega Santizo (Cap), Marvin Tomás Ávila Sánchez, Claudio Josué Albizuris Aguilár, Mario Giovany Acevedo Menzie (74.Minor Ignacio López Campollo), Guillermo Ramírez Ortega, Carlos Fernando Figueroa Martínez (57.Marco Pablo Pappa Ponce), Carlos Rafael Castillo Rosales, Jean Jonathan Márquez Orellana. Trainer: Benjamín Eduardo Monterroso Díaz.
Goals: 1-0 Kenny Cooper (54), 2-0 Fredua Koranteng Adu (69).
Cautions: Ricardo Anthony Clark, Pablo Mastroeni / Yony Wilson Flores Monroy.

GROUP 2

20.08.2008	Toronto	Canada - Jamaica	1-1(0-0)
20.08.2008	Ciudad de México	Mexico - Honduras	2-1(0-1)
06.09.2008	Ciudad de México	Mexico - Jamaica	3-0(2-0)
06.09.2008	Montreal	Canada - Honduras	1-2(1-0)
10.09.2008	Tuxtla Gutiérrez	Mexico - Canada	2-1(0-0)
10.09.2008	San Pedro Sula	Honduras - Jamaica	2-0(0-0)
11.10.2008	Kingston	Jamaica - Mexico	1-0(1-0)
11.10.2008	San Pedro Sula	Honduras - Canada	3-1(1-0)
15.10.2008	Kingston	Jamaica - Honduras	1-0(1-0)
15.10.2008	Edmonton	Canada - Mexico	2-2(1-1)
19.11.2008	San Pedro Sula	Honduras - Mexico	1-0(0-0)
19.11.2008	Kingston	Jamaica - Canada	3-0(1-0)

FINAL STANDINGS

1.	**Honduras**	6	4	0	2	9	-	5	12
2.	**Mexico**	6	3	1	2	9	-	6	10
3.	Jamaica	6	3	1	2	6	-	6	10
4.	Canada	6	0	2	4	6	-	13	2

Honduras and Mexico qualified for the Fourth Round.

20.08.2008, BMO Field, Toronto; Attendance: 22,000
Referee: Carlos Alberto Batres González (Guatemala)
CANADA - JAMAICA 1-1(0-0)
CAN: Patrick Stewart Onstad, Richard Cory Hastings, Michael Klukowski, Patrice Bernier (65.Iain Edward Hume), Paul Andrew Stalteri (Cap), Julien Bobby De Guzmán, Atiba Hutchinson, Dwayne Anthony De Rosario, Adrian Serioux, Tomasz Radziński, Robert Douglas Friend (77.Ali Ngon Gerba). Trainer: Dale William Dink Mitchell.
JAM: Donovan Ricketts, Ian Goodison, Jermaine Taylor, Ricardo Gardner (Cap), O'Brian Woodbine, Wolry Wolfe (87.Omar Cummings), Demar Phillips (90+2.Jermaine Hue), Evan Taylor, Rudolph Austin, Deon Burton, Andrew Williams (63.Luton Shelton). Trainer: René Rodrigues Simões (Brazil).
Goals: 1-0 Julien Bobby De Guzmán (47), 1-1 Andrew Williams (52).
Cautions: Dwayne Anthony De Rosario, Adrian Serioux, Atiba Hutchinson /

20.08.2008, Estadio Azteca, Ciudad de México; Attendance: 81,100
Referee: Joel Antonio Aguilar Chicas (El Salvador)
MEXICO - HONDURAS 2-1(0-1)
MEX: Oswaldo Javier Sánchez Ibarra, José Jonny Magallón Oliva, Ricardo Osorio Mendoza, Rafael Márquez Álvarez (Cap), Carlos Arnoldo Salcido Flores, José Andrés Guardado Hernández, Pável Pardo Segura, Fernando Enrique Arce Ruiz (70.Cuauhtémoc Blanco Bravo), Leandro Augusto Oldoni, Giovanni dos Santos Ramírez (56.Guillermo Luis Franco Farquarson), Carlos Alberto Vela Garrido (61.Omar Bravo Torrrecillas). Trainer: Sven-Göran Eriksson (Sweden).
HON: Noel Eduardo Valladares Bonilla, Víctor Salvador Bernárdez Blanco, Maynor Alexis Figueroa Róchez, Sergio Giovany Mendoza Escobar, Emilio Arturo Izaguirre Girón, Wilson Roberto Palacios Suazo, Edgard Anthony Álvarez Reyes (81.Oscar Boniek García Ramírez), Amado Guevara (Cap), Julio César de León (85.Carlos Yaír Costly Molina), Danilo Elvis Turcios Funes (69.Mario Iván Guerrero Ramírez), Óscar David Suazo Velázquez. Trainer: Reinaldo Rueda Rivera (Colombia).
Goals: 0-1 Julio César De León (35), 1-1 Pável Pardo Segura (73), 2-1 Pável Pardo Segura (65).
Cautions: Fernando Enrique Arce Ruiz, José Jonny Magallón Oliva / Danilo Elvis Turcios Funes, Maynor Alexis Figueroa Róchez, Oscar Boniek García Ramírez.
Sent off: Maynor Alexis Figueroa Róchez (76).

06.09.2008, Estadio Azteca, Ciudad de México; Attendance: 96,000
Referee: Baldomero Toledo (United States)
MEXICO - JAMAICA   **3-0(2-0)**
MEX: Oswaldo Javier Sánchez Ibarra, José Jonny Magallón Oliva, Ricardo Osorio Mendoza, Rafael
Márquez Álvarez (Cap), Carlos Arnoldo Salcido Flores, José Andrés Guardado Hernández, Pável Pardo
Segura (61.Gerardo Torrado Díez de Bonilla), Fernando Enrique Arce Ruiz, Giovanni dos Santos
Ramírez (71.Cuauhtémoc Blanco Bravo), Luis Ernesto Pérez Gómez, Carlos Alberto Vela Garrido
(78.Vicente José Matías Vuoso). Trainer: Sven-Göran Eriksson (Sweden).
JAM: Donovan Ricketts, Ian Goodison, Jermaine Taylor, Ricardo Gardner (Cap), Tyrone Marshall,
Evan Taylor (53.Keneil Moodie), Ricardo Fuller, Demar Phillips (46.Wolry Wolfe), Rodolph Austin,
Deon Burton (71.Luton Shelton), Andrew Williams. Trainer: René Rodrigues Simões (Brazil).
Goals: 1-0 José Andrés Guardado Hernández (3), 2-0 Fernando Enrique Arce Ruiz (33), 3-0 José Jonny
Magallón Oliva (63).
Cautions: Carlos Arnoldo Salcido Flores, Rafael Márquez Álvarez / Evan Taylor, Rodolph Austin,
Demar Phillips.

06.09.2008, Saputo Stadium, Montreal; Attendance: 13,032
Referee: Walter Quesada Cordero (Costa Rica)
CANADA - HONDURAS   **1-2(1-0)**
CAN: Lars Justin Hirschfeld, Richard Cory Hastings, Michael Klukowski, Patrice Bernier, Paul
Andrew Stalteri (Cap), Julien Bobby De Guzmán, Atiba Hutchinson, Dwayne Anthony De Rosario,
Adrian Seiroux, Tomasz Radziński (21.Iain Edward Hume; 83.James Gerald Brennan), Ali Ngon Gerba
(62.Robert Douglas Friend). Trainer: Dale William Dink Mitchell.
HON: Noel Eduardo Valladares Bonilla, Víctor Salvador Bernárdez Blanco, Osman Danilo Chávez
Guity, Sergio Giovany Mendoza Escobar (84.Oscar Boniek García Ramírez), Emilio Arturo Izaguirre
Girón, Wilson Roberto Palacios Suazo, Hendry Thomas, Amado Guevara, Carlos Yaír Costly Molina,
Ramón Fernando Núñez Reyes (75.Miguel Angel Castillo Flores), Óscar David Suazo Velázquez.
Trainer: Reinaldo Rueda Rivera (Colombia).
Goals: 1-0 Adrian Seiroux (5), 1-1 Ramón Fernando Núñez Reyes (47), 1-2 Ramón Fernando Núñez
Reyes (56).
Cautions: Patrice Bernier.
Sent off: Patrice Bernier (73).

10.09.2008, Estadio „Víctor Manuel Reyna", Tuxtla Gutiérrez; Attendance: 26,900
Referee: Neal Brizan (Trinidad & Tobago)
MEXICO - CANADA   **2-1(0-0)**
MEX: Oswaldo Javier Sánchez Ibarra, José Jonny Magallón Oliva, Ricardo Osorio Mendoza, Rafael
Márquez Álvarez (Cap), Fausto Manuel Pinto Rosas, José Andrés Guardado Hernández, Gerardo
Torrado Díez de Bonilla, Luis Ernesto Pérez Gómez, Fernando Enrique Arce Ruiz (89.Cuauhtémoc
Blanco Bravo), Giovanni dos Santos Ramírez (57.Omar Bravo Torrrecillas), Carlos Alberto Vela
Garrido (70.Carlos Augusto Ochoa Mendoza). Trainer: Sven-Göran Eriksson (Sweden).
CAN: Lars Justin Hirschfeld, Michael Klukowski, Richard Cory Hastings, Paul Andrew Stalteri (Cap),
James Gerald Brennan (65.Ali Ngon Gerba), Issey Morgan Nakajima-Farran (62.Iain Edward Hume),
Julien Bobby De Guzmán, Atiba Hutchinson, Dwayne Anthony De Rosario, Adrian Seiroux, Robert
Douglas Friend (81.Olivier Occean). Trainer: Dale William Dink Mitchell.
Goals: 1-0 Omar Bravo Torrrecillas (59), 2-0 Rafael Márquez Álvarez (73), 2-1 Ali Ngon Gerba (79).
Cautions: José Andrés Guardado Hernández, Cuauhtémoc Blanco Bravo / Dwayne Anthony De
Rosario, Michael Klukowski, Adrian Seiroux.

10.09.2008, Estadio Olimpico Metropolitano, San Pedro Sula; Attendance: 39,000
Referee: Roberto Moreno (Panama)
HONDURAS - JAMAICA   **2-0(0-0)**
HON: Noel Eduardo Valladares Bonilla, Víctor Salvador Bernárdez Blanco, Maynor Alexis Figueroa

Róchez, Sergio Giovany Mendoza Escobar, Emilio Arturo Izaguirre Girón, Wilson Roberto Palacios Suazo, Hendry Thomas, Amado Guevara (88.Milton Omar Núñez García), Carlos Yaír Costly Molina (70.Saúl Asael Martínez), Ramón Fernando Núñez Reyes, Óscar David Suazo Velázquez (67.Danilo Elvis Turcios Funes). Trainer: Reinaldo Rueda Rivera (Colombia).
JAM: Donovan Ricketts, Ian Goodison, Jermaine Taylor (16.Jevaughn Watson), Ricardo Gardner, Tyrone Marshall, O'Brian Woodbine, Shavar Thomas, Wolry Wolfe (67.Ricardo Fuller), Luton Shelton, Rodolph Austin, Andrew Williams (53.Jermaine Hue). Trainer: René Rodrigues Simões (Brazil).
Goals: 1-0 Ramón Fernando Núñez Reyes (65), 2-0 Amado Guevara (73 penalty).
Cautions: Shavar Thomas, O'Brian Woodbine.

11.10.2008, Independence Park, Kingston; Attendance: 27,000
Referee: Walter Quesada Cordero (Costa Rica)
JAMAICA - MEXICO   **1-0(1-0)**
JAM: Donovan Ricketts, Ian Goodison, Claude Davis (75.Damian Steward), Ricardo Gardner (Cap), Tyrone Marshall, Oneil Thompson (79.Jermaine Johnson), Jamal Campbell-Ryce, Demar Phillips, Rodolph Austin, Ricardo Fuller (70.Omar Cummings), Luton Shelton. Trainer: Theodore Whitmore.
MEX: Oswaldo Javier Sánchez Ibarra, José Jonny Magallón Oliva, Ricardo Osorio Mendoza (55.Aarón Galindo Rubio), Rafael Márquez Álvarez (Cap), Carlos Arnoldo Salcido Flores, Gerardo Torrado Díez de Bonilla, Fernando Enrique Arce Ruiz, Luis Ernesto Pérez Gómez (67.Omar Arellano Riverón), Omar Bravo Torrrecillas (57.Vicente José Matías Vuoso), Giovanni dos Santos Ramírez, Carlos Alberto Vela Garrido. Trainer: Sven-Göran Eriksson (Sweden).
Goal: 1-0 Ricardo Fuller (34).
Cautions: Ricardo Fuller, Rodolph Austin, Tyrone Marshall, Oneil Thompson / Rafael Márquez Álvarez, Carlos Arnoldo Salcido Flores, Carlos Alberto Vela Garrido.

11.10.2008, Estadio Olimpico Metropolitano, San Pedro Sula; Attendance: 36,000
Referee: Jair Marrufo (United States)
HONDURAS - CANADA   **3-1(1-0)**
HON: Noel Eduardo Valladares Bonilla, Víctor Salvador Bernárdez Blanco, Osman Danilo Chávez Guity, Sergio Giovany Mendoza Escobar, Maynor Alexis Figueroa Róchez, Hendry Thomas, Amado Guevara, Wilson Roberto Palacios Suazo, Carlos Yaír Costly Molina, Walter Julián Martínez Ramos (70.Carlos Will Mejía García), Ramón Fernando Núñez Reyes (46.Danilo Elvis Turcios Funes; 90.Emilio Arturo Izaguirre Girón). Trainer: Reinaldo Rueda Rivera (Colombia).
CAN: Lars Justin Hirschfeld, Michael Klukowski, André Robert Hainault, Kevin James McKenna, Paul Andrew Stalteri (Cap), Patrice Bernier (46.Iain Edward Hume), Marcel De Jong (76.Richard Cory Hastings), Atiba Hutchinson, Kevin Jorge Harmse, Tomasz Radziński, Ali Ngon Gerba (46.Robert Douglas Friend). Trainer: Dale William Dink Mitchell.
Goals: 1-0 Walter Julián Martínez Ramos (8), 1-1 André Robert Hainault (52), 2-1 Carlos Yaír Costly Molina (65), 3-1 Hendry Thomas (90).
Cautions: Osman Danilo Chávez Guity, Carlos Yaír Costly Molina, Sergio Giovany Mendoza Escobar, Carlos Will Mejía García / Iain Edward Hume.

15.10.2008, Independence Park, Kingston; Attendance: 25,000
Referee: Neal Brizan (Trinidad & Tobago)
JAMAICA - HONDURAS   **1-0(1-0)**
JAM: Donovan Ricketts, Ian Goodison, Claude Davis (61.Damian Steward), Ricardo Gardner (Cap), Tyrone Marshall, Oneil Thompson, Ricardo Fuller (78.Dane Richards), Demar Phillips, Omar Daley (71.Omar Cummings), Jamal Campbell-Ryce, Luton Shelton. Trainer: Theodore Whitmore.
HON: Noel Eduardo Valladares Bonilla, Víctor Salvador Bernárdez Blanco, Sergio Giovany Mendoza Escobar, Osman Danilo Chávez Guity, Maynor Alexis Figueroa Róchez, Wilson Roberto Palacios Suazo, Hendry Thomas, Amado Guevara (72.Ramón Fernando Núñez Reyes), Carlos Yaír Costly Molina, Danilo Elvis Turcios Funes (61.Carlos Will Mejía García), Milton Omar Núñez García (50.Walter Julián Martínez Ramos). Trainer: Reinaldo Rueda Rivera (Colombia).

Goal: 1-0 Luton Shelton (16).
Cautions: Jamal Campbell-Ryce, Demar Phillips, Omar Daley / Hendry Thomas, Maynor Alexis Figueroa Róchez, Wilson Roberto Palacios Suazo.

15.10.2008, Commonwealth Stadium, Edmonton; Attendance: 14,145
Referee: Enrico Wijngaarde (Suriname)
CANADA - MEXICO   **2-2(1-1)**
CAN: Lars Justin Hirschfeld, Michael Klukowski, André Robert Hainault, Paul Andrew Stalteri (Cap), Patrice Bernier, Richard Cory Hastings (89.Charles Patrick Gbeke), Marcel De Jong (39.Krzysztof Pozniak), Kevin Jorge Harmse, Adrian Serioux, Tomasz Radziński, Ali Ngon Gerba. Trainer: Dale William Dink Mitchell.
MEX: Oswaldo Javier Sánchez Ibarra, José Jonny Magallón Oliva, Ricardo Osorio Mendoza, Carlos Arnoldo Salcido Flores, Aarón Galindo Rubio, Fernando Enrique Arce Ruiz (82.Carlos Augusto Ochoa Mendoza), José Andrés Guardado Hernández, Luis Ernesto Pérez Gómez (55.Vicente José Matías Vuoso), Giovanni dos Santos Ramírez, Carlos Alberto Vela Garrido (67.Omar Bravo Torrrecillas). Trainer: Sven-Göran Eriksson (Sweden).
Goals: 1-0 Ali Ngon Gerba, (13), 1-1 Carlos Arnoldo Salcido Flores (35), 2-1 Tomasz Radziński (50), 2-2 Vicente José Matías Vuoso (64).
Cautions: Michael Klukowski, Paul Andrew Stalteri, Tomasz Radziński, Kevin Jorge Harmse.

19.11.2008, Estadio Olimpico Metropolitano, San Pedro Sula; Attendance: 45,000
Referee: Carlos Alberto Batres González (Guatemala)
HONDURAS - MEXICO   **1-0(0-0)**
HON: Noel Eduardo Valladares Bonilla, Víctor Salvador Bernárdez Blanco, Sergio Giovany Mendoza Escobar, Maynor Alexis Figueroa Róchez, Wilson Roberto Palacios Suazo, Hendry Thomas (46.Danilo Elvis Turcios Funes), Amado Guevara (Cap), Mario Iván Guerrero Ramírez, Emil José Martínez Cruz (71.Ramón Fernando Núñez Reyes), Carlos Yaír Costly Molina, Óscar David Suazo Velázquez. Trainer: Reinaldo Rueda Rivera (Colombia).
MEX: Oswaldo Javier Sánchez Ibarra, Aarón Galindo Rubio, Carlos Arnoldo Salcido Flores, Rafael Márquez Álvarez (Cap), Ricardo Osorio Mendoza, José Andrés Guardado Hernández, Pável Pardo Segura, Gerardo Torrado Díez de Bonilla, Antônio Naelson Matías „Zinha" (57.Carlos Alberto Vela Garrido), Fernando Enrique Arce Ruiz (73.Nery Alberto Castillo Confalonieri), Vicente José Matías Vuoso (82.Omar Bravo Torrrecillas). Trainer: Sven-Göran Eriksson (Sweden).
Goal: 1-0 Ricardo Osorio Mendoza (52 own goal)
Cautions: Wilson Roberto Palacios Suazo, Carlos Yaír Costly Molina, Amado Guevara / Fernando Enrique Arce Ruiz, Antônio Naelson Matías „Zinha", Rafael Márquez Álvarez, Gerardo Torrado Díez de Bonilla.
Sent off: Gerardo Torrado Díez de Bonilla (89), Carlos Alberto Vela Garrido (90+1).

19.11.2008, Independence Park, Kingston; Attendance: 28,000
Referee: Joel Antonio Aguilar Chicas (El Salvador)
JAMAICA - CANADA   **3-0(1-0)**
JAM: Donovan Ricketts, Ian Goodison, Claude Davis, Ricardo Gardner (Cap), Tyrone Marshall, Marlon King (79.Dane Richards), Demar Phillips, Jamal Campbell-Ryce, Rodolph Austin (81.Jermaine Johnson), Ricardo Fuller (71.Omar Cummings), Luton Shelton. Trainer: John Charles Bryan Barnes (England).
CAN: Lars Justin Hirschfeld, Adrian Cann, André Robert Hainault, Marcel De Jong, Paul Andrew Stalteri (Cap) (65.Andrzej Mateusz Ornoch), Krzysztof Pozniak, Kevin Jorge Harmse, Nikolas William Ledgerwood, William David Johnson, Issey Morgan Nakajima-Farran (69.Christopher Williams), Charles Patrick Gbeke. Trainer: Dale William Dink Mitchell.
Goals: 1-0 Luton Shelton (28), 2-0 Marlon King (58 penalty), 3-0 Omar Cummings (71).
Cautions: Jamal Campbell-Ryce.

GROUP 3

20.08.2008	Port-au-Prince	Haiti - Suriname	2-2(0-1)
20.08.2008	San José	Costa Rica – El Salvador	1-0(0-0)
06.09.2008	San Salvador	El Salvador - Haiti	5-0(2-0)
06.09.2008	San José	Costa Rica - Suriname	7-0(2-0)
10.09.2008	Paramaribo	Suriname – El Salvador	0-2(0-2)
10.09.2008	Port-au-Prince	Haiti – Costa Rica	1-3(1-1)
11.10.2008	Paramaribo	Suriname – Costa Rica	1-4(0-2)
11.10.2008	Port-au-Prince	Haiti – El Salvador	0-0
15.10.2008	San José	Costa Rica - Haiti	2-0(1-0)
15.10.2008	San Salvador	El Salvador - Suriname	3-0(2-0)
19.11.2008	Paramaribo	Suriname - Haiti	1-1(1-1)
19.11.2008	San Salvador	El Salvador – Costa Rica	1-3(1-2)

FINAL STANDINGS

1.	**Costa Rica**	6	6	0	0	20	-	3	18
2.	**El Salvador**	6	3	1	2	11	-	4	10
3.	Haiti	6	0	3	3	4	-	13	3
4.	Suriname	6	0	2	4	4	-	19	2

Costa Rica and El Salvador qualified for the Fourth Round.

20.08.2008, Stade „Sylvio Cator", Port-au-Prince; Attendance: 7,800
Referee: Mauricio Navarro (Canada)
HAITI - SURINAME   **2-2(1-1)**
HAI: Gabard Fenelon (Cap), Frantz Bertin, Frantz Gilles (54.Fritzon Jean-Baptiste), Brunel Fucien, Mones Chéry, Jean Jacques Pierre (74.Lesly Fellinga), Jean-Sony Alcenat, Mackorel Sampeur, Peter Germain, Fabrice Noël, Ricardo Pierre-Louis (46.Peterson Joseph). Trainer: Wagneau Eloi.
SUR: Ronny Aloema, Derrik Garden, Marlon Felter (Cap), Ferdinand Jap A Joe, Emilio Limon (66.Lorenzo Wiebers), Rinaldo Lupson (59.Hesron Jeroe), Clifton Sandvliet, Vangellino Sastromedjo, Germaine Sergio van Dijk, Romano Sordam (78.Melvin Valies), Wensley Christoph. Trainer: Kenneth Jaliens.
Goals: 0-1 Wensley Christoph (31), 0-2 Wensley Christoph (46), 1-2 Frantz Bertin (90), 2-2 Brunel Fucien (90+5).
Cautions: Mackorel Sampeur / Wensley Christoph, Ferdinand Jap A Joe.

20.08.2008, Estadio „Ricardo Saprissa", San José; Attendance: 27,000
Referee: Marco Antonio Rodríguez Moreno (Mexico)
COSTA RICA – EL SALVADOR   **1-0(0-0)**
CRC: Ricardo González Fonseca, Cristian Montero Fallas (67.Jervis Drummond Johnson), Júnior Enrique Díaz Campbell, Gonzalo Segares González, Wálter Centeno Corea (Cap), Harold Wallace McDonald, Celso Borges Mora, Alonso Solís Calderón (87.Leonardo González Arce), Álvaro Alberto Saborío Chacón, Alejandro Alpizar Delgado, Bryan Ruiz González (46.Froylán Ledezma Stevens). Trainer: Rodrigo Kenton Johnson.
SLV: Miguel Ángel Montes Moreno, Luis Alonso Anaya Merino, Marvin René González Leiva, Alfredo Alberto Pacheco (Cap) (80.William Osael Romero Castillo), Manuel Alejandro Salazar Rivas, Christian Giovanni Castillo Martínez, Shawn Hasani Martin Henríquez, Ramón Alfredo Sánchez Paredes, Eliseo Antonio Quintanilla Ortíz, Salvador Arturo Coreas Pérez (84.Williams Enrique Reyes Rodríguez), Rudis Alberto Rivera Corrales (73.Rodolfo Antonio Zelaya García). Trainer: Carlos de los Cobos Martínez (Mexico).
Goal: 1-0 Álvaro Alberto Saborío Chacón (48 penalty).
Cautions: Júnior Enrique Díaz Campbell, Cristian Montero Fallas, Álvaro Alberto Saborío Chacón, Froylán Ledezma Stevens / Manuel Alejandro Salazar Rivas, Shawn Hasani Martin Henríquez, Ramón Alfredo Sánchez Paredes, Miguel Ángel Montes Moreno, Eliseo Antonio Quintanilla Ortíz.

148

Sent off: Álvaro Alberto Saborío Chacón (81).

06.09.2008, Estadio „Ricardo Saprissa", San José; Attendance: 27,000
Referee: Marco Antonio Rodríguez Moreno (Mexico)
EL SALVADOR - HAITI   **5-0(2-0)**
SLV: Juan José Gómez, Luis Alonso Anaya Merino, Marvin René González Leiva, Ramón Ulises Flores Aguirre, Alfredo Alberto Pacheco, Manuel Alejandro Salazar Rivas, Christian Giovanni Castillo Martínez, Ramón Alfredo Sánchez Paredes (75.Óscar Armando Jiménez Campos), William Jeovanny Torres Alegría, Williams Enrique Reyes Rodríguez (54.César Alexander Larios Flores), Rodolfo Antonio Zelaya García (60.Salvador Arturo Coreas Pérez). Trainer: Carlos de los Cobos Martínez (Mexico).
HAI: Gabard Fenelon, Frantz Bertin, Brunel Fucien, Mones Chéry, Mackorel Sampeur, Frantz Gilles, Jean-Sony Alcenat, Peter Germain (63.Alain Vubert), Charles Davidson (46.Windsor Noncent), Pierre-Richard Bruny, Abel Thermeus (46.Leonel Saint-Preux). Trainer: Wagneau Eloi.
Goals: 1-0 Rodolfo Antonio Zelaya García (8), 2-0 Rodolfo Antonio Zelaya García (24), 3-0 Rodolfo Antonio Zelaya García (53), 4-0 César Alexander Larios Flores (53), 5-0 William Jeovanny Torres Alegría (79).
Cautions: Mackorel Sampeur, Leonel Saint-Preux.
Sent off: Pierre-Richard Bruny.

06.09.2008, Estadio „Ricardo Saprissa", San José; Attendance: 11,000
Referee: Steven Depiero (Canada)
COSTA RICA - SURINAME   **7-0(2-0)**
CRC: Ricardo González Fonseca, Gonzalo Segares González, Júnior Enrique Díaz Campbell, Wálter Centeno Corea (Cap), José Freddy Fernández Beita, José Luis López Ramírez (83.Alonso Solís Calderón), Celso Borges Mora, Armando Alonso Rodríguez, Harold Wallace McDonald, Alejandro Alpizar Delgado (68.William Sunsing Hidalgo), Froylán Ledezma Stevens (55.Bryan Ruiz González). Trainer: Rodrigo Kenton Johnson.
SUR: Ronny Aloema, Derrik Garden, Marlon Felter, Ferdinand Jap A Joe, Rinaldo Lupson, Claudio Pinas, Gary Sordjo (46.Hesron Jeroe), Lorenzo Wiebers (54.Romano Sordam), Vangellino Sastromedjo (71.Germaine Sergio Van Dijk), Emilio Limon, Wensley Christoph. Trainer: Kenneth Jaliens.
Goals: 1-0 Froylán Ledezma Stevens (9), 2-0 Froylán Ledezma Stevens (41), 3-0 Alejandro Alpizar Delgado (47), 4-0 Armando Alonso Rodríguez (78), 5-0 Celso Borges Mora (81), 6-0 Alonso Solís Calderón (86), 7-0 Bryan Ruiz González (88).
Cautions: Froylán Ledezma Stevens / Rinaldo Lupson, Emilio Limon.
Sent off: Rinaldo Lupson (45+2).

10.09.2008, „André Kamperveen" Stadion, Paramaribo; Attendance: 4,500
Referee: Benito Armando Archundia Téllez (Mexico)
SURINAME – EL SALVADOR   **0-2(0-2)**
SUR: Ronny Aloema, Derrik Garden, Marlon Felter (Cap) (75.Lorenzo Wiebers), Ferdinand Jap A Joe, Hesron Jeroe, Romano Sordam, Emilio Limon, Clifton Sandvliet (78.Melvin Valies), Vangellino Sastromedjo, Claudio Pinas, Wensley Christoph (61.Gary Sordjo). Trainer: Kenneth Jaliens.
SLV: Juan José Gómez, Luis Alonso Anaya Merino, Marvin René González Leiva, Alfredo Alberto Pacheco (Cap), Manuel Alejandro Salazar Rivas, Christian Giovanni Castillo Martínez (62.Salvador Arturo Coreas Pérez), William Jeovanny Torres Alegría (29.Óscar Armando Jiménez Campos), Shawn Hasani Martin Henríquez, Ramón Alfredo Sánchez Paredes, Eliseo Antonio Quintanilla Ortíz, Rodolfo Antonio Zelaya García (67.César Alexander Larios Flores). Trainer: Carlos de los Cobos Martínez (Mexico).
Goals: 0-1 Shawn Hasani Martin Henríquez (1), 0-2 Marlon Felter (12 own goal).
Cautions: Derrik Garden, Hesron Jeroe, Ferdinand Jap A Joe / Ramón Alfredo Sánchez Paredes.

10.09.2008, Stade „Sylvio Cator", Port-au-Prince; Attendance: 14,700
Referee: Carlos Alberto Batres González (Guatemala)
HAITI - COSTA RICA   **1-3(1-1)**
HAI: Gabard Fenelon, Frantz Bertin (Cap), Lesly Fellinga, Meshack Jérôme, Jean-Sony Alcenat, Fabrice Noël, Charles Davidson (64.Jean Michel Alexandre Boucicaut), James Marcellin, Alain Vubert, Sony Norde (80.Leonel Saint-Preux), Abel Thermeus (75.Fritzon Jean-Baptiste). Trainer: Wagneau Eloi.
CRC: Ricardo González Fonseca, Gonzalo Segares González, José Freddy Fernández Beita, Júnior Enrique Díaz Campbell, Wálter Centeno Corea (Cap) (70.Leonardo González Arce), Celso Borges Mora, Harold Wallace McDonald, Armando Alonso Rodríguez, José Luis López Ramírez (56.Alonso Solís Calderón), Bryan Ruiz González, William Sunsing Hidalgo (46.Alejandro Alpizar Delgado). Trainer: Rodrigo Kenton Johnson.
Goals: 0-1 Brian Ruiz (12), 1-1 Alain Vubert (40), 1-2 Brian Ruiz (75), 1-3 Alejandro Alpizar Delgado (86).
Cautions: Charles Davidson, Jean-Sony Alcenat, Sony Norde / Gonzalo Segares González, Júnior Enrique Díaz Campbell, José Freddy Fernández Beita, Ricardo González Fonseca.

11.10.2008, „André Kamperveen" Stadion, Paramaribo; Attendance: 3,000
Referee: Courtney Campbell (Jamaica)
SURINAME – COSTA RICA   **1-4(0-2)**
SUR: Ronny Aloema, Malcolm Weibolt, Marlon Felter, Hesron Jeroe, Eugene Apanta (65.Claudio Pinas), Cleven Wanabo (46.Sergio Aroepa), Vangellino Sastromedjo (61.Jerome Strijder), Clifton Sandvliet, Germaine Sergio van Dijk, Emilio Limon, Wensley Christoph. Trainer: Kenneth Jaliens.
CRC: Keylor Antonio Navas Gamboa, José Freddy Fernández Beita, Cristian Montero Fallas, José Luis López Ramírez, Celso Borges Mora, Wálter Centeno Corea (Cap) (80.Víctor Núñez Rodríguez), Leonardo González Arce, Armando Alonso Rodríguez, Harold Wallace McDonald, Bryan Ruiz González (73.Alonso Solís Calderón), William Sunsing Hidalgo (59.Álvaro Alberto Saborío Chacón). Trainer: Rodrigo Kenton Johnson.
Goals: 0-1 Wálter Centeno Corea (11), 0-2 Celso Borges Mora (43), 0-3 Armando Alonso Rodríguez (47), 1-3 Clifton Sandvliet (48), 1-4 Alonso Solís (77).
Cautions: Marlon Felter, Sergio Aroepa / Alonso Solís Calderón.

11.10.2008, Stade „Sylvio Cator", Port-au-Prince; Attendance: 10,000
Referee: Neal Brizan (Trinidad & Tobago)
HAITI – EL SALVADOR   **0-0**
HAI: Dominique Jean-Zéphirin, Franz Bertin, Judelin Aveska, Lesly Fellinga, Brunel Fucien (46.Ricardo Pierre-Louis), Charles Davidson (72.Leonel Saint-Preux), Mackorel Sampeur, Jean Michel Alexandre Boucicaut, Pierre-Richard Bruny (Cap), Sony Norde (63.Mones Chéry), Abel Thermeus. Trainer: Wagneau Eloi.
SLV: Miguel Ángel Montes Moreno, Luis Alonso Anaya Merino, Marvin Gonzàlez, Alfredo Alberto Pacheco, Christian Giovanni Castillo Martínez (90.William Osael Romero Castillo), Óscar Armando Jiménez Campos, Manuel Alejandro Salazar Rivas, Shawn Hasani Martin Henríquez, Salvador Arturo Coreas Pérez, Eliseo Antonio Quintanilla Ortíz (90.Mario Edgardo Aguilar Posadas), Rudis Alberto Rivera Corrales (83.Rodolfo Antonio Zelaya García). Trainer: Carlos de los Cobos Martínez (Mexico).
Cautions: Mackorel Sampeur, Charles Davidson, Abel Thermeus / Shawn Hasani Martin Henríquez.

15.10.2008, Estadio „Ricardo Saprissa", San José; Attendance: 5,500
Referee: Ricardo Salazar (United States)
COSTA RICA - HAITI   **2-0(1-0)**
CRC: Keylor Antonio Navas Gamboa, Gonzalo Segares González, José Freddy Fernández Beita, Júnior Enrique Díaz Campbell, Wálter Centeno Corea (Cap) (46.José Luis López Ramírez), Armando Alonso Rodríguez, Celso Borges Mora, Roy Myrie Medrano, Alonso Solís Calderón (83.Víctor Núñez Rodríguez), Álvaro Alberto Saborío Chacón (57.Bryan Ruiz González), William Sunsing Hidalgo.

Trainer: Rodrigo Kenton Johnson.
HAI: Dominique Jean-Zéphirin, Judelin Aveska, Lesly Fellinga, Franz Bertin, Meshack Jérôme, Pierre-Richard Bruny (Cap), Mackorel Sampeur, Jean Michel Alexandre Boucicaut (51.Leonel Saint-Preux), Ednerson Raymond (57.Alain Vubert), Sony Norde (65.Ricardo Pierre-Louis), Abel Thermeus. Trainer: Wagneau Eloi.
Goals: 1-0 Júnior Enrique Díaz Campbell (17), 2-0 Víctor Núñez Rodríguez (90+1).
Cautions: Alonso Solís Calderón / Judelin Aveska, Meshack Jérôme, Pierre-Richard Bruny.

15.10.2008, Estadio Cuscatlán, San Salvador; Attendance: 20,000
Referee: Carlos Alberto Batres González (Guatemala)
EL SALVADOR - SURINAME   **3-0(2-0)**
SLV: Miguel Ángel Montes Moreno, Luis Alonso Anaya Merino, Marvin Gonzàlez, Alfredo Alberto Pacheco (Cap), Manuel Alejandro Salazar Rivas, Christian Giovanni Castillo Martínez (81.Salvador Arturo Coreas Pérez), Shawn Hasani Martin Henríquez, Ramón Alfredo Sánchez Paredes, Rodolfo Antonio Zelaya García (66.Williams Enrique Reyes Rodríguez), Eliseo Antonio Quintanilla Ortíz (67.William Jeovanny Torres Alegría), Rudis Alberto Rivera Corrales. Trainer: Carlos de los Cobos Martínez (Mexico).
SUR: Ronny Aloema, Derrik Garden, Marlon Felter, Ferdinand Jap A Joe, Hesron Jeroe (85.Malcolm Weibolt), Sergio Aroepa, Eugene Apanta, Germaine Sergio van Dijk, Clifton Sandvliet (78.Claudio Pinas), Vangellino Sastromedjo (65.Cleven Wanabo), Wensley Christoph. Trainer: Kenneth Jaliens.
Goals: 1-0 Rodolfo Antonio Zelaya García (8), 2-0 Eliseo Antonio Quintanilla Ortíz (27), 3-0 Derrik Garden (81 own goal).
Cautions: Eliseo Antonio Quintanilla Ortíz / Eugene Apanta, Germaine Sergio van Dijk.

19.11.2008, „André Kamperveen" Stadion, Paramaribo; Attendance: 800
Referee: Marco Antonio Rodríguez Moreno (Mexico)
SURINAME - HAITI   **1-1(1-1)**
SUR: Ronny Aloema, Derrik Garden, Marlon Felter (Cap), Sergio Aroepa (63.Emilio Limon), Ferdinand Jap A Joe, Hesron Jeroe, Germaine Van Dijk (29.Romano Sordam), Vangellino Sastromedjo, Clifton Sandvliet, Romeo Jomena (74.Sigfried Uralima), Wensley Christoph. Trainer: Kenneth Jaliens.
HAI: Yves-Marie Clervin, Frantz Gilles, Peter Germain (74.Alain Vubert), Meshack Jérôme, Ismael Gregory, Guiliano Phillipe (46.Jean Monuma), Pierre-Richard Bruny (Cap), Mackorel Sampeur (86.Yvener Guerrier), Ednerson Raymond, Jean Michel Alexandre Boucicaut, Leonel Saint-Preux. Trainer: Jaime Rendón (Colombia).
Goals: 0-1 Leonel Saint-Preux (28), 1-1 Wensley Christoph (40).
Cautions: Hesron Jeroe / Leonel Saint-Preux.

19.11.2008, Estadio Cuscatlán, San Salvador; Attendance: 20,000
Referee: Silviu Petrescu (Canada)
EL SALVADOR - COSTA RICA   **1-3(1-2)**
SLV: Juan José Gómez, Luis Miguel Hernández Campos, Marvin René González Leiva, Alfredo Alberto Pacheco (Cap), Manuel Alejandro Salazar Rivas, Christian Giovanni Castillo Martínez (58.Williams Enrique Reyes Rodríguez), Ramón Alfredo Sánchez Paredes, Ramón Ulises Flores Aguirre (45+1.William Jeovanny Torres Alegría), Salvador Arturo Coreas Pérez, Eliseo Antonio Quintanilla Ortíz (64.William Osael Romero Castillo), Rudis Alberto Rivera Corrales. Trainer: Carlos de los Cobos Martínez (Mexico).
CRC: Ricardo González Fonseca, Gonzalo Segares González (13.Pablo Andrés Brenes Quesada), Cristian Montero Fallas, Wálter Centeno Corea (Cap), José Freddy Fernández Beita, Celso Borges Mora, Roy Myrie Medrano, Oscar Emilio Rojas Ruíz, Álvaro Alberto Saborío Chacón (56.José Luis López Ramírez), Froylán Ledezma Stevens (73.Armando Alonso Rodríguez), William Sunsing Hidalgo. Trainer: Rodrigo Kenton Johnson.
Goals: 1-0 Rudis Alberto Rivera Corrales (18), 1-1 Roy Myrie (23), 1-2 José Freddy Fernández Beita (29), 1-3 Roy Myrie (90+4).

Cautions: Ramón Ulises Flores Aguirre, Manuel Alejandro Salazar Rivas / Wálter Centeno Corea, Ricardo González Fonseca, Froylán Ledezma Stevens, Cristian Montero Fallas, Armando Alonso Rodríguez.

FOURTH ROUND

11.02.2009	Columbus	United States - Mexico	2-0(1-0)
11.02.2009	San Salvador	El Salvador - Trinidad & Tobago	2-2(0-2)
11.02.2009	San José	Costa Rica - Honduras	2-0(0-0)
28.03.2009	Ciudad de México	Mexico – Costa Rica	2-0(1-0)
28.03.2009	Port of Spain	Trinidad & Tobago - Honduras	1-1(0-0)
28.03.2009	San Salvador	El Salvador - United States	2-2(1-0)
01.04.2009	Nashville	United States - Trinidad & Tobago	3-0(1-0)
01.04.2009	San Pedro Sula	Honduras - Mexico	3-1(2-0)
01.04.2009	San José	Costa Rica – El Salvador	1-0(0-0)
03.06.2009	San José	Costa Rica – United States	3-1(2-0)
06.06.2009	Bacolet	Trinidad & Tobago – Costa Rica	2-3(1-1)
06.06.2009	Chicago	United States - Honduras	2-1(1-1)
06.06.2009	San Salvador	El Salvador - Mexico	2-1(1-0)
10.06.2009	San Pedro Sula	Honduras – El Salvador	1-0(1-0)
10.06.2009	Ciudad de México	Mexico - Trinidad & Tobago	2-1(1-1)
12.08.2009	Ciudad de México	Mexico – United States	2-1(1-1)
12.08.2009	Port of Spain	Trinidad & Tobago – El Salvador	1-0(1-0)
12.08.2009	San Pedro Sula	Honduras – Costa Rica	4-0(1-0)
05.09.2009	Sandy	United States – El Salvador	2-1(2-1)
05.09.2009	San Pedro Sula	Honduras - Trinidad & Tobago	4-1(2-0)
05.09.2009	San José	Costa Rica - Mexico	0-3(0-1)
09.09.2009	Port of Spain	Trinidad & Tobago – United States	0-1(0-0)
09.09.2009	San Salvador	El Salvador – Costa Rica	1-0(0-0)
09.09.2009	Ciudad de México	Mexico - Honduras	1-0(0-0)
10.10.2009	Ciudad de México	Mexico – El Salvador	4-1(1-0)
10.10.2009	San José	Costa Rica - Trinidad & Tobago	4-0(1-0)
10.10.2009	San Pedro Sula	Honduras – United States	2-3(0-0)
14.10.2009	San Salvador	El Salvador - Honduras	0-1(0-0)
14.10.2009	Port of Spain	Trinidad & Tobago - Mexico	2-2(1-0)
14.10.2009	Washington DC	United States – Costa Rica	2-2(0-2)

FINAL STANDINGS

1.	**UNITED STATES**	10	6	2	2	19	-	13	20
2.	**MEXICO**	10	6	1	3	18	-	12	19
3.	**HONDURAS**	10	5	1	4	17	-	11	16
4.	**Costa Rica**	10	5	1	4	15	-	15	16
5.	El Salvador	10	2	2	6	9	-	15	8
6.	Trinidad & Tobago	10	1	3	6	10	-	22	6

United States, Mexico and Honduras qualified for the World Cup Final Tournament 2010; Costa Rica qualified for the Intercontinental Play-Offs against the 5th placed team from South America.

11.02.2009, Columbus Crew Stadium, Columbus; Attendance: 23,776
Referee: Carlos Alberto Batres González (Guatemala)
UNITED STATES - MEXICO   **2-0(1-0)**
USA: Tim Howard, Francis Daniel Hejduk, Carlos Manuel Bocanegra (Cap), Oguchialu Chijioke Onyewu, Heath Gregory Pearce, Clinton Drew Dempsey, Michael Sheehan Bradley, Sacha Kljestan (86.Ricardo Anthony Clark), DaMarcus Lamont Beasley, Landon Timothy Donovan, Brian Ching (83.Josmer Volmy Altidore). Trainer: Robert Bradley.
MEX: Oswaldo Javier Sánchez Ibarra, Aarón Galindo Rubio, Rafael Márquez Álvarez, Ricardo Osorio Mendoza, Carlos Arnoldo Salcido Flores, Pável Pardo Segura, Leandro Augusto Oldoni Stachelski, Alberto Medina Briseño (59.Antônio Naelson Matías „Zinha"), Nery Alberto Castillo Confalonieri (64.José Israel Martínez Salas), Giovani dos Santos Ramírez (71.Omar Bravo Torrecillas), Carlos Augusto Ochoa Mendoza. Trainer: Sven-Göran Eriksson (Sweden).
Goals: 1-0 Michael Sheehan Bradley (43), 2-0 Michael Sheehan Bradley (90+2).
Cautions: Tim Howard / Carlos Arnoldo Salcido Flores.
Sent off: Rafael Márquez Álvarez (65).

11.02.2009, Estadio Cuscatlán, San Salvador; Attendance: 25,000
Referee: Marco Antonio Rodríguez Moreno (Mexico)
EL SALVADOR - TRINIDAD & TOBAGO   **2-2(0-2)**
SLV: Juan José Gómez, Alexander Escobar Rosales, Marvin René González Leiva, Luis Miguel Hernández Campos (33.William Jeovanny Torres Alegría), Alfredo Alberto Pacheco, Shawn Hasani Martin Henríquez (60.Salvador Arturo Coreas Pérez), Ramón Alfredo Sánchez Paredes, Christian Giovanni Castillo Martínez, Eliseo Antonio Quintanilla Ortíz, William Osael Romero Castillo, Rudis Alberto Rivera Corrales (46.Rodolfo Antonio Zelaya García). Trainer: Carlos de los Cobos Martínez (Mexico).
TRI: Clayton Ince, Aklie Edwards, Dennis Lawrence, Keyeno Thomas (12.Makan Hislop), Silvio Spann, Carlos Edwards, Keon Daniel, Christopher Birchall (59.Clyde Leon), Dwight Eversley Yorke (Cap), Stern John (77.Cornell Glen), Kenwyne Jones. Trainer: Francisco Maturana (Colombia).
Goals: 0-1 Carlos Edwards (7), 0-2 Dwight Eversley Yorke (27 penalty), 1-2 William Osael Romero Castillo (82), 2-2 William Osael Romero Castillo (90+3).
Cautions: Keon Daniel, Dwight Eversley Yorke, Christopher Birchall, Carlos Edwards, Clayton Ince.
Sent off: Dwight Eversley Yorke (90).

11.02.2009, Estadio „Ricardo Saprissa", San José; Attendance: 18,000
Referee: Joel Antonio Aguilar Chicas (El Salvador)
COSTA RICA - HONDURAS   **2-0(0-0)**
CRC: Ricardo González Fonseca, Míchael Umaña Corrales, Júnior Enrique Díaz Campbell, Roy Myrie Medrano, José Freddy Fernández Beita, Wálter Centeno Corea (Cap), Celso Borges Mora, Armando Alonso Rodríguez (72.Christian Oviedo Calvo), Andy Alexander Furtado Dixón, Álvaro Alberto Saborío Chacón (53.Carlos Hernández Valverde), William Sunsing Hidalgo (75.Pablo Herrera Barrantes). Trainer: Rodrigo Kenton Johnson.
HON: Noel Eduardo Valladares Bonilla, Víctor Salvador Bernárdez Blanco, Maynor Alexis Figueroa Róchez, Oscar Boniek García Ramírez, Mario Iván Guerrero Ramírez, Amado Guevara, Walter Julián Martínez Ramos (40.Marvin Antonio Chávez), Emil José Martínez Cruz, Mario César Rodríguez Madrid (50.Ramón Fernando Núñez Reyes), Hendry Thomas, Óscar David Suazo Velázquez. Trainer: Reinaldo Rueda Rivera (Colombia).
Goals: 1-0 Andy Alexander Furtado Dixón (48), 2-0 Andy Alexander Furtado Dixón (59).
Cautions: Júnior Enrique Díaz Campbell, Wálter Centeno Corea / Mario César Rodríguez Madrid, Víctor Salvador Bernárdez Blanco.

28.03.2009, Estadio Azteca, Ciudad de México; Attendance: 90,000
Referee: Terry Vaughn (United States)
MEXICO - COSTA RICA   **2-0(1-0)**
MEX: Francisco Guillermo Ochoa Magaña, Aarón Galindo Rubio, Leobardo López García, Ricardo Osorio Mendoza (79.José Jonny Magallón Oliva), Fausto Manuel Pinto Rosas, José Andrés Guardado Hernández (79.Gerardo Torrado Díez de Bonilla), Pável Pardo Segura, Fernando Enrique Arce Ruiz, Leandro Augusto Oldoni Stachelski, Omar Bravo Torrecillas, Vicente José Matías Vuoso (85.Omar Arellano Riverón). Trainer: Sven-Göran Eriksson (Sweden).
CRC: Ricardo González Fonseca, Míchael Umaña Corrales, Júnior Enrique Díaz Campbell, Roy Myrie Medrano (60.Armando Alonso Rodríguez), José Freddy Fernández Beita (Cap), Óscar Esteban Granados Maroto (46.Álvaro Alberto Saborío Chacón), Celso Borges Mora, Óscar Emilio Rojas Ruíz, Bryan Ruiz González, Andy Alexander Furtado Dixón, William Sunsing Hidalgo (51.Pablo Andrés Brenes Quesada). Trainer: Rodrigo Kenton Johnson.
Goals: 1-0 Omar Bravo Torrecillas (20), 2-0 Pável Pardo Segura (53 penalty).
Cautions: Vicente José Matías Vuoso, Leandro Augusto Oldoni Stachelski / Óscar Esteban Granados Maroto, Roy Myrie Medrano, Celso Borges Mora, Andy Alexander Furtado Dixón.

28.03.2009, „Hasely Crawford" Stadium, Port of Spain; Attendance: 23,500
Referee: Walter Quesada Cordero (Costa Rica)
TRINIDAD & TOBAGO - HONDURAS   **1-1(0-0)**
TRI: Jan-Michael Williams, Keyeno Thomas, Dennis Lawrence (Cap), Aklie Edwards, Clyde Leon, Densill Theobald (61.Khaleem Hyland), Stern John, Jason Scotland (61.Kenwyne Jones), Keon Daniel (66.Russell Latapy), Carlos Edwards, Anthony Wolfe. Trainer: Francisco Maturana (Colombia).
HON: Noel Eduardo Valladares Bonilla, Jorge Samuel Caballero, Osman Danilo Chávez Guity, Maynor Alexis Figueroa Róchez, Oscar Boniek García Ramírez, Amado Guevara, Ramón Fernando Núñez Reyes (77.Marvin Antonio Chávez), Wilson Roberto Palacios Suazo, Hendry Thomas, Julio César de León, Carlos Alberto Pavón Plummer (82.Carlos Yaír Costly Molina). Trainer: Reinaldo Rueda Rivera (Colombia).
Goals: 0-1 Carlos Alberto Pavón Plummer (51), 1-1 Khaleem Hyland (88).

28.03.2009, Estadio Cuscatlán, San Salvador; Attendance: 30,350
Referee: Benito Armando Archundia Téllez (Mexico)
EL SALVADOR - UNITED STATES   **2-2(1-0)**
SLV: Miguel Ángel Montes Moreno (74.Juan José Gómez), Manuel Alejandro Salazar Rivas, Marvin René González Leiva, José Mardoqueo Heníquez Dubón, Alfredo Alberto Pacheco, Julio Enrique Martínez Rivera, Ramón Alfredo Sánchez Paredes, Christian Giovanni Castillo Martínez, Eliseo Antonio Quintanilla Ortíz (82.Dennis Jonathan Alas Morales), William Osael Romero Castillo, Rodolfo Antonio Zelaya García (78.Carlos Ernesto Ayala Amaya). Trainer: Carlos de los Cobos Martínez (Mexico).
USA: Bradley Edwin Guzan, Francis Daniel Hejduk, Danny Califf, Carlos Manuel Bocanegra (Cap), Heath Gregory Pearce (61.Josmer Volmy Altidore), Sacha Kljestan (72.José Francisco Torres Mezzell), Michael Sheehan Bradley (90+5.Maurice Edu), Landon Timothy Donovan, DaMarcus Lamont Beasley, Brian Ching, Clinton Drew Dempsey. Trainer: Robert Bradley.
Goals: 1-0 Eliseo Antonio Quintanilla Ortíz (15), 2-0 Christian Giovanni Castillo Martínez (72), 2-1 Josmer Volmy Altidore (77), 2-2 Francis Daniel Hejduk (88).
Cautions: Christian Giovanni Castillo Martínez, Eliseo Antonio Quintanilla Ortíz, Julio Enrique Martínez Rivera / Michael Sheehan Bradley.

01.04.2009, LP Field, Nashville; Attendance: 27,959
Referee: Roberto Moreno (Panama)
UNITED STATES - TRINIDAD & TOBAGO   **3-0(1-0)**
USA: Tim Howard, Francis Daniel Hejduk, Carlos Manuel Bocanegra (Cap), Oguchialu Chijioke Onyewu, DaMarcus Lamont Beasley, Clinton Drew Dempsey (84.Sacha Kljestan), Michael Sheehan Bradley, Pablo Mastroeni, Landon Timothy Donovan, Brian Ching (81.José Francisco Torres Mezzell), Josmer Volmy Altidore. Trainer: Robert Bradley.
TRI: Clayton Ince, Aklie Edwards, Anthony Wolfe (46.Makan Hislop), Keyeno Thomas, Dennis Lawrence (Cap), Christopher Birchall (56.Khaleem Hyland), Carlos Edwards, Clyde Leon, Keon Daniel (71.Jason Scotland), Kenwyne Jones, Stern John. Trainer: Francisco Maturana (Colombia).
Goals: 1-0 Josmer Volmy Altidore (13), 2-0 Josmer Volmy Altidore (71), 3-0 Josmer Volmy Altidore (89).
Cautions: Aklie Edwards.

01.04.2009, Estadio Olimpico Metropolitano, San Pedro Sula; Attendance: 28,000
Referee: Paul Ward (Canada)
HONDURAS - MEXICO   **3-1(2-0)**
HON: Noel Eduardo Valladares Bonilla, Osman Danilo Chávez Guity, Maynor Alexis Figueroa Róchez, Emilio Arturo Izaguirre Girón, Mauricio Alberto Sabillón Peña, Amado Guevara, Ramón Fernando Núñez Reyes (74.Danilo Elvis Turcios Funes), Wilson Roberto Palacios Suazo, Julio César de León (90.Marvin Antonio Chávez), Carlos Yaír Costly Molina (82.Hendry Thomas), Carlos Alberto Pavón Plummer. Trainer: Reinaldo Rueda Rivera (Colombia).
MEX: Francisco Guillermo Ochoa Magaña, José Jonny Magallón Oliva, Fausto Manuel Pinto Rosas, Leobardo López García (26.Aarón Galindo Rubio), Carlos Arnoldo Salcido Flores, Luis Ernesto Pérez Gómez (46.Vicente José Matías Vuoso), Pável Pardo Segura (Cap), José Andrés Guardado Hernández, Leandro Augusto Oldoni Stachelski, Carlos Alberto Vela Garrido, Omar Bravo Torrecillas (70.Nery Alberto Castillo Confalonieri). Trainer: Sven-Göran Eriksson (Sweden).
Goals: 1-0 Carlos Yaír Costly Molina (17), 2-0 Carlos Alberto Pavón Plummer (43), 3-0 Carlos Yaír Costly Molina (79), 3-1 Nery Alberto Castillo Confalonieri (80 penalty)
Cautions: Julio César de León, Carlos Yaír Costly Molina / Carlos Arnoldo Salcido Flores, Pável Pardo Segura, Carlos Alberto Vela Garrido.
Sent off: Carlos Arnoldo Salcido Flores (88).

01.04.2009, Estadio „Ricardo Saprissa", San José; Attendance: 19,200
Referee: Jair Marrufo (United States)
COSTA RICA – EL SALVADOR   **1-0(0-0)**
CRC: Keylor Antonio Navas Gamboa, Míchael Umaña Corrales, Júnior Enrique Díaz Campbell, Roy Myrie Medrano, Michael Barrantes Rojas (46.Pablo Andrés Brenes Quesada), Wálter Centeno Corea (Cap), Armando Alonso Rodríguez (56.Pablo Herrera Barrantes), Celso Borges Mora, Bryan Ruiz González, Rolando Fonseca Jiménez, Andy Alexander Furtado Dixón (62.Carlos Hernández Valverde). Trainer: Rodrigo Kenton Johnson.
SLV: Miguel Ángel Montes Moreno, Manuel Alejandro Salazar Rivas, Marvin René González Leiva, José Mardoqueo Heníquez Dubón, Alfredo Alberto Pacheco, Julio Enrique Martínez Rivera, Ramón Alfredo Sánchez Paredes, Carlos Romeo Monteagudo Alfaro (68.Rudis Alberto Rivera Corrales), Dennis Jonathan Alas Morales (71.William Jeovanny Torres Alegría), William Osael Romero Castillo, Rodolfo Antonio Zelaya García (77.Mark Léster Blanco Pineda). Trainer: Carlos de los Cobos Martínez (Mexico).
Goal: 1-0 Wálter Centeno Corea (69).
Cautions: Míchael Umaña Corrales / José Mardoqueo Heníquez Dubón, Rodolfo Antonio Zelaya García, Carlos Romeo Monteagudo Alfaro.

03.06.2009, Estadio „Ricardo Saprissa", San José; Attendance: 19,200
Referee: Neal Brizan (Trinidad & Tobago)
COSTA RICA - UNITED STATES   **3-1(2-0)**
CRC: Keylor Antonio Navas Gamboa, Ángel Esteban Sirias Áviles, Míchael Umaña Corrales, Júnior Enrique Díaz Campbell, José Freddy Fernández Beita, Harold Wallace McDonald (55.Pablo Herrera Barrantes), Wálter Centeno Corea (Cap), Celso Borges Mora, Bryan Ruiz González, Andy Francisco Herrón Aguilar (71.Cristian Bolaños Navarro), Álvaro Alberto Saborío Chacón (76.Carlos Hernández Valverde). Trainer: Rodrigo Kenton Johnson.
USA: Tim Howard, Marvell Wynne, Oguchialu Chijioke Onyewu, Carlos Manuel Bocanegra (Cap), DaMarcus Lamont Beasley, Pablo Mastroeni (63.Fredua Koranteng Adu), Michael Sheehan Bradley, José Francisco Torres Mezzell (46.Sacha Kljestan), Clinton Drew Dempsey (80.Charles Desmond Davies), Landon Timothy Donovan, Josmer Volmy Altidore. Trainer: Robert Bradley.
Goals: 1-0 Álvaro Alberto Saborío Chacón (2), 2-0 Celso Borges Mora (13), 3-0 Pablo Herrera Barrantes (68), 3-1 Landon Timothy Donovan (90+2 penalty).
Cautions: José Freddy Fernández Beita, Pablo Herrera Barrantes, Júnior Enrique Díaz Campbell / Michael Sheehan Bradley, Sacha Kljestan.

06.06.2009, „Dwight Eversley Yorke" Stadium, Bacolet; Attendance: 8,000
Referee: Courtney Campbell (Jamaica)
TRINIDAD & TOBAGO - COSTA RICA   **2-3(1-1)**
TRI: Clayton Ince, Marvin Andrews, Dennis Lawrence, Avery John, Hayden Tinto (46.Collin Samuel), Dwight Eversley Yorke (Cap), Trent Noel, Silvio Spann (60.Cornell Glen), Carlos Edwards, Jason Scotland (73.Christopher Birchall), Kenwyne Jones. Trainer: Russell Nigel Latapy.
CRC: Keylor Antonio Navas Gamboa, Ángel Esteban Sirias Áviles (84.Óscar Esteban Granados Maroto), Míchael Umaña Corrales, Dennis Marshall Maxwell, Gonzalo Segares González, Pablo Herrera Barrantes, Wálter Centeno Corea (Cap), Celso Borges Mora, Bryan Ruiz González (51.Cristian Bolaños Navarro), Andy Francisco Herrón Aguilar (61.Armando Alonso Rodríguez), Álvaro Alberto Saborío Chacón. Trainer: Rodrigo Kenton Johnson.
Goals: 1-0 Carlos Edwards (29), 1-1 Álvaro Alberto Saborío Chacón (40), 1-2 Celso Borges Mora (52), 2-2 Collin Samuel (63), 2-3 Celso Borges Mora (68).
Cautions: Cornell Glen / Bryan Ruiz González.

06.06.2009, Soldier Field, Chicago; Attendance: 55,647
Referee: Mauricio Rafael Morales Ovalle (Mexico)
UNITED STATES - HONDURAS   **2-1(1-1)**
USA: Tim Howard, Jonathan Michael Paul Spector, Oguchialu Chijioke Onyewu, Carlos Manuel Bocanegra (Cap) (71.Jay Michael DeMerit), Jonathan Bornstein, Clinton Drew Dempsey, Ricardo Anthony Clark, Pablo Mastroeni (46.Benny Feilhaber), Landon Timothy Donovan, Conor Casey (75.DaMarcus Lamont Beasley), Josmer Volmy Altidore. Trainer: Robert Bradley.
HON: Noel Eduardo Valladares Bonilla, Mario Roberto Beata Reyes, Osman Danilo Chávez Guity, Mauricio Alberto Sabillón Peña, Maynor Alexis Figueroa Róchez, Amado Guevara, Ramón Fernando Núñez Reyes (78.Walter Julián Martínez Ramos), Wilson Roberto Palacios Suazo (66.Danilo Elvis Turcios Funes), Hendry Thomas, Carlos Yaír Costly Molina, Carlos Alberto Pavón Plummer (66.Georgie Wilson Welcome Collins). Trainer: Reinaldo Rueda Rivera (Colombia).
Goals: 0-1 Carlos Yaír Costly Molina (5), 1-1 Landon Timothy Donovan (43 penalty), 2-1 Carlos Manuel Bocanegra (68).
Cautions: Conor Casey, Landon Timothy Donovan / Mario Roberto Beata Reyes.

06.06.2009, Estadio Cuscatlán, San Salvador; Attendance: 33,000
Referee: Walter Quesada Cordero (Costa Rica)
EL SALVADOR - MEXICO 2-1(1-0)
SLV: Miguel Ángel Montes Moreno, Manuel Alejandro Salazar Rivas, Marvin René González Leiva, Alexander Escobar Rosales, Alfredo Alberto Pacheco (74.Rudis Alberto Rivera Corrales), Julio Enrique Martínez Rivera, Ramón Alfredo Sánchez Paredes, Christian Giovanni Castillo Martínez, William Osael Romero Castillo, Eliseo Antonio Quintanilla Ortíz (90.José Mardoqueo Heníquez Dubón), Rodolfo Antonio Zelaya García (90+4.Salvador Arturo Coreas Pérez). Trainer: Carlos de los Cobos Martínez (Mexico).
MEX: Óscar Pérez Rojas, Aarón Galindo Rubio, Ricardo Osorio Mendoza, Francisco Javier Rodríguez Pinedo, Óscar Adrián Rojas Castillón, José Andrés Guardado Hernández (77.Alberto Medina Briseño), Pável Pardo Segura (46.Israel Castro Macías), Gerardo Torrado Díez de Bonilla, Fernando Enrique Arce Ruiz (46.Cuauhtémoc Blanco Bravo), Nery Alberto Castillo Confalonieri, Guillermo Luis Franco Farquarson. Trainer: Javier Aguirre Onaindía.
Goals: 1-0 Julio Enrique Martínez Rivera (11), 1-1 Cuauhtémoc Blanco Bravo (71 penalty), 2-1 Eliseo Antonio Quintanilla Ortíz (86 penalty).
Cautions: Rodolfo Antonio Zelaya García / Pável Pardo Segura, Guillermo Luis Franco Farquarson, Gerardo Torrado Díez de Bonilla.

10.06.2009, Estadio Olimpico Metropolitano, San Pedro Sula; Attendance: 28,000
Referee: Baldomero Toledo (United States)
HONDURAS – EL SALVADOR 1-0(1-0)
HON: Noel Eduardo Valladares Bonilla, Osman Danilo Chávez Guity, Emilio Arturo Izaguirre Girón, Mauricio Alberto Sabillón Peña, Maynor Alexis Figueroa Róchez, Amado Guevara, Ramón Fernando Núñez Reyes (74.Walter Julián Martínez Ramos), Wilson Roberto Palacios Suazo, Julio César de León (86.Hendry Thomas), Carlos Yaír Costly Molina (90+1.Víctor Salvador Bernárdez Blanco), Carlos Alberto Pavón Plummer. Trainer: Reinaldo Rueda Rivera (Colombia).
SLV: Miguel Ángel Montes Moreno, Manuel Alejandro Salazar Rivas, Marvin René González Leiva, Alexander Escobar Rosales, Alfredo Alberto Pacheco (90.William Jeovanny Torres Alegría), Julio Enrique Martínez Rivera, Ramón Alfredo Sánchez Paredes, Christian Giovanni Castillo Martínez, Salvador Arturo Coreas Pérez, Eliseo Antonio Quintanilla Ortíz, Rudis Alberto Rivera Corrales (78.Williams Enrique Reyes Rodríguez). Trainer: Carlos de los Cobos Martínez (Mexico).
Goal: 1-0 Carlos Alberto Pavón Plummer (13).
Cautions: Julio César de León, Wilson Roberto Palacios Suazo, Ramón Fernando Núñez Reyes, Carlos Alberto Pavón Plummer / Manuel Alejandro Salazar Rivas, Salvador Arturo Coreas Pérez, Ramón Alfredo Sánchez Paredes.

10.06.2009, Estadio Azteca, Ciudad de México; Attendance: 92,000
Referee: José Benigno Pineda Fernández (Honduras)
MEXICO - TRINIDAD & TOBAGO 2-1(1-1)
MEX: Óscar Pérez Rojas, Ricardo Osorio Mendoza, Francisco Javier Rodríguez Pinedo, Óscar Adrián Rojas Castillón, Carlos Arnoldo Salcido Flores, Israel Castro Macías, José Andrés Guardado Hernández, Nery Alberto Castillo Confalonieri (35.Miguel Sabah Rodríguez), Cuauhtémoc Blanco Bravo, Carlos Esquivel Silva (52.Alberto Medina Briseño), Guillermo Luis Franco Farquarson (75.Giovani dos Santos Ramírez). Trainer: Javier Aguirre Onaindía.
TRI: Clayton Ince, Carlos Edwards, Marvin Andrews, Makan Hislop, Radanfah Abu Bakr, Hayden Tinto, Dwight Eversley Yorke (Cap), Christopher Birchall, Trent Noel (72.Silvio Spann), Keon Daniel (80.Kerry Baptiste), Kenwyne Jones (54.Devon Jorsling). Trainer: Russell Nigel Latapy.
Goals: 1-0 Guillermo Luis Franco Farquarson (2), 1-1 Hayden Tinto (45+1), 2-1 Óscar Adrián Rojas Castillón (48).
Cautions: Radanfah Abu Bakr.

12.08.2009, Estadio Azteca, Ciudad de México; Attendance: 104,499
Referee: Roberto Moreno (Panama)
MEXICO - UNITED STATES 2-1(1-1)
MEX: Francisco Guillermo Ochoa Magaña, José Jonny Magallón Oliva, Carlos Arnoldo Salcido Flores, Ricardo Osorio Mendoza, Efraín Juárez Valdéz, Gerardo Torrado Díez de Bonilla, José Andrés Guardado Hernández (71.Nery Alberto Castillo Confalonieri), Israel Castro Macías, Cuauhtémoc Blanco Bravo (55.Carlos Alberto Vela Garrido), Guillermo Luis Franco Farquarson (80.Miguel Sabah Rodríguez), Giovani dos Santos Ramírez. Trainer: Javier Aguirre Onaindía.
USA: Tim Howard, Steven Cherundolo, Oguchialu Chijioke Onyewu, Jay Michael DeMerit, Carlos Manuel Bocanegra (Cap), Clinton Drew Dempsey, Ricardo Anthony Clark (58.Stuart Holden), Michael Sheehan Bradley, Landon Timothy Donovan, Charles Desmond Davies (76.Josmer Volmy Altidore), Brian Ching (58.Benny Feilhaber). Trainer: Robert Bradley.
Goals: 0-1 Charles Desmond Davies (9), 1-1 Israel Castro Macías (19), 2-1 Miguel Sabah Rodríguez (82).
Cautions: Gerardo Torrado Díez de Bonilla, Giovani dos Santos Ramírez / Oguchialu Chijioke Onyewu, Jay Michael DeMerit, Carlos Manuel Bocanegra, Benny Feilhaber.

12.08.2009, „Hasely Crawford" Stadium, Port of Spain; Attendance: 25,784
Referee: Terry Vaughn (United States)
TRINIDAD & TOBAGO – EL SALVADOR 1-0(1-0)
TRI: Clayton Ince, Dennis Lawrence (Cap), Keston Williams, Radanfah Abu Bakr, Silvio Spann, Clyde Leon (63.Christopher Birchall), Trent Noel, Keon Daniel (72.Dwight Eversley Yorke), Carlos Edwards, Cornell Glen (83.Jason Scotland), Kenwyne Jones. Trainer: Russell Nigel Latapy.
SLV: Miguel Ángel Montes Moreno, Luis Miguel Hernández Campos, Manuel Alejandro Salazar Rivas, Marvin René González Leiva, Deris Ariel Umanzor Guevara, Ramón Ulises Flores Aguirre (66.Williams Enrique Reyes Rodríguez), Ramón Alfredo Sánchez Paredes, Christian Giovanni Castillo Martínez, William Osael Romero Castillo (46.José Arturo Álvarez Hernández), Eliseo Antonio Quintanilla Ortíz, Rodolfo Antonio Zelaya García (83.Rudis Alberto Rivera Corrales). Trainer: Carlos de los Cobos Martínez (Mexico).
Goal: Cornell Glen (7).
Cautions: Clyde Leon, Kenwyne Jones, Dennis Lawrence, Christopher Birchall / Christian Giovanni Castillo Martínez, Eliseo Antonio Quintanilla Ortíz.

12.08.2009, Estadio Olimpico Metropolitano, San Pedro Sula; Attendance: 30,000
Referee: Marco Antonio Rodríguez Moreno (Mexico)
HONDURAS - COSTA RICA 4-0(1-0)
HON: Noel Eduardo Valladares Bonilla, Osman Danilo Chávez Guity, Emilio Arturo Izaguirre Girón, Mauricio Alberto Sabillón Peña, Maynor Alexis Figueroa Róchez, Amado Guevara, Ramón Fernando Núñez Reyes (60.Julio César de León), Wilson Roberto Palacios Suazo, Danilo Elvis Turcios Funes (85.Hendry Thomas), Carlos Yaír Costly Molina, Carlos Alberto Pavón Plummer (72.Melvin Yovany Valladares Castillo). Trainer: Reinaldo Rueda Rivera (Colombia).
CRC: Keylor Antonio Navas Gamboa (23.Ricardo González Fonseca), Darío Alejandro Delgado Mora, Ángel Esteban Sirias Áviles, Júnior Enrique Díaz Campbell, José Freddy Fernández Beita, Harold Wallace McDonald (63.Froylán Ledezma Stevens), Wálter Centeno Corea (Cap), Armando Alonso Rodríguez, Celso Borges Mora, Andy Francisco Herrón Aguilar (43.Cristian Bolaños Navarro), Álvaro Alberto Saborío Chacón. Trainer: Rodrigo Kenton Johnson.
Goals: 1-0 Carlos Yaír Costly Molina (30), 2-0 Carlos Alberto Pavón Plummer (51), 3-0 Melvin Yovany Valladares Castillo (89), 4-0 Carlos Yaír Costly Molina (90+2).
Cautions: Wilson Roberto Palacios Suazo, Carlos Yaír Costly Molina, Osman Danilo Chávez Guity, Danilo Elvis Turcios Funes / Andy Francisco Herrón Aguilar, Harold Wallace McDonald, Cristian Bolaños Navarro.

158

05.09.2009, Rio Tinto Stadium, Sandy; Attendance: 19,066
Referee: José Pineda (Honduras)
UNITED STATES – EL SALVADOR   **2-1(2-1)**
USA: Tim Howard, Jonathan Michael Paul Spector, Chad Marshall, Carlos Manuel Bocanegra (Cap), Jonathan Bornstein, Benny Feilhaber (80.Kyle Robert Beckerman), Michael Sheehan Bradley, Landon Timothy Donovan, Clinton Drew Dempsey, Charles Desmond Davies (73.Stuart Holden), Josmer Volmy Altidore (85.José Francisco Torres Mezzell). Trainer: Robert Bradley.
SLV: Miguel Ángel Montes Moreno, Manuel Alejandro Salazar Rivas, José Mardoqueo Heníquez Dubón, Marvin René González Leiva, Deris Ariel Umanzor Guevara, Ramón Ulises Flores Aguirre (63.Williams Enrique Reyes Rodríguez), Ramón Alfredo Sánchez Paredes, Christian Giovanni Castillo Martínez, José Arturo Álvarez Hernández (50.William Osael Romero Castillo), Eliseo Antonio Quintanilla Ortíz (75.Rudis Alberto Rivera Corrales), Rodolfo Antonio Zelaya García. Trainer: Carlos de los Cobos Martínez (Mexico).
Goals: 0-1 Christian Giovanni Castillo Martínez (31), 1-1 Clinton Drew Dempsey (41), Josmer Volmy Altidore (45+2).
Cautions: Ramón Ulises Flores Aguirre, Rodolfo Antonio Zelaya García.

05.09.2009, Estadio Olimpico Metropolitano, San Pedro Sula; Attendance: 38,000
Referee: Mark Geiger (United States)
HONDURAS - TRINIDAD & TOBAGO   **4-1(2-0)**
HON: Noel Eduardo Valladares Bonilla, Erick Zenón Norales Casildo, Emilio Arturo Izaguirre Girón, Mauricio Alberto Sabillón Peña, Maynor Alexis Figueroa Róchez, Amado Guevara (72.Edgard Anthony Álvarez Reyes), Ramón Fernando Núñez Reyes, Hendry Thomas, Danilo Elvis Turcios Funes (77.Melvin Yovany Valladares Castillo), Jerry Nelson Palacios Suazo (59.Óscar David Suazo Velázquez), Carlos Alberto Pavón Plummer. Trainer: Reinaldo Rueda Rivera (Colombia).
TRI: Clayton Ince, Carlos Edwards, Marvin Andrews (Cap), Radanfah Abu Bakr, Jlloyd Samuel, Keon Daniel (78.Kerry Baptiste), Densill Theobald (75.Lyndon Andrews), Trent Noel, Silvio Spann (46.Hayden Tinto), Cornell Glen, Kenwyne Jones. Trainer: Russell Nigel Latapy.
Goals: 1-0 Carlos Alberto Pavón Plummer (20), 2-0 Carlos Alberto Pavón Plummer (28), 3-0 Amado Guevara (62), 4-0 Óscar David Suazo Velázquez (83), 4-1 Kerry Baptiste (88).
Cautions: Hendry Thomas / Silvio Spann, Trent Noel.

05.09.2009, Estadio „Ricardo Saprissa", San José; Attendance: 20,000
Referee: Neal Brizan (Trinidad & Tobago)
COSTA RICA - MEXICO   **0-3(0-1)**
CRC: Keylor Antonio Navas Gamboa, Darío Alejandro Delgado Mora, Júnior Enrique Díaz Campbell, Míchael Umaña Corrales, Carlos Johnson Carpio, Christian Oviedo Calvo (63.Froylán Ledezma Stevens), Armando Alonso Rodríguez (74.Pablo Herrera Barrantes), Celso Borges Mora (Cap), Carlos Hernández Valverde (50.Ángel Esteban Sirias Áviles), Bryan Ruiz González, Álvaro Alberto Saborío Chacón. Trainer: Rodrigo Kenton Johnson.
MEX: Francisco Guillermo Ochoa Magaña, José Jonny Magallón Oliva, Carlos Arnoldo Salcido Flores, Ricardo Osorio Mendoza, José Antonio Castro González, Efraín Juárez Valdéz, Gerardo Torrado Díez de Bonilla (Cap), Israel Castro Macías, Cuauhtémoc Blanco Bravo (74.Miguel Sabah Rodríguez), Guillermo Luis Franco Farquarson (69.José Andrés Guardado Hernández), Giovani dos Santos Ramírez (80.Nery Alberto Castillo Confalonieri). Trainer: Javier Aguirre Onaindía.
Goals: 0-1 Giovani dos Santos Ramírez (45), 0-2 Guillermo Luis Franco Farquarson (52), 0-3 José Andrés Guardado Hernández (70).
Cautions: Christian Oviedo Calvo, Álvaro Alberto Saborío Chacón, Armando Alonso Rodríguez / Guillermo Luis Franco Farquarson, Gerardo Torrado Díez de Bonilla, Ricardo Osorio Mendoza.

09.09.2009, „Hasely Crawford" Stadium, Port of Spain; Attendance: 4,700
Referee: Joel Antonio Aguilar Chicas (El Salvador)
TRINIDAD & TOBAGO - UNITED STATES   **0-1(0-0)**
TRI: Clayton Ince, Carlos Edwards, Radanfah Abu Bakr, Dennis Lawrence (Cap), Jlloyd Samuel, Hayden Tinto (66.Keon Daniel), Clyde Leon, Trent Noel (84.Jason Scotland), Silvio Spann (72.Kerry Baptiste), Cornell Glen, Kenwyne Jones. Trainer: Russell Nigel Latapy.
USA: Tim Howard, Jonathan Michael Paul Spector, Oguchialu Chijioke Onyewu, Carlos Manuel Bocanegra (Cap), Jonathan Bornstein, Clinton Drew Dempsey (82.Stuart Holden), Ricardo Anthony Clark, Michael Sheehan Bradley, Landon Timothy Donovan, Charles Desmond Davies (77.Brian Ching), Josmer Volmy Altidore (63.Benny Feilhaber). Trainer: Robert Bradley.
Goal: 0-1 Ricardo Anthony Clark (62).
Cautions: Jlloyd Samuel.

09.09.2009, Estadio Cuscatlán, San Salvador; Attendance: 18,000
Referee: Benito Armando Archundia Téllez (Mexico)
EL SALVADOR - COSTA RICA   **1-0(0-0)**
SLV: Miguel Ángel Montes Moreno, Manuel Alejandro Salazar Rivas, José Mardoqueo Heníquez Dubón, Marvin René González Leiva, Deris Ariel Umanzor Guevara (81.Rudis Alberto Rivera Corrales), William Osael Romero Castillo, Ramón Alfredo Sánchez Paredes, Christian Giovanni Castillo Martínez (68.Alfredo Alberto Pacheco), José Arturo Álvarez Hernández (76.Salvador Arturo Coreas Pérez), Eliseo Antonio Quintanilla Ortíz, Rodolfo Antonio Zelaya García. Trainer: Carlos de los Cobos Martínez (Mexico).
CRC: Ricardo González Fonseca, Ángel Esteban Sirias Áviles, Míchael Umaña Corrales, Júnior Enrique Díaz Campbell, Pablo Herrera Barrantes, Dennis Marshall Maxwell, Christian Oviedo Calvo, Cristian Bolaños Navarro (64.Wálter Centeno Corea), Celso Borges Mora (Cap), Bryan Ruiz González (76.William Sunsing Hidalgo), Froylán Ledezma Stevens (81.Giovanni Alejandro Sequeira Solano). Trainer: Rodrigo Kenton Johnson.
Goal: Rudis Alberto Rivera Corrales (90+1).
Cautions: Rodolfo Antonio Zelaya García, Rudis Alberto Rivera Corrales / Cristian Bolaños Navarro, Míchael Umaña Corrales.

09.09.2009, Estadio Azteca, Ciudad de México; Attendance: 97,897
Referee: Courtney Campbell (Jamaica)
MEXICO - HONDURAS   **1-0(0-0)**
MEX: Francisco Guillermo Ochoa Magaña, José Jonny Magallón Oliva, Carlos Arnoldo Salcido Flores, Ricardo Osorio Mendoza, José Antonio Castro González (63.Pablo Edson Barrera Acosta), Israel Castro Macías, Efraín Juárez Valdéz, José Andrés Guardado Hernández, Giovani dos Santos Ramírez (80.Óscar Adrián Rojas Castillón), Cuauhtémoc Blanco Bravo, Miguel Sabah Rodríguez (71.Juan Carlos Cacho Gutiérrez). Trainer: Javier Aguirre Onaindía.
HON: Noel Eduardo Valladares Bonilla, Osman Danilo Chávez Guity, Emilio Arturo Izaguirre Girón, Mauricio Alberto Sabillón Peña (46.Oscar Boniek García Ramírez), Maynor Alexis Figueroa Róchez, Amado Guevara, Ramón Fernando Núñez Reyes (71.Julio César de León), Wilson Roberto Palacios Suazo, Danilo Elvis Turcios Funes, Óscar David Suazo Velázquez (59.Carlos Yaír Costly Molina), Carlos Alberto Pavón Plummer. Trainer: Reinaldo Rueda Rivera (Colombia).
Goal: 1-0 Cuauhtémoc Blanco Bravo (76 penalty).
Cautions: Efraín Juárez Valdéz / Danilo Elvis Turcios Funes, Osman Danilo Chávez Guity, Carlos Yaír Costly Molina, Amado Guevara.

10.10.2009, Estadio Azteca, Ciudad de México; Attendance: 104,000
Referee: Carlos Alberto Batres González (Guatemala)
MEXICO – EL SALVADOR **4-1(1-0)**
MEX: Francisco Guillermo Ochoa Magaña, Carlos Arnoldo Salcido Flores, Rafael Márquez Álvarez, Ricardo Osorio Mendoza, Efraín Juárez Valdéz, Gerardo Torrado Díez de Bonilla, Israel Castro Macías, Cuauhtémoc Blanco Bravo (78.Juan Francisco Palencia Hernández), Carlos Alberto Vela Garrido, José Andrés Guardado Hernández (89.Pablo Edson Barrera Acosta), Guillermo Luis Franco Farquarson (86.Miguel Sabah Rodríguez). Trainer: Javier Aguirre Onaindía.
SLV: Miguel Ángel Montes Moreno, Manuel Alejandro Salazar Rivas, José Mardoqueo Heníquez Dubón, Marvin René González Leiva, Deris Ariel Umanzor Guevara, Julio Enrique Martínez Rivera, Ramón Alfredo Sánchez Paredes, Christian Giovanni Castillo Martínez, José Arturo Álvarez Hernández (60.Rudis Alberto Rivera Corrales), Eliseo Antonio Quintanilla Ortíz (80.Juan Carlos Moscoso Palma), William Osael Romero Castillo (48.Salvador Arturo Coreas Pérez). Trainer: Carlos de los Cobos Martínez (Mexico).
Goals: 1-0 Marvin René González Leiva (25 own goal), 2-0 Cuauhtémoc Blanco Bravo (71), 3-0 Juan Francisco Palencia Hernández (85), 3-1 Julio Enrique Martínez Rivera (89), 4-1 Carlos Alberto Vela Garrido (90).
Cautions: Rafael Márquez Álvarez, Juan Francisco Palencia Hernández / Julio Enrique Martínez Rivera, José Mardoqueo Heníquez Dubón.

10.10.2009, Estadio „Ricardo Saprissa", San José; Attendance: 10,000
Referee: Jair Marrufo (United States)
COSTA RICA - TRINIDAD & TOBAGO **4-0(1-0)**
CRC: Keylor Antonio Navas Gamboa, Pablo Herrera Barrantes (77.Víctor Nuñez Rodríguez), Luis Antonio Marín Murillo, Dennis Marshall Maxwell, Cristian Montero Fallas, Ángel Esteban Sirias Áviles, Michael Barrantes Rojas, Wálter Centeno Corea (Cap) (66.Cristian Bolaños Navarro), Randall Azofeifa Corrales, Bryan Ruiz González (58.Rolando Fonseca Jiménez), Álvaro Alberto Saborío Chacón. Trainer: René Rodrigues Simões (Brazil).
TRI: Marvin Phillip, Jake Thomson, Julius James, Radanfah Abu Bakr, Kern Cupid, Carlos Edwards (Cap), Trent Noel (72.Devon Jorsling), Clyde Leon, Keon Daniel (63.Hayden Tinto), Kerry Baptiste (69.Dennis Lawrence), Kenwyne Jones. Trainer: Russell Nigel Latapy.
Goals: 1-0 Julius James (26 own goal), 2-0 Wálter Centeno Corea (51), 3-0 Álvaro Alberto Saborío Chacón (61), 4-0 Álvaro Alberto Saborío Chacón (64).
Cautions: Dennis Marshall Maxwell / Radanfah Abu Bakr, Jake Thomson.
Sent off: Julius James (66).

10.10.2009, Estadio Olimpico Metropolitano, San Pedro Sula; Attendance: 37,000
Referee: Roberto Moreno (Panama)
HONDURAS - UNITED STATES **2-3(0-0)**
HON: Noel Eduardo Valladares Bonilla, Osman Danilo Chávez Guity, Emilio Arturo Izaguirre Girón, Mauricio Alberto Sabillón Peña, Maynor Alexis Figueroa Róchez, Edgard Anthony Álvarez Reyes (63.Óscar David Suazo Velázquez), Wilson Roberto Palacios Suazo, Hendry Thomas (74.Ramón Fernando Núñez Reyes), Julio César de León (79.Walter Julián Martínez Ramos), Carlos Yaír Costly Molina, Carlos Alberto Pavón Plummer. Trainer: Reinaldo Rueda Rivera (Colombia).
USA: Tim Howard, Jonathan Michael Paul Spector, Oguchialu Chijioke Onyewu, Carlos Manuel Bocanegra (Cap), Jonathan Bornstein, Stuart Holden (90+3.Steven Cherundolo), Ricardo Anthony Clark, Michael Sheehan Bradley, Landon Timothy Donovan, Charles Desmond Davies (79.Josmer Volmy Altidore), Conor Casey (84.Benny Feilhaber). Trainer: Robert Bradley.
Goals: 1-0 Julio César de León (47), 1-1 Conor Casey (55), 1-2 Conor Casey (66), 1-3 Landon Timothy Donovan (71), 2-3 Julio César de León (78).
Cautions: Osman Danilo Chávez Guity, Maynor Alexis Figueroa Róchez / Jonathan Bornstein, Jonathan Michael Paul Spector.

14.10.2009, Estadio Cuscatlán, San Salvador; Attendance: 28,000
Referee: Ricardo Salazar (United States)
EL SALVADOR - HONDURAS   **0-1(0-0)**
SLV: Miguel Ángel Montes Moreno, Manuel Alejandro Salazar Rivas, Alexander Escobar Rosales, Marvin René González Leiva (66.Rudis Alberto Rivera Corrales), Deris Ariel Umanzor Guevara, Ramón Ulises Flores Aguirre, Ramón Alfredo Sánchez Paredes, Christian Giovanni Castillo Martínez, José Arturo Álvarez Hernández, Eliseo Antonio Quintanilla Ortíz (39.William Osael Romero Castillo), Williams Enrique Reyes Rodríguez (72.Dennis Jonathan Alas Morales). Trainer: Carlos de los Cobos Martínez (Mexico).
HON: Noel Eduardo Valladares Bonilla, Emilio Arturo Izaguirre Girón, Erick Zenón Norales Casildo, Johnny Eulogio Palacios Cacho, Mauricio Alberto Sabillón Peña, Edgard Anthony Álvarez Reyes (65.Danilo Elvis Turcios Funes), Amado Guevara, Wilson Roberto Palacios Suazo, Julio César de León, Carlos Alberto Pavón Plummer (76.Carlos Yaír Costly Molina), Óscar David Suazo Velázquez (84.Hendry Thomas). Trainer: Reinaldo Rueda Rivera (Colombia).
Goal: 0-1 Carlos Alberto Pavón Plummer (64).
Cautions: William Osael Romero Castillo, Alexander Escobar Rosales / Óscar David Suazo Velázquez, Wilson Roberto Palacios Suazo, Erick Zenón Norales Casildo, Noel Eduardo Valladares Bonilla.

14.10.2009, „Hasely Crawford" Stadium, Port of Spain; Attendance: 2,000
Referee: Walter Quesada Cordero (Costa Rica)
TRINIDAD & TOBAGO - MEXICO   **2-2(1-0)**
TRI: Marvin Phillip, Robert Primus, Kern Cupid, Dennis Lawrence, Jake Thomson, Trent Noel (78.Densill Theobald), Carlos Edwards (Cap), Clyde Leon, Hayden Tinto (56.Hughtun Hector), Kerry Baptiste, Devon Jorsling (76.Kenwyne Jones). Trainer: Russell Nigel Latapy.
MEX: Francisco Guillermo Ochoa Magaña, José Jonny Magallón Oliva, Carlos Arnoldo Salcido Flores, Héctor Alfredo Moreno Herrera, José Antonio Castro González, Gerardo Torrado Díez de Bonilla, Israel Castro Macías, José Andrés Guardado Hernández (46.Pablo Edson Barrera Acosta), Juan Francisco Palencia Hernández (54.Cuauhtémoc Blanco Bravo), Carlos Alberto Vela Garrido, Miguel Sabah Rodríguez (54.Enrique Alejandro Esqueda Tirado). Trainer: Javier Aguirre Onaindía.
Goals: 1-0 Kerry Baptiste (32 penalty), 1-1 Enrique Alejandro Esqueda Tirado (57), 2-1 Kerry Baptiste (61), 2-2 Carlos Arnoldo Salcido Flores (65).

14.10.2009, „Robert F. Kennedy" Memorial Stadium, Washington; Attendance: 26,243
Referee: Benito Armando Archundia Téllez (Mexico)
UNITED STATES - COSTA RICA   **2-2(0-2)**
USA: Tim Howard, Steven Cherundolo, Oguchialu Chijioke Onyewu, Carlos Manuel Bocanegra (Cap), Jonathan Bornstein, Stuart Holden (69.Robert Hampton Rogers III), Benny Feilhaber (63.José Francisco Torres Mezzell) , Michael Sheehan Bradley, Landon Timothy Donovan, Josmer Volmy Altidore, Conor Casey (79.Kenny Cooper). Trainer: Robert Bradley.
CRC: Keylor Antonio Navas Gamboa, Pablo Herrera Barrantes, Luis Antonio Marín Murillo, Dennis Marshall Maxwell (90+2.Douglas Sequeira Solano), Cristian Montero Fallas, Ángel Esteban Sirias Áviles (73.Júnior Enrique Díaz Campbell), Michael Barrantes Rojas, Wálter Centeno Corea (Cap), Randall Azofeifa Corrales, Bryan Ruiz González (82.Cristian Bolaños Navarro), Álvaro Alberto Saborío Chacón. Trainer: René Rodrigues Simões (Brazil).
Goals: 0-1 Bryan Ruiz González (20), 0-2 Bryan Ruiz González (23), 1-2 Michael Sheehan Bradley (72), 2-2 Jonathan Bornstein (90+5).
Cautions: Josmer Volmy Altidore / Cristian Montero Fallas, Álvaro Alberto Saborío Chacón.

162

AFRICA

For the World Cup 2010 organized in South Africa, 5 teams besides South Africa qualify for the Final Round. The qualifiers for the World Cup 2010 were combined with the qualifiers for the 27th African Cup of nations (hosted 2010 by Angola). The CAF qualification process began with a preliminary round played on 13 October and 17 November 2007:

FIRST ROUND

13.10.2007	Antananarivo	Madagascar - Comoros	6-2(2-1)
13.10.2007	Freetown	Sierra Leone – Guinea-Bissau	1-0(1-0)
13.10.2007	Djibouti	Djibouti - Somalia	1-0(0-0)
17.11.2007	Moroni	Comoros - Madagascar	0-4(0-1)
17.11.2007	Bissau	Guinea-Bissau – Sierra Leone	0-0

Madagascar, Sierra Leone and Djibouti qualified for the second round.

13.10.2007, Stade Municipal de Mahamasina, Antananarivo; Attendance: 7,754
Referee: Wellington Kaoma (Zimbabwe)
MADAGASCAR - COMOROS   **6-2(2-1)**
MAD: Jean Chrysostome Raharison, Mamy Gervais Randrianarisoa, Faneva Imà Andriantsima, Mamisoa Razafindrakoto (Cap), Sedera Mathieu Randriamparany, Lalaina Nomenjanahary, Rija Juvence Rakotomandimby (83.Jean Tsima Randriamihaja), Valentin Mazinot, Jean de l'Or Carolus Tsaralaza, Jean Mandilimana (46.Eric-Julien Faneva Rakotondrabe), Hubert Robson Razakanantema (60.Pamphile Rabefitia). Trainer: Franz Gerber (Germany).
COM: Hachim Nayef, Said Ahamada, Salim Mramboini (38.Mohamed Mahamoud), Djamal Mohamed, Yacine Saandi, Madi Anziz (81.Ahmed Said), Jean Housseini, Ibor Bakar (62.Issouf Djabir), Izzdine Zainoudine (Cap), Daoud Midtadi, Said Ben Boina. Trainer: Ali Mbae Camara.
Goals: 0-1 Daoud Midtadi(6), 1-1 Faneva Imà Andriantsima (30), 2-1 Faneva Imà Andriantsima (40), 3-1 Faneva Imà Andriantsima (49 penalty), 3-2 Ibor Bakar (53 penalty), 4-2 Faneva Imà Andriantsima (57), 5-2 Rija Juvence Rakotomandimby (65), 6-2 Jean de l'Or Carolus Tsaralaza (79).
Cautions: Jean de l'Or Carolus Tsaralaza / Djamal Mohamed.

13.10.2007, National Stadium, Freetown; Attendance: 25,000
Referee: Sule Mana (Nigeria)
SIERRA LEONE – GUINEA-BISSAU   **1-0(1-0)**
SLE: Christian Caulker, Kemokai Kallon (76.Mustapha Pa Safa Sama), Ibrahim Obreh Kargbo, Alphajor Mahmadu Bah (46.Sheriff Awilo Suma), Kewullay Conteh, Mohamed Kallon (Cap), Julius Gibrilla Woobay, Foday Ishmail Kamara, Umaru Bangura, Warren John Kanu, Paul Kpaka (81.Mohamed Sesay). Trainer: James Peters (Nigeria).
GNB: Flaviano Nanque, Bruno Fernandes, Mamadi Baldé, Braima Injai (Cap), Emiliano Te, Vladimir Mendes, Bacari Diallo, Muhamed Sano, Demba Jassi (58.Ibrahima Baldé), Sanussi Camara (72.Agostinho Soares), Vladimir Mendonça (83.Suleimane Seidi). Trainer: Baciro Candé.
Goal: 1-0 Kewullay Conteh (17)
Cautions: Mamadi Baldé, Sanussi Camara.

13.10.2007, „El Hadj Hassan Gouled" Stadium, Djibouti; Attendance: 10,000
Referee: Khalid Abdel Rahman (Sudan)
DJIBOUTI - SOMALIA   **1-0(0-0)**
DJI: Guedi Hassan, Ahmed Abdi, Akdiuahi Yassin (85.Salim Kadar), Mahamood Omar (Cap), Daher Mohamed, Guirreh Ayanleh, Abdourahman Mohamed (90.Ibrahim Moustapha), Ali Mawlid, Hussein Yassin, Miad Charmare, Houssein Saad (88.Ahmed Hassan Daher). Trainer: Ahmed Houssein.
SOM: Sheikh Osman Abdulkadir, Ali Egal Yasin, Omar Abdulkadir, Ahmed Ibrahim, Sadow Kasim,

Moalim Bader, Mohamed Ali Abdiaziz, Abdi Mohamed, Ismail Abdirahman (61.Abdi Abdifatah), Yusuf Abdulahi (75.Mohamed Abdiwahid), Rage Bashir. Trainer: Hussein Abdulla.
Goal: 1-0 Hussein Yassin (84).
Cautions: Hussein Yassin, Salim Kadar / Ali Egal Yasin.

17.11.2007, Moroni; Attendance: 1,610
Referee: Jerome Damon (South Africa)
COMOROS - MADAGASCAR   **0-4(0-1)**
COM: Mohamed Assane, Issouf Djabir, Sidi Yakout (72.Ahmed Said), Said Ali, Omar Himidi (72.Mzitrani Nourdine), Kary Zainoudine, Haniou Damine, Daoud Midtadi, Madi Takfidine, Izzdine Zainoudine (Cap), Ali Anmadidinse (23.Mohamed Mouigni). Trainer: Ali Mbae Camara.
MAD: Jean Chrysostome Raharison, Mamy Gervais Randrianarisoa, Faneva Imà Andriantsima (70.Hubert Robson Razakanantema), Sedera Mathieu Randriamparany, Paul Johan, Tojonavalona Rajaonarisoa, Lalaina Nomenjanahary, Rija Juvence Rakotomandimby, Valentin Mazinot, Jean de l'Or Carolus Tsaralaza (80.Eric-Julien Faneva Rakotondrabe), Paulin Voavy (80.Taima Randrianimata). Trainer: Franz Gerber (Germany).
Goals: 0-1 Lalaina Nomenjanahary (37), 0-2 Lalaina Nomenjanahary (51), 0-3 Rija Juvence Rakotomandimby (61), 0-4 Hubert Robson Razakanantema (73).
Cautions: Paulin Voavy, Jean de l'Or Carolus Tsaralaza, Paul Johan / Izzdine Zainoudine, Kary Zainoudine, Mohamed Assane.

17.11.2007, Stade du 24 septembre, Bissau; Attendance: 12,000
Referee: Joseph Lamptey (Ghana)
GUINEA-BISSAU – SIERRA LEONE   **0-0**
GNB: Flaviano Nanque, Bruno Fernandes (85.Ibrahima Baldé), Mamadi Baldé, Braima Injai (Cap), Emiliano Te, Vladimir Mendes, Bacari Diallo, Dionisio Fernandes, Muhamed Sano, Sanussi Camara (63.Vladimir Mendonça), Suleimane Baid. Trainer: Baciro Candé.
SLE: Christian Caulker, Mustapha Pa Safa Sama (53.Ibrahim Marcel Koroma), Kemokai Kallon (66.Foday Ishmail Kamara), Ibrahim Obreh Kargbo, Alphajor Mahmadu Bah, Kewullay Conteh, Mohamed Kallon (Cap), Julius Gibrilla Woobay, Umaru Bangura, Warren John Kanu, Paul Kpaka (73.Foday Ishmail Kamara). Trainer: James Peters (Nigeria).
Cautions: Bruno Fernandes, Braima Injai, Vladimir Mendonça / Julius Gibrilla Woobay, Alphajor Mahmadu Bah, Ibrahim Marcel Koroma, Mohamed Kallon, Christian Caulker.

The 48 teams were drawn in 12 groups. Each group winners and 8 best runners-up advanced to the third round. Ethiopia (Group 8, exclusion by the FIFA) and Eritrea (Group 11, withdraw) left prematurely the qualification. Due to this fact, that two qualifying groups were reduced to only three teams, the comparison of the 8 best runners-up do not include results of this teams against teams who finished fourth in their groups.

GROUP 1

31.05.2008	Yaoundé	Cameroon – Cape Verde	2-0(1-0)
31.05.2008	Dar-es-Salaam	Tanzania - Mauritius	1-1(0-1)
07.06.2008	Praia	Cape Verde - Tanzania	1-0(0-0)
08.06.2008	Curepipe	Mauritius - Cameroon	0-3(0-2)
14.06.2008	Dar-es-Salaam	Tanzania - Cameroon	0-0
15.06.2008	Curepipe	Mauritius – Cape Verde	0-1(0-1)
21.06.2008	Yaoundé	Cameroon - Tanzania	2-1(0-0)
22.06.2008	Praia	Cape Verde - Mauritius	3-1(1-0)
06.09.2008	Curepipe	Mauritius - Tanzania	1-4(1-4)
06.09.2008	Praia	Cape Verde - Cameroon	1-2(1-0)
11.10.2008	Yaoundé	Cameroon - Mauritius	5-0(1-0)
11.10.2008	Dar-es-Salaam	Tanzania – Cape Verde	3-1(2-1)

FINAL STANDINGS

1. Cameroon	6	5	1	0	14	-	2	16
2. Cape Verde	6	3	0	3	7	-	8	9
3. Tanzania	6	2	2	2	9	-	6	8
4. Mauritius	6	0	1	5	3	-	17	1

31.05.2008, Stade Omnisports „Ahmadou-Ahidjo", Yaoundé; Attendance: 20,000
Referee: Kokou Djaoupé (Togo)
CAMEROON – CAPE VERDE   **2-0(1-0)**
CMR: Idriss Carlos Kameni, Geremi Sorele Njitap Fotso, Rigobert Song Bahanag (Cap), Timothée Atouba, Alexandre Dimitri Song Billong, Jean II Makoun, Modeste M'bami, Stéphane Mbia Etoundi, Alain Mosely Nkong (89.Achille Emana Edzimbi), Pierre Achille Webó Kouamo (81.Gustave Anicet Bebbe Mbangue), Samuel Eto'o. Trainer: Otto Pfister (Germany).
CPV: Ernesto da Conceição Soares, Gilberto Reis, Fernando Maria Neves „Nando", Ricardo Jorge Ferreira Pinto da Silva, Emerson dos Santos da Luz „Gabei", Cláudio Zélito Fonseca Fernandes Aguiar „Lito" (Cap) (80.Silvino Gomes Soares), Adriano Barbosa Miranda da Luz „Néné" (66.Edson Lopes da Cruz „Karr"), Odysseu Guy Ramos, Ronny Souto Amado, Eduardo Fernandes Pereira Gomes „Dady" (65.Elton Rodrigues „Toy Adão"), Cecilio Lopes. Trainer: Ricardo Roberto Barreto da Rocha (Brazil).
Goals: 1-0 Rigobert Song Bahanag (8), 2-0 Samuel Eto'o (57 penalty).
Cautions: Timothée Atouba, Alexandre Dimitri Song Billong / Adriano Barbosa Miranda da Luz „Néné", Fernando Maria Neves „Nando".

31.05.2008, National Stadium, Dar-es-Salaam; Attendance: 35,000
Referee: Kenias Marange (Zimbabwe)
TANZANIA - MAURITIUS   **1-1(0-1)**
TAN: Ivo Mapunda, Nadir Haroub, Amir Maftah (64.Jerson Tegete), Farouk Ramadhan Nzee, Geoffrey Bonny Namwandu, Nizzar Khalfan (85.Athuman Iddy), Fredy Mbuna, Henry Joseph Shindika (Cap), Ulimboka Mwakingwe, Emmanuel Gabriel Mwakyusa (66.Kigi Makasi), Danny Mrwanda. Trainer: Marcio Maximo Barcellos (Brazil).
MRI: Désiré-François Ammomoothoo, Christopher Bazerque, Almondo Fricain, Stéphane L'Enflé

(Cap), Vincent Labonté (84.Fabien Pithia), Johan Marmitte, Charles Content, Ashley Lemince, Fabrice Pauline (55.Jean-Pierre Andy Sophie), Arassen Ragaven (58.Sewraj Dawoochand), Westley Marquette. Tráiner: Ashok Chundunsing.
Goals: 0-1 Westley Marquette (39), 1-1 Danny Mrwanda (69).
Cautions: Henry Joseph Shindika, Nadir Haroub / Arassen Ragaven, Fabrice Pauline, Christopher Bazerque.
Sent off: Westley Marquette (59).

07.06.2008, Estadio da Varzea, Praia; Attendance: 6,000
Referee: Abdellah El Achiri (Morocco)
CAPE VERDE - TANZANIA   **1-0(0-0)**
CPV: Ernesto da Conceição Soares, Gilberto Reis, Fernando Maria Neves „Nando", Ricardo Jorge Ferreira Pinto da Silva, Emerson dos Santos da Luz „Gabei", Marco Paulo Silva Soares (58.Elves Macedo „Babanco"), Cláudio Zélito Fonseca Fernandes Aguiar „Lito" (Cap), Odysseu Guy Ramos, Ronny Souto Amado, Eduardo Fernandes Pereira Gomes „Dady" (83.Edson Lopez Cruz), Silvino Gomes Soares (66.Hernâni José Oliveira Santos Borges). Trainer: Ricardo Roberto Barreto da Rocha (Brazil).
TAN: Ivo Mapunda, Nadir Haroub, Amir Maftah, Shadrack Nsajigwa, Salum Swedi, Geoffrey Bonny Namwandu, Athuman Iddy (78.Kigi Makasi), Nizzar Khalfan (66.Ulimboka Mwakingwe), Henry Joseph Shindika (Cap), Emmanuel Gabriel Mwakyusa (71.Uhuru Selemani), Danny Mrwanda. Trainer: Marcio Maximo Barcellos (Brazil).
Goal: 1-0 Elves Macedo „Babanco" (73).
Cautions: Nizzar Khalfan, Danny Mrwanda, Henry Joseph Shindika / Cláudio Zélito Fonseca, Fernandes Aguiar „Lito".

08.06.2008, Stade „Georges V", Curepipe; Attendance: 4,500
Referee: Hélder Martins de Carvalho (Angola)
MAURITIUS - CAMEROON   **0-3(0-2)**
MRI: Désiré-François Ammomoothoo, Christopher Bazerque, Almondo Fricain, Stéphane L'Enflé (Cap), Vincent Labonté, Johan Marmitte, Charles Content, Jimmy Cundasamy, Ashley Lemince (51.Ricardo Naboth), Jean-Pierre Andy Sophie, Arassen Ragaven (42.Sewraj Dawoochand). Trainer: Ashok Chundunsing.
CMR: Idriss Carlos Kameni, André Stéphane Bikey Amugu, Rigobert Song Bahanag (Cap), Timothée Atouba, Geremi Sorele Njitap Fotso, Modeste M'bami (85.Gilles Augustin Binya), Alexandre Dimitri Song Billong, Jean II Makoun, Stéphane Mbia Etoundi, Samuel Eto'o (66.Gustave Anicet Bebbe Mbangue), Pierre Achille Webó Kouamo (87.Alain Mosely Nkong). Trainer: Otto Pfister (Germany).
Goals: 0-1 André Stéphane Bikey Amugu (11), 0-2 Samuel Eto'o (27), 0-3 Gustave Anicet Bebbe Mbangue (87).
Cautions: Sewraj Dawoochand / Pierre Achille Webó Kouamo, Samuel Eto'o.

14.06.2008, National Stadium, Dar-es-Salaam; Attendance: 55,000
Referee: Coffi Codjia (Benin)
TANZANIA - CAMEROON   **0-0**
TAN: Ivo Mapunda, Nadir Haroub, Amir Maftah, Shadrack Nsajigwa, Salum Swedi, Geoffrey Bonny Namwandu, Athuman Iddy (89.Kigi Makasi), Nizzar Khalfan (78.Abdi Kassim), Shaban Nditi, Danny Mrwanda, Mrisho Ngasa. Trainer: Marcio Maximo Barcellos (Brazil).
CMR: Idriss Carlos Kameni, André Stéphane Bikey Amugu, Rigobert Song Bahanag (Cap), Timothée Atouba, Geremi Sorele Njitap Fotso, Stéphane Mbia Etoundi (71.Alain Mosely Nkong), Alexandre Dimitri Song Billong, Modeste M'bami, Jean II Makoun (62.Gustave Anicet Bebbe Mbangue), Samuel Eto'o, Pierre Achille Webó Kouamo (71.Achille Emana Edzimbi). Trainer: Otto Pfister (Germany).
Cautions: Amir Maftah / André Stéphane Bikey Amugu.

15.06.2008, Stade „George V", Curepipe; Attendance: 1,480
Referee: Wellington Kaoma (Zambia)
MAURITIUS – CAPE VERDE   **0-1(0-1)**

MRI: Didier Gopaul, Christopher Bazerque, Almondo Fricain, Stéphane L'Enflé (Cap), Vincent Labonté, Johan Marmitte (84.Bruno Ravina), Charles Content, Jimmy Cundasamy, Sewraj Dawoochand (46.Arassen Ragaven), Ricardo Naboth, Jean-Pierre Andy Sophie. Trainer: Ashok Chundunsing.
CPV: Ernesto da Conceição Soares, Gilberto Reis, Fernando Maria Neves „Nando", Ricardo Jorge Ferreira Pinto da Silva, Emerson dos Santos da Luz „Gabei", Marco Paulo Silva Soares, Cláudio Zélito Fonseca Fernandes Aguiar „Lito" (Cap) (87.Fernando Lopes dos Santos Varela), Elves Macedo „Babanco" (46.Edson Lopes da Cruz „Karr"), Odysseu Guy Ramos, Ronny Souto Amado, Eduardo Fernandes Pereira Gomes „Dady" (82.Elton Rodrigues „Toy Adão"). Trainer: Ricardo Roberto Barreto da Rocha (Brazil).
Goal: 0-1 Eduardo Fernandes Pereira Gomes „Dady" (43 penalty).
Cautions: Christopher Bazerque, Didier Gopaul / Gilberto Reis, Ernesto da Conceição Soares.

21.06.2008, Stade Omnisports „Ahmadou-Ahidjo", Yaoundé; Attendance: 25,000
Referee: John Mendy (Gambia)
CAMEROON - TANZANIA 2-1(0-0)
CMR: Idriss Carlos Kameni, André Stéphane Bikey Amugu, Rigobert Song Bahanag (Cap), Timothée Atouba (75.Haman Sadjo), Geremi Sorele Njitap Fotso, Stéphane Mbia Etoundi (46.Joël Dieudonné Martin Epalle Newaka), Alexandre Dimitri Song Billong, Modeste M'bami, Jean II Makoun (65.Achille Emana Edzimbi), Samuel Eto'o, Pierre Achille Webó Kouamo. Trainer: Otto Pfister (Germany).
TAN: Ivo Mapunda, Nadir Haroub, Amir Maftah, Shadrack Nsajigwa, Salum Swedi (86.Kevin Yondani), Geoffrey Bonny Namwandu, Nizzar Khalfan, Shaban Nditi, Henry Joseph Shindika (Cap), Danny Mrwanda, Mrisho Ngasa (69.Jerson Tegete). Trainer: Marcio Maximo Barcellos (Brazil).
Goals: 1-0 Samuel Eto'o (65), 1-1 Danny Mrwanda (72), 2-1 Samuel Eto'o (89).
Cautions: Stéphane Mbia Etoundi, Samuel Eto'o / Henry Joseph Shindika, Danny Mrwanda, Mrisho Ngasa.

22.06.2008, Estadio da Varzea, Praia; Attendance: 2,850
Referee: Koman Coulibaly (Mali)
CAPE VERDE - MAURITIUS 3-1(1-0)
CPV: Ernesto da Conceição Soares, Gilberto Reis, Fernando Maria Neves „Nando" (82.Ianique Santos Tavares „Stopira"), Ricardo Jorge Ferreira Pinto da Silva, Emerson dos Santos da Luz „Gabei", Marco Paulo Silva Soares, Cláudio Zélito Fonseca Fernandes Aguiar „Lito" (Cap), Elves Macedo „Babanco" (68.Fernando Lopes dos Santos Valter), Odysseu Guy Ramos, Ronny Souto Amado (63.Elton Rodrigues „Toy Adão"), Eduardo Fernandes Pereira Gomes „Dady". Trainer: Ricardo Roberto Barreto da Rocha (Brazil).
MRI: Didier Gopaul, Almondo Fricain, Allyson Kersley Jolicoeur (46.Louis Pithia), Stéphane L'Enflé (Cap), Vincent Labonté, Johan Marmitte *(sent off 49)*, Bruno Ravina, Charles Content (70.Johan Cundasamy), Ashley Lemince, Jimmy Cundasamy, Ricardo Naboth (46.Jean-Pierre Andy Sophie). Trainer: Ashok Chundunsing.
Goals: 1-0 Eduardo Fernandes Pereira Gomes „Dady" (45+1), 2-0 Eduardo Fernandes Pereira Gomes „Dady" (58), 2-1 Jean-Pierre Andy Sophie (67), 3-1 Marco Paulo Silva Soares (78).
Cautions: Vincent Labonté, Johan Cundasamy,Ashley Lemince, Stéphane L'Enflé.
Sent off: Johan Marmitte (49).

06.09.2008, Stade „George V", Curepipe; Attendance: 100
Referee: Alfred Ndinya (Kenya)
MAURITIUS - TANZANIA 1-4(1-4)
MRI: Désiré-François Ammomoothoo, Christopher Bazerque, Johan Cundasamy, Stéphane L'Enflé (Cap), Vincent Labonté (46.Allyson Kersley Jolicoeur), Ashley Lemince, Jimmy Cundasamy, Sewraj Dawoochand (63.Fabien Pithia), Louis Pithia, Westley Marquette, Jean-Pierre Andy Sophie. Trainer: Ashok Chundunsing.
TAN: Ivo Mapunda, Nadir Haroub, Juma Jabu, Shadrack Nsajigwa, Salum Swedi, Geoffrey Bonny Namwandu, Nizzar Khalfan, Kigi Makasi (60.Musa Mgosi Hassan), Shaban Nditi (79.Jabir Stima), Mrisho Ngasa, Jerson Tegete (74.Adam Kingwande). Trainer: Marcio Maximo Barcellos (Brazil).

167

Goals: 0-1 Kigi Makasi (12), 1-1 Westley Marquette (13), 1-2 Nizzar Khalfan (20), 1-3 Jerson Tegete (30), 1-4 Jerson Tegete (35).
Cautions: Geoffrey Bonny Namwandu.

06.09.2008, Estadio da Varzea, Praia; Attendance: 5,000
Referee: Jean-Claude Labrosse (Seychelles)
CAPE VERDE - CAMEROON   **1-2(1-0)**
CPV: Ernesto da Conceição Soares, Janício de Jesus Gomes Martins, Fernando Maria Neves „Nando", Ricardo Jorge Ferreira Pinto da Silva, Pedro Miguel Cardoso Monteiro „Pedro Pelé" (84.Elton Rodrigues „Toy Adão"), Marco Paulo Silva Soares (55.Emerson dos Santos da Luz „Gabei"), Cláudio Zélito Fonseca Fernandes Aguiar „Lito" (Cap), Odysseu Guy Ramos, Ronny Souto Amado, Eduardo Fernandes Pereira Gomes „Dady", Gilson Manuel Silva Alves „Já" (75.Cecilio Lopes). Trainer: Ricardo Roberto Barreto da Rocha (Brazil).
CMR: Idriss Carlos Kameni, André Stéphane Bikey Amugu, Rigobert Song Bahanag (Cap), Timothée Atouba, Stéphane Mbia Etoundi (62.Franck Steve Songo'o), Alexandre Dimitri Song Billong, Modeste M'bami (46.Somen Tchoyi), Jean II Makoun, Gilles Augustin Binya, Albert Meyong Zé, Pierre Achille Webó Kouamo (46.Achille Emana Edzimbi). Trainer: Otto Pfister (Germany).
Goals: 1-0 Cláudio Zélito Fonseca Fernandes Aguiar „Lito" (39), 1-1 Achille Emana Edzimbi (51), 1-2 Somen Tchoyi (65).
Cautions: Emerson dos Santos da Luz „Gabei" / Alexandre Dimitri Song Billong.
Sent off: Alexandre Dimitri Song Billong (90+2).

11.10.2008, Stade Omnisports „Ahmadou-Ahidjo", Yaoundé; Attendance: 12,000
Referee: Mohamed Ould Lemghambodj (Mauritania)
CAMEROON - MAURITIUS   **5-0(1-0)**
CMR: Idriss Carlos Kameni, André Stéphane Bikey Amugu, Rigobert Song Bahanag (Cap), Geremi Sorele Njitap Fotso, Modeste M'bami (70.Guy Stephane Essame), Jean II Makoun, Daniel Armand Ngom Kome, Gilles Augustin Binya, Somen Tchoyi (59.Eric Djemba-Djemba), Achille Emana Edzimbi (46.Albert Meyong Zé), Samuel Eto'o. Trainer: Otto Pfister (Germany).
MRI: Désiré-François Ammomoothoo, Almondo Fricain (73.Jean-Pierre Cerveaux), Johan Cundasamy, Stéphane L'Enflé (Cap), Vincent Labonté, Bruno Ravina, Gilbert Bayaram (63.Jean-Pierre Andy Sophie), Thierry Collet, Jimmy Cundasamy, Jerry Louis, Westley Marquette (80.Fabrice Pauline). Trainer: Ashok Chundunsing.
Goals: 1-0 Samuel Eto'o (26), 2-0 Samuel Eto'o (46 penalty), 3-0 Albert Meyong Zé (56), 4-0 Jean II Makoun (70), 5-0 Albert Meyong Zé (72).
Cautions: Daniel Armand Ngom Kome / Thierry Collet.

11.10.2008, National Stadium, Dar-es-Salaamy; Attendance: 10,000
Referee: Jerome Damon (South Africa)
TANZANIA – CAPE VERDE   **3-1(2-1)**
TAN: Ivo Mapunda, Nadir Haroub, Hamadi Nurdin Bakari, Juma Jabu, Shadrack Nsajigwa, Salum Swedi, Athuman Iddy, Haruna Moshi (68.Kigi Makasi), Henry Joseph Shindika (Cap) (90+2 Jabi Stima), Mrisho Ngasa, Jerson Tegete (72.Musa Mgosi Hassan). Trainer: Marcio Maximo Barcellos (Brazil).
CPV: Ernesto da Conceição Soares, Janício de Jesus Gomes Martins, Fernando Maria Neves „Nando" (71.Henrique Mateus Lopes), Fernando Lopes dos Santos Valter, Pedro Miguel Cardoso Monteiro „Pedro Pelé", Emerson dos Santos da Luz „Gabei", Marco Paulo Silva Soares, Cláudio Zélito Fonseca Fernandes Aguiar „Lito" (Cap), Odysseu Guy Ramos (31.José Semedo), Ronny Souto Amado (46.Héldon Augusto Almeida Ramos „Nhuc"), Eduardo Fernandes Pereira Gomes „Dady". Trainer: Ricardo Roberto Barreto da Rocha (Brazil).
Goals: 1-0 Athuman Iddy (5), 2-0 Jerson Tegete (27), 2-1 José Semedo (35), 3-1 Mrisho Ngasa (74).
Cautions: Salum Swedi, Juma Jabu / Emerson dos Santos da Luz „Gabei", José Semedo.

168

31.05.2008	Windhoek	Namibia - Kenya	2-1(1-1)
01.06.2008	Conakry	Guinea - Zimbabwe	0-0
07.06.2008	Nairobi	Kenya - Guinea	2-0(1-0)
08.06.2008	Harare	Zimbabwe - Namibia	2-0(1-0)
14.06.2008	Windhoek	Namibia - Guinea	1-2(1-2)
14.06.2008	Nairobi	Kenya - Zimbabwe	2-0(1-0)
22.06.2008	Harare	Zimbabwe - Kenya	0-0
22.06.2008	Conakry	Guinea - Namibia	4-0(2-0)
06.09.2008	Nairobi	Kenya - Namibia	1-0(1-0)
07.09.2008	Harare	Zimbabwe - Guinea	0-0
11.10.2008	Windhoek	Namibia - Zimbabwe	4-2(3-0)
12.10.2008	Conakry	Guinea - Kenya	3-2(1-0)

FINAL STANDINGS

1. Guinea	6	3	2	1	9 - 5	11
2. Kenya	6	3	1	2	8 - 5	10
3. Zimbabwe	6	1	3	2	4 - 6	6
4. Namibia	6	2	0	4	7 - 12	6

31.05.2008, Independence Stadium, Windhoek; Attendance: 6,000
Referee: Muhmed Ssegonga (Uganda)
NAMIBIA - KENYA **2-1(1-1)**
NAM: Athiel Mbaha, Jeremiah Baisako, Richard Gariseb, Michael Pienaar (Cap), Hartman Toromba, Brian Brendell (60.Rudolph Bester), Quinton Norman Jacobs (70.Tulongeni Tuyeni), Jamuovandu Ngatjizeko, Costa Khaiseb, Lazarus Kaimbi (46.Pineas Jacob), Wilko Risser. Trainer: Arie Schans (Holland).
KEN: Arnold Origi Otieno, Edgar Ochieng Odhiambo, Ibrahim Shikanda, Kennedy Ayong Omogi, Llyod Wahome Kinguru, Austin Charles Makacha, Titus Mulama, Kevin Ochieng Opondo (55.Patrick Omoya Onyango), Allan Wetende Wanga (81.Osborne Monday), Robert Mambo Mumba, Dennis Oliech (72.Francis Ouma). Trainer: Francis Kimanzi.
Goals: 1-0 Wilko Risser (14), 1-1 Austin Charles Makacha (40), 2-1 Costa Khaiseb (89).
Cautions: Costa Khaiseb / Austin Charles Makacha.

01.06.2008, Stade 28 Septembre, Conakry; Attendance: 12,000
Referee: Djamel Haimoudi (Algeria)
GUINEA - ZIMBABWE **0-0**
GUI: Kémoko Camara, Dianbobo Baldé, Alsény Camara, Oumar Kalabane, Ibrahima Diallo, Samuel Johnson, Mohamed Sacko (86.Boubacar Diallo), Pascal Feindouno (Cap), Ismaël Bangoura (71.Amara Karba Bangoura), Karamoko Cissé (71.Alhassane Keïta), Fodé Mansaré. Trainer: Robert Nouzaret (France).
ZIM: Energy Murambadoro, Onismor Bhasera, David Kutyauripo, Zvenyika Makonese, James Matola, Cephas Chimedza, Harlington Shereni (62.Clemence Matawu), Esrom Nyandoro, Benjamin Mwaruwari, Gilbert Mushangazhike (64.Takesure Chinyama), Joseph Ngwenya (85.Tinashe Washington Nengomasha). Trainer: Jose Claudinei Georgini „Valinhos" (Brazil).
Cautions: Samuel Johnson / Gilbert Mushangazhike.

07.06.2008, Nyayo National Stadium, Nairobi; Attendance: 35,000
Referee: Lambert Eyene (Cameroon)
KENYA - GUINEA **2-0(1-0)**
KEN: Arnold Origi Otieno, John Njoroge Mwangi, Edgar Ochieng Odhiambo, George Owino, Anthony Kimani Wanjohi, Austin Charles Makacha, Titus Mulama (49.Kevin Ochieng Opondo), Patrick Omoya Onyango (83.Allan Wetende Wanga), McDonald Mariga Wanyama, Robert Mambo Mumba, Dennis

Oliech. Trainer: Francis Kimanzi.

GUI: Kémoko Camara, Dianbobo Baldé, Alsény Camara, Oumar Kalabane, Ibrahima Diallo, Amara Karba Bangoura, Samuel Johnson (30.Algassimou Baldé), Mohamed Sacko, Pascal Feindouno (Cap), Ismaël Bangoura, Fodé Mansaré. Trainer: Robert Nouzaret (France).

Goals: 1-0 Dennis Oliech (3), 2-0 Dennis Oliech (50).

Cautions: Dennis Oliech, Patrick Omoya Onyango / Algassimou Baldé, Fodé Mansaré, Ibrahima Diallo.

08.06.2008, Rufaro Stadium, Harare; Attendance: 27,979
Referee: Verson Lwanja (Malawi)

ZIMBABWE - NAMIBIA   **2-0(1-0)**

ZIM: Energy Murambadoro, Onismor Bhasera, David Kutyauripo, Zvenyika Makonese, James Matola, Cephas Chimedza (78.Vusumuzi Nyoni), Harlington Shereni, Esrom Nyandoro, Benjamin Mwaruwari (Cap) (83.Takesure Chinyama), Gilbert Mushangazhike, Joseph Ngwenya (54.Clemence Matawu). Trainer: Jose Claudinei Georgini „Valinhos" (Brazil).

NAM: Athiel Mbaha, Steven Goaxab, Richard Gariseb, Ivan Namaseb (77.Pineas Jacob), Oliver Risser, Hartman Toromba, Brian Brendell (59.Floris Diergaardt), Jamuovandu Ngatjizeko, Costa Khaiseb, Quinton Norman Jacobs (59.Jeremiah Baisako), Wilko Risser. Trainer: Arie Schans (Holland).

Goals: 1-0 Gilbert Mushangazhike (26), 2-0 Gilbert Mushangazhike (85).

14.06.2008, Independence Stadium, Windhoek; Attendance: 5,000
Referee: Emmanuel Imiere (Nigeria)

NAMIBIA - GUINEA   **1-2(1-2)**

NAM: Esau Tjiouro, Richard Gariseb, Ivan Namaseb (62.Arend von Stryk), Michael Pienaar (Cap), Oliver Risser, Hartman Toromba, Quinton Norman Jacobs (70.Jeremiah Baisako), Jamuovandu Ngatjizeko, Costa Khaiseb, Rudolph Bester (75.Floris Diergaardt), Wilko Risser. Trainer: Arie Schans (Holland).

GUI: Kémoko Camara, Dianbobo Baldé, Morlaye Cissé (87.Mangué Camara), Oumar Kalabane, Ibrahima Diallo, Kamil Zayatte, Mohamed Sacko, Pascal Feindouno (Cap), Ismaël Bangoura, Ibrahima Bangoura (76.Alsény Camara), Fodé Mansaré (60.Amara Karba Bangoura). Trainer: Robert Nouzaret (France).

Goals: 0-1 Ismaël Bangoura (22), 1-1 Rudolph Bester (41), 1-2 Pascal Feindouno (45+1).

Cautions: Dianbobo Baldé, Mohamed Sacko, Ismaël Bangoura.

14.06.2008, Nyayo National Stadium, Nairobi; Attendance: 27,500
Referee: Badara Diatta (Senegal)

KENYA - ZIMBABWE   **2-0(1-0)**

KEN: Arnold Origi Otieno, John Njoroge Mwangi, Edgar Ochieng Odhiambo, George Owino, Anthony Kimani Wanjohi, Austin Charles Makacha, Titus Mulama (51.Allan Wetende Wanga), Patrick Omoya Onyango, McDonald Mariga Wanyama (59.Kevin Ochieng Opondo), Robert Mambo Mumba (72.Osborne Monday), Dennis Oliech. Trainer: Francis Kimanzi.

ZIM: Energy Murambadoro, Onismor Bhasera (82.Sam Mutenheri), David Kutyauripo, Zvenyika Makonese, James Matola (80.Clemence Matawu), Cephas Chimedza (78.Vusumuzi Nyoni), Harlington Shereni, Esrom Nyandoro, Benjamin Mwaruwari (Cap), Gilbert Mushangazhike, Joseph Ngwenya. Trainer: Jose Claudinei Georgini „Valinhos" (Brazil).

Goals: 1-0 McDonald Mariga Wanyama (13), 2-0 Dennis Oliech (88).

Cautions: Patrick Omoya Onyango / Esrom Nyandoro, James Matola.

22.06.2008, Rufaro Stadium, Harare; Attendance: 23,000
Referee: Alex Kotey (Ghana)

ZIMBABWE - KENYA   **0-0**

ZIM: Energy Murambadoro (55.Washington Arubi), Onismor Bhasera, David Kutyauripo, Zvenyika Makonese, James Matola, Cephas Chimedza, Clemence Matawu, Esrom Nyandoro, Benjamin Mwaruwari (Cap), Gilbert Mushangazhike (73.Kingston Nkatha), Joseph Ngwenya (23.Honour Gombami). Trainer: Jose Claudinei Georgini „Valinhos" (Brazil).

KEN: Noah Ayuko, John Njoroge Mwangi, Edgar Ochieng Odhiambo, George Owino, Anthony Kimani Wanjohi, Andrew Oyombe (52.Osborne Monday), Austin Charles Makacha, Kevin Ochieng Opondo (87.Joseph Shikokoti Ebenzi), Robert Mambo Mumba, Dennis Oliech, Francis Ouma (80.Allan Wetende Wanga). Trainer: Francis Kimanzi.
Cautions: Dennis Oliech, Noah Ayuko.

22.06.2008, Stade 28 Septembre, Conakry; Attendance: 15,000
Referee: Herminio Monteiro Lopes (Cape Verde)
GUINEA - NAMIBIA   **4-0(2-0)**
GUI: Kémoko Camara, Dianbobo Baldé, Morlaye Cissé, Oumar Kalabane (79.Mangué Camara), Ibrahima Diallo, Kamil Zayatte, Mohamed Sacko (85.Minka Yadi Camara), Pascal Feindouno (Cap) (89.Amara Karba Bangoura), Ismaël Bangoura, Ibrahima Bangoura, Fodé Mansaré. Trainer: Robert Nouzaret (France).
NAM: Esau Tjiouro (46.Maximilian Mbaeva), Jeremiah Baisako, Richard Gariseb, Ivan Namaseb (59.Wilko Risser), Michael Pienaar (Cap), Oliver Risser, Hartman Toromba, Brian Brendell (68.Rudolph Bester), Jamuovandu Ngatjizeko, Costa Khaiseb, Pineas Jacob. Trainer: Arie Schans (Holland).
Goals: 1-0 Pascal Feindouno (23), 2-0 Ismaël Bangoura (27), 3-0 Ismaël Bangoura (55), 4-0 Ismaël Bangoura (60).
Cautions: Dianbobo Baldé / Jeremiah Baisako.

06.09.2008, Moi International Sports Centre, Nairobi; Attendance: 40,000
Referee: Jean-Marie Hicuburundi (Burundi)
KENYA - NAMIBIA   **1-0(1-0)**
KEN: Noah Ayuko, John Njoroge Mwangi, Edgar Ochieng Odhiambo, George Owino, Mohammed Jamal (90+1.Joseph Shikokoti Ebenzi), Austin Charles Makacha, James Ndeto Mulinge, McDonald Mariga Wanyama, Allan Wetende Wanga (70.Francis Ouma), Robert Mambo Mumba, Patrick Omoya Onyango (88.Kevin Ochieng Opondo). Trainer: Francis Kimanzi.
NAM: Athiel Mbaha, Steven Goaxab, Richard Gariseb (46.Ivan Namaseb), George Hummel, Oliver Risser (14.Lazarus Kaimbi), Hartman Toromba, Collin Benjamin (Cap), Quinton Norman Jacobs, Sydney Convinus Plaatjies, Paulus Shipanga (64.Rudolph Bester), Wilko Risser. Trainer: Tom Saintfiet (Belgium).
Goal: 1-0 Mohammed Jamal (44 penalty).
Cautions: Collin Benjamin.

07.09.2008, Rufaro Stadium, Harare; Attendance: 23,000
Referee: Raphael Divine Evehe (Cameroon)
ZIMBABWE - GUINEA   **0-0**
ZIM: Tapuwa Kapini, Onismor Bhasera, David Kutyauripo, Zvenyika Makonese, James Matola, Edward Sadomba, Tinashe Washington Nengomasha (37.Clemence Matawu), Esrom Nyandoro, Joseph Ngwenya, Gilbert Mushangazhike (68.Cuthbert Malajila), Joel Lupahla (71.Ovidy Karuru). Trainer: Jose Claudinei Georgini „Valinhos" (Brazil).
GUI: Naby-Moussa Yattara, Mamadi Kaba (63.Aboubacar M'Baye Camara), Morlaye Cissé, Kamil Zayatte, Ibrahima Diallo, Mamadou Dioulde Bah, Mohamed Sacko, Pascal Feindouno (Cap), Ismaël Bangoura (80.Larsen Touré), Ibrahima Bangoura (46.Amara Karba Bangoura), Fodé Mansaré. Trainer: Robert Nouzaret (France).
Cautions: Mamadou Dioulde Bah, Naby-Moussa Yattara.
Sent off: Amara Karba Bangoura (73).

11.10.2008, Independence Stadium, Windhoek; Attendance: 4,000
Referee: Koman Coulibaly (Mali)
NAMIBIA - ZIMBABWE   **4-2(3-0)**
NAM: Athiel Mbaha, Richard Gariseb, George Hummel, Ivan Namaseb, Hartman Toromba, Collin Benjamin (Cap), Quinton Norman Jacobs, Sydney Convinus Plaatjies (56.Lazarus Kaimbi), Paulus Shipanga, Rudolph Bester (68.Jamuovandu Ngatjizeko), Wilko Risser (82.Jerome Louise). Trainer: Tom Saintfiet (Belgium).
ZIM: Tapuwa Kapini, Onismor Bhasera, David Kutyauripo, Zvenyika Makonese, James Matola, Edward Sadomba, Tinashe Washington Nengomasha, Pride Tafirenyika (70.Ovidy Karuru), Quincy Antipas (46.Clemence Matawu), Gilbert Mushangazhike, Joel Lupahla (70.Cuthbert Malajila). Trainer: Jose Claudinei Georgini „Valinhos" (Brazil).
Goals: 1-0 Wilko Risser (18), 2-0 Rudolph Bester (30), 3-0 Paulus Shipanga (43), 3-1 Esrom Nyandoro (51), 4-1 Wilko Risser (53), 4-2 Cuthbert Malajila (83).
Cautions: Quinton Norman Jacobs, Wilko Risser.

12.10.2008, Stade 28 Septembre, Conakry; Attendance: 16,400
Referee: Eddy Allen Maillet Guyto (Seychelles)
GUINEA - KENYA   **3-2(1-0)**
GUI: Naby-Moussa Yattara, Dianbobo Baldé, Oumar Kalabane, Kamil Zayatte (79.Mohamed Sacko), Ibrahima Sory Camara, Ibrahima Diallo, Mamadou Dioulde Bah, Alhassane Keïta, Pascal Feindouno (Cap), Ismaël Bangoura (89.Minka Yadi Camara), Fodé Mansaré (90+3.Aboubacar M'Baye Camara). Trainer: Robert Nouzaret (France).
KEN: Noah Ayuko, John Njoroge Mwangi, Edgar Ochieng Odhiambo, George Owino, Mohammed Jamal (55.Allan Wetende Wanga), Austin Charles Makacha (81.Kevin Ochieng Opondo), James Ndeto Mulinge, Osborne Monday, McDonald Mariga Wanyama, Dennis Oliech, Patrick Omoya Onyango (75.Francis Ouma). Trainer: Francis Kimanzi.
Goals: 1-0 Ismaël Bangoura (31), 2-0 Mamadou Bah (51), 2-1 Francis Ouma (70), 3-1 Kamil Zayatte (72), 3-2 Dennis Oliech (90+3).

GROUP 3

31.05.2008	Kampala	Uganda - Niger		1-0(0-0)
01.06.2008	Luanda	Angola - Benin		3-0(0-0)
07.06.2008	Niamey	Niger - Angola		1-2(1-1)
08.06.2008	Cotonou	Benin - Uganda		4-1(2-1)
14.06.2008	Kampala	Uganda - Angola		3-1(2-0)
15.06.2008	Niamey	Niger - Benin		0-2(0-0)
22.06.2008	Cotonou	Benin - Niger		2-0(1-0)
23.06.2008	Luanda	Angola - Uganda		0-0
07.09.2008	Cotonou	Benin - Angola		3-2(1-1)
07.09.2008	Niamey	Niger - Uganda		3-1(0-1)
12.10.2008	Kampala	Uganda - Benin		2-1(0-1)
12.10.2008	Luanda	Angola - Niger		3-1(0-1)

FINAL STANDINGS

1. Benin	6	4	0	2	12 - 8	12
2. Angola	6	3	1	2	11 - 8	10
3. Uganda	6	3	1	2	8 - 9	10
4. Niger	6	1	0	5	5 - 11	3

31.05.2008, „Nelson Mandela" National Stadium, Kampala; Attendance: 25,000
Referee: Raphael Divine Evehe (Cameroon)
UGANDA - NIGER **1-0(0-0)**
UGA: Dennis Masinde Onyango, Abubakari Tabula, Timothy Batabaire, Joseph Nestroy Kizito, Simoen Masaba, Ibrahim Sekagya (Cap) (67.Andrew Mwesigwa), David Obua, Assani Bajope (52.Samson Caesar Okhuti), Noah Babadi Kasule (61.Sulaiman Tenywa Bonseu), Joseph Kabagambe, Eugene Ssepuuya. Trainer: László Csaba (Hungary).
NIG: Kassaly Daouda, Ismaël Eragae Alassane, Emaniel Djibril Dankawa, Amadou Kader, Karim Oumarou, Ouwo Moussa Maazou (75.Abdoul Aziz Hamza), Idrissa Laouali, Souleymane Dela Sakou (63.Saidou Idrissa), Harouna Ide Loga, Kamilou Daouda, Lassina Abdoul Karim Konate. Trainer: Hameye Amadou.
Goal: 1-0 Ibrahim Sekagya (53).
Cautions: Eugene Ssepuuya / Idrissa Laouali.

31.05.2008, Estádio Coqueiros, Luanda; Attendance: 6,000
Referee: Jerome Damon (South Africa)
ANGOLA - BENIN **3-0(0-0)**
ANG: Luís Mamona João „Lama", Manuel Alexandre Jamuana, Carlos Manuel Gonçalves Alonso „Kali", Yamba Asha João, Manuel Rui Marques, Paulo Batista Nsimba „Zé Kalanga" (78.António Manuel Viana Mendonça), André Venceslau Valentim Macanga (Cap), Norberto Mauro Mulenessa „Maurito" (46.Ricardo Job), Felisberto Sebastião de Graça Amaral „Gilberto", Flávio Amado da Silva, Arsenio Sebastião Cabungula "Love" (67.Pedro Manuel Torres „Mantorras"). Trainer: Luís Oliveira Gonçalves.
BEN: Yoann Djidonou, Abdoul Khaled Akiola Adénon, Damien Chrysostome, Anicet Adjamossi, Moustapha Agnidé (50.Razak Omotoyossi), Jocelyn Ahouéya, Romuald Boco, Oscar Olou, Stéphane Sessegnon, Oumar Tchomogo, Abou Gariga Maïga (82.Daniel Gbaguidi). Trainer: Wabi Gomez.
Goals: 1-0 Flávio Amado da Silva (62), 2-0 Ricardo Job (81), 3-0 António Manuel Viana Mendonça (86).
Cautions: André Venceslau Valentim Macanga, Ricardo Job / Stéphane Sessegnon, Razak Omotoyossi

07.06.2008, Stade „Général Seyni Kountché", Niamey; Attendance: 23,000
Referee: Slim Jedidi (Tunisia)
NIGER - ANGOLA **1-2(1-1)**

NIG: Kassaly Daouda, Ismaël Eragae Alassane (61.Yaou Dan Jouma), Koffi Dan Kowa, Amadou Kader, Abdoulkarim Moussa Konate (58.Saidou Idrissa), Karim Oumarou, Ouwo Moussa Maazou, Abdoul Aziz Hamza, Idrissa Laouali, Souleymane Dela Sakou (Cap), Kamilou Daouda (82.Hamidou Djibo). Trainer: Hameye Amadou.

ANG: Luís Mamona João „Lama", Manuel Alexandre Jamuana, Carlos Manuel Gonçalves Alonso „Kali", Yamba Asha João, Manuel Rui Marques, Paulo Batista Nsimba „Zé Kalanga" (64.Ricardo Job), André Venceslau Valentim Macanga (Cap), Felisberto Sebastião de Graça Amaral „Gilberto", António Manuel Viana Mendonça (81.Norberto Mauro Mulenessa „Maurito"), Flávio Amado da Silva, Arsenio Sebastião Cabungula "Love" (79.Fernando Agostinho Da Costa „Xara"). Trainer: Luís Oliveira Gonçalves.

Goals: 1-0 Ismaël Eragae Alassane (3), 1-1 Flávio Amado da Silva (30), 1-2 Yamba Asha João (71).

Cautions: Karim Oumarou, Idrissa Laouali.

08.06.2008, Stade de l'Amitié, Cotonou; Attendance: 10,200
Referee: Ousmane Karembe (Mali)
BENIN - UGANDA   **4-1(2-1)**
BEN: Yoann Djidonou, Abdoul Khaled Akiola Adénon, Damien Chrysostome, Anicet Adjamossi, Moustapha Agnidé (32.Oscar Olou), Jocelyn Ahouéya, Romuald Boco, Mouritala Ogunbiyi, Stéphane Sessegnon (82.Abou Gariga Maïga), Razak Omotoyossi, Oumar Tchomogo (Cap) (58.Wassiou Oladipupo). Trainer: Michel Dussuyer (France).

UGA: Dennis Masinde Onyango, Abubakari Tabula, Timothy Batabaire, Simoen Masaba, Andrew Mwesigwa, David Obua, Assani Bajope, James Kidega (54.Samson Caesar Okhuti), Joseph Kabagambe (27.Dan Wagaluka), Eugene Ssepuuya (80.Geoffrey Sserunkuma), Michael Sserumagga. Trainer: László Csaba (Hungary).

Goals: 0-1 Eugene Ssepuuya (8), 1-1 Razak Omotoyossi (16), 2-1 Oumar Tchomogo (21), 3-1 Stéphane Sessegnon (70), 4-1 Razak Omotoyossi (87).

14.06.2008, „Nelson Mandela" National Stadium, Kampala; Attendance: 20,000
Referee: Eddy Allen Maillet Guyto (Seychelles)
UGANDA - ANGOLA   **3-1(2-0)**
UGA: Dennis Masinde Onyango, Abubakari Tabula, Timothy Batabaire, Joseph Nestroy Kizito, Andrew Mwesigwa, David Obua (90.Assani Bajope), Ibrahim Sekagya (Cap), Johnson Bagoole, Joseph Kabagambe (38.Dan Wagaluka), Eugene Ssepuuya (58.Geoffrey Sserunkuma), Michael Sserumagga. Trainer: László Csaba (Hungary).

ANG: Luís Mamona João „Lama", Carlos Manuel Gonçalves Alonso „Kali", Manuel Antonio Cange „Locó" (46.Ricardo Job), Yamba Asha João, Manuel Rui Marques, Paulo Batista Nsimba „Zé Kalanga", André Venceslau Valentim Macanga (Cap), Norberto Mauro Mulenessa „Maurito" (59.Pedro Manuel Torres „Mantorras"), Fernando Agostinho Da Costa „Xara" (26.Arsenio Sebastião Cabungula "Love"), António Manuel Viana Mendonça, Flávio Amado da Silva. Trainer: Luís Oliveira Gonçalves.

Goals: 1-0 Eugene Ssepuuya (6), 2-0 Andrew Mwesigwa (18), 3-0 Dan Wagaluka (73), 3-1 Pedro Manuel Torres „Mantorras" (90+1).

Cautions: Joseph Kabagamb, Abubakari Tabula.

15.06.2008, Stade „Général Seyni Kountché", Niamey; Attendance: 5,000
Referee: Djamel Haimoudi (Algeria)
NIGER - BENIN   **0-2(0-0)**
NIG: Kassaly Daouda, Ismaël Eragae Alassane (28.Chikoto Mohamed), Emaniel Djibril Dankawa, Amadou Kader (46.Amadou Bouzou), Karim Oumarou, Ouwo Moussa Maazou, Souleymane Dela Sakou (Cap), Abdoul Aziz Hamza, Harouna Ide Loga, Lassina Abdoul Karim Konate, Kamilou Daouda (68.Saidou Idrissa). Trainer: Dan Anghelescu (Romania).

BEN: Yoann Djidonou, Abdoul Khaled Akiola Adénon, Damien Chrysostome, Anicet Adjamossi, Jocelyn Ahouéya, Romuald Boco, Seidath Kenabe Tchomogo (70.Oscar Olou), Mouritala Ogunbiyi, Stéphane Sessegnon, Razak Omotoyossi (70.Abou Gariga Maïga), Oumar Tchomogo (Cap) (84.Noël Séka). Trainer: Michel Dussuyer (France).

174

Goals: 0-1 Oumar Tchomogo (54), 0-2 Razak Omotoyossi (70).
Cautions: Souleymane Dela Sakou, Harouna Ide Loga / Abdoul Khaled Akiola Adénon.

22.06.2008, Stade de l'Amitié, Cotonou; Attendance: 25,000
Referee: Jean-Claude Niyongabo (Burundi)
BENIN - NIGER   **2-0(1-0)**
BEN: Yoann Djidonou, Abdoul Khaled Akiola Adénon, Damien Chrysostome, Anicet Adjamossi, Jocelyn Ahouéya, Romuald Boco, Seidath Kenabe Tchomogo, Mouritala Ogunbiyi (90+2.Wassiou Oladipupo), Stéphane Sessegnon (80.Noël Séka), Razak Omotoyossi, Oumar Tchomogo (Cap) (68.Abou Gariga Maïga). Trainer: Michel Dussuyer (France).
NIG: Kassaly Daouda, Emaniel Djibril Dankawa, Chikoto Mohamed, Amadou Kader, Karim Oumarou, Pascal Anicet (71.Abdoul Aziz Hamza), Lassina Abdoul Karim Konate, Souleymane Dela Sakou (Cap) (60.Ouwo Moussa Maazou), Idrissa Laouali, Mahamadou Oumarou, Saidou Idrissa (67.Kamilou Daouda). Trainer: Dan Anghelescu (Romania).
Goals: 1-0 Jocelyn Ahouéya (45), 2-0 Pascal Anicet (53 own goal).
Cautions: Stéphane Sessegnon / Emaniel Djibril Dankawa, Idrissa Laouali, Kamilou Daouda.

23.06.2008, Estádio Coqueiros, Luanda; Attendance: 16,000
Referee: Sule Mana (Nigeria)
ANGOLA - UGANDA   **0-0**
ANG: Luís Mamona João „Lama", Manuel Alexandre Jamuana, Manuel Antonio Cange „Locó", Yamba Asha João, Manuel Rui Marques, Paulo Batista Nsimba „Zé Kalanga" (57.Ricardo Job), André Venceslau Valentim Macanga (Cap), Pedro Manuel Torres „Mantorras" (52.Arsenio Sebastião Cabungula "Love"), Felisberto Sebastião de Graça Amaral „Gilberto", António Manuel Viana Mendonça, Flávio Amado da Silva (79.Vado). Trainer: Luís Oliveira Gonçalves.
UGA: Dennis Masinde Onyango, Abubakari Tabula, Timothy Batabaire, Andrew Mwesigwa, Joseph Nestroy Kizito, David Obua, Simoen Masaba (90.Dan Wagaluka), Ibrahim Sekagya (Cap), Johnson Bagoole, Eugene Ssepuuya (62.Geoffrey Massa), Michael Sserumagga (75.Assani Bajope). Trainer: László Csaba (Hungary).
Cautions: Eugene Ssepuuya, Andrew Mwesigwa, Dennis Masinde Onyango.

07.09.2008, Stade de l'Amitié, Cotonou; Attendance: 30,000
Referee: Mohamed Benouza (Algeria)
BENIN - ANGOLA   **3-2(1-1)**
BEN: Yoann Djidonou, Abdoul Khaled Akiola Adénon, Damien Chrysostome, Anicet Adjamossi, Moustapha Agnidé (44.Djiman Koukou), Jocelyn Ahouéya, Romuald Boco, Nouhoum Kobénam (80.Seidath Kenabe Tchomogo), Oscar Olou, Razak Omotoyossi, Mickaël Poté. Trainer: Michel Dussuyer (France).
ANG: Luís Mamona João „Lama", Manuel Alexandre Jamuana, Carlos Manuel Gonçalves Alonso „Kali", Manuel Antonio Cange „Locó", Luis Manuel Ferreira Delgado (61.Amandio Costa „Amaro"), Adérito Waldemar Alves De Carvalho „Dedé", Mateus Galiano da Costa (61.Arsenio Sebastião Cabungula "Love"), André Venceslau Valentim Macanga (Cap) (75.Ricardo Job), José Carlos da Silva Santana, Felisberto Sebastião de Graça Amaral „Gilberto", Flávio Amado da Silva. Trainer: Luís Oliveira Gonçalves.
Goals: 1-0 Abdoul Khaled Akiola Adénon (2), 1-1 Flávio Amado da Silva (12), 2-1 Razak Omotoyossi (52),
3-1 Razak Omotoyossi (66), 3-2 Manuel Antonio Cange „Locó" (84).
Cautions: Moustapha Agnidé, Anicet Adjamossi / Luis Manuel Ferreira Delgado.

07.09.2008, Stade „Général Seyni Kountché", Niamey; Attendance: 5,000
Referee: Joseph Lamptey (Ghana)
NIGER - UGANDA   **3-1(0-1)**
NIG: Kassaly Daouda, Emaniel Djibril Dankawa, Hassane Modi Baraze, Chikoto Mohamed, Moussa Mallam, Souleymane Dela Sakou (Cap) (57.Jimmy Bulus), Idrissa Laouali, Lassina Abdoul Karim Konate, Mahamadou Oumarou (89.Lawaly Mamane), Saidou Idrissa (53.Alhassane Dante Issoufou), Kamilou Daouda. Trainer: Dan Anghelescu (Romania).
UGA: Dennis Masinde Onyango, Abubakari Tabula, Timothy Batabaire, Andrew Mwesigwa, Joseph Nestroy Kizito, David Obua, Ibrahim Sekagya (Cap), Johnson Bagoole, Dan Wagaluka (80.Joseph Kabagambe), Geoffrey Massa (56.Samson Caesar Okhuti), Michael Sserumagga (60.Anthony Mawejje). Trainer: Robert Williamson (Scotland).
Goals: 0-1 David Obua (33), 1-1 Alhassane Dante Issoufou (68), 2-1 Alhassane Dante Issoufou (86), 3-1 Kamilou Daouda (88).
Cautions: Emaniel Djibril Dankawa, Alhassane Dante Issoufou / Geoffrey Massa, Andrew Mwesigwa, Ibrahim Sekagya, Dennis Masinde Onyango.

12.10.2008, „Nelson Mandela" National Stadium, Kampala; Attendance: 2,913
Referee: Essam Abd El Fatah (Egypt)
UGANDA - BENIN   **2-1(0-1)**
UGA: Posnet Richard Omony, Timothy Batabaire, Joseph Nestroy Kizito, Simoen Masaba, Ibrahim Sekagya (Cap), Johnson Bagoole, Vincent Kayizi (72.Dan Wagaluka), Michael Sebalinga (46.Samson Caesar Okhuti), Geoffrey Massa, Eugene Ssepuuya (57.Geoffrey Sserunkuma), Michael Sserumagga. Trainer: Robert Williamson (Scotland).
BEN: Yoann Djidonou, Abdoul Khaled Akiola Adénon, Damien Chrysostome, Anicet Adjamossi, Jocelyn Ahouéya, Romuald Boco (77.Nouhoum Kobénam), Oscar Olou, Mouritala Ogunbiyi (63.Abou Gariga Maïga), Stéphane Sessegnon, Razak Omotoyossi, Mickaël Poté. Trainer: Michel Dussuyer (France).
Goals: 0-1 Razak Omotoyossi (30),
Cautions: Johnson Bagoole, Joseph Nestroy Kizito / Stéphane Sessegnon.

12.10.2008, Estádio Coqueiros, Luanda; Attendance: 3,200
Referee: Michel Gasingwa (Rwanda)
ANGOLA - NIGER   **3-1(0-1)**
ANG: Luís Mamona João „Lama", Marco Airosa, Carlos Manuel Gonçalves Alonso „Kali", Yamba Asha João, João Pereira „Jamba", André Venceslau Valentim Macanga (Cap) (89.Adérito Waldemar Alves De Carvalho „Dedé"), Felisberto Sebastião de Graça Amaral „Gilberto", Paulo Batista Nsimba „Zé Kalanga", Mateus Galiano da Costa (46.Arsenio Emanuel „Nelo"), Flávio Amado da Silva, Manucho (46.Arsenio Sebastião Cabungula "Love"). Trainer: Alvaro de Almeida.
NIG: Kassaly Daouda, Amadou Kader (87.Chikoto Mohamed), Hassane Modi Baraze, Karim Paraiso, Moussa Mallam, Lassina Abdoul Karim Konate (*sent off 64*), Idrissa Laouali, Pascal Anicet, Alhassane Dante Issoufou (73.Ouwo Moussa Maazou), Mahamadou Oumarou (66.Naso Lahi), Kamilou Daouda. Trainer: Dan Anghelescu (Romania).
Goals: 0-1 Moussa Mallam (19), 1-1 Kassaly Daouda (53 own goal), 2-1 Felisberto Sebastião de Graça Amaral „Gilberto" (66), 3-1 Paulo Batista Nsimba „Zé Kalanga" (70).
Cautions: André Venceslau Valentim Macanga / Lassina Abdoul Karim Konate, Amadou Kader.
Sent off: Lassina Abdoul Karim Konate (64).

GROUP 4

01.06.2008	Malabo	Equatorial Guinea – Sierra Leone		2-0(0-0)
01.06.2008	Abuja	Nigeria – South Africa		2-0(2-0)
07.06.2008	Atteridgeville	South Africa – Equatorial Guinea		4-1(2-0)
07.06.2008	Freetown	Sierra Leone - Nigeria		0-1(0-0)
14.06.2008	Freetown	Sierra Leone – South Africa		1-0(1-0)
15.06.2008	Malabo	Equatorial Guinea - Nigeria		0-1(0-1)
21.06.2008	Atteridgeville	South Africa – Sierra Leone		0-0
21.06.2008	Abuja	Nigeria - Equatorial Guinea		2-0(1-0)
06.09.2008	Port Elizabeth	South Africa - Nigeria		0-1(0-0)
06.09.2008	Freetown	Sierra Leone - Equatorial Guinea		2-1(1-0)
11.10.2008	Malabo	Equatorial Guinea – South Africa		0-1(0-1)
11.10.2008	Abuja	Nigeria – Sierra Leone		4-1(3-1)

FINAL STANDINGS

1. **Nigeria**	6	6	0	0	11	-	1	18
2. South Africa	6	2	1	3	5	-	5	7
3. Sierra Leone	6	2	1	3	4	-	8	7
4. Equatorial-Guinea	6	1	0	5	4	-	10	3

01.06.2008, Nuevo Estadio, Malabo; Attendance: 13,000
Referee: Coffi Codjia (Benin)
EQUATORIAL GUINEA – SIERRA LEONE   **2-0(0-0)**
EQG: Emanul Danilo Clementino Silva, Laurence Doe, Ronan Carolino Falcão, Ibrahima El Adji Touré (19.Francisco Mbome Duclair), David Álvarez Aguirre „Kily", José Luis Rondo Polo, Yago Alonso-Fueyo Sako „Yago Yao", André Moreira Neles „André Balada" (73.Pablo Armando Esono „Edjo Armando"), Iván Zarandona Esono (80.Juvenal Edjogo-Owono Montalbán), Benjamín Zarandona Esono, Juan Ramón Epitié Dyowe Roig. Trainer: Jordan de Freitas (Brazil).
SLE: Christian Caulker, Ibrahim Obreh Kargbo, Mustapha Pa Safa Sama (79.Foday Ishmail Kamara), Alphajor Mahmadu Bah (82.Mustapha Bangura), Umaru Bangura, Samuel Barlay, Warren John Kanu, Mohamed Kallon (Cap), Julius Gibrilla Woobay, Alhatie Jabbie (69.Sheriff Awilo Suma), Kaiansu Kamara. Trainer: Ahmed Kanu.
Goals: 1-0 Ronan Carolino Falcão (47), 2-0 Juan Ramón Epitié Dyowe Roig(57).
Cautions: Emanul Danilo Clementino Silva / Mustapha Pa Safa Sama, Mohamed Kallon.

31.05.2008, National Stadium, Abuja; Attendance: 50,000
Referee: Koman Coulibaly (Mali)
NIGERIA – SOUTH AFRICA   **2-0(2-0)**
NGA: Vincent Enyeama, Yusuf Mohammed, Joseph Ikpo Yobo (Cap), Obinna Nwaneri, Taye Ismaila Taïwo, Yusuf Ayila (68.Oluwaseyi George Olofinjana), John Michael Nchekwube Obinna, Kalu Uche (69.Nwankwo Christian Nwosu Kanu), John Chukwudi Utaka, Ikechukwu Uche, Abdulrasaq Yakubu Aiyegbeni (60.Victor Chinedu Anichebe). Trainer: Shaibu Amodu.
RSA: Rowen Fernández, Bevan Fransman, Peter Tsepo Masilela (82.Innocent Mdledle), Aaron Tebomo Mokoena, Lance Davids, Ntuthuko Macbeth Sibaya, Kagiso Evidence Dikgacoi, Bryce Moon, Surprise Mohlomolleng Moriri, Steven Jerome Pienaar (78.Excellent Musa Walaza), Delron Sebastian Buckley (60.Lawley Thembinkosi Fanteni). Trainer: Joel Natalino Santana (Brazil).
Goals: 1-0 Ikechukwu Uche (8), 2-0 Obinna Nwaneri (45).
Cautions: Kagiso Evidence Dikgacoi, Aaron Tebomo Mokoena, Ntuthuko Macbeth Sibaya.

07.06.2008, Super Stadium, Atteridgeville; Attendance: 10,000
Referee: Abdou Diouf (Senegal)
SOUTH AFRICA – EQUATORIAL GUINEA   **4-1(2-0)**
RSA: Itumeleng Isaack Khune, Bevan Fransman (26.Bongani Khumalo), Peter Tsepo Masilela, Aaron Tebomo Mokoena (78.Lance Davids), Steven Jerome Pienaar (83.Delron Sebastian Buckley), Kagiso Evidence Dikgacoi, Bryce Moon, Ntuthuko Macbeth Sibaya, Teko Tsholofelo Modise, Surprise Mohlomolleng Moriri, Lawley Thembinkosi Fanteni. Trainer: Joel Natalino Santana (Brazil).
EQG: Emanul Danilo Clementino Silva, Laurence Doe, Ronan Carolino Falcão, David Álvarez Aguirre „Kily" (68.Pablo Armando Esono „Edjo Armando"), José Luis Rondo Polo, Yago Alonso-Fueyo Sako „Yago Yao", Javier Ángel Balboa Osa, Francisco Mbome Duclair, Benjamín Zarandona Esono (37.Juvenal Edjogo-Owono Montalbán), Iván Zarandona Esono (70.Silvestre Boté Mesaka), Juan Ramón Epitié Dyowe Roig. Trainer: Jordan de Freitas (Brazil).
Goals: 1-0 Kagiso Evidence Dikgacoi (10), 2-0 Surprise Mohlomolleng Moriri (34), 3-0 Lawley Thembinkosi Fanteni (60), 3-1 Juvenal Edjogo-Owono Montalbán (78 penalty), 4-1 Kagiso Evidence Dikgacoi (89).
Cautions: Teko Tsholofelo Modise / Iván Zarandona Esono.

07.06.2008, National Stadium, Freetown; Attendance: 25,000
Referee: Sam Korti (Liberia)
SIERRA LEONE - NIGERIA   **0-1(0-0)**
SLE: Christian Caulker, Ibrahim Obreh Kargbo, Ibrahim Marcel Koroma, Alphajor Mahmadu Bah (69.Foday Ishmail Kamara), Umaru Bangura, Samuel Barlay, Warren John Kanu (52.Kemokai Kallon), Julius Gibrilla Woobay, Mustapha Bangura, Kaiansu Kamara (75.Alfi Conteh-Lacalle), Sheriff Awilo Suma. Trainer: Ahmed Kanu.
NGA: Vincent Enyeama, Yusuf Mohammed, Joseph Ikpo Yobo, Obinna Nwaneri, Taye Ismaila Taïwo, John Chukwudi Utaka (55.Osaze Peter Odemwingie), Yusuf Ayila, John Michael Nchekwube Obinna (62.Oluwaseyi George Olofinjana), Ikechukwu Uche, Nwankwo Christian Nwosu Kanu (Cap) (87.Kalu Uche), Abdulrasaq Yakubu Aiyegbeni. Trainer: Shaibu Amodu.
Goal: 0-1 Joseph Ikpo Yobo (89).
Cautions: John Michael Nchekwube Obinna, Osaze Peter Odemwingie.

14.06.2008, National Stadium, Freetown; Attendance: 15,000
Referee: Lassina Paré (Burkina Faso)
SIERRA LEONE – SOUTH AFRICA   **1-0(1-0)**
SLE: Christian Caulker, Ibrahim Obreh Kargbo, Ibrahim Marcel Koroma, Umaru Bangura, Samuel Barlay (84.Alpha Sumoi Lansana), Warren John Kanu, Julius Gibrilla Woobay, Mustapha Bangura (74.Paul Kpaka), Mohamed Kallon (Cap), Kaiansu Kamara (89.Foday Ishmail Kamara), Sheriff Awilo Suma. Trainer: Ahmed Kanu.
RSA: Itumeleng Isaack Khune, Mokete Reuben Tsotetsi, Peter Tsepo Masilela, Bongani Khumalo, Teko Tsholofelo Modise, Ntuthuko Macbeth Sibaya (Cap), Kagiso Evidence Dikgacoi, Surprise Mohlomolleng Moriri, Steven Jerome Pienaar, Bryce Moon (68.Katlego Evidence Mashego), Lawley Thembinkosi Fanteni (81.Mpho Lerato Chabangu). Trainer: Joel Natalino Santana (Brazil).
Goal: 1-0 Mohamed Kallon (21 penalty).
Cautions: Warren John Kanu, Kaiansu Kamara /Steven Jerome Pienaar.

15.06.2008, Nuevo Estadio, Malabo; Attendance: 15,200
Referee: John Mendy (Gambia)
EQUATORIAL GUINEA - NIGERIA   **0-1(0-1)**
EQG: Emanul Danilo Clementino Silva, Laurence Doe, Ronan Carolino Falcão, David Álvarez Aguirre „Kily", Yago Alonso-Fueyo Sako „Yago Yao", Javier Ángel Balboa Osa, Francisco Mbome Duclair (78.Benjamín Zarandona Esono), Juvenal Edjogo-Owono Montalbán (80.Silvestre Boté Mesaka), Iván Zarandona Esono, Rodolfo Bodipo Diaz, Juan Ramón Epitié Dyowe Roig. Trainer: Jordan de Freitas (Brazil).

NGA: Vincent Enyeama, Chukwudi Odiah, Joseph Ikpo Yobo (Cap), Obinna Nwaneri, Taye Ismaila Taïwo, Kalu Uche, Yusuf Ayila, Oluwaseyi George Olofinjana, Osaze Peter Odemwingie (60.Victor Chinedu Anichebe), Ikechukwu Uche (58.Victor Nsofor Obinna), Abdulrasaq Yakubu Aiyegbeni. Trainer: Shaibu Amodu.
Goal: 0-1 Joseph Ikpo Yobo (4).
Cautions: David Álvarez Aguirre „Kily" / Obinna Nwaneri, Yusuf Ayila.

21.06.2008, Super Stadium, Atteridgeville; Attendance: 12,000
Referee: Raphael Divine Evehe (Cameroon)
SOUTH AFRICA – SIERRA LEONE   **0-0**
RSA: Itumeleng Isaack Khune, Bevan Fransman, Peter Tsepo Masilela, Aaron Tebomo Mokoena, Teko Tsholofelo Modise, Kagiso Evidence Dikgacoi, Ntuthuko Macbeth Sibaya (70.Mpho Lerato Chabangu), Bryce Moon, Steven Jerome Pienaar (83.Delron Sebastian Buckley), Surprise Mohlomolleng Moriri, Lawley Thembinkosi Fanteni (62.Katlego Evidence Mashego). Trainer: Joel Natalino Santana (Brazil).
SLE: Christian Caulker, Ibrahim Obreh Kargbo, Ibrahim Marcel Koroma, Umaru Bangura, Samuel Barlay, Warren John Kanu (72.Albert Cole), Julius Gibrilla Woobay, Mohamed Kallon (Cap), Kaiansu Kamara (89.Alpha Sumoi Lansana), Paul Kpaka (56.Alphajor Mahmadu Bah), Sheriff Awilo Suma. Trainer: Ahmed Kanu.
Cautions: Bevan Fransman, Aaron Tebomo Mokoena, Teko Tsholofelo Modise / Julius Gibrilla Woobay, Kaiansu Kamara, Mohamed Kallon.

21.06.2008, National Stadium, Abuja; Attendance: 20,000
Referee: Jamel Ambaya (Libya)
NIGERIA - EQUATORIAL GUINEA   **2-0(1-0)**
NGA: Vincent Enyeama, Chukwudi Odiah, Joseph Ikpo Yobo, Obinna Nwaneri, Taye Ismaila Taïwo, Kalu Uche, Yusuf Ayila, Nwankwo Christian Nwosu Kanu (Cap) (68.John Michael Nchekwube Obinna), Abdulrasaq Yakubu Aiyegbeni (81.Ikechukwu Uche), Victor Chinedu Anichebe (40.Victor Nsofor Obinna). Trainer: Shaibu Amodu.
EQG: Emanul Danilo Clementino Silva, Laurence Doe, Ronan Carolino Falcão, David Álvarez Aguirre „Kily", Silvestre Boté Mesaka, Yago Alonso-Fueyo Sako „Yago Yao", Javier Ángel Balboa Osa, Francisco Mbome Duclair, Juvenal Edjogo-Owono Montalbán (65.Ibrahima El Adji Touré), Iván Zarandona Esono, Rodolfo Bodipo Diaz (65.Juan Ramón Epitié Dyowe Roig). Trainer: Jordan de Freitas (Brazil).
Goals: 1-0 Abdulrasaq Yakubu Aiyegbeni (45), 2-0 Ikechukwu Uche (84).
Cautions: Rodolfo Bodipo Diaz, Ibrahima El Adji Touré.

06.09.2008, Telkom Park Stadium, Port Elizabeth; Attendance: 25,000
Referee: Verson Lwanja (Malawi)
SOUTH AFRICA - NIGERIA   **0-1(0-0)**
RSA: Itumeleng Isaack Khune, Siboniso Pa Gaxa, Mbulelo Mabizela, Nasief Morris, Bradley Fitzroy Carnell, Teko Tsholofelo Modise, Kagiso Evidence Dikgacoi, Ntuthuko Macbeth Sibaya (75.Surprise Mohlomolleng Moriri), Lawrence Siphiwe Tshabalala (75.Sibusiso Wiseman Zuma), Siyabonga Solace Nkosi, Benedict McCarthy. Trainer: Joel Natalino Santana (Brazil).
NGA: Bamidele Mathew Aiyenugba, Chukwudi Odiah, Daniel Olusola Shittu, Obinna Nwaneri, Taye Ismaila Taïwo, Oluwaseyi George Olofinjana, Yusuf Ayila, John Chukwudi Utaka, Kalu Uche (67.Christian Udubuesi Obodo), Ikechukwu Uche (84.Joseph Akpala), Abdulrasaq Yakubu Aiyegbeni (Cap). Trainer: Shaibu Amodu.
Goal: 0-1 Ikechukwu Uche (69).
Cautions: Bradley Fitzroy Carnell / Kalu Uche.

06.09.2008, National Stadium, Freetown; Attendance: 22,000
Referee: Noumandiez Doué (Ivory Coast)
SIERRA LEONE - EQUATORIAL GUINEA   **2-1(1-0)**
SLE: Christian Caulker, Kewullay Conteh, Ibrahim Obreh Kargbo, Ahmed Deen, Alphajor Mahmadu Bah (61.Albert Cole), Umaru Bangura, Ibrahim Marcel Koroma, Mohamed Kallon (Cap), Mustapha Bangura (89.Sam Obi Metzger Jr.), Paul Kpaka (70.Sallrew Bunao), Sheriff Awilo Suma. Trainer: Ahmed Kanu.
EQG: Emanul Danilo Clementino Silva, Laurence Doe, Ronan Carolino Falcão (46.Juan Mbeia Roku), David Álvarez Aguirre „Kily" (76.Óscar Bonsu Amoa Beng), José Luis Rondo Polo, Silvestre Boté Mesaka, Yago Alonso-Fueyo Sako „Yago Yao", Francisco Mbome Duclair, Juvenal Edjogo-Owono Montalbán, Benjamín Zarandona Esono, Rodolfo Bodipo Diaz. Trainer: Vicente Engonga Maté (Spain).
Goals: 1-0 Kewullay Conteh (30), 2-0 Sheriff Awilo Suma (73), 2-1 Rodolfo Bodipo Diaz (83 penalty).
Cautions: Ibrahim Marcel Koroma, Mustapha Bangura / Juvenal Edjogo-Owono Montalbán.

11.10.2008, Nuevo Estadio, Malabo; Attendance: 6,500
Referee: Kokou Djaoupé (Togo)
EQUATORIAL GUINEA – SOUTH AFRICA   **0-1(0-1)**
EQG: Emanul Danilo Clementino Silva, Damian Enzema (87.Carlos Mengue), David Álvarez Aguirre „Kily", José Luis Rondo Polo, Óscar Bonsu Amoa Beng (42.Justo Nguema), José Bokung, Francisco Mbome Duclair, Anselmo Eyegue Nfondo, Juvenal Edjogo-Owono Montalbán, Iván Zarandona Esono, Juan Mbela Roku (53.Juan Simeón Esono). Trainer: Vicente Engonga Maté (Spain).
RSA: Itumeleng Isaack Khune, Siboniso Pa Gaxa, Nasief Morris, Aaron Tebomo Mokoena (Cap), Bradley Fitzroy Carnell, Kagiso Evidence Dikgacoi, Lance Davids, Lawrence Siphiwe Tshabalala, Teko Tsholofelo Modise (77.Samuel Lefa Tsutsulupa), Benedict McCarthy (88.Lawley Thembinkosi Fanteni), Siyabonga Solace Nkosi (71.Bernard Melvin Parker). Trainer: Joel Natalino Santana (Brazil).
Goal: 0-1 Lawrence Siphiwe Tshabalala (9).
Cautions: Juan Mbela Roku / Siboniso Pa Gaxa, Siyabonga Solace Nkosi.

11.10.2008, National Stadium, Abuja; Attendance: 25,000
Referee: Wellington Kaoma (Zambia)
NIGERIA – SIERRA LEONE   **4-1(3-1)**
NGA: Bamidele Mathew Aiyenugba, Chukwudi Odiah, Joseph Ikpo Yobo (Cap), Daniel Olusola Shittu, Taye Ismaila Taïwo, Sani Haruna Kaita, Kalu Uche, Christian Udubuesi Obodo, Victor Nsofor Obinna (66.Joseph Akpala), Ikechukwu Uche (81.Abdulrasaq Yakubu Aiyegbeni), Osaze Peter Odemwingie (68.Chinedu Obasi Ogbuke). Trainer: Shaibu Amodu.
SLE: Christian Caulker, Kewullay Conteh, Ibrahim Obreh Kargbo, Ahmed Deen (54.Mustapha Bangura), Alphajor Mahmadu Bah, Alhassan Bangura, Umaru Bangura, Warren John Kanu, Mohamed Kallon (Cap) (43.Paul Kpaka), Kaiansu Kamara, Sheriff Awilo Suma. Trainer: Ahmed Kanu.
Goals: 1-0 Christian Udubuesi Obodo (21), 1-1 Joseph Ikpo Yobo (31 own goal), 2-1 Victor Nsofor Obinna (35), 3-1 Osaze Peter Odemwingie (45), Chukwudi Odiah (51).
Cautions: Christian Udubuesi Obodo / Mohamed Kallon, Alphajor Mahmadu Bah, Ibrahim Obreh Kargbo.

GROUP 5

01.06.2008	Kumasi	Ghana - Libya		3-0(1-0)
07.06.2008	Tripoli	Libya - Gabon		1-0(1-0)
08.06.2008	Bloemfontein	Lesotho - Ghana		2-3(0-2)
14.06.2008	Libreville	Gabon - Ghana		2-0(1-0)
15.06.2008	Bloemfontein	Lesotho - Libya		0-1(0-0)
20.06.2008	Tripoli	Libya - Lesotho		4-0(1-0)
22.06.2008	Accra	Ghana - Gabon		2-0(1-0)
28.06.2008	Libreville	Gabon - Lesotho		2-0(1-0)
05.09.2008	Tripoli	Libya - Ghana		1-0(0-0)
07.09.2008	Bloemfontein	Lesotho - Gabon		0-3(0-0)
11.10.2008	Sekondi-Takiradi	Ghana - Lesotho		3-0(2-0)
11.10.2008	Libreville	Gabon - Libya		1-0(0-0)

FINAL STANDINGS

1. **Ghana**	6	4	0	2	11 - 5	12
2. **Gabon**	6	4	0	2	8 - 3	12
3. Libya	6	4	0	2	7 - 4	12
4. Lesotho	6	0	0	6	2 - 16	0

01.06.2008, Baba Yara Stadium, Kumasi; Attendance: 27,908
Referee: Eddy Allen Maillet Guyto (Seychelles)
GHANA - LIBYA **3-0(1-0)**
GHA: Richard Paul Franck Kingson, John Paintsil, Harrison Afful, Eric Pappoe Addo, John Mensah (78.Francis Dickoh), Anthony Annan, Laryea Kingston, Michael Kojo Essien, Manuel „Junior" Agogo (76.Eric Bekoe), Prince Tagoe, Sulleyman Ali Muntari (77.Haminu Dramani). Trainer: Sellas Tethe.
LBY: Samir Abdussalam Aboud, Younes Al Shibani, Mohamed El Magrabi, Walid Ali El Shebai, Osama Musbah Al Hamadi, Nader Abdussalam Al Tarhouni, Osama Mohamed El Fezzani (77.Mohamed Noureddin Zubya), Walid Jalal (67.Ahmed Faraj El Masli), Khaled Mohamed Hussein (67.Nader Mohammed Kara), Abdulnaser Mohammed Slil, Ahmed Saad Soleiman Osman. Trainer: Faouzi El Benzarti (Tunisia).
Goals: 1-0 Prince Tagoe (17), 2-0 Manuel „Junior" Agogo (54), 3-0 Laryea Kingston (64).
Cautions: Sulleyman Ali Muntari / Osama Mohamed El Fezzani.

07.06.2008, Stade „11 Juin", Tripoli; Attendance: 30,000
Referee: Ibrahim Chaibou (Niger)
LIBYA - GABON **1-0(1-0)**
LBY: Samir Abdussalam Aboud, Younes Al Shibani, Mohamed El Magrabi, Walid Ali El Shebai (90.Omar Dawood), Osama Musbah Al Hamadi, Hesham Ahmed Shaban, Khaled Mohamed Hussein (71.Mohamed Ali Esnani), Nader Abdussalam Al Tarhouni, Tarik Ibrahim Muhammed El Taib (Cap) (66.Salem Ibrahim Al Rewani), Osama Mohamed El Fezzani, Ahmed Saad Soleiman Osman. Trainer: Faouzi El Benzarti (Tunisia).
GAB: Didier Janvier Ovono Ebang, Bernard Obiang Bibang, Bruno Ecuélé Manga, Moïse Akou Apanga Brou, Ernest Akouassaga, Bruno Zita Mbanangoye (68.Stéphane N'Guéma), Shiva N'Zigou (90.Arsène Copa), Ulrich Paul Kessany (Cap), Cédric Moubamba, Eric Mouloungui, Fabrice Do Marcolino (78.Georges Akierémy Owondo). Trainer: Alain Giresse (France).
Goal: 1-0 Moise Akou Apanga Brou (5 own goal).
Cautions: Osama Mohamed El Fezzani, Ahmed Saad Soleiman Osman, Younes Al Shibani / Cédric Moubamba.

08.06.2008, Vodacom Park Stadium, Bloemfontein (South Africa); Attendance: 8,000
Referee: Michel Gasingwa (Rwanda)
LESOTHO - GHANA   **2-3(0-2)**
LES: Sam Ketsekile, Thabo Masualle, Thapelo Mokhele, Bokang Mothoana, Mohapi Ntobo, Khoto
Sesinyi, Thabane Rankara (78.Thapelo Tale), Moli Lesesa (55.Sello Muso), Lehlohonolo Simon Seema
(Cap), Reitumetse Moloisane (88.Bushi Moletsane), Lebajoa Mphongoa. Trainer: Zaviša Milošavljević
(Serbia).
GHA: Richard Paul Franck Kingson, John Paintsil, Harrison Afful, Eric Pappoe Addo, John Mensah,
Anthony Annan, Laryea Kingston, Michael Kojo Essien (83.Emmanuel Badu Agyeman), Prince Tagoe
(71.Quincy James Owusu-Abeyie), Manuel „Junior" Agogo, Haminu Dramani. Trainer: Sellas Tethe.
Goals: 0-1 Laryea Kingston (15), 0-2 Manuel „Junior" Agogo (41), 0-3 Manuel „Junior" Agogo (63), 1-3
Sello Muso (90+1), 2-3 Lehlohonolo Simon Seema (90+2).
Cautions: Bokang Mothoana, Moli Lesesa / John Paintsil.

14.06.2008, Stade Omnisports „Président Omar Bongo", Libreville; Attendance: 13,000
Referee: Mohamed Benouza (Algeria)
GABON - GHANA   **2-0(1-0)**
GAB: Didier Janvier Ovono Ebang, Bernard Obiang Bibang, Bruno Ecuélé Manga, Moïse Akou Apanga
Brou, Ernest Akouassaga, Stéphane N'Guéma, Arsène Copa (50.Shiva N'Zigou), Ulrich Paul Kessany
(Cap), Cédric Moubamba, Eric Mouloungui (60.Fabrice Do Marcolino), Roguy Méyé (90.Thierry
Issiémou). Trainer: Alain Giresse (France).
GHA: Richard Paul Franck Kingson, John Paintsil, Harrison Afful, Eric Pappoe Addo (46.Francis
Dickoh), John Mensah, Anthony Annan, Laryea Kingston (66.Haminu Dramani), Michael Kojo Essien,
Sulleyman Ali Muntari, Eric Bekoe (53.Manuel „Junior" Agogo), Prince Tagoe. Trainer: Sellas Tethe.
Goals: 1-0 Roguy Méyé (45+1), 2-0 Stéphane N'Guéma (59).
Cautions: Laryea Kingston.

15.06.2008, Seisa Ramabodu Stadium, Bloemfontain; Attendance: 3,500
Referee: Kenias Marange (Zimbabwe)
LESOTHO - LIBYA   **0-1(0-0)**
LES: Sam Ketsekile, Thabo Masualle, Thapelo Mokhele, Bokang Mothoana, Mohapi Ntobo, Sello Muso
(83.Motlalepula Mofolo), Khoto Sesinyi, Bushi Moletsane (82.Reitumetse Moloisane), Lehlohonolo
Simon Seema (Cap), Lebajoa Mphongoa, Thapelo Tale (46.Thabane Rankara). Trainer: Zaviša
Milošavljević (Serbia).
LBY: Samir Abdussalam Aboud, Younes Al Shibani, Omar Dawood, Mohamed El Magrabi, Walid Ali
El Shebai, Hesham Ahmed Shaban (55.Ali El Hasi), Nader Mohammed Kara (70.Reyad Salam Ellafi),
Nader Abdussalam Al Tarhouni, Khaled Mohamed Hussein, Salem Ibrahim Al Rewani (79.Mohamed
Noureddin Zubya), Ahmed Saad Soleiman Osman. Trainer: Faouzi El Benzarti (Tunisia).
Goal: 0-1 Ahmed Saad Soleiman Osman (85).
Cautions: Bokang Mothoana /   Hesham Ahmed Shaban, Ahmed Saad Soleiman Osman, Nader
Abdussalam Al Tarhouni.

20.06.2008, 11 June Stadium, Tripoli; Attendance: 30,000
Referee: Aouaz Trabelsi (Tunisia)
LIBYA - LESOTHO   **4-0(1-0)**
LBY: Samir Abdussalam Aboud, Younes Al Shibani, Omar Dawood, Mohamed El Magrabi, Ali El Hasi
(34.Hesham Ahmed Shaban), Walid Ali El Shebai, Tarik Ibrahim Muhammed El Taib (Cap), Nader
Abdussalam Al Tarhouni, Khaled Mohamed Hussein, Salem Ibrahim Al Rewani (73.Nader Mohammed
Kara), Osama Mohamed El Fezzani (90.Mohamed Noureddin Zubya). Trainer: Faouzi El Benzarti
(Tunisia).
LES: Sam Ketsekile, Thapelo Mokhele, Mohapi Ntobo, Sello Muso (87.Mpitsa Marai), Khoto Sesinyi
(60.Langana Nkhethoa), Thabane Rankara (67.Ngo Makama), Bushi Moletsane, Tatolo Mphuthing,
Lehlohonolo Simon Seema (Cap), Reitumetse Moloisane, Lebajoa Mphongoa. Trainer: Zaviša

Milošavljević (Serbia).
Goals: 1-0 Ahmed Saad Soleiman Osman (3), 2-0 Omar Dawood (50), 3-0 Younes Al Shibani (68), 4-0 Hesham Ahmed Shaban (80).
Cautions: Salem Ibrahim Al Rewani / Thapelo Mokhele, Mohapi Ntobo, Thapelo Mokhele, Mohapi Ntobo.

22.06.2008, Ohene Djan Sports Stadium, Accra; Attendance: 29,040
Referee: Jerome Damon (South Africa)
GHANA - GABON   **2-0(1-0)**
GHA: Richard Paul Franck Kingson, John Paintsil, Harrison Afful, John Mensah, Issah Gabriel Ahmed (60.John Boye), Anthony Annan, Laryea Kingston (61.Quincy James Owusu-Abeyie), Michael Kojo Essien, Sulleyman Ali Muntari, Manuel „Junior" Agogo (76.Haminu Dramani), Prince Tagoe. Trainer: Sellas Tethe.
GAB: Didier Janvier Ovono Ebang, Bernard Obiang Bibang, Bruno Ecuélé Manga, Erwing Nguéma, Ernest Akouassaga, Cédric Moubamba, Thierry Issiémou, Ulrich Paul Kessany (Cap), Bruno Zita Mbanangoye (82.Shiva N'Zigou), Stéphane N'Guéma, Roguy Méyé (75.Georges Akierémy Owondo). Trainer: Alain Giresse (France).
Goals: 1-0 Prince Tagoe (31), 2-0 Sulleyman Ali Muntari (75).
Cautions: Michael Kojo Essien, Anthony Annan / Thierry Issiémou, Stéphane N'Guéma, Ulrich Paul Kessany.

28.06.2008, Stade Omnisports „Président Omar Bongo", Libreville; Attendance: 15,000
Referee: John Mendy (Gambia)
GABON - LESOTHO   **2-0(1-0)**
GAB: Didier Janvier Ovono Ebang, Rodrigue Moundounga, Bruno Ecuélé Manga, Moïse Akou Apanga Brou, Ernest Akouassaga (84.Bernard Obiang Bibang), Ulrich Paul Kessany (Cap) (66.Bruno Zita Mbanangoye), Cédric Moubamba, Arsène Copa (46.Etienne Alain Djissikadié), Fabrice Do Marcolino, Roguy Méyé, Stéphane N'Guéma. Trainer: Alain Giresse (France).
LES: Sam Ketsekile, Thapelo Mokhele, Bokang Mothoana, Mohapi Ntobo, Khoto Sesinyi, Thabane Rankara (82.Thapelo Tale), Moli Lesesa, Tatolo Mphuthing, Lehlohonolo Simon Seema (Cap), Ngo Makama (71.Lebajoa Mphongoa), Reitumetse Moloisane (31.Sello Muso). Trainer: Zaviša Milošavljević (Serbia).
Goals: 1-0 Fabrice Do Marcolino (45), 2-0 Fabrice Do Marcolino (63).
Cautions: Tatolo Mphuthing, Lehlohonolo Simon Seema.

05.09.2008, 11 June Stadium, Tripoli; Attendance: 45,000
Referee: Koman Coulibaly (Mali)
LIBYA - GHANA   **1-0(0-0)**
LBY: Samir Abdussalam Aboud, Younes Al Shibani, Omar Dawood, Mohamed El Magrabi, Hesham Ahmed Shaban, Khaled Mohamed Hussein, Nader Abdussalam Al Tarhouni, Osama Mohamed El Fezzani, Salem Ibrahim Al Rewani (81.Nader Mohammed Kara), Ahmed Saad Soleiman Osman, Ahmed Faraj El Masli (67.Walid Ali El Shebai). Trainer: Faouzi El Benzarti (Tunisia).
GHA: Richard Paul Franck Kingson, John Paintsil (89.Eric Bekoe), Harrison Afful, Jonathan Quartey, Eric Pappoe Addo, Anthony Annan, Laryea Kingston (53.Quincy James Owusu-Abeyie), Michael Kojo Essien (18.Stephen Appiah), Manuel „Junior" Agogo, Haminu Dramani, Sulleyman Ali Muntari. Trainer: Milovan Rajevac (Serbia).
Goal: 1-0 Ahmed Saad Soleiman Osman (86).
Cautions: Salem Ibrahim Al Rewani, Ahmed Saad Soleiman Osman / Laryea Kingston, Manuel „Junior" Agogo.

07.09.2008, Seisa Ramabodu Stadium, Bloemfontain; Attendance: 1,500
Referee: Essam Abd El Fatah (Egypt)
LESOTHO - GABON   **0-3(0-0)**
LES: Lekunutu Ts'eounyane, Thapelo Mokhel, Sello Muso (41.Mpitsa Marai), Khoto Sesinyi, Thabane Rankara, Nkau Lerotholi, Moli Lesesa, Mpho Matsinyane (48.Bushi Moletsane), Tatolo Mphuthing, Reitumetse Moloisane, Lebajoa Mphongoa (76.Tsepo Lekhoana). Trainer: Zaviša Milošavljević (Serbia).
GAB: Didier Janvier Ovono Ebang, Ernest Akouassaga, Bruno Ecuélé Manga, Moïse Akou Apanga Brou, Etienne Alain Djissikadié, Rodrigue Moundounga, Ulrich Paul Kessany (46.Bruno Zita Mbanangoye), Cédric Moubamba, Eric Mouloungui, Stéphane N'Guéma (67.Gilles Daniel Mbang Ondo), Roguy Méyé. Trainer: Alain Giresse (France).
Goals: 0-1 Bruno Ecuélé Manga (56), 0-2 Roguy Méyé (72), 0-3 Bruno Zita Mbanangoye (90+4).
Cautions: Lebajoa Mphongoa, Moli Lesesa / Bruno Zita Mbanangoye.
Sent off: Thapelo Mokhele (32), Eric Mouloungui (32).

11.10.2008, Sekondi-Takiradi Stadium, Sekondi; Attendance: 20,000
Referee: Khalid Abdel Rahman (Sudan)
GHANA - LESOTHO   **3-0(2-0)**
GHA: Richard Paul Franck Kingson, John Paintsil, John Mensah, Eric Pappoe Addo, Harrison Afful, Anthony Annan, Daniel Yeboah, Stephen Appiah (Cap) (85.Eric Bekoe), Sulleyman Ali Muntari (83.Haminu Dramani), Matthew Amoah, Manuel „Junior" Agogo (62.Prince Tagoe). Trainer: Milovan Rajevac (Serbia).
LES: Sam Ketsekile, Thabo Masualle, Bokang Mothoana, Mohapi Ntobo, Khoto Sesinyi, Thabane Rankara (82.Thulo Ranchobe), Tsepo Lekhoana, Nkau Lerotholi, Ramashalane Taeli (65.Bushi Moletsane), Lehlohonolo Simon Seema (Cap), Reitumetse Moloisane (46.Sello Muso). Trainer: Zaviša Milošavljević (Serbia).
Goals: 1-0 Stephen Appiah (19), 2-0 Manuel „Junior" Agogo (24), 3-0 Matthew Amoah (62).

11.10.2008, Stade Omnisports „Président Omar Bongo", Libreville; Attendance: 26,000
Referee: Daniel Bennett (South Africa)
GABON - LIBYA   **1-0(0-0)**
GAB: Didier Janvier Ovono Ebang, Rodrigue Moundounga, Bruno Ecuélé Manga, Moïse Akou Apanga Brou, Georges Ambourouet, Ulrich Paul Kessany (77.Fabrice Do Marcolino), Cédric Moubamba, Etienne Alain Djissikadié (69.Bruno Zita Mbanangoye), Stéphane N'Guéma, Daniel Cousin, Roguy Méyé. Trainer: Alain Giresse (France).
LBY: Samir Abdussalam Aboud, Younes Al Shibani, Omar Dawood (20.Walid Jalal), Mohamed El Magrabi, Hesham Ahmed Shaban, Walid Ali El Shebai (64.Mohamed Ali Esnani), Nader Abdussalam Al Tarhouni, Khaled Mohamed Hussein, Osama Mohamed El Fezzani (84.Ahmed Mahmoud Zuway), Ahmed Saad Soleiman Osman, Ahmed Faraj El Masli. Trainer: Faouzi El Benzarti (Tunisia).
Goal: 1-0 Bruno Zita Mbanangoye (82).
Cautions: Cédric Moubamba, Roguy Méyé / Walid Ali El Shebai, Khaled Mohamed Hussein, Osama Mohamed El Fezzani, Hesham Ahmed Shaban.

GROUP 6

31.05.2008	Dakar	Senegal - Algeria		1-0(0-0)
01.06.2008	Monrovia	Liberia - Gambia		1-1(0-1)
06.06.2008	Blida	Algeria - Liberia		3-0(2-0)
08.06.2008	Banjul	Gambia - Senegal		0-0
14.06.2008	Banjul	Gambia - Algeria		1-0(1-0)
15.06.2008	Monrovia	Liberia - Senegal		2-2(0-0)
20.06.2008	Blida	Algeria - Gambia		1-0(1-0)
21.06.2008	Dakar	Senegal - Liberia		3-1(2-0)
05.09.2008	Blida	Algeria - Senegal		3-2(0-0)
06.09.2008	Banjul	Gambia - Liberia		3-0(2-0)
11.10.2008	Dakar	Senegal - Gambia		1-1(0-0)
11.10.2008	Monrovia	Liberia - Algeria		0-0

FINAL STANDINGS

1. Algeria	6	3	1	2	7 - 4	10
2. Gambia	6	2	3	1	6 - 3	9
3. Senegal	6	2	3	1	9 - 7	9
4. Liberia	6	0	3	3	4 - 12	3

31.05.2008, Stade „Léopold Sédar Senghor", Dakar; Attendance: 50,000
Referee: Alex Kotey (Ghana)
SENEGAL - ALGERIA **1-0(0-0)**
SEN: Tony Mario Sylva, Pape Malickou Diakhaté, Abdoulaye Diagne-Faye, Ibrahima Faye, Moustapha Bayal Sall, Papa Malick Bâ (76.Mbaye Lèye), Diomansy Mehdi Kamara, Babacar M'Baye Guèye (69.Frédéric Mendy), Henri Camara, Papa Waigo N'Diaye, El Hadji Ousseynou Diouf (63.Ousmane N'Doye). Trainer: Lamine N'Diaye.
ALG: Lounès Gaouaoui, Slimane Raho, Samir Zaoui, Anthar Yahia (80.Rafik Halliche), Nadir Belhadj, Brahim Hemdani (69.Lamouri Ben Kadda Djediat), Yazid Mansouri (Cap), Khaled Lemmouchia, Karim Ziani, Rafik Saïfi, Rafik Djebbour (75.Hameur Bouazza). Trainer: Rabah Saâdane.
Goal: 1-0 Abdoulaye Diagne-Faye (79).
Cautions: Samir Zaoui, Nadir Belhadj, Lounès Gaouaoui.

01.06.2008, „Samuel Doe" Sports Complex, Monrovia; Attendance: 35,000
Referee: Yakhouba Keïta (Guinea)
LIBERIA - GAMBIA **1-1(0-1)**
LBR: Melvin King, Jimmy Dixon, James Koko Lomell, Murphy Kumonple Nagbe, Esaiah Pello Benson, Theo Lewis Weeks, Dulee Johnson (57.Francis Doe Forkey), Zah Rahan Krangar (76.George Gebro), Stephen Nagbe Mennoh (46.Oliver Paul Makor), Anthony Snoti Laffor, James Zortiah. Trainer: Antoine Hey (Germany).
GAM: Robert Badjie, Abdou Jammeh, Mathew Mendy, Ousman Koli, Pa Saikou Kujabi, Tijan Jaiteh, Ebrima Ebou Sillah, Mustapha Jarjue, Aziz Corr Nyang (63.Demba Savage), Njogu Demba-Nyrén (78.Modou Jagne). Trainer: Paul Put (Belgium).
Goals: 0-1 Mustapha Jarjue (17), 1-1 Oliver Paul Makor (82).
Cautions: Esaiah Pello Benson / Ousman Koli, Pa Saikou Kujabi.

06.06.2008, SStade „Mustapha Tchaker", Blida; Attendance: 35,000
Referee: Ould Lamghambodj Mohamed (Mauritania)
ALGERIA - LIBERIA **3-0(2-0)**
ALG: Lounès Gaouaoui, Slimane Raho, Samir Zaoui, Anthar Yahia (70.Rafik Halliche), Nadir Belhadj (86.Abderraouf Zarabi), Karim Ziani, Yazid Mansouri (Cap), Khaled Lemmouchia, Yacine Bezzaz (51.Lamouri Ben Kadda Djediat), Rafik Saïfi, Rafik Djebbour. Trainer: Rabah Saâdane.
LBR: Melvin King, Jimmy Dixon, James Koko Lomell (51.Kelvin Sebwe), George Gebro (68.Christian

Essel), Murphy Kumonple Nagbe, Esaiah Pello Benson, Zah Rahan Krangar (33.Ben Teekloh), Anthony Snoti Laffor, Theo Lewis Weeks, James Zortiah, Oliver Paul Makor. Trainer: Antoine Hey (Germany).
Goals: 1-0 Rafik Djebbour (15), 2-0 Karim Ziani (18), 3-0 Karim Ziani (47 penalty).
Cautions: Nadir Belhad / Esaiah Pello Benson.

08.06.2008, Independence Stadium, Bakau; Attendance: 24,500
Referee: Aldrin Ncobo (South Africa)
GAMBIA - SENEGAL   **0-0**
GAM: Robert Badjie, Abdou Jammeh, Mathew Mendy, Ousman Koli (48.Ebrahim Savaneh), Pa Saikou Kujabi, Tijan Jaiteh, Ebrima Ebou Sillah, Ebrima Sohna, Mustapha Jarjue (90.Modou Jagne), Aziz Corr Nyang (72.Edrissa Sonko), Njogu Demba-Nyrén. Trainer: Paul Put (Belgium).
SEN: Tony Mario Sylva, Pape Malickou Diakhaté, Ibrahima Faye, Moustapha Bayal Sall, Kader Mangane, Abdoulaye Diagne-Faye, Diomansy Mehdi Kamara, Frédéric Mendy (61.Issiar Dia), Henri Camara (43.Guirane N'Daw), El Hadji Ousseynou Diouf, Papa Waigo N'Diaye. Trainer: Lamine N'Diaye.
Cautions: Pa Saikou Kujabi, Tijan Jaiteh / Kader Mangane, El Hadji Ousseynou Diouf, Frédéric Mendy, Papa Waigo N'Diaye.
Sent off: Kader Mangane (38).

14.06.2008, Independence Stadium, Banjul; Attendance: 2,000
Referee: Koman Coulibaly (Mali)
GAMBIA - ALGERIA   **1-0(1-0)**
GAM: Bala Musa Bajaha, Abdou Jammeh, Mathew Mendy, Tijan Jaiteh, Ebrima Ebou Sillah (73.Abdoulie Mansally), Ebrima Sohna, Mustapha Jarjue, Aziz Corr Nyang (87.Assan Jatta), Pa Modou Jagne, Ousman Jallow (85.Yankuba Ceesay), Njogu Demba-Nyrén. Trainer: Paul Put (Belgium).
ALG: Lounès Gaouaoui, Slimane Raho, Samir Zaoui, Anthar Yahia, Abderraouf Zarabi, Karim Ziani, Yazid Mansouri (Cap), Khaled Lemmouchia, Lamouri Ben Kadda Djediat, Mohamed Seguer (66.Nabil Hemani), Rafik Djebbour (66.Yacine Bezzaz). Trainer: Rabah Saâdane.
Goal: 1-0 Mustapha Jarjue (19 penalty).
Cautions: Njogu Demba-Nyrén / Khaled Lemmouchia, Yazid Mansouri, Yacine Bezzaz.

15.06.2008, „Samuel Doe" Sports Complex, Monrovia; Attendance: 18,000
Referee: Kokou Djaoupé (Togo)
LIBERIA - SENEGAL   **2-2(0-0)**
LBR: Melvin King, Jimmy Dixon, Solomon Grimes, James Koko Lomell (53.Francis Doe Forkey), Ben Teekloh (80.Boikai Eddie Foday), Murphy Kumonple Nagbe (Cap), Theo Lewis Weeks, Anthony Snoti Laffor (70.Zah Rahan Krangar), James Zortiah, Dioh Williams, Oliver Paul Makor. Trainer: Antoine Hey (Germany).
SEN: Tony Mario Sylva, Pape Malickou Diakhaté, Ibrahima Faye (40.Guirane N'Daw), Ibrahima Sonko, Moustapha Bayal Sall, Papa Malick Bâ, Frédéric Mendy (77.Diomansy Mehdi Kamara), Henri Camara, El Hadji Ousseynou Diouf, Papa Waigo N'Diaye (46.Cheikh Matar Guèye), Issiar Dia. Trainer: Lamine N'Diaye.
Goals: 0-1 (47), 0-2 (55), 1-2 Dioh Williams (74), 2-2 Oliver Paul Makor (85).
Cautions: Ben Teekloh, Oliver Paul Makor, Theo Lewis Weeks / Ibrahima Faye, Issiar Dia, Cheikh Matar Guèye.

20.06.2008, Stade „Mustapha Tchaker", Blida; Attendance: 24,000
Referee: Gilles Ndume (Gabon)
ALGERIA - GAMBIA   **1-0(1-0)**
ALG: Lounès Gaouaoui, Slimane Raho, Madjid Bougherra, Anthar Yahia, Abderraouf Zarabi, Karim Ziani, Yazid Mansouri (Cap), Khaled Lemmouchia, Yacine Bezzaz (70.Lamouri Ben Kadda Djediat), Rafik Saïfi (83.Nabil Hemani), Rafik Djebbour. Trainer: Rabah Saâdane.
GAM: Bala Musa Bajaha, Abdou Jammeh, Mathew Mendy, Pa Saikou Kujabi, Tijan Jaiteh (86.Abdoulie Mansally), Yankuba Ceesay, Ebrima Ebou Sillah, Ebrima Sohna, Mustapha Jarjue, Ousman Jallow,

Njogu Demba-Nyrén (79.Assan Jatta). Trainer: Paul Put (Belgium).
Goal: 1-0 Anthar Yahia (33).
Cautions: Rafik Saïfi, Anthar Yahia, Yazid Mansouri / Yankuba Ceesay, Mustapha Jarjue.

21.06.2008, Stade „Léopold Sédar Senghor", Dakar; Attendance: 40,000
Referee: Ibrahim Chaibou (Niger)
SENEGAL - LIBERIA   **3-1(2-0)**
SEN: Tony Mario Sylva (Cap), Pape Malickou Diakhaté, Ibrahima Sonko, Guirane N'Daw, Kader Mangane, Issiar Dia (61.Henri Camara), Diomansy Mehdi Kamara (6.Frédéric Mendy), Mbaye Lèye, Ousmane N'Doye, Cheikh Matar Guèye (37.Papa Waigo N'Diaye), El Hadji Ousseynou Diouf. Trainer: Lamine N'Diaye.
LBR: Melvin King, Jimmy Dixon, Solomon Grimes, James Koko Lomell, Ben Teekloh, George Gebro (67.Boikai Eddie Foday), Murphy Kumonple Nagbe (19.George Baysah), Theo Lewis Weeks (54.Zah Rahan Krangar), James Zortiah, Francis Doe Forkey, Dioh Williams. Trainer: Antoine Hey (Germany).
Goals: 1-0 Ibrahima Sonko (8), 2-0 El Hadji Ousseynou Diouf (32), 3-0 Henri Camara (65), 3-1 Dioh Williams (89).
Cautions: Theo Lewis Weeks, Francis Doe Forkey.

05.09.2008, Stade „Mustapha Tchaker", Blida; Attendance: 35,000
Referee: Eddy Allen Maillet Guyto (Seychelles)
ALGERIA - SENEGAL   **3-2(0-0)**
ALG: Lounès Gaouaoui, Slimane Raho, Madjid Bougherra, Anthar Yahia, Nadir Belhadj, Karim Ziani, Brahim Hemdani, Chérif Abdeslam, Yacine Bezzaz (79.Samir Zaoui), Kamel Ghilas (69.Lamouri Ben Kadda Djediat), Rafik Saïfi (89.Nabil Hemani). Trainer: Rabah Saâdane.
SEN: Tony Mario Sylva (Cap), Ibrahima Faye (77.Pape Amodou Sougou), Abdoulaye Diagne-Faye, Pape Malickou Diakhaté, Cheikh Matar Guèye (81.Pascal Mendy), Issiar Dia, Ousmane N'Doye (70.Frédéric Mendy), Guirane N'Daw, Kader Mangane, Henri Camara, El Hadji Ousseynou Diouf. Trainer: Lamine N'Diaye.
Goals: 1-0 Yacine Bezzaz (8), 1-1 Issiar Dia (54), 2-1 Rafik Saïfi (67), 3-1 Anthar Yahia (73), 3-2 Pape Amodou Sougou (90).
Cautions: Anthar Yahia, Madjid Bougherra, Karim Ziani / Pascal Mendy, Pape Amodou Sougou.

06.09.2008, Independence Stadium, Bakau; Attendance: 10,000
Referee: Jamel Ambaya (Libya)
GAMBIA - LIBERIA   **3-0(2-0)**
GAM: Bala Musa Bajaha, Abdou Jammeh, Mathew Mendy, Pa Saikou Kujabi, Tijan Jaiteh, Ebrima Ebou Sillah (87.Cherno Samba), Ebrima Sohna, Mustapha Jarjue, Aziz Corr Nyang (78.Ebrahim Savaneh), Ousman Jallow, Njogu Demba-Nyrén (88.Omar Koroma). Trainer: Paul Put (Belgium).
LBR: Anthony Tokpah, Jimmy Dixon, George Baysah, Willis Forko (33.James Koko Lomell), Ben Teekloh, Esaiah Felo Benson, Dulee Johnson (46.Boikai Eddie Foday), Stephen Nagbe Mennoh (61.Zah Rahan Krangar), James Zortiah, Oliver Paul Makor, Dioh Williams. Trainer: Antoine Hey (Germany).
Goals: 1-0 Njogu Demba-Nyrén (10), 2-0 Ousman Jallow (26), 3-0 Njogu Demba-Nyrén (76).
Cautions: Mathew Mendy, Abdou Jammeh / George Baysah, Ben Teekloh.

11.10.2008, Stade „Léopold Sédar Senghor", Dakar; Attendance: 50,000
Referee: Kacem Bennaceur (Tunisia)
SENEGAL - GAMBIA   **1-1(0-0)**
SEN: Tony Mario Sylva (Cap), Pape Malickou Diakhaté, Cheikh Matar Guèye, Guirane N'Daw, Salif Diao (55.Rémi Gomis), Abdoulaye Diagne-Faye (81.Ibrahima Sonko), Kader Mangane, Khalilou Fadiga (60.Ousmane N'Doye), Henri Camara, El Hadji Ousseynou Diouf, Issiar Dia. Trainer: Lamine N'Diaye.
GAM: Bala Musa Bajaha, Abdou Jammeh, Mathew Mendy, Tijan Jaiteh, Ebrima Ebou Sillah (73.Abdoulie Mansally), Ebrima Sohna, Mustapha Jarjue, Aziz Corr Nyang (88.Cherno Samba), Ousman Jallow, Pa Modou Jagne, Njogu Demba-Nyrén (85.Omar Koroma). Trainer: Paul Put (Belgium).
Goals: 1-0 Kader Mangane (67), 1-1 Aziz Corr Nyang (85).

Cautions: Mathew Mendy.

11.10.2008, „Samuel Doe" Sports Complex, Monrovia; Attendance: 2,000
Referee: Ahmed Auda (Egypt)
LIBERIA - ALGERIA   **0-0**
LBR: Anthony Tokpah, George Baysah, Solomon Grimes, James Koko Lomell (46.Mardie Rennie), Varmah Kpoto, Anthony Snoti Laffor (90.Tonia Tisdell), Leon Power, Theo Lewis Weeks, James Zortiah, Oliver Paul Makor (Cap), Dioh Williams (86.Preston Corporal). Trainer: Antoine Hey (Germany).
ALG: Lounès Gaouaoui, Slimane Raho, Madjid Bougherra, Samir Zaoui, Nadir Belhadj, Chérif Abdeslam, Yazid Mansouri, Lamouri Ben Kadda Djediat, Karim Ziani, Kamel Ghilas (66.Yacine Bezzaz), Rafik Saïfi. Trainer: Rabah Saâdane.
Cautions: George Baysah / Chérif Abdeslam, Karim Ziani, Lamouri Ben Kadda Djediat.

GROUP 7

31.05.2008	Gaborone	Botswana - Madagascar	0-0
01.06.2008	Abidjan	Ivory Coast - Mozambique	1-0(0-0)
08.06.2008	Antananarivo	Madagascar - Ivory Coast	0-0
08.06.2008	Maputo	Mozambique - Botswana	1-2(0-1)
14.06.2008	Gaborone	Botswana - Ivory Coast	1-1(1-0)
15.06.2008	Antananarivo	Madagascar - Mozambique	1-1(0-1)
22.06.2008	Maputo	Mozambique - Madagascar	3-0(1-0)
22.06.2008	Abidjan	Ivory Coast - Botswana	4-0(2-0)
07.09.2008	Antananarivo	Madagascar - Botswana	1-0(1-0)
07.09.2008	Maputo	Mozambique - Ivory Coast	1-1(0-0)
11.10.2008	Abidjan	Ivory Coast - Madagascar	3-0(1-0)
11.10.2008	Gaborone	Botswana - Mozambique	0-1(0-1)

FINAL STANDINGS

1. **Ivory Coast**	6	3	3	0	10 - 2	12
2. **Mozambique**	6	2	2	2	7 - 5	8
3. Madagascar	6	1	3	2	2 - 7	6
4. Botswana	6	1	2	3	3 - 8	5

31.05.2008, National Stadium, Gaborone; Attendance: 11,087
Referee: Wellington Kaoma (Zambia)
BOTSWANA - MADAGASCAR   **0-0**
BOT: Modiri Marumo (Cap), Ndiapo Letsholathebe, Michael Mogaladi (58.Dirang Moloi), Mompati Thuma, Ernest Amos, Nelson Gabolwewe, Boitumelo Mafoko, Joel Mogorosi (75.Malepa Boleleng), Pontsho Moloi, Tshepo Motlhabankwe, Diphetogo Selolwane (58.Mpho Mabogo). Trainer: Stanley Tshosane.
MAD: Jean Chrysostome Raharison, Mamy Gervais Randrianarisoa, Mamisoa Razafindrakoto (Cap), Pascal Razakanantenaina (82.Eric-Julien Faneva Rakotondrabe), Jean Tholix, Damien Mahavony, Sedera Mathieu Randriamparany, Milison Niasexe (56.Yvan Rajoarimanana), Guy Hubert Mamihasindrahona, Faneva Imà Andriantsima, Stéphane Praxis Rabemananjara (79.Dimitri Carlos Zozimar). Trainer: Mickael Andrianasy.

31.05.2008, Stade „Félix Houphouët-Boigny", Abidjan; Attendance: 20,000
Referee: Ahmed Auda (Egypt)
IVORY COAST - MOZAMBIQUE   **1-0(0-0)**
CIV: Boubacar Barry, Guy Roland Demel, Abdoulaye Méïté (46.Alexandre Igor Lolo), Marco André Zoro Kpolo, Arthur Etienne Boka, Emmanuel Eboué, Siaka Tiéné, Alain Didier Zokora Deguy (Cap), Kanga Gauthier Akalé, Boubacar Sanogo (85.Emerse Faé), Kandia Traoré (67.Sekou Cissé). Trainer: Vahid Halilhodž ċ (Bosnia-Herzegovina).
MOZ: João Raphael Kapango, Alberto Massinga Fanuel, Dario Ivan Khan (*sent off 89*), Daniel Almiro Lobo „Miro" (82.Carlos Gonçalves „Fumo"), Simão Mate Junior, Martinho Martins Mukana „Paíto", Elias Gaspar Pelembe „Dominguês" (88.Maurício Ernesto Pequenino), Celso Halilo de Abdul „Mano", Nasser Amade Carimo „Nelinho", Dário Alberto Jesus Monteiro, Manuel José Luis Bucuane „Tico-Tico" (65.Eugenio Fernando Bila „Genito"). Trainer: Ignatus Martinus Nooij (Holland).
Goal: 1-0 Sekou Cissé (75).
Cautions: Marco André Zoro Kpolo, Siaka Tiéné / Manuel José Luis Bucuane „Tico-Tico",Martinho Martins Mukana „Paíto", Dario Ivan Khan, Simão Mate Junior.
Sent off: Dario Ivan Khan (89).

08.06.2008, Mahamasina Stadium, Antanarivo; Attendance: 15,000
Referee: Jean-Claude Labrosse (Seychelles)
MADAGASCAR - IVORY COAST   **0-0**
MAD: Jean Chrysostome Raharison, Mamy Gervais Randrianarisoa, Mamisoa Razafindrakoto (Cap), Sedera Mathieu Randriamparany, Jean Tholix, Faneva Imà Andriantsima (79.Stéphane Praxis Rabemananjara), Lalaina Nomenjanahary (85.Milison Niasexe), Guy Hubert Mamihasindrahona, Pascal Razakanantenaina, Paulin Voavy, Yvan Rajoarimanana (90.Jean de l'Or Carolus Tsaralaza). Trainer: Mickael Andrianasy.
CIV: Boubacar Barry, Guy Roland Demel (74.Sekou Cissé), Abdoulaye Méïté, Kolo Habib Touré (Cap), Arthur Etienne Boka, Emmanuel Eboué, Siaka Tiéné, Emerse Faé (64.Emmanuel Koné), Alain Didier Zokora Deguy, Kanga Gauthier Akalé (82.Kandia Traoré), Boubacar Sanogo. Trainer: Vahid Halilhodž č (Bosnia-Herzegovina).
Cautions: Faneva Imà Andriantsima, Jean Tholix, Mamisoa Razafindrakoto / Guy Roland Demel, Emmanuel Eboué.

08.06.2008, Machava Stadium, Maputo; Attendance: 30,000
Referee: Mbongseni Fakudze (Swaziland)
MOZAMBIQUE - BOTSWANA   **1-2(0-1)**
MOZ: João Raphael Kapango, Alberto Massinga Fanuel, Daniel Almiro Lobo „Miro", Simão Mate Junior, Martinho Martins Mukana „Paíto", Elias Gaspar Pelembe „Dominguês", Eugenio Fernando Bíla „Genito" (46.Maurício Ernesto Pequenino), Nasser Amade Carimo „Nelinho", Dário Alberto Jesus Monteiro, Celso Halilo de Abdul „Mano", Manuel José Luis Bucuane „Tico-Tico". Trainer: Ignatus Martinus Nooij (Holland).
BOT: Modiri Marumo (Cap), Ndiapo Letsholathebe, Michael Mogaladi, Mompati Thuma, Ernest Amos, Nelson Gabolwewe, Boitumelo Mafoko, Pontsho Moloi (71.Joel Mogorosi), Tshepo Motlhabankwe, Malepa Boleleng (49.Keoagetse Radipotsane), Diphetogo Selolwane. Trainer: Stanley Tshosane.
Goals: 0-1 Diphetogo Selolwane (30), 1-1 Daniel Almiro Lobo „Miro" (60), 1-2 Boitumelo Mafoko (82).
Cautions: Dário Alberto Jesus Monteiro / Malepa Boleleng, Keoagetse Radipotsane, Boitumelo Mafoko.

14.06.2008, National Stadium, Gaborone; Attendance: 21,400
Referee: Muhmed Ssegonga (Uganda)
BOTSWANA - IVORY COAST   **1-1(1-0)**
BOT: Modiri Marumo (Cap), Ndiapo Letsholathebe, Michael Mogaladi, Mompati Thuma, Ernest Amos, Nelson Gabolwewe, Boitumelo Mafoko, Pontsho Moloi (56.Joel Mogorosi), Tshepo Motlhabankwe, Malepa Boleleng, Diphetogo Selolwane (80.Moemedi Moatiharing). Trainer: Stanley Tshosane.
CIV: Boubacar Barry, Alexandre Igor Lolo, Abdoulaye Méïté, Kolo Habib Touré, Arthur Etienne Boka, Siaka Tiéné (89.Emerse Faé), Emmanuel Koné, Alain Didier Zokora Deguy, Sekou Cissé (85.Kandia Traoré), Kanga Gauthier Akalé (77.Emmanuel Eboué), Boubacar Sanogo. Trainer: Vahid Halilhodž č (Bosnia-Herzegovina).
Goals: 1-0 Diphetogo Selolwane (25), 1-1 Abdoulaye Méïté (65).
Cautions: Pontsho Moloi, Michael Mogaladi, Nelson Gabolwewe.

15.06.2008, Mahamasina Stadium, Antananarivo; Attendance: 15,501
Referee: Abdul Basit Ebrahim (South Africa)
MADAGASCAR - MOZAMBIQUE   **1-1(0-1)**
MAD: Jean Chrysostome Raharison, Jean Tsima Randriamihaja, Mamisoa Razafindrakoto (Cap), Mamy Gervais Randrianarisoa, Sedera Mathieu Randriamparany, Faneva Imà Andriantsima, Lalaina Nomenjanahary (47.Stéphane Praxis Rabemananjara), Guy Hubert Mamihasindrahona (39.Pascal Razakanantenaina), Dimitri Carlos Zozimar (60.Yvan Rajoarimanana), Damien Mahavony, Paulin Voavy. Trainer: Mickael Andrianasy.
MOZ: João Raphael Kapango, Alberto Massinga Fanuel, Daniel Almiro Lobo „Miro", Simão Mate Junior (47.Nasser Amade Carimo „Nelinho"), Dario Ivan Khan (Cap) (46.Whiskey), Martinho Martins Mukana „Paíto", Carlos Parruque Danito Nhapossa (77.Momed Antonio Hagy), Elias Gaspar Pelembe

„Dominguês", Dário Alberto Jesus Monteiro, Celso Halilo de Abdul „Mano", Manuel José Luis Bucuane „Tico-Tico". Trainer: Ignatus Martinus Nooij (Holland).
Goals: 0-1 Dário Alberto Jesus Monteiro (33), 1-1 Guy Hubert Mamihasindrahona (90+1 penalty).
Cautions: Sedera Mathieu Randriamparany, Pascal Razakanantenaina / Dário Alberto Jesus Monteiro, Alberto Massinga Fanuel, João Raphael Kapango,Nasser Amade Carimo „Nelinho",Daniel Almiro Lobo „Miro".

22.06.2008, Estadio Nacional da Machava, Maputo; Attendance: 20,000
Referee: Eddy Allen Maillet Guyto (Seychelles)
MOZAMBIQUE - MADAGASCAR   **3-0(1-0)**
MOZ: Marcelino Armando Cumbane, Alberto Massinga Fanuel, Dario Ivan Khan, Daniel Almiro Lobo „Miro", Simão Mate Junior, Momed Antonio Hagy, Martinho Martins Mukana „Paíto" (35.Carlos Parruque Danito Nhapossa), Elias Gaspar Pelembe „Dominguês", Maurício Ernesto Pequenino (78.Sonito), Celso Halilo de Abdul „Mano", Manuel José Luis Bucuane „Tico-Tico" (Cap) (75.Josemar Tiago Machaisse). Trainer: Ignatus Martinus Nooij (Holland).
MAD: Jean Chrysostome Raharison, Mamy Gervais Randrianarisoa, Mamisoa Razafindrakoto (Cap), Pascal Razakanantenaina (46.Jean de l'Or Carolus Tsaralaza), Jean Tholix, Guy Hubert Mamihasindrahona (73.Hubert Robson Razakananantena), Lalaina Nomenjanahary, Rija Juvence Rakotomandimby, Sedera Mathieu Randriamparany, Faneva Imà Andriantsima, Yvan Rajoarimanana (86.Stéphane Praxis Rabemananjara). Trainer: Franck Rajaonarisamba.
Goals: 1-0 Manuel José Luis Bucuane „Tico-Tico" (23), 2-0 Carlos Parruque Danito Nhapossa (52), 3-0 Elias Gaspar Pelembe „Dominguês" (64).
Cautions: Sedera Mathieu Randriamparany, Mamisoa Razafindrakoto.

22.06.2008, Stade „Félix Houphouёt-Boigny", Abidjan; Attendance: 15,000
Referee: Kacem Bennaceur (Tunisia)
IVORY COAST - BOTSWANA   **4-0(2-0)**
CIV: Boubacar Barry, Abdoulaye Méïté (84.Marco André Zoro Kpolo), Kolo Habib Touré (Cap), Arthur Etienne Boka, Emmanuel Eboué, Siaka Tiéné, Emmanuel Koné, Alain Didier Zokora Deguy, Sekou Cissé (71.Salomon Kalou), Kanga Gauthier Akalé (75.Emerse Faé), Boubacar Sanogo. Trainer: Vahid Halilhodž ċ (Bosnia-Herzegovina).
BOT: Modiri Marumo (Cap), Ndiapo Letsholathebe, Mompati Thuma, Ernest Amos, Nelson Gabolwewe, Boitumelo Mafoko, Pontsho Moloi, Tshepo Motlhabankwe (55.Joel Mogorosi), Keoagetse Radipotsane, Malepa Boleleng (63.Dirang Moloi), Diphetogo Selolwane. Trainer: Stanley Tshosane.
Goals: 1-0 Boubacar Sanogo (16), 2-0 Alain Didier Zokora Deguy (22), 3-0 Sekou Cissé (46), 4-0 Sekou Cissé (70).
Cautions: Ndiapo Letsholathebe.

07.09.2008, Mahamasina Stadium, Antananarivo; Attendance: 20,000
Referee: Rajindraparsad Seechurn (Mauritius)
MADAGASCAR - BOTSWANA   **1-0(1-0)**
MAD: Jean Chrysostome Raharison, Urbain Andriamampionona, Mamy Gervais Randrianarisoa, Eric-Julien Faneva Rakotondrabe (Cap), Claudio Ramiadamanana, Jean Tholix, Guy Hubert Mamihasindrahona, Heritiana Thierry Ratsimbazafy, Yvan Rajoarimanana (84.Rija Juvence Rakotomandimby), Paulin Voavy (86.Jean de l'Or Carolus Tsaralaza), Stéphane Praxis Rabemananjara (70.Tovohery Rabenandrasana). Trainer: Franck Rajaonarisamba.
BOT: Modiri Marumo (Cap), Michael Mogaladi, Mosimanegape Ramoshibidu (53.Nelson Gabolwewe), Mompati Thuma, Boitumelo Mafoko, Joel Mogorosi, Pontsho Moloi, Abednico Powel (53.Tshepo Motlhabankwe), Mogogi Gabonamong, Jerome Ramatlhakwane, Diphetogo Selolwane. Trainer: Stanley Tshosane.
Goals: 1-0 Stéphane Praxis Rabemananjara (70).
Cautions: Eric-Julien Faneva Rakotondrabe.

07.09.2008, Estadio Nacional da Machava, Maputo; Attendance: 35,000
Referee: Abdellah El Achiri (Morocco)
MOZAMBIQUE - IVORY COAST   **1-1(0-0)**
MOZ: João Raphael Kapango, Alberto Massinga Fanuel, Dario Ivan Khan, Daniel Almiro Lobo „Miro", Simão Mate Junior, Momed Antonio Hagy (86.Carlos Parruque Danito Nhapossa), Elias Gaspar Pelembe „Dominguês", Dário Alberto Jesus Monteiro, Eugenio Fernando Bila „Genito", Celso Halilo de Abdul „Mano", Manuel José Luis Bucuane „Tico-Tico" (Cap) (90.Nito). Trainer: Ignatus Martinus Nooij (Holland).
CIV: Boubacar Barry, Guy Roland Demel, Kolo Habib Touré (Cap), Arthur Etienne Boka, Emmanuel Eboué, Gnegneri Yaya Touré (88.Kafoumba Coulibaly), Emerse Faé, Alain Didier Zokora Deguy, Salomon Kalou (82.Kanga Gauthier Akalé), Bakari Koné (84.Siaka Tiéné), Boubacar Sanogo. Trainer: Vahid Halilhodž è (Bosnia-Herzegovina).
Goals: 0-1 Bakari Koné (48), 1-1Daniel Almiro Lobo „Miro" (52).
Cautions: Eugenio Fernando Bila „Genito" / Emerse Faé, Alain Didier Zokora Deguy.

11.10.2008, Stade Champroux, Abidjan; Attendance: 24,000
Referee: Mohamed Benouza (Algeria)
IVORY COAST - MADAGASCAR   **3-0(1-0)**
CIV: Boubacar Barry, Guy Roland Demel, Kolo Habib Touré (Cap) (71.Marco André Zoro Kpolo), Alexandre Igor Lolo, Arthur Etienne Boka, Emmanuel Eboué (62.Emerse Faé), Gnegneri Yaya Touré, Alain Didier Zokora Deguy, Salomon Kalou (88.Kanga Gauthier Akalé), Bakari Koné, Boubacar Sanogo. Trainer: Vahid Halilhodž è (Bosnia-Herzegovina).
MAD: Jean Chrysostome Raharison, Urbain Andriamampionona (50.Guy Hubert Mamihasindrahona), Eric-Julien Faneva Rakotondrabe (Cap), Mamy Gervais Randrianarisoa, Sedera Mathieu Randriamparany, Heritiana Thierry Ratsimbazafy, Lalaina Nomenjanahary (62.Tovohery Rabenandrasana), Mamisoa Razafindrakoto, Yvan Rajoarimanana (74.Ibrahim Amada), Paulin Voavy, Stéphane Praxis Rabemananjara. Trainer: Franck Rajaonarisamba.
Goals: 1-0 Boubacar Sanogo (41), 2-0 Boubacar Sanogo (55), 3-0 Salomon Kalou (55).
Cautions: Salomon Kalou, Marco André Zoro Kpolo / Paulin Voavy, Eric-Julien Faneva Rakotondrabe, Mamy Gervais Randrianarisoa.

11.10.2008, National Stadium, Gaborone; Attendance: 2,000
Referee: Cheikh Ahmed Tidiane Seck (Senegal)
BOTSWANA - MOZAMBIQUE   **0-1(0-1)**
BOT: Modiri Marumo (Cap), Gobonyeone Selefa, Nelson Gabolwewe, Mompati Thuma, Boitumelo Mafoko (76.Dirang Moloi), Joel Mogorosi, Pontsho Moloi, Tshepo Motlhabankwe, Mogogi Gabonamong, Jerome Ramatlhakwane (49.Malepa Boleleng), Diphetogo Selolwane. Trainer: Stanley Tshosane.
MOZ: Marcelino Armando Cumbane, Alberto Massinga Fanuel, Daniel Almiro Lobo „Miro", Simão Mate Junior, Hagy (47.Carlos Bernardo Chimomole „Carlitos"), Whiskey, Elias Gaspar Pelembe „Dominguês", Dário Alberto Jesus Monteiro, Eugenio Fernando Bila „Genito" (90+2.Nasser Amade Carimo „Nelinho"), Celso Halilo de Abdul „Mano", Manuel José Luis Bucuane „Tico-Tico" (Cap) (78.Carlos Parruque Danito Nhapossa). Trainer: Ignatus Martinus Nooij (Holland).
Goal: 0-1 Eugenio Fernando Bila „Genito" (6).
Cautions: Mogogi Gabonamong, Diphetogo Selolwane / Whiskey.

GROUP 8

31.05.2008	Kigali	Rwanda - Mauritania	3-0(1-0)
31.05.2008	Casablanca	Morocco - Ethiopia	3-0(2-0)
07.06.2008	Nouakchott	Mauritania – Morocco	1-4(0-2)
08.06.2008	Addis Abeba	Ethiopia - Rwanda	1-2(1-0)
13.06.2008	Nouakchott	Mauritania - Ethiopia	0-1(0-0)
14.06.2008	Kigali	Rwanda - Morocco	3-1(1-0)
21.06.2008	Casablanca	Morocco - Rwanda	2-0(1-0)
22.06.2008	Addis Abeba	Ethiopia - Mauritania	6-1(1-1)
06.09.2008	Nouakchott	Mauritania – Rwanda	0-1(0-0)
11.10.2008	Rabat	Morocco - Mauritania	4-1(1-0)

Note: Ethiopia could not play to end its qualifiying matches after beeing suspended by the FIFA from competitive internationals.

FINAL STANDINGS

1. Morocco	4	3	0	1	11 - 5	9
2. Rwanda	4	3	0	1	7 - 3	9
3. Mauritania	6	0	0	6	3 - 19	0

31.05.2008, Stade Regional de Nyamirambo, Kigali; Attendance: 12,000
Referee: Noumandiez Doué (Ivory Coast)
RWANDA - MAURITANIA   **3-0(1-0)**
RWA: Jean-Claude Ndori, Eric Gasana, Patrick Mutesa Mafisango, Ismail Nshutinamagara, Elias Ntaganda (63.Alua Gaseruka), Boubakary Sadou, Hamad Ndikumana, Jean-Baptiste Mugiraneza (65.Haruna Niyonzima), Olivier Karekezi (Cap), Labama Bokota (77.Bobo Bola), Saïd Abed Makasi. Trainer: Branko Tucak (Croatia).
MTN: Souleymane Diallo (39.M'baye Lamine Niang), Moise Kandé, Ibrahima Mamadou Sy, Abdelaziz Kamara (Cap), Yacoub Ba, Yacoub Fall, Yoann-Jean-Noël Langlet, Brahim Old Boubacar Sidina, Ahmed Ould Teguedi (87.Daouda Sow), Dominique Da Silva, Ismael Diakité (61.Boubacar Jiddou). Trainer: Alain Moizan (France).
Goals: 1-0 Olivier Karekezi (15), Saïd Abed Makasi (67 penalty), Labama Bokota (72).
Cautions: Jean-Baptiste Mugiraneza, Eric Gasana, Alua Gaseruka / Abdelaziz Kamara, Ibrahima Mamadou Sy.

31.05.2008, Stade „Mohammed V", Casablanca; Attendance: 5,000
Referee: Badara Diatta (Senegal)
MOROCCO - ETHIOPIA   **3-0(2-0)**
MAR: Nadir Lamyaghri, Michaël Basser Chrétien, Mourad Aïni, Amin El Erbati, Badr El Kaddouri, Youssef Safri, Houcine Kharja, Soufiane Alloudi, Nabil El Zhar (63.Moubarak Boussoufa), Hicham Aboucherouane, Abdessalam Benjelloun (90+2.Rachid Hamdani). Trainer: Roger Lemerre (France).
ETH: Jemal Sadat, Abebaw Butako, Adane Girma, Siyoum Girom, Samson Mulugeta, Behailu Demeke (58.Andualem Nigussie), Aneley Berhane, Mirhet Mulugeta, Said Saladin, Fikru Tefera Lemessa (*sent off 51*), Tafese Tesfaye. Trainer: Abraham Teklehaymanot.
Goals: 1-0 Abdessalam Benjelloun (4), 2-0 Hicham Aboucherouane (11), 3-0 Houssein Kharja (85).
Cautions: Moubarak Boussoufa / Siyoum Girom.
Sent off: Fikru Tefera Lemessa (51).

07.06.2008, Stade Olympique, Nouakchott; Attendance: 9,500
Referee: Joseph Lamptey (Ghana)
MAURITANIA – MOROCCO   **1-4(0-2)**
MTN: Souleymane Diallo, Pascal-Dominique Gourville (65.Taghiyoullah Abderrahman Denna), Moise Kandé (Cap), Seydou Nourou M'bodji, Abdelaziz Kamara, Yacoub Ba, Yoann-Jean-Noël Langlet, Mohamed Ould Lamine, Brahim Old Boubacar Sidina (46.Ismael Diakité), Ahmed Ould Teguedi,

193

Boubacar Jiddou (64.Dominique Da Silva). Trainer: Alain Moizan (France).

MAR: Nadir Lamyaghri, Michaël Basser Chrétien, Mourad Aïni, Amin El Erbati, Younes Mankari, Youssef Safri, Houcine Kharja, Tarik Sektioui (21.Nabil El Zhar), Soufiane Alloudi, Hicham Aboucherouane (78.Rachid Hamdani), Abdessalam Benjelloun (81.Brahim El Bahri). Trainer: Roger Lemerre (France).

Goals: 0-1 Tarik Sektioui (9), 0-2 Abdessalam Benjelloun (37), 0-3 Youssef Safri (58), 0-4 Houcine Kharja (79), 1-4 Ahmed Ould Teguedi (82 penalty)

Cautions: Pascal-Dominique Gourville, Moise Kandé, Taghiyoullah Abderrahman Denna, Dominique Da Silva / Youssef Safri, Michaël Basser Chrétien, Soufiane Alloudi, Brahim El Bahri.

08.06.2008, Addis Abeba Stadium, Addis Abeba; Attendance: 18,000
Referee: Alfred Ndinya (Kenya)
ETHIOPIA - RWANDA   **1-2(1-0)**
ETH: Jemal Sadat, Abebaw Butako, Adane Girma (83.Mohamed Mesud), Degu Debebe, Siyoum Girom, Samson Mulugeta, Mirhet Mulugeta, Said Saladin, Andualem Nigussie, Tafese Tesfaye (53.Solomon Kebede), Zinabu Yared (31.Behailu Demeke). Trainer: Abraham Teklehaymanot.
RWA: Jean-Claude Ndori, Eric Gasana, Alua Gaseruka (88.Abedi Mulenda), Patrick Mutesa Mafisango, Elias Ntaganda, Boubakary Sadou (46.Ismail Nshutinamagara), Hamad Ndikumana, Haruna Niyonzima, Labama Bokota (77.Jean-Baptiste Mugiraneza), Olivier Karekezi (Cap), Saïd Abed Makasi. Trainer: Branko Tucak (Croatia).
Goals: 1-0 Tafese Tesfaye (44), 1-1 Saïd Abed Makasi (59), Olivier Karekezi (82).
Cautions: Boubakary Sadou, Ismail Nshutinamagara, Haruna Niyonzima.

13.06.2008, Stade Olympique, Nouakchott; Attendance: 5,000
Referee: Jamel Ambaya (Libya)
MAURITANIA - ETHIOPIA   **0-1(0-0)**
MTN: Souleymane Diallo, Moise Kandé, Abdelaziz Kamara, Yacoub Ba (85.Lemine Balla Cherif), Yacoub Fall, Yoann-Jean-Noël Langlet, Mohamed Ould Lamine, Mamadou Bilal Sidibé, Ahmed Ould Teguedi, Ahmed Sidibé (Cap) (66.Marabott Sow), Ely Cheik Ould Voulani (76.Khatry Abdallahi Ould Khourou). Trainer: Mohamed Ould.
ETH: Samson Asefa, Abebaw Butako, Adane Girma (63.Michael Desta), Degu Debebe, Samson Mulugeta, Behailu Demeke, Aneley Berhane, Mohamed Mesud, Mirhet Mulugeta, Said Saladin, Andualem Nigussie (83.Solomon Kebede). Trainer: Abraham Teklehaymanot.
Goal: 0-1 Said Saladin (90+3).

14.06.2008, Stade Regional de Nyamirambo, Kigali; Attendance: 12,000
Referee: Raphael Divine Evehe (Cameroon)
RWANDA - MOROCCO   **3-1(1-0)**
RWA: Jean-Claude Ndori, Eric Gasana, Alua Gaseruka, Patrick Mutesa Mafisango, Ismail Nshutinamagara, Elias Ntaganda, Hamad Ndikumana, Haruna Niyonzima (Cap), Labama Bokota (81.Jean-Baptiste Mugiraneza), Olivier Karekezi, Saïd Abed Makasi. Trainer: Branko Tucak (Croatia).
MAR: Nadir Lamyaghri, Michaël Basser Chrétien (57.Badr El Kaddouri), Amin El Erbati , Mourad Aïni, Mohammed Oulhadj (36.Hicham Aboucherouane), Younes Mankari, Youssef Safri, Houcine Kharja, Soufiane Alloudi, Nabil El Zhar, Abdessalam Benjelloun (83.Brahim El Bahri). Trainer: Roger Lemerre (France).
Goals: Youssef Safri (78)
Cautions: Ismail Nshutinamagara / Younes Mankari, Nabil El Zhar.
Sent off: Eric Gasana (73), Soufiane Alloudi (73).

21.06.2008, Stade „Mohammed V", Casablanca; Attendance: 2,500
Referee: Mohamed Benouza (Algeria)
MOROCCO - RWANDA   **2-0(1-0)**
MAR: Nadir Lamyaghri, Michaël Basser Chrétien, Mourad Aïni (90+1.Adil Hermach), Amin El Erbati, Badr El Kaddouri, Youssef Safri, Houcine Kharja, Ahmed Ajeddou (80.Mohamed Madihi), Nabil El

Zhar, Abdessalam Benjelloun, Hicham Aboucherouane (46.Bouchaib El Moubarki). Trainer: Roger Lemerre (France).
RWA: Jean-Claude Ndori (60.Jean-Luc Ndayishimiye), Alua Gaseruka, Patrick Mutesa Mafisango, Elias Ntaganda, Aimable Rucogoza, Hamad Ndikumana, Haruna Niyonzima, Labama Bokota (68.Jean-Claude Iranzi), Jean-Baptiste Mugiraneza (78.Bobo Bola), Olivier Karekezi (Cap), Saïd Abed Makasi. Trainer: Branko Tucak (Croatia).
Goals: 1-0 Youssef Safri (12 penalty), 2-0 Nabil El Zhar (49).
Cautions: Badr El Kaddouri / Jean-Baptiste Mugiraneza, Aimable Rucogoza, Elias Ntaganda.
Sent off: Elias Ntaganda (16).

22.06.2008, Addis Abeba Stadium, Addis Abeba; Attendance: 13,000
Referee: Verson Lwanja (Malawi)
ETHIOPIA - MAURITANIA 6-1(1-1)
ETH: Samson Asefa, Abebaw Butako (73.Michael Desta), Adane Girma, Degu Debebe, Samson Mulugeta, Aneley Berhane (80.Damte Hunegnaw), Mohamed Mesud (83.Behailu Demeke), Mirhet Mulugeta, Said Saladin, Fikru Tefera Lemessa, Andualem Nigussie. Trainer: Abraham Teklehaymanot.
MTN: Souleymane Diallo, Moise Kandé, Seydou Nourou M'bodji, Abdelaziz Kamara, Yacoub Ba, Yacoub Fall, Mohamed Ould Lamine, Ahmed Ould Teguedi (78.Djibi Ahmed Samba), Brahim Old Boubacar Sidina (65.Mohamed Ould Cheikhani), Khatry Abdallahi Ould Khourou (46.Marabott Sow), Ely Cheik Ould Voulani. Trainer: Mohamed Ould.
Goals: 1-0 Fikru Tefera Lemessa (38), 1-1 Ely Cheik Ould Voulani (44), 2-1 Andualem Nigussie (55), 3-1 Andualem Nigussie (63), 4-1 Mohamed Mesud (83), 5-1 Fikru Tefera Lemessa (89), 6-1 Adane Girma (90).
Cautions: Mirhet Mulugeta / Brahim Old Boubacar Sidina, Yacoub Ba.
Sent off: Yacoub Ba (37).

06.09.2008, Stade Olympique, Nouakchott; Attendance: 1,000
Referee: Kacem Bennaceur (Tunisia)
MAURITANIA – RWANDA 0-1(0-0)
MTN: M'baye Lamine Niang, Mohamed Ould Cheikhani, Babacar Dieng, Mohamed Hamoud (70.Mohamed Lamine Ahmed Khatry), Boubou N'diaye, Mohamed Ould Lamine, Brahim Old Boubacar Sidina, Ahmed Ould Teguedi, Karamoko Moussa Traoré (72.Oumar Fall), Ely Cheik Ould Voulani (68.Khatry Abdallahi Ould Khourou). Trainer: Mohamed Ould.
RWA: Jean-Claude Ndori, Bonaventure Hategekimana, Patrick Mutesa Mafisango, Ismail Nshutinamagara, Hamad Ndikumana, Abedi Mulenda (59.Bobo Bola), Haruna Niyonzima, Henri Munyaneza (72.Mwemere Ngirinshuti), Abdoul Uwimana, Olivier Karekezi (Cap), Saïd Abed Makasi (85.Jean Bosco Uwacu). Trainer: Branko Tucak (Croatia).
Goal: 0-1 Bobo Bola (79).
Cautions: Ahmed Ould Teguedi / Henri Munyaneza, Olivier Karekezi, Bonaventure Hategekimana.

11.10.2008, Prince „Moulay Abdellah", Rabat; Attendance: 1,472
Referee: Sharaf Aboubacar (Ivory Coast)
MOROCCO - MAURITANIA 4-1(1-0)
MAR: Nadir Lamyaghri, Michaël Basser Chrétien, Abdesslam Ouaddou, Amin El Erbati (70.Youssef Rabeh), Salaheddine Sbai, Nabil El Zhar (79.Moncef Zerka), Youssef Safri, Houcine Kharja, Nabil Dirar, Youssouf Hadji (65.Marouane Zemmama), Marouane Chamakh. Trainer: Roger Lemerre (France).
MTN: Souleymane Diallo, Mohamed Ould Cheikhani, Babacar Dieng, Yacoub Fall, Mohamed Hamoud, Mohamed Ould Lamine, Boubou N'diaye, Brahim Old Boubacar Sidina, Ahmed Ould Teguedi (67.Djibi Ahmed Samba), Karamoko Moussa Traoré (65.Oumar Fall), Ely Cheik Ould Voulani. Trainer: Mohamed Ould.
Goals: 1-0 Youssef Safri (35), 2-0 Youssouf Hadji (56), 3-0 Youssouf Hadji (60), 4-0 Marouane Zemmama (66), 4-1 Ahmed Ould Teguedi (67)
Cautions: Amin El Erbati, Youssouf Hadji / Brahim Old Boubacar Sidina, Karamoko Moussa Traoré, Oumar Fall.

195

GROUP 9

01.06.2008	Bujumbura	Burundi - Seychelles	1-0(0-0)
01.06.2008	Radès	Tunisia – Burkina Faso	1-2(1-0)
07.06.2008	Victoria	Seychelles - Tunisia	0-2(0-0)
07.06.2008	Ouagadougou	Burkina Faso - Burundi	2-0(2-0)
14.06.2008	Victoria	Seychelles - Burkina Faso	2-3(0-1)
15.06.2008	Bujumbura	Burundi - Tunisia	0-1(0-0)
21.06.2008	Ouagadougou	Burkina Faso - Seychelles	4-1(2-1)
21.06.2008	Radès	Tunisia - Burundi	2-1(2-1)
06.09.2008	Victoria	Seychelles - Burundi	1-2(0-1)
06.09.2008	Ouagadougou	Burkina Faso - Tunisia	0-0
11.10.2008	Radès	Tunisia - Seychelles	5-0(4-0)
12.10.2008	Bujumbura	Burundi - Burkina Faso	1-3(1-1)

FINAL STANDINGS

1. **Burkina Faso**	6	5	1	0	14	-	5	16
2. **Tunisia**	6	4	1	1	11	-	3	13
3. Burundi	6	2	0	4	5	-	9	6
4. Seychelles	6	0	0	6	4	-	17	0

01.06.2008, Prince „Louis Rwagasore" Stadium, Bujumbura; Attendance: 4,000
Referee: Emmanuel Imiere (Nigeria)
BURUNDI - SEYCHELLES   **1-0(0-0)**
BDI: Vladimir Niyonkuru, David Habarugira, Hassan Hakizimana, Henry Mbazumutima, Valery Twite Nahayo (61.Fuadi Ndayisenga), Floribert Tambwe Ndayisaba (Cap), Alain Ndizéyé (75.Faty Papy), Karim Nizigiyimana, Kassim Bizimana (34.Claude Nahimana), Dugary Ndabashinzé, Yamin Selema Ndikumana. Trainer: Adel Amrouche (Algeria).
SEY: Eric Nelson Sopha, Godfrey Denis Armel, Nigel Freminot, Harry Libanotis (90.Steve Henriette), Alex Nibourette (58.Achilles Henriette), Neddy Rose, Don Annacoura, Denis Barbe (Cap), David Dorby, Nelson Laurence (80.Michel Joubert), Philip Zialor. Trainer: Jan Mak (Holland).
Goal: 1-0 Selemani Ndikumana (81).
Cautions: Alain Ndizéyé, Karim Nizigiyimana, Claude Nahimana / Neddy Rose.

01.06.2008, Stade Olympique 7 Novembre, Radès; Attendance: 15,000
Referee: Jamel Ambaya (Libya)
TUNISIA – BURKINA FASO   **1-2(1-0)**
TUN: Hamdi Kasraoui, Radhi Ben Abdelmajid Jaïdi (Cap), Saber Ben Frej (72.Chadi Hammami), Yassin Mikari, Radhouène Felhi, Jawhar Mnari, Chaker Zouaghi, Tijani Belaid, Mejdi Traoui (40.Chaouki Ben Saada), Mohamed Amine Chermiti, Issam Jemâa (80.Wissem Ben Yahia). Trainer: Roger Lemerre (France).
BFA: Daouda Diakité, Paul Kéba Koulibaly, Mamadou Tall, Mady Saïdou Panandétiguiri, Charles Kaboré, Mahamoudou Kéré (Cap), Soumaïla Tassembédo (83.Yssouf Koné), Narcisse Yaméogo, Jonathan Pitroipa (90.Florent Rouamba), Patrick Zoundi (63.Issouf Ouattara), Beli Moumouni Dagano. Trainer: Paulo Jorge Rebelo Duarte (Portugal).
Goals: 1-0 Tijani Belaid (38), 1-1 Yssouf Koné (85), 1-2 Yssouf Koné (87).
Cautions: Radhi Ben Abdelmajid Jaïdi, Saber Ben Frej / Mady Saidou Panandétiguiri, Mahamoudou Kéré, Mamadou Tall.

07.06.2008, Stade Linité, Victoria; Attendance: 2,033
Referee: Justino Faduco (Mozambique)
SEYCHELLES - TUNISIA   **0-2(0-0)**
SEY: Eric Nelson Sopha, Godfrey Denis Armel (73.Jonathan Bibi), Nigel Freminot, Alex Nibourette, Neddy Rose, Don Annacoura, Denis Barbe (Cap), David Dorby (80.Rennick Esther), Michel Joubert,

Nelson Laurence, Philip Zialor (66.Achilles Henriette). Trainer: Jan Mak (Holland).
TUN: Aymen Mathlouthi Balbouli, Radhi Ben Abdelmajid Jaïdi (Cap), Yassin Mikari, Radhouène Felhi (82.Saïf Ghezal), Chadi Hammami, Jawhar Mnari, Mohamed Ali Nafkha (75.Wissem Ben Yahia), Tijani Belaid (63.Youssef Mouihbi), Mehdi Ben Dhifallah, Chaouki Ben Saada, Issam Jemâa. Trainer: Roger Lemerre (France).
Goals: 0-1 Issam Jemâa (9), 0-2 Chaouki Ben Saada (43).
Cautions: Radhouène Felhi, Yassin Mikari.

07.06.2008, Stade du 4-Août, Ouagadougou; Attendance: 10,000
Referee: Gil Ndume (Gabon)
BURKINA FASO - BURUNDI   **2-0(2-0)**
BFA: Daouda Diakité, Paul Kéba Koulibaly, Mamadou Tall, Mady Saïdou Panandétiguiri, Charles Kaboré, Mahamoudou Kéré (Cap) (62.Florent Rouamba), Jonathan Pitroipa, Soumaïla Tassembédo, Patrick Zoundi (50.Abdoul Aziz Nikiéma), Yssouf Koné, Beli Moumouni Dagano. Trainer: Paulo Jorge Rebelo Duarte (Portugal).
BDI: Vladimir Niyonkuru, David Habarugira, Hassan Hakizimana, Henry Mbazumutima (80.Christian Nduwimana), Valery Twite Nahayo (Cap), Floribert Tambwe Ndayisaba, Alain Ndizéyé (75.Faty Papy), Karim Nizigiyimana, Fuadi Ndayisenga (30.Claude Nahimana), Dugary Ndabashinzé, Yamin Selema Ndikumana. Trainer: Adel Amrouche (Algeria).
Goals: 1-0 Beli Moumouni Dagano (23 penalty), 2-0 Beli Moumouni Dagano (44 penalty).
Cautions: Dugary Ndabashinzé.
Sent off: Yamin Selema Ndikumana (20).

14.06.2008, Stade Linité, Victoria; Attendance: 1,000
Referee: Rajindraparsad Seechurn (Mauritius)
SEYCHELLES - BURKINA FASO   **2-3(0-1)**
SEY: Eric Nelson Sopha, Nigel Freminot (86.Michel Joubert), Steve Henriette, Alex Nibourette, Bernard St. Ange (81.Achilles Henriette), Don Annacoura, Denis Barbe (Cap), David Dorby, Henny Dufrene, Lorenzo Mathiot (66.Jonathan Bibi), Philip Zialor. Trainer: Jan Mak (Holland).
BFA: Daouda Diakité, Paul Kéba Koulibaly, Mamadou Tall, Mady Saïdou Panandétiguiri, Charles Kaboré, Mahamoudou Kéré (Cap), Abdoul Aziz Nikiéma (50.Jonathan Pitroipa), Soumaïla Tassembédo, Narcisse Yaméogo, Beli Moumouni Dagano (84.Florent Rouamba), Issouf Ouattara (67.Yssouf Koné). Trainer: Paulo Jorge Rebelo Duarte (Portugal).
Goals: 0-1 Beli Moumouni Dagano (25), 1-1 Philip Zialor (47), 2-1 Don Annacoura (52), 2-2 Beli Moumouni Dagano (57), 2-3 Beli Moumouni Dagano (78).
Cautions: Mady Saïdou Panandétiguiri.

15.06.2008, Prince „Louis Rwagasore" Stadium, Bujumbura; Attendance: 7,000
Referee: Jerome Damon (South Africa)
BURUNDI - TUNISIA   **0-1(0-0)**
BDI: Vladimir Niyonkuru, David Habarugira, Hassan Hakizimana, Henry Mbazumutima, Valery Twite Nahayo, Floribert Tambwe Ndayisaba, Alain Ndizéyé (52.Faty Papy), Karim Nizigiyimana, Fuadi Ndayisenga (73.Jean-Paul Habarugira), Kassim Bizimana (59.Claude Nahimana), Dugary Ndabashinzé. Trainer: Adel Amrouche (Algeria).
TUN: Aymen Mathlouthi Balbouli, Fatah Garbi, Saïf Ghezal, Radhi Ben Abdelmajid Jaïdi (Cap), Chadi Hammami, Jawhar Mnari, Mohamed Ali Nafkha, Tijani Belaid (56.Youssef Mouihbi), Mehdi Ben Dhifallah (77.Wissem Ben Yahia), Chaouki Ben Saada, Issam Jemâa (65.Hichem Essifi). Trainer: Roger Lemerre (France).
Goal: 0-1 Radhi Ben Abdelmajid Jaïdi (70).
Cautions: Alain Ndizéyé, Valery Twite Nahayo, Jean-Paul Habarugira / Radhi Ben Abdelmajid Jaïdi, Saïf Ghezal, Mehdi Ben Dhifallah.

21.06.2008, Stade du 4-Août, Ouagadougou; Attendance: 12,500
Referee: Joseph Lamptey (Ghana)
BURKINA FASO - SEYCHELLES 4-1(2-1)
BFA: Daouda Diakité, Bakary Koné, Paul Kéba Koulibaly, Mamadou Tall, Charles Kaboré, Soumaïla Tassembédo (79.Yssouf Koné), Mahamoudou Kéré (Cap), Narcisse Yaméogo (87.Bureima Maïga), Jonathan Pitroipa, Beli Moumouni Dagano, Issouf Ouattara (69.Alain Traoré). Trainer: Paulo Jorge Rebelo Duarte (Portugal).
SEY: Eric Nelson Sopha (Cap), Godfrey Denis Armel (81.Nelson Laurence), Jonathan Bibi (39.Bernard St. Ange), Nigel Freminot, Steve Henriette, Alex Nibourette, Neddy Rose, Henny Dufrene, Achilles Henriette, Colin Laporte, Michel Joubert (88.David Dorby). Trainer: Jan Mak (Holland).
Goals: 1-0 Charles Kaboré (21), 2-0 Mahamoudou Kéré (28), 2-1 Bernard St. Ange (44), 3-1 Issouf Ouattara (54), 4-1 Yssouf Koné (89).
Cautions: Jonathan Pitroipa / Godfrey Denis Armel, Nigel Freminot.

21.06.2008, Stade 7 November, Radès; Attendance: 6,000
Referee: Yasser Abn El Raaof Younis (Egypt)
TUNISIA - BURUNDI 2-1(2-1)
TUN: Aymen Mathlouthi Balbouli, Saïf Ghezal, Yassin Mikari (83.Fatah Garbi), Radhouène Felhi, Chadi Hammami, Jawhar Mnari (Cap), Mohamed Ali Nafkha, Mehdi Ben Dhifallah (70.Hichem Essifi), Chaouki Ben Saada, Mohamed Amine Chermiti (59.Tijani Belaid), Issam Jemâa. Trainer: Roger Lemerre (France).
BDI: Janvier Ndikuman, David Habarugira, Hassan Hakizimana, Henry Mbazumutima (80.Jean-Paul Habarugira), Valery Twite Nahayo, Floribert Tambwe Ndayisaba, Karim Nizigiyimana, Fuadi Ndayisenga (20.Vladimir Niyonkuru), Faty Papy, Claude Nahimana (88.Christian Nduwimana), Dugary Ndabashinzé. Trainer: Adel Amrouche (Algeria).
Goals: 1-0 Chaouki Ben Saada (30 penalty), 2-0 Issam Jemâa (44), 2-1 Henry Mbazumutima (45).
Cautions: Chadi Hammami / David Habarugira, Valery Twite Nahayo, Hassan Hakizimana.
Sent off: Janvier Ndikumana (20).

06.09.2008, Stade Linité, Victoria; Attendance: 3,000
Referee: Kokou Djaoupé (Togo)
SEYCHELLES - BURUNDI 1-2(0-1)
SEY: Ricky Rose, Godfrey Denis Armel (64.Lorenzo Mathiot), Jonathan Bibi, Nigel Freminot, Alex Nibourette, Neddy Rose (83.Andy Mougal), Don Annacoura, Denis Barbe (Cap), David Dorby, Henny Dufrene, Rennick Esther (46.Philip Zialor). Trainer: Ulrich Mathiot.
BDI: Vladimir Niyonkuru, David Habarugira, Henry Mbazumutima, Ismail Mutambara, Floribert Tambwe Ndayisaba, Alain Ndizéyé (Cap) (71.Fidèle Nibumona), Emmanuel Ngama (77.Mohamed Saidi), Karim Nizigiyimana, Sadiki Nsengiyumva, Faty Papy, Claude Nahimana. Trainer: Adel Amrouche (Algeria).
Goals: 0-1 Henry Mbazumutima (28), 0-2 Claude Nahimana (58), 1-2 Philip Zialor (63).
Cautions: Don Annacoura, Denis Barbe / Alain Ndizéyé, Faty Papy.

06.09.2008, Stade du 4-Août, Ouagadougou; Attendance: 10,000
Referee: Mathews Katjimune (Namibia)
BURKINA FASO - TUNISIA 0-0
BFA: Daouda Diakité, Bakary Koné, Paul Kéba Koulibaly (60.Issouf Ouattara), Mamadou Tall, Madi Saidou Panandétiguiri, Charles Kaboré, Mahamoudou Kéré (Cap), Narcisse Yaméogo, Jonathan Pitroipa (90.Joël Venceslas Kouassi), Beli Moumouni Dagano, Patrick Zoundi (79.Yssouf Koné). Trainer: Paulo Jorge Rebelo Duarte (Portugal).
TUN: Aymen Mathlouthi Balbouli, Yamen Ben Zekry, Saïf Ghezal, Karim Haggui (Cap), Anis Boussaidi, Hocine Ragued, Tijani Belaid (74.Chaouki Ben Saada), Fahid Ben Khalfallah, Anis Boujelbene (82.Jawhar Mnari), Youssef Mouihbi (43.Mejdi Traoui), Mohamed Selliti. Trainer: Humberto Manuel Jesus Coelho (Portugal).
Cautions: Madi Saidou Panandétiguiri / Mohamed Selliti, Karim Haggui.

11.10.2008, Stade Olympique 7 Novembre, Radès; Attendance: 10,000
Referee: Badara Diatta (Senegal)
TUNISIA - SEYCHELLES **5-0(4-0)**
TUN: Aymen Mathlouthi Balbouli, Saïf Ghezal, Karim Haggui (Cap), Saber Ben Frej, Yassin Mikari, Hocine Ragued, Tijani Belaid, Fahid Ben Khalfallah (61.Chaouki Ben Saada), Hichem Essifi (69.Mejdi Mosrati), Wissem Ben Yahia (81.Oussama Darragi), Issam Jemâa. Trainer: Humberto Manuel Jesus Coelho (Portugal).
SEY: Eric Nelson Sopha (Cap), Godfrey Denis Armel, Bertrand Esther, Nigel Freminot, Alex Nibourette, Neddy Rose, Denis Barbe (Cap), Verna Rose (46.Jonathan Bibi), Colin Esther, Lorenzo Mathiot (53.Andy Mougal), Philip Zialor (70.Nelson Laurence). Trainer: Ulrich Mathiot.
Goals: 1-0 Hichem Essifi (5), 2-0 Yassin Mikari (18), 3-0 Saber Ben Frej (20), 4-0 Fahid Ben Khalfallah (43), 5-0 Hichem Essifi (68).
Cautions: Neddy Rose.

12.10.2008, Stade „Prince Louis Rwagasore", Bujumbura; Attendance: 10,000
Referee: Muhmed Ssegonga (Uganda)
BURUNDI - BURKINA FASO **1-3(1-1)**
BDI: Vladimir Niyonkuru, David Habarugira, Hassan Hakizimana, Henry Mbazumutima, Ismail Mutambara, Valery Twite Nahayo (Cap), Floribert Tambwe Ndayisaba (64.Alain Ndizéyé), Dugary Ndabashinzé (64.Karim Nizigiyimana), Faty Papy, Abdallah Irambona (34.Claude Nahimana), Yamin Selema Ndikumana. Trainer: Adel Amrouche (Algeria).
BFA: Daouda Diakité, Ibrahim Gnanou (26.Mady Saïdou Panandétiguiri), Joël Venceslas Kouassi, Paul Kéba Koulibaly, Salif Dianda, Charles Kaboré, Florent Rouamba, Soumaïla Tassembédo, Issouf Ouattara (54.Jonathan Pitroipa), Aristide Bancé (59.Patrick Zoundi), Beli Moumouni Dagano (Cap). Trainer: Paulo Jorge Rebelo Duarte (Portugal).
Goals: 0-1 Aristide Bancé (18), 1-1 Claude Nahimana (43), 1-2 Beli Moumouni Dagano (54), 1-3 Beli Moumouni Dagano (76).
Cautions: Valery Twite Nahayo, Ismail Mutambara / Issouf Ouattara.

GROUP 10

01.06.2008	Bamako	Mali - Congo	4-2(3-1)
07.06.2008	N'Djamena	Chad - Mali	1-2(1-2)
08.06.2008	Brazzaville	Congo - Sudan	1-0(0-0)
14.06.2008	N'Djamena	Chad - Congo	2-1(1-1)
14.06.2008	Khartoum	Sudan - Mali	3-2(1-0)
22.06.2008	Brazzaville	Congo - Chad	2-0(1-0)
22.06.2008	Bamako	Mali - Sudan	3-0(1-0)
06.09.2008	Cairo (EGY)	Sudan - Chad	1-2(0-1)
07.09.2008	Brazzaville	Congo - Mali	1-0(0-0)
10.09.2008	Cairo (EGY)	Chad - Sudan	1-3(1-1)
11.10.2008	Bamako	Mali - Chad	2-1(1-0)
11.10.2008	Omdurman	Sudan - Congo	2-0(1-0)

FINAL STANDINGS

1. Mali	6	4	0	2	13 - 8	12
2. Sudan	6	3	0	3	9 - 9	9
3. Congo	6	3	0	3	7 - 8	9
4. Chad	6	2	0	4	7 - 11	6

01.06.2008, Stade „26 Mars", Bamako; Attendance: 40,000
Referee: Kacem Bennaceur (Tunisia)
MALI - CONGO **4-2(3-1)**
MLI: Mahamadou Sidibé, Adama Coulibaly, Adama Tamboura, Cédric Kanté, Drissa Diakité, Mahamadou Diarra (Cap), Mohamed Lamine Sissoko Gillan (75.Bakary Diakité), Soumaïla Coulibaly (70.Mamadou Bagayoko), Mamadou Diallo (80.Mahamane El Hadji Traoré), Seydou Keïta, Frédéric Oumar Kanouté. Trainer: Stephen Okechukwu Keshi (Nigeria).
CGO: Barel Morial Mouko, Bruce Abdoulaye, Christel Kimbembe, Leonce Kevin Andzouana, Fabry Makita-Passy, Oscar Ewolo, Gervais Batota, Denis Tsoumou, Armel Mamouna-Ossila (60.Wilfrid Urbain Elvis Endzanga), Dyzaiss-Lys Mouithys Mickalad, Harris Brandt Tchilimbou (46.Jean-Vivien Bantsimba). Trainer: Ivica Todorov (Serbia).
Goals: 1-0 Seydou Keïta (2), 1-1 Dyzaiss-Lys Mouithys Mickalad (5), 2-1 Adama Coulibaly (32), 3-i Soumaïla Coulibaly (42), 4-1 Seydou Keïta (61), 4-2 Dyzaiss-Lys Mouithys Mickalad (74).
Cautions: Mohamed Lamine Sissoko Gillan, Drissa Diakité / Fabry Makita-Passy.

07.06.2008, Stade Omnisports „Idriss Mahamat Ouya", N'Djamena; Attendance: 15,000
Referee: Crespin Aguidissou (Benin)
CHAD - MALI **1-2(1-2)**
CHA: Armel Koulara, Mondesir Alladjim, Sitamadji Allarassem, Leger Djimé, Syriakata Hassan, Cesar Madalangue (58.Djimalde Dossengar), Djondja Jules Mbairemadji, Nekiambe Marius Mbaiam (77.Mahamat Alhadj), Hillaire Kedigui, Misdongarde Betoligar, Ezechiel Ndouasel (66.Ahmat Brahim). Trainer: Natoltiga Okalah.
MLI: Soumaïla Diakité, Adama Coulibaly, Cédric Kanté, Adama Tamboura, Drissa Diakité, Mahamadou Diarra (Cap), Soumaïla Coulibaly, Seydou Keïta, Mamadou Bagayoko (75.Mahamadou Dissa), Mamadou Diallo (63.Ténéma N'Diaye), Frédéric Oumar Kanouté. Trainer: Stephen Okechukwu Keshi (Nigeria).
Goals: 0-1 Frédéric Oumar Kanouté (5), 0-2 Frédéric Oumar Kanouté (21), 1-2 Hillaire Kedigui (37).
Cautions: Ezechiel Ndouasel, Djondja Jules Mbairemadji, Syriakata Hassan, Misdongarde Betoliga / Soumaïla Diakité, Mamadou Diallo, Adama Tamboura, Mahamadou Diarra.
Sent off: Djondja Jules Mbairemadji (90+1).

08.06.2008, Centre Sportif „Alphonse Massamba", Brazzaville; Attendance: 25,000
Referee: Sule Mana (Nigeria)
CONGO - SUDAN   **1-0(0-0)**
CGO: Barel Morial Mouko, Bruce Abdoulaye, Christel Kimbembe, Leonce Kevin Andzouana, Fabry Makita-Passy, Denis Tsoumou, Gervais Batota, Delvin Chanel Ndinga, Jean-Vivien Bantsimba (41.Ladislas Douniama), Armel Mamouna-Ossila (46.Wilfrid Urbain Elvis Endzanga), Dyzaiss-Lys Mouithys Mickalad (84.Jean-Claude Mpassy-Nzoumba). Trainer: Ivica Todorov (Serbia).
SUD: Mustafa Hafez, Ahmed Adam Al Basha, Omer Mohamed Bakhit, Mohamed Osman Tahir (53.Mudathir El Tahir), Amir Damar Koku, Mousa Al Tayeb, Mohammed Ali El Khider, Alaa Eldin Yousif Ahmed Hado, Haitham Mostafa Ahmed Karar, Saifeldin Ali Idris Masawi, Haytham Kamal Tambal. Trainer: Mohammed Abdallah Mazda.
Goal: 1-0 Wilfrid Urbain Elvis Endzanga (70).
Cautions: Mohammed Ali El Khider, Omer Mohamed Bakhit.

14.06.2008, Stade Omnisports „Idriss Mahamat Ouya", N'Djamena; Attendance: 8,000
Referee: Noumandiez Doué (Ivory Coast)
CHAD - CONGO   **2-1(1-1)**
CHA: Armel Koulara, Mondesir Alladjim (39.Djideo Abdoulaye), Sitamadji Allarassem, Armand Djérabé, Leger Djimé, Djimalde Dossengar, Syriakata Hassan, Nekiambe Marius Mbaiam, Hillaire Kedigui (56.Esaie Djikoloum), Misdongarde Betoligar, Ezechiel Ndouasel (76.Ahmat Brahim). Trainer: Natoltiga Okalah.
CGO: Barel Morial Mouko, Bruce Abdoulaye, Christel Kimbembe, Leonce Kevin Andzouana, Fabry Makita-Passy, Oscar Ewolo, Gervais Batota (73.Armel Mamouna-Ossila), Denis Tsoumou, Wilfrid Urbain Elvis Endzanga, Harris Brandt Tchilimbou (78.Edson Dico Minga), Dyzaiss-Lys Mouithys Mickalad (52.Ladislas Douniama). Trainer: Ivica Todorov (Serbia).
Goals: 0-1 Gervais Batota (30), 1-1 Hillaire Kedigui (44 penalty), 2-1 Syriakata Hassan (48).
Cautions: Syriakata Hassan, Djimalde Dossengar, Misdongarde Betoligar / Bruce Abdoulaye, Denis Tsoumou.

14.06.2008, Al Hilal Stadium, Khartoum; Attendance: 15,000
Referee: Essam Abd El Fatah (Egypt)
SUDAN - MALI   **3-2(1-0)**
SUD: Mustafa Hafez, Ahmed Adam Al Basha (54.Mohamed Osman Tahir), Omer Mohamed Bakhit, Mudathir El Tahir (78.Nasr Eldin Omer El Shigail), Amir Damar Koku, Mousa Al Tayeb, Mohammed Ali El Khider, Alaa Eldin Yousif Ahmed Hado, Haitham Mostafa Ahmed Karar, Saifeldin Ali Idris Masawi, Alaa Eldin Hado Babiker (69.Haytham Kamal Tambal). Trainer: Mohammed Abdallah Mazda.
MLI: Soumaïla Diakité, Adama Coulibaly, Cédric Kanté, Adama Tamboura, Drissa Diakité, Mahamadou Diarra (Cap), Soumaïla Coulibaly (24.Bakary Diakité), Seydou Keïta, Mamadou Bagayoko (58.Mahamadou Dissa), Mahamane El Hadji Traoré (72.Djibril Sidibé), Frédéric Oumar Kanouté. Trainer: Stephen Okechukwu Keshi (Nigeria).
Goals: 1-0 Alaa Eldin Yousif Ahmed Hado (45+1), 1-1 Frédéric Oumar Kanouté (63), 2-1 Mohamed Osman Tahir (72 penalty), 3-1 Haytham Kamal Tambal (80), 3-2 Frédéric Oumar Kanouté (90+4).
Cautions: Amir Damar Koku, Omer Mohamed Bakhit / Soumaïla Diakité, Drissa Diakité.

22.06.2008, Centre Sportif „Alphonse Massamba", Brazzaville; Attendance: 8,000
Referee: Abdou Diouf (Senegal)
CONGO - CHAD   **2-0(1-0)**
CGO: Barel Morial Mouko, Bruce Abdoulaye, Christel Kimbembe (46.Theddy Ongoly), Leonce Kevin Andzouana, Fabry Makita-Passy, Oscar Ewolo, Franchel Ibara, Denis Tsoumou (43.Delvin Chanel Ndinga), Ladislas Douniama (54.Harris Brandt Tchilimbou), Wilfrid Urbain Elvis Endzanga, Dyzaiss-Lys Mouithys Mickalad. Trainer: Ivica Todorov (Serbia).
CHA: Armel Koulara, Mondesir Alladjim, Sitamadji Allarassem, Armand Djérabé, Leger Djimé (74.Ahmat Brahim), Djimalde Dossengar, Djideo Abdoulaye (57.Esaie Djikoloum), Nekiambe Marius

Mbaiam, David Mbaihouloum (87.Karl Marx Barthelemy), Hillaire Kedigui, Ezechiel Ndouasel. Trainer: Natoltiga Okalah.
Goals: 1-0 Dyzaiss-Lys Mouithys Mickalad (14), 2-0 Franchel Ibara (64).
Cautions: Wilfrid Urbain Elvis Endzanga, Franchel Ibara, Leonce Kevin Andzouana / Nekiambe Marius Mbaiam, David Mbaihoulou, Hillaire Kedigui.

22.06.2008, Stade 26 mars, Bamako; Attendance: 25,000
Referee: Noumandiez Doué (Ivory Coast)
MALI - SUDAN   **3-0(1-0)**
MLI: Mahamadou Sidibé, Adama Coulibaly, Moussa Coulibaly, Souleymane Diamouténé, Amadou Sidibé, Mahamadou Diarra (Cap), Seydou Keïta, Djibril Sidibé (80.Kalifa Cissé), Souleymane Dembélé (80.Mamadou Diallo), Mahamane El Hadji Traoré, Frédéric Oumar Kanouté. Trainer: Stephen Okechukwu Keshi (Nigeria).
SUD: Mustafa Hafez, Nasr Eldin Omer El Shigail, Ammar Ramadan Abdelaziz Mirig, Mudathir El Tahir (31.Mohamed Osman Tahir), Mousa Al Tayeb, Hassan Sayed (65.Anas Farah), Mohammed Ali El Khider, Alaa Eldin Yousif Ahmed Hado, Haitham Mostafa Ahmed Karar, Saifeldin Ali Idris Masawi, Haytham Kamal Tambal. Trainer: Mohammed Abdallah Mazda.
Goals: 1-0 Frédéric Oumar Kanouté (23), 2-0 Seydou Keïta (58), 3-0 Seydou Keïta (66).
Cautions: Seydou Keïta / Saifeldin Ali Idris Masawi, Ammar Ramadan Abdelaziz Mirig, Mousa Al Tayeb.

06.09.2008, Military Academy Stadium, Cairo (Egypt); Attendance: 4,000
Referee: Aouaz Trabelsi (Tunisia)
SUDAN - CHAD   **1-2(0-1)**
SUD: Elmuez Mahgoub Abdalla, Bader Eldin Abdalla Eldoud Galag, Omer Mohamed Bakhit (66.Ahmed Adil), Mousa Al Tayeb, Mugahid Ahmed Mohammed (57.Hamouda Ahmed El Bashir), Mohammed Ali El Khider, Khalid Hassan Ali Jolit, Haitham Mostafa Ahmed Karar, Faisal Agab Sido, Saifeldin Ali Idris Masawi (46.Alaa Eldin Yousif Ahmed Hado), Haytham Kamal Tambal. Trainer: Mohammed Abdallah Mazda.
CHA: Armel Koulara, Mondesir Alladjim, Sitamadji Allarassem, Armand Djérabé, Leger Djimé, Djimalde Dossengar, Syriakata Hassan, Ahmat Brahim (58.Mahamat Saleh Habib), Nekiambe Marius Mbaiam (81.Esaie Djikoloum), Azrack-Yassine Mahamat, Sidick Aboubacar. Trainer: Natoltiga Okalah.
Goals: 0-1 Nekiambe Marius Mbaiam (29), 1-1 Haytham Kamal Tambal (77), 1-2 Syriakata Hassan (81).
Cautions: Mohammed Ali El Khider, Alaa Eldin Yousif Ahmed Hado, Khalid Hassan Ali Jolit / Azrack-Yassine Mahamat.

07.09.2008, Centre Sportif „Alphonse Massamba", Brazzaville; Attendance: 16,000
Referee: Djamel Haimoudi (Algeria)
CONGO - MALI   **1-0(0-0)**
CGO: Barel Morial Mouko, Bruce Abdoulaye, Francis N'Ganga, Brunel Okana-Stasi (79.Frabrice N'Guessi Ondama), Fabry Makita-Passy, Veijeany Christopher Samba, Oscar Ewolo, Franchel Ibara, Denis Tsoumou (46.Delvin Chanel Ndinga), Rolf-Christel Guié-Mien (72.Wilfrid Urbain Elvis Endzanga), Dyzaiss-Lys Mouithys Mickalad. Trainer: Ivica Todorov (Serbia).
MLI: Mahamadou Sidibé, Adama Coulibaly, Souleymane Diamouténé, Aboubacar Tambadou, Seydou Keïta, Soumaïla Coulibaly (46.Modibo Maïga), Amadou Sidibé, Mohamed Lamine Sissoko Gillan, Mamadou Diallo (72.Cheik Tidiane Diabaté), Mahamadou Diarra (Cap), Mamady Sidibé (79.Djibril Sidibé). Trainer: Stephen Okechukwu Keshi (Nigeria).
Goal: 1-0 Wilfrid Urbain Elvis Endzanga (87).
Cautions: Bruce Abdoulaye, Delvin Chanel Ndinga / Aboubacar Tambadou.

10.09.2008, Stade Omnisports „Idriss Mahamat Ouya", N'Djamena; Attendance: 10,000
Referee: Badara Diatta (Senegal)
CHAD - SUDAN **1-3(1-1)**
CHA: Armel Koulara, Mondesir Alladjim, Sitamadji Allarassem, Armand Djérabé, Leger Djimé, Djimalde Dossengar, Syriakata Hassan (79.David Mbaihouloum), Cesar Madalangue (63.Sidick Aboubacar), Nekiambe Marius Mbaiam, Azrack-Yassine Mahamat, Ezechiel Ndouasel (86.Hillaire Kedigui). Trainer: Natoltiga Okalah.
SUD: Elmuez Mahgoub Abdalla, Ahmed Adil (58.Haytham Kamal Tambal), Bader Eldin Abdalla Eldoud Galag, Amir Damar Koku, Mousa Al Tayeb, Khalid Hassan Ali Jolit, Alaa Eldin Yousif Ahmed Hado, Haitham Mostafa Ahmed Karar, Mudathir El Tahir (65.Nasr Eldin Omer El Shigail), Faisal Agab Sido (86.Mugahid Ahmed Mohammed), Saifeldin Ali Idris Masawi. Trainer: Mohammed Abdallah Mazda.
Goals: 0-1 Ahmed Adil (4), 1-1 Leger Djimé (34), 1-2 Faisal Agab Sido (48 penalty), 1-3 Saifeldin Ali Idris Masawi Idris Masawi (76).
Cautions: Ezechiel Ndouasel, Sitamadji Allarassem, Sidick Aboubacar / Alaa Eldin Yousif Ahmed Hado, Amir Damar Koku, Saifeldin Ali Idris Masawi.
Sent off: Nekiambe Marius Mbaiam (90+2).

11.10.2008, Stade 26 mars, Bamako; Attendance: 40,000
Referee: Yakhouba Keïta (Guinea)
MALI - CHAD **2-1(1-0)**
MLI: Mahamadou Sidibé, Adama Coulibaly (55.Cédric Kanté), Souleymane Diamouténé, Adama Tamboura, Drissa Diakité, Mahamadou Diarra (Cap) (28.Sidi Yaya Keïta), Soumaïla Coulibaly, Seydou Keïta, Mohamed Lamine Sissoko Gillan, Ténéma N'Diaye, Frédéric Oumar Kanouté (67.Cheick Tidiane Diabaté). Trainer: Stephen Okechukwu Keshi (Nigeria).
CHA: Armel Koulara, Mondesir Alladjim, Sitamadji Allarassem, Armand Djérabé, Leger Djimé, Djimalde Dossengar, Syriakata Hassan, Azrack-Yassine Mahamat (70.Tigaye Masrabaye), Mahamat Alhadj (88.Sidick Aboubacar), Mahamat Saleh Habib (59.Hamadou Jules), Misdongarde Betoligar. Trainer: Natoltiga Okalah.
Goals: 1-0 Sidi Yaya Keïta (44), 1-1 Betolngar Misdongarde (64), 2-1 Sidi Yaya Keïta (83).
Cautions: Mohamed Lamine Sissoko Gillan, Cheick Tidiane Diabaté / Djimalde Dossengar, Tigaye Masrabaye.

11.10.2008, Al Merreikh Stadium, Ondurman; Attendance: 27,000
Referee: Jamel Ambaya (Libya)
SUDAN - CONGO **2-0(1-0)**
SUD: Elmuez Mahgoub Abdalla, Omer Mohamed Bakhit (*sent off 66*), Bader Eldin Abdalla Eldoud Galag, Mousa Al Tayeb, Mohammed Ali El Khider, Haitham Mostafa Ahmed Karar, Rtshard Justin Lado, Mohamed Osman Tahir, Mugahid Ahmed Mohammed (46.Nasr Eldin Omer El Shigail), Faisal Agab Sido, Haytham Kamal Tambal (70.Mudathir El Tahir). Trainer: Mohammed Abdallah Mazda.
CGO: Barel Morial Mouko, Patrick Mouaya, Francis N'Ganga, Brunel Okana-Stasi (66.Franky Sembolo), Fabry Makita-Passy, Prince Oniangue, Veijeany Christopher Samba, Oscar Ewolo (35.Delvin Chanel Ndinga), Christ Malonga-Nsayi (79.Leonce Kevin Andzouana), Rolf-Christel Guié-Mien, Dyzaiss-Lys Mouithys Mickalad. Trainer: Ivica Todorov (Serbia).
Goals: 1-0
Cautions: Rtshard Justin Lado, Omer Mohamed Bakhit / Barel Morial Mouko.
Sent off: Dyzaiss-Lys Mouithys Mickalad (51), Omer Mohamed Bakhit (66).

GROUP 11

31.05.2008	Accra (GHA)	Togo - Zambia	1-0(1-0)
08.06.2008	Lobamba	Swaziland - Togo	2-1(0-0)
15.06.2008	Lobamba	Swaziland - Zambia	0-0
21.06.2008	Chililabombwe	Zambia - Swaziland	1-0(0-0)
10.09.2008	Chililabombwe	Zambia - Togo	1-0(1-0)
11.10.2008	Accra (GHA)	Togo - Swaziland	6-0(3-0)

FINAL STANDINGS

1. **Zambia**	4	2	1	1	2 - 1	7
2. **Togo**	4	2	0	2	8 - 3	6
3. Swaziland	4	1	1	2	2 - 8	4

31.05.2008, Ohene Djan Sports Stadium, Accra (Ghana); Attendance: 15,000
Referee: Lassina Paré (Burkina Faso)
TOGO - ZAMBIA **1-0(1-0)**
TOG: Cédric Mensah, Éric Akoto (34.Komlan Amewou), Abdoul Gafarou Mamah, Daré Nibombé, Komi Massamesso Tchangai (27.Jafar Djabouro Moumouni), Yao Mawuko Sènaya, Jacques Alaixys Romao, Kwami Komlan Kacla Akoete Eninful, Sheyi Emmanuel Adebayor, Robert Malm (74.Yao Séyram Junior Sènaya), Adékambi Olufadé. Trainer: Henri Stambouli (France).
ZAM: Kennedy Mweene, Chintu Kampamba, William Chinyama, Joseph Musonda, Billy Mwanza, Isaac Chansa, Francis Kasonde (64.James Chamanga), Felix Katongo, Christopher Katongo (Cap), Rodgers Kola (46.Emmanuel Mayuka), Clifford Mulenga. Trainer: Hervé Renard (France).
Goal: 1-0 Adékambi Olufadé (16).
Cautions: Felix Katongo, Isaac Chansa, Billy Mwanza.
Sent off: Isaac Chansa (90).

08.06.2008, Somholo National Stadium, Lobamba; Attendance: 5,819
Referee: Jean-Claude Niyongabo (Burundi)
SWAZILAND - TOGO **2-1(0-0)**
SWZ: Njabuliso Simelane, Themba Manana (54.Absalom Dlamini), Zakhele Manyatsi, Mxolisi Mthethwa, Dennis Fakudze, Collen Salelwako (90+1.Phinda Dlamini), Tony Thulani Tsabedze (Cap), Siza Dlamini, Sihawu Dlamini, Dennis Mcebo Masina, Gcina Mazibuko. Trainer: Ephraim Mashaba (South Africa).
TOG: Cédric Mensah, Abdoul Gafarou Mamah, Daré Nibombé, Komi Massamesso Tchangai, Jacques Alaixys Romao, Komlan Amewou, Kwami Komlan Kacla Akoete Eninful (27.Yao Mawuko Sènaya), Moustapha Salifou, Yao Séyram Junior Sènaya (77.Jonathan Ayité), Sheyi Emmanuel Adebayor, Adékambi Olufadé. Trainer: Henri Stambouli (France).
Goals: 1-0 Siza Dlamini (55), 2-0 Collen Salelwako (73), 2-1 Adékambi Olufadé (88).
Cautions: Absalom Dlamini, Tony Thulani Tsabedze / Kwami Komlan Kacla Akoete Eninful, Abdoul Gafarou Mamah.

15.06.2008, Somholo National Stadium, Lobamba; Attendance: 7,462
Referee: Alex Kotey (Ghana)
SWAZILAND - ZAMBIA **0-0**
SWZ: Njabuliso Simelane, Zakhele Manyatsi, Mxolisi Mthethwa, Dennis Fakudze (Cap), Raphael Ntimane, Collen Salelwako (56.Phinda Dlamini), Tony Thulani Tsabedze, Siza Dlamini, Sihawu Dlamini, Dennis Mcebo Masina (89.Malungisa Dlamini), Gcina Mazibuko (80.Absalom Dlamini). Trainer: Ephraim Mashaba (South Africa).
ZAM: Kennedy Mweene, Chintu Kampamba, William Chinyama, Joseph Musonda, Billy Mwanza, James Chamanga (78.Rodgers Kola), Felix Katongo, Christopher Katongo (Cap), Emmanuel Mayuka, Stophira Sunzu (40.Henry Nyambe Mulenga), Clifford Mulenga (62.Jacob Mulenga). Trainer: Hervé Renard (France).

21.06.2008, Konkola Stadium, Chililabombwe; Attendance: 14,458
Referee: Kenias Marange (Zimbabwe)
ZAMBIA - SWAZILAND   **1-0(0-0)**
ZAM: Kennedy Mweene, Chintu Kampamba, Joseph Musonda, Billy Mwanza, Henry Nyambe Mulenga (57.Rodgers Kola), Isaac Chansa (46.Clifford Mulenga), Rainford Kalaba, Felix Katongo, Christopher Katongo (Cap), Stophira Sunzu (73.James Chamanga), Jacob Mulenga. Trainer: Hervé Renard (France).
SWZ: Njabuliso Simelane, Phinda Dlamini (70.Absalom Dlamini), Mxolisi Mthethwa, Zakhele Manyatsi, Dennis Fakudze (Cap), Raphael Ntimane, Tony Thulani Tsabedze (73.Malungisa Dlamini), Siza Dlamini, Sihawu Dlamini, Dennis Mcebo Masina, Gcina Mazibuko (46.Lwazi Maziya). Trainer: Ephraim Mashaba (South Africa).
Goal: 1-0 Christopher Katongo (86 penalty).
Cautions: Chintu Kampamba / Siza Dlamini.
Sent off: Zakhele Manyatsi.

10.09.2008, Konkola Stadium, Chililabombwe; Attendance: 10,500
Referee: Jerome Damon (South Africa)
ZAMBIA - TOGO   **1-0(1-0)**
ZAM: Kennedy Mweene, Hichani Himoonde, Joseph Musonda, Elijah Tana, Noah Sikombe Chivuta, Kebby Hachipuka (85.Chintu Kampamba), Rainford Kalaba, Felix Katongo, Christopher Katongo (Cap), Jacob Mulenga (46.James Chamanga), Collins Ntofontofo Mbezuma (76.Rodgers Kola). Trainer: Hervé Renard (France).
TOG: Cédric Mensah (54.Abdoul Nassirou Omouroun), Serge Ognadon Akakpo, Abdoul Gafarou Mamah, Daré Nibombé (Cap), Ousseni Labo (75.Yao Mawuko Sènaya), Jacques Alaixys Romao, Komlan Amewou, Kwami Komlan Kacla Akoete Eninful, Moustapha Salifou, Alikem Segbefia (61.Arafat Djako), Yao Séyram Junior Sènaya. Trainer: Kodjovi Mawuéna.
Goal: 1-0 Felix Katongo (31).
Cautions: Kebby Hachipuka, Noah Sikombe Chivuta / Yao Séyram Junior Sènaya.

11.10.2008, Ohene Djan Sports Stadium, Accra (Ghana); Attendance: 8,000
Referee: Raphael Divine Evehe (Cameroon)
TOGO - SWAZILAND   **6-0(3-0)**
TOG: Kossi Agassa, Serge Ognadon Akakpo, Abdoul Gafarou Mamah, Daré Nibombé, Ousseni Labo, Jacques Alaixys Romao, Moustapha Salifou (84.Sapol Mani), Mamam Cherif Touré, Sheyi Emmanuel Adebayor, Floyd Ayité (86.Komlan Amewou), Adékambi Olufadé (83.Thomas Dossevi). Trainer: Kodjovi Mawuéna.
SWZ: Njabuliso Simelane, Phinda Dlamini, Mxolisi Mthethwa, Mlungisi Ngubane (5.Lwazi Maziya), Dennis Fakudze (Cap), Raphael Ntimane, Mfanufikile Ndzimande, Tony Thulani Tsabedze, Sihawu Dlamini, Dennis Mcebo Masina, Gcina Mazibuko (30.Malungisa Dlamini). Trainer: Ephraim Mashaba (South Africa).
Goals: 1-0 Moustapha Salifou (16), 2-0 Sheyi Emmanuel Adebayor (29), 3-0 Adékambi Olufadé (44), 4-0 Sheyi Emmanuel Adebayor (47), 5-0 Sheyi Emmanuel Adebayor (72), 6-0 Sheyi Emmanuel Adebayor (85).

31.05.2008	Blantyre	Malawi - Djibouti	8-1(2-1)
01.06.2008	Cairo	Egypt – D.R. Congo	2-1(0-1)
06.06.2008	Djibouti	Djibouti - Egypt	0-4(0-1)
08.06.2008	Kinshasa	D.R. Congo - Malawi	1-0(0-0)
13.06.2008	Djibouti	Djibouti - D.R. Congo	0-6(0-3)
14.06.2008	Blantyre	Malawi - Egypt	1-0(0-0)
22.06.2008	Kinshasa	D.R. Congo - Djibouti	5-1(2-0)
22.06.2008	Cairo	Egypt - Malawi	2-0(1-0)
05.09.2008	Djibouti	Djibouti - Malawi	0-3(0-1)
07.09.2008	Kinshasa	D.R. Congo - Egypt	0-1(0-1)
11.10.2008	Blantyre	Malawi - D.R. Congo	2-1(0-1)
12.10.2008	Cairo	Egypt - Djibouti	4-0(1-0)

FINAL STANDINGS

1. **Egypt**	6	5	0	1	13 - 2	15
2. **Malawi**	6	4	0	2	14 - 5	12
3. D.R. Congo	6	3	0	3	14 - 6	9
4. Djibouti	6	0	0	6	2 - 30	0

31.05.2008, Kamuzu Stadium, Blantyre; Attendance: 35,000
Referee: Mathews Katjimune (Namibia)
MALAWI - DJIBOUTI **8-1(2-1)**
MWI: Valence Kamzere, Elvis Bryson Kafoteka, Peter Mponda (Cap) (34.Joseph Kamwendo), Jacob Ngwira, James Sangala, Moses Chavula, Tawonga Chimodzi (57.Noel Mkandawire), Fisher Kenani Kondowe, Hellings Mwakasungula (58.Robert Ng'ambi), Russel Mwafulirwa, Essau Boxer Kanyenda. Trainer: Kinnah Phiri.
DJI: Ali Yassin, Daher Mohamed, Hassan Nour, Mahamood Omar (Cap), Daoud Wais, Hassan Ahmed (87.Hassan Khalif Ahmed), Miad Charmare, Ahmed Hassan Daher (59.Houssein Saad), Abchir Houssein, Meraneh Mohamed (41.Mohamed Liban), Said Riyad. Trainer: Mohamed Abar.
Goals: 1-0 Elvis Bryson Kafoteka (3), 2-0 Essau Boxer Kanyenda (19), 2-1 Ahmed Hassan Daher (23), 3-1 Essau Boxer Kanyenda (46), 4-1 Essau Boxer Kanyenda (48), 5-1 Joseph Kamwendo (66), 6-1 Moses Chavula (73), 7-1 Robert Ng'ambi (78), 8-1 Noel Mkandawire (83).
Cautions: Essau Boxer Kanyenda, Elvis Bryson Kafoteka, Hellings Mwakasungula, Joseph Kamwendo / Meraneh Mohamed, Abchir Houssein, Hassan Nour, Daoud Wais.

01.06.2008, International Stadium, Cairo; Attendance: 40,000
Referee: Rajindraparsad Seechurn (Mauritius)
EGYPT – D.R. CONGO **2-1(0-1)**
EGY: Essam Kamal Tawfik El-Hadary, Ahmed Al-Muhammadi (62.Ahmed Eid Abdel Malek), Mahmoud Fathallah, Hani Mohammed Said Zakaria, Wael Gomaa Kamel El Hooty, Ahmed Samir Farag (76.Abdel Aziz Tawfik), Hosny Abd Rabo Abd El Motaleb Ibrahim, Ahmed Hassan Kamel, Hossam El Sayed Ghaly (49.Mahmoud Abdel Razek Fadlallah „Shikabala"), Amr Hassan Zaki, Emad Mohamed Abd El Naby Ibrahim „Emad Motaeb". Trainer: Hassan Shehata.
COD: Robert Muteba Kidiaba, Gladys Bokese, Larrys Mabiala, Hérita N'Kongolo Ilunga, Rodrigue Dikaba, Youssouf Mulumbu (61.Cédric Mongongu), Tshiolola Tshinyama, Marcel Kimemba Mbayo (55.Serge Lofo Bongeli), Lomana Trésor LuaLua, Dieumerci Mbokani Bezua (67.Ngabu Yannick Bapupa), Shabani Christophe Nonda. Trainer: Patrice Neveu (France).
Goals: 0-1 Hérita N'Kongolo Ilunga (43), 1-1 Amr Hassan Zaki (69), 2-1 Ahmed Eid Abdel Malek (80).
Cautions: Marcel Kimemba Mbayo.

06.06.2008, „El Hadj Hassan Gouled" Stadium, Djibouti; Attendance: 6,000
Referee: Amanuel Eyob (Eritrea)
DJIBOUTI - EGYPT **0-4(0-1)**
DJI: Guedi Hassan, Aden Charmakeh, Daher Mohamed, Daoud Wais, Hassan Ahmed (37.Houssein Saad), Miad Charmare (Cap), Abchir Houssein (71.Hassan Mohamed), Ahmed Ibrahim, Meraneh Mohamed (47.Abdi Mohamed Elmi), Said Riyad, Hussein Yassin. Trainer: Mohamed Abar.
EGY: Essam Kamal Tawfik El-Hadary, Abdel Aziz Tawfik (44.Ahmed Eid Abdel Malek), Mahmoud Fathallah, Hani Mohammed Said Zakaria, Wael Gomaa Kamel El Hooty, Ahmed Samir Farag, Ahmed Hassan Kamel, Hosny Abd Rabo Abd El Motaleb Ibrahim, Mahmoud Abdel Razek Fadlallah „Shikabala", Mohamed Fadl Zahran (46.Ahmed Al-Muhammadi), Amr Hassan Zaki (65.Hassan Mostafa Hassan Abd El Rahman). Trainer: Hassan Shehata.
Goals: 0-1 Amr Hassan Zaki (40), 0-2 Hosny Abd Rabo Abd El Motaleb Ibrahim (47 penalty), 0-3 Ahmed Hassan Kamel (55), 0-4 Ahmed Eid Abdel Malek (65).
Cautions: Hussein Yassin, Meraneh Mohamed / Hassan Mostafa Hassan Abd El Rahman.

08.06.2008, Stade des Martyrs, Kinshasa; Attendance: 35,000
Referee: Badr Abdel Gadir (Sudan)
D.R. CONGO - MALAWI **1-0(0-0)**
COD: Robert Muteba Kidiaba, Gladys Bokese, Larrys Mabiala, Hérita N'Kongolo Ilunga (63.Christopher Oualembo), Rodrigue Dikaba, Youssouf Mulumbu, Tshiolola Tshinyama, Zola Matumona, Dieumerci Mbokani Bezua, Trésor Mputu Mabi (87.Ngabu Yannick Bapupa), Shabani Christophe Nonda (67.Risasi Yannick Yenga). Trainer: Patrice Neveu (France).
MWI: Swadick Sanudi, Elvis Bryson Kafoteka, Peter Mponda (Cap), James Sangala, Moses Chavula, Tawonga Chimodzi (35.Noel Mkandawire), Jacob Ngwira, Fisher Kenani Kondowe (70.Jimmy Zakazaka), Hellings Mwakasungula, Russel Mwafulirwa, Essau Boxer Kanyenda. Trainer: Kinnah Phiri.
Goal: 1-0 Zola Matumona (76).
Cautions: Swadick Sanudi.

13.06.2008, „El Hadj Hassan Gouled" Stadium, Djibouti; Attendance: 3,000
Referee: Thapelo Disang (Botswana)
DJIBOUTI - D.R. CONGO **0-6(0-3)**
DJI: Guedi Hassan, Ahmed Mohamed, Salim Kadar (51.Mohamed Abdi Omar), Daoud Wais, Abchir Houssein (84.Hassan Ahmed), Hassan Nour, Mahmood Omar (Cap), Hassan Khalif Ahmed (49.Kadir Moussa), Abdillahi Mohamed, Miad Charmare, Ahmed Ibrahim. Trainer: Mohamed Abar.
COD: Robert Muteba Kidiaba, Gladys Bokese, Larrys Mabiala, Christopher Oualembo, Rodrigue Dikaba, Youssouf Mulumbu (82.Risasi Yannick Yenga), Tshiolola Tshinyama, Zola Matumona, Dieumerci Mbokani Bezua (51.Lakuya Biscotte Mbala Mbuta), Trésor Mputu Mabi, Shabani Christophe Nonda. Trainer: Patrice Neveu (France).
Goals: 0-1 Dieumerci Mbokani Bezua (24), 0-2 Shabani Christophe Nonda (30), 0-3 Zola Matumona (39), 0-4 Dieumerci Mbokani Bezua (47), 0-5 Zola Matumona (51), 0-6 Trésor Mputu Mabi (80).
Cautions: Hassan Nour / Dieumerci Mbokani Bezua, Shabani Christophe Nonda, Zola Matumona.

14.06.2008, Kamuzu Stadium, Blantyre; Attendance: 40,000
Referee: Yakhouba Keïta (Guinea)
MALAWI - EGYPT **1-0(0-0)**
MWI: Swadick Sanudi, Elvis Bryson Kafoteka, Peter Mponda (Cap), James Sangala, Moses Chavula, Fisher Kenani Kondowe (54.Robert Ng'ambi), Hellings Mwakasungula, Noel Mkandawire (54.Jimmy Zakazaka), Joseph Kamwendo, Russel Mwafulirwa (79.Chiukepo Msowoya), Essau Boxer Kanyenda. Trainer: Kinnah Phiri.
EGY: Essam Kamal Tawfik El-Hadary, Ahmed Al-Muhammadi (69.Abdallah El-Said), Mahmoud Fathallah, Hani Mohammed Said Zakaria, Wael Gomaa Kamel El Hooty, Ahmed Samir Farag, Ahmed Hassan Kamel, Hosny Abd Rabo Abd El Motaleb Ibrahim, Mahmoud Abdel Razek Fadlallah „Shikabala" (77.Amr Hassan Zaki), Ahmed Eid Abdel Malek (56.Islam Awad), Ahmed Abdel Raouf.

Trainer: Hassan Shehata.
Goal: 1-0 Chiukepo Msowoya (90+3).
Cautions: James Sangala / Islam Awad.

22.06.2008, Stade des Martyrs, Kinshasa; Attendance: 15,000
Referee: Khalil Rouaissi (Morocco)
D.R. CONGO - DJIBOUTI   **5-1(2-0)**
COD: Robert Muteba Kidiaba, Gladys Bokese, Larrys Mabiala, Rodrigue Dikaba, Youssouf Mulumbu, Tshiolola Tshinyama, Zola Matumona, Kosi Saka, Marcel Kimemba Mbayo (57.Dieumerci Mbokani Bezua), Trésor Mputu Mabi (67.Lakuya Biscotte Mbala Mbuta), Shabani Christophe Nonda (79.Risasi Yannick Yenga). Trainer: Patrice Neveu (France).
DJI: Guedi Hassan, Aden Charmakeh, Waberi Hachi, Salim Kadar, Mahmood Omar (Cap) (55.Mohamed Abdi Omar), Abdillahi Mohamed (76.Mohamed Liban), Abchir Houssein, Hassan Daher, Abdi Mohamed Elmi (78.Moussa Hirir), Meraneh Mohamed, Ahmed Ibrahim. Trainer: Mohamed Abar.
Goals: 1-0 Shabani Christophe Nonda (10), 2-0 Shabani Christophe Nonda (45+3), 3-0 Shabani Christophe Nonda (52), 4-0 Tshiolola Tshinyama (60), 5-0 Dieumerci Mbokani Bezua (64), 5-1 Moussa Hirir (90+1).
Cautions: Kosi Saka / Abchir Houssein, Hassan Daher, Salim Kadar, Mahmood Omar, Aden Charmakeh.

22.06.2008, International Stadium, Cairo; Attendance: 20,000
Referee: Badara Diatta (Senegal)
EGYPT - MALAWI   **2-0(1-0)**
EGY: Essam Kamal Tawfik El-Hadary, Mahmoud Fathallah, Hani Mohammed Said Zakaria, Wael Gomaa Kamel El Hooty, Ahmed Samir Farag, Ahmed Hassan Kamel, Hossam El Sayed Ghaly (21.Ahmed Al-Muhammadi), Hosny Abd Rabo Abd El Motaleb Ibrahim, Mahmoud Abdel Razek Fadlallah „Shikabala" (62.Hassan Mostafa Hassan Abd El Rahman), Emad Mohamed Abd El Naby Ibrahim „Emad Motaeb", Amr Hassan Zaki (84.Tarek Mahmoud El Sayed). Trainer: Hassan Shehata.
MWI: Swadick Sanudi, Elvis Bryson Kafoteka, Peter Mponda (Cap), James Sangala, Moses Chavula, David John Banda (46.Robert Ng'ambi), Fisher Kenani Kondowe, Joseph Kamwendo (69.Jimmy Zakazaka), Hellings Mwakasungula, Russel Mwafulirwa (46.Chiukepo Msowoya), Essau Boxer Kanyenda. Trainer: Kinnah Phiri.
Goals: 1-0 Emad Mohamed Abd El Naby Ibrahim „Emad Motaeb" (17), 2-0 Emad Mohamed Abd El Naby Ibrahim „Emad Motaeb" (50).
Cautions: Wael Gomaa Kamel El Hooty, Ahmed Al-Muhammadi / Moses Chavula, David John Banda.

05.09.2008, „El Hadj Hassan Gouled" Stadium, Djibouti; Attendance: 700
Referee: Hélder Martins de Carvalho (Angola)
DJIBOUTI - MALAWI   **0-3(0-1)**
DJI: Guedi Hassan, Egueh Magdi, Salim Kadar (88.Moussa Hirir), Mahmood Omar (Cap), Daoud Wais, Abdourahman Mohamed, Hassan Daher (70.Waberi Hachi), Abdi Mohamed Elmi, Mohamed Mohamed, Meraneh Mohamed (81.Moussa Warsama), Hussein Yassin. Trainer: Mohamed Abar.
MWI: Swadick Sanudi, Elvis Bryson Kafoteka, Peter Mponda (Cap), James Sangala, Moses Chavula, Jacob Ngwira, Fisher Kenani Kondowe, Joseph Kamwendo (46.Noel Mkandawire), Tawonga Chimodzi (80.Robert Ng'ambi), Jimmy Zakazaka (57.Atusaye Nyondo), Chiukepo Msowoya. Trainer: Kinnah Phiri.
Goals: 0-1 Chiukepo Msowoya (30), 0-2 Moses Chavula (63), 0-3 Atusaye Nyondo (67).
Cautions: Hussein Yassin / Fisher Kenani Kondowe.

07.09.2008, Stade des Martyrs, Kinshasa; Attendance: 80,000
Referee: Daniel Bennett (South Africa)
D.R. CONGO - EGYPT **0-1(0-1)**
COD: Robert Muteba Kidiaba (46.Parfait Mandanda), Larrys Mabiala, Cédric Mongongu, André-Joël Sami, Hérita N'Kongolo Ilunga, Youssouf Mulumbu, Tshiolola Tshinyama, Zola Matumona, Lomana Trésor LuaLua (10.Trésor Mputu Mabi), Dieumerci Mbokani Bezua, Shabani Christophe Nonda (Cap) (78.Blaise Lelo Mbele). Trainer: Patrice Neveu (France).
EGY: Essam Kamal Tawfik El-Hadary, Ahmed Al-Muhammadi, Mahmoud Fathallah, Hani Mohammed Said Zakaria, Wael Gomaa Kamel El Hooty, Ahmed Samir Farag, Hosny Abd Rabo Abd El Motaleb Ibrahim, Ahmed Hassan Kamel (75.Ahmed Fahim Shaaban), Mohamed Aboutrika (85.Ahmed Hossam Hussein Abdelamid „Mido"), Amr Hassan Zaki, Emad Mohamed Abd El Naby Ibrahim „Emad Motaeb" (61.Mohamed Soliman „Humoos"). Trainer: Hassan Shehata.
Goal: 0-1 Mohamed Aboutrika (31).
Cautions: Zola Matumona / Amr Hassan Zaki, Ahmed Hassan Kamel, Essam Kamal Tawfik El-Hadary.

11.10.2008, Kamuzu Stadium, Blantyre; Attendance: 50,000
Referee: Coffi Codjia (Benin)
MALAWI - D.R. CONGO **2-1(0-1)**
MWI: Swadick Sanudi, Elvis Bryson Kafoteka, Peter Mponda (Cap), James Sangala (63.Wisdom Ndhlovu), Moses Chavula, Fisher Kenani Kondowe, Joseph Kamwendo (48.Chiukepo Msowoya), Hellings Mwakasungula, Robert Ng'ambi (62.Jimmy Zakazaka), Essau Boxer Kanyenda, Russel Mwafulirwa. Trainer: Kinnah Phiri.
COD: Robert Muteba Kidiaba, Gladys Bokese, Larrys Mabiala, Cédric Mongongu (88.Miala Nkulukuta), Hérita N'Kongolo Ilunga, Youssouf Mulumbu, Tshiolola Tshinyama, Marcel Kimemba Mbayo (65.Serge Lofo Bongeli), Lomana Trésor LuaLua, Dieumerci Mbokani Bezua (46.Blaise Lelo Mbele), Trésor Mputu Mabi. Trainer: Patrice Neveu (France).
Goals: 0-1 Lomana Trésor LuaLua (13), 1-1 Robert Ng'ambi (56), 2-1 Chiukepo Msowoya (83).
Cautions: James Sangala, Essau Boxer Kanyenda / Trésor Mputu Mabi.

12.10.2008, Military Academy Stadium, Cairo; Attendance: 10,000
Referee: Lassina Paré (Burkina Faso)
EGYPT - DJIBOUTI **4-0(1-0)**
EGY: Essam Kamal Tawfik El-Hadary (74.Amir Abdel Hamid Mohamed), Ahmed Al-Muhammadi (64.Ahmed Abdel Ghani), Hani Mohammed Said Zakaria, Wael Gomaa Kamel El Hooty, Ahmad Shedid Qinawi, Ahmed Hassan Kamel, Hosny Abd Rabo Abd El Motaleb Ibrahim, Mohamed Shawky Ali Sallam, Ahmed Eid Abdel Malek (58.Mohamed Soliman „Humoos"), Mohamed Aboutrika, Emad Mohamed Abd El Naby Ibrahim „Emad Motaeb". Trainer: Hassan Shehata.
DJI: Guedi Hassan, Waberi Hachi (74.Ahmed Mahdi), Hassan Ahmed, Daher Mohamed, Ahmed Hassan Daher (90.Hussein Yassin), Hassan Daher (84.Salim Kadar), Abchir Houssein, Mohamed Liban, Abdi Mohamed Elmi, Meraneh Mohamed (Cap), Said Riyad. Trainer: Mohamed Abar.
Goals: 1-0 Emad Mohamed Abd El Naby Ibrahim „Emad Motaeb" (19), 2-0 Ahmed Hassan Kamel (50), 3-0 Mohamed Aboutrika (66), 4-0 Said Riyad (90 own goal).
Cautions: Meraneh Mohamed, Salim Kadar, Ahmed Mahdi.

RANKING OF THE RUNNERS-UP

(only the results of the matches against the current group first and third of each group were considered)

1. Rwanda	4	3	0	1	7 - 3	9
2. Kenya	4	2	1	1	6 - 3	7
3. Tunisia	4	2	1	1	4 - 3	7
4. Togo	4	2	0	2	8 - 3	6
5. Gabon	4	2	0	2	3 - 3	6
6. Sudan	4	2	0	2	5 - 6	6
7. Malawi	4	2	0	2	3 - 4	6
8. Mozambique	4	1	2	1	5 - 3	5
9. Gambia	4	1	2	1	2 - 2	5
10. Angola	4	1	1	2	6 - 6	4
11. Cape Verde	4	1	0	3	3 - 7	3
12. South Africa	4	0	1	3	0 - 4	1

THIRD ROUND

On 22 October 2008, in Zürich, the remaining 20 teams were drawn in 5 groups of 4 teams to play the third round (28.03.2009 – 14.11.2009) of the african preliminaries. The winner of each groups will qualify to the World Cup finals. Moreover, the best three teams of each group will qualify for the African Cup of Nations 2010.

Before drawing in Zürich, the 20 teams (based on the FIFA World Rankings) were divided in four seeding pots, with one team to be drawn in each group:

Pot A: Cameroon, Egypt, Nigeria, Ghana, Ivory Coast
Pot B: Tunisia, Morocco, Guinea, Mali, Zambia
Pot C: Burkina Faso, Algeria, Gabon, Kenya, Rwanda
Pot D: Benin, Togo, Mozambique, Sudan, Malawi

After the drawing, the five qualifier groups were as following:

GROUP A
Cameroon, Morocco, Gabon, Togo.

GROUP B
Nigeria, Tunisia, Kenya, Mozambique.

GROUP C
Egypt, Algeria, Zambia, Rwanda.

GROUP D
Ghana, Mali, Benin, Sudan.

GROUP E
Ivory Coast, Guinea, Burkina Faso, Malawi.

THIRD ROUND

GROUP A

28.03.2009	Accra (Ghana)	Togo - Cameroon	1-0(1-0)
28.03.2009	Casablanca	Morocco - Gabon	1-2(0-2)
06.06.2009	Libreville	Gabon - Togo	3-0(1-0)*
07.06.2009	Yaoundé	Cameroon - Morocco	0-0
20.06.2009	Rabat	Morocco - Togo	0-0
05.09.2009	Libreville	Gabon - Cameroon	0-2(0-0)
06.09.2009	Lomé	Togo - Morocco	1-1(1-0)
09.09.2009	Yaoundé	Cameroon - Gabon	2-1(1-0)
10.10.2009	Yaoundé	Cameroon - Togo	3-0(1-0)
10.10.2009	Libreville	Gabon - Morocco	3-1(1-0)
14.11.2009	Fes	Morocco - Cameroon	0-2(0-1)
14.11.2009	Lomé	Togo - Gabon	1-0(0-0)

*awarded 3-0 for Gabon by the FIFA.

FINAL STANDINGS

1. CAMEROON	6	4	1	1	9 - 2	13
2. Gabon	6	3	0	3	9 - 7	9
3. Togo	6	2	2	2	3 - 7	8
4. Morocco	6	0	3	3	3 - 8	3

Cameroon qualified for the 19th World Cup Final Tournament.

28.03.2009, Ohene Djan Stadium, Accra (Ghana); Attendance: 26,450
Referee: Essam Abd El Fatah (Egypt)
TOGO - CAMEROON   **1-0(1-0)**
TOG: Kodjovi Dodji Obilale, Abdoul-Gafar Mamah, Daré Nibombé, Serge Ognadon Akakpo, Richmond Forson, Jacques Alaixys Romao, Komlan Amewou, Mamam Cherif Touré (63.Kassim Guyazou), Moustapha Salifou (81.Yao Séyram Junior Sènaya), Thomas Dossevi (88.Floyd Ayité), Sheyi Emmanuel Adebayor. Trainer: Jean Thissen (Belgium).
CMR: Idriss Carlos Kameni, André Stéphane Bikey Amugu, Rigobert Song Bahanag (Cap), Benoît Pierre David Assou-Ekotto, Geremi Sorele Njitap Fotso, Modeste M'bami (59.Stéphane Mbia Etoundi), Jean II Makoun, Daniel Armand Ngom Kome (46.Eric Daniel Djemba-Djemba), Somen Tchoyi, Pierre Achille Webó Kouamo (46.Paul Claudel Alo'o Efoulou), Samuel Eto'o. Trainer: Otto Pfister (Germany).
Goal: 1-0 Sheyi Emmanuel Adebayor (11).
Cautions: Sheyi Emmanuel Adebayor, Komlan Amewou, Kodjovi Dodji Obilale, Abdoul-Gafar Mamah / André Stéphane Bikey Amugu, Geremi Sorele Njitap Fotso.

28.03.2009, Stade „Mohamed V", Casablanca; Attendance: 38,000
Referee: Badara Diatta (Senegal)
MOROCCO - GABON   **1-2(0-2)**
MAR: Karim Zaza, Badr El Kaddouri, Amin El Erbati, Chemcedine El Araichi, Talal El Karkouri, Youssef Safri, Nabil Dirar (56.Adel Taarabt), Houssine Kharja, Youssouf Hadji, Marouane Chamakh (61.Moubarak Boussoufa), Mounir El Hamdaoui. Trainer: Roger Lemerre (France).
GAB: Didier Janvier Ovono Ebang, Ernest Akouassaga (88.Erwin Nguéma Obame), Georges Ambourouet, Bruno Ecuélé Manga, Rodrigue Moundounga, Etienne Alain Djissikadié Mpaga, Paul Ulrich Kessany Zategwa, Bruno Mbanangoyé Zita, Pierre-Emerick Aubameyang (72.Fabrice Do Marcolino), Roguy Méyé, Stéphane N'Guéma (46.Jean Stéphane Achi Yessi). Trainer: Alain Giresse (France).
Goals: 0-1 Pierre-Emerick Aubameyang (34), 0-2 Roguy Méyé (45), 1-2 Mounir El Hamdaoui (83).
Cautions: Youssef Safri / Pierre-Emerick Aubameyang, Ernest Akouassaga, Ro.drigue Moundounga

06.06.2009, Stade Omnisports „Président Omar Bongo", Libreville; Attendance: 20,000
Referee: Verson Lwanja (Malawi)
GABON - TOGO   **3-0(1-0)***
GAB: Didier Janvier Ovono Ebang, Georges Ambourouet (68.Etienne Alain Djissikadié Mpaga), Moïse Akou Brou Apanga, Bruno Ecuélé Manga, Rodrigue Moundounga, Paul Ulrich Kessany Zategwa, Bruno Mbanangoyé Zita, Pierre-Emerick Aubameyang (79.Willy Aubameyang), Cédric Moubamba, Roguy Méyé, Stéphane N'Guéma. Trainer: Alain Giresse (France).
TOG: Kossi Agassa, Kwami Komlan Kacla Akoete Eninful, Abdoul-Gafar Mamah, Serge Ognadon Akakpo, Richmond Forson (46.Éric Akoto), Jacques Alaixys Romao, Komlan Amewou, Mamam Cherif Touré (28.Adékambi Olufadé), Moustapha Salifou (66.Mohamed Abdel Kader Coubadja Touré), Thomas Dossevi (*sent off 35*), Sheyi Emmanuel Adebayor. Trainer: Jean Thissen (Belgium).
Goals: 1-0 Bruno Ecuélé Manga (11), 2-0 Roguy Méyé (67), 3-0 Moïse Akou Brou Apanga (81).
Cautions: Thomas Dossevi, Sheyi Emmanuel Adebayor.
Sent off: Thomas Dossevi.
*The match was awarded 3-0 for Gabon because Togo used a player being suspended.

07.06.2009, Stade Omnisports „Ahmadou-Ahidjo", Yaoundé; Attendance: 35,000
Referee: Rajindraparsad Seechurn (Mauritius)
CAMEROON - MOROCCO   **0-0**
CMR: Idriss Carlos Kameni, Nicolas Alexis Julio N'Koulou N'Doubena, Rigobert Song Bahanag (Cap), Aurélian Bayard Chedjou Fongang (54.Daniel Armand Ngom Kome), Geremi Sorele Njitap Fotso, Jean II Makoun, Eyong Tarkang Enoh, Achille Emana Edzimbi (68.Marcus Nwambo Mokaké), Paul Claudel Alo'o Efoulou (77.Stéphane Mbia Etoundi), Pierre Achille Webó Kouamo, Samuel Eto'o. Trainer: Thomas Nkono.
MAR: Nadir Lamyaghri, Mehdi Benatia, Amin El Erbati, Michaël Basser Chrétien, Badr El Kaddouri, Kamel Chafni, Karim El Ahmadi (70.Younes Mankari), Houssine Kharja (85.Walid Regragui), Youssouf Hadji, Marouane Zemmama (62.Rafik Abdessamad), Mounir El Hamdaoui. Trainer: Roger Lemerre (France).

20.06.2009, Complexe Sportif „Moulay Abdellah", Rabat; Attendance: 22,000
Referee: Wellington Kaoma (Zambia)
MOROCCO - TOGO   **0-0**
MAR: Nadir Lamyaghri, Mehdi Benatia, Amin El Erbati, Michaël Basser Chrétien, Badr El Kaddouri, Kamel Chafni (69.Rafik Abdessamad), Karim El Ahmadi, Houssine Kharja, Youssouf Hadji, Marouane Zemmama (87.Walid Regragui), Mounir El Hamdaoui (62.Nabil Baha). Trainer: Roger Lemerre (France).
TOG: Kodjovi Dodji Obilale, Akimsola Boussari, Abdoul-Gafar Mamah, Assimiou Touré, Mohammed Zanzan Atte-Oudeyi, Yao Séyram Junior Sènaya (76.Adékambi Olufadé), Jacques Alaixys Romao, Komlan Amewou, Moustapha Salifou (83.Arafat Djako), Euloge Ahodikpé, Mohamed Abdel Kader Coubadja Touré. Trainer: Jean Thissen (Belgium).
Cautions: Abdoul-Gafar Mamah, Komlan Amewou, Jacques Alaixys Romao.

05.09.2009, Stade „Omar Bongo", Libreville; Attendance: 10,000
Referee: Alfred Ndinya (Kenya)
GABON - CAMEROON   **0-2(0-0)**
GAB: Didier Janvier Ovono Ebang, Ernest Akouassaga, Georges Ambourouet, Moïse Akou Brou Apanga (46.Fabrice Do Marcolino), Rodrigue Moundounga, Paul Ulrich Kessany Zategwa (82.Etienne Alain Djissikadié Mpaga), Bruno Mbanangoyé Zita, Cédric Moubamba, Pierre-Emerick Aubameyang (73.Eric Mouloungui), Daniel Cousin, Roguy Méyé. Trainer: Alain Giresse (France).
CMR: Idriss Carlos Kameni, Sébastien Bassong Nguena (27.Rigobert Song Bahanag), Nicolas Alexis Julio N'Koulou N'Doubena, Benoît Pierre David Assou-Ekotto, Geremi Sorele Njitap Fotso, Stéphane Mbia Etoundi, Jean II Makoun, Achille Emana Edzimbi, Somen Tchoyi (46.Paul Claudel Alo'o Efoulou), Pierre Achille Webó Kouamo (77.Eyong Tarkang Enoh), Samuel Eto'o (Cap). Trainer: Paul Le Guen (France).

Goals: 0-1 Achille Emana Edzimbi (65), 0-2 Samuel Eto'o (67).
Cautions: Paul Ulrich Kessany Zategwa / Achille Emana Edzimbi, Benoît Pierre David Assou-Ekotto.

06.09.2009, Stade de Kégué, Lomé; Attendance: 24,651
Referee: Muhmed Ssegonga (Uganda)
TOGO - MOROCCO   **1-1(1-0)**
TOG: Kodjovi Dodji Obilale (58.Kossi Agassa), Sénah Mango, Daré Nibombé, Assimiou Touré, Serge Ognadon Akakpo, Jacques Alaixys Romao, Moustapha Salifou, Euloge Ahodikpé, Thomas Dossevi (78.Yao Séyram Junior Sènaya), Mohamed Abdel Kader Coubadja Touré, Sheyi Emmanuel Adebayor. Trainer: Jean Thissen (Belgium).
MAR: Nadir Lamyaghri, Jamal Allioui, Mehdi Benatia, Amin El Erbati, Hicham Mahdoufi, Youssef Safri, Houssine Kharja (64.Abdessalam Benjelloun), Youssouf Hadji (87.Jaouad Zairi), Marouane Zemmama, Moubarak Boussoufa (76.Adel Taarabt), Marouane Chamakh. Trainer: Hassan Moumen.
Goals: 1-0 Moustapha Salifou (3), 1-1 Adel Taarabt (90+3).
Cautions: Daré Nibombé, Euloge Ahodikpé, Sheyi Emmanuel Adebayor, Mohamed Abdel Kader Coubadja Touré / Marouane Chamakh.

09.09.2009, Stade Omnisports „Ahmadou-Ahidjo", Yaoundé; Attendance: 38,000
Referee: Kacem Bennaceur (Tunisia)
CAMEROON - GABON   **2-1(1-0)**
CMR: Idriss Carlos Kameni, Nicolas Alexis Julio N'Koulou N'Doubena, Rigobert Song Bahanag, Benoît Pierre David Assou-Ekotto, Geremi Sorele Njitap Fotso, Alexandre Dimitri Song Billong, Jean II Makoun (80.Aurélian Bayard Chedjou Fongang), Joël Landry Tsafack N'Guémo, Achille Emana Edzimbi (85.Daniel Armand Ngom Kome), Pierre Achille Webó Kouamo (73.Paul Claudel Alo'o Efoulou), Samuel Eto'o (Cap). Trainer: Paul Le Guen (France).
GAB: Didier Janvier Ovono Ebang, Ernest Akouassaga, Georges Ambourouet, Moïse Akou Brou Apanga, Rodrigue Moundounga, Bruno Mbanangoyé Zita (70.Etienne Alain Djissikadié Mpaga), Cédric Moubamba, Thierry Issiémou, Stéphane N'Guéma (77.Eric Mouloungui), Roguy Méyé, Pierre-Emerick Aubameyang (60.Daniel Cousin). Trainer: Alain Giresse (France).
Goals: 1-0 Jean II Makoun (25), 2-0 Samuel Eto'o (64), 2-1 Daniel Cousin (90).
Cautions: Benoît Pierre David Assou-Ekotto.

10.10.2009, Stade Omnisports „Ahmadou-Ahidjo", Yaoundé; Attendance: 37,400
Referee: Wellington Kaoma (Zambia)
CAMEROON - TOGO   **3-0(1-0)**
CMR: Idriss Carlos Kameni, Henri Bedimo Nsame, Nicolas Alexis Julio N'Koulou N'Doubena, Rigobert Song Bahanag, Geremi Sorele Njitap Fotso, Alexandre Dimitri Song Billong, Jean II Makoun (78.Eyong Tarkang Enoh), Joël Landry Tsafack N'Guémo (70.Stéphane Mbia Etoundi), Achille Emana Edzimbi, Pierre Achille Webó Kouamo (70.Somen Tchoyi), Samuel Eto'o (Cap). Trainer: Paul Le Guen (France).
TOG: Kodjovi Dodji Obilale, Daré Nibombé, Assimiou Touré, Serge Ognadon Akakpo, Emmanuel Mathias, Jacques Alaixys Romao, Komlan Amewou, Moustapha Salifou (16.Serge Gakpé), Euloge Ahodikpé (55.Thomas Dossevi), Floyd Ayité, Sheyi Emmanuel Adebayor (58.Jonathan Ayité). Trainer: Hubert Velud (France).
Goals: 1-0 Geremi Sorele Njitap Fotso (29), 2-0 Jean II Makoun (46), 3-0 Achille Emana Edzimbi (54).
Cautions: Kodjovi Dodji Obilale, Daré Nibombé.

10.10.2009, Stade Omnisports „Président Omar Bongo", Libreville; Attendance: 14,000
Referee: Noumandiez Doué (Ivory Coast)
GABON - MOROCCO   **3-1(1-0)**
GAB: Didier Janvier Ovono Ebang, Georges Ambourouet, Moïse Akou Brou Apanga, Bruno Ecuélé Manga, Rodrigue Moundounga, Etienne Alain Djissikadié Mpaga, Paul Ulrich Kessany Zategwa, Cédric Moubamba, Stéphane N'Guéma (58.Eric Mouloungui), Pierre-Emerick Aubameyang (86.Roguy Méyé), Daniel Cousin (82.Thierry Issiémou). Trainer: Alain Giresse (France).

MAR: Nadir Lamyaghri, Mehdi Benatia, Amin El Erbati, Chakib Benzoukane, Hicham Mahdoufi (82.Karim El Ahmadi), Youssef Safri, Houssine Kharja, Adel Taarabt, Marouane Zemmama (65.Jaouad Zairi), Marouane Chamakh, Mounir El Hamdaoui (46.Hicham Aboucherouane). Trainer: Hassan Moumen.

Goals: 1-0 Elamine Erbati (43 own goal), 2-0 Eric Mouloungui (65), 3-0 Daniel Cousin (70), 3-1 Adel Taarabt (88).

Cautions: Stéphane N'Guéma, Moïse Akou Brou Apanga / Youssef Safri, Chakib Benzoukane, Amin El Erbati, Marouane Chamakh, Houssine Kharja.

14.11.2009, Stade de Fès, Fès; Attendance: 17,000
Referee: Daniel Bennett (South Africa)
MOROCCO - CAMEROON   **0-2(0-1)**
MAR: Nadir Lamyaghri, Mehdi Benatia, Issam El Adoua, Zakaria Zerouali (70.Khalid Sekkat), Adil Hermach, Nabil Dirar (54.Nabil Baha), Karim El Ahmadi, Mohammed Oulhadj, Mohamed Chihani, Adel Taarabt, Abdessalam Benjelloun (58.Mustapha El Allaoui). Trainer: Hassan Moumen.

CMR: Idriss Carlos Kameni, Nicolas Alexis Julio N'Koulou N'Doubena, Rigobert Song Bahanag, Benoît Pierre David Assou-Ekotto, Geremi Sorele Njitap Fotso, Alexandre Dimitri Song Billong, Jean II Makoun, Joël Landry Tsafack N'Guémo (78.Somen Tchoyi), Achille Emana Edzimbi (68.Stéphane Mbia Etoundi), Pierre Achille Webó Kouamo (81.Eyong Tarkang Enoh), Samuel Eto'o (Cap). Trainer: Paul Le Guen (France).

Goals: 0-1 Pierre Achille Webó Kouamo (19), 0-2 Samuel Eto'o (52).

Cautions: Zakaria Zerouali, Mehdi Benatia / Rigobert Song Bahanag, Pierre Achille Webó Kouamo, Joël Landry Tsafack N'Guémo.

14.11.2009, Stade de Kégué, Lomé; Attendance: 10,000
Referee: Rajindraparsad Seechurn (Mauritius)
TOGO - GABON   **1-0(0-0)**
TOG: Baba Tchagouni, Kwami Komlan Kacla Akoete Eninful, Abdoul-Gafar Mamah, Assimiou Touré, Serge Ognadon Akakpo, Jacques Alaixys Romao, Komlan Amewou, Serge Gakpé (83.Liyabé Kpatoumbi), Thomas Dossevi (61.Floyd Ayité), Sheyi Emmanuel Adebayor, Jonathan Ayité (68.Moustapha Salifou). Trainer: Hubert Velud (France).

GAB: Didier Janvier Ovono Ebang, Georges Ambourouet, Moïse Akou Brou Apanga, Bruno Ecuélé Manga, Rodrigue Moundounga, Paul Ulrich Kessany Zategwa, Bruno Mbanangoyé Zita, Cédric Moubamba (65.Thierry Issiémou), Eric Mouloungui (84.Fabrice Do Marcolino), Daniel Cousin (Cap) (40.Pierre-Emerick Aubameyang), Roguy Méyé. Trainer: Alain Giresse (France).

Goal: 1-0 Floyd Ayité (71).

Cautions: Assimiou Touré, Sheyi Emmanuel Adebayor.

GROUP B

28.03.2009	Nairobi	Kenya - Tunisia		1-2(0-1)
29.03.2009	Maputo	Mozambique - Nigeria		0-0
06.06.2009	Radès	Tunisia - Mozambique		2-0(1-0)
07.06.2009	Abuja	Nigeria - Kenya		3-0(1-0)
20.06.2009	Nairobi	Kenya - Mozambique		2-1(1-0)
20.06.2009	Radès	Tunisia - Nigeria		0-0
06.09.2009	Maputo	Mozambique - Kenya		1-0(0-0)
06.09.2009	Abuja	Nigeria - Tunisia		2-2(1-1)
11.10.2009	Abuja	Nigeria - Mozambique		1-0(0-0)
11.10.2009	Radès	Tunisia - Kenya		1-0(1-0)
14.11.2009	Nairobi	Kenya - Nigeria		2-3(1-0)
14.11.2009	Maputo	Mozambique - Tunisia		1-0(0-0)

FINAL STANDINGS

1. NIGERIA	6	3	3	0	9 - 4	12
2. Tunisia	6	3	2	1	7 - 4	11
3. Mozambique	6	2	1	3	3 - 5	7
4. Kenya	6	1	0	5	5 - 11	3

Nigeria qualified for the 19th World Cup Final Tournament.

28.03.2009, Nyayo National Stadium, Nairobi; Attendance: 27,000
Referee: Raphael Divine Evehe (Cameroon)
KENYA - TUNISIA **1-2(0-1)**
KEN: Noah Ayuko, John Njoroge Mwangi (68.Victor Mugabe Wanyama), James Mulinge Ndeto Munandi, Pascal Ochieng, Musa Otieno Ongao (Cap), George Owino, Hillary Echesa Odada (46.Boniface Ambani), Robert Mambo Mumba, McDonald Mariga Wanyama, Dennis Oliech, Francis Ouma (51.Patrick Oboya Onyango). Trainer: Antoine Hey (Germany).
TUN: Hamdi Kasraoui, Karim Haggui, Radhi Ben Abdelmajid Jaïdi, Anis Boussaïdi, Aïmen Demai (46.Oussama Darragi), Ammar Jemal, Hocine Ragued, Wissem Ben Yahia, Tijani Belaid (75.Saïf Ghezal), Fahid Ben Khalfallah (56.Mohamed Ali Ghariani), Issam Jemâa. Trainer: Humberto Manuel Jesus Coelho (Portugal).
Goal: 0-1 Ammar Jemal (6), 1-1 Dennis Oliech (70), 1-1 Issam Jemâa (79).
Cautions: Tijani Belaid, Mohamed Ali Ghariani.

29.03.2009, Estádio da Machava, Maputo; Attendance: 35,000
Referee: Amanuel Eyob (Eritrea)
MOZAMBIQUE - NIGERIA **0-0**
MOZ: João Raphael Kapango, Daniel Almiro Lobo „Miro" (82.Carlos Parruque Danito Nhapossa), Alberto Massinga Fanuel, Dario Ivan Khan, Celso Halilo de Abdul „Mano", Mohamed Antonio Hagy, Martinho Martins Mukana „Paíto" (89.Samuel Luis Campira Chapanga), Eugenio Fernando Bila „Genito" (50.Luis), Simão Mate Junior, Elias Gaspar Pelembe „Domingués", Dário Alberto Jesus Monteiro. Trainer: Ignatus Martinus Nooij (Holland).
NGA: Vincent Enyeama, Chukwudi Odiah (86.Onyekachi Apam), Daniel Olusola Shittu, Obinna Nwaneri (Cap), Taye Ismaila Taïwo, Sani Haruna Kaita, Osaze Peter Odemwingie, John Michael Nchekwube Obinna, Victor Nsofor Obinna (75.Oluwafemi Ajilore), Ikechukwu Uche, Obafemi Akinwunmi Martins. Trainer: Shaibu Amodu.
Cautions: Elias Gaspar Pelembe „Domingués" / Obinna Nwaneri, Sani Haruna Kaita.

215

06.06.2009, Stade Olympique 7 Novembre, Radès; Attendance: 30,000
Referee: Kokou Djaoupé (Togo)
TUNISIA - MOZAMBIQUE   **2-0(1-0)**
TUN: Hamdi Kasraoui, Khaled Souissi, Karim Haggui, Radhi Ben Abdelmajid Jaïdi, Yassin Mikari, Hocine Ragued, Wissem Ben Yahia, Khaled Korbi (46.Chadi Hammami), Fahid Ben Khalfallah, Samuel Allagui (54.Lassad Hassen Nouioui; 78.Oussama Darragi), Mohamed Ali Ghariani. Trainer: Humberto Manuel Jesus Coelho (Portugal).
MOZ: João Raphael Kapango, Daniel Almiro Lobo „Miro", Alberto Massinga Fanuel, Dario Ivan Khan, Celso Halilo de Abdul „Mano", Mohamed Antonio Hagy (81.Carlos Parruque Danito Nhapossa), Martinho Martins Mukana „Paíto" (50.Eugenio Fernando Bila „Genito"), Simão Mate Junior, Elias Gaspar Pelembe „Dominguês", Dário Alberto Jesus Monteiro (90.Hélder Pelembe), Manuel José Luis Bucuane „Tico-Tico". Trainer: Ignatus Martinus Nooij (Holland).
Goals: 1-0 Wissem Ben Yahia (21), 2-0 Oussama Darragi (89).
Cautions: Wissem Ben Yahia, Yassin Mikari, Mohamed Ali Ghariani, Oussama Darragi / João Raphael Kapango, Daniel Almiro Lobo „Miro".

07.06.2009, National Stadium, Abuja; Attendance: 60,000
Referee: Abdellah El Achiri (Morocco)
NIGERIA - KENYA   **3-0(1-0)**
NGA: Vincent Enyeama, Yusuf Mohammed, Samuel Okeremute Sodje (71.Onyekachi Apam), Ayodele Adeleye, Uwa Elderson Echiéjilé, Kalu Uche, Oluwaseyi George Olofinjana (Cap), Dickson Paul Etuhu (46.Nwankwo Christian Nwosu Kanu), Osaze Peter Odemwingie, Ikechukwu Uche, Michael Eneramo (55.Victor Nsofor Obinna). Trainer: Shaibu Amodu.
KEN: Arnold Origi Otieno, John Njoroge Mwangi, Pascal Ochieng, Musa Otieno Ongao (Cap), Julius Owino, George Owino, McDonald Mariga Wanyama, Austin Charles Makacha, Robert Mambo Mumba (53.Allan Wanga Wetende), Patrick Oboya Onyango (54.Victor Mugabe Wanyama), Dennis Oliech (84.Peter Opiyo Odhiambo). Trainer: Antoine Hey (Germany).
Goals: 1-0 Ikechukwu Uche (2), 2-0 Victor Nsofor Obinna (73 penalty), 3-0 Victor Nsofor Obinna (78).
Cautions: Uwa Elderson Echiéjilé / Dennis Oliech, George Owino.

20.06.2009, Kasarani Sports Complex, Nairobi; Attendance: 15,000
Referee: Yakhouba Keita (Guinea)
KENYA - MOZAMBIQUE   **2-1(1-0)**
KEN: Arnold Origi Otieno, John Njoroge Mwangi, Pascal Ochieng, Musa Otieno Ongao (Cap), Julius Owino, George Owino, Robert Mambo Mumba (90.Taiwo Leo Awuonda Atieno), McDonald Mariga Wanyama, Austin Charles Makacha, Patrick Oboya Onyango (58.Victor Mugabe Wanyama), Dennis Oliech (46.Allan Wanga Wetende). Trainer: Antoine Hey (Germany).
MOZ: Marcelino Armando Cumbane (19.Albino Cossa „Bino"), Samuel Luis Campira Chapanga, Alberto Massinga Fanuel, Dario Ivan Khan, Mohamed Antonio Hagy, Martinho Martins Mukana „Paíto", Eugenio Fernando Bila „Genito" (81.Josimar Tiago Machaisse), Simão Mate Junior, Elias Gaspar Pelembe „Dominguês", Dário Alberto Jesus Monteiro (73.Carlos Gonçalves „Fumo"), Manuel José Luis Bucuane „Tico-Tico". Trainer: Ignatus Martinus Nooij (Holland).
Goals: 1-0 Julius Owino (8), 1-1 Elias Gaspar Pelembe „Domingues" (49), 2-1 McDonald Mariga Wanyama (72 penalty).
Cautions: Mohamed Antonio Hagy, Dario Ivan Khan, Alberto Massinga Fanuel.

20.06.2009, Stade Olympique 7 Novembre, Radès; Attendance: 45,000
Referee: Koman Coulibaly (Mali)
TUNISIA - NIGERIA   **0-0**
TUN: Hamdi Kasraoui, Khaled Souissi, Saïf Ghezal, Karim Haggui, Anis Boussaïdi (58.Tijani Belaid), Ammar Jemal, Hocine Ragued, Khaled Korbi, Oussama Darragi (87.Wissem Ben Yahia), Samuel Allagui (64.Mohamed Amine Chermiti), Ali Zitouni. Trainer: Humberto Manuel Jesus Coelho (Portugal).
NGA: Vincent Enyeama, Olubayo Adefemi, Joseph Ikpo Yobo (Cap), Ayodele Adeleye, Taye Ismaila

Taïwo, Oluwaseyi George Olofinjana, John Michael Nchekwube Obinna, Kalu Uche (68.Nwankwo Christian Nwosu Kanu), Osaze Peter Odemwingie, Ikechukwu Uche (84.John Chukwudi Utaka), Victor Nsofor Obinna (68.Michael Eneramo). Trainer: Shaibu Amodu.

06.09.2009, Estádio da Machava, Maputo; Attendance: 35,000
Referee: Koman Coulibaly (Mali)
MOZAMBIQUE - KENYA   **1-0(0-0)**
MOZ: João Raphael Kapango, Daniel Almiro Lobo „Miro" (79.Mohamed Antonio Hagy), Dario Ivan Khan, Celso Halilo de Abdul „Mano", Edson André Sitoe „Mexer", Martinho Martins Mukana „Paíto", Eugenio Fernando Bila „Genito" (65.Josimar Tiago Machaisse), Simão Mate Junior, Elias Gaspar Pelembe „Domingués", Dário Alberto Jesus Monteiro, Manuel José Luis Bucuane „Tico-Tico" (83.Jeremias Jorge Sitoe „Jerry"). Trainer: Ignatus Martinus Nooij (Holland).
KEN: Willis Ochieng Oganyo, John Njoroge Mwangi (78.Taiwo Leo Awuonda Atieno), Pascal Ochieng, Musa Otieno Ongao (Cap), Julius Owino, George Owino, Austin Charles Makacha (71.Allan Wanga Wetende), Robert Mambo Mumba, McDonald Mariga Wanyama, Patrick Oboya Onyango (58.Victor Mugabe Wanyama), Dennis Oliech. Trainer: Antoine Hey (Germany).
Goal: 1-0 Manuel José Luis Bucuane „Tico-Tico" (66).
Cautions: Simão Mate Junior / Robert Mambo Mumba.

06.09.2009, National Stadium, Abuja; Attendance: 52,000
Referee: Daniel Bennett (South Africa)
NIGERIA - TUNISIA   **2-2(1-1)**
NGA: Vincent Enyeama, Olubayo Adefemi, Joseph Ikpo Yobo (Cap), Ayodele Adeleye, Taye Ismaila Taïwo, Oluwaseyi George Olofinjana (57.Michael Eneramo), John Michael Nchekwube Obinna, Kalu Uche, Osaze Peter Odemwingie, Ikechukwu Uche (65.Victor Nsofor Obinna), Chinedu Obasi Ogbuke (67.Nwankwo Christian Nwosu Kanu). Trainer: Shaibu Amodu.
TUN: Aymen Mathlouthi Balbouli, Khaled Souissi, Saïf Ghezal, Karim Haggui, Yassin Mikari, Hocine Ragued, Khaled Korbi (60.Haïthem Mrabet), Nabil Taïder (75.Radhouène Felhi), Oussama Darragi, Chaouki Ben Saada (80.Zouheir Dhaouadi), Issam Jemâa. Trainer: Humberto Manuel Jesus Coelho (Portugal).
Goals: 1-0 Osaze Peter Odemwingie (23), 1-1 Nabil Taïder (24), 2-1 Michael Eneramo (80), 2-2 Oussama Darragi (89).
Cautions: Ikechukwu Uche, Olubayo Adefemi, Michael Eneramo / Aymen Mathlouthi Balbouli, Karim Haggui.

11.10.2009, National Stadium, Abuja; Attendance: 13,000
Referee: Khalid Abdel Rahman (Sudan)
NIGERIA - MOZAMBIQUE   **1-0(0-0)**
NGA: Vincent Enyeama, Yusuf Mohammed (31.Daniel Olusola Shittu, Joseph Ikpo Yobo (Cap), Obinna Nwaneri, Uwa Elderson Echiéjilé, Yusuf Ayila Atanda, Oluwaseyi George Olofinjana, Oluwafemi Ajilore, Osaze Peter Odemwingie, Michael Eneramo (61.Victor Nsofor Obinna), Abdulrasaq Yakubu Aiyegbeni (55.Obafemi Akinwunmi Martins). Trainer: Shaibu Amodu.
MOZ: João Raphael Kapango, Daniel Almiro Lobo „Miro", Samuel Luis Campira Chapanga, Celso Halilo de Abdul „Mano" (90+4.Alberto Massinga Fanuel), Edson André Sitoe „Mexer", Mohamed Antonio Hagy (88.Carlos Parruque Danito Nhapossa), Martinho Martins Mukana „Paíto", Eugenio Fernando Bila „Genito" (79.Josimar Tiago Machaisse), Elias Gaspar Pelembe „Domingués", Dário Alberto Jesus Monteiro, Manuel José Luis Bucuane „Tico-Tico". Trainer: Ignatus Martinus Nooij (Holland).
Goal: 1-0 Victor Nsofor Obinna (90).
Cautions: Samuel Luis Campira Chapanga.

217

11.10.2009, Stade Olympique 7 Novembre, Radès; Attendance: 50,000
Referee: Badara Diatta (Senegal)
TUNISIA - KENYA   **1-0(1-0)**
TUN: Aymen Mathlouthi Balbouli, Khaled Souissi, Saïf Ghezal, Ammar Jemal, Yassin Mikari, Hocine
Ragued (61.Jamel Saihi), Khaled Korbi, Nabil Taïder (46.Fahid Ben Khalfallah), Oussama Darragi
(76.Sofian Chahed), Chaouki Ben Saada, Issam Jemâa. Trainer: Humberto Manuel Jesus Coelho
(Portugal).
KEN: Willis Ochieng Oganyo, Jockins Otieno Atudo, John Njoroge Mwangi, Musa Otieno Ongao (Cap),
Julius Owino (44.Taiwo Leo Awuonda Atieno), George Owino, Victor Mugabe Wanyama (67.Allan
Wanga Wetende), Peter Opiyo Odhiambo, Patrick Osiako, Robert Mambo Mumba (84.Austin Charles
Makacha), Patrick Oboya Onyango. Trainer: Antoine Hey (Germany).
Goal: 1-0 Issam Jemâa (1).

14.11.2009, Nyayo National Stadium, Nairobi; Attendance: 20,000
Referee: Eddy Allen Maillet Guyto (Seychelles)
KENYA - NIGERIA   **2-3(1-0)**
KEN: Willis Ochieng Oganyo, John Njoroge Mwangi, Edgar Ochieng Odhiambo, Musa Otieno Ongao
(Cap), George Owino, Julius Owino, Peter Opiyo Odhiambo, Victor Mugabe Wanyama (73.Allan Wanga
Wetende), Emmanuel Ake Muttendango (78.Hillary Echesa Odada), Dennis Oliech, Patrick Oboya
Onyango (51.Patrick Osiako). Trainer: Twahir Muhiddin.
NGA: Vincent Enyeama, Onyekachi Apam, Joseph Ikpo Yobo (Cap), Obinna Nwaneri, Uwa Elderson
Echiéjilé, Oluwaseyi George Olofinjana (30.Yusuf Ayila Atanda), Oluwafemi Ajilore (46.Obafemi
Akinwunmi Martins), John Michael Nchekwube Obinna, Osaze Peter Odemwingie, Michael Eneramo
(61.Victor Nsofor Obinna), Abdulrasaq Yakubu Aiyegbeni. Trainer: Shaibu Amodu.
Goals: 1-0 Dennis Oliech (15), 1-1 Obafemi Akinwunmi Martins (60), 1-2 Abdulrasaq Yakubu
Aiyegbeni (64), 2-2 Allan Wanga Wetende (77), 2-3 Obafemi Akinwunmi Martins (81).
Cautions: Musa Otieno Ongao, Patrick Oboya Onyango, Edgar Ochieng Odhiambo, Peter Opiyo
Odhiambo / Uwa Elderson Echiéjilé, Osaze Peter Odemwingie.

14.11.2009, Estádio da Machava, Maputo; Attendance: 30,000
Referee: Noumandiez Doué (Ivory Coast)
MOZAMBIQUE - TUNISIA   **1-0(0-0)**
MOZ: João Raphael Kapango, Daniel Almiro Lobo „Miro" (78.Mohamed Antonio Hagy), Samuel Luis
Campira Chapanga, Dario Ivan Khan, Edson André Sitoe „Mexer", Martinho Martins Mukana „Paíto",
Eugenio Fernando Bila „Genito" (65.Carlos Gonçalves „Fumo"), Simão Mate Junior, Elias Gaspar
Pelembe „Dinguês", Dário Alberto Jesus Monteiro, Manuel José Luis Bucuane „Tico-Tico". Trainer:
Ignatus Martinus Nooij (Holland).
TUN: Aymen Mathlouthi Balbouli, Khaled Souissi, Saïf Ghezal, Karim Haggui, Yassin Mikari, Hocine
Ragued, Khaled Korbi, Fahid Ben Khalfallah (46.Ali Zitouni), Chaouki Ben Saada (76.Zouheir
Dhaouadi), Mohamed Amine Chermiti (63.Oussama Darragi), Issam Jemâa. Trainer: Humberto Manuel
Jesus Coelho (Portugal).
Goal: 1-0 Dário Alberto Jesus Monteiro (83).
Cautions: Elias Gaspar Pelembe „Dinguês",Manuel José Luis Bucuane „Tico-Tico", João Raphael
Kapango / Khaled Souissi.

GROUP C

28.03.2009	Kigali	Rwanda - Algeria		0-0
29.03.2009	Cairo	Egypt - Zambia		1-1(1-0)
06.06.2009	Chililabombwe	Zambia - Rwanda		1-0(0-0)
07.06.2009	Blida	Algeria - Egypt		3-1(0-0)
20.06.2009	Chililabombwe	Zambia - Algeria		0-2(0-1)
05.07.2009	Cairo	Egypt - Rwanda		3-0(0-0)
05.09.2009	Kigali	Rwanda - Egypt		0-1(0-0)
06.09.2009	Blida	Algeria - Zambia		1-0(0-0)
10.10.2009	Chililabombwe	Zambia - Egypt		0-1(0-0)
11.10.2009	Blida	Algeria - Rwanda		3-1(2-1)
14.11.2009	Kigali	Rwanda - Zambia		0-0
14.11.2009	Cairo	Egypt - Algeria		2-0(1-0)

FINAL STANDINGS

1. Algeria	6	4	1	1	9 - 4		13
2. Egypt	6	4	1	1	9 - 4		13
3. Zambia	6	1	2	3	2 - 5		5
4. Rwanda	6	0	2	4	1 - 8		2

PLAY-OFF

18.11.2009	Omdurman (Sudan)	**ALGERIA** - Egypt	1-0(1-0)

Algeria qualified for the 19th World Cup Final Tournament.

28.03.2009, Stade Amahoro, Kigali; Attendance: 22,000
Referee: Coffi Codjia (Benin)
RWANDA - ALGERIA   **0-0**
RWA: Jean-Claude Ndori, Bonaventure Hategekimana, Patrick Mutesa Mafisango, Elias Ntaganda (46.Jean-Baptiste Mugiraneza), Hamad Ndikumana, Boubakary Sadou, Eric Gasana Mbuyu Twite, Haruna Niyonzima, Olivier Karekezi, Jimmy Mulisa (46.Jimmy Gatété), Saïd Abed Makasi (90+2.Pekeyake Tuyisenge). Trainer: Branko Tucak (Croatia).
LG: Lounès Gaouaoui, Slimane Raho, Madjid Bougherra, Rafik Halliche, Nadir Belhadj, Karim Matmour, Yazid Mansouri (Cap), Khaled Lemmouchia, Kamel Ghilas (60.Hameur Bouazza), Rafik Saïfi (60.Rafik Djebbour), Abdelkader Ghezzal (90+1.Lazhar Hadj Aïssa). Trainer: Rabah Saâdane.
Cautions: Patrick Mutesa Mafisango / Rafik Saïfi.

29.03.2009, International Stadium, Cairo; Attendance: 70,000
Referee: Koman Coulibaly (Mali)
EGYPT - ZAMBIA   **1-1(1-0)**
EGY: Essam Kamal Tawfik El-Hadary, Ahmed Al-Muhammadi Abdel Fattah, Wael Gomaa Kamel El Hooty, Hani Mohammed Said Zakaria (72.Hosni Abd Rabo Abd El Motalem Ibrahim), Mohamed Barakat Ahmed Bastamy, Ahmed Fathi, Ahmed Hassan Kamel (Cap), Mohamed Shawky Ali Sallam, Mohamed Abdullah Zidan (57.Mohamed Aboutrika), Amr Hassan Zaki, Emad Mohamed Abd El Naby Ibrahim „Emad Moteab" (68.Ahmed Hossam Hussein Abdelamid „Mido"). Trainer: Hassan Shehata.
ZAM: Kennedy Mweene, Dennis Banda, Emmanuel Mbola, Misheck Lungu (54.Joseph Musonda), Henry Nyambe Mulenga, Francis Kasonde, Noah Sikombe Chivuta, Rainford Kalaba (85.Chintu Kampamba), Felix Katongo (88.Fwayo Tembo), Christopher Katongo, Jacob Mulenga. Trainer: Hervé Renard (France).
Goals: 1-0 Amr Hassan Zaki (27), 1-1 Francis Kasonde (56).
Cautions: Hani Mohammed Said Zakaria, Mohamed Shawky Ali Sallam / Emmanuel Mbola, Rainford Kalaba.

06.06.2009, Konkola Stadium, Chililabombwe; Attendance: 28,000
Referee: Cheikh Ahmed Tidane Seck (Senegal)
ZAMBIA - RWANDA   **1-0(0-0)**
ZAM: Kennedy Mweene, Dennis Banda, Emmanuel Mbola, Joseph Musonda, Henry Nyambe Mulenga, Francis Kasonde, Noah Sikombe Chivuta (36.Collins Ntofontofo Mbezuma; 73.James Chamanga), Rainford Kalaba, Felix Katongo, Christopher Katongo, Given Singuluma (61.Jacob Mulenga). Trainer: Hervé Renard (France).
RWA: Jean-Claude Ndori, Patrick Mutesa Mafisango, Elias Ntaganda, Aloua Gaseruka (81.Saïd Abed Makasi), Hamad Ndikumana, Boubakary Sadou, Eric Gasana Mbuyu Twite, Jean-Baptiste Mugiraneza (66.Jean Bosco Ngaboyisibo), Haruna Niyonzima (46.Bonaventure Hategekimana), Olivier Karekezi, Labama Bokota. Trainer: Branko Tucak (Croatia).
Goal: 1-0 Rainford Kalaba (78).
Cautions: Dennis Banda / Jean-Baptiste Mugiraneza, Boubakary Sadou, Saïd Abed Makasi.

07.06.2009, Stade „Mustapha Tchaker", Blida; Attendance: 26,500
Referee: Daniel Bennett (South Africa)
ALGERIA - EGYPT   **3-1(0-0)**
ALG: Lounès Gaouaoui, Madjid Bougherra, Rafik Halliche, Anthar Yahia, Nadir Belhadj, Karim Ziani, Yazid Mansouri (Cap), Khaled Lemmouchia, Karim Matmour (85.Hameur Bouazza), Abdelkader Ghezzal (90.Kamel Ghilas), Rafik Djebbour (83.Yacine Bezzaz). Trainer: Rabah Saâdane.
EGY: Essam Kamal Tawfik El-Hadary, Ahmed Fathi, Wael Gomaa Kamel El Hooty, Hani Mohammed Said Zakaria, Ahmed Said (66.Ahmed Hassan Kamel), Sayed Moawad Abdelwahed, Mohamed Shawky Ali Sallam, Hosni Abd Rabo Abd El Motalem Ibrahim, Mohamed Aboutrika, Amr Hassan Zaki (81.Ahmed Abdel Raouf Mohamed Adam), Mohamed Abdullah Zidan (81.Ahmed Eid Abdel Malek). Trainer: Hassan Shehata.
Goals: 1-0 Karim Matmour (60), 2-0 Abdelkader Ghezzal (63), 3-0 Rafik Djebbour (77), 3-1 Mohamed Aboutrika (86).
Cautions: Anthar Yahia, Nadir Belhadj, Abdelkader Ghezzal, Rafik Djebbour, Yazid Mansouri / Amr Hassan Zaki, Ahmed Hassan Kamel.

20.06.2009, Konkola Stadium, Chililabombwe; Attendance: 9,000
Referee: Raphael Divine Evehe (Cameroon)
ZAMBIA - ALGERIA   **0-2(0-1)**
ZAM: Kennedy Mweene, Dennis Banda, Emmanuel Mbola, Joseph Musonda, Henry Nyambe Mulenga, Francis Kasonde (46.Noah Sikombe Chivuta), Rainford Kalaba, Felix Katongo, Christopher Katongo (71.Emmanuel Mayuka), Jacob Mulenga, Given Singuluma (46.Fwayo Tembo). Trainer: Hervé Renard (France).
ALG: Lounès Gaouaoui, Madjid Bougherra, Rafik Halliche, Anthar Yahia, Nadir Belhadj, Karim Matmour, Khaled Lemmouchia, Yazid Mansouri (Cap), Karim Ziani (85.Yacine Bezzaz), Abdelkader Ghezzal (61.Rafik Saïfi), Rafik Djebbour (82.Hameur Bouazza). Trainer: Rabah Saâdane.
Goals: 0-1 Madjid Bougherra (21), 0-2 Rafik Saïfi (66).
Cautions: Rainford Kalaba / Karim Ziani, Karim Matmour.

05.07.2009, Cairo Military Academy Stadium, Cairo; Attendance: 18,000
Referee: Emmanuel Imiere (Nigeria)
EGYPT - RWANDA   **3-0(0-0)**
EGY: Essam Kamal Tawfik El-Hadary (Cap), Ahmed Al-Muhammadi Abdel Fattah, Wael Gomaa Kamel El Hooty, Hani Mohammed Said Zakaria, Mahmoud Fathallah Abdo, Sayed Moawad Abdelwahed (73.Abdel Aziz Tawfik Hassan), Mohamed Shawky Ali Sallam (42.Ahmed Abdel Raouf Mohamed Adam), Mohamed Soliman „Humoos", Hosni Abd Rabo Abd El Motalem Ibrahim, Mohamed Aboutrika, Mohamed Abdullah Zidan (53.Ahmed Eid Abdel Malek). Trainer: Hassan Shehata.
RWA: Jean-Claude Ndori, Cyrille Agnini Kouame (78.Jean Bosco Ngaboyisibo), Patrick Mutesa Mafisango, Elias Ntaganda (78.Jean-Paul Eale Lutula), Hamad Ndikumana, Boubakary Sadou, Eric

Gasana Mbuyu Twite, Didier Kapet Kouin, Jean-Baptiste Mugiraneza, Haruna Niyonzima, Olivier Karekezi. Trainer: Branko Tucak (Croatia).
Goals: 1-0 Mohamed Aboutrika (64), 2-0 Hosni Abd Rabo Abd El Motalem Ibrahim (74 penalty), 3-0 Mohamed Aboutrika (90).
Cautions: Eric Gasana Mbuyu Twite, Patrick Mutesa Mafisango.
Sent off: Eric Gasana Mbuyu Twite (88).

05.09.2009, Stade Amahoro, Kigali; Attendance: 20,000
Referee: Joseph Lamptey (Ghana)
RWANDA - EGYPT   **0-1(0-0)**
RWA: Jean-Claude Ndori, Louis Aniweta (79.Hussein Sibomana), Hamad Ndikumana, Boubakary Sadou, Edwin Ouon, Didier Kapet Kouin, Jean Bosco Ngaboyisibo, Haruna Niyonzima, Jimmy Gatété (81.Daddy Birori), Olivier Karekezi, Saïd Abed Makasi (60.Labama Bokota). Trainer: Branko Tucak (Croatia).
EGY: Essam Kamal Tawfik El-Hadary, Ahmed Fathi, Wael Gomaa Kamel El Hooty, Hani Mohammed Said Zakaria, Ahmed Said, Sayed Moawad Abdelwahed, Mohamed Shawky Ali Sallam, Hosni Abd Rabo Abd El Motalem Ibrahim, Ahmed Hassan Kamel (Cap) (59.Ahmed Eid Abdel Malek), Al-Sayed Hamdy (33.Mohamed El-Gabbas), Ahmed Abdel Raouf Mohamed Adam (70.Mohamed Barakat Ahmed Bastamy). Trainer: Hassan Shehata.
Goal: 0-1 Ahmed Hassan Kamel (67).
Cautions: Louis Aniweta / Ahmed Fathi, Mohamed Shawky Ali Sallam.

06.09.2009, Stade „Mustapha Tchaker", Blida; Attendance: 30,000
Referee: Rajindraparsad Seechurn (Mauritius)
ALGERIA - ZAMBIA   **1-0(0-0)**
ALG: Lounès Gaouaoui, Madjid Bougherra, Rafik Halliche, Anthar Yahia (46.Mourad Meghni), Nadir Belhadj, Karim Matmour, Khaled Lemmouchia, Yazid Mansouri (Cap), Karim Ziani, Rafik Saïfi (76.Kamel Ghilas), Rafik Djebbour (65.Abdelkader Ghezzal). Trainer: Rabah Saâdane.
ZAM: Kennedy Mweene, Dennis Banda, Hichani Himoonde, Emmanuel Mbola, Joseph Musonda, Noah Sikombe Chivuta (76.Henry Banda), Stophira Sunzu, Felix Katongo, Jonas Sakuwaha (68.James Chamanga), Christopher Katongo (76.Given Singuluma), Jacob Mulenga. Trainer: Hervé Renard (France).
Goal: 1-0 Yazid Mansouri (73).
Cautions: Yazid Mansouri / Christopher Katongo, Felix Katongo.

10.10.2009, Konkola Stadium, Chililabombwe; Attendance: 10,000
Referee: Kokou Djaoupé (Togo)
ZAMBIA - EGYPT   **0-1(0-0)**
ZAM: Kennedy Mweene, Dennis Banda, Hichani Himoonde, Emmanuel Mbola, Joseph Musonda (84.Jonas Sakuwaha), Noah Sikombe Chivuta (74.Emmanuel Mayuka), Andrew Mutambo Sinkala, Stophira Sunzu, Rainford Kalaba, Christopher Katongo, Collins Ntofontofo Mbezuma (68.Given Singuluma). Trainer: Hervé Renard (France).
EGY: Essam Kamal Tawfik El-Hadary, Ahmed Fathi, Ahmed Said (85.Sherif Abdel-Fadil), Hani Mohammed Said Zakaria, Wael Gomaa Kamel El Hooty, Sayed Moawad Abdelwahed, Mohamed Barakat Ahmed Bastamy (58.Ahmed Abdel Raouf Mohamed Adam), Ahmed Hassan Kamel (Cap), Hosni Abd Rabo Abd El Motalem Ibrahim, Mohamed Aboutrika, Amr Hassan Zaki (79.Ahmed Eid Abdel Malek). Trainer: Hassan Shehata.
Goal: 0-1 Hosni Abd Rabo Abd El Motalem Ibrahim (69).
Cautions: Rainford Kalaba, Given Singuluma / Ahmed Said, Wael Gomaa Kamel El Hooty.

11.10.2009, Stade „Mustapha Tchaker", Blida; Attendance: 22,000
Referee: Yakhouba Keita (Guinea)
ALGERIA - RWANDA   **3-1(2-1)**
ALG: Lounès Gaouaoui, Madjid Bougherra, Rafik Halliche, Anthar Yahia, Nadir Belhadj, Mourad

221

Meghni, Karim Matmour (73.Hassan Yebda), Khaled Lemmouchia, Karim Ziani, Rafik Saïfi (Cap) (72.Rafik Djebbour), Abdelkader Ghezzal (85.Kamel Ghilas). Trainer: Rabah Saâdane.
RWA: Jean-Luc Ndayishimiye, Louis Aniweta, Cyrille Agnini Kouame, Edwin Ouon, Patrick Mutesa Mafisango, Hamad Ndikumana, Boubakary Sadou, Jean-Baptiste Mugiraneza, Jean Bosco Ngaboyisibo, Haruna Niyonzima, Jean-Paul Eale Lutula (90+1.Jimmy Gatété). Trainer: Branko Tucak (Croatia).
Goals: 0-1 Patrick Mutesa Mafisango (19), 1-1 Abdelkader Ghezzal (22), 2-1 Nadir Belhadj (45+2), 3-1 Karim Ziani (90 penalty).
Cautions: Hamad Ndikumana, Jean Bosco Ngaboyisibo, Boubakary Sadou, Jean-Paul Eale Lutula, Edwin Ouon.

14.11.2009, Stade Amahoro, Kigali; Attendance: 18,000
Referee: Jamel Ambaya (Libya)
RWANDA - ZAMBIA   **0-0**
RWA: Jean-Luc Ndayishimiye, Louis Aniweta, Mow Kalisa, Patrick Mutesa Mafisango, Didier Lapet Kouin (65.Jimmy Gatété), Eric Gasana Mbuyu Twite, Jean-Baptiste Mugiraneza, Haruna Niyonzima, Abbas Rassou, Labama Bokota (65.Saïd Abed Makasi), Jean-Paul Eale Lutula (46.Olivier Karekezi). Trainer: Branko Tucak (Croatia).
ZAM: Kennedy Mweene, Dennis Banda, Chintu Kampamba, Emmanuel Mbola, Joseph Musonda, Noah Sikombe Chivuta (67.Francis Kasonde), William Njovu, James Chamanga (46.Felix Katongo), Rainford Kalaba (75.Given Singuluma), Christopher Katongo, Jacob Mulenga. Trainer: Hervé Renard (France).
Cautions: Haruna Niyonzima, Jean-Baptiste Mugiraneza, Louis Aniweta / Rainford Kalaba, Kennedy Mweene, Emmanuel Mbola.
Sent off: Jean-Baptiste Mugiraneza (90+4).

14.11.2009, International Stadium, Cairo; Attendance: 75,000
Referee: Jerome Damon (South Africa)
EGYPT - ALGERIA   **2-0(1-0)**
EGY: Essam Kamal Tawfik El-Hadary, Ahmed Al-Muhammadi Abdel Fattah, Ahmed Fathi, Hani Mohammed Said Zakaria, Abdel Zaher El-Saqua, Sayed Moawad Abdelwahed, Ahmed Hassan Kamel (Cap), Mohamed Soliman „Humoos" (56.Mohamed Barakat Ahmed Bastamy), Mohamed Aboutrika, Amr Hassan Zaki (65.Emad Mohamed Abd El Naby Ibrahim „Emad Moteab"), Mohamed Abdullah Zidan (78.Ahmed Eid Abdel Malek). Trainer: Hassan Shehata.
ALG: Lounès Gaouaoui, Madjid Bougherra, Rafik Halliche (72.Abdelkader Laïfaoui), Anthar Yahia, Nadir Belhadj, Karim Matmour (46.Yacine Bezzaz), Yazid Mansouri (Cap), Karim Ziani, Khaled Lemmouchia, Mourad Meghni, Rafik Saïfi (63.Abdelkader Ghezzal). Trainer: Rabah Saâdane.
Goals: 1-0 Amr Hassan Zaki (2), 2-0 Emad Mohamed Abd El Naby Ibrahim „Emad Moteab" (90+5).
Cautions: Lounès Gaouaoui, Khaled Lemmouchia.

PLAY-OFF

18.11.2009, Al Merreikh Stadium, Omdurman (Sudan); Attendance: 35,000
Referee: Eddy Allen Maillet Guyto (Seychelles)
ALGERIA - EGYPT   **1-0(1-0)**
ALG: Faouzi Chaouchi, Madjid Bougherra, Rafik Halliche, Anthar Yahia (67.Samir Zaoui), Mourad Meghni (57.Karim Matmour), Hassan Yebda, Yazid Mansouri (Cap), Karim Ziani, Nadir Belhadj, Rafik Saïfi (89.Kamel Ghilas), Abdelkader Ghezzal. Trainer: Rabah Saâdane.
EGY: Essam Kamal Tawfik El-Hadary, Ahmed Al-Muhammadi Abdel Fattah, Wael Gomaa Kamel El Hooty, Hani Mohammed Said Zakaria, Abdel Zaher El-Saqua (75.Ahmed Eid Abdel Malek), Sayed Moawad Abdelwahed, Ahmed Hassan Kamel (Cap), Ahmed Fathi (46.Hosni Abd Rabo Abd El Motalem Ibrahim), Mohamed Aboutrika, Emad Mohamed Abd El Naby Ibrahim „Emad Moteab", Amr Hassan Zaki (46.Mohamed Abdullah Zidan). Trainer: Hassan Shehata.
Goals: 1-0 Anthar Yahia (40).
Cautions: Nadir Belhadj, Abdelkader Ghezzal, Karim Ziani, Hassan Yebda / Wael Gomaa Kamel El Hooty, Hosni Abd Rabo Abd El Motalem Ibrahim.

GROUP D

28.03.2009	Omdurman	Sudan - Mali	1-1(1-1)
29.03.2009	Kumasi	Ghana - Benin	1-0(1-0)
07.06.2009	Cotonou	Benin - Sudan	1-0(1-0)
07.06.2009	Bamako	Mali - Ghana	0-2(0-0)
20.06.2009	Omdurman	Sudan - Ghana	0-2(0-1)
21.06.2009	Bamako	Mali - Benin	3-1(1-1)
06.09.2009	Cotonou	Benin - Mali	1-1(0-0)
06.09.2009	Accra	Ghana - Sudan	2-0(1-0)
11.10.2009	Cotonou	Benin – Ghana	1-0(0-0)
11.10.2009	Bamako	Mali - Sudan	1-0(0-0)
14.11.2009	Omdurman	Sudan - Benin	1-2(1-1)
15.11.2009	Kumasi	Ghana - Mali	2-2(0-1)

FINAL STANDINGS

1. GHANA	6	4	1	1	9 - 3	13
2. Benin	6	3	1	2	6 - 6	10
3. Mali	6	2	3	1	8 - 7	9
4. Sudan	6	0	1	5	2 - 9	1

Ghana qualified for the 19th World Cup Final Tournament.

28.03.2009, Al Merreikh Stadium, Omdurman; Attendance: 35,000
Referee: Eddy Allen Maillet Guyto (Seychelles)
SUDAN - MALI   **1-1(1-1)**
SUD: Hafez Ahmad Mustafa Hamed, Ahmed Adam Al Basha, Tariq Mukhtar Kafi, Hassan Ishaq Hassan (58.Mohamed Tahir Osman), Nasr Eldin Omer Ahmed Al Shigail, Ballah Gabir Kortokaila, Bader El Din Abdalla El Doud Galag (74.Ragei Abdelati Abdalla), Haitham Mostafa Ahmed Karar, Mosa El Nour, Mudather Eltaib Ibrahim El Tahir (82.El Zeldin El Ghaib), Haytham Kamal Tambal. Trainer: Stephen Phillip Constantine (England).
MLI: Mahamadou Sidibé, Adama Coulibaly, Souleymane Diamouténé, Bakary Soumaré, Adama Tamboura, Soumaïla Coulibaly (85.Souleymane Dembélé), Sidi Yaya Keïta, Seydou Keïta, Mahamane El Hadji Traoré (87.Bakaye Traoré), Mustapha Yatabaré (63.Modibo Maïga), Frédéric Oumar Kanouté (Cap). Trainer: Stephen Okechukwu Keshi (Nigeria).
Goals: 0-1 Frédéric Oumar Kanouté (19), 1-1 Mudather Eltaib Ibrahim El Tahir (23).
Cautions: Mosa El Nour.

29.03.2009, Baba Yara Stadium, Kumasi; Attendance: 39,000
Referee: Daniel Bennett (South Africa)
GHANA - BENIN   **1-0(1-0)**
GHA: Richard Paul Franck Kingson, John Paintsil, Samuel Diadie Inkoom, Jonathan Quartey, Eric Pappoe Addo, Anthony Annan, Stephen Appiah (74.Asamoah Gyan), Michael Kojo Essien, Matthew Amoah (60.Kojo „Kwadwo" Asamoah), Prince Tagoe, Sulleyman Ali Muntari (87.Isaac Vorsah). Trainer: Milovan Rajevac (Serbia).
BEN: Yoann Djidonou, Abdoul Khaled Akiola Adénon, Damien Koffi Anderson Chrysostome, Anicet Adjamossi, Idrissou Moustapha Agnidé (78.Nouhoum Kobénam), Jocelyn Ahouéya (74.Djiman Koukou), Stéphane Sessegnon, Seidath Kenabe Tchomogo, Romuald Boco, Razak Omotoyossi, Mickaël Poté. Trainer: Michel Dussuyer (France).
Goal: 1-0 Prince Tagoe (1).
Cautions: Jonathan Quartey, Richard Paul Franck Kingson / Anicet Adjamossi.

07.06.2009, Stade de l'Amitié, Cotonou; Attendance: 26,000
Referee: Kenias Marange (Zimbabwe)
BENIN - SUDAN   **1-0(1-0)**
BEN: Yoann Djidonou, Abdoul Khaled Akiola Adénon, Damien Koffi Anderson Chrysostome, John Glélé (83.Félicien Singbo), Jocelyn Ahouéya, Stéphane Sessegnon, Seidath Kenabe Tchomogo, Mouritala Ogunbiyi (62.Nouhoum Kobénam), Romuald Boco, Razak Omotoyossi (87.Djiman Koukou), Mickaël Poté. Trainer: Michel Dussuyer (France).
SUD: El Muez Mahjoub Abdallah, Ahmed Adam Al Basha, Tariq Mukhtar Kafi, Ballah Gabir Kortokaila, Saeed Mustafa Balla Gaber, Hassan Ishaq Hassan (78.Mohamed Tahir Osman), Saifeldin Ali Idris Farah Masawi, Mugahid Ahmed Mohammed (62.Moshraf Zakaria Ahmad), Ahmed Adil Hamad (68.El Zeldin El Ghaib), Mudather Eltaib Ibrahim El Tahir, Amin Sami Abdalla. Trainer: Stephen Phillip Constantine (England).
Goal: 1-0 Razak Omotoyossi (22).
Cautions: Razak Omotoyossi, Abdoul Khaled Akiola Adénon / Ahmed Adil Hamad, Moshraf Zakaria Ahmad.

07.06.2009, Stade 26 mars, Bamako; Attendance: 40,000
Referee: Raphael Divine Evehe (Cameroon)
MALI - GHANA   **0-2(0-0)**
MLI: Mahamadou Sidibé (Cap), Lassana Fané, Souleymane Diamouténé, Bakary Soumaré, Drissa Diakité, Adama Tamboura (90+1.Souleymane Dembélé), Alphousseyni Keïta, Seydou Keïta, Modibo Maïga, Mamadou Diallo (84.Yacouba Diarra), Frédéric Oumar Kanouté. Trainer: Stephen Okechukwu Keshi (Nigeria).
GHA: Richard Paul Franck Kingson, John Paintsil, Harrison Afful, John Mensah, Eric Pappoe Addo, Anthony Annan, Michael Kojo Essien (90.Moussa Narry), Kojo „Kwadwo" Asamoah, Prince Tagoe (80.Haminu Dramani), Nana Opoku Agyemang-Prempeh (87.Isaac Vorsah), Matthew Amoah. Trainer: Milovan Rajevac (Serbia).
Goals: 0-1 Kojo „Kwadwo" Asamoah (67), 0-2 Mathew Amoah (79).
Cautions: X / Nana Opoku Agyemang-Prempeh, John Paintsil.
 # , Seydou KEITA (MLI) 72'

20.06.2009, Al Merreikh Stadium, Omdurman; Attendance: 30,000
Referee: Jamel Ambaya (Libya)
SUDAN - GHANA   **0-2(0-1)**
SUD: Hafez Ahmad Mustafa Hamed, Tariq Mukhtar Kafi, Moshraf Zakaria Ahmad, Ballah Gabir Kortokaila, Saeed Mustafa Balla Gaber, Hamouda Ahmed El Bashir, Hassan Ishaq Hassan (32.Mousa Zuma Al Tayeb), Haitham Mostafa Ahmed Karar (60.Alaa Eldin Yousif Ahmed Hado), Ahmed Adil Hamad (64.Abdelhamid Amari), Mudather Eltaib Ibrahim El Tahir, Amin Sami Abdalla. Trainer: Stephen Phillip Constantine (England).
GHA: Richard Paul Franck Kingson, Samuel Diadie Inkoom, Harrison Afful, John Mensah, Eric Pappoe Addo, Michael Kojo Essien, Anthony Annan, Nana Opoku Agyemang-Prempeh (54.Isaac Vorsah), Mathew Amoah (85.Manuel „Junior" Agogo), Prince Tagoe (80.Haminu Dramani), Kojo „Kwadwo" Asamoah. Trainer: Milovan Rajevac (Serbia).
Goals: 0-1 Mathew Amoah (6), 0-2 Mathew Amoah (52).
Cautions: Tariq Mukhtar Kafi, Saeed Mustafa Balla Gaber, Alaa Eldin Yousif Ahmed Hado / Kojo „Kwadwo" Asamoah, John Mensah.

21.06.2009, Stade 26 mars, Bamako; Attendance: 40,000
Referee: Essam Abd El Fatah (Egypt)
MALI - BENIN   **3-1(1-1)**
MLI: Mahamadou Sidibé (Cap), Lassana Fané, Souleymane Diamouténé, Bakary Soumaré, Adama Tamboura, Drissa Diakité, Bakaye Traoré (78.Alphousseyni Keïta), Jimmy Boubou Kébé (22.Souleymane Dembélé), Modibo Maïga, Mahamane El Hadji Traoré (62.Mamadou Diallo), Frédéric

Oumar Kanouté. Trainer: Stephen Okechukwu Keshi (Nigeria).
BEN: Yoann Djidonou, Abdoul Khaled Akiola Adénon, Damien Koffi Anderson Chrysostome, Anicet Adjamossi, Jocelyn Ahouéya, Nouhoum Kobénam (80.Jean Louis Pascal Angan), Stéphane Sessegnon, Félicien Singbo, Seidath Kenabe Tchomogo (90.Romuald Boco), Mouritala Ogunbiyi, Mickaël Poté (70.Abou Gariga Maïga). Trainer: Michel Dussuyer (France).
Goals: 0-1 Seidath Kenabe Tchomogo (15), 1-1 Modibo Maïga (29), 2-1 Mamadou Diallo (76), 3-1 Frédéric Oumar Kanouté (84).
Cautions: Lassana Fané, Bakary Soumaré, Souleymane Dembélé, Drissa Diakité / Abdoul Khaled Akiola Adénon, Anicet Adjamossi, Stéphane Sessegnon.

06.09.2009, Stade de l'Amitié, Cotonou; Attendance: 33,000
Referee: Jerome Damon (South Africa)
BENIN - MALI   **1-1(0-0)**
BEN: Yoann Djidonou, Damien Koffi Anderson Chrysostome, Réda Johnson, Jocelyn Ahouéya, Félicien Singbo (39.Moufoutaou Adou), Jean Louis Pascal Angan, Seidath Kenabe Tchomogo (79.Djiman Koukou), Mouritala Ogunbiyi, Romuald Boco, Razak Omotoyossi, Mickaël Poté (79.Mohamed Aoudou). Trainer: Michel Dussuyer (France).
MLI: Mahamadou Sidibé (Cap), Adama Coulibaly, Adama Tamboura, Drissa Diakité, Bakaye Traoré, Soumaïla Coulibaly (55.Modibo Maïga), Bakary Soumaré, Seydou Keïta, Mahamane El Hadji Traoré (63.Mamadou Diallo), Mamadou Samassa (83.Alphousseyni Keïta), Frédéric Oumar Kanouté. Trainer: Stephen Okechukwu Keshi (Nigeria).
Goals: 0-1 Mamadou Samassa (72), 1-1 Mohamed Aoudou (87).
Cautions: Félicien Singbo, Jocelyn Ahouéya / Seydou Keïta, Alphousseyni Keïta, Mamadou Diallo.

06.09.2009, Ohene Djan Stadium, Accra; Attendance: 38,000
Referee: Essam Abd El Fatah (Egypt)
GHANA - SUDAN   **2-0(1-0)**
GHA: Richard Paul Franck Kingson, John Paintsil, Harrison Afful, Eric Pappoe Addo, John Mensah, Anthony Annan, Samuel Diadie Inkoom, Michael Kojo Essien, Matthew Amoah (86.Asamoah Gyan), Stephen Appiah (74.Laryea Kingston), Sulleyman Ali Muntari (88.Haminu Dramani). Trainer: Milovan Rajevac (Serbia).
SUD: Hafez Ahmad Mustafa Hamed, Ahmed Adam Al Basha, Hassan Abakar (81.Omar Mosaab Maaz), Mohamed Abdalla (68.Ragei Abdelati Abdalla), Moshraf Zakaria Ahmad, Nasr Eldin Omer Ahmed Al Shigail (64.Saeed Mustafa Balla Gaber), Alaa Eldin Yousif Ahmed Hado, Saifeldin Ali Idris Farah Masawi, Ahmed Idris, Mudather Eltaib Ibrahim El Tahir, Amin Sami Abdalla. Trainer: Stephen Phillip Constantine (England).
Goals: 1-0 Sulleyman Ali Muntari (14), Michael Kojo Essien (53).
Cautions: Sulleyman Ali Muntari, Stephen Appiah / Saifeldin Ali Idris Farah Masawi, Saeed Mustafa Balla Gaber.

11.10.2009, Stade de l'Amitié, Cotonou; Attendance: 20,000
Referee: Verson Lwanja (Malawi)
BENIN – GHANA   **1-0(0-0)**
BEN: Yoann Djidonou, Abdoul Khaled Akiola Adénon, Damien Koffi Anderson Chrysostome, Jocelyn Ahouéya, Stéphane Sessegnon, Félicien Singbo (39.Moufoutaou Adou), Seidath Kenabe Tchomogo (79.Djiman Koukou), Mouritala Ogunbiyi, Romuald Boco, Razak Omotoyossi (82.Mohamed Aoudou), Mickaël Poté. Trainer: Michel Dussuyer (France).
GHA: Richard Paul Franck Kingson, John Paintsil, Jonathan Quartey, Eric Pappoe Addo, Laryea Kingston, Stephen Appiah (80.Isaac Vorsah), Michael Kojo Essien, Samuel Kyere (70.Haminu Dramani), Asamoah Gyan (86.Derek Owusu Boateng), Matthew Amoah. Trainer: Milovan Rajevac (Serbia).
Goal: 1-0 Mohamed Aoudou (89).
Cautions: Matthew Amoah, Eric Pappoe Addo.

11.10.2009, Stade 26 mars, Bamako; Attendance: 15,000
Referee: Mohamed Benouza (Algeria)
MALI - SUDAN   **1-0(0-0)**
MLI: Mahamadou Sidibé, Adama Coulibaly, Adama Tamboura, Bakary Soumaré, Bakaye Traoré (76.Ténéma N'Diaye), Drissa Diakité, Mahamadou Diarra (Cap), Seydou Keïta, Frédéric Oumar Kanouté, Modibo Maïga (64.Sigamary Diarra), Mamadou Samassa. Trainer: Stephen Okechukwu Keshi (Nigeria).
SUD: Hafez Ahmad Mustafa Hamed, Tariq Mukhtar Kafi, Hassan Abakar, Mohamed Abdalla (31.Ragei Abdelati Abdalla), Moshraf Zakaria Ahmad, Alaa Eldin Yousif Ahmed Hado, Saeed Mustafa Balla Gaber, Ahmed Idris (87.Omar Mosaab Maaz), Mohamed Tahir Osman, Mudather Eltaib Ibrahim El Tahir (81.Nadir Elimam), Amin Sami Abdalla (*sent off 90*). Trainer: Stephen Phillip Constantine (England).
Goal: 1-0 Frédéric Oumar Kanouté (89).
Cautions: Mahamadou Diarra / Alaa Eldin Yousif Ahmed Hado, Hassan Abakar.
Sent off: Alaa Eldin Yousif Ahmed Hado (41), Amin Sami Abdalla (90).

14.11.2009, Al Merreikh Stadium, Omdurman; Attendance: 600
Referee: Slim Jedidi (Tunisia)
SUDAN - BENIN   **1-2(1-1)**
SUD: Ruei Ruei, Ahmed Adam Al Basha, Tariq Mukhtar Kafi, Hassan Abakar (46.Omar Mosaab Maaz), Mohamed Abdalla, Moshraf Zakaria Ahmad, Saeed Mustafa Balla Gaber, Ahmed Idris, Saifeldin Ali Idris Farah Masawi, Mohamed Tahir Osman (42.Ragei Abdelati Abdalla), Mudather Eltaib Ibrahim El Tahir (70.Bakri Makeen). Trainer: Stephen Phillip Constantine (England).
BEN: Rachad Chitou, Abdoul Khaled Akiola Adénon, Damien Koffi Anderson Chrysostome, Nouhoum Kobénam (83.Jocelyn Ahouéya), Stéphane Sessegnon, Félicien Singbo, Seidath Kenabe Tchomogo, Jean Louis Pascal Angan (46.Djiman Koukou), Mouritala Ogunbiyi, Romuald Boco, Razak Omotoyossi (70.Mohamed Aoudou). Trainer: Michel Dussuyer (France).
Goals: 0-1 Razak Omotoyossi (34 penalty), 1-1 Hassan Abakar (45+1 penalty), 1-2 Djiman Koukou (62).
Cautions: Moshraf Zakaria Ahmad / Abdoul Khaled Akiola Adénon.

15.11.2009, Baba Yara Stadium, Kumasi; Attendance: 39,000
Referee: Badara Diatta (Senegal)
GHANA - MALI   **2-2(0-1)**
GHA: Richard Paul Franck Kingson, John Paintsil, Samuel Diadie Inkoom, Eric Pappoe Addo, Jonathan Quartey, Anthony Annan, Stephen Appiah (61.Kojo „Kwadwo" Asamoah), Michael Kojo Essien (82.Emmanuel Agyemang-Badu), Matthew Amoah, Asamoah Gyan, Sulleyman Ali Muntari (79.Lee Addy). Trainer: Milovan Rajevac (Serbia).
MLI: Mahamadou Sidibé (Cap), Adama Coulibaly, Adama Tamboura, Lassana Fané, Bakary Soumaré, Drissa Diakité, Lassine Diarra, Mamadou Diallo (66.Mustapha Yatabaré), Sidi Yaya Keïta (90+2.Ousmane Berthé), Mamadou Bagayoko, Modibo Maïga (39.Ténéma N'Diaye). Trainer: Stephen Okechukwu Keshi (Nigeria).
Goals: 0-1 Lassana Fané (23), 1-1 Mathew Amoah (65), 1-2 Ténéma N'Diaye (68), 2-2 Anthony Annan (83).
Cautions: Lassana Fané, Ténéma N'Diaye.

GROUP E

28.03.2009	Ouagadougou	Burkina Faso - Guinea	4-2(2-0)
29.03.2009	Abidjan	Ivory Coast - Malawi	5-0(3-0)
06.06.2009	Blantyre	Malawi – Burkina Faso	0-1(0-0)
07.06.2009	Conakry	Guinea - Ivory Coast	1-2(0-1)
20.06.2009	Ouagadougou	Burkina Faso - Ivory Coast	2-3(1-1)
21.06.2009	Conakry	Guinea - Malawi	2-1(2-0)
05.09.2009	Blantyre	Malawi - Guinea	2-1(0-1)
05.09.2009	Abidjan	Ivory Coast – Burkina Faso	5-0(1-0)
10.10.2009	Blantyre	Malawi - Ivory Coast	1-1(0-0)
11.10.2009	Accra (Ghana)	Guinea – Burkina Faso	1-2(0-1)
14.11.2009	Ouagadougou	Burkina Faso - Malawi	1-0(0-0)
14.11.2009	Abidjan	Ivory Coast - Guinea	3-0(2-0)

FINAL STANDINGS

1. IVORY COAST	6	5	1	0	19 - 4	16
2. Burkina Faso	6	4	0	2	10 - 11	12
3. Malawi	6	1	1	4	4 - 11	4
4. Guinea	6	1	0	5	7 - 14	3

Ivory Cost qualified for the 19th World Cup Final Tournament.

28.03.2009, Stade du 4-Août, Ouagadougou; Attendance: 30,000
Referee: Mohamed Benouza (Algeria)
BURKINA FASO - GUINEA   **4-2(2-0)**
BFA: Daouda Diakité, Bakary Koné, Mahamoudou Kéré, Paul Kéba Koulibaly, Mamadou Tall, Mady Saïdou Panandétiguiri, Charles Kaboré, Alain Traoré (78.Yssouf Koné), Jonathan Pitroipa (62.Wilfried Sanou), Patrick Zoundi (38.Narcisse Yaméogo), Beli Moumouni Dagano (Cap). Trainer: Paulo Jorge Rebelo Duarte (Portugal).
GUI: Naby-Moussa Yattara, Dianbobo Baldé (46.Mamadou Alimou Diallo), Habib-Jean Baldé, Oumar Kalabane, Kamil Zayatte, Ibrahima Sorry Camara, Mamadou Diouldé Bah, Kévin Constant, Pascal Feindouno, Alhassane Keïta Otchico (62.Karamoko Cissé), Souleymane Youla (62.Larsen Touré). Trainer: Robert Nouzaret (France).
Goals: 1-0 Mahamoudou Kéré (23), 2-0 Alain Traoré (30), 3-0 Beli Moumouni Dagano (55 penalty), 3-1 Pascal Feindouno(65 penalty), 4-1 Beli Moumouni Dagano (71), 4-2 Kamil Zayatte (86).
Cautions: Mamadou Tall, Mahamoudou Kéré / Oumar Kalabane, Dianbobo Baldé, Naby-Moussa Yattara.

29.03.2009, Stade „Félix Houphouet-Boigny", Abidjan; Attendance: 34,000
Referee: Djamel Haimoudi (Algeria)
IVORY COAST - MALAWI   **5-0(3-0)**
CIV: Boubacar Barry, Abdoulaye Méïté (85.Souleymane Bamba), Kolo Habib Touré, Emmanuel Eboué, Siaka Tiéné, Emmanuel Koné, Christian Koffi Ndri „Romaric", Alain Didier Zokora Deguy, Bakari Koné (75.Abdul Kader Keïta), Didier Yves Drogba Tébily (78.Boubacar Sanogo), Salomon Kalou. Trainer: Vahid Halilhodž ċ (Bosnia-Herzegovina).
MWI: Swadick Sanudi, Elvis Bryson Kafoteka (90+1.Wisdom Ndholvu), Allan Kamanga, Peter Mponda (Cap), Moses Chavula, Hellings Mwakasungula (80.David John Banda), Robert Ng'ambi, Joseph Kamwendo, Peter Wadabwa, Chiukepo Msowoya, Jimmy Zakazaka. Trainer: Kinnah Phiri.
Goals: 1-0 Christian Koffi Ndri „Romaric" (1), 2-0 Didier Yves Drogba Tébily (6 penalty), 3-0 Didier Yves Drogba Tébily (27), 4-0 Salomon Kalou (59), 5-0 Bakari Koné (70).
Cautions: Emmanuel Koné / Elvis Bryson Kafoteka.

06.06.2009, Kamuzu Stadium, Blantyre; Attendance: 25,000
Referee: Kacem Bennaceur (Tunisia)
MALAWI – BURKINA FASO   **0-1(0-0)**
MWI: Swadick Sanudi, Allan Kamanga, Peter Mponda (Cap), James Sangala, Moses Chavula, Hellings Mwakasungula, Robert Ng'ambi, Joseph Kamwendo (74.Atusaye Nyondo), Essau Boxer Kanyenda, Chiukepo Msowoya, Jimmy Zakazaka (60.Peter Wadabwa). Trainer: Kinnah Phiri.
BFA: Daouda Diakité, Ibrahim Gnanou, Bakary Koné, Paul Kéba Koulibaly, Mady Saïdou Panandétiguiri, Charles Kaboré, Florent Rouamba, Alain Traoré (72.Roméo Bébé Kambou), Narcisse Yaméogo (86.Aristide Bancé), Patrick Zoundi (60.Jonathan Pitroipa), Beli Moumouni Dagano (Cap). Trainer: Paulo Jorge Rebelo Duarte (Portugal).
Goal: 0-1 Beli Moumouni Dagano (68).
Cautions: Allan Kamanga / Florent Rouamba, Paul Kéba Koulibaly.

07.06.2009, Stade 28 Septembre, Conakry; Attendance: 14,000
Referee: Essam Abd El Fatah (Egypt)
GUINEA - IVORY COAST   **1-2(0-1)**
GUI: Kémoko Camara, Habib-Jean Baldé, Mamadou Alimou Diallo (55.Dianbobo Baldé), Oumar Kalabane, Kamil Zayatte, Ibrahima Sorry Camara, Mamadou Diouldé Bah, Pascal Feindouno, Ismaël Bangoura, Sambégou Bangoura (90+1.Karamoko Cissé), Alhassane Keïta Otchico (63.Amara Karba Bangoura). Trainer: Robert Nouzaret (France).
CIV: Boubacar Barry, Guy Roland Demel, Kolo Habib Touré, Emmanuel Eboué, Siaka Tiéné, Gnegneri Yaya Touré (84.Emmanuel Koné), Christian Koffi Ndri „Romaric" (86.Benjamin Angoua Brou), Alain Didier Zokora Deguy, Salomon Kalou (80.Sekou Cissé), Bakari Koné, Didier Yves Drogba Tébily. Trainer: Vahid Halilhodž è (Bosnia-Herzegovina).
Goals: 0-1 Bakari Koné (44), 1-1Sambégou Bangoura (65), 1-2 Christian Koffi Ndri „Romaric" (72).
Cautions: Ibrahima Sorry Camara, Oumar Kalabane, Habib-Jean Baldé / Bakari Koné, Gnegneri Yaya Touré, Sekou Cissé.

20.06.2009, Stade du 4-Août, Ouagadougou; Attendance: 33,056
Referee: Jerome Damon (South Africa)
BURKINA FASO - IVORY COAST   **2-3(1-1)**
BFA: Daouda Diakité, Bakary Koné, Mahamoudou Kéré (Cap), Paul Kéba Koulibaly (35.Ibrahim Gnanou), Mamadou Tall, Mady Saïdou Panandétiguiri, Charles Kaboré, Jonathan Pitroipa, Patrick Zoundi (71.Aristide Bancé), Beli Moumouni Dagano, Wilfried Sanou (58.Alain Traoré). Trainer: Paulo Jorge Rebelo Duarte (Portugal).
CIV: Boubacar Barry, Abdoulaye Méïté, Guy Roland Demel (66.Siaka Tiéné), Kolo Habib Touré, Emmanuel Eboué, Gnegneri Yaya Touré, Christian Koffi Ndri „Romaric", Alain Didier Zokora Deguy, Salomon Kalou (90+2.Sekou Cissé), Bakari Koné (82.Souleymane Bamba), Didier Yves Drogba Tébily. Trainer: Vahid Halilhodž è (Bosnia-Herzegovina).
Goals: 0-1 Gnegneri Yaya Touré (14), 1-1 Jonathan Pitroipa (27), 1-2 Mamadou Tall (54 own goal), 1-3 Didier Yves Drogba Tébily (70), 2-3 Aristide Bancé (78).
Cautions: Charles Kaboré / Boubacar Barry.

21.06.2009, Stade 28 Septembre, Conakry; Attendance: 14,000
Referee: Khalid Abdel Rahman (Sudan)
GUINEA - MALAWI   **2-1(2-0)**
GUI: Kémoko Camara, Dianbobo Baldé, Mamadou Alimou Diallo, Kamil Zayatte, Ibrahima Sorry Camara, Kanfory Sylla, Mamadou Diouldé Bah, Pascal Feindouno (86.Mohamed Sacko), Ismaël Bangoura, Sambégou Bangoura (47.Ibrahima Bangoura), Ibrahim Yattara (74.Karamoko Cissé). Trainer: Aboubacar Sidiki Camara.
MWI: Swadick Sanudi, Elvis Bryson Kafoteka, Allan Kamanga, Peter Mponda (Cap), James Sangala (87.Wisdom Ndholvu), Moses Chavula, Hellings Mwakasungula, Robert Ng'ambi (46.Chiukepo Msowoya), Fisher Kenani Kondowe (40.David John Banda), Joseph Kamwendo, Essau Boxer Kanyenda.

Trainer: Kinnah Phiri.
Goals: 1-0 Pascal Feindouno (25), 2-0 Pascal Feindouno (43), 2-1 Chiukepo Msowoya (88).

05.09.2009, Kamuzu Stadium, Blantyre; Attendance: 15,000
Referee: Coffi Codjia (Benin)
MALAWI - GUINEA   **2-1(0-1)**
MWI: Swadick Sanudi, Elvis Bryson Kafoteka, Allan Kamanga, Peter Mponda (Cap), James Sangala, David John Banda (46.Chiukepo Msowoya), Moses Chavula, Hellings Mwakasungula, Peter Wadabwa, Joseph Kamwendo (71.Robert Ng'ambi), Russel Mwafulirwa (83.Victor Nyirenda). Trainer: Kinnah Phiri.
GUI: Kémoko Camara, Dianbobo Baldé, Oumar Kalabane, Ibrahima Sorry Camara, Alsény Camara, Kamil Zayatte, Kanfory Sylla, Pascal Feindouno (85.Ibrahima Bangoura), Ismaël Bangoura, Kaba Diawara, Fodé Mansaré (68.Souleymane Youla). Trainer: Aboubacar Sidiki Camara.
Goals: 0-1 Oumar Kalabane (38), 1-1 Chiukepo Msowoya (46), 2-1 Chiukepo Msowoya (59).
Cautions: Elvis Bryson Kafoteka, Hellings Mwakasungula.

05.09.2009, Stade „Félix Houphouët-Boigny", Abidjan; Attendance: 38,209
Referee: Eddy Allen Maillet Guyto (Seychelles)
IVORY COAST – BURKINA FASO   **5-0(1-0)**
CIV: Boubacar Barry, Souleymane Bamba, Kolo Habib Touré, Emmanuel Eboué, Arthur Etienne Boka, Siaka Tiéné (81.Emmanuel Koné), Gnegneri Yaya Touré, Alain Didier Zokora Deguy, Abdul Kader Keïta (88.Gervais Yao Kouassi „Gervinho"), Salomon Kalou, Didier Yves Drogba Tébily (85.Boubacar Sanogo). Trainer: Vahid Halilhodž č (Bosnia-Herzegovina).
BFA: Daouda Diakité, Bakary Koné, Mahamoudou Kéré (Cap), Paul Kéba Koulibaly, Mamadou Tall, Mady Saïdou Panandétiguiri, Charles Kaboré (88.Mohamed Koffi), Jonathan Pitroipa, Alain Traoré, Patrick Zoundi (54.Aristide Bancé), Beli Moumouni Dagano. Trainer: Paulo Jorge Rebelo Duarte (Portugal).
Goals: 1-0 Mady Saïdou Panandétiguiri (9 own goal), 2-0 Didier Yves Drogba Tébily (48), 3-0 Gnegneri Yaya Touré (54), 4-0 Didier Yves Drogba Tébily (64), 5-0 Abdul Kader Keïta (68).
Cautions: Siaka Tiéné / Beli Moumouni Dagano, Charles Kaboré.

10.10.2009, Kamuzu Stadium, Blantyre; Attendance: 25,000
Referee: Abdellah El Achiri (Morocco)
MALAWI - IVORY COAST   **1-1(0-0)**
MWI: Swadick Sanudi, Allan Kamanga, Peter Mponda (Cap), Maupo Msowoya, Jacob Ngwira, James Sangala, David John Banda (69.Robert Ng'ambi), Peter Wadabwa, Joseph Kamwendo, Russel Mwafulirwa (86.Atusaye Nyondo), Victor Nyirenda (69.Chiukepo Msowoya). Trainer: Kinnah Phiri.
CIV: Boubacar Barry, Souleymane Bamba, Guy Roland Demel, Emmanuel Eboué, Arthur Etienne Boka, Jean-Jacques Gosso, Emerse Faé (69.Gervais Yao Kouassi „Gervinho"), Emmanuel Koné (79.Gnegneri Yaya Touré), Alain Didier Zokora Deguy, Salomon Kalou, Sekou Cissé (65.Didier Yves Drogba Tébily). Trainer: Vahid Halilhodž č (Bosnia-Herzegovina).
Goals: 1-0 Jacob Ngwira (64), 1-1 Didier Yves Drogba Tébily (67).
Cautions: Russel Mwafulirwa, James Sangala, Peter Mponda / Souleymane Bamba.

11.10.2009, Ohene Djan Stadium, Accra (Ghana); Attendance: 5,000
Referee: Jamel Ambaya (Libya)
GUINEA – BURKINA FASO   **1-2(0-1)**
GUI: Kémoko Camara, Mamadou Alimou Diallo, Ibrahima Sorry Camara, Alsény Camara, Kamil Zayatte, Ibrahima Diallo (71.Alhassane Keïta Otchico), Mamadou Diouldé Bah, Pascal Feindouno, Ismaël Bangoura, Kaba Diawara (61.Ibrahima Bangoura), Fodé Mansaré (67.Kévin Constant). Trainer: Aboubacar Sidiki Camara.
BFA: Daouda Diakité, Bakary Koné, Mahamoudou Kéré (Cap), Paul Kéba Koulibaly, Mamadou Tall, Mady Saïdou Panandétiguiri, Florent Rouamba, Narcisse Yaméogo, Jonathan Pitroipa (86.Ibrahim Gnanou), Habib Bamogo (59.Mohamed Koffi), Beli Moumouni Dagano (72.Aristide Bancé). Trainer:

Paulo Jorge Rebelo Duarte (Portugal).
Goals: 0-1 Beli Moumouni Dagano (37 penalty), 0-2 Habib Bamogo (59), 1-2 (82).
Cautions: Mamadou Alimou Diallo, Fodé Mansaré / Mady Saïdou Panandétiguiri, Mahamoudou Kéré.

14.11.2009, Stade du 4-Août, Ouagadougou; Attendance: 20,000
Referee: Essam Abd El Fatah (Egypt)
BURKINA FASO - MALAWI   **1-0(0-0)**
BFA: Daouda Diakité, Ibrahim Gnanou, Mahamoudou Kéré (Cap) (67.Mohamed Koffi), Paul Kéba Koulibaly, Mamadou Tall, Charles Kaboré, Florent Rouamba, Narcisse Yaméogo (59.Patrick Zoundi), Jonathan Pitroipa (28.Abdoul-Aziz Nikiéma), Habib Bamogo, Beli Moumouni Dagano. Trainer: Paulo Jorge Rebelo Duarte (Portugal).
MWI: Swadick Sanudi, Allan Kamanga, Peter Mponda (Cap), Jacob Ngwira (34.David John Banda), James Sangala, Moses Chavula, Hellings Mwakasungula, Peter Wadabwa, Joseph Kamwendo, Chiukepo Msowoya (46.Essau Boxer Kanyenda), Russel Mwafulirwa (66.Victor Nyirenda). Trainer: Kinnah Phiri.
Goal: 1-0 Beli Moumouni Dagano (47).
Cautions: Hellings Mwakasungula, Allan Kamanga, David John Banda.

14.11.2009, Stade „Félix Houphouët-Boigny", Abidjan; Attendance: 28,000
Referee: Kenias Marange (Zimbabwe)
IVORY COAST - GUINEA   **3-0(2-0)**
CIV: Aristide Benoît Zogbo, Benjamin Angoua Brou, Souleymane Bamba, Emmanuel Eboué, Siaka Tiéné, Gnegneri Yaya Touré, Christian Koffi Ndri „Romaric" (70.Jean-Jacques Gosso), Alain Didier Zokora Deguy, Abdul Kader Keïta (78.Seydou Doumbia), Aruna Dindane (82.Sekou Cissé), Gervais Yao Kouassi „Gervinho". Trainer: Vahid Halilhodž è (Bosnia-Herzegovina).
GUI: Kémoko Camara, Ibrahima Sory Bangoura, Mamadou Alimou Diallo, Kamil Zayatte, Ibrahima Sorry Camara, Alsény Camara, Kévin Constant (65.Ismaël Bangoura), Pascal Feindouno, Ibrahima Bangoura (46.Mamadou Diouldé Bah), Alhassane Keïta Otchico, Souleymane Youla (83.Kaba Diawara). Trainer: Aboubacar Sidiki Camara.
Goals: 1-0 Gervais Yao Kouassi „Gervinho" (16), 2-0 Gervais Yao Kouassi „Gervinho" (31), 3-0 Siaka Tiéné (67).
Cautions: Siaka Tiéné / Alsény Camara, Mamadou Alimou Diallo.

ASIA

For the World Cup 2010 organized in South Africa, the Asian Football Confederation had been allocated four places to qualify directly for the Final Round. At the same time, a fifth team had the chance to play against the Oceania Zone Winner in a two leg tie to reach the Final Round.

43 Asian nations entered to play this World Cup qualifiers. Laos, Brunei and the Philippines did not take part in competition. For the first time, Australia (having moved from the Oceania Football Confederation in 2006) and Timor-Lense has competed in the World Cup qualifiers as a member of the Asian Football Confederation. Before the draw, teams were divided into three groups (pots):

Top Seeds: Australia, Korea Republic, Saudi Arabia, Japan, Iran (this teams entered only the 3rd Round).

Pot A: Bahrain, Uzbekistan, Kuwait, Korea D.P.R., China P.R., Jordan, Iraq, Lebanon, Oman, United Arab Emirates, Qatar, Syria, Palestine, Thailand, Turkmenistan, Tajikistan, Indonesia, Hong Kong, Yemen.

Pot B: Vietnam, Kyrgyzistan, Maldives, India, Singapore, Sri Lanka, Malaysia, Chinese Taipei, Bangladesh, Macau, Pakistan, Afghanistan, Mongolia, Guam, Nepal, Cambodia, Bhutan, Myanmar, Timor-Leste.

Teams from Pot A and Pot B played the 1st Round (Knock-out Round).

FIRST ROUND

22.10./28.10.2007	Pakistan - **Iraq**	0-7(0-2)	0-0
13.10./28.10.2007	**Uzbekistan** – Chinese Taipei	9-0(5-0)	2-0(0-0)
08.10./15.10.2007	**Thailand** - Macau	6-1(2-1)	7-1(3-0)
21.10./28.10.2007	Sri Lanka - **Qatar**	0-1(0-0)	0-5(0-2)
21.10./28.10.2007	**China P.R.** - Myanmar	7-0(2-0)	4-0(4-0)
	Bhutan - **Kuwait**	Bhutan withdrew	
18.10./28.10.2007	Kyrgyzstan - **Jordan**	2-0(1-0)	0-2(0-1)
			5-6 penalties
08.10./28.10.2007	Vietnam – **United Arab Emirates**	0-1(0-0)	0-5(0-2)
21.10./28.10.2007	**Bahrain** - Malaysia	4-1(2-1)	0-0
21.10./28.10.2007	Timor-Leste – **Hong Kong**	2-3(1-2)	1-8(0-2)
08.10./26.10.2007	**Syria** - Afghanistan	3-0(0-0)	2-1(1-1)
08.10./28.10.2007	**Yemen** - Maldives	3-0(1-0)	0-2(0-1)
08.10./28.10.2007	Bangladesh - **Tajikistan**	1-1(0-0)	0-5(0-0)
21.10./28.10.2007	Mongolia – **Korea D.P.R.**	1-4(0-3)	1-5(1-3)
08.10./28.10.2007	**Oman** - Nepal	2-0(2-0)	2-0(1-0)
08.10./28.10.2007	Palestine - **Singapore**	0-4(0-1)	0-3/awarded
08.10./30.10.2007	**Lebanon** - India	4-1(1-1)	2-2(0-1)
11.10./28.10.2007	Cambodia - **Turkmenistan**	0-1(0-0)	1-4(1-1)
	Guam – **Indonesia**	Guam withdrew	

22.10.2007, Punjab Stadium, Lahore; Attendance: 2,500
Referee: Kadyrbek Chynybekov (Kyrgyzstan)
PAKISTAN - IRAQ   **0-7(0-2)**
PAK: Muhammad Shahzad, Tanveer Ahmed (60.Yasir Sabir), Muhammad Naveed Akram, Samar Ishaq, Zesh Rehman, Abbas Ali, Ahmed Adeel (27.Imran Niazi), Adnan Farooq Ahmed, Amjad Iqbal (87.Shahid Ahmed), Muhammed Essa Khan, Farooq Shah. Trainer: Mohiuddin Akhtar.
IRQ: Noor Sabri Abbas Hassan, Jassim Mohammed Ghulam Al Hamd, Khaldoun Ibrahim Mohammed, Bassim Abbas Kati, Ali Hussein Rehema Al Muttairi, Ahmed Manajid Abbas, Karrar

Jassim Mohammed (65.Emad Mohammed Ridha), Mahdi Karim Ajeel, Qusai Munir Aboodi (72.Haitham Kadhim Tahir), Nashat Akram Ali, Ahmad Salah Alwan (56.Hawar Mulla Mohammed Taher Zibari). Trainer: Egil Roger Olsen (Norway).
Goals: 0-1 Nashat Akram Ali (19), 0-2 Mahdi Karim Ajeel (24), 0-3 Mahdi Karim Ajeel (49), 0-4 Jassim Mohammed Ghulam Al Hamd (71), 0-5 Emad Mohammed Ridha (83), 0-6 Mahdi Karim Ajeel (88), 0-7 Mahdi Karim Ajeel (90).

28.10.2007, Abbasiyyin Stadium, Damascus (Syria); Attendance: 8,000
Referee: Saad Kameel Al Fadhli (Kuwait)
IRAQ - PAKISTAN   **0-0**
PAK: Ahmed Iltaf, Tanveer Ahmed, Samar Ishaq, Zesh Rehman, Abbas Ali, Shahid Ahmed (78.Imran Niazi), Adnan Farooq Ahmed, Amjad Iqbal (68.Muhammad Irfan), Muhammed Essa Khan, Muhammad Qasim, Farooq Shah. Trainer: Mohiuddin Akhtar.
IRQ: Noor Sabri Abbas Hassan, Nabeel Abbas Lafta, Haidar Abdul-Amir Hussain, Khaldoun Ibrahim Mohammed, Ali Hussein Rehema Al Muttairi, Ahmed Manajid Abbas (66.Ahmad Salah Alwan), Mahdi Karim Ajeel, Hawar Mulla Mohammed Taher Zibari, Qusai Munir Aboodi (37.Haitham Kadhim Tahir), Nashat Akram Ali, Emad Mohammed Ridha (83.Alaa Abdul-Zahra Khashan). Trainer: Egil Roger Olsen (Norway).
Cautions: Adnan Farooq Ahmed, Muhammad Qasim, Muhammed Essa Khan.

13.10.2007, Central Army Stadium, Tashkent; Attendance: 7,000
Referee: Ali Hamad Madhad Saif Al Badwawi (United Arab Emirates)
UZBEKISTAN – CHINESE TAIPEI   **9-0(5-0)**
UZB: Ignatiy Nesterov, Asror Aliqulov, Islom Inomov (73.Bakhtier Ashurmatov), Aleksey Nikolaev (46.Vitaliy Denisov), Ilkhom Suyunov, Odil Ahmedov, Server Djeparov, Timur Kapadze, Ulugbek Bakaev (63.Shavkat Salomov), Maksim Shatskikh (Cap), Viktor Karpenko. Trainer: Rauf Inileev.
TPE: Lu Kun-chi, Kao Hao-chieh (17.Chen Chang-min), Kuo Chun-yi, Chen Yu-lin, Cheng Yung-jen (Cap), Feng Pao-hsing, Liang Chien-wei, Chen Po-liang, Chen Yi-wei, Huang Cheng-tsung (71.Lo Chih-an), Wu Pai-ho (73.Lo Chih-en). Trainer: Imai Toshiaki (Japan).
Goals: 1-0 Maksim Shatskikh (4), 2-0 Maksim Shatskikh (16), 3-0 Timur Kapadze (26), 4-0 Maksim Shatskikh (34), 5-0 Viktor Karpenko (43), 6-0 Ulugbek Bakaev (54), 7-0 Maksim Shatskikh (57), 8-0 Shavkat Salomov (68), 9-0 Maksim Shatskikh (77).
Cautions: Chen Yu-lin.

28.10.2007, Chungshan Soccer Stadium, Taipei; Attendance: 800
Referee: Tayeb Shamsuzzaman (Bangladesh)
CHINESE TAIPEI – UZBEKISTAN   **0-2(0-0)**
TPE: Lu Kun-chi (90+2.Hsu Jen-feng), Chen Chang-min, Hsieh Meng-hsuan, Chen Po-liang (85.Huang Cheng-tsung), Cheng Yung-jen (Cap) (76.Liang Chien-wei), Feng Pao-hsing, Kuo Chun-yi, Lin Tsung-jen, Hueng Wei-yi, Lo Chih-en, Lo Chih-an. Trainer: Trainer: Imai Toshiaki (Japan).
UZB: Ignatiy Nesterov, Bakhtier Ashurmatov, Islom Inomov, Hayrulla Karimov, Ilkhom Suyunov, Odil Ahmedov, Server Djeparov (Cap) (41.Shavkat Salomov), Azizbek Haydarov (72.Hamza Karimov), Timur Kapadze, Viktor Klishin, Pavel Solomin (74.Anvar Gafurov). Trainer: Rauf Inileev.
Goals: 0-1 Islom Inomov (81), 0-2 Ilkhom Suyunov (90).
Cautions: Lu Kun-chi, Huang Cheng-tsung / Hayrulla Karimov, Hamza Karimov.

08.10.2007, Suphachalasai Stadium, Bangkok; Attendance: 11,254
Referee: Kadyrbek Chynybekov (Kyrgyzstan)
THAILAND - MACAU   **6-1(2-1)**
THA: Sinthaweechai Hathairattanakool, Nattaporn Phanrit (66.Natthaphong Samana), Patiparn Phetphun, Prat Samakrat, Suree Sukha, Nirut Surasiang, Tawan Sripan, Datsakorn Thonglao, Sarayoot Chaikamdee (81.Pichitphong Choeichiu), Teerasil Dangda, Teeratep Winothai (67.Suriya Domtaisong).

Trainer: Chanvit Phalajivin.
MAC: Leong Chon Kit, Sou Fai Wong (55.Che Chi Man), Kong Cheng Hou, Lam Ka Koi (Cap), Emmanuel Libano Noruega (86.Chan Pak Chun), Cheang Cheng Ineong „Paulo", Geofredo De Sousa Cheung, Chan Man Hei (71.Leong Chong In), Leong Lap San, Luis Manuel Amorim Da Silva Hung, Chan Kin Seng. Trainer: Masanaga Kageyama (Japan).
Goals: 1-0 Sarayoot Chaikamdee (12), 2-0 Teerasil Dangda (21), 2-1 Kin Seng Chan (23), 3-1 Sarayoot Chaikamdee (49), 4-1 Teeratep Winothai (55 penalty), 5-1 Patiparn Phetphun (82), 6-1 Datsakorn Thonglao (90+1).
Cautions: Emmanuel Libano Noruega.

15.10.2007, Sports Field and Pavilion at MUST, Macau; Attendance: 500
Referee: Abdulrahman Racho (Syria)
MACAU - THAILAND   **1-7(0-3)**
MAC: Leong Chon Kit, Sou Fai Wong (83.Francisco Souza da Cunha), Lam Ka Pou, Kong Cheng Hou, Lam Ka Koi (Cap), Emmanuel Libano Noruega (57.Che Chi Man), Cheang Cheng Ineong „Paulo", Geofredo De Sousa Cheung, Chan Man Hei, Leong Lap San (63.Leong Chong In), Chan Kin Seng. Trainer: Masanaga Kageyama (Japan).
THA: Sivaruk Tedsungnoen, Jetsada Jitsawad, Kiatprawut Saiwaew (70.Apichet Puttan), Natthaphong Samana, Suree Sukha, Nirut Surasiang, Jakkrit Bunkham (44 Kittisak Tanasuwan), Pichitphong Choeichiu (63 Hadtaporn Suwan), Datsakorn Thonglao, Sarayoot Chaikamdee, Teerasil Dangda. Trainer: Chanvit Phalajivin.
Goals: 0-1 Teerasil Dangda (22), 0-2 Suree Sukha (39), 0-3 Nirut Surasiang (43), 0-4 Datsakorn Thonglao (48), 0-5 Sarayoot Chaikamdee (53), 0-6 Sarayoot Chaikamdee (57), 0-7 Sarayoot Chaikamdee (86), 1-7 Kin Seng Chan (90+2).

21.10.2007, Sugathadasa Stadium, Colombo; Attendance: 6,500
Referee: Malik Abdul Bashir (Singapore)
SRI LANKA - QATAR   **0-1(0-0)**
SRI: Sugath Dammika Thilakaratne, Thilina Suranda Bandara Liyana Arachchilage, Sellaperuma Arachige Dunil Lakshan Nirantha Perera, Ramlan Tuwan Gafoor Raheem, Rohana Dinesh Ruwan Thilaka Well Don, Ediri Bandanage Channa, Azmeer Lathif Mohamed, Mohamed Rawme Mohideen (69.Chandradasa Karunaratne), Wellala Hettige Chathura Gunrathna, Siyaguna Kosgodage Chathura Maduranga Weerasingha, Kasun Nadika Weerarathna Jayasuriya (90+2.Pasqual Handi Nadeeka Pushpakumara). Trainer: Jang Jung (Korea Republic).
QAT: Abdulaziz Ali Abdullah, Mustafa Abdi Abdullah, Salman Mesabeh Al Meamari, Ahmad Dad Shahi, Hamed Shami Zaher, Saad Sattam Al Shammari (Cap), Wesam Rizik Abdulmajid (82.Mujib Hamed Gamer), Waleed Muhyideen Aldeen Ahmad (76.Waleed Hamzah Rasoul Pakhshe), Talal Hassan Ali Al Bloushi, Sayed Ali Baba Al Basheer (90.Mirghani Babiker Al Zain), Andrés Sebastián Soria Quintana. Trainer: Jorge Daniel Fossati Lurachi (Uruguay).
Goal: 0-1 Andrés Sebastián Soria Quintana (69).
Cautions: Ramlan Tuwan Gafoor Raheem, Kasun Nadika Weerarathna Jayasuriya / Talal Hassan Ali Al Bloushi, Andrés Sebastián Soria Quintana.

28.10.2007, „Jassim Bin Hamad" Stadium, Doha; Attendance: 3,000
Referee: Khalil Ibrahim Al Ghamdi (Saudi Arabia)
QATAR - SRI LANKA   **5-0(2-0)**
QAT: Rajab Hamza Kassim, Mustafa Abdi Abdullah, Ibrahim Abdullah Al Ghanim, Ali Nasser Saleh, Bilal Mohammed Rajab, Saad Sattam Al Shammari (Cap), Wesam Rizik Abdulmajid (73.Majed Mohammed Hassan), Talal Hassan Ali Al Bloushi, Majdi Abdulla Siddiq (57.Waleed Muhyideen Aldeen Ahmad), Sayed Ali Baba Al Basheer (59.Waleed Hamzah Rasoul Pakhshe), Andrés Sebastián Soria Quintana. Trainer: Jorge Daniel Fossati Lurachi (Uruguay).
SRI: Viraj Asanka, Thilina Suranda Bandara Liyana Arachchilage, Ramlan Tuwan Gafoor Raheem, Rohana Dinesh Ruwan Thilaka Well Don, Ediri Bandanage Channa, Chandradasa Karunaratne

(67.Pasqual Handi Nadeeka Pushpakumara), Azmeer Lathif Mohamed, Wellala Hettige Chathura Gunrathna, Kasun Nadika Weerarathna Jayasuriya, Mohamed Izzadeen Mohamed Naufer (46.Mohamed Ramees Mohamed Hassan), Chathura Lakruwan Samarasekera (46.Sellaperuma Arachige Dunil Lakshan Nirantha Perera). Trainer: Jang Jung (Korea Republic).
Goals: 1-0 Andrés Sebastián Soria Quintana (4), 2-0 Sayed Ali Baba Al Basheer (16), 3-0 Sayed Ali Baba Al Basheer (54), 4-0 Andrés Sebastián Soria Quintana (75), 5-0 Saad Sattam Al Shammari (85).
Cautions: Andrés Sebastián Soria Quintana, Wesam Rizik Abdulmajid / Ramlan Tuwan Gafoor Raheem, Wellala Hettige Chathura Gunrathna, Chandradasa Karunaratne, Rohana Dinesh Ruwan Thilaka Well Don
Sent off: Ramlan Tuwan Gafoor Raheem (57).

21.10.2007, Century Lotus Stadium, Foshan; Attendance: 21,000
Referee: Abdulhameed Ebrahim (Bahrain)
CHINA P.R. - MYANMAR   **7-0(2-0)**
CHN: Zong Lei, Du Wei, Li Weifeng, Zhang Shuai, Sun Xiang, Zhao Junzhe, Du Zhenyu, Wang Dong (58.Liu Jian), Xiao Zhanbo (46.Zheng Bin), Qu Bo, Yang Lin (61.Li Jinyu). Trainer: Vladimir Petrović (Serbia).
MYA: Aung Aung Oo, Kyaw Khing Win, Khin Maung Lwin, Moe Win, U Min Thu, Zaw Lin Thun, Zaw Htet Aung (65.Thura Aung), Aung Myo Thant (68.Yaza Win Thein), Myo Min Tun, Soe Myat Min (60.Tun Tun Win), Yan Paing. Trainer: Marcos Antonio Falopa (Brazil).
Goals: 1-0 Qu Bo (17), 2-0 Du Zhenyu (22), 3-0 Yang Lin (58), 4-0 Liu Jian (63), 5-0 Li Jinyu (76), 6-0 Li Weifeng (79), 7-0 Qu Bo (81).
Cautions: Moe Win, Yan Paing, Khin Maung Lwin.

28.10.2007, KLFA Stadium, Kuala Lumpur (Malaysia); Attendance: 200
Referee: Abdullah Balideh (Qatar)
MYANMAR - CHINA P.R.   **0-4(0-4)**
MYA: Kyaw Zin Htet, Thura Aung, Kyaw Khing Win, Khin Maung Lwin, U Min Thu, Zaw Lin Thun (46.Zaw Htet Aung), Moe Win, Aung Myo Thant (62.Yaza Win Thein), Myo Min Tun (46.Soe Myat Min), Tun Tun Win, Yan Paing. Trainer: Marcos Antonio Falopa (Brazil).
CHN: Yang Zhi, Wang Xiao, Zhang Shuai, Zhang Yaokun, Liu Jian, Wu Weian (60.Xiao Zhanbo), Zhang Xiaofei, Zheng Bin (36.Wang Dong), Zhou Haibin (60.Qu Bo), Hao Junmin, Li Jinyu. Trainer: Vladimir Petrović (Serbia).
Goals: 0-1 Wu Weian (13), 0-2 Liu Jian (14), 0-3 Zheng Bin (35), 0-4 Zhang Yaokun (39 penalty).
Cautions: Myo Min Tun, Soe Myat Min / Liu Jian

18.10.2007, Spartak Stadium, Bishkek; Attendance: 18,000
Referee: Subrata Sarkar (India)
KYRGYZSTAN - JORDAN   **2-0(1-0)**
KGZ: Maxim Agapov, Vyacheslav Amin (Cap), Igor Kudrenko, Talant Samsaliev, Ruslan Sydykov, Vadim Kharchenko, Azamat Ishenbaev (61.Aibek Bokoev), Sergey Kniazev, Timur Valiev (80.Davron Askarov), Cholponbek Esenkul Uulu, Andrey Krasnov (57.Roman Kornilov). Trainer: Boris Podkorytov.
JOR: Amer Shafi Sabbah Mahmoud, Hatem Mohammed Aqel, Bashar Bani Mustafa Yaseen, Faisal Ibrahim Suleiman (Cap), Mohammad Khamees, Khaled Saad Al Maltaah (58.Thaer Fayed Bawab), Qusai Mohammed Mahmoud Abu Alieh, Amer Deeb Mohammad Khalil, Hassouneh Qasem Al Shaikh, Abdullah Khalid Deeb Salim (66.Awad Deeb Ragheb), Mahmoud Omar Shelbaieh. Trainer: Eduardo Manuel Martinho Vingada (Portugal).
Goals: 1-0 Cholponbek Esenkul Uulu (45), 2-0 Aibek Bokoev (76).
Cautions: Igor Kudrenko, Sergey Kniazev, Aibek Bokoev.

28.10.2007, Amman International Stadium, Amman; Attendance: 12,000
Referee: Abdulhameed Ebrahim (Bahrain)
JORDAN - KYRGYZSTAN   **2-0(1-0); 6-5 penalties**
JOR: Lo'ai Salem Atallah El Amaireh, Hatem Mohammed Aqel, Bashar Bani Mustafa Yaseen, Faisal Ibrahim Suleiman (107.Majed Mahmoud Mohamed), Mohammad Khamees, Qusai Mohammed Mahmoud Abu Alieh, Moayad Omar Suleimani Abu Keshek, Amer Deeb Mohammad Khalil, Hassouneh Qasem Al Shaikh, Abdullah Khalid Deeb Salim (73.Siraj Ahmad Yousif Saleh Al Tall), Mahmoud Omar Shelbaieh (80.Thaer Fayed Bawab). Trainer: Eduardo Manuel Martinho Vingada (Portugal).
KGZ: Maxim Agapov, Vyacheslav Amin (Cap), Igor Kudrenko, Talant Samsaliev, Ruslan Sydykov, Aibek Bokoev (68.Davron Askarov), Vadim Kharchenko, Azamat Ishenbaev (63.Timur Valiev), Sergey Kniazev (74.Ildar Amirov), Valeriy Berezovskiy, Cholponbek Esenkul Uulu. Trainer: Boris Podkorytov.
Goals: 1-0 Mahmoud Omar Shelbaieh (34), Hatem Mohammed Aqel (51 penalty).
Penalties: Qusai Mohammed Mahmoud Abu Alieh 1-0, Igor Kudrenko 1-1, Thaer Fayed Bawab 2-1, Vadim Kharchenko 2-2, Moayad Omar Suleimani Abu Keshek 3-2, Talant Samsaliev 3-3, Amer Deeb Mohammad Khalil 4-3, Ruslan Sydykov 4-4, Hatem Mohammed Aqel 5-4, Cholponbek Esenkul Uulu 5-5, Bashar Bani Mustafa Yaseen 6-5, Vyacheslav Amin (missed).
Cautions: Bashar Bani Mustafa Yaseen, Abdullah Khalid Deeb Salim, Amer Deeb Mohammad Khalil, Qusai Mohammed Mahmoud Abu Alieh, Mohammad Khamees / Sergey Kniazev, Igor Kudrenko, Ruslan Sydykov, Ildar Amirov, Cholponbek Esenkul Uulu, Maxim Agapov, Valeriy Berezovskiy.
Sent off: Valeriy Berezovskiy (120+1).

08.10.2007, My Dinh National Stadium, Hanoi; Attendance: 20,000
Referee: Yuichi Nishimura (Japan)
VIETNAM – UNITED ARAB EMIRATES   **0-1(0-0)**
VIE: Dương Hồng Sơn, Đoàn Việt Cường, Mai Tiến Thành (64.Lê Tấn Tài), Nguyễn Huy Hoàng, Phùng Văn Nhiên (85.Châu Phong Hứa), Vũ Như Thành, Nguyễn Minh Phương (Cap), Nguyễn Vũ Phong, Phan Văn Tài Em, Lê Công Vinh, Nguyễn Anh Đức (80.Phan Thành Bình). Trainer: Alfred Riedl (Austria).
UAE: Majed Nasser Al Maqdami, Saleh Abdulla Obaid Al Areefi, Rashid Abdulrahman Al Hosani (Cap), Bashir Saeed Sanqour Al Hammadi, Haidar Alo Ali Mohammed, Saif Mohamed Al Bishr (64.Ahmed Mohammed Mubarak Al Mahri „Dada"), Amir Mubarak Al Hammadi (73.Abdulla Belal Saeed Al Noubi), Nawaf Mubarak Al Darmaki, Helal Saeed Obaid Al Dhanhani Mesmari, Ismail Matar Ibrahim Khamis Al Mukhaini Al Junaibi, Mohamed Saeed Rashed Saiwed Al Shehhi. Trainer: Bruno Metsu (France).
Goal: 0-1 Bashir Saeed Sanqour Al Hammadi (79).
Cautions: Phan Văn Tài Em / Haidar Alo Ali Mohammed, Amir Mubarak Al Hammadi, Nawaf Mubarak Al Darmaki.

28.10.2007, „Mohammed Bin Zayed" Stadium, Abu Dhabi; Attendance: 12,000
Referee: Subkhiddin Mohd Salleh (Malaysia)
UNITED ARAB EMIRATES – VIETNAM   **5-0(2-0)**
UAE: Waleed Salem Al Badrani, Saleh Abdulla Obaid Al Areefi, Rashid Abdulrahman Al Hosani (Cap), Bashir Saeed Sanqour Al Hammadi, Haidar Alo Ali Mohammed, Ahmed Mohammed Mubarak Al Mahri „Dada" (75.Saif Mohamed Al Bishr), Nawaf Mubarak Al Darmaki, Amir Mubarak Al Hammadi (82.Saeed Hassan Salem Alkas), Helal Saeed Obaid Al Dhanhani Mesmari (60.Ali Abbas Al Hawasin), Ismail Matar Ibrahim Khamis Al Mukhaini Al Junaibi, Mohamed Saeed Rashed Saiwed Al Shehhi. Trainer: Bruno Metsu (France).
VIE: Dương Hồng Sơn, Quang Thanh Huynh, Nguyễn Huy Hoàng, Phùng Văn Nhiên, Vũ Như Thành (75.Nguyễn Thành Long Giang), Lê Tấn Tài, Nguyễn Minh Phương (Cap), Nguyễn Vũ Phong (79.Mai Tiến Thành), Phan Văn Tài Em, Trần Trường Giang (53.Phan Thành Bình), Lê Công Vinh. Trainer:

Alfred Riedl (Austria).
Goals: 1-0 Ismail Matar Ibrahim Khamis Al Mukhaini Al Junaibi (13), 2-0 Ahmed Mohammed Mubarak Al Mahri „Dada" (40), 3-0 Mohamed Saeed Rashed Saiwed Al Shehhi (53), 4-0 Nawaf Mubarak Al Darmaki (90), 5-0 Saeed Hassan Salem Alkas (90+2 penalty).
Cautions: Amir Mubarak Al Hammadi / Lê Tấn Tài, Nguyễn Huy Hoàng.
Sent off: Nguyễn Huy Hoàng (90+2).

21.10.2007, National Stadium, Manama; Attendance: 4,000
Referee: Yang Zhiqiang (China P.R.)
BAHRAIN - MALAYSIA   **4-1(2-1)**
BHR: Sayed Mohammed Jaffer Sabet, Sayed Mohamed Adnan, Salman Isa Ghuloom, Ebrahim Ali Hasan Al Mishkhas (Cap), Faouzi Mubarak Aaish, Mahmood Abdulrahman Mohammed Noor, Babatunde Fatai-Baba Fatadi, Mohamed Ahmed Hubail (70.Mohamed Husain Bahzad), Abdullah Omar Ismail, Sayed Mahmood Jalal Al Wadaei (70.A'ala Ahmed Hubail), Jaycee John Akwani Okwunwanne (79.Ismaeel Abdullatif Hasan). Trainer: Milan Máčala (Czech Republic).
MAS: Syed Adney Syed Hussein, Mohd Aidil Zafuan Abdul Radzak, Mohd Daudsu Jamaluddin, Norhafiz Zamani Misbah (Cap), Mohd Amirul Hadi Zainal, Sumardi Hajalan, Nanthakumar Kalliappan, Mohd Zaquan Adha Abdul Radzak (57.Mohamad Syamsol Sabtu), Indra Putra Mahayuddin, Azi Shahril Azmi (32.Mohd Bunyamin Umar), Mohammad Safee Sali (75.Mohd Khyril Muhymeen Zambri). Trainer: Satiananthan Bhashkran.
Goals: 1-0 Babatunde Fatai-Baba Fatadi (4), 2-0 Jaycee John Akwani Okwunwanne (15), 2-1 Mohd Bunyamin Umar (45+2), 3-1 Mahmood Abdulrahman Mohammed Noor (55), 4-1 A'ala Ahmed Hubail (90 penalty).
Cautions: Azi Shahril Azmi, Mohd Aidil Zafuan Abdul Radzak.

28.10.2007, Shah Alam Stadium, Petaling Jaya; Attendance: 2,000
Referee: Lee Gi-Young (Korea Republic)
MALAYSIA - BAHRAIN   **0-0**
MAS: Syed Adney Syed Hussein, Mohd Aidil Zafuan Abdul Radzak, Mohd Daudsu Jamaluddin, Norhafiz Zamani Misbah (Cap), Mohd Amirul Hadi Zainal (46.Mohd Khyril Muhymeen Zambri), Sumardi Hajalan (69.Norshahrul Idlan Talaha), Nanthakumar Kalliappan, Mohd Bunyamin Umar, Mohd Zaquan Adha Abdul Radzak (83.Saramsak Kram), Indra Putra Mahayuddin, Mohammad Safee Sali. Trainer: Satiananthan Bhashkran.
BHR: Sayed Mohammed Jaffer Sabet, Sayed Mohamed Adnan, Salman Isa Ghuloom (90.Mohamed Ahmed Hubail), Mohamed Husain Bahzad (90+1.Ebrahim Ali Hasan Al Mishkhas), Abdullah Al Marzooqi, Mahmood Abdulrahman Mohammed Noor, Babatunde Fatai-Baba Fatadi (74.Faouzi Mubarak Aaish), Abdullah Omar Ismail, Sayed Mahmood Jalal Al Wadaei (Cap), A'ala Ahmed Hubail, Jaycee John Akwani Okwunwanne. Trainer: Milan Máčala (Czech Republic).
Cautions: Indra Putra Mahayuddin, Mohd Bunyamin Umar, Mohammad Safee Sali / Sayed Mohammed Jaffer Sabet, Abdullah Al Marzooqi.
Sent off: Mohd Aidil Zafuan Abdul Radzak (12), Mahmood Abdulrahman Mohammed Noor (12).

21.10.2007, Gianyar Stadium, Gianyar (Indonesia); Attendance: 1,500
Referee: Rosdi Shaharul (Malaysia)
TIMOR-LESTE – HONG KONG   **2-3(1-2)**
TLS: Diamantino Leong, Juliao Dos Santos, Alfredo Esteves, Eduardo Pereira, Miguel Soares, Eusebio De Almeida, Luis Maria, Antonio Marques (37.Juvito da Silva), Helder Mota Ricardo (57.Salvador do Rego), José João Pereira, Emilio da Silva. Trainer: João Paulo Pereira.
HKG: Ho Kwok Chuen, Chan Wai Ho, Cristiano Preigchadt Cordeiro, Lau Chi Keung, Lee Chi Ho, Poon Yiu Cheuk, Cheung Sai Ho (82.Lam Ka Wai), Lee Sze Ming (46.Cheung Kin Fung), Chan Siu Ki, Cheng Siu Wai, Chu Siu Kei (68.Leung Chun Pong). Trainer: Lai Sun Cheung.
Goals: 0-1 Cheng Siu Wai (25), 0-2 Alfredo Esteves (35 own goal), 1-2 Emilio da Silva (41), 1-3

Cheng Siu Wai (50), 2-3 Emilio da Silva (69).
Cautions: Alfredo Esteves / Cheung Sai Ho.

28.10.2007, Hong Kong Stadium, Hong Kong; Attendance: 1,542
Referee: Mohsen Torky (Iran)
HONG KONG – TIMOR-LESTE   **8-1(2-0)**
HKG: Fan Chun Yip, Lee Wai Lun, Lee Chi Ho, Man Pei Tak (74.Chan Wai Ho), Poon Yiu Cheuk, Cheung Sai Ho, Leung Chun Pong, Lo Kwan Yee (55..Lee Sze Ming), Chan Siu Ki, Cheng Siu Wai, Chu Siu Kei (68.Lam Ka Wai). Trainer: Lai Sun Cheung.
TLS: Diamantino Leong, Juliao Dos Santos (46.Marcelo Da Cruz), Alfredo Esteves, Eduardo Pereira (84.Juvito da Silva), Miguel Soares, Eusebio De Almeida, Luis Maria, Helder Mota Ricardo, José João Pereira (72.Salvador do Rego), Emilio da Silva, Adelio Guterres. Trainer: João Paulo Pereira.
Goals: 1-0 Lo Kwan Yee (2), 2-0 Chan Siu Ki (5), 3-0 Cheung Sai Ho (49), 3-1 Emilio da Silva (54), 4-1 Cheng Siu Wai (67), 5-1 Cheng Siu Wai (70), 6-1 Chan Siu Ki (78), 7-1 Lam Ka Wai (83), 8-1 Chan Siu Ki (85).
Cautions: Helder Mota Ricardo, Emilio da Silva.

08.10.2007, Abbasiyyin Stadium, Damascus; Attendance: 3,000
Referee: Khalil Ibrahim Al Ghamdi (Saudi Arabia)
SYRIA - AFGHANISTAN   **3-0(0-0)**
SYR: Mosab Balhous, Khaled Mansor Al Baba, Wael Ayan, Ali Dyab, Feras Fissal Esmaeel, Omar Hemidi, Jehad Al Hussain Fadel, Mohamed Al Zeno (89.Mootassem Alaya), Bakri Tarrab (68.Bwrhan Sahiwni), Maher Al Sayed, Zyad Barakat Chaabo (56.Majed Al Haj). Trainer: Fajer Ebrahim.
AFG: Shamsuddin Amiri, Bashir Ahmad Saadat (Cap), Zohib Islam Amiri (80.Mohammed Yousuf Sameh), Qudratullah Hussaini, Djelaluddin Sharityar, Raza Mahmoudi, Sayed Masood Hashimi (86.Ali Ahmad Yarzada), Sayed Bashir Azimi, Obaidullah Karimi, Ata Yamrali, Hafizullah Qadami (71.Hashmatullah Barekzai). Trainer: Mohammed Yousef Kargar.
Goals: 1-0 Mohamed Al Zeno (73), 2-0 Maher Al Sayed (81 penalty), 3-0 Mohamed Al Zeno (87 penalty).
Cautions: Zohib Islam Amiri.

26.10.2007, Pamir Stadium, Dushanbe (Tajikistan); Attendance: 2,000
Referee: Ravshan Irmatov (Uzbekistan)
AFGHANISTAN - SYRIA   **1-2(1-1)**
AFG: Shamsuddin Amiri, Bashir Ahmad Saadat (Cap) (85.Israfeel Kohistani), Zohib Islam Amiri, Qudratullah Hussaini, Ali Ahmad Yarzada, Raza Mahmoudi, Sayed Bashir Azimi, Harez-Arian Habib, Yusuf Barak, Obaidullah Karimi (88.Hashmatullah Barekzai), Ata Yamrali (84.Sayed Masood Hashimi). Trainer: Mohammed Yousef Kargar.
SYR: Mosab Balhous, Khaled Mansor Al Baba (75.Abdulkader Dakka), Ali Dyab, Feras Fissal Esmaeel, Omar Hemidi, Jehad Al Hussain Fadel, Mohamed Al Zeno, Aatef Abdulelah Jenyat, Bwrhan Sahiwni, Mootassem Alaya (71.Wael Ayan), Zyad Barakat Chaabo (83.Abdul Fattah Al Agha). Trainer: Fajer Ebrahim.
Goals: 1-0 Obaidullah Karimi (16), 1-1 Aatef Abdulelah Jenyat (17), 1-2 Feras Fissal Esmaeel (64).

08.10.2007, „Ali Mohsen Al-Muraisi" Stadium, Sana'a; Attendance: 3,000
Referee: Mohamad Mansour (Lebanon)
YEMEN - MALDIVES   **3-0(1-0)**
YEM: Salem Abdullah Awad Saeed, Mohammed Saleh Yousef Salem, Zaher Mohammed Farid Al Fadhli, Ahmed Salem Al Wadi, Awsam Nasser Omar Al Sayed, Akram Hamood Abdo Al Worafi (77.Tamer Mohammed Ali Hanash), Rian Haikl (83.Abdulkarem Al Qetwi), Ala'a Mohammed Abdullah Al Sassi, Saleh Ahmed Qasem Al Shehri, Fekri Yahia Al Hubaishi, Nasser Ghazi (Cap) (54.Haitham Abdo Saeed Thabit). Trainer: Mohsen Al Harthi (Oman).

MDV: Hassan Rameez, Assad Abdul Ghani (Cap), Mohamed Sabah Ibrahim, Ibrahim Amil (82.Shinaz Hilmy), Mohamed Shinan, Mohamed Umair (60.Mukhthar Naseer), Akram Abdul Gani, Mohamed Jameel, Ismail Mohamed, Ali Ashad, Ali Ashfaq (70.Ali Umar). Trainer: Jozef Jankech (Slovakia).
Goals: 1-0 Mohammed Saleh Yousef Salem (44), 2-0 Fekri Yahia Al Hubaishi (66), 3-0 Haitham Abdo Saeed Thabit (80).
Cautions: Ahmed Salem Al Wadi, Fekri Yahia Al Hubaishi / Mohamed Jameel, Hassan Rameez.

28.10.2007, Galolhu National Stadium, Malé; Attendance: 8,900
Referee: Subrata Sarkar (India)
MALDIVES - YEMEN   **2-0(1-0)**
MDV: Hassan Rameez, Assad Abdul Ghani, Mohamed Sabah Ibrahim, Mohamed Jameel, Mohamed Shinan, Akram Abdul Ghani (62.Shinaz Hilmy), Mukhthar Naseer, Ali Ashfaq, Ibrahim Fazeel (59.Ismail Mohamed), Shamweel Qasim (76.Ali Ashad), Ali Umar. Trainer: Jozef Jankech (Slovakia).
YEM: Salem Abdullah Awad Saeed, Zaher Mohammed Farid Al Fadhli, Awsam Nasser Omar Al Sayed, Ahmed Salem Al Wadi, Mohammed Saleh Yousef Salem (71.Fuad Al Ammari), Ali Al Omqy, Saleh Ahmed Qasem Al Shehri, Akram Hamood Abdo Al Worafi (78.Abdulkarem Al Quetwi), Haitham Abdo Saeed Thabit (61.Khaled Hassan Hussein Baleid), Fekri Yahia Al Hubaishi, Rian Haikl. Trainer: Mohsen Al Harthi (Oman).
Goals: 1-0 Qasim Shamweel (14), 2-0 Ali Ashfaq (67).
Cautions: Ali Umar / Ahmed Salem Al Wadi, Saleh Ahmed Qasem Al Shehri.

08.10.2007, Bangabandhu National Stadium, Dhaka; Attendance: 700
Referee: Abdullah Mohamed Al Hilali (Oman)
BANGLADESH - TAJIKISTAN   **1-1(0-0)**
BAN: Biplop Bhattacharjee, Mohammed Hassan Al Mamun (90.Amit Khan Shuvra), Aziz Al Arman, Rajani Kanta Barman, Mohammed Waly Faisal, Kazi Nazrul Islam Nazir, Mohamed Monower Hossain (55.Anamul Hoque Sharif), Mohamed Abul Hossain, Mohamed Zumratul Mithu, Mohamed Jahid Hassan Ameli, Mohamed Shaifur Rahman Moni. Trainer: Syed Nayeemuddin (India).
TJK: Alexandr Mukanin, Farrukh Choriev, Safarali Karimov, Hasan Rustamov, Farkhod Vasiev, Rahmonali Barotov (64.Faitk Vaskulov), Numondzhon Khakimov (87.Daler Tukhtasunov), Khurshed Makhmudov, Ilhomdzhon Ortikov (46.Dilshod Vasiev), Shukhrat Dzhabarov (Cap), Kamil Saidov. Trainer: Makhmadjon Khabibulloev.
Goals: 1-0 Mohamed Zumratul Mithu (50), 1-1 Numondzhon Khakimov (58 penalty).
Cautions: Mohamed Shaifur Rahman Moni, Mohammed Hassan Al Mamun, Mohamed Abul Hossain / Ilhomdzhon Ortikov.

28.10.2007, Central Stadium, Dushanbe; Attendance: 10,000
Referee: Kadyrbek Chynybekov (Kyrgyzstan)
TAJIKISTAN - BANGLADESH   **5-0(0-0)**
TJK: Alexandr Mukanin, Subkhon Khujamov, Alexsei Negmatov (46.Rahmonali Barotov), Naim Nosirov, Zafardzhon Zuvaydov, Fatkhullo Fatkhuloev (46.Dilshod Vasiev), Numondzhon Khakimov, Akmal Kholomatov (Cap), Khurshed Makhmudov (79.Samad Shohzukhurov), Ibrahim Rabimov, Dzhamikhon Muhidinov. Trainer: Makhmadjon Khabibulloev.
BAN: Biplop Bhattacharjee, Mohammed Hassan Al Mamun, Aziz Al Arman, Rajani Kanta Barman, Mohammed Waly Faisal, Mohamed Ariful Islam, Amit Khan Shuvra (74.Mahmudul Hasan), Mohamed Abul Hossain (74.Anamul Hoque Sharif), Mohamed Zumratul Mithu (87.Mohamed Robin), Mohamed Jahid Hassan Ameli, Mohamed Shaifur Rahman Moni. Trainer: Syed Nayeemuddin (India).
Goals: 1-0 Numondzhon Khakimov (46), 2-0 Numondzhon Khakimov (47), 3-0 Dzhamikhon Muhidinov (49), 4-0 Farkhod Vasiev (70), 5-0 Numondzhon Khakimov (76 penalty).

21.10.2007, National Sports Stadium, Ulaanbaatar; Attendance: 4,870
Referee: Hiroyoshi Takayama (Japan)
MONGOLIA – KOREA D.P.R.   **1-4(0-3)**
MGL: Yura Sainkhuu, Enkhjargal Tserenjav, Garidmagnai Bayasgalan (85.Agvaan Batbold),
Lkhümbengarav Donorovyn, Munkhbat Chimeddorj, Odkhuu Selenge, Ganbat Bat-Yalalt (68.Anar
Batchuluun), Davaa-Ochir Gongorjav, Tsend-Ayush Khurelbaatar (57 Sukhbaatar Bayarzaya), Murun
Altankhuyag, Tugsbayar Ganbaatar. Trainer: Ishdorj Otgonbayar.
PRK: Ri Myong-Guk (46.Ju Kwang-Min), Jon Kwang-Ik, Pak Nam-Chol I, Ri Jun-Il, Yun Yong-Il,
Kim Kyong-Il (30.So Kwang-Chol), Pak Song-Chol, Ri Chol-Myong (76.Jong Su-Hyok), Kim Kum-Il,
Jong Chol-Min, Pak Chol-Min. Trainer: Jo Tong-Sop.
Goals: 0-1 Pak Chol-Min (14), 0-2 Jong Chol-Min (24), 0-3 Jong Chol-Min (32), 0-4 Jong Chol-Min
(78), 1-4 Odkhuu Selenge (90+3).
Cautions: Munkhbat Chimeddorj, Odkhuu Selenge, Lkhümbengarav Donorovyn.

28.10.2007, „Kim Il Sung“ Stadium, P'yŏngyang; Attendance: 5,000
Referee: Ram Gosh (Bangladesh)
KOREA D.P.R. – MONGOLIA   **5-1(3-1)**
PRK: Ju Kwang-Min, Cha Jong-Hyok, Jon Kwang-Ik, Pak Nam-Chol II, Ri Jun-Il (65.Ri Kwang-
Hyok), Yun Yong-Il, Kim Kuk-Jin (46.Hung-ryong Ri), Pak Song-Chol, Ri Chol-Myong, Jong Chol-
Min (79.So Kwang-Chol), Pak Chol-Min. Trainer: Jo Tong-Sop.
MGL: Nasanjargal Sharav, Bayarzaya Sukhbaatar, Enkhjargal Tserenjav, Garidmagnai Bayasgalan,
Lkhümbengarav Donorovyn, Munkhbat Chimeddorj, Odkhuu Selenge, Ganbat Bat-Yalalt (49.Battulga
Zorigt), Davaa-Ochir Gongorjav, Murun Altankhuyag (88.Erdene-Ochir Ganzorig), Tugsbayar
Ganbaatar (90+3.Tsend-Ayush Khurelbaatar). Trainer: Ishdorj Otgonbayar.
Goals: 1-0 Pak Chol-Min (3), 2-0 Kim Kuk-Jin (10), 3-0 Jong Chol-Min (36), 3-1 Lkhümbengarav
Donorovyn (41), 4-1 Pak Chol-Min (79), 5-1 Jon Kwang-Il (90+1).
Cautions: Pak Chol-Min / Lkhümbengarav Donorovyn, Battulga Zorigt.
Sent off: Ri Chol-Myong (58).

08.10.2007, „Sultan Qaboos“ Sports Complex, Muscat; Attendance: 15,000
Referee: Fareed Ali Mohammed Al Marzooqi (United Arab Emirates)
OMAN - NEPAL   **2-0(2-0)**
OMA: Ali Abdulla Al Habsi, Mohammed Abdullah Mubarak Al Balushi „Al Sheiba“, Hassan Yousuf
Mudhafar Al Gheilani, Mohamed Rabia Jamaan Al Noobi, Mohammed Saleh Abdallah Al Ghassani
(62.Younis Khalifa Al Mushaifri; 86.Hussain Ali Farah Al Hadhri), Ahmed Hadid Thuwaini Al
Mukhaini (79.Mohammed Al Hooti), Khalifa Ayil Salim Al Naufali, Fawzi Bashir Rajab Bait
Doorbeen, Ahmed Mubarak Obaid Al Mahaijri, Ismail Sulaiman Al Ajmi, Imad Ali Sulaiman Al
Hosani. Trainer: Gabriel Humberto Calderón (Argentina).
NEP: Ritesh Thapa, Rakesh Shrestha (Cap), Lok Bandhu Gurung, K.C.Anjan, Sagar Thapa, Sanjib
Budathoki, Tashi Tsering (37.Rajesh Khadagi), Pradeep Maharjan, Nirajan Rayamajhi (90+2.Nabin
Neupane), Ju Manu Rai, Anil Gurung (80.Bishow Bairag Samal). Trainer: Shyam Thapa.
Goals: 1-0 Fawzi Bashir Rajab Bait Doorbeen (5), 2-0 Hassan Yousuf Mudhafar Al Gheilani (23).
Cautions: Ahmed Hadid Thuwaini Al Mukhaini / Ritesh Thapa, Nirajan Rayamajhi.

28.10.2007, Dasarath Rangasala Stadium, Kathmandu; Attendance: 10,000
Referee: Satop Tongkhan (Thailand)
NEPAL - OMAN   **0-2(0-1)**
NEP: Ritesh Thapa, Rakesh Shrestha (Cap), Lok Bandhu Gurung (73.Rajesh Khadagi), K.C. Anjan,
Sagar Thapa, Sanjib Budathoki, Pradeep Maharjan, Tashi Tsering (87.Raju Tamang), Nirajan
Rayamajhi, Ju Manu Rai (72.Santosh Shahukhala), Anil Gurung. Trainer: Shyam Thapa.
OMA: Ali Abdulla Al Habsi, Mohammed Abdullah Mubarak Al Balushi „Al Sheiba“, Hassan Yousuf
Mudhafar Al Gheilani, Nabil Ashoor Ramadhan Bait Faraj Allah, Mohamed Rabia Jamaan Al Noobi,

Mohammed Saleh Abdallah Al Ghassani, Younis Mubarak Al Mahaijri (46.Imad Ali Sulaiman Al Hosani), Fawzi Bashir Rajab Bait Doorbeen, Ahmed Mubarak Obaid Al Mahaijri, Hashim Saleh Mohamed Al Balushi (79.Ahmed Mani Al Noobi), Mohamed Mubarak Al Hinai (69.Badar Mubarak Al Maimani). Trainer: Gabriel Humberto Calderón (Argentina).
Goals: 0-1 Hashim Saleh Mohamed Al Balushi (28), 0-2 Mohamed Mubarak Al Hinai (54).
Cautions: Hashim Saleh Mohamed Al Balushi.

08.10.2007, „Ahmed bin Ali" Stadium, Doha (Qatar); Attendance: 75
Referee: Mohsen Hassan Basma (Syria)
PALESTINE - SINGAPORE   **0-4(0-1)**
PLE: Mohammed Shbair, Ramzi Saleh, Majed Mostafa Abu Seidu, Ismail Al Amour (46.Mohammed Al Shery), Roberto Bishara, Omar Jarun, Ali Nassar, Ibrahim Al Sweirki (62.Taysir Amar), Edgardo Montero, Fady Abu Latifa, Fahed Al Attal (82.Ahmed Keshkesh). Trainer: Nelson Docmac (Chile).
SIN: Lionel Lewis, Faizal Abdul Hamid (78.Ismail Yunos), Daniel Mark Bennett, Precious Emuejeraye, Baihakki Khaizan, Fahrudin Mustafić, Khairul Amri Mohamad Kamal, Shi Jiayi (74.Mohammad Shahril Ishak), John Wilkinson, Indra Sahdan Daud (Cap) (59.Agu Casmir), Noh Alam Shah Kamarezaman. Trainer: Radojko Avramović (Serbia).
Goals: 0-1 Shi Jiayi (44), 0-2 Shi Jiayi (53), 0-3 John Wilkinson (73), 0-4 Noh Alam Shah Kamarezaman (86).
Cautions: Ismail Al Amour, Majed Mostafa Abu Seidu / Khairul Amri Mohamad Kamal, Faizal Abdul Hamid, Ismail Yunos.

28.10.2007
SINGAPORE - PALESTINE   **3-0**
Palestine failed to appear for the second leg. The Palestine Football Federation appealed to have the match rescheduled on the grounds that its players did not receive permits to leave the Gaza Strip, but FIFA did not accept the appeal. The game was awarded 3-0 for Singapore.

08.10.2007, Saida International Stadium, Saida; Attendance: 500
Referee: Saad Kameel Al Fadhli (Kuwait)
LEBANON - INDIA   **4-1(1-1)**
LIB: Lary Mehanna, Faisal Antar, Ahmad El Choum (46.Amer Khan), Ramez Dayoub, Mohammad Halawi, Mohamad Korhani, Khodor Salame, Roda Antar, Abbas Ahmed Atwi, Mahmoud El Ali (80.Abbas Ahmed Atwi), Paul Emile Rustom (60.Mohammed Ghaddar). Trainer: Emile Rustom.
IND: Subrata Pal, Mahesh Gawli, Naduparambil Pappachan Pradeep (73.Mehraj Ud Din Wadoo), Manju Shivananju, Irungbam Surkumar Singh, Gouramangi Moirangthem Singh, Steven Benedict Dias, Climax Lawrence, Renedy Potsangbam Singh (65.Krishnan Nair Ajayan), Baichung Bhutia, Sunil Chhetri. Trainer: Robert Douglas Houghton (England).
Goals: 0-1 Sunil Chhetri (30), 1-1 Roda Antar (33), 2-1 Mohammed Ghaddar (62), 3-1 Mahmoud El Ali (63), 4-1 Mohammed Ghaddar (76).

30.10.2007, Fatorda Stadium, Goa; Attendance: 10,000
Referee: Salem Mahmoud Mujghef (Jordan)
INDIA - LEBANON   **2-2(1-0)**
IND: Subrata Pal, Mahesh Gawli, Naduparambil Pappachan Pradeep, Gouramangi Moirangthem Singh, Irungbam Surkumar Singh, Steven Benedict Dias, Climax Lawrence (69.Mehraj Ud Din Wadoo), Sameer Subash Naik (73.Sandip Nandy), Krishnan Nair Ajayan (58 Clifford Miranda), Baichung Bhutia, Sunil Chhetri. Trainer: Robert Douglas Houghton (England).
LIB: Lary Mehanna, Ali Al Saadi (54.Amer Khan), Faisal Antar, Ramez Dayoub, Mohammad Halawi, Hussain Hamdan (46.Mohammed Ghaddar), Mohamad Korhani, Khodor Salame, Ali Yaacoub, Abbas Ahmed Atwi, Mahmoud El Ali (76.Paul Emile Rustom). Trainer: Emile Rustom.
Goals: 1-0 Sunil Chhetri (29), 1-1 Mohammed Ghaddar (72 penalty), 1-2 Mohammed Ghaddar (85), 2-

2 Steven Benedict Dias (90+2).
Cautions: Ramez Dayoub, Lary Mehanna, Mahmoud El Ali.
Sent off: Subrata Pal (72).

11.10.2007, National Olympic Stadium, Phnom Penh; Attendance: 3,000
Referee: Ram Gosh (Bangladesh)
CAMBODIA - TURKMENISTAN   **0-1(0-0)**
CAM: Oum Chandara, Kim Chanbunrith, Om Thavrak, Tieng Tiny, Chan Rithy, Sun Sovannarith, Pok
Chantan (Cap) (73.Keo Kosal), Samel Nasa (87.Hok Sotitya), Kouch Sokumpheak, Teab Vathanak
(83.Nuth Sinuon), Khim Borey. Trainer: Scott O'Donell (Australia).
TKM: Nikita Gorbunow, Begli Annageldiýew, Omar Berdiýew, Gochguly Gochguliýew,
Yagmyrmyrat Annamyradow, Nazar Baýramov, Didar Hajyýew, Murad Khamraýew (77.Artur
Gevorkyan), Arif Mirzoýew (82.Döwletmyrat Ataýew), Muslim Agaýew, Mamedaly Karadanow
(88.Mekan Nasyrow). Trainer: Rahim Kurbanmamedov.
Goal: 0-1 Mamedaly Karadanow (85).

28.10.2007, Olympic Stadium, Aşgabat; Attendance: 5,000
Referee: Rustam Saidov (Uzbekistan)
TURKMENISTAN - CAMBODIA   **4-1(1-1)**
TKM: Baýramnyýaz Berdiýew, Begli Annageldiýew, Omar Berdiýew, Gochguly Gochguliýew,
Yagmyrmyrat Annamyradow, Nazar Baýramov, Didar Hajyýew, Murad Khamraýew (59.Döwletmyrat
Ataýew), Mekan Nasyrow, Muslim Agaýew (46.Artur Gevorkyan), Mamedaly Karadanow (77.Arif
Mirzoýew). Trainer: Rahim Kurbanmamedov.
CAM: Oum Chandara, Kim Chanbunrith, Om Thavrak, Tieng Tiny, Chan Rithy, Sun Sovannarith, Pok
Chantan (Cap), Samel Nasa (77.Hok Sotitya), Kouch Sokumpheak, Teab Vathanak (69.Nuth Sinuon),
Khim Borey (74.Chan Chaya). Trainer: Scott O'Donell (Australia).
Goals: 0-1 Samel Nasa (12), 1-1 Mekan Nasyrow (41), 1-2 Artur Gevorkyan (50), 1-3 Artur
Gevorkyan (66), 1-4 Mamedaly Karadanow (74).
Cautions: Muslim Agaýew, Mamedaly Karadanow / Pok Chantan, Tieng Tiny.

SECOND ROUND

Among the 19 winners of the 1st Round, the 11 ranked teams avanced directly to the 3rd Round. The
other 8 teams played in the 2nd Round:

10.11./18.11.2007	Hong Kong - **Turkmenistan**	0-0	0-3(0-1)
09.11./18.11.2007	Indonesia - **Syria**	1-4(1-3)	0-7(0-2)
09.11./18.11.2007	**Singapore** - Tajikistan	2-0(2-0)	1-1(1-1)
09.11./18.11.2007	Yemen - **Thailand**	1-1(1-1)	0-1(0-1)

10.11.2007, Hong Kong Stadium, Hong Kong; Attendance: 2,823
Referee: Salem Mahmoud Mujghef (Jordan)
HONG KONG - TURKMENISTAN   **0-0**
HKG: Fan Chun Yip (Cap), Chan Wai Ho, Lee Wai Lun, Lee Chi Ho, Poon Yiu Cheuk, Lam Ka Wai
(84.Lee Sze Ming), Leung Chun Pong (62.Lau Chi Keung), Lo Kwan Yee, Chan Siu Ki, Cheng Siu
Wai, Chu Siu Kei (56.Lo Chi Kwan). Trainer: Lai Sun Cheung.
TKM: Pavel Kharchik (69.Baýramnyýaz Berdiýew), Begli Annageldiýew, Omar Berdiýew, Gochguly
Gochguliýew (Cap), Alik Haydarov, Nazar Baýramov, Artur Gevorkyan (71.Yewgeniy Zemskov),
Didar Hajyýew, Mekan Nasyrow (88.Murad Khamraýew), Vladimir Baýramow, Guwançmuhammet
Öwekow. Trainer: Rahim Kurbanmamedov.
Cautions: Nazar Baýramov, Omar Berdiýew, Murad Khamraýew.

18.11.2007, Olympic Stadium, Aşgabat; Attendance: 30,000
Referee: Abdullah Mohamed Al Hilali (Oman)
TURKMENISTAN - HONG KONG   **3-0(1-0)**
TKM: Baýramnyýaz Berdiýew, Begli Annageldiýew, Omar Berdiýew, Gochguly Gochguliýew (Cap), Alik Haydarov, Nazar Baýramov, Didar Hajyýew, Vyacheslav Krendelev, Mekan Nasyrow (76.Artur Gevorkyan), Vladimir Baýramow (67.Arif Mirzoýew), Guwançmuhammet Öwekow (86 Azat Muhadov). Trainer: Rahim Kurbanmamedov.
HKG: Fan Chun Yip (Cap), Chan Wai Ho (71.Lee Sze Ming), Cheung Kin Fung, Lau Chi Keung, Lee Wai Lun (62.Man Pei Tak), Lee Chi Ho, Lam Ka Wai, Lo Chi Kwan (62.Chu Siu Kei), Lo Kwan Yee, Chan Siu Ki, Cheng Siu Wai. Trainer: Lai Sun Cheung.
Goals: 1-0 Mekan Nasyrow (42), 2-0 Nazar Baýramov (53), 3-0 Arif Mirzoýew (80).
Cautions: Didar Hajyýew / Lee Chi Ho, Lau Chi Keung, Chan Siu Ki.

09.11.2007, Gelora Bung Karno Stadium, Jakarta; Attendance: 35,000
Referee: Mohsen Torky (Iran)
INDONESIA - SYRIA   **1-4(1-3)**
IDN: Markus Horison Ririhina, Maman Abdurrachman, Mahyadi Panggabean (46.Fandy Mochtar), Muhammaed Ridwan, Charis Yulianto, Ponaryo Astaman, Ian Kabes, Eka Ramdani (Cap), Budi Sudarsono, Firman Utina (78.Rudi Widodo), Bambang Pamungkas (64.Ellie Aiboy). Trainer: Ivan Kolev (Bulgaria).
SYR: Mosab Balhous, Abdulkader Dakka, Ali Dyab, Feras Fissal Esmaeel, Omar Hemidi, Jehad Al Hussain Fadel, Mohamed Al Zeno (69.Raja Rafe), Aatef Abdulelah Jenyat (58.Wael Ayan), Bakri Tarrab, Mootassem Alaya, Zyad Barakat Chaabo (88.Zain Al Fandi). Trainer: Fajer Ebrahim.
Goals: 0-1 Feras Fissal Esmaeel (17), 0-2 Mohamed Al Zeno (34), 1-2 Budi Sudarsono (39), 1-3 Zyad Barakat Chaabo (43), 1-4 Raja Rafe (90+3).
Cautions: Mahyadi Panggabean, Ponaryo Astaman, Firman Utina / Feras Fissal Esmaeel, Mosab Balhous.

18.11.2007, Abbasiyyin Stadium, Damascus; Attendance: 5,000
Referee: Sun Baojie (China P.R.)
SYRIA - INDONESIA   **7-0(2-0)**
SYR: Mosab Balhous, Wael Ayan (79.Abdul Fattah Al Agha), Abdulkader Dakka, Ali Dyab, Feras Fissal Esmaeel, Omar Hemidi, Jehad Al Hussain Fadel, Mohamed Al Zeno (57.Raja Rafe), Bakri Tarrab, Mootassem Alaya (50.Bwrhan Sahiwni), Zyad Barakat Chaabo. Trainer: Fajer Ebrahim.
IDN: Dian Agus Prasetyo, Fandy Mochtar, Purwaka Pratomo, Muhammad Robby, Ricardo Salampessy, Ardan Aras (67.Imanuel Wanggai), Atep (73.Mahmud Bachtiar), Ian Kabes (57.Suswanto), Eka Ramdani (Cap), Corneles Geddi, Airlangga Sutjipto. Trainer: Ivan Kolev (Bulgaria).
Goals: 1-0 Zyad Barakat Chaabo (40), 2-0 Zyad Barakat Chaabo (44), 3-0 Raja Rafe (60), 4-0 Raja Rafe (72), 5-0 Jehad Al Hussain Fadel (81 penalty), 6-0 Zyad Barakat Chaabo (87), 7-0 Raja Rafe (90).
Cautions: Imanuel Wanggai.

09.11.2007, National Stadium, Singapore; Attendance: 6,606
Referee: Kwon Jong-Chul (Korea Republic)
SINGAPORE - TAJIKISTAN   **2-0(2-0)**
SIN: Lionel Lewis, Faizal Abdul Hamid, Daniel Mark Bennett, Precious Emuejeraye, Baihakki Khaizan, Fahrudin Mustafić, Khairul Amri Mohamad Kamal (87 Fazrul Nawaz Shahul Hameed), John Wilkinson (90+1.Muhammad Ridhuan), Indra Sahdan Daud (Cap) (82 Mohammad Shahril Ishak), Aleksandar Đurić, Noh Alam Shah Kamarezaman. Trainer: Radojko Avramović (Serbia).
TJK: Alexandr Mukanin (Cap) (62.Alisher Dodov), Farrukh Choriev (46 Shukhrat Dzhabarov), Subkhon Khujamov, Naim Nosirov, Zafardzhon Zuvaydov, Rahmonali Barotov, Numondzhon

Khakimov, Jamshed Ismailov (60.Dilshod Vasiev), Khurshed Makhmudov, Ibrahim Rabimov, Dzhamikhon Muhidinov. Trainer: Makhmadjon Khabibulloev.
Goals: 1-0 Aleksandar Đurić (23), 2-0 Aleksandar Đurić (44).
Cautions: Noh Alam Shah Kamarezaman / Ibrahim Rabimov, Zafardzhon Zuvaydov, Subkhon Khujamov.

18.11.2007, Central Stadium, Dushanbe; Attendance: 21,500
Referee: Mark Alexander Shield (Australia)
TAJIKISTAN - SINGAPORE   **1-1(1-1)**
TJK: Alisher Dodov, Naim Nosirov, Zafardzhon Zuvaydov, Farkhod Vasiev, Rahmonali Barotov, Numondzhon Khakimov (74.Dzhomikhon Mukhiddinov), Jamshed Ismailov (59.Samad Shohzukhurov), Akmal Kholomatov (Cap), Khurshed Makhmudov (59.Dilshod Vasiev), Ibrahim Rabimov, Kamil Saidov. Trainer: Makhmadjon Khabibulloev.
SIN: Faizal Abdul Hamid, Daniel Mark Bennett, Precious Emuejeraye, Baihakki Khaizan, Fahrudin Mustafić, Khairul Amri Mohamad Kamal (72.Mohammad Shahril Ishak), John Wilkinson, Indra Sahdan Daud (Cap) (62.Shi Jiayi), Aleksandar Đurić, Noh Alam Shah Kamarezaman (86.Noh Rahman). Trainer: Radojko Avramović (Serbia).
Goals: 1-0 Jamshed Ismailov (2), 1-1 Noh Alam Shah Kamarezaman (27).
Cautions: Zafardzhon Zuvaydov, Akmal Kholomatov / Noh Alam Shah Kamarezaman, John Wilkinson, Noh Rahman.

09.11.2007, „Ali Muhsin Al-Muriasi" Stadium, Sana'a; Attendance: 12,000
Referee: Khalil Ibrahim Al Ghamdi (Saudi Arabia)
YEMEN - THAILAND   **1-1(1-1)**
YEM: Salem Abdullah Awad Saeed, Zaher Mohammed Farid Al Fadhli, Awsam Nasser Omar Al Sayed, Mohammed Saleh Yousef Salem, Mohammed Ali Al Ammari, Ali Al Omqy, Abdulkarem Al Quetwi, Akram Hamood Abdo Al Worafi (78.Ali Mohammed Mubarak Yousef), Ali Mohammed Al Nono (83.Fekri Yahia Al Hubaishi), Rian Haikl, Abdullah Yaslam (67.Yasser Ahmed Mohammed Basuhai). Trainer: Mohsen Al Harthi (Oman).
THA: Sinthaweechai Hathairattanakool, Jetsada Jitsawad, Natthaphong Samana, Niweat Siriwong, Suree Sukha, Nirut Surasiang (Cap), Jakkrit Bunkham, Datsakorn Thonglao, Sarayoot Chaikamdee, Teerasil Dangda (82.Pipat Thonkanya), Suchao Nuchnum (46.Pichitphong Choeichiu). Trainer: Chanvit Phalajivin.
Goals: 0-1 Sarayoot Chaikamdee (35), 1-1 Ali Mohammed Al Nono (43).
Cautions: Zaher Mohammed Farid Al Fadhli, Ali Al Omqy, Mohammed Saleh Yousef Salem / Suree Sukha, Datsakorn Thonglao.
Sent off: Ali Al Omqy (90+2).

18.11.2007, Suphachalasai Stadium, Bangkok; Attendance: 29,000
Referee: Kazuhiko Matsumura (Japan)
THAILAND - YEMEN   **1-0(1-0)**
THA: Sinthaweechai Hathairattanakool, Punnarat Klinsukon, Kiatprawut Saiwaew, Niweat Siriwong, Suree Sukha, Nirut Surasiang, Tawan Sripan (Cap), Datsakorn Thonglao, Sarayoot Chaikamdee, Teerasil Dangda (64.Teeratep Winothai), Sutee Suksomkit. Trainer: Chanvit Phalajivin.
YEM: Salem Abdullah Awad Saeed, Zaher Mohammed Farid Al Fadhli, Awsam Nasser Omar Al Sayed, Ahmed Salem Al Wadi, Mohammed Saleh Yousef Salem, Mohammed Ali Al Ammari, Abdulkarem Al Quetwi, Akram Hamood Abdo Al Worafi (87.Abdullah Yaslam), Fekri Yahia Al Hubaishi (65.Yasser Ahmed Mohammed Basuhai), Ali Mohammed Al Nono, Rian Haikl (78.Haitham Abdo Saeed Thabit). Trainer: Mohsen Al Harthi (Oman).
Goal: 1-0 Sarayoot Chaikamdee (16).
Cautions: Suree Sukha, Nirut Surasiang, Datsakorn Thonglao / Akram Hamood Abdo Al Worafi, Rian Haikl, Ahmed Salem Al Wadi, Ali Mohammed Al Nono, Mohammed Saleh Yousef Salem.
Sent off: Ahmed Salem Al Wadi (90+1).

THIRD ROUND

The 20 teams (Top Seeds, 11 teams from the 1st Round and 4 teams from the 2nd Round) were divided into 4 pots:
Pot A: Australia, Korea Republic, Saudi Arabia, Japan, Iran.
Pot B: Bahrain, Uzbekistan, Kuwait, Korea D.P.R., China P.R.
Pot C: Jordan, Iraq, Lebanon, Oman, United Arab Emirates.
Pot D: Qatar, Syria, Thailand, Turkmenistan, Singapore.

By the draw on 25 November 2007 in Durban (South Africa), the 20 teams were drawn in 5 qualifying groups. Each group winners and runners-up advanced to the 4th Round.

GROUP 1

06.02.2008	Melbourne	Australia - Qatar	3-0(3-0)
06.02.2008	Dubai (UAE)	Iraq – China P.R.	1-1(0-0)
26.03.2008	Kunming	China P.R. - Australia	0-0
26.03.2008	Doha	Qatar - Iraq	2-0(1-0)
01.06.2008	Brisbane	Australia - Iraq	1-0(0-0)
02.06.2008	Doha	Qatar – China P.R.	0-0
07.06.2008	Tianjin	China P.R. - Qatar	0-1(0-1)
07.06.2008	Dubai (UAE)	Iraq - Australia	1-0(1-0)
14.06.2008	Tianjin	China P.R. - Iraq	1-2(1-1)
14.06.2008	Doha	Qatar - Australia	1-3(0-1)
22.06.2008	Sydney	Australia – China P.R.	0-1(0-1)
22.06.2008	Dubai (UAE)	Iraq - Qatar	0-1(0-0)

FINAL STANDINGS

1.	**Australia**	6	3	1	2	7 - 3	10
2.	**Qatar**	6	3	1	2	5 - 6	10
3.	Iraq	6	2	1	3	4 - 6	7
4.	China P.R.	6	1	3	2	3 - 4	6

06.02.2008, Telstra Dome, Melbourne; Attendance: 50,969
Referee: Subkhiddin Mohd Salleh (Malaysia)
AUSTRALIA - QATAR   **3-0(3-0)**
AUS: Mark Schwarzer, Craig Andrew Moore (78. Brett Holman), Lucas Edward Neill (Cap), Brett Michael Emerton, Luke Wilkshire, Jason Čulina, Mark Bresciano, David Raymond Carney, Timothy Joel Cahill (67.Carl Valeri), Joshua Blake Kennedy (70.John Aloisi), Scott Douglas McDonald. Trainer: Peter Tim Verbeek (Holland).
QAT: Mohamed Ahmed Saqer, Mustafa Abdi Abdullah (46.Wesam Rizik Abdulmajid), Ibrahim Abdullah Al Ghanim, Abdullah Obaid Koni, Marcone Amaral Costa Júnior, Saad Sattam Al Shammari (Cap), Talal Hassan Ali Al Bloushi (78.Waleed Jassim Abdullah), Fábio César Montezine, Majdi Abdulla Siddiq (46.Mesaad Ali Al Hamad), Ali Hassan Afif Yahya, Khalfan Ibrahim Al Khalfan. Trainer: Jorge Daniel Fossati Lurachi (Uruguay).
Goals: 1-0 Joshua Blake Kennedy (11), 2-0 Timothy Joel Cahill (17), 3-0 Mark Bresciano (33).
Cautions: Craig Andrew Moore / Abdullah Obaid Koni.

06.02.2008, Al Rashid Stadium, Dubai (United Arab Emirates); Attendance: 11,000
Referee: Mohsen Torky (Iran)
IRAQ – CHINA P.R.   **1-1(0-0)**
IRQ: Noor Sabri Abbas Hassan, Haidar Abdul-Amir Hussain (90+2.Jassim Mohammed Haji), Jassim Mohammed Ghulam Al Hamd, Bassim Abbas Kati, Salam Shakir, Karrar Jassim Mohammed, Mahdi Karim Ajeel (75.Ahmed Abd Ali Mohammed), Hawar Mulla Mohammed Taher Zibari, Qusai Munir

Aboodi, Nashat Akram Ali, Younis Mahmoud Khalef (6.Mustafa Karim Abdullah). Trainer: Egil Roger Olsen (Norway).
CHN: Zong Lei, Feng Xiaoting, Li Weifeng, Zhang Shuai, Xu Yunlong, Sun Xiang (62.Du Zhenyu), Zheng Zhi, Liu Jian (72.Wang Dong), Zhou Haibin (81.Sun Jihai), Qu Bo, Zhu Ting. Trainer: Vladimir Petrović (Serbia).
Goals: 1-0 Hawar Mulla Mohammed Taher Zibari (51 penalty), 1-1 Zheng Zhi (75).
Cautions: Karrar Jassim Mohammed, Nashat Akram Ali, Mustafa Karim Abdullah, Qusai Munir Aboodi / Li Weifeng, Sun Xiang, Zhu Ting, Zhang Shuai, Sun Jihai.
Sent off: Nashat Akram Ali (68).

26.03.2008, Tuodong Stadium, Kunming; Attendance: 32,000
Referee: Mohamed Omar Al Saeedi (United Arab Emirates)
CHINA P.R. - AUSTRALIA   **0-0**
CHN: Zong Lei, Feng Xiaoting, Li Weifeng, Zhang Shuai, Sun Xiang, Sun Jihai, Zheng Zhi (68.Shao Jiayi), Zhou Haibin (62.Xiao Zhanbo), Han Peng (73.Qu Bo), Jiang Ning, Zhu Ting. Trainer: Vladimir Petrović (Serbia).
AUS: Mark Schwarzer, Lucas Edward Neill (Cap), Jade Bronson North, Michael Beauchamp, Luke Wilkshire, Vincenzo Grella, Jason Čulina, Carl Valeri, Mark Bresciano, David Raymond Carney, Archibald Gerald Thompson (10.Brett Holman). Trainer: Peter Tim Verbeek (Holland).
Cautions: Feng Xiaoting / David Raymond Carney, Brett Holman, Mark Schwarzer.

26.03.2008, „Jassem bin Hamad" Stadium, Doha; Attendance: 13,000
Referee: Yuichi Nishimura (Japan)
QATAR - IRAQ   **2-0(1-0)**
QAT: Mohamed Ahmed Saqer, Abdullah Obaid Koni (Cap), Ibrahim Abdul Majid, Marcone Amaral Costa Júnior, Wesam Rizik Abdulmajid (77.Mustafa Abdi Abdullah), Talal Hassan Ali Al Bloushi, Mesaad Ali Al Hamad, Fábio César Montezine (85.Saad Sattam Al Shammari), Hussain Yasser Abdulrahman (88.Majed Mohammed Hassan), Márcio Passos de Albuquerque „Emerson", Andrés Sebastián Soria Quintana. Trainer: Jorge Daniel Fossati Lurachi (Uruguay).
IRQ: Noor Sabri Abbas Hassan, Haidar Abdul-Amir Hussain, Jassim Mohammed Ghulam Al Hamd, Ali Hussein Rehema Al Muttairi, Karrar Jassim Mohammed (73.Salih Sadir Al Sadoun), Mahdi Karim Ajeel (83.Alaa Abdul-Zahra Khashan), Hawar Mulla Mohammed Taher Zibari, Qusai Munir Aboodi, Haitham Kadhim Tahir, Younis Mahmoud Khalef, Emad Mohammed Ridha (63.Mohammed Ali Karim). Trainer: Egil Roger Olsen (Norway).
Goals: 1-0 Fábio César Montezine (1), 2-0 Fábio César Montezine (62).
Cautions: Hussain Yasser Abdulrahman / Karrar Jassim Mohammed, Jassim Mohammed Ghulam Al Hamd.

01.06.2008, Suncorp Stadium, Brisbane; Attendance: 48,678
Referee: Ravshan Irmatov (Uzbekistan)
AUSTRALIA - IRAQ   **1-0(0-0)**
AUS: Mark Schwarzer, Jade Bronson North, Michael Beauchamp Brett Michael Emerton, Luke Wilkshire, Vincenzo Grella, Jason Čulina, Mark Bresciano (62.Carl Valeri), David Raymond Carney, Harold Kewell (Cap) (77.Bruce José Djité), Scott Douglas McDonald (65.Brett Holman). Trainer: Peter Tim Verbeek (Holland).
IRQ: Noor Sabri Abbas Hassan, Haidar Abdul-Amir Hussain, Saad Attiya Hafidh, Bassim Abbas Kati, Ali Hussein Rehema Al Muttairi, Mahdi Karim Ajeel (68.Salih Sadir Al Sadoun), Hawar Mulla Mohammed Taher Zibari (84.Mustafa Karim Abdullah), Qusai Munir Aboodi, Nashat Akram Ali, Younis Mahmoud Khalef, Emad Mohammed Ridha. Trainer: Egil Roger Olsen (Norway).
Goal: 1-0 Harold Kewell (47).
Cautions: Vincenzo Grella, Luke Wilkshire / Ali Hussein Rehema Al Muttairi, Haidar Abdul-Amir Hussain.

02.06.2008, „Jassem bin Hamad" Stadium, Doha; Attendance: 9,000
Referee: Mohsen Hassan Basma (Syria)
QATAR – CHINA P.R. **0-0**
QAT: Mohamed Ahmed Saqer, Abdullah Obaid Koni (Cap), Ibrahim Abdul Majid, Marcone Amaral Costa Júnior, Bilal Mohammed Rajab, Wesam Rizik Abdulmajid, Talal Hassan Ali Al Bloushi (89.Yousef Ahmed Ali), Mesaad Ali Al Hamad (71.Sayed Ali Baba Al Basheer), Hussain Yasser Abdulrahman, Khalfan Ibrahim Al Khalfan (57.Fábio César Montezine), Andrés Sebastián Soria Quintana. Trainer: Jorge Daniel Fossati Lurachi (Uruguay).
CHN: Song Zhenyu, Li Weifeng, Wang Xiao, Zhang Yaokun, Sun Xiang, Sun Jihai (90.Wu Hao), Zheng Zhi, Xiao Zhanbo (55.Liu Jian), Zhou Haibin, Han Peng (85.Qu Bo), Zhu Ting. Trainer: Vladimir Petrović (Serbia).
Cautions: Song Zhenyu, Han Peng, Zhou Haibin, Wu Hao.

07.06.2008, Tianjin Olympic Centre Stadium, Tianjin; Attendance: 50,000
Referee: Tallat Najm (Lebanon)
CHINA P.R. - QATAR **0-1(0-1)**
CHN: Song Zhenyu, Li Weifeng, Wang Xiao, Cao Yang, Sun Xiang (46.Du Zhenyu), Zheng Zhi, Huang Bowen, Liu Jian, Hao Junmin, Gao Lin (62.Han Peng), Zhu Ting (62.Qu Bo). Trainer: Vladimir Petrović (Serbia).
QAT: Mohamed Ahmed Saqer, Abdullah Obaid Koni (Cap), Ibrahim Abdul Majid, Marcone Amaral Costa Júnior, Bilal Mohammed Rajab, Wesam Rizik Abdulmajid, Talal Hassan Ali Al Bloushi, Mesaad Ali Al Hamad, Fábio César Montezine (85.Mohammed Gholam Al Bloushi), Yousef Ahmed Ali (62.Majed Mohammed Hassan), Andrés Sebastián Soria Quintana (90+2.Mustafa Abdi Abdullah). Trainer: Jorge Daniel Fossati Lurachi (Uruguay).
Goal: 0-1 Andrés Sebastián Soria Quintana (14 penalty).
Cautions: Huang Bowen, Liu Jian, Du Zhenyu, Cao Yang, Li Weifeng / Talal Hassan Ali Al Bloushi, Yousef Ahmed Ali, Andrés Sebastián Soria Quintana.
Sent off: Sun Jihai (80, on the bench).

07.06.2008, Al Rashid Stadium, Dubai (United Arab Emirates); Attendance: 8,000
Referee: Kazuhiko Matsumura (Japan)
IRAQ - AUSTRALIA **1-0(1-0)**
IRQ: Noor Sabri Abbas Hassan, Haidar Abdul-Amir Hussain, Saad Attiya Hafidh, Bassim Abbas Kati, Ali Hussein Rehema Al Muttairi, Mahdi Karim Ajeel (68.Mohammed Ali Karim), Hawar Mulla Mohammed Taher Zibari (68.Salih Sadir Al Sadoun), Qusai Munir Aboodi, Nashat Akram Ali (78.Haitham Kadhim Tahir), Younis Mahmoud Khalef, Emad Mohammed Ridha. Trainer: Egil Roger Olsen (Norway).
AUS: Mark Schwarzer, Christopher John Coyne (64.Joshua Blake Kennedy), Jade Bronson North, Michael Beauchamp, Brett Michael Emerton, Luke Wilkshire, Vincenzo Grella (46.Brett Holman), Jason Čulina, Carl Valeri, David Raymond Carney, Harold Kewell (Cap) (70.Scott Douglas McDonald). Trainer: Peter Tim Verbeek (Holland).
Goal: 1-0 Emad Mohammed Ridha (28).
Cautions: Saad Attiya Hafidh, Younis Mahmoud Khalef / Vincenzo Grella.

14.06.2008, Tianjin Olympic Centre Stadium, Tianjin; Attendance: 39,000
Referee: Malik Abdul Bashir (Singapore)
CHINA P.R. - IRAQ **1-2(1-1)**
CHN: Song Zhenyu, Zhang Yaokun, Cao Yang (46.Feng Xiaoting), Xu Yunlong, Sun Xiang, Zheng Zhi, Du Zhenyu (62.Liu Jian), Xiao Zhanbo (75.Hao Junmin), Zhou Haibin, Han Peng, Zhu Ting. Trainer: Vladimir Petrović (Serbia).
IRQ: Noor Sabri Abbas Hassan, Haidar Abdul-Amir Hussain, Saad Attiya Hafidh, Bassim Abbas Kati, Ali Hussein Rehema Al Muttairi, Hawar Mulla Mohammed Taher Zibari (86.Mohammed Ali Karim), Qusai Munir Aboodi, Nashat Akram Ali, Salih Sadir Al Sadoun (66.Haitham Kadhim Tahir), Younis

Mahmoud Khalef (12.Mahdi Karim Ajeel), Emad Mohammed Ridha. Trainer: Adnan Hamd.
Goals: 1-0 Zhou Haibin (33), 1-1 Emad Mohammed Ridha (41), 1-2 Nashat Akram Ali (65).
Cautions: Bassim Abbas Kati, Saad Attiya Hafidh.

14.06.2008, „Jassem bin Hamad" Stadium, Doha; Attendance: 12,000
Referee: Lee Gi-Young (Korea Republic)
QATAR - AUSTRALIA   **1-3(0-1)**
QAT: Mohamed Ahmed Saqer, Abdullah Obaid Koni (Cap) (33.Ibrahim Abdullah Al Ghanim), Ibrahim Abdul Majid (65.Khalfan Ibrahim Al Khalfan), Marcone Amaral Costa Júnior, Bilal Mohammed Rajab, Wesam Rizik Abdulmajid, Talal Hassan Ali Al Bloushi, Mesaad Ali Al Hamad, Fábio César Montezine, Yousef Ahmed Ali (46.Majed Mohammed Hassan), Andrés Sebastián Soria Quintana. Trainer: Jorge Daniel Fossati Lurachi (Uruguay).
AUS: Mark Schwarzer, Jade Bronson North, Michael Beauchamp, Brett Michael Emerton, Luke Wilkshire, Jason Čulina, Carl Valeri, Mark Bresciano, David Raymond Carney, Brett Holman, Harold Kewell (Cap) (85.Bruce José Djité). Trainer: Peter Tim Verbeek (Holland).
Goals: 0-1 Brett Michael Emerton (17), 0-2 Brett Michael Emerton (56), 0-3 Harold Kewell (74), 1-3 Khalfan Ibrahim Al Khalfan (89).
Cautions: Yousef Ahmed Ali, Wesam Rizik Abdulmajid, Fábio César Montezine / David Raymond Carney, Carl Valeri, Mark Bresciano, Mark Schwarzer, Luke Wilkshire.

22.06.2008, Olympic Stadium, Sydney; Attendance: 70,054
Referee: Khalil Ibrahim Al Ghamdi (Saudi Arabia)
AUSTRALIA – CHINA P.R.   **0-1(0-1)**
AUS: Michael Petkovic, Nikolai David Topor-Stanley, Jade Bronson North, Matthew Thomas Spiranovic, Ruben Anton Zadkovich, James Robert Holland (63.David Joel Williams), Michael John Jedinak (79.Neil Martin Kilkenny), James Troisi (83.Kristian Ronald Sarkies), Carl Valeri, Harold Kewell (Cap), (Bruce José Djité). Trainer: Peter Tim Verbeek (Holland).
CHN: Song Zhenyu, Li Weifeng, Zhang Yaokun, Xu Yunlong (69.Wu Hao), Sun Xiang, Du Zhenyu, Liu Jian, Wang Dong, Xiao Zhanbo (73.Zheng Zhi), Gao Lin (87.Han Peng), Qu Bo. Trainer: Vladimir Petrović (Serbia).
Goal: 0-1 Sun Xiang (12).

22.06.2008, Al-Rashid Stadium, Dubai (United Arab Emirates); Attendance: 10,000
Referee: Ali Hamad Madhad Saif Al Badwawi (United Arab Emirates)
IRAQ - QATAR   **0-1(0-0)**
Noor Sabri Abbas Hassan, Haidar Abdul-Amir Hussain, Bassim Abbas Kati, Ali Hussein Rehema Al Muttairi, Salam Shakir, Mahdi Karim Ajeel (78.Younis Mahmoud Khalef), Hawar Mulla Mohammed Taher Zibari, Qusai Munir Aboodi, Nashat Akram Ali (86.Mustafa Karim Abdullah), Salih Sadir Al Sadoun (66.Haitham Kadhim Tahir), Emad Mohammed Ridha. Trainer: Adnan Hamd.
QAT: Mohamed Ahmed Saqer, Ibrahim Abdul Majid, Marcone Amaral Costa Júnior, Bilal Mohammed Rajab, Wesam Rizik Abdulmajid (Cap), Talal Hassan Ali Al Bloushi, Mesaad Ali Al Hamad, Fábio César Montezine (71.Khalfan Ibrahim Al Khalfan), Majdi Abdulla Siddiq (46.Hussain Yasser Abdulrahman), Sayed Ali Baba Al Basheer (80.Ibrahim Abdullah Al Ghanim), Andrés Sebastián Soria Quintana. Trainer: Jorge Daniel Fossati Lurachi (Uruguay).
Goal: 0-1 Sayed Ali Baba Al Basheer (76).
Cautions: Haitham Kadhim Tahir / Wesam Rizik Abdulmajid, Hussain Yasser Abdulrahman, Khalfan Ibrahim Al Khalfan, Mohamed Ahmed Saqer.

GROUP 2

06.02.2008	Saitama	Japan - Thailand	4-1(1-1)
06.02.2008	Muscat	Oman - Bahrain	0-1(0-1)
26.03.2008	Bangkok	Thailand - Oman	0-1(0-1)
26.03.2008	Madinat 'Isa	Bahrain - Japan	1-0(0-0)
02.06.2008	Yokohama	Japan - Oman	3-0(2-0)
02.06.2008	Bangkok	Thailand - Bahrain	2-3(2-2)
07.06.2008	Muscat	Oman - Japan	1-1(1-0)
07.06.2008	Madinat 'Isa	Bahrain - Thailand	1-1(0-0)
14.06.2008	Bangkok	Thailand - Japan	0-3(0-2)
14.06.2008	Madinat 'Isa	Bahrain - Oman	1-1(1-0)
22.06.2008	Saitama	Japan - Bahrain	1-0(0-0)
22.06.2008	Muscat	Oman - Thailand	2-1(0-1)

FINAL STANDINGS

1.	**Japan**	6	4	1	1	12	-	3	13
2.	**Bahrain**	6	3	2	1	7	-	5	11
3.	Oman	6	2	2	2	5	-	7	8
4.	Thailand	6	0	1	5	5	-	14	1

06.02.2008, Saitama Stadium, Saitama; Attendance: 35,130
Referee: Khalil Ibrahim Al Ghamdi (Saudi Arabia)
JAPAN - THAILAND   **4-1(1-1)**
JPN: Yoshikatsu Kawaguchi, Yuji Nakazawa, Yuichi Komano, Atsuto Uchida, Yuki Abe, Yasuhito Endō, Koji Yamase (68.Seiichiro Maki), Keita Suzuki, Kengo Nakamura, Yoshito Okubo (87.Naotake Hanyu), Naohiro Takahara (81.Ryuji Bando). Trainer: Takeshi Okada.
THA: Sinthaweechai Hathairattanakool, Nattaporn Phanrit, Patiparn Phetphun, Apichet Puttan, Natthaphong Samana, Nirut Surasiang (Cap), Narongchai Vachiraban, Sarayoot Chaikamdee (81.Pipat Thonkanya), Suchao Nuchnum (83.Anon Sangsanoi), Sutee Suksomkit, Teeratep Winothai (72.Pichitphong Choeichiu). Trainer: Chanvit Phalajivin.
Goals: 1-0 Yasuhito Endō (21), 1-1 Teeratep Winothai (22), 2-1 Yoshito Okubo (54), 3-1 Yuji Nakazawa (66), 4-1 Seiichiro Maki (90+1).
Cautions: Narongchai Vachiraban, Apichet Puttan, Teeratep Winothai.
Sent off: Narongchai Vachiraban (64).

06.02.2008, „Sultan Qaboos" Sports Complex, Muscat; Attendance: 28,000
Referee: Lee Gi-Young (Korea Republic)
OMAN - BAHRAIN   **0-1(0-1)**
OMA: Ali Abdulla Al Habsi, Mohammed Abdullah Mubarak Al Balushi „Al Sheiba", Hassan Yousuf Mudhafar Al Gheilani, Mohamed Rabia Jamaan Al Noobi (Cap), Talal Khalfan Al Farsi (80.Hashim Saleh Mohamed Al Balushi), Khalifa Ayil Salim Al Naufali, Fawzi Bashir Rajab Bait Doorbeen, Ahmed Mubarak Obaid Al Mahaijri, Ismail Sulaiman Al Ajmi, Badar Mubarak Al Maimani (74.Mohamed Mubarak Al Hinai), Imad Ali Sulaiman Al Hosani, Trainer: Gabriel Humberto Calderón (Argentina).
BHR: Sayed Mohammed Jaffer Sabet, Sayed Mohamed Adnan, Hussain Ali Baba Mohammed, Salman Isa Ghuloom, Mohamed Husain Bahzad, Babatunde Fatai-Baba Fatadi, Abdullah Omar Ismail, Sayed Mahmood Jalal Al Wadaei (Cap), Mohamed Ahmed Yusuf Salmeen (78.Faouzi Mubarak Aaish), Ismaeel Abdullatif Hasan, A'ala Ahmed Hubail (89.Abdulla Adnan Saleh Salman Al Dakheel). Trainer: Milan Máčala (Czech Republic).
Goal: 0-1 A'ala Ahmed Hubail (14).
Cautions: Ahmed Mubarak Obaid Al Mahaijri, Talal Khalfan Al Farsi, Khalifa Ayil Salim Al Naufali / Sayed Mahmood Jalal Al Wadaei, Hussain Ali Baba Mohammed, Mohamed Ahmed Yusuf Salmeen, Babatunde Fatai-Baba Fatadi.

26.03.2008, Rajamangala National Stadium, Bangkok; Attendance: 40,000
Referee: Mohsen Torky (Iran)
THAILAND - OMAN   **0-1(0-1)**
THA: Sinthaweechai Hathairattanakool, Punnarat Klinsukon (58.Kiatprawut Saiwaew), Nattaporn Phanrit, Patiparn Phetphun, Suree Sukha, Nirut Surasiang, Tawan Sripan (Cap), Datsakorn Thonglao, Teerasil Dangda, Sutee Suksomkit (71.Tana Chanabut), Teeratep Winothai. Trainer: Chanvit Phalajivin.

OMA: Ali Abdulla Al Habsi, Mohammed Abdullah Mubarak Al Balushi „Al Sheiba", Hassan Yousuf Mudhafar Al Gheilani, Mohamed Rabia Jamaan Al Noobi (Cap), Talal Khalfan Al Farsi, Ahmed Hadid Thuwaini Al Mukhaini, Khalifa Ayil Salim Al Naufali, Fawzi Bashir Rajab Bait Doorbeen, Ahmed Mubarak Obaid Al Mahaijri, Ismail Sulaiman Al Ajmi, Imad Ali Sulaiman Al Hosani (81.Mohammed Al Lawati). Trainer: Gabriel Humberto Calderón (Argentina).
Goal: 0-1 Ismail Sulaiman Al Ajmi (1).
Cautions: Datsakorn Thonglao / Hassan Yousuf Mudhafar Al Gheilani, Imad Ali Sulaiman Al Hosani, Fawzi Bashir Rajab Bait Doorbeen, Ahmed Mubarak Obaid Al Mahaijri, Talal Khalfan Al Farsi, Mohamed Rabia Jamaan Al Noobi, Khalifa Ayil Salim Al Naufali, Ahmed Hadid Thuwaini Al Mukhaini.
Sent off: Talal Khalfan Al Farsi (90+4).

26.03.2008, National Stadium, Manama; Attendance: 26,000
Referee: Mark Alexander Shield (Australia)
BAHRAIN - JAPAN   **1-0(0-0)**
BHR: Sayed Mohammed Jaffer Sabet, Sayed Mohamed Adnan, Salman Isa Ghuloom (81.Faouzi Mubarak Aaish), Mohamed Husain Bahzad, Abdullah Al Marzooqi, Babatunde Fatai-Baba Fatadi, Abdullah Omar Ismail, Sayed Mahmood Jalal Al Wadaei, Mohamed Ahmed Yusuf Salmeen (73.Hamad Rakea Al Enezi), A'ala Ahmed Hubail, Ismaeel Abdullatif Hasan (87.Abdulla Adnan Saleh Salman Al Dakheel). Trainer: Milan Máčala (Czech Republic).
JPN: Yoshikatsu Kawaguchi, Yuki Abe (82.Keiji Tamada), Yuji Nakazawa, Yasuyuki Konno, Yuichi Komano, Keita Suzuki, Kengo Nakamura, Michihiro Yasuda (72.Satoru Yamagishi), Koji Yamase (56.Yasuhito Endō), Seiichiro Maki, Yoshito Okubo. Trainer: Takeshi Okada.
Goal: 1-0 A'ala Ahmed Hubail (78).
Cautions: Babatunde Fatai-Baba Fatadi, Sayed Mahmood Jalal Al Wadaei, Hamad Rakea Al Enezi / Yuki Abe.

02.06.2008, International Stadium, Yokohama; Attendance: 46,764
Referee: Abdul Malik Bashir (Singapore)
JAPAN - OMAN   **3-0(2-0)**
JPN: Seigo Narazaki, Yuto Nagatomo (83.Yasuyuki Konno), Marcus Tulio Tanaka, Yuji Nakazawa, Yuichi Komano, Yasuhito Endō, Makoto Hasebe, Daisuke Matsui, Shunsuke Nakamura, Yoshito Okubo (72.Shinji Kagawa), Keiji Tamada (79.Seiichiro Maki). Trainer: Takeshi Okada.
OMA: Ali Abdulla Al Habsi, Hassan Yousuf Mudhafar Al Gheilani, Issam Al Sinani, Nabil Ashoor Ramadhan Bait Faraj Allah, Ashraf Eid Taysir, Mohammed Al Mashaikhi (55.Hashim Saleh Mohamed Al Balushi), Ahmed Hadid Thuwaini Al Mukhaini, Fawzi Bashir Rajab Bait Doorbeen (Cap), Ismail Sulaiman Al Ajmi, Mohamed Mubarak Al Hinai (75.Hassan Rabia Al Housni), Imad Ali Sulaiman Al Hosani. Trainer: Julio César Ribas (Uruguay).
Goals: 1-0 Yuji Nakazwa (10), 2-0 Yoshito Okubo (22), 3-0 Shunsuke Nakamura (49).
Cautions: Makoto Hasebe, Shinji Kagawa / Mohammed Al Mashaikhi, Hassan Yousuf Mudhafar Al Gheilani, Imad Ali Sulaiman Al Hosani.

02.06.2008, Rajamangala National Stadium, Bangkok; Attendance: 15,000
Referee: Sun Baojie (China P.R.)
THAILAND - BAHRAIN 2-3(2-2)
THA: Sivaruk Tedsungnoen, Nattaporn Phanrit, Prat Samakrat (46.Nirut Surasiang), Natthaphong Samana, Niweat Siriwong, Suree Sukha (77.Ekaphan Inthasen), Pichitphong Choeichiu, Tawan Sripan (Cap), Datsakorn Thonglao, Sarayoot Chaikamdee (57.Tana Chanabut), Teeratep Winothai. Trainer: Chanvit Phalajivin.
BHR: Sayed Mohammed Jaffer Sabet, Sayed Mohamed Adnan, Salman Isa Ghuloom, Mohamed Husain Bahzad (Cap) (69.Hamad Rakea Al Enezi), Abdullah Al Marzooqi, Faouzi Mubarak Aaish, Mahmood Abdulrahman Mohammed Noor, Abdullah Omar Ismail, Mohamed Ahmed Yusuf Salmeen, Ismaeel Abdullatif Hasan (80.Jaycee John Akwani Okwunwanne), A'ala Ahmed Hubail (89.Jamal Rashid Rahman). Trainer: Milan Máčala (Czech Republic).
Goals: 0-1 Sarayoot Chaikamdee (22), 1-1 Salman Isa Ghuloom (25), 1-2 Ismaeel Abdullatif Hasan (34), 2-2 Teeratep Winothai (45), 2-3 Sayed Mohamed Adnan (57).
Cautions: Suree Sukha / Abdullah Al Marzooqi, Mohamed Husain Bahzad.

07.06.2008, Royal Oman Police Stadium, Muscat; Attendance: 6,500
Referee: Subkhiddin Mohd Salleh (Malaysia)
OMAN - JAPAN 1-1(1-0)
OMA: Ali Abdulla Al Habsi, Issam Al Sinani, Mohamed Rabia Jamaan Al Noobi, Talal Khalfan Al Farsi, Ahmed Hadid Thuwaini Al Mukhaini, Khalifa Ayil Salim Al Naufali, Fawzi Bashir Rajab Bait Doorbeen (85.Younis Mubarak Al Mahaijri), Ahmed Mubarak Obaid Al Mahaijri (69.Mohammed Al Mashaikhi), Ismail Sulaiman Al Ajmi, Hashim Saleh Mohamed Al Balushi, Mohamed Mubarak Al Hinai (Cap) (46.Nabil Ashoor Ramadhan Bait Faraj Allah). Trainer: Hamad Khalifa Hamed Al Azani.
JPN: Seigo Narazaki, Yuji Nakazawa, Yuichi Komano, Atsuto Uchida (90+2.Yasuyuki Konno), Marcus Tulio Tanaka, Yasuhito Endō, Makoto Hasebe, Shunsuke Nakamura, Daisuke Matsui (78.Koji Yamase), Yoshito Okubo, Keiji Tamada (90+1.Kisho Yano). Trainer: Takeshi Okada.
Goals: 1-0 Ahmed Mubarak Obaid Al Mahaijri (12), 1-1 Yasuhito Endō (53 penalty).
Cautions: Fawzi Bashir Rajab Bait Doorbeen.
Sent off: Khalifa Ayil Salim Al Naufali (73), Yoshito Okubo (73).

07.06.2008, National Stadium, Manama; Attendance: 21,000
Referee: Mohsen Hassan Basma (Syria)
BAHRAIN - THAILAND 1-1(0-0)
BHR: Sayed Mohammed Jaffer Sabet, Sayed Mohamed Adnan, Salman Isa Ghuloom (90+3.Abdulla Adnan Saleh Salman Al Dakheel), Abdullah Al Marzooqi, Faouzi Mubarak Aaish, Mahmood Abdulrahman Mohammed Noor, Babatunde Fatai-Baba Fatadi, Abdullah Omar Ismail, Mohamed Ahmed Yusuf Salmeen (Cap), Ismaeel Abdullatif Hasan (70.Hamad Rakea Al Enezi), A'ala Ahmed Hubail (80.Rashed Jamal Salem Mohamed Saleem). Trainer: Milan Máčala (Czech Republic).
THA: Sinthaweechai Hathairattanakool, Wattana Chaiwuth (83.Suchao Nuchnum), Nattaporn Phanrit, Natthaphong Samana, Niweat Siriwong, Suree Sukha, Pichitphong Choeichiu (85.Rangsan Viwatchaichok), Tawan Sripan (Cap), Datsakorn Thonglao, Sarayoot Chaikamdee (75.Tana Chanabut), Teeratep Winothai. Trainer: Chanvit Phalajivin.
Goals: 0-1 Datsakorn Thonglao (65), 1-1 Salman Isa Ghuloom (67).
Cautions: Faouzi Mubarak Aaish / Natthaphong Samana, Wattana Chaiwuth, Tana Chanabut, Tawan Sripan, Rangsan Viwatchaichok.
Sent off: Babatunde Fatai-Baba Fatadi (56), Teeratep Winothai (90).

14.06.2008, Rajamangala National Stadium, Bangkok; Attendance: 25,000
Referee: Ali Hamad Madhad Saif Al Badwawi (United Arab Emirates)
THAILAND - JAPAN 0-3(0-2)
THA: Sinthaweechai Hathairattanakool, Wattana Chaiwuth (71.Nirut Surasiang), Nattaporn Phanrit, Kiatprawut Saiwaew, Niweat Siriwong, Suree Sukha, Pichitphong Choeichiu (85.Sutee Suksomkit),

Tawan Sripan (Cap), Datsakorn Thonglao, Sarayoot Chaikamdee (48.Tana Chanabut), Teerasil Dangda. Trainer: Chanvit Phalajivin.
JPN: Seigo Narazaki, Yuji Nakazawa, Yuichi Komano, Marcus Tulio Tanaka, Atsuto Uchida, Yasuhito Endō, Shinji Kagawa (82.Yasuyuki Konno), Daisuke Matsui (70.Kisho Yano), Shunsuke Nakamura (70.Kengo Nakamura), Keiji Tamada, Makoto Hasebe. Trainer: Takeshi Okada.
Goals: 0-1 Marcus Tulio Tanaka (23), 0-2 Yuji Nakazawa (39), 0-3 Kengo Nakamura (88).
Cautions: Kiatprawut Saiwaew, Datsakorn Thonglao, Suree Sukha, Nirut Surasiang / Yuichi Komano, Daisuke Matsui.

14.06.2008, National Stadium, Manama; Attendance: 25,000
Referee: Saad Kameel Al Fadhli (Kuwait)
BAHRAIN - OMAN   **1-1(1-0)**
BHR: Sayed Mohammed Jaffer Sabet, Sayed Mohamed Adnan, Salman Isa Ghuloom (72.Mahmood Abdulrahman Mohammed Noor), Mohamed Husain Bahzad (85.Hamad Rakea Al Enezi), Abdullah Al Marzooqi, Faouzi Mubarak Aaish, Abdullah Omar Ismail, Sayed Mahmood Jalal Al Wadaei (Cap), Mohamed Ahmed Yusuf Salmeen, A'ala Ahmed Hubail, Ismaeel Abdullatif Hasan (67.Rashed Jamal Salem Mohamed Saleem). Trainer: Milan Máčala (Czech Republic).
OMA: Ali Abdulla Al Habsi, Hassan Yousuf Mudhafar Al Gheilani, Issam Al Sinani, Nabil Ashoor Ramadhan Bait Faraj Allah, Mohamed Rabia Jamaan Al Noobi (Cap), Talal Khalfan Al Farsi, Ahmed Hadid Thuwaini Al Mukhaini, Ahmed Mubarak Obaid Al Mahaijri, Ismail Sulaiman Al Ajmi, Hashim Saleh Mohamed Al Balushi, Imad Ali Sulaiman Al Hosani. Trainer: Hamad Khalifa Hamed Al Azani.
Goals: 1-0 Faouzi Mubarak Aaish (41), 1-1 Ismail Sulaiman Al Ajmi (72).
Cautions: A'ala Ahmed Hubail, Ismaeel Abdullatif Hasan, Abdullah Al Marzooqi / Ahmed Hadid Thuwaini Al Mukhaini, Ahmed Mubarak Obaid Al Mahaijri, Mohamed Rabia Jamaan Al Noobi.

22.06.2008, Saitama Stadium, Saitama; Attendance: 51,180
Referee: Ravshan Irmatov (Uzbekistan)
JAPAN - BAHRAIN   **1-0(0-0)**
JPN: Seigo Narazaki, Atsuto Uchida, Yuji Nakazawa, Marcus Tulio Tanaka, Michihiro Yasuda (73.Yasuyuki Konno), Kengo Nakamura, Yasuhito Endō, Shunsuke Nakamura, Keisuke Honda (80.Seiichiro Maki), Hisato Sato (64.Koji Yamase), Keiji Tamada. Trainer: Takeshi Okada.
BHR: Sayed Mohammed Jaffer Sabet, Sayed Mohamed Adnan, Abbas Sayed Ali Mansoor Ayyad (72.Rashed Isa Al Allan), Salman Isa Ghuloom, Mohamed Husain Bahzad, Faouzi Mubarak Aaish, Mahmood Abdulrahman Mohammed Noor, Hamad Rakea Al Enezi, Abdullah Omar Ismail, Sayed Mahmood Jalal Al Wadaei (Cap), Ismaeel Abdullatif Hasan (78.Rashed Jamal Salem Mohamed Saleem). Trainer: Milan Máčala (Czech Republic).
Goal: 1-0 (Atsuto Uchida 90).
Cautions: Keisuke Honda / , Sayed Mahmood Jalal Al Wadaei, Sayed Mohamed Adnan.

22.06.2008, Royal Oman Police Stadium, Muscat; Attendance: 3,000
Referee: Salem Mahmoud Mujghef (Jordan)
OMAN - THAILAND   **2-1(0-1)**
OMA: Ali Abdulla Al Habsi, Hassan Yousuf Mudhafar Al Gheilani, Issam Al Sinani, Nabil Ashoor Ramadhan Bait Faraj Allah, Talal Khalfan Al Farsi, Mohammed Al Mashaikhi, Khalifa Ayil Salim Al Naufali (73.Ashraf Eid Taysir), Fawzi Bashir Rajab Bait Doorbeen, Ismail Sulaiman Al Ajmi (81.Mohamed Mubarak Al Hinai), Hashim Saleh Mohamed Al Balushi (Cap), Imad Ali Sulaiman Al Hosani. Trainer: Hamad Khalifa Hamed Al Azani.
THA: Sivaruk Tedsungnoen, Wattana Chaiwuth, Jetsada Jitsawad, Nattaporn Phanrit, Kiatprawut Saiwaew (85.Natthaphong Samana), Phukhom Sutinun, Pichitphong Choeichiu (75.Arthit Sunthornphit), Tawan Sripan (Cap), Teerasil Dangda, Anon Sangsanoi (61.Tana Chanabut), Sutee Suksomkit. Trainer: Chanvit Phalajivin.
Goals: 0-1 Totchtawan Sripan (3 penalty), 1-1 Imad Ali Sulaiman Al Hosani (58), 1-2 Imad Ali Sulaiman Al Hosani (65).
Cautions: Kiatprawut Saiwaew, Sivaruk Tedsungnoen, Wattana Chaiwuth.

GROUP 3

06.02.2008	Seoul	Korea Republic - Turkmenistan	4-0(1-0)
06.02.2008	Amman	Jordan – Korea D.P.R.	0-1(0-1)
26.03.2008	Shanghai (CHN)	Korea D.P.R. – Korea Republic	0-0
26.03.2008	Aşgabat	Turkmenistan - Jordan	0-2(0-1)
31.05.2008	Seoul	Korea Republic - Jordan	2-2(1-0)
02.06.2008	Aşgabat	Turkmenistan – Korea D.P.R.	0-0
07.06.2008	P'yŏngyang	Korea D.P.R. - Turkmenistan	1-0(0-0)
07.06.2008	Amman	Jordan – Korea Republic	0-1(0-1)
14.06.2008	P'yŏngyang	Korea D.P.R. - Jordan	2-0(1-0)
14.06.2008	Aşgabat	Turkmenistan – Korea Republic	1-3(0-1)
22.06.2008	Seoul	Korea Republic – Korea D.P.R.	0-0
22.06.2008	Amman	Jordan - Turkmenistan	2-0(0-0)

FINAL STANDINGS

1.	**Korea Republic**	6	3	3	0	10	-	3	12
2.	**Korea D.P.R.**	6	3	3	0	4	-	0	12
3.	Jordan	6	2	1	3	6	-	6	7
4.	Turkmenistan	6	0	1	5	1	-	12	1

06.02.2008, Seoul World Cup Stadium, Seoul; Attendance: 25,738
Referee: Jasim Karim (Bahrain)
KOREA REPUBLIC - TURKMENISTAN   **4-0(1-0)**
KOR: Jung Sung-Ryong, Oh Beom-Seok, Kwak Tae-Hwi, Kang Min-Soo, Lee Young-Pyo, Cho Yong-Hyung (86.Park Won-Jae), Park Ji-Sung, Kim Nam-Il (Cap) (78.Lee Kwan-Woo), Seol Ki-Hyeon, Park Chu-Young, Yeom Ki-Hun (41.Kim Do-Heon). Trainer: Huh Jung-Moo.
TKM: Baýramnyýaz Berdiýew, Begli Annageldiýew, Gochguly Gochguliýew (Cap), Yagmyrmyrat Annamyradow (54.Nazar Çöliýew), Nazar Baýramov, Didar Hajyýew, Vyacheslav Krendelev, Mekan Nasyrow (78.Artur Gevorkyan), Vladimir Baýramow, Azat Muhadov, Guwançmuhammet Öwekow (60.Mamedaly Karadanow). Trainer: Rahim Kurbanmamedov.
Goals: 1-0 Kwak Tae-Hwi (43), 2-0 Seol Ki-Hyeon (57), 3-0 Seol Ki-Hyeon (83), 4-0 Park Ji-Sung (70).
Cautions: Azat Muhadov.

06.02.2008, Amman International Stadium, Amman; Attendance: 16,000
Referee: Tayeb Shamsuzzaman (Bangladesh)
JORDAN – KOREA D.P.R.   **0-1(0-1)**
JOR: Lo'ai Salem Atallah El Amaireh, Waseem Al Bzoor, Hatem Mohammed Aqel, Faisal Ibrahim Suleiman (46.Rafat Ali Ahmad Jaber), Basem Fathi Omar Othman, Qusai Mohammed Mahmoud Abu Alieh, Moayad Omar Suleimani Abu Keshek (70.Odai Yousef Ismail Al Saify), Amer Deeb Mohammad Khalil, Hassouneh Qasem Al Shaikh (78.Awad Deeb Ragheb), Abdullah Khalid Deeb Salim, Mahmoud Omar Shelbaieh. Trainer: Eduardo Manuel Martinho Vingada (Portugal).
PRK: Ri Myong-Guk, Nam Song-Chol, Pak Chol-Jin (60.Cha Jong-Hyok), Ri Jun-Il, Ri Kwang-Chon, An Jong-Ho, Han Song-Chol, Kim Yong-Jun (40.Ryang Yong-Gi; 90+2.Pak Nam-Chol II), Mun In-Guk, Jong Tae-Se, Yong-Jo Hong. Trainer: Han Hyong-Yi.
Goal: 0-1 Hong Yong-Jo (44).
Cautions: Odai Yousef Ismail Al Saify, Amer Deeb Mohammad Khalil, Hatem Mohammed Aqel / Ri Myong-Guk, Jong Tae-Se.

26.03.2008, Hongkou Football Stadium, Shanghai (China P.R.); Attendance: 20,000
Referee: Saad Kameel Al Fadhli (Kuwait)
KOREA D.P.R. – KOREA REPUBLIC   **0-0**
PRK: Ri Myong-Guk, Nam Song-Chol, Ri Jun-Il, Ri Kwang-Hyok, An Yong-Hak, Han Song-Chol (27.Cha Jong-Hyok), Kim Yong-Jun, Mun In-Guk, Pak Song-Chol, Jong Tae-Se (90+2.Pak Nam-Chol

II), Yong-Jo Hong. Trainer: Kim Jong-Hun.
KOR: Jung Sung-Ryong, Oh Beom-Seok, Lee Jung-Soo, Kang Min-Soo, Lee Young Pyo, Cho Won-Hee, Kim Nam-Il (Cap) (28.Kim Do-Heon), Seol Ki- Hyeon (81.Han Tae-You), Park Chu-Young, Park Ji Sung, Cho Jae-Jin (46.Yeom Ki-Hun). Trainer: Huh Jung-Moo.
Cautions: Cho Won-Hee.

26.03.2008, Olympic Stadium, Aşgabat; Attendance: 20,000
Referee: Satop Tongkhan (Thailand)
TURKMENISTAN - JORDAN   **0-2(0-1)**
TKM: Baýramnyýaz Berdiýew, Begli Annageldiýew, Maksim Belyh, Gochguly Gochguliýew (Cap), Yagmyrmyrat Annamyradow, Nazar Baýramov, Didar Hajyýew, Vyacheslav Krendelev, Mekan Nasyrow (58.Artur Gevorkyan), Vladimir Baýramow (60 Mamedaly Karadanow), Guwançmuhammet Öwekow (70.Arif Mirzoýew). Trainer: Rahim Kurbanmamedov.
JOR: Lo'ai Salem Atallah El Amaireh, Waseem Al Bzoor, Hatem Mohammed Aqel, Bashar Bani Mustafa Yaseen, Ala'a Hasan Mohammad Matalqa, Ala Al Bashir (46.Hassouneh Qasem Al Shaikh), Amer Deeb Mohammad Khalil, Baha'a Abdulrahman Suleiman, Odai Yousef Ismail Al Saify, Abdullah Khalid Deeb Salim (80.Khaled Saad Al Maltaah), Mahmoud Omar Shelbaieh (78.Thaer Fayed Bawab). Trainer: Eduardo Manuel Martinho Vingada (Portugal).
Goals: 0-1 Waseem Al Bzoor (33), 0-2 Thaer Fayed Bawab (86).
Cautions: Yagmyrmyrat Annamyradow / Bashar Bani Mustafa Yaseen, Ala Al Bashir.

31.05.2008, Seoul World Cup Stadium, Seoul; Attendance: 50,000
Referee: Mark Alexander Shield (Australia)
KOREA REPUBLIC - JORDAN   **2-2(1-0)**
KOR: Kim Yong-Dae, Oh Beom-Seok, Lee Jung-Soo, Kwak Hee-Joo, Lee Young Pyo, Cho Won-Hee, Kim Nam-Il (Cap) (74.Cho Yong-Hyung), Lee Chung-Yong (54.Kim Do-Heon), Ahn Jung-Hwan (85.Ko Ki-Gu), Park Ji-Sung, Park Chu-Young. Trainer: Huh Jung-Moo.
JOR: Lo'ai Salem Atallah El Amaireh, Mohammad Munir Al Mutasim (52.Hassan Mahmoud Abdel Fattah), Hatem Mohammed Aqel, Mohammad Khamees, Ala'a Hasan Mohammad Matalqa, Amer Deeb Mohammad Khalil, Hassouneh Qasem Al Shaikh, Baha'a Abdulrahman Suleiman, Odai Yousef Ismail Al Saify, Thaer Fayed Bawab (73.Mustafa Shehadeh Mustafa Aburomeh), Abdullah Khalid Deeb Salim (67.Moayad Omar Suleimani Abu Keshek). Trainer: Eduardo Manuel Martinho Vingada (Portugal).
Goals: 1-0 Park Ji-Sung (39), 2-0 Park Chu-Young (48 penalty), 2-1 Hassan Mahmoud Abdel Fattah (73), 2-2 Hassan Mahmoud Abdel Fattah (81).
Cautions: Cho Yong-Hyung / Mohammad Munir Al Mutasim, Hassouneh Qasem Al Shaikh, Amer Deeb Mohammad Khalil, Thaer Fayed Bawab, Hassan Mahmoud Abdel Fattah.

02.06.2008, Olympic Stadium, Aşgabat; Attendance: 20,000
Referee: Khalil Ibrahim Al Ghamdi (Saudi Arabia)
TURKMENISTAN – KOREA D.P.R.   **0-0**
TKM: Baýramnyýaz Berdiýew, Begli Annageldiýew, Omar Berdiýew, Gochguly Gochguliýew (Cap), Yagmyrmyrat Annamyradow, Nazar Baýramov (82.Witaliý Alikperow), Didar Hajyýew, Vyacheslav Krendelev, Mekan Nasyrow (51.Artur Gevorkyan), Vladimir Baýramow, Gahrymanberdi Çoňkaýew (55.Arif Mirzoýew). Trainer: Rahim Kurbanmamedov.
PRK: Ri Myong-Guk, Cha Jong-Hyok (57.Han Song-Chol), Nam Song-Chol, Pak Chol-Jin, Ri Jun-Il, Ri Kwang-Chon, An Yong-Hak, Kim Yong-Jun (64.Pak Nam-Chol II), Mun In-Guk, Jong Tae-Se, Yong-Jo Hong. Trainer: Kim Jong-Hun.
Cautions: Vladimir Baýramow, Arif Mirzoýew / Jong Tae-Se.

07.06.2008, „Kim Il-sung" Stadium, P'yŏngyang; Attendance: 25,000
Referee: Saad Kameel Al Fadhli (Kuwait)
KOREA D.P.R. - TURKMENISTAN **1-0(0-0)**
PRK: Ri Myong-Guk, Cha Jong-Hyok, Nam Song-Chol, Pak Chol-Jin (28.Han Song-Chol). Ri Kwang-Chon, Ri Jun-Il, An Yong-Hak (60.Kim Yong-Jun), Mun In-Guk, Pak Nam-Chol II. Choe Kum-Chol, Yong-Jo Hong (87.Kim Myong-Won). Trainer: Kim Jong-Hun.
TKM: Baýramnyýaz Berdiýew (Cap), Witaliý Alikperow (.ahrymanberdi Çoňkaýew), Begli Annageldiýew, Maksim Belyh, Omar Berdiýew, Yagmyrmyrat Annamyradow, Nazar Baýramov, Didar Hajyýew, Vyacheslav Krendelev, Mekan Nasyrow (75.Arif Mirzoýew), Vladimir Baýramow. Trainer: Rahim Kurbanmamedov.
Goal: 1-0 Choe Kum-Chol (72).
Cautions: An Yong-Hak / Maksim Belyh, Nazar Baýramov, Omar Berdiýew.

07.06.2008, „King Abdullah" Stadium, Amman; Attendance: 8,000
Referee: Masoud Moradi Hasanali (Iran)
JORDAN – KOREA REPUBLIC **0-1(0-1)**
JOR: Lo'ai Salem Atallah El Amaireh, Mohammad Munir Al Mutasim, Hatem Mohammed Aqel, Mohammad Khamees, Ala'a Hasan Mohammad Matalqa, Hassouneh Qasem Al Shaikh, Baha'a Abdulrahman Suleiman, Odai Yousef Ismail Al Saify (56.Moayad Omar Suleimani Abu Keshek), Thaer Fayed Bawab (71.Mustafa Shehadeh Mustafa Aburomeh), Hassan Mahmoud Abdel Fattah, Abdullah Khalid Deeb Salim (60.Khaled Saad Al Maltaah). Trainer: Eduardo Manuel Martinho Vingada (Portugal).
KOR: Jung Sung-Ryong, Oh Beom-Seok, Cho Won-Hee, Kang Min-Soo, Kwak Hee-Joo, Lee Young Pyo (66.Lee Jung-Soo), Kim Nam-Il (Cap), Park Ji-Sung, Park Chu-Young, Seol Ki-Hyun (46.Cho Yong-Hyung), Lee Keun-Ho (79.Ahn Jung-Hwan). Trainer: Huh Jung-Moo.
Goal: 0-1 Park Chu-Young (24 penalty).
Cautions: Lo'ai Salem Atallah El Amaireh, Mohammad Munir Al Mutasim, Khaled Saad Al Maltaah / Kang Min-Soo, Park Ji-Sung.

14.06.2008, Yanggakdo Stadium, P'yŏngyang; Attendance: 25,000
Referee: Talaat Najm (Lebanon)
KOREA D.P.R. - JORDAN **2-0(1-0)**
PRK: Ri Myong-Guk, Cha Jong-Hyok, Nam Song-Chol, Ri Kwang-Chon, Ri Jun-Il, An Yong-Hak, Han Song-Chol, Mun In-Guk, Pak Nam-Chol II (88.Choe Kum-Chol), Jong Tae-Se, Yong-Jo Hong. Trainer: Kim Jong-Hun.
JOR: Lo'ai Salem Atallah El Amaireh, Hatem Mohammed Aqel, Mohammad Khamees, Ala'a Hasan Mohammad Matalqa, Qusai Mohammed Mahmoud Abu Alieh (63.Mohannad Othman Mohammad Maharmeh), Moayad Omar Suleimani Abu Keshek (56.Mahmoud Omar Shelbaieh), Amer Deeb Mohammad Khalil, Hassouneh Qasem Al Shaikh, Baha'a Abdulrahman Suleiman, Odai Yousef Ismail Al Saify (46.Thaer Fayed Bawab), Hassan Mahmoud Abdel Fattah. Trainer: Eduardo Manuel Martinho Vingada (Portugal).
Goals: 1-0 Hong Yong-Jo (44), 2-0 Hong Yong-Jo (72).
Cautions: Yong-Jo Hong, Nam Song-Chol, Jong Tae-Se, Han Song-Chol / Baha'a Abdulrahman Suleiman, Hassouneh Qasem Al Shaikh.

14.06.2008, Nazar Baýramov; Attendance: 11,000
Referee: Hiroyoshi Takayama (Japan)
TURKMENISTAN – KOREA REPUBLIC **1-3(0-1)**
TKM: Baýramnyýaz Berdiýew, Witaliý Alikperow (31.Guwançmuhammet Öwekow), Begli Annageldiýew, Omar Berdiýew, Gochguly Gochguliýew (Cap), Yagmyrmyrat Annamyradow, Nazar Baýramov, Didar Hajyýew, Vyacheslav Krendelev, Mekan Nasyrow (86.Yewgeniy Zemskov), Vladimir Baýramow (36.Mamedaly Karadanow). Trainer: Rahim Kurbanmamedov.
KOR: Jung Sung-Ryong, Oh Beom-Seok (27.Lee Jung-Soo), Cho Yong-Hyung, Cho Won-Hee

(46.Choi Hyo-Jin), Kang Min-Soo, Kim Nam-Il (Cap), Kim Do-Heon, Lee Keun-Ho (79.Lee Chung-Yong), Park Chu-Yong, Seol Ki-Hyeon. Trainer: Huh Jung-Moo.
Goals: 0-1 (Kim Do-Heon 14), 1-1 Guwançmuhammet Öwekow (77 penalty), 1-2 Kim Do-Heon (86), 1-3 Kim Do-Heon (90+3 penalty).
Cautions: Vladimir Baýramow, Yagmyrmyrat Annamyradow, Baýramnyýaz Berdiýew / Oh Beom-Seok, Cho Yong-Hyung, Jung Sung-Ryong, Kim Nam-Il.

22.06.2008, Seoul World Cup Stadium, Seoul; Attendance: 48,519
Referee: Subkhiddin Mohd Salleh (Malaysia)
KOREA REPUBLIC – KOREA D.P.R.   **0-0**
KOR: Jung Sung-Ryong, Lee Jung-Soo, Kang Min-Soo, Kim Chi-Woo, Choi Hyo-Jin, Oh Jang-Eun (77.Lee Keun-Ho), Kim Jung-Woo (71.Kim Nam-Il), Kim Do-Heon, Lee Chung-Yong, Ahn Jung-Hwan (Cap) (59.Park Chu-Young), Ko Ki-Gu. Trainer : Huh Jung-Moo.
PRK: Ri Myong-Guk, Cha Jong-Hyok, Nam Song-Chol, Pak Chol-Jin, Ri Jun-Il, Ri Kwang-Chon, An Yong-Hak, Kim Yong-Jun (63.Pak Nam-Chol II), Mun In-Guk, Jong Tae-Se, Yong-Jo Hong (10.Choe Kum-Chol). Trainer: Kim Jong-Hun.
Cautions: Ahn Jung-Hwan / Jong Tae-Se.

22.06.2008, Amman International Stadium, Amman; Attendance: 150
Referee: Benjamin Jon Williams (Australia)
JORDAN - TURKMENISTAN   **2-0(0-0)**
JOR: Lo'ai Salem Atallah El Amaireh, Mohammad Munir Al Mutasim, Hatem Mohammed Aqel, Bashar Bani Mustafa Yaseen, Basem Fathi Omar Othman, Qusai Mohammed Mahmoud Abu Alieh, Amer Deeb Mohammad Khalil, Mustafa Shehadeh Mustafa Aburomeh (80.Odai Yousef Ismail Al Saify), Baha'a Abdulrahman Suleiman (66.Ala Waleed Mufleh Al Bashir), Hassan Mahmoud Abdel Fattah, Abdullah Khalid Deeb Salim (61.Mohannad Othman Mohammad Maharmeh). Trainer: Eduardo Manuel Martinho Vingada (Portugal).
TKM: Baýramnyýaz Berdiýew, Begli Annageldiýew, Maksim Belyh, Gochguly Gochguliýew, Rustam Saparow, Serdar Geldiýew, Vyacheslav Krendelev, Döwletmyrat Ataýew (72.Witaliý Alikperow), Gahrymanberdi Çoňkaýew (61.Arif Mirzoýew), Mamedaly Karadanow, Yewgeniy Zemskov (78.Guvanç Abylow). Trainer: Rahim Kurbanmamedov.
Goals: 1-0 Hassan Mahmoud Abdel Fattah (66), 2-0 Hassan Mahmoud Abdel Fattah (67).
Cautions: Baha'a Abdulrahman Suleiman / Döwletmyrat Ataýew, Begli Annageldiýew.

GROUP 4

06.02.2008	Beirut	Lebanon - Uzbekistan	0-1(0-1)
06.02.2008	Riyadh	Saudi Arabia - Singapore	2-0(1-0)
26.03.2008	Tashkent	Uzbekistan – Saudi Arabia	3-0(1-0)
26.03.2008	Singapore	Singapore - Lebanon	2-0(2-0)
02.06.2008	Singapore	Singapore - Uzbekistan	3-7(2-5)
02.06.2008	Riyadh	Saudi Arabia - Lebanon	4-1(1-1)
07.06.2008	Tashkent	Uzbekistan - Singapore	3-0/awarded
07.06.2008	Riyadh	Lebanon – Saudi Arabia	1-2(0-1)
14.06.2008	Singapore	Singapore – Saudi Arabia	0-3/awarded
14.06.2008	Tashkent	Uzbekistan - Lebanon	3-0(0-0)
22.06.2008	Beirut	Lebanon - Singapore	1-2(0-0)
22.06.2008	Riyadh	Saudi Arabia - Uzbekistan	4-0(1-0)

FINAL STANDINGS

1.	**Uzbekistan**	6	5	0	1	17	-	7	15
2.	**Saudi Arabia**	6	5	0	1	15	-	5	15
3.	Singapore	6	2	0	4	7	-	16	6
4.	Lebanon	6	0	0	6	3	-	14	0

06.02.2008, „Camille Chamoun" Sports City Stadium, Beirut; Attendance: 800
Referee: Abdullah Mohamed Al Hilali (Oman)
LEBANON - UZBEKISTAN   **0-1(0-1)**
LIB: Lary Mehanna, Hussein Amine, Ahmad El Choum, Bilal Najarin (33.Ali Al Saadi), Ramez Dayoub, Ali Fouad El Atat, Mohamad Korhani, Roda Antar, Abbas Ahmed Atwi (63.Abbas Ahmed Atwi), Mohammed Ghaddar, Paul Emile Rustom (74.Mahmoud El Ali). Trainer: Emile Rustom.
UZB: Ignatiy Nesterov, Asror Aliqulov, Vitaliy Denisov, Aziz Ibrahimov (78.Hayrulla Karimov), Islom Inomov, Ilkhom Suyunov, Odil Ahmedov, Server Djeparov, Timur Kapadze, Marat Bikmaev (60.Viktor Karpenko), Maksim Shatskikh (Cap) (82.Ulugbek Bakaev). Trainer: Rauf Inileev.
Goal: 0-1 Odil Ahmedov (44).
Cautions: Odil Ahmedov.

06.02.2008, „King Fahd" International Stadium, Riyadh; Attendance: 10,000
Referee: Mohsen Hassan Basma (Syria)
SAUDI ARABIA - SINGAPORE   **2-0(1-0)**
KSA: Tisir Al Antaif, Rashed Al Rahib, Abdoh Ibrahim Otaif (79.Manaf Abou Shaqer), Osama Abdul Razzaq Al Hawsawi, Abdrabah Waled, Mohammed Massad, Khaled Aziz Al Thaker, Saud Ali Khariri, Mohammad Bander Al Shalhoub (87.Omar Al Ghamdi), Saad Mish'al Al Harthi (66.Malek Mouath Al Hawsawi), Yasser Saeed Al Qahtani (Cap). Trainer: Hélio César Pinto dos Anjos (Brazil).
SIN: Lionel Lewis (Cap), Daniel Mark Bennett, Precious Emuejeraye, Baihakki Khaizan, Noh Rahman, Fahrudin Mustafić, Mohammad Shahril Ishak, Khairul Amri Mohamad Kamal (46.Muhammad Ridhuan), Shi Jiayi, John Wilkinson, Aleksandar Đurić (86.Indra Sahdan Daud). Trainer: Radojko Avramović (Serbia).
Goals: 1-0 Yasser Saeed Al Qahtani (38), 2-0 Malek Mouath Al Hawsawi (81).
Cautions: Abdrabah Waled, Malek Mouath Al Hawsawi / Fahrudin Mustafić, Noh Rahman, Indra Sahdan Daud.

26.03.2008, Markaziy Harbiy Sportklubi Army Stadium, Tashkent; Attendance: 17,000
Referee: Subkhiddin Mohd Salleh (Malaysia)
UZBEKISTAN – SAUDI ARABIA   **3-0(1-0)**
UZB: Ignatiy Nesterov, Asror Aliqulov, Bakhtier Ashurmatov, Islom Inomov, Ilkhom Suyunov (79.Aleksey Nikolaev), Odil Ahmedov, Server Djeparov (72.Aleksandr Geynrikh), Azizbek Haydarov (64.Aziz Ibrahimov), Timur Kapadze, Maksim Shatskikh (Cap), Viktor Karpenko. Trainer: Rauf Inileev.

KSA: Tisir Al Antaif, Kamel Al Mousa Fallatah, Hassan Mouath Fallatah, Osama Abdul Razzaq Al Hawsawi, Abdrabah Waled, Khaled Aziz Al Thaker, Ahmed Al Mousa (46.Abdoh Ibrahim Otaif), Saud Ali Khariri, Mohammad Bander Al Shalhoub, Malek Mouath Al Hawsawi (82.Abdulrahman Al Qahtani), Yasser Saeed Al Qahtani (Cap) (39.Saad Mish'al Al Harthi). Trainer: Hélio César Pinto dos Anjos (Brazil).
Goals: 1-0 Timur Kapadze (46), 2-0 Maksim Shatskikh (66), 3-0 Server Djeparov (68).
Cautions: Abdrabah Waled, Osama Abdul Razzaq Al Hawsawi.

26.03.2008, National Stadium, Singapore; Attendance: 10,118
Referee: Hiroyoshi Takayama (Japan)
SINGAPORE - LEBANON 2-0(2-0)
SIN: Lionel Lewis, Daniel Mark Bennett, Precious Emuejeraye, Baihakki Khaizan, Noh Rahman, Fahrudin Mustafić, Shi Jiayi, John Wilkinson, Indra Sahdan Daud (Cap) (65.Mohammad Shahril Ishak), Aleksandar Đurić (80.Hariss Harun), Fazrul Nawaz Shahul Hameed (46.Khairul Amri Mohamad Kamal). Trainer: Radojko Avramović (Serbia).
LIB: Lary Mehanna, Ali Al Saadi (60.Ahmad El Choum), Hussein Amine, Khalid Hamiyeh (56.Nasrat Zaki Al Jamal), Bilal Najarin, Abbas Ahmed Atwi, Amer Khan, Mohamad Korhani, Ali Yaacoub, Mahmoud El Ali, Mohammed Ghaddar (77.Paul Emile Rustom). Trainer: Emile Rustom.
Goals: 1-0 Aleksandar Đurić (8), 2-0 Fazrul Nawaz Shahul Hameed (24).
Cautions: Fazrul Nawaz Shahul Hameed, Lionel Lewis, Shi Jiayi / Mohammed Ghaddar, Amer Khan.

02.06.2008, National Stadium, Singapore; Attendance: 28,750
Referee: Ali Hamad Madhad Saif Al Badwawi (United Arab Emirates)
SINGAPORE - UZBEKISTAN 3-7(2-5)
SIN: Lionel Lewis (Cap), Daniel Mark Bennett, Precious Emuejeraye, Baihakki Khaizan, Noh Rahman (72.Juma'at Jantan), Fahrudin Mustafić, Mohammad Shahril Ishak (76.Muhammad Ridhuan), Khairul Amri Mohamad Kamal, Shi Jiayi, John Wilkinson, Aleksandar Đurić (46.Qiu Li). Trainer: Radojko Avramović (Serbia).
UZB: Ignatiy Nesterov, Asror Aliqulov, Vitaliy Denisov (46.Aziz Ibrahimov), Islom Inomov, Hayrulla Karimov (74.Aleksey Nikolaev), Ilkhom Suyunov, Odil Ahmedov, Server Djeparov, Timur Kapadze (59.Zaynitdin Tadjiyev), Maksim Shatskikh (Cap), Viktor Karpenko. Trainer: Rauf Inileev.
Goals: 0-1 Timur Kapadze (10), 1-1 Aleksandar Đurić (16), 1-2 Viktor Karpenko (22), 2-2 Fahrudin Mustafić (31 penalty), 2-3 Server Djeparov (34), 2-4 Vitaliy Denisov (42), 2-5 Server Djeparov (44), 2-6 Aziz Ibrahimov (62), 3-6 John Wilkinson (73), 3-7 Maksim Shatskikh (88).
Cautions: Noh Rahman, Qiu Li, Muhammad Ridhuan / Islom Inomov, Hayrulla Karimov.

02.06.2008, „King Fahd" International Stadium, Riyadh; Attendance: 8,000
Referee: Saad Kamil Al Faadhli (Kuwait)
SAUDI ARABIA - LEBANON 4-1(1-1)
KSA: Waleed Abdullah Ali, Zaid Al Mowalad (66.Hassan Mouath Fallatah), Osama Abdul Razzaq Al Hawsawi, Abdoh Ibrahim Otaif (60.Abdulrahman Al Qahtani), Abdullah Shuhail, Redha Hassan Tukar Fallatah, Khaled Aziz Al Thaker, Ahmed Ibrahim Otaif (80.Omar Al Ghamdi), Mohammad Bander Al Shalhoub, Malek Mouath Al Hawsawi, Yasser Saeed Al Qahtani (Cap). Trainer: Hélio César Pinto dos Anjos (Brazil).
LIB: Lary Mehanna, Ali Al Saadi, Hussein Amine, Abbas Kenaan, Bilal Najarin, Amer Khan (81.Abbas Ahmed Atwi), Mohamad Korhani (69.Ahmad El Choum), Ali Yaacoub, Mahmoud Mohammed Younis, Mahmoud El Ali (55.Nasrat Zaki Al Jamal), Mohammed Ghaddar. Trainer: Emile Rustom.
Goals: 0-1 Mahmoud El Ali (43), 1-1 Yasser Saeed Al Qahtani (44), 2-1 Osama Abdul Razzaq Al Hawsawi (62), 3-1 Redha Hassan Tukar Fallatah (84), 4-1 Yasser Saeed Al Qahtani (90).
Cautions: Ahmed Ibrahim Otaif / Mohamad Korhani.

07.06.2008, Markaziy Harbiy Sportklubi Army Stadium, Tashkent; Attendance: 12,867
Referee: Kim Dong-Jin (Korea Republic)
UZBEKISTAN - SINGAPORE   **1-0(0-0)**
                                                                     3-0/awarded
UZB: Temur Juraev, Asror Aliqulov, Anvar Gafurov (38.Timur Kapadze), Anzur Ismailov, Aleksey Nikolaev, Odil Ahmedov, Server Djeparov, Aziz Ibrahimov (54.Vitaliy Denisov), Maksim Shatskikh (Cap), Zaynitdin Tadjiyev (65.Aleksandr Geynrikh), Viktor Karpenko. Trainer: Rauf Inileev.
SIN: Lionel Lewis, Daniel Mark Bennett, Precious Emuejeraye, Baihakki Khaizan, Fahrudin Mustafić (84.Mohammad Shahril Ishak), Mohd Bin Abdul, Khairul Amri Mohamad Kamal (78.Fazrul Nawaz Shahul Hameed), Shi Jiayi, John Wilkinson, Indra Sahdan Daud (Cap) (67.Qiu Li), Aleksandar Đurić. Trainer: Radojko Avramović (Serbia).
Goal: 1-0 Aleksandr Geynrikh (80).
Cautions: Aleksey Nikolaev / Fahrudin Mustafić.
Singapore fielded the ineligible player (Qiu Li). FIFA awarded the game 1-0 for Uzbekistan.

07.06.2008, „King Fahd" International Stadium, Riyadh (Saudi Arabia)(match was moved from Beirut to Riyadh (Saudi Arabia)); Attendance: 2,000
Referee: Satop Tongkhan (Thailand)
LEBANON – SAUDI ARABIA   **1-2(0-1)**
LIB: Lary Mehanna, Ali Al Saadi (86.Abbas Kenaan), Hussein Amine, Ahmad El Choum, Bilal Najarin (46.Mootaz Jounaidi), Abbas Ahmed Atwi, Ramez Dayoub, Amer Khan, Ali Yaacoub (72.Khalid Hamiyeh), Mahmoud Mohammed Younis, Mohammed Ghaddar. Trainer: Emile Rustom.
KSA: Waleed Abdullah Ali, Zaid Al Mowalad, Hassan Mouath Fallatah (84.Osama Mabrouk Awad Al Harbi Al Muwallad), Osama Abdul Razzaq Al Hawsawi, Redha Hassan Tukar Fallatah (Cap), Khaled Aziz Al Thaker, Ahmed Al Mousa, Saud Ali Khariri, Mohammad Bander Al Shalhoub (64.Abdoh Ibrahim Otaif), Nasser Ali Al Shamrani, Malek Mouath Al Hawsawi (77.Saad Mish'al Al Harthi). Trainer: Hélio César Pinto dos Anjos (Brazil).
Goals: 0-1 Redha Hassan Tukar Fallatah (45+2), 0-2 Redha Hassan Tukar Fallatah (60), 1-2 Mohammed Ghaddar (90+3).
Cautions: Ahmed Al Mousa, Saud Ali Khariri, Khaled Aziz Al Thaker.

14.06.2008, National Stadium, Singapore; Attendance: 23,000
Referee: Benjamin Jon Williams (Australia)
SINGAPORE – SAUDI ARABIA   **0-1(0-2);**
                                                                     0-3/awarded
SIN: Hassan Sunny, Daniel Mark Bennett, Precious Emuejeraye, Baihakki Khaizan, Noh Rahman, Mohd Bin Abdul (63.Ismail Yunos), Mohammad Shahril Ishak, Khairul Amri Mohamad Kamal (46.Qiu Li), John Wilkinson, Indra Sahdan Daud (Cap), Aleksandar Đurić (78.Fazrul Nawaz Shahul Hameed). Trainer: Radojko Avramović (Serbia).
KSA: Waleed Abdullah Ali, Osama Mabrouk Awad Al Harbi Al Muwallad (84.Abdulla Al Dossari), Abdoh Ibrahim Otaif, Osama Abdul Razzaq Al Hawsawi, Abdullah Shuhail, Redha Hassan Tukar Fallatah (Cap), Khaled Aziz Al Thaker, Ahmed Ibrahim Otaif, Mohammad Bander Al Shalhoub (72.Ahmed Al Fraidi), Saad Mish'al Al Harthi, Malek Mouath Al Hawsawi (88.Omar Al Ghamdi). Trainer: Nasser Al Johar.
Goals: 0-1 Abdoh Ibrahim Otaif (37), 0-2 Ahmed Al Fraidi (76).
Cautions: Noh Rahman, Ismail Yunos / Khaled Aziz Al Thaker, Osama Mabrouk Awad Al Harbi Al Muwallad, Redha Hassan Tukar Fallatah.
Singapore fielded the ineligible player (Qiu Li). FIFA awarded the game 3-0 for Saudi Arabia.

14.06.2008, Markaziy Harbiy Sportklubi Army Stadium, Tashkent; Attendance: 7,000
Referee: Matthew Christopher Breeze (Australia)
UZBEKISTAN - LEBANON   **3-0(0-0)**
UZB: Ignatiy Nesterov, Asror Aliqulov, Vitaliy Denisov (46.Odil Ahmedov), Anzur Ismailov, Ilkhom Suyunov, Server Djeparov, Azizbek Haydarov, Timur Kapadze (41.Viktor Karpenko), Aleksandr Geynrikh, Aziz Ibrahimov (46.Marat Bikmaev), Maksim Shatskikh (Cap). Trainer: Rauf Inileev.
LIB: Hassan Moghnieh, Ali Al Saadi, Hussein Amine, Ahmad El Choum (82.Nasrat Zaki Al Jamal), Khalid Hamiyeh, Mootaz Jounaidi, Abbas Ahmed Atwi, Ali Yaacoub, Mahmoud Mohammed Younis (84.Abbas Kenaan), Mohammed Ghaddar, Paul Emile Rustom (70.Mahmoud El Ali). Trainer: Emile Rustom.
Goals: 1-0 Odil Ahmedov (51), 2-0 Odil Ahmedov (62), 3-0 Server Djeparov (90+4).
Cautions: Aleksandr Geynrikh / Abbas Ahmed Atwi, Hassan Moghnieh, Mootaz Jounaidi, Mahmoud Mohammed Younis.

22.06.2008, „Camille Chamoun" Sports City Stadium, Beirut; Attendance: 500
Referee: Masoud Moradi Hasanali (Iran)
LEBANON - SINGAPORE   **1-2(0-0)**
LIB: Hassan Moghnieh, Ali Al Saadi (90+4.Hussein Amine), Khalid Hamiyeh, Abbas Kenaan (88.Mootaz Jounaidi), Abbas Ahmed Atwi (79.Ali Fouad El Atat), Ramez Dayoub, Amer Khan, Ali Yaacoub, Mahmoud Mohammed Younis, Nasrat Zaki Al Jamal, Mahmoud El Ali. Trainer: Emile Rustom.
SIN: Hassan Sunny, Daniel Mark Bennett, Precious Emuejeraye, Baihakki Khaizan, Ismail Yunos, Fahrudin Mustafić, Mohammad Shahril Ishak (77.Shi Jiayi), Muhammad Ridhuan (62.Fazrul Nawaz Shahul Hameed), John Wilkinson, Indra Sahdan Daud (Cap) (60.Khairul Amri Mohamad Kamal), Aleksandar Đurić. Trainer: Radojko Avramović (Serbia).
Goals: 1-0 Baihakki Khaizan (62 own goal), 1-1 Ramez Dayoub (72 own goal), 1-2 John Wilkinson (73).
Cautions: Amer Khan, Mahmoud Mohammed Younis / John Wilkinson, Fahrudin Mustafić, Daniel Mark Bennett.

22.06.2008, „King Fahd" International Stadium, Riyadh; Attendance: 5,000
Referee: Yuichi Nishimura (Japan)
SAUDI ARABIA - UZBEKISTAN   **4-0(1-0)**
KSA: Mansour Al Naje, Osama Mabrouk Awad Al Harbi Al Muwallad (61.Abdulla Al Dossari), Abdoh Ibrahim Otaif (76.Fisal Al Sultan), Osama Abdul Razzaq Al Hawsawi, Abdullah Shuhail, Redha Hassan Tukar Fallatah (Cap), Ahmed Ibrahim Otaif, Saud Ali Khariri, Mohammad Bander Al Shalhoub, Saad Mish'al Al Harthi (90+1.Abdrabah Waled), Malek Mouath Al Hawsawi. Trainer: Nasser Al Johar.
UZB: Ignatiy Nesterov, Sadriddin Abdullaev (76.Farhod Tadjiyev), Asror Aliqulov (Cap), Anzur Ismailov, Shavkat Raimkulov (61.Pavel Solomin), Ilkhom Suyunov, Odil Ahmedov, Azizbek Haydarov, Aziz Ibrahimov (72.Sakhob Jurayev), Zaynitdin Tadjiyev, Viktor Karpenko. Trainer: Rauf Inileev.
Goals: 1-0 Abdoh Ibrahim Otaif (7), 2-0 Malek Mouath Al Hawsawi (37), 3-0 Saad Mish'al Al Harthi (56), 4-0 Malek Mouath Al Hawsawi (88).
Cautions: Azizbek Haydarov, Shavkat Raimkulov, Ilkhom Suyunov.

GROUP 5

06.02.2008	Tehran	Iran - Syria	0-0
06.02.2008	Abu Dhabi	United Arab Emirates - Kuwait	2-0(1-0)
26.03.2008	Damascus	Syria - United Arab Emirates	1-1(1-0)
26.03.2008	Kuwait City	Kuwait - Iran	2-2(1-2)
02.06.2008	Tehran	Iran - United Arab Emirates	0-0
02.06.2008	Damascus	Syria - Kuwait	1-0(0-0)
07.06.2008	Al Ain	United Arab Emirates - Iran	0-1(0-1)
08.06.2008	Al Salmiya	Kuwait - Syria	4-2(2-2)
14.06.2008	Damascus	Syria - Iran	0-2(0-0)
14.06.2008	Al Salmiya	Kuwait - United Arab Emirates	2-3(0-2)
22.06.2008	Tehran	Iran - Kuwait	2-0(1-0)
22.06.2008	Al Ain	United Arab Emirates - Syria	1-3(0-1)

FINAL STANDINGS

1.	**Iran**	6	3	3	0	7	-	2	12
2.	**United Arab Emirates**	6	2	2	2	7	-	7	8
3.	Syria	6	2	2	2	7	-	8	8
4.	Kuwait	6	1	1	4	8	-	12	4

06.02.2008, Azadi Stadium, Tehran; Attendance: 45,000
Referee: Abdul Malik Bashir (Singapore)
IRAN - SYRIA   **0-0**
IRN: Seyyed Mehdi Rahmati, Seyed Hadi Aghily Anvar, Seyed Jalal Hosseini Khoshkbejari, Hossein Kaebi, Andranik Teymourian, Mehrzad Madanchi Ardakani (76.Javad Kazemian), Ali Reza Vahedi-Nikbakht, Mohammad Ali Karimi Pashaki, Medhi Mahdavikia (83.Eman Mobali), Mehdi Rajabzadeh, Ali Samereh (56.Mohsen Khalili). Trainer: Mansour Ebrahimzadeh.
SYR: Mosab Balhous, Abdulkader Dakka, Ali Dyab, Feras Fissal Esmaeel, Omar Hemidi, Adel Abdullah, Jehad Al Hussain Fadel (67.Raja Rafe), Aatef Abdulelah Jenyat, Bakri Tarrab, Feras Al Khatib (90+2.Ahmad Deeb), Zyad Barakat Chaabo (86.Youness Sulaiman Hamida). Trainer: Fajer Ebrahim.
Cautions: Mehdi Rajabzadeh, Mohsen Khalili / Omar Hemidi, Abdulkader Dakka, Feras Fissal Esmaeel.

06.02.2008, „Mohammed Bin Zayed Stadium", Abu Dhabi; Attendance: 19,000
Referee: Ravshan Irmatov (Uzbekistan)
UNITED ARAB EMIRATES - KUWAIT   **2-0(1-0)**
UAE: Majed Nasser Al Maqdami, Rashid Abdulrahman Al Hosani (Cap), Bashir Saeed Sanqour Al Hammadi El Hammadi, Haidar Alo Ali Mohammed, Ahmed Mohammed Mubarak Al Mahri „Dada", Obaid Khalifa Mubarak Mesari, Helal Saeed Obaid Al Dhanhani Mesmari, Subait Khater Fayel Khamis Al Mekhaini (87.Abdullah Malallah Al Shamali), Faisal Khalil Sebait Mubarak Al Junaibi (89.Ahmad Khalil Sebait Mubarak Al Junaibi), Ismail Matar Ibrahim Khamis Al Mukhaini Al Junaibi, Mohamed Saeed Rashed Saiwed Al Shehhi. Trainer: Bruno Metsu (France).
KUW: Khalid Al Fadhli, Yaqoub Abdullah Al Tahir, Nohayr Mohsen Al Shimmari, Ebrahim Saleh (46 Ahmed Saad Ajab Al Azemi), Mohammed Rashid Sinad Al Fadhli, Adeel Humoud Al Shimmari, Mohamad Jarragh (67.Salih Shaikh Al Hendi), Waleed Ali Jumah, Yousef Zayed, Fahad Al Hamad (61.Fahad Aidh Al Rashidi), Bader Al Mutawa. Trainer: Rodion Hamid Gačanin (Croatia).
Goals: 1-0 Mohamed Saeed Rashed Saiwed Al Shehhi (14), 2-0 Faisal Khalil Sebait Mubarak Al Junaibi (53).
Cautions: Haidar Alo Ali Mohammed / Ebrahim Saleh.

26.03.2008, Abbasiyyin Stadium, Damascus; Attendance: 35,000
Referee: Sun Baojie (China P.R.)
SYRIA - UNITED ARAB EMIRATES   **1-1(1-0)**

SYR: Mosab Balhous, Abdulkader Dakka, Ali Dyab, Feras Fissal Esmaeel (70.Mahmoud Al Amenah), Omar Hemidi, Adel Abdullah, Jehad Al Hussain Fadel, Aatef Abdulelah Jenyat, Bakri Tarrab, Feras Al Khatib (78.Mohamed Al Zeno), Zyad Barakat Chaabo (90+2.Maher Al Sayed). Trainer: Fajer Ebrahim.
UAE: Majed Nasser Al Maqdami, Rashid Abdulrahman Al Hosani (Cap), Fayez Jumah Khamis, Bashir Saeed Sanqour Al Hammadi, Ahmed Mohammed Mubarak Al Mahri „Dada", Darwish Ahmed Ghoulom (82.Abdullah Malallah Al Shamali), Obaid Khalifa Mubarak Mesari, Helal Saeed Obaid Al Dhanhani Mesmari, Subait Khater Fayel Khamis Al Mekhaini (88.Ahmad Khalil Sebait Mubarak Al Junaibi), Ismail Matar Ibrahim Khamis Al Mukhaini Al Junaibi (90+2.Faisal Khalil Sebait Mubarak Al Junaibi), Mohamed Saeed Rashed Saiwed Al Shehhi. Trainer: Bruno Metsu (France).
Goals: 1-0 Zyad Barakat Chaabo (2), 1-1 Ismail Matar Ibrahim Khamis Al Mukhaini Al Junaibi (54).
Cautions: Rashid Abdulrahman Al Hosani, Helal Saeed Obaid Al Dhanhani Mesmari.

26.03.2008, Al Kuwait Sports Club Stadium, Kuwait City; Attendance: 15,000
Referee: Matthew Christopher Breeze (Australia)
KUWAIT - IRAN   **2-2(1-2)**
KUW: Khalid Al Fadhli, Yaqoub Abdullah Al Tahir, Musaed Neda Al Enazi, Ali Al Maqseed (46.Waleed Ali Jumah), Hussain Fadhel Ali, Ebrahim Saleh (72.Fahad Aidh Al Rashidi), Mohammed Rashid Sinad Al Fadhli, Jarrah Al Ataiqi, Mohamad Jarragh, Khaled Ahmad Khalaf Matar (46.Bader Al Mutawa), Ahmed Saad Ajab Al Azemi. Trainer: Rodion Hamid Gačanin (Croatia).
IRN: Seyyed Mehdi Rahmati, Majid Gholamnejad, Seyed Jalal Hosseini Khoshkbejari, Mohsen Bengar, Andranik Teymourian, Hashem Beikzadeh, Mehrzad Madanchi Ardakani (58.Milad Meydavoudi), Ebrahim Sadeghi Senjani, Ali Reza Vahedi-Nikbakht (71.Mojtaba Jabbari), Mohammad Ali Karimi Pashaki, Masoud Shojaei Soleimani (88.Mohsen Khalili). Trainer: Ali Daei.
Goals: 0-1 Ali Reza Vahedi-Nikbakht (2), 0-2 Seyed Jalal Hosseini Khoshkbejari (5), 1-2 Ahmed Saad Ajab Al Azemi (39), 2-2 Fahad Aidh Al Rashidi (82).
Cautions: Mohammed Rashid Sinad Al Fadhli, Ebrahim Saleh, Yaqoub Abdullah Al Tahir / Masoud Shojaei Soleimani, Mehrzad Madanchi Ardakani, Andranik Teymourian.
Sent off: Musaed Neda Al Enazi (90+2).

02.06.2008, Azadi Stadium, Tehran; Attendance: 50,000
Referee: Lee Gi-Young (Korea Republic)
IRAN - UNITED ARAB EMIRATES   **0-0**
IRN: Seyyed Mehdi Rahmati, Seyed Hadi Aghily Anvar, Seyed Jalal Hosseini Khoshkbejari, Sattar Zare, Hossein Kaebi, Javad Nekounam, Andranik Teymourian, Ehsan Hajsafi (39.Ali Reza Vahedi-Nikbakht), Gholamreza Rezaei (72.Milad Meydavoudi), Masoud Shojaei Soleimani, Gholam Reza Enayati (58.Mohsen Khalili). Trainer: Ali Daei.
UAE: Majed Nasser Al Maqdami, Saleh Abdulla Obaid Al Areefi, Rashid Abdulrahman Al Hosani, Bashir Saeed Sanqour Al Hammadi El Hammadi, Haidar Alo Ali Mohammed, Saif Mohamed Al Bishr (68.Faisal Khalil Sebait Mubarak Al Junaibi), Abdul Rahim Jumaa Anbar Mubarak Al Araimi Al Jenaibi (Cap), Ahmed Mohammed Mubarak Al Mahri „Dada" (89.Ahmad Khalil Sebait Mubarak Al Junaibi), Helal Saeed Obaid Al Dhanhani Mesmari, Subait Khater Fayel Khamis Al Mekhaini (83.Mohammed Ibrahim Hussain Al Bloushi), Ismail Matar Ibrahim Khamis Al Mukhaini Al Junaibi. Trainer: Bruno Metsu (France).
Cautions: Andranik Teymourian, Hossein Kaebi / Rashid Abdulrahman Al Hosani, Saif Mohamed Al Bishr, Majed Nasser Al Maqdami.

02.06.2008, Abbasiyyin Stadium, Damascus; Attendance: 25,000
Referee: Salem Mahmoud Mujghef (Jordan)
SYRIA - KUWAIT   **1-0(0-0)**
SYR: Mosab Balhous, Anas Al Khoja, Ali Dyab, Omar Hemidi, Rafat Mohammad, Adel Abdullah, Mahmoud Al Amenah (80.Feras Fissal Esmaeel), Jehad Al Hussain Fadel, Aatef Abdulelah Jenyat (89.Abdulkader Dakka), Feras Al Khatib, Zyad Barakat Chaabo (46.Raja Rafe). Trainer: Mohamad Qwayed.
KUW: Nawaf Khaled Al Khaldi, Yaqoub Abdullah Al Tahir, Ali Al Maqseed, Hussain Fadhel Ali,

Mohammed Rashid Sinad Al Fadhli (87.Khaled Al Shammari), Jarrah Al Ataiqi, Salih Shaikh Al Hendi (76.Khaled Ahmad Khalaf Matar), Mohamad Jarragh (60.Khalaf Al Mutairi), Waleed Ali Jumah, Ahmed Saad Ajab Al Azemi, Fahad Aidh Al Rashidi. Trainer: Rodion Hamid Gačanin (Croatia).
Goal: 1-0 Jehad Al Hussain Fadel (52).
Cautions: Feras Al Khatib, Aatef Abdulelah Jenyat, Mosab Balhous / Jarrah Al Ataiqi, Mohammed Rashid Sinad Al Fadhli.

07.06.2008, „Khalifa Bin Zayed" Stadium, Al Ain; Attendance: 9,000
Referee: Yuichi Nishimura (Japan)
UNITED ARAB EMIRATES - IRAN   **0-1(0-1)**
UAE: Majed Nasser Al Maqdami, Saleh Abdulla Obaid Al Areefi, Fayez Jumah Khamis, Bashir Saeed Sanqour Al Hammadi, Haidar Alo Ali Mohammed, Abdul Rahim Jumaa Anbar Mubarak Al Araimi Al Jenaibi (Cap), Ahmed Mohammed Mubarak Al Mahri „Dada" (66.Ahmad Khalil Sebait Mubarak Al Junaibi), Helal Saeed Obaid Al Dhanhani Mesmari (79.Mohammed Ibrahim Hussain Al Bloushi), Subait Khater Fayel Khamis Al Mekhaini (46.Ismail Salem Al Hammadi), Faisal Khalil Sebait Mubarak Al Junaibi, Ismail Matar Ibrahim Khamis Al Mukhaini Al Junaibi. Trainer: Bruno Metsu (France).
IRN: Seyyed Mehdi Rahmati, Seyed Hadi Aghily Anvar, Seyed Jalal Hosseini Khoshkbejari, Sattar Zare, Hossein Kaebi, Javad Nekounam, Gholamreza Rezaei (87.Mojtaba Jabbari), Ebrahim Sadeghi Senjani, Ferrydoon Zandi (73.Ehsan Hajsafi), Masoud Shojaei Soleimani, Mohsen Khalili (83.Ali Reza Vahedi-Nikbakht). Trainer: Ali Daei.
Goal: 0-1 Ferrydoon Zandi (8).
Cautions: Ismail Matar Ibrahim Khamis Al Mukhaini Al Junaibi / Gholamreza Rezaei, Ehsan Hajsafi.

08.06.2008, Thamir Stadium, Al Salmiya; Attendance: 10,000
Referee: Abdullah Mohamed Al Hilali (Oman)
KUWAIT - SYRIA   **4-2(2-2)**
KUW: Nawaf Khaled Al Khaldi, Yaqoub Abdullah Al Tahir, Ali Al Maqseed, Khaled Al Shammari (55.Waleed Ali Jumah), Hussain Fadhel Ali, Jarrah Al Ataiqi, Salih Shaikh Al Hendi, Adeel Humoud Al Shimmari, Mohamad Jarragh, Ahmed Saad Ajab Al Azemi (71.Khaled Ahmad Khalaf Matar), Khalaf Al Mutairi (77.Ahmed Al Fadhli). Trainer: Rodion Hamid Gačanin (Croatia).
SYR: Mosab Balhous, Anas Al Khoja (77.Mahmoud Al Amenah), Ali Dyab, Feras Fissal Esmaeel, Rafat Mohammad (67.Lowai Shanko), Elias Morkos, Adel Abdullah, Jehad Al Hussain Fadel, Aatef Abdulelah Jenyat, Feras Al Khatib, Raja Rafe (61.Sanharib Sabah Malki). Trainer: Mohamad Qwayed.
Goals: 1-0 Ahmed Saad Ajab Al Azemi (2), 1-1 Feras Al Khatib (10), 2-1 Ahmed Saad Ajab Al Azemi (19), Feras Al Khatib (45+2), 3-2 Anas Al Khoja (57 own goal), 4-2 Ahmed Saad Ajab Al Azemi (63).
Cautions: Hussain Fadhel Ali, Ali Al Maqseed, Ahmed Saad Ajab Al Azemi / Adel Abdullah, Elias Morkos.
Sent off: Nawaf Khaled Al Khaldi (72).

14.06.2008, Abbasiyyin Stadium, Damascus; Attendance: 25,000
Referee: Satop Tongkhan (Thailand)
SYRIA - IRAN   **0-2(0-0)**
SYR: Mosab Balhous, Abdulkader Dakka, Ali Dyab, Omar Hemidi, Adel Abdullah, Jehad Al Hussain Fadel (67.Mahmoud Al Amenah), Aatef Abdulelah Jenyat, Bakri Tarrab, Feras Al Khatib, Zyad Barakat Chaabo (46.Raja Rafe), Lowai Shanko (75.Sanharib Sabah Malki). Trainer: Mohamad Qwayed.
IRN: Seyyed Mehdi Rahmati, Seyed Hadi Aghily Anvar, Seyed Jalal Hosseini Khoshkbejari, Sattar Zare, Hossein Kaebi, Javad Nekounam, Gholamreza Rezaei (90.Ali Reza Vahedi-Nikbakht), Ebrahim Sadeghi Senjani, Ferrydoon Zandi (67.Mojtaba Jabbari), Masoud Shojaei Soleimani (90+3.Andranik Teymourian), Mohsen Khalili. Trainer: Ali Daei.
Goals: 0-1 Gholamreza Rezaei (64), 0-2 Mohsen Khalili (90+5).
Cautions: Abdulkader Dakka / Masoud Shojaei Soleimani.

14.06.2008, Thamer Stadium, Salmiya; Attendance: 20,000
Referee: Subkhiddin Mohd Salleh (Malaysia)
KUWAIT - UNITED ARAB EMIRATES   **2-3(0-2)**
KUW: Hameed Youssef Al Qallaf, Yaqoub Abdullah Al Tahir, Musaed Neda Al Enazi
(75.Mohammed Rashid Sinad Al Fadhli), Ali Al Maqseed, Hussain Fadhel Ali, Salih Shaikh Al Hendi,
Adeel Humoud Al Shimmari, Mohamad Jarragh, Waleed Ali Jumah (46.Khaled Ahmad Khalaf Matar),
Ahmed Saad Ajab Al Azemi, Khalaf Al Mutairi (67.Fahad Aidh Al Rashidi). Trainer: Rodion Hamid
Gačanin (Croatia).
UAE: Majed Nasser Al Maqdami, Saleh Abdulla Obaid Al Areefi, Rashid Abdulrahman Al Hosani,
Bashir Saeed Sanqour Al Hammadi, Haidar Alo Ali Mohammed, Abdul Rahim Jumaa Anbar Mubarak
Al Araimi Al Jenaibi (Cap), Ahmed Mohammed Mubarak Al Mahri „Dada" (63.Saif Mohamed Al
Bishr), Helal Saeed Obaid Al Dhanhani Mesmari, Subait Khater Fayel Khamis Al Mekhaini
(79.Abdullah Malallah Al Shamali), Ismail Matar Ibrahim Khamis Al Mukhaini Al Junaibi
(90+2.Ismail Salem Al Hammadi), Mohamed Saeed Rashed Saiwed Al Shehhi. Trainer: Bruno Metsu
(France).
Goals: 0-1 Ismail Matar Ibrahim Khamis Al Mukhaini Al Junaibi (23), 0-2 Ismail Matar Ibrahim
Khamis Al Mukhaini Al Junaibi (39), 1-2 Ahmed Saad Ajab Al Azemi (52), 2-2 Ahmed Saad Ajab Al
Azemi (79), 2-3 Saif Mohamed Al Bishr (90+1).
Cautions: Yaqoub Abdullah Al Tahir, Hameed Youssef Al Qallaf, Hussain Fadhel Ali / Subait Khater
Fayel Khamis Al Mekhaini, Haidar Alo Ali Mohammed, Saif Mohamed Al Bishr.

22.06.2008, Azadi Stadium, Tehran; Attendance: 20,000
Referee: Sun Baojie (China P.R.)
IRAN - KUWAIT   **2-0(1-0)**
IRN: Seyyed Mehdi Rahmati, Seyed Hadi Aghily Anvar, Seyed Jalal Hosseini Khoshkbejari, Sattar
Zare, Hossein Kaebi, Javad Nekounam, Andranik Teymourian, Gholamreza Rezaei, Ebrahim Sadeghi
Senjani (60.Majid Gholamnejad), Ferrydoon Zandi (90.Mojtaba Shiri), Milad Meydavoudi
(79.Mohamadreza Khalatbari). Trainer: Ali Daei.
KUW: Nawaf Khaled Al Khaldi, Musaed Neda Al Enazi, Fayez Bandar Al Enezi, Ali Al Maqseed,
Khaled Al Shammari, Mohammed Rashid Sinad Al Fadhli, Jarrah Al Ataiqi, Salih Shaikh Al Hendi,
Adeel Humoud Al Shimmari (64.Fahad Aidh Al Rashidi), Khaled Ahmad Khalaf Matar (69.Mashari Al
Azmi), Ahmed Saad Ajab Al Azemi (46.Hamad Al Enezi). Trainer: Rodion Hamid Gačanin (Croatia).
Goals: 1-0 Javad Nekounam (17), 2-0 Gholamreza Rezaei (90+2).
Cautions: Hossein Kaebi, Javad Nekounam / Khaled Al Shammari, Adeel Humoud Al Shimmari.

22.06.2008, „Khalifa Bin Zayed" Stadium, Al Ain; Attendance: 7,000
Referee: Mark Alexander Shield (Australia)
UNITED ARAB EMIRATES - SYRIA   **1-3(0-1)**
UAE: Majed Nasser Al Maqdami, Saleh Abdulla Obaid Al Areefi, Rashid Abdulrahman Al Hosani,
Bashir Saeed Sanqour Al Hammadi, Tariq Hasan Abdulla Tarish (55.Fayez Jumah Khamis), Abdul
Rahim Jumaa Anbar Mubarak Al Araimi Al Jenaibi (Cap), Ahmed Mohammed Mubarak Al Mahri
„Dada" (55.Ismail Salem Al Hammadi), Helal Saeed Obaid Al Dhanhani Mesmari, Subait Khater Fayel
Khamis Al Mekhaini, Ismail Matar Ibrahim Khamis Al Mukhaini Al Junaibi, Mohamed Saeed Rashed
Saiwed Al Shehhi (63.Adel Abdul Aziz). Trainer: Bruno Metsu (France).
SYR: Mosab Balhous, Samer Awad (76.Youness Sulaiman Hamida), Ali Dyab, Bassel Hamamieh,
Omar Hemidi, Adel Abdullah, Mahmoud Al Amenah (76.Raja Rafe), Jehad Al Hussain Fadel, Feras Al
Khatib, Sanharib Sabah Malki, Lowai Shanko (65.Feras Fissal Esmaeel). Trainer: Mohamad Qwayed.
Goals: 0-1 Jehad Al Hussain Fadel (34), 0-2 Jehad Al Hussain Fadel (51), 1-2 Ismail Matar Ibrahim
Khamis Al Mukhaini Al Junaibi (83 penalty), 1-3 Sanharib Sabah Malki (90+3).
Cautions: Majed Nasser Al Maqdami, Bashir Saeed Sanqour Al Hammadi / Bassel Hamamieh, Omar
Hemidi, Mosab Balhous.

FOURTH ROUND

By the draw on 27 June 2008 in Kuala Lumpur (Malaysia), the 10 teams were drawn in 2 qualifying groups. Each group winners and runners-up qualified directly to the World Cup Final Tournament. The two third-placed teams will play a double-leg tie to advance for the play-off against the Oceania Zone Winner.

GROUP 1

06.09.2008	Madinat 'Isa	Bahrain - Japan	2-3(0-2)
06.09.2008	Doha	Qatar - Uzbekistan	3-0(1-0)
10.09.2008	Tashkent	Uzbekistan - Australia	0-1(0-1)
10.09.2008	Doha	Qatar - Bahrain	1-1(1-0)
15.10.2008	Brisbane	Australia - Qatar	4-0(2-0)
15.10.2008	Saitama	Japan - Uzbekistan	1-1(1-1)
19.11.2008	Madinat 'Isa	Bahrain - Australia	0-1(0-0)
19.11.2008	Doha	Qatar - Japan	0-3(0-1)
11.02.2009	Yokohama	Japan - Australia	0-0
11.02.2009	Tashkent	Uzbekistan - Bahrain	0-1(0-0)
28.03.2009	Saitama	Japan - Bahrain	1-0(0-0)
28.03.2009	Tashkent	Uzbekistan - Qatar	4-0(2-0)
01.04.2009	Sydney	Australia - Uzbekistan	2-0(0-0)
01.04.2009	Madinat 'Isa	Bahrain - Qatar	1-0(0-0)
06.06.2009	Tashkent	Uzbekistan - Japan	0-1(0-1)
06.06.2009	Doha	Qatar - Australia	0-0
10.06.2009	Sydney	Australia - Bahrain	2-0(0-0)
10.06.2009	Yokohama	Japan - Qatar	1-1(1-0)
17.06.2009	Melbourne	Australia - Japan	2-1(0-1)
17.06.2009	Madinat 'Isa	Bahrain - Uzbekistan	1-0(0-0)

FINAL STANDINGS

1.	**AUSTRALIA**	8	6	2	0	12	-	1	20
2.	**JAPAN**	8	4	3	1	11	-	6	15
3.	**Bahrain**	8	3	1	4	6	-	8	10
4.	Qatar	8	1	3	4	5	-	14	6
5.	Uzbekistan	8	1	1	6	5	-	10	4

Australia & Japan qualified for the Final Tournament; Bahrain qualified for the Play-Offs.

06.09.2008, National Stadium, Manama; Attendance: 20,000
Referee: Abdul Malik Bashir (Singapore)
BAHRAIN - JAPAN   **2-3(0-2)**
BHR: Sayed Mohammed Jaffer Sabet, Sayed Mohamed Adnan, Salman Isa Ghuloom, Mohamed Husain Bahzad, Abdullah Al Marzooqi, Faouzi Mubarak Aaish, Abdullah Omar Ismail, Sayed Mahmood Jalal Al Wadaei (Cap), Mohamed Ahmed Yusuf Salmeen (82.Jamal Rashid Rahman), Ismaeel Abdullatif Hasan (62.Mahmood Abdulrahman Mohammed Noor), A'ala Ahmed Hubail (62.Jaycee John Akwani Okwunwanne). Trainer: Milan Máčala (Czech Republic).
JPN: Seigo Narazaki, Atsuto Uchida, Yuji Nakazawa, Marcus Tulio Tanaka, Yuki Abe, Makoto Hasebe (84.Yasuyuki Konno), Yasuhito Endō, Shunsuke Nakamura, Daisuke Matsui (70.Kengo Nakamura), Tatsuya Tanaka, Keiji Tamada (78.Hisato Satō). Trainer: Takeshi Okada.
Goals: 0-1 Shunsuke Nakamura (18), 0-2 Yasuhito Endō (44 penalty), 0-3 Kengo Nakamura (85), 1-3 Salman Isa Ghuloom (87), 2-3 Marcus Tulio Tanaka (88 own goal).
Cautions: Mohamed Husain Bahzad, Faouzi Mubarak Aaish, Abdullah Omar Ismail / Daisuke Matsui.
Sent off: Mohamed Husain Bahzad (66).

06.09.2008, „Jassim Bin Hamad" Stadium, Doha; Attendance: 8,000
Referee: Subkhiddin Mohd Salleh (Malaysia)
QATAR - UZBEKISTAN   **3-0(1-0)**
QAT: Mohamed Ahmed Saqer, Abdullah Obaid Koni, Ibrahim Abdul Majid (64.Mohammed Gholam
Al Bloushi), Marcone Amaral Costa Júnior Costa Júnior, Bilal Mohammed Rajab, Saad Sattam Al
Shammari (Cap), Talal Hassan Ali Al Bloushi, Fábio César Montezine (77.Khalfan Ibrahim Al
Khalfan), Majdi Abdulla Siddiq, Sayed Ali Baba Al Basheer (71.Majed Mohammed Hassan), Andrés
Sebastián Soria Quintana. Trainer: Jorge Daniel Fossati Lurachi (Uruguay).
UZB: Ignatiy Nesterov, Asror Aliqulov, Bakhtier Ashurmatov, Vitaliy Denisov, Islom Inomov, Ilkhom
Suyunov, Odil Ahmedov, Azizbek Haydarov (46.Aleksandr Geynrikh), Server Djeparov, Timur
Kapadze (66.Vagiz Galiullin), Maksim Shatskikh (Cap) (79.Ulugbek Baqayev). Trainer: Rauf Inileev.
Goals: 1-0 Majdi Abdulla Siddiq (37), 2-0 Majed Mohammed Hassan (73), 3-0 Talal Hassan Ali Al
Bloushi (86).
Cautions: Talal Hassan Ali Al Bloushi / Asror Aliqulov, Timur Kapadze, Aleksandr Geynrikh,
Bakhtier Ashurmatov.

10.09.2008, Pakhtakor Stadion, Tashkent; Attendance: 34,000
Referee: Saad Kamil Al Faadhli (Kuwait)
UZBEKISTAN - AUSTRALIA   **0-1(0-1)**
UZB: Ignatiy Nesterov, Asror Aliqulov, Islom Inomov, Anzur Ismailov, Ilkhom Suyunov, Odil
Ahmedov, Jasur Hasanov, Vagiz Galiullin (43.Timur Kapadze), Server Djeparov, Ulugbek Baqayev
(69.Zaynitdin Tadjiyev), Maksim Shatskikh (Cap). Trainer: Rauf Inileev.
AUS: Mark Schwarzer, Lucas Edward Neill (Cap), Christopher John Coyne, Luke Wilkshire, Scott
Chipperfield, Jacob Geoffrey Burns, Brett Michael Emerton, Harold Kewell (90.Bruce José Djité), Carl
Valeri, Brett Holman (77.Mile Sterjovski), Mark Bresciano (73.David Raymond Carney). Trainer:
Peter Tim Verbeek (Holland).
Goals: 0-1 Scott Chipperfield (26).
Cautions: Islom Inomov / Carl Valeri, David Raymond Carney.

10.09.2008, „Jassim Bin Hamad" Stadium, Doha; Attendance: 7,000
Referee: Kim Dong-Jin (Korea Republic)
QATAR - BAHRAIN   **1-1(1-0)**
QAT: Mohamed Ahmed Saqer, Abdullah Obaid Koni (Cap), Ibrahim Abdul Majid (74.Hassan Khalid
Al Haydos), Marcone Amaral Costa Júnior Costa Júnior (84.Saad Sattam Al Shammari), Bilal
Mohammed Rajab, Wesam Rizik Abdulmajid, Hussein Yasser Abdulrahman, Majdi Abdulla Siddiq,
Fábio César Montezine, Khalfan Ibrahim Al Khalfan (58.Majed Mohammed Hassan), Andrés Sebastián
Soria Quintana. Trainer: Jorge Daniel Fossati Lurachi (Uruguay).
BHR: Sayed Mohammed Jaffer Sabet, Sayed Mohamed Adnan, Salman Isa Ghuloom, Abdullah Al
Marzooqi, Mahmood Abdulrahman Mohammed Noor, Babatunde Fatai-Baba Fatadi, Abdullah Omar
Ismail, Sayed Mahmood Jalal Al Wadaei (Cap), Mohamed Ahmed Yusuf Salmeen (67.Rashed Isa Al
Allan), Jaycee John Akwani Okwunwanne (89.Rashed Jamal Salem Mohamed Saleem), Abdulla
Adnan Saleh Salman Al Dakheel (46.Hussain Ali Baba Mohammed). Trainer: Milan Máčala (Czech
Republic).
Goals: 1-0 Andrés Sebastián Soria Quintana (6), 1-1 Babatunde Fatai-Baba Fatadi (67).
Cautions: Mohamed Ahmed Saqer, Ibrahim Abdul Majid / Abdullah Al Marzooqi, Abdullah Omar
Ismail, Sayed Mahmood Jalal Al Wadaei, Mohamed Ahmed Yusuf Salmeen.
Sent off: Abdullah Al Marzooqi (36).

15.10.2008, Suncorp Stadium, Milton, Brisbane; Attendance: 34,230
Referee: Khalil Ibrahim Al Ghamdi (Saudi Arabia)
AUSTRALIA - QATAR   **4-0(2-0)**
AUS: Mark Schwarzer, Lucas Edward Neill (Cap), David Raymond Carney, Craig Andrew Moore, Luke Wilkshire, Scott Chipperfield (46.Mile Sterjovski), Jason Čulina, Brett Michael Emerton (87.Jacob Geoffrey Burns), Timothy Joel Cahill, Joshua Blake Kennedy, Scott Douglas McDonald (69.Brett Holman). Trainer: Peter Tim Verbeek (Holland).
QAT: Abdulaziz Ali Abdullahh, Abdullah Obaid Koni, Mustafa Abdi Abdullah, Ibrahim Abdul Majid, Saad Sattam Al Shammari (Cap) (46.Ahmad Khalifa Hashim), Talal Hassan Ali Al Bloushi, Fábio César Montezine (72.Younes Ali Rahmati), Majdi Abdulla Siddiq, Khalfan Ibrahim Al Khalfan, Majed Mohammed Hassan, Andrés Sebastián Soria Quintana (72.Yousef Ahmed Ali). Trainer: Bruno Metsu (France).
Goals: 1-0 Timothy Joel Cahill (9), 2-0 Brett Michael Emerton (17 penalty), 3-0 Brett Michael Emerton (59), 4-0 Joshua Blake Kennedy (76).
Cautions: Brett Michael Emerton / Abdullah Obaid Koni, Talal Hassan Ali Al Bloushi, Yousef Ahmed Ali.

15.10.2008, Saitama Stadium, Saitama; Attendance: 55,142
Referee: Ali Hamad Madhad Saif Al Badwawi (United Arab Emirates)
JAPAN - UZBEKISTAN   **1-1(1-1)**
JPN: Seigo Narazaki, Yuki Abe, Marcus Tulio Tanaka, Yuji Nakazawa, Atsuto Uchida, Yasuhito Endō, Makoto Hasebe, Shinji Kagawa (76.Junichi Inamoto), Shunsuke Nakamura, Yoshito Okubo (62.Shinji Okazaki), Keiji Tamada (81.Shinzo Koroki). Trainer: Takeshi Okada.
UZB: Ignatiy Nesterov, Asror Aliqulov, Vitaliy Denisov, Anvar Gafurov, Anzur Ismailov, Odil Ahmedov (72.Azizbek Haydarov), Jasur Hasanov, Timur Kapadze, Server Djeparov, Ildar Magdeyev (57.Ruslan Melziddinov), Maksim Shatskikh (Cap) (72.Aleksandr Geynrikh). Trainer: Mirdjalal Qasimov.
Goals: 0-1 Maksim Shatskikh (27), 1-1 Keiji Tamada (40).
Cautions: Ruslan Melziddinov, Anzur Ismailov.

19.11.2008, National Stadium, Manama; Attendance: 10,000
Referee: Masoud Moradi Hasanali (Iran)
BAHRAIN - AUSTRALIA   **0-1(0-0)**
BHR: Sayed Mohammed Jaffer Sabet, Sayed Mohamed Adnan, Hussain Ali Baba Mohammed (75.Jamal Rashid Rahman), Salman Isa Ghuloom, Mohamed Husain Bahzad (Cap), Mahmood Abdulrahman Mohammed Noor (79.Rashid Abdulrahman Saif Abdulla Al Dossari), Faouzi Mubarak Aaish, Babatunde Fatai-Baba Fatadi, Mohamed Ahmed Hubail, Jaycee John Akwani Okwunwanne, A'ala Ahmed Hubail (87.Abdulla Adnan Saleh Salman Al Dakheel). Trainer: Milan Máčala (Czech Republic).
AUS: Mark Schwarzer, Lucas Edward Neill (Cap), David Raymond Carney, Christopher John Coyne (69.Jade Bronson North), Luke Wilkshire, Jason Čulina, Carl Valeri, Timothy Joel Cahill (86.Mile Sterjovski), Mark Bresciano, Joshua Blake Kennedy, Harold Kewell (71.Brett Holman). Trainer: Peter Tim Verbeek (Holland).
Goal: 0-1 Mark Bresciano (90+3).
Cautions: Christopher John Coyne.

19.11.2008, „Jassim Bin Hamad" Stadium, Doha; Attendance: 13,000
Referee: Sun Baojie (China P.R.)
QATAR - JAPAN   **0-3(0-1)**
QAT: Mohamed Ahmed Saqer, Meshal Abdullah Mobarak Budawood (Cap), Ahmad Khalifa Hashim (59.Sayed Ali Baba Al Basheer), Ibrahim Abdul Majid, Bilal Mohammed Rajab, Talal Hassan Ali Al Bloushi, Mesaad Ali Al Hamad, Fábio César Montezine (68.Mohammed Abdulrab Al Yazidi), Majdi Abdulla Siddiq (80.Majed Mohammed Hassan), Khalfan Ibrahim Al Khalfan, Andrés Sebastián Soria

Quintana. Trainer: Bruno Metsu (France).
JPN: Yoshikatsu Kawaguchi, Shuhei Terada, Atsuto Uchida, Marcus Tulio Tanaka, Yasuhito Endō, Tatsuya Tanaka (71.Daisuke Matsui), Shunsuke Nakamura, Keiji Tamada (90+2.Hisato Satō), Yuto Nagatomo, Yoshito Okubo (86.Shinji Okazaki), Makoto Hasebe. Trainer: Takeshi Okada.
Goals: 0-1 Tatsuya Tanaka (19), 0-2 Keiji Tamada (47), 0-3 Marcus Tulio Tanaka (68).
Cautions: Bilal Mohammed Rajab, Majed Mohammed Hassan, Ibrahim Abdul Majid.

11.02.2009, International Stadium, Yokohama; Attendance: 66,000
Referee: Mohsen Hassan Basma (Syria)
JAPAN - AUSTRALIA   **0-0**
JPN: Ryōta Tsuzuki, Yuto Nagatomo, Marcus Tulio Tanaka, Yuji Nakazawa, Atsuto Uchida, Yasuhito Endō, Makoto Hasebe, Daisuke Matsui (57.Yoshito Okubo), Shunsuke Nakamura, Keiji Tamada, Tatsuya Tanaka (83.Shinji Okazaki). Trainer: Takeshi Okada.
AUS: Mark Schwarzer, Lucas Edward Neill (Cap), Craig Andrew Moore, Luke Wilkshire, Scott Chipperfield, Vincenzo Grella, Jason Čulina, Carl Valeri, Timothy Joel Cahill (85.Joshua Blake Kennedy), Brett Holman (64.Richard Garcia), Mark Bresciano (90.David Raymond Carney). Trainer: Peter Tim Verbeek (Holland).
Cautions: Scott Chipperfield, Luke Wilkshire, Carl Valeri.

11.02.2009, Pahtakor Stadium, Tashkent; Attendance: 30,000
Referee: Subkhiddin Mohd Salleh (Malaysia)
UZBEKISTAN - BAHRAIN   **0-1(0-0)**
UZB: Ignatiy Nesterov, Anvar Gafurov, Anzur Ismailov, Islom Tukhtahujaev, Sakhob Jurayev, Odil Ahmedov, Jasur Hasanov (59.Vitaliy Denisov), Timur Kapadze (55.Maksim Shatskikh), Ildar Magdeyev, Server Djeparov (Cap), Farhod Tadjiyev (69.Anvarjon Soliyev). Trainer: Mirdjalal Qasimov.
BHR: Sayed Mohammed Jaffer Sabet, Sayed Mohamed Adnan, Hussain Ali Baba Mohammed, Salman Isa Ghuloom, Mahmood Abdulrahman Mohammed Noor, Babatunde Fatai-Baba Fatadi (70.Abdulla Abdi Omar Yasser), Mohamed Ahmed Hubail, Abdullah Omar Ismail, Mohamed Ahmed Yusuf Salmeen, Ismaeel Abdullatif Hasan (77.Abdulla Adnan Saleh Salman Al Dakheel), Jaycee John Akwani Okwunwanne (89.Dawood Salman Saad). Trainer: Milan Máčala (Czech Republic).
Goal: 0-1 Mahmood Abdulrahman Mohammed Noor (90+4).
Cautions: Ildar Magdeyev, Ignatiy Nesterov, Anvar Gafurov, Anzur Ismailov / Mahmood Abdulrahman Mohammed Noor, Babatunde Fatai-Baba Fatadi, Mohamed Ahmed Hubail, Abdulla Abdi Omar Yasser.

28.03.2009, Saitama Stadium, Saitama; Attendance: 57,276
Referee: Kim Dong-Jin (Korea Republic)
JAPAN - BAHRAIN   **1-0(0-0)**
JPN: Seigo Narazaki, Atsuto Uchida, Yuji Nakazawa, Marcus Tulio Tanaka, Yuto Nagatomo, Makoto Hasebe (76.Hideo Hashimoto), Yasuhito Endō, Shunsuke Nakamura, Tatsuya Tanaka (86.Shinji Okazaki), Yoshito Okubo, Keiji Tamada (79.Daisuke Matsui). Trainer: Takeshi Okada.
BHR: Sayed Mohammed Jaffer Sabet, Sayed Mohamed Adnan, Salman Isa Ghuloom, Abdullah Al Marzooqi, Mahmood Abdulrahman Mohammed Noor, Faouzi Mubarak Aaish (90+1.Ismaeel Abdullatif Hasan), Babatunde Fatai-Baba Fatadi, Mohamed Ahmed Hubail, Abdullah Omar Ismail (75.Abdulla Abdi Omar Yasser), Mohamed Ahmed Yusuf Salmeen, Jaycee John Akwani Okwunwanne. Trainer: Milan Máčala (Czech Republic).
Goal: 1-0 Shunsuke Nakamura (47).
Cautions: Tatsuya Tanaka / Jaycee John Akwani Okwunwanne, Abdullah Omar Ismail.

28.03.2009, Pakhtakor Stadium, Tashkent; Attendance: 18,000
Referee: Masoud Moradi Hasanali (Iran)
UZBEKISTAN - QATAR   **4-0(2-0)**
UZB: Ignatiy Nesterov, Anvar Gafurov, Hayrulla Karimov, Islom Tukhtahujaev, Sakhob Jurayev, Odil Ahmedov, Jasur Hasanov, Viktor Karpenko (61.Stanislav Andreyev), Server Djeparov (46.Timur Kapadze), Maksim Shatskikh (Cap) (56.Anvarjon Soliyev), Farhod Tadjiyev. Trainer: Mirdjalal Qasimov.
QAT: Mohamed Ahmed Saqer, Meshal Abdullah Mobarak Budawood (Cap), Marcone Amaral Costa Júnior Costa Júnior (14.Moussa Haroun Jama), Ahmed Mohammed Mousa Ali, Bilal Mohammed Rajab, Hussein Yasser Abdulrahman, Talal Hassan Ali Al Bloushi, Mesaad Ali Al Hamad, Mohammed Abdulrab Al Yazidi, Khalfan Ibrahim Al Khalfan (65.Majdi Abdulla Siddiq), Andrés Sebastián Soria Quintana (64.Ibrahima Moussa N'Diaye). Trainer: Bruno Metsu (France).
Goals: 1-0 Farhod Tadjiyev (34), 2-0 Farhod Tadjiyev (45+2), 3-0 Farhod Tadjiyev (53), 4-0 Anvarjon Soliyev (62).
Cautions: Farhod Tadjiyev / Meshal Abdullah Mobarak Budawood.
Sent off: Bilal Mohammed Rajab (32).

01.04.2009, Olympic Stadium, Sydney; Attendance: 57,292
Referee: Ali Hamad Madhad Saif Al Badwawi (United Arab Emirates)
AUSTRALIA - UZBEKISTAN   **2-0(0-0)**
AUS: Mark Schwarzer, Lucas Edward Neill (Cap), Michael Beauchamp, Luke Wilkshire, Scott Chipperfield, Jason Čulina, Carl Valeri (80.Michael John Jedinak), Harold Kewell (74.Brett Holman), Mark Bresciano, Richard Garcia, Scott Douglas McDonald (59.Joshua Blake Kennedy). Trainer: Peter Tim Verbeek (Holland).
UZB: Ignatiy Nesterov, Anvar Gafurov, Aziz Ibrahimov (65.Azizbek Haydarov), Anzur Ismailov, Hayrulla Karimov (75.Islom Tukhtahujaev), Sakhob Jurayev, Odil Ahmedov, Jasur Hasanov, Server Djeparov (Cap), Timur Kapadze, Farhod Tadjiyev (58.Anvarjon Soliyev). Trainer: Mirdjalal Qasimov.
Goals: 1-0 Joshua Blake Kennedy (66), 2-0 Harold Kewell (73 penalty).
Cautions: Luke Wilkshire, Lucas Edward Neill / Sakhob Jurayev, Anvar Gafurov.

01.04.2009, National Stadium, Manama; Attendance: 20,000
Referee: Sun Baojie (China P.R.)
BAHRAIN - QATAR   **1-0(0-0)**
BHR: Sayed Mohammed Jaffer Sabet, Sayed Mohamed Adnan, Hussain Ali Baba Mohammed (70.Abdullah Omar Ismail), Salman Isa Ghuloom, Abdullah Al Marzooqi, Faouzi Mubarak Aaish (84.Mahmood Abdulrahman Mohammed Noor), Babatunde Fatai-Baba Fatadi, Mohamed Ahmed Hubail, Mohamed Ahmed Yusuf Salmeen (Cap), Jaycee John Akwani Okwunwanne (89.Ahmed Hassan Taleb), A'ala Ahmed Hubail. Trainer: Milan Máčala (Czech Republic).
QAT: Mohamed Ahmed Saqer, Meshal Abdullah Mobarak Budawood (Cap), Moussa Haroun Jama, Ibrahim Abdul Majid, Talal Hassan Ali Al Bloushi, Mesaad Ali Al Hamad, Mohammed Abdulrab Al Yazidi, Khalfan Ibrahim Al Khalfan (85.Hussein Yasser Abdulrahman), Ali Hassan Afif Yahya (71.Yousef Ahmed Ali), Andrés Sebastián Soria Quintana, Ibrahima Moussa N'Diaye (76.Majed Mohammed Hassan). Trainer: Bruno Metsu (France).
Goal: 1-0 Faouzi Mubarak Aaish (52).
Cautions: Hussain Ali Baba Mohammed, Sayed Mohamed Adnan, Babatunde Fatai-Baba Fatadi, Faouzi Mubarak Aaish / Moussa Haroun Jama, Mohammed Abdulrab Al Yazidi, Khalfan Ibrahim Al Khalfan.

06.06.2009, Pakhtakor Markaziy Stadium, Tashkent; Attendance: 30,000
Referee: Subkhiddin Mohd Salleh (Malaysia)
UZBEKISTAN - JAPAN   **0-1(0-1)**
UZB: Ignatiy Nesterov, Anzur Ismailov, Hamza Karimov, Ilkhom Suyunov (85.Sakhob Jurayev), Islom Tukhtahujaev, Odil Ahmedov, Jasur Hasanov, Server Djeparov (Cap), Timur Kapadze,

Aleksandr Geynrikh (75.Shakhboz Erkinov), Farhod Tadjiyev (61.Anvarjon Soliyev). Trainer: Mirdjalal Qasimov.
JPN: Seigo Narazaki, Yuji Nakazawa, Yūichi Komano, Marcus Tulio Tanaka, Yasuhito Endō, Shinji Okazaki, Shunsuke Nakamura (90.Yuki Abe), Kengo Nakamura (66.Keisuke Honda), Yuto Nagatomo, Yoshito Okubo (69.Kisho Yano), Makoto Hasebe. Trainer: Takeshi Okada.
Goal: 0-1 Shinji Okazaki (9).
Cautions: Aleksandr Geynrikh / Shunsuke Nakamura, Yuto Nagatomo, Yasuhito Endō.
Sent off: Makoto Hasebe (89).

06.06.2009, Al Sadd Club Stadium, Doha; Attendance: 7,000
Referee: Abdul Malik Bin Abdul Bashir (Singapore)
QATAR - AUSTRALIA 0-0
QAT: Qasem Abdulhamed Burhan, Ahmed Ali Faris Al Binali (62.Majdi Abdulla Siddiq), Ibrahim Abdul Majid, Bilal Mohammed Rajab, Hamed Shami Zaher, Talal Hassan Ali Al Bloushi, Mesaad Ali Al Hamad, Mohammed Abdulrab Al Yazidi, Majed Mohammed Hassan (83.Yousef Ahmed Ali), Ali Hassan Afif Yahya (77.Hassan Khalid Al Haydos), Andrés Sebastián Soria Quintana (Cap). Trainer: Bruno Metsu (France).
AUS: Mark Schwarzer, Lucas Edward Neill (Cap), Christopher John Coyne, Scott Chipperfield, Jason Čulina, Vincenzo Grella (73.Jade Bronson North), Carl Valeri, Mark Bresciano (77.Brett Holman), Timothy Joel Cahill (90+3.Richard Garcia), Joshua Blake Kennedy, Harold Kewell. Trainer: Peter Tim Verbeek (Holland).
Cautions: Hamed Shami Zaher, Andrés Sebastián Soria Quintana, Talal Hassan Ali Al Bloushi / Lucas Edward Neill.

10.06.2009, Olympic Stadium, Sydney; Attendance: 39,540
Referee: Abdullah Mohamed Masoud Al Hilali (Oman)
AUSTRALIA - BAHRAIN 2-0(0-0)
AUS: Mark Schwarzer, Mark Daniel Milligan, Christopher John Coyne (73.Jade Bronson North), David Raymond Carney, Luke Wilkshire, Jason Čulina, Michael John Jedinak (63.Vincenzo Grella), Mile Sterjovski, Harold Kewell, Brett Holman (84.Nicholas Alberto Carle), Scott Douglas McDonald. Trainer: Peter Tim Verbeek (Holland).
BHR: Sayed Mohammed Jaffer Sabet, Hussain Ali Baba Mohammed, Salman Isa Ghuloom (90+2.Ali Abdulwahab Hussain Al Safi), Abdullah Al Marzooqi, Abdulla Abdi Omar Yasser (87.Ahmed Hassan Taleb), Faouzi Mubarak Aaish (76.Ismaeel Abdullatif Hasan), Mahmood Abdulrahman Mohammed Noor, Mohamed Ahmed Hubail, Abdullah Omar Ismail, Mohamed Ahmed Yusuf Salmeen (Cap), Jaycee John Akwani Okwunwanne. Trainer: Milan Máčala (Czech Republic).
Goals: 1-0 Mile Sterjovski (55), 2-0 David Raymond Carney (88).
Cautions: Michael John Jedinak, Mark Daniel Milligan, Luke Wilkshire / Faouzi Mubarak Aaish.

10.06.2009, International Stadium, Yokohama; Attendance: 60,256
Referee: Subkhiddin Mohd Salleh (Malaysia)
JAPAN - QATAR 1-1(1-0)
JPN: Seigo Narazaki, Yuji Nakazawa, Marcus Tulio Tanaka, Atsuto Uchida, Hideo Hashimoto, Yuki Abe (58.Daisuke Matsui), Shunsuke Nakamura (81.Keisuke Honda), Kengo Nakamura, Yasuyuki Konno, Shinji Okazaki, Keiji Tamada (67.Shinzo Koroki). Trainer: Takeshi Okada.
QAT: Qasem Abdulhamed Burhan, Ahmed Ali Faris Al Binali, Ibrahim Abdul Majid, Bilal Mohammed Rajab (Cap), Hamed Shami Zaher, Mohammed Yasser Mohammady, Mohammed Abdulrab Al Yazidi, Fábio César Montezine (70.Mesaad Ali Al Hamad), Majdi Abdulla Siddiq, Majed Mohammed Hassan (54.Yousef Ahmed Ali), Ali Hassan Afif Yahya (57.Hassan Khalid Al Haydos). Trainer: Bruno Metsu (France).
Goals: 1-0 Ahmed Ali Al Binali (3 own goal), 1-1 Ali Hassan Afif Yahya (53 penalty).
Cautions: Yuji Nakazawa / Hamed Shami Zaher.

17.06.2009, Melbourne Cricket Ground, Melbourne; Attendance:
Referee: Khalil Ibrahim Al Ghamdi (Saudi Arabia)
AUSTRALIA - JAPAN   **2-1(0-1)**
AUS: Mark Schwarzer, Lucas Edward Neill, Shane Peter Stefanutto, Rhys Williams (79.Jacob Geoffrey Burns), Jade Bronson North, Jason Čulina, Vincenzo Grella, Mile Sterjovski, Nicholas Alberto Carle (79.Scott Douglas McDonald), Timothy Joel Cahill (86.Dario Vidošić), Joshua Blake Kennedy. Trainer: Peter Tim Verbeek (Holland).
JPN: Seigo Narazaki, Atsuto Uchida, Marcus Tulio Tanaka, Yuki Abe, Yuto Nagatomo, Hideo Hashimoto (84.Shinzo Koroki), Yasuyuki Konno, Kengo Nakamura, Daisuke Matsui (67.Kisho Yano), Shinji Okazaki, Keiji Tamada. Trainer: Takeshi Okada.
Goals: 0-1 Marcus Tulio Tanaka (39), 1-1 Timothy Joel Cahill (59), 1-2 Timothy Joel Cahill (77).

17.06.2009, National Stadium, Manama; Attendance: 14,100
Referee: Masoud Moradi Hasanali (Iran)
BAHRAIN - UZBEKISTAN   **1-0(0-0)**
BHR: Sayed Mohammed Jaffer Sabet, Sayed Mohamed Adnan, Mohamed Husain Bahzad, Salman Isa Ghuloom, Abdullah Al Marzooqi, Abdulla Abdi Omar Yasser (46.Mahmood Abdulrahman Mohammed Noor), Mohamed Ahmed Hubail, Abdullah Omar Ismail, Mohamed Ahmed Yusuf Salmeen (Cap) (88.Ahmed Hassan Taleb), Ismaeel Abdullatif Hasan, A'ala Ahmed Hubail (80.Ali Abdulwahab Hussain Al Safi). Trainer: Milan Máčala (Czech Republic).
UZB: Ignatiy Nesterov, Anvar Gafurov, Anzur Ismailov, Islom Tukhtahujaev, Sakhob Jurayev, Odil Ahmedov, Stanislav Andreyev (46.Jasur Hasanov), Server Djeparov (Cap), Timur Kapadze (73.Anvarjon Soliyev), Viktor Karpenko, Zaynitdin Tadjiyev (62.Aleksandr Geynrikh). Trainer: Mirdjalal Qasimov.
Goal: 1-0 Mahmood Abdulrahman Mohammed Noor (76).
Cautions: Mohamed Ahmed Yusuf Salmeen / Viktor Karpenko, Sakhob Jurayev, Anzur Ismailov.
Sent off: Abdullah Al Marzooqi (78).

GROUP 2

06.09.2008	Abu Dhabi	United Arab Emirates – Korea D.P.R.	1-2(0-0)
06.09.2008	Riyadh	Saudi Arabia - Iran	1-1(1-0)
10.09.2008	Shanghai (CHN)	Korea D.P.R. – Korea Republic	1-1(0-0)
10.09.2008	Abu Dhabi	United Arab Emirates – Saudi Arabia	1-2(1-0)
15.10.2008	Seoul	Korea Republic - United Arab Emirates	4-1(2-0)
15.10.2008	Tehran	Iran – Korea D.P.R.	2-1(1-0)
19.11.2008	Dubai	United Arab Emirates - Iran	1-1(1-0)
19.11.2008	Riyadh	Saudi Arabia – Korea Republic	0-2(0-0)
11.02.2009	P'yŏngyang	Korea D.P.R. – Saudi Arabia	1-0(1-0)
11.02.2009	Tehran	Iran – Korea Republic	1-1(0-0)
28.03.2009	P'yŏngyang	Korea D.P.R. - United Arab Emirates	2-0(0-0)
28.03.2009	Tehran	Iran – Saudi Arabia	1-2(0-0)
01.04.2009	Seoul	Korea Republic – Korea D.P.R.	1-0(0-0)
01.04.2009	Riyadh	Saudi Arabia - United Arab Emirates	3-2(1-2)
06.06.2009	P'yŏngyang	Korea D.P.R. - Iran	0-0
06.06.2009	Dubai	United Arab Emirates – Korea Republic	0-2(0-2)
10.06.2009	Seoul	Korea Republic – Saudi Arabia	0-0
10.06.2009	Tehran	Iran - United Arab Emirates	1-0(0-0)
17.06.2009	Seoul	Korea Republic - Iran	1-1(0-0)
17.06.2009	Riyadh	Saudi Arabia – Korea D.P.R.	0-0

FINAL STANDINGS

1.	**KOREA REPUBLIC**	8	4	4	0	12	-	4	16
2.	**KOREA D.P.R.**	8	3	3	2	7	-	5	12
3.	**Saudi Arabia**	8	3	3	2	8	-	8	12
4.	Iran	8	2	5	1	8	-	7	11
5.	United Arab Emirates	8	0	1	7	6	-	17	1

Korea Republic & Korea D.P.R. qualified for the Final Tournament; Saudi Arabia qualified for the Play-Offs.

06.09.2008, „Mohammed Bin Zayed" Stadium, Abu Dhabi; Attendance: 10,000
Referee: Ravshan Irmatov (Uzbekistan)
UNITED ARAB EMIRATES – KOREA D.P.R.   **1-2(0-0)**
UAE: Mohamed Obaid Majid Al Tawila, Saleh Abdulla Obaid Al Areefi, Bashir Saeed Sanqour Al Hammadi, Rashid Abdulrahman Al Hosani (Cap), Haidar Alo Ali Mohammed, Abdul Rahim Jumaa Anbar Mubarak Al Araimi Al Jenaibi, Subait Khater Fayel Khamis Al Mekhaini (54.Mohammed Ibrahim Hussain Al Bloushi), Hilal Said Al Saeedi (67.Abdullah Malallah Al Shamali), Ismail Salem Al Hammadi, Ismail Matar Ibrahim Khamis Al Mukhaini Al Junaibi, Mohamed Saeed Rashed Saiwed Al Shehhi (63.Ahmed Mohammed Mubarak Al Mahri „Dada"). Trainer: Bruno Metsu (France).
PRK: Ri Myong-Guk, Cha Jong-Hyok, Nam Song-Chol (Cap), Pak Chol-Jin, Ri Kwang-Chon, Ri Jun-Il, Kim Yong-Jun (29.An Chol-Hyok), An Yong-Hak, Mun In-Guk, Choe Kum-Chol, Hong Yong-Jo (71.Kim Kum-Il). Trainer: Kim Jong-Hun.
Goals: 0-1 Choe Kum-Chol (72), 0-2 An Chol-Hyok (81), 1-2 Bashir Saeed Sanqour Al Hammadi (86).
Cautions: Abdullah Malallah Al Shamali / An Chol-Hyok.

06.09.2008, „King Fahd" International Stadium, Riyadh; Attendance: 50,000
Referee: Mark Alexander Shield (Australia)
SAUDI ARABIA - IRAN   **1-1(1-0)**
KSA: Mansour Al Naje, Abdoh Ibrahim Otaif, Osama Abdul Razzaq Al Hawsawi, Abdullah Shuhail, Redha Hassan Tukar Fallatah, Hussein Abdulghani Al Sulaimani (Cap), Khaled Aziz Al Thaker, Ahmed Ibrahim Otaif, Mohammad Bander Al Shalhoub (67.Omar Al Ghamdi), Saad Mish'al Al Harthi, Faisal Al Sultan (70.Yasser Saeed Al Qahtani). Trainer: Nasser Al Johar.
IRN: Seyyed Mehdi Rahmati, Majid Gholamnejad, Seyed Hadi Aghily Anvar, Seyed Jalal Hosseini

Khoshkbejari, Sattar Zare, Masoud Shojaei Soleimani, Javad Nekounam (Cap), Ferydoon Zandi (59.Rasoul Khatibi), Andranik Teymourian (75.Mojtaba Jabari Kordgeshlagi), Vahid Hashemian, Gholamreza Rezaei (59.Mehrzad Madanchi Ardakani). Trainer: Ali Daei.

Goals: 1-0 Saad Mish'al Al Harthi (29), 1-1 Javad Nekounam (81).

Cautions: Faisal Al Sultan, Saad Mish'al Al Harthi, Redha Hassan Tukar Fallatah / Seyed Hadi Aghily Anvar, Mehrzad Madanchi Ardakani.

10.09.2008, Hongkou Stadium, Shanghai (China P.R.); Attendance: 3,000
Referee: Mohsen Hassan Basma (Syria)
KOREA D.P.R. – KOREA REPUBLIC   **1-1(0-0)**
PRK: Ri Myong-Guk, Cha Jong-Hyok, Kim Yong-Jun (71.Choe Kum-Chol; 89.Kim Kum-Il), Nam Song-Chol (Cap), Pak Chol-Jin, Ri Kwang-Chon, Ri Jun-Il, An Yong-Hak, Mun In-Guk, Jong Tae-Se, Hong Yong-Jo. Trainer: Kim Jong-Hun.
KOR: Jung Sung-Ryong, Oh Beom-Seok (78.Choi Hyo-Jin), Kim Dong-Jin, Kim Jin-Kyu, Kang Min-Soo, Kim Chi-Woo, Kim Nam-Il (Cap), Kim Do-Heon, Ki Sung-Yueng, Choi Sung-Kuk (61.Lee Chun-Soo), Cho Jae-Jin (61.Seo Dong-Hyeon). Trainer: Huh Jung-Moo.
Goals: 1-0 Hong Yong-Jo (64 penalty), 1-1 Ki Sung-Yueng (69).
Cautions: Kim Nam-Il.

10.09.2008, „Mohammed Bin Zayed" Stadium, Abu Dhabi; Attendance: 15,000
Referee: Yuichi Nishimura (Japan)
UNITED ARAB EMIRATES – SAUDI ARABIA   **1-2(1-0)**
UAE: Majed Nasser Al Maqdami, Haidar Alo Ali Mohammed (89.Faris Jumaa Hassan Al Saadi), Rashid Abdulrahman Al Hosani (Cap), Bashir Saeed Sanqour Al Hammadi, Adel Abdul Aziz, Subait Khater Fayel Khamis Al Mekhaini, Hilal Said Al Saeedi, Ismail Salem Al Hammadi (87.Mohammed Ibrahim Hussain Al Bloushi), Faisal Khalil Sebait Mubarak Al Junaibi, Ismail Matar Ibrahim Khamis Al Mukhaini Al Junaibi, Mohamed Saeed Rashed Saiwed Al Shehhi (78.Ahmed Mohammed Mubarak Al Mahri „Dada"). Trainer: Bruno Metsu (France).
KSA: Walid Abdullah Ali, Majid Al Marshadi, Abdoh Ibrahim Otaif, Osama Abdul Razzaq Al Hawsawi, Abdullah Shuhail, Hussein Omar Abdul Ghani Sulaimani, Khaled Aziz Al Thaker, Ahmed Ibrahim Otaif, Mohammad Bander Al Shalhoub (63.Ahmed Al Fraidi), Saad Al Harthi (46.Yasser Saeed Al Qahtani), Faisal Al Sultan (82.Saud Ali Khariri). Trainer: Nasser Al Johar.
Goals: 1-0 Subait Khater Fayel Khamis Al Mekhaini (23), 1-1 Abdoh Ibrahim Otaif (69), 1-2 Ahmed Al Fraidi (73).
Cautions: Subait Khater Fayel Khamis Al Mekhaini, Faisal Khalil Sebait Mubarak Al Junaibi, Hilal Said Al Saeedi / Khaled Aziz Al Thaker, Mohammad Bander Al Shalhoub, Saad Al Harthi, 46.Yasser Saeed Al Qahtani.

15.10.2008, Seoul World Cup Stadium, Seoul; Attendance: 30,000
Referee: Matthew Christopher Breeze (Australia)
KOREA REPUBLIC - UNITED ARAB EMIRATES   **4-1(2-0)**
KOR: Jung Sung-Ryong, Kwak Tae-Hwi, Cho Yong-Hyung, Lee Young-Pyo, Kim Dong-Jin, Kim Jung-Woo, Park Ji-Sung (Cap), Ki Sung-Yueng (79.Cho Won-Hee), Lee Chung-Yong (55.Kim Hyeung-Bum), Lee Keun-Ho (87.Shin Young-Rok), Jeong Shung-Hoon. Trainer: Huh Jung-Moo.
UAE: Majed Nasser Al Maqdami, Haidar Alo Ali Mohammed, Bashir Saeed Sanqour Al Hammadi (Cap), Fayez Jumah Khamis, Yousif Jaber Naser Al Hammadi (79.Ahmed Mohammed Mubarak Al Mahri „Dada"), Mohamed Othman Salem Mubarak Al Zaabi (46.Ismail Salem Al Hammadi), Obaid Khalifa Mubarak Mesari (90.Tariq Hasan Abdulla Tarish), Amir Mubarak Al Hammadi, Nawaf Mubarak Al Darmaki, Ismail Matar Ibrahim Khamis Al Mukhaini Al Junaibi, Mohamed Saeed Rashed Saiwed Al Shehhi. Trainer: Dominique Bathenay (France).
Goals: 1-0 Lee Keun Ho (20), 2-0 Park Ji Sung (26), 2-1 Ismail Salem Al Hammadi (72), 3-1 Lee Keun Ho (80), 4-1 Kwak Tae Hee (89).
Cautions: Kim Jung-Woo / Fayez Jumah Khamis, Bashir Saeed Sanqour Al Hammadi.

15.10.2008, Azadi Stadium, Tehran; Attendance: 60,000
Referee: Abdullah Mohamed Masoud Al Hilali (Oman)
IRAN – KOREA D.P.R.   **2-1(1-0)**
IRN: Seyyed Mehdi Rahmati, Hossein Kaebi, Seyed Hadi Aghily Anvar, Seyed Jalal Hosseini Khoshkbejari, Sattar Zare, Masoud Shojaei Soleimani, Javad Nekounam, Mehdi Mahdavikia, Mojtaba Jabari Kordgeshlagi (74.Ferydoon Zandi), Rasoul Khatibi (80.Mohammad Seyed Salehi), Gholamreza Rezaei (90.Maziyar Zare). Trainer: Ali Daei.
PRK: Ri Myong-Guk, Cha Jong-Hyok, Kim Yong-Jun (46.Choe Kum-Chol), Nam Song-Chol (Cap), Pak Chol-Jin, Ri Kwang-Chon, Ri Jun-Il, An Yong-Hak, Mun In-Guk (90+2.Pak Nam-Chol II), Jong Tae-Se, Hong Yong-Jo. Trainer: Kim Jong-Hun.
Goals: 1-0 Mehdi Mahdavikia (9), 2-0 Javad Nekounam (63), 2-1 Jong Tae-Se (72).
Cautions: Nam Song-Chol.

19.11.2008, „Al-Maktoum" Stadium, Dubai; Attendance: 8,000
Referee: Subkhiddin Mohd Salleh (Malaysia)
UNITED ARAB EMIRATES - IRAN   **1-1(1-0)**
UAE: Majed Nasser Al Maqdami, Fayez Jumah Khamis, Adel Abdul Aziz, Mohammed Qassim Al Bloushi, Abdul Rahim Jumaa Anbar Mubarak Al Araimi Al Jenaibi (Cap), Nawaf Mubarak Al Darmaki (78.Ahmed Ali Moadhed), Haidar Alo Ali Mohammed, Ismail Salem Al Hammadi, Abdullah Malallah Al Shamali (86.Mohammed Ali Ahmed Al Wehaibi), Ismail Matar Ibrahim Khamis Al Mukhaini Al Junaibi, Mohamed Saeed Rashed Saiwed Al Shehhi (70.Ahmad Khalil Sebait Mubarak Al Junaibi). Trainer: Dominique Bathenay (France).
IRN: Seyyed Mehdi Rahmati, Hossein Kaebi, Pirouz Ghorbani, Seyed Jalal Hosseini Khoshkbejari, Sattar Zare (76.Mehrzad Madanchi Ardakani), Javad Nekounam, Karim Bagheri (Cap), Masoud Shojaei Soleimani, Mehdi Mahdavikia (56.Majid Gholamnejad), Vahid Hashemian (72.Mohammad Seyed Salehi), Gholamreza Rezaei. Trainer: Ali Daei.
Goals: 1-0 Abdul Rahim Jumaa Anbar Mubarak Al Araimi Al Jenaibi (19), 1-1 Karim Bagheri (81).
Cautions: Haidar Alo Ali Mohammed, Ahmed Ali Moadhed, Ismail Matar Ibrahim Khamis Al Mukhaini Al Junaibi / Gholamreza Rezaei.

19.11.2008, „King Fahd" International Stadium, Riyadh; Attendance: 60,000
Referee: Abdul Malik Bashir (Singapore)
SAUDI ARABIA – KOREA REPUBLIC   **0-2(0-0)**
KSA: Walid Abdullah Ali, Abdulla Al Dossari, Osama Mabrouk Awad Al Harbi Al Muwallad, Abdoh Ibrahim Otaif (79.Malek Mouath Al Hawsawi), Osama Abdul Razzaq Al Hawsawi, Redha Hassan Tukar Fallatah (Cap), Khaled Aziz Al Thaker, Naif Ahmad Taib Hazazi, Ahmed Ibrahim Otaif, Mohammad Bander Al Shalhoub (57.Ahmed Al Fraidi), Faisal Al Sultan (86.Hassan Al Rahib). Trainer: Nasser Al Johar.
KOR: Lee Woon-Jae, Cho Yong-Hyung, Lee Young-Pyo, Kang Min-Soo, Oh Beom-Seok, Kim Jung-Woo, Park Ji-Sung (Cap), Ki Sung-Yueng, Lee Chung-Yong (90+2.Cho Won-Hee), Lee Keun-Ho (87.Yeom Ki-Hun), Jeong Shung-Hoon (73.Park Chu-Young). Trainer: Huh Jung-Moo.
Goals: 0-1 Lee Keun-Ho (77), 0-2 Park Chu-Young (90+2).
Cautions: Naif Ahmad Taib Hazazi, Khaled Aziz Al Thaker / Lee Young-Pyo.
Sent off: Naif Ahmad Taib Hazazi (58).

11.02.2009, „Kim Il-Sung" Stadium, P'yŏngyang; Attendance: 48,000
Referee: Ravshan Irmatov (Uzbekistan)
KOREA D.P.R. – SAUDI ARABIA   **1-0(1-0)**
PRK: Ri Myong-Guk, Cha Jong-Hyok, Ji Yun-Nam, Pak Chol-Jin, Ri Kwang-Chon, Ri Jun-Il, An Yong-Hak (67.An Chol-Hyok; 85.Kim Myong-Won), Mun In-Guk, Pak Nam-Chol II, Jong Tae-Se, Hong Yong-Jo (Cap). Trainer: Kim Jong-Hun.
KSA: Walid Abdullah Ali, Abdulla Al Dossari, Majid Al Marshadi, Osama Abdul Razzaq Al Hawsawi, Abdullah Shuhail, Mohammed Noor Al Hawsawi (Cap), Ahmed Al Fraidi (77.Ahmed Al Mousa), Taisir Jaber Al Jassam (82.Abdoh Ibrahim Otaif), Sultan Abdulaziz Al Numari (38.Hassan Al

273

Rahib), Ahmed Ibrahim Otaif, Yasser Saeed Al Qahtani. Trainer: Nasser Al Johar.
Goal: 1-0 Mun In-Guk (28).
Cautions: Ri Kwang-Chon / Yasser Saeed Al Qahtani, Abdullah Shuhail.

11.02.2009, Azadi Stadium, Tehran; Attendance: 75,000
Referee: Benjamin Jon Williams (Australia)
IRAN – KOREA REPUBLIC   **1-1(0-0)**
IRN: Seyyed Mehdi Rahmati, Hossein Kaebi, Seyed Jalal Hosseini Khoshkbejari, Seyed Hadi Aghily
Anvar, Hassan Ashjari, Hossein Kazemi, Javad Nekounam, Karim Bagheri (Cap), Masoud Shojaei
Soleimani (73.Majid Gholamnejad), Vahid Hashemian (82.Siavash Akbarpour), Mohammad Reza
Khalatbary (89.Arash Borhani). Trainer: Ali Daei.
KOR: Lee Woon-Jae, Cho Yong-Hyung, Kang Min-Soo, Oh Beom-Seok, Lee Young-Pyo (69.Kim
Dong-Jin), Kim Jung-Woo, Ki Sung-Yueng, Lee Chung-Yong, Park Ji-Sung (Cap) (83.Park Chu-
Young), Lee Keun-Ho, Jeong Shung-Hoon (40.Yeom Ki-Hun). Trainer: Huh Jung-Moo.
Goals: 1-0 Javad Nekounam (58), 1-1 Park Ji-Sung (81).
Cautions: Hossein Kaebi / Kim Jung-Woo, Ki Sung-Yueng.

28.03.2009, „Kim Il-Sung" Stadium, P'yŏngyang; Attendance: 50,000
Referee: Matthew Christopher Breeze (Australia)
KOREA D.P.R. - UNITED ARAB EMIRATES   **2-0(0-0)**
PRK: Ri Myong-Guk, Cha Jong-Hyok, Ji Yun-Nam, Pak Chol-Jin, Ri Kwang-Chon, Ri Jun-Il, An
Yong-Hak, Mun In-Guk, Pak Nam-Chol II, Jong Tae-Se, Hong Yong-Jo (Cap) (88.Choe Kum-Chol).
Trainer: Kim Jong-Hun.
UAE: Majed Nasser Al Maqdami, Walid Abbas Al Bloushi, Mohammed Qassim Al Bloushi, Hamdan
Ismail Mohamed Al Kamali, Haidar Alo Ali Mohammed (86.Fayez Jumah Khamis), Saif Mohammed
Al Bishr (65.Mohammed Saeed Al Shehi), Abdul Rahim Jumaa Anbar Mubarak Al Araimi Al Jenaibi
(Cap), Nawaf Mubarak Al Darmaki, Ismail Salem Al Hammadi, Ahmad Khalil Sebait Mubarak Al
Junaibi, Abdullah Malallah Al Shamali (54.Mohammed Ibrahim Hussain Al Bloushi). Trainer:
Dominique Bathenay (France).
Goals: 1-0 Pak Nam-Chol II (51), 2-0 Mun In-Guk (90+3).
Cautions: An Yong-Hak / Nawaf Mubarak Al Darmaki.

28.03.2009, Azadi Stadium, Tehran; Attendance: 100,000
Referee: Yuichi Nishimura (Japan)
IRAN – SAUDI ARABIA   **1-2(0-0)**
IRN: Seyyed Mehdi Rahmati, Hossein Kaebi, Seyed Jalal Hosseini Khoshkbejari, Seyed Hadi Aghily
Anvar, Hassan Ashjari, Mehdi Mahdavikia, Hossein Kazemi, Javad Nekounam, Masoud Shojaei
Soleimani, Mohammad Reza Khalatbary (81.Mehrzad Madanchi Ardakani), Gholamreza Rezaei
(55.Vahid Hashemian). Trainer: Ali Daei.
KSA: Walid Abdullah Ali, Abdulla Al Dossari, Osama Mabrouk Awad Al Harbi Al Muwallad,
Mohammad Al Nakhli, Osama Abdul Razzaq Al Hawsawi, Abdoh Ibrahim Otaif (90+5.Redha Hassan
Tukar Fallatah), Mohammed Noor Al Hawsawi (Cap), Saheb Jassim Al Abdullah (73.Taisir Jaber Al
Jassam), Nasser Ali Al Shamrani (73.Saleh Bashir Al Dosari), Ahmed Ibrahim Otaif, Naif Ahmad Taib
Hazazi. Trainer: José Vítor dos Santos Peseiro (Portugal).
Goals: 0-1 Masoud Shojaei Soleimani (57), 1-1 Naif Ahmad Taib Hazazi (79), 1-2 Osama Mabrouk
Awad Al Harbi Al Muwallad (87).
Cautions: Vahid Hashemian, Javad Nekounam / Abdoh Ibrahim Otaif, Mohammed Noor Al Hawsawi.

01.04.2009, Seoul World Cup Stadium, Seoul; Attendance: 48,000
Referee: Abdullah Mohamed Al Hilali (Oman)
KOREA REPUBLIC – KOREA D.P.R.   **1-0(0-0)**
KOR: Lee Woon-Jae, Lee Young-Pyo (58.Kim Dong-Jin), Hwang Jae-Won (53.Lee Jung-Soo), Oh
Beom-Seok, Kang Min-Soo, Cho Won-Hee, Park Ji-Sung (Cap), Ki Sung-Yueng, Lee Chung-Yong,
Park Chu-Young, Lee Keun-Ho (78.Kim Chi-Woo). Trainer: Huh Jung-Moo.

PRK: Ri Myong-Guk, Cha Jong-Hyok, Ji Yun-Nam (80.Nam Song-Chol), Pak Chol-Jin, Ri Kwang-Chon, Ri Jun-Il, Kim Yong-Jun (83.Choe Kum-Chol), Mun In-Guk, Pak Nam-Chol II, Jong Tae-Se, Hong Yong-Jo (Cap). Trainer: Kim Jong-Hun.
Goal: 1-0 Kim Chi-Woo (87).
Cautions: Kim Dong-Jin / Mun In-Guk.

01.04.2009, „King Fahd" International Stadium, Riyadh; Attendance: 70,000
Referee: Subkhiddin Mohd Salleh (Malaysia)
SAUDI ARABIA - UNITED ARAB EMIRATES 3-2(1-2)
KSA: Walid Abdullah Ali, Abdulla Al Dossari, Osama Mabrouk Awad Al Harbi Al Muwallad, Mohammad Al Nakhli, Abdoh Ibrahim Otaif (81.Mohammad Bander Al Shalhoub), Osama Abdul Razzaq Al Hawsawi, Mohammed Noor Al Hawsawi (Cap), Saheb Jassim Al Abdullah (46.Hussein Omar Abdul Ghani Sulaimani), Nasser Ali Al Shamrani (61.Saleh Bashir Al Dosari), Ahmed Ibrahim Otaif, Naif Ahmad Taib Hazazi. Trainer: José Vítor dos Santos Peseiro (Portugal).
UAE: Majed Nasser Al Maqdami, Mohammed Fayez Al Alawi (60.Walid Abbas Al Bloushi), Mohammed Qassim Al Bloushi, Hamdan Ismail Mohamed Al Kamali, Fayez Jumah Khamis, Abdul Rahim Jumaa Anbar Mubarak Al Araimi Al Jenaibi (Cap), Mohammed Ibrahim Hussain Al Bloushi (64.Mahmoud Khamis Saeed Al Hammadi), Nawaf Mubarak Al Darmaki (86.Sultan Saleh Bargash Jaralla Al Menhali), Ismail Salem Al Hammadi, Ismail Matar Ibrahim Khamis Al Mukhaini Al Junaibi, Mohammed Saeed Al Shehi. Trainer: Dominique Bathenay (France).
Goals: 1-0 Abdoh Ibrahim Otaif (4 penalty), 1-1 Mohammed Saeed Al Shehi (38), 1-2 Ismail Matar Ibrahim Khamis Al Mukhaini Al Junaibi (45+1), 2-2 Fayez Jumah Khamis (70 own goal), 3-2 Naif Ahmad Taib Hazazi (85).
Cautions: Mohammad Al Nakhli, Osama Mabrouk Awad Al Harbi Al Muwallad, Walid Abdullah Ali / Ismail Salem Al Hammadi.

06.06.2009, Yanggakdo Stadium, P'yŏngyang; Attendance: 30.000
Referee: Sun Baojie (China P.R.)
KOREA D.P.R. - IRAN 0-0
PRK: Ri Myong-Guk, Cha Jong-Hyok, Ji Yun-Nam, Pak Chol-Jin, Ri Kwang-Chon, Ri Jun-Il, An Yong-Hak, Mun In-Guk (88.Kim Yong-Jun), Pak Nam-Chol II, Jong Tae-Se, Hong Yong-Jo (Cap). Trainer: Kim Jong-Hun.
IRN: Seyyed Mehdi Rahmati, Hossein Kaebi, Seyed Jalal Hosseini Khoshkbejari, Seyed Hadi Aghily Anvar, Mohammad Nosrati (88.Mohammad Reza Khalatbary), Mehdi Mahdavikia, Sahand-Pejman Nouri, Andranik Teymourian, Masoud Shojaei Soleimani, Mohammad Ali Karimi Pashaki, Vahid Hashemian (65.Mohsen Khalili; 70.Mehrzad Madanchi Ardakani). Trainer: Afshin Ghotbi.
Cautions: Masoud Shojaei Soleimani.

06.06.2009, „Al-Maktoum" Stadium, Dubai; Attendance: 4,000
Referee: Abdullah Dor Mohammad Balideh (Qatar)
UNITED ARAB EMIRATES – KOREA REPUBLIC 0-2(0-2)
UAE: Majed Nasser Al Maqdami, Walid Abbas Al Bloushi, Mohammed Qassim Al Bloushi, Faris Jumaa Hassan Al Saadi, Salim Masoud Al Abri, Mohammed Ali Ahmed Al Wehaibi, Abdulsalam Jumaa Al Junaibi (Cap) (83.Ahmed Ali Moadhed), Nawaf Mubarak Al Darmaki, Hilal Said Al Saeedi, Ismail Salem Al Hammadi (8.Mahmoud Khamis Saeed Al Hammadi), Mohammed Saeed Al Shehi. Trainer: Dominique Bathenay (France).
KOR: Lee Woon-Jae, Lee Jung-Soo, Cho Yong-Hyung, Lee Young-Pyo (59.Kim Dong-Jin), Oh Beom-Seok, Kim Jung-Woo, Ki Sung-Yueng, Park Ji-Sung (Cap), Lee Chung-Yong, Lee Keun-Ho (51.Cho Won-Hee), Park Chu-Young (82.Bae Ki-Jong). Trainer: Huh Jung-Moo.
Goals: 0-1 Park Chu-Young (9), 0-2 Ki Sung-Yueng (37).
Cautions: Majed Nasser Al Maqdami, Salim Masoud Al Abri / Lee Young-Pyo, Kim Jung-Woo, Oh Beom-Seok.
Sent off: Kim Jung-Woo (49), Hilal Said Al Saeedi (85).

275

10.06.2009, Seoul World Cup Stadium, Seoul; Attendance: 32,510
Referee: Benjamin Jon Williams (Australia)
KOREA REPUBLIC – SAUDI ARABIA   **0-0**
KOR: Lee Woon-Jae, Lee Jung-Soo, Cho Yong-Hyung, Kim Dong-Jin, Kim Hyung-Il, Ki Sung-Yueng, Cho Won-Hee, Park Ji-Sung (Cap), Lee Chung-Yong, Lee Keun-Ho (84.Choi Tae-Uk), Park Chu-Young (73.Yang Dong-Hyun). Trainer: Huh Jung-Moo.
KSA: Walid Abdullah Ali, Abdulla Al Dossari, Naif Fallatah Al Qadhi, Abdoh Ibrahim Otaif (52.Abdulrahman Al Qahtani), Osama Abdul Razzaq Al Hawsawi, Abdullah Shuhail, Hussein Omar Abdul Ghani Sulaimani, Mohammed Noor Al Hawsawi (Cap), Nasser Ali Al Shamrani (68.Naif Ahmad Taib Hazazi), Ahmed Ibrahim Otaif, Yasser Saeed Al Qahtani (82.Khaled Aziz Al Thaker). Trainer: José Vítor dos Santos Peseiro (Portugal).
Cautions: Park Chu-Young, Cho Yong-Hyung, Kim Hyung-Il / Ahmed Ibrahim Otaif.
Sent off: Ahmed Ibrahim Otaif (80).

10.06.2009, Azadi Stadium, Tehran; Attendance: 38,000
Referee: Ravshan Irmatov (Uzbekistan)
IRAN - UNITED ARAB EMIRATES   **1-0(0-0)**
IRN: Seyyed Mehdi Rahmati, Hossein Kaebi, Seyed Jalal Hosseini Khoshkbejari, Seyed Hadi Aghily Anvar, Mehdi Mahdavikia (46.Mohammad Reza Khalatbary), Sahand-Pejman Nouri, Andranik Teymourian, Masoud Shojaei Soleimani (79.Khosro Heydari), Javad Nekounam, Mohammad Ali Karimi Pashaki, Vahid Hashemian (58.Arash Borhani). Trainer: Afshin Ghotbi.
UAE: Majed Nasser Al Maqdami, Walid Abbas Al Bloushi, Mohammed Qassim Al Bloushi, Faris Jumaa Hassan Al Saadi, Mohammed Ali Ahmed Al Wehaibi (88.Mahmoud Khamis Saeed Al Hammadi), Salim Masoud Al Abri, Abdulsalam Jumaa Al Junaibi (Cap), Obaid Khalifa Mubarak Mesari, Amir Mubarak Al Hammadi, Nawaf Mubarak Al Darmaki (85.Saif Mohammed Al Bishr), Mohammed Saeed Al Shehi. Trainer: Dominique Bathenay (France).
Goal: 1-0 Mohammad Ali Karimi Pashaki (53).
Cautions: Mohammad Reza Khalatbary, Mohammad Ali Karimi Pashaki / , Faris Jumaa Hassan Al Saadi, Mahmoud Khamis Saeed Al Hammadi.

17.06.2009, Seoul World Cup Stadium, Seoul; Attendance: 40,000
Referee: Yuichi Nishimura (Japan)
KOREA REPUBLIC - IRAN   **1-1(0-0)**
KOR: Lee Woon-Jae, Lee Jung-Soo, Cho Yong-Hyung, Kim Dong-Jin (70.Lee Young-Pyo), Oh Beom-Seok, Ki Sung-Yueng (75.Yang Dong-Hyun), Kim Jung-Woo, Park Ji-Sung (Cap), Lee Chung-Yong (46.Cho Won-Hee), Lee Keun-Ho, Park Chu-Young. Trainer: Huh Jung-Moo.
IRN: Seyyed Mehdi Rahmati, Hossein Kaebi, Seyed Jalal Hosseini Khoshkbejari, Seyed Hadi Aghily Anvar, Mohammad Nosrati (86.Mohammad Reza Khalatbary), Mehdi Mahdavikia (87.Vahid Hashemian), Javad Nekounam, Sahand-Pejman Nouri, Andranik Teymourian, Masoud Shojaei Soleimani, Mohammad Ali Karimi Pashaki (75.Arash Borhani). Trainer: Afshin Ghotbi.
Goals: 0-1 Masoud Shojaei Soleimani (52), 1-1 Park Ji-Sung (82).
Cautions: Ki Sung-Yueng, Park Ji-Sung / Javad Nekounam, Hossein Kaebi, Andranik Teymourian, Masoud Shojaei Soleimani.

17.06.2009, „King Fahd" International Stadium, Riyadh; Attendance: 65,000
Referee: Mohsen Hassan Basma (Syria)
SAUDI ARABIA – KOREA D.P.R.   **0-0**
KSA: Walid Abdullah Ali, Abdulla Al Dossari, Naif Fallatah Al Qadhi, Osama Abdul Razzaq Al Hawsawi, Abdullah Shuhail, Hussein Omar Abdul Ghani Sulaimani (Cap), Khaled Aziz Al Thaker (75.Saheb Jassim Al Abdullah), Mohammed Noor Al Hawsawi, Abdulrahman Al Qahtani (69.Mohammad Bander Al Shalhoub), Naif Ahmad Taib Hazazi, Yasser Saeed Al Qahtani (86.Nasser Ali Al Shamrani). Trainer: José Vítor dos Santos Peseiro (Portugal).
PRK: Ri Myong-Guk, Cha Jong-Hyok, Ji Yun-Nam, Pak Chol-Jin, Ri Kwang-Chon, Ri Jun-Il, An Yong-Hak, Mun In-Guk (74.Kim Kum-Il), Pak Nam-Chol II, Jong Tae-Se (89.Kim Yong-Jun), Hong

Yong-Jo (Cap) (60.An Chol-Hyok). Trainer: Kim Jong-Hun.
Cautions: Ri Myong-Guk.
Sent off: Kim Yong-Jun (90+4).

FIFTH ROUND

| 05.09.2009 | Manama | Bahrain – Saudi Arabia | 0-0 |
| 09.00.2009 | Riyadh | Saudi Arabia – Bahrain | 2-2(1-1) |

05.09.2009, National Stadium, Manama; Attendance: 16,000
Referee: Yuichi Nishimura (Japan)
BAHRAIN – SAUDI ARABIA   **0-0**
BHR: Sayed Mohammed Jaffer Sabet, Sayed Mohamed Adnan, Hussain Ali Baba Mohamed, Salman Issa Ghuloom (81.Mahmood Abdulrahman Mohammed Noor), Faouzi Mubarak Aaish, Mohamed Ahmed Hubail, Abdullah Omar Ismail, Sayed Mahmood Jalal Al Wadaei, Mohamed Ahmed Yusuf Salmeen, Ismaeel Abdullatif Hasan, Husain Ali Ahmed Ahmed Abdulla (70.Jaycee John Akwani Okwunwanne). Trainer: Milan Máčala (Czech Republic).
KSA: Walid Abdullah Ali, Abdullah Al Dossari, Hamad Al Montashari, Osama Abdul Razzaq Al Hawsawi, Abdullah Shuhail, Hussein Omar Abdul Ghani Sulaimani, Ahmed Ibrahim Otaif (87.Abdullatif Al Ghannam), Saud Ali Khariri, Mohammed Noor Al Hawsawi, Malek Mouath Al Hawsawi (65.Nasser Ali Al Shamrani), Yasser Saeed Al Qahtani. Trainer: José Vítor dos Santos Peseiro (Portugal).
Cautions: Mohamed Ahmed Yusuf Salmeen.

09.09.2009, „King Fahd" International Stadium, Riyadh; Attendance: 50,000
Referee: Ravshan Irmatov (Uzbekistan)
SAUDI ARABIA - BAHRAIN   **2-2(1-1)**
KSA: Walid Abdullah Ali, Hamad Al Montashari, Osama Abdul Razzaq Al Hawsawi, Abdullah Shuhail (82.Hassan Mouath Fallatah), Hussein Omar Abdul Ghani Sulaimani, Taisir Jaber Al Jassam (78.Malek Mouath Al Hawsawi), Abdullatif Al Ghannam (63.Ahmed Ibrahim Otaif), Nasser Ali Al Shamrani, Saud Ali Khariri, Mohammed Noor Al Hawsawi, Yasser Saeed Al Qahtani. Trainer: José Vítor dos Santos Peseiro (Portugal).
BHR: Sayed Mohammed Jaffer Sabet, Sayed Mohamed Adnan, Hussain Ali Baba Mohamed, Salman Issa Ghuloom, Faouzi Mubarak Aaish (76.Mahmood Abdulrahman Mohammed Noor), Babatunde Fatai-Baba Fatadi, Mohamed Ahmed Hubail, Abdullah Omar Ismail, Sayed Mahmood Jalal Al Wadaei, Husain Ali Ahmed Ahmed Abdulla (65.Ismaeel Abdullatif Hasan), Jaycee John Akwani Okwunwanne (82.Ali Abdulwahab Hussain Al Safi). Trainer: Milan Máčala (Czech Republic).
Goals: 1-0 Nasser Ali Al Shamrani (13), 1-1 Jaycee John Akwani Okwunwanne (42), 2-1 Hamad Al Montashari (90+1), 2-2 Ismaeel Abdullatif Hasan (90+3).
Cautions: Walid Abdullah Ali, Hamad Al Montashari / Babatunde Fatai-Baba Fatadi.

Bahrain qualified for the Intercontinental Play-off against the Oceania Zone winner (New Zealand).

OCEANIA

The first phase of the qualifiers coincided with the 2007 South Pacific Games tournament, organized in Samoa in August 2007. The top-3 teams (New Caledonia, Fiji and Vanuatu) joined New Zealand in the second phase which was also the 2008 OFC (Oceania Football Confederation) Nations Cup. Finally, the winner played a home and away play-off with the fifth-placed Asian nation for a place in the World Cup final tournament.

FIRST PHASE
(2007 South Pacific Games)

GROUP A

25.08.2007	Apia	Tahiti – New Caledonia	0-1(0-1)
25.08.2007	Apia	Fiji - Tuvalu	16-0(10-0)
27.08.2007	Apia	Tuvalu - New Caledonia	0-1(0-0)
27.08.2007	Apia	Fiji – Cook Islands	4-0(2-0)
29.08.2007	Apia	Tuvalu - Tahiti	1-1(0-1)
29.08.2007	Apia	New Caledonia – Cook Islands	3-0(1-0)
01.09.2007	Apia	Cook Islands - Tuvalu	4-1(1-0)
01.09.2007	Apia	Tahiti - Fiji	0-4(0-2)
03.09.2007	Apia	New Caledonia - Fiji	1-1(1-0)
03.09.2007	Apia	Cook Islands - Tahiti	0-1(0-0)

FINAL STANDINGS

1.	**Fiji**	4	3	1	0	25	-	1		10
2.	**New Caledonia**	4	3	1	0	6	-	1		10
3.	Tahiti	4	1	1	2	2	-	6		4
4.	Cook Islands	4	1	0	3	4	-	9		3
5.	Tuvalu	4	0	1	3	2	-	22		1

Note: Tuvalu are not members of FIFA and so were not eligible to qualify for the World Cup.

25.08.2007, Toleafoa „Joseph S. Blatter" Complex, Apia (Samoa); Attendance: 400
Referee: Michael Hester (New Zealand)
TAHITI – NEW CALEDONIA   **0-1(0-1)**
TAH: Xavier Samin, Jean-Yves Li Wa Ut, Stéphane Gelima, Billy Mataitai (78.Temarii Tinorua), Raimana Li Fung Kee, Raimoana Bennett, Auguste Washetine, Taufa Neuffer, Axel Williams (67.Jerome Tetavahi), Teva Zaveroni, Angelo Tchen. Trainer: Gerard Kautai.
NCL: Marc Ounemoa, Andre Naxue, Andre Sinedo, Georges Wadenges, Marius Mapou, Pierre Wajoka (Cap), Luther Wahnyamalla (60.Patrick Diake), José Hmaé, Iamel Babeu (46.Jean-Louis Toto), Poulidor Toto. Trainer: Didier Chambaron (France).
Goal: 0-1 Pierre Wajoka (9 penalty).
Cautions: Stéphane Gelima, Taufa Neuffer, Angelo Tchen / Luther Wahnyamalla, Jean-Louis Toto,
Sent off: José Hmaé (40).

25.08.2007, Toleafoa „Joseph S. Blatter" Complex, Apia (Samoa); Attendance: 200
Referee: Fiti Aimaasu (Samoa)
FIJI - TUVALU   **16-0(10-0)**
FIJ: Benaminio Mateinaaqara, Ronil Kumar (64.Alvin Avinesh), Lorima Dau, Pita Baleitoga (52.Taniela Waqa), Osea Vakatalesau, Thomas Vulivuli, Peni Finau, Salesh Kumar, Malakai Tiwa (52.Ratu Inosi Vatuvicila), Pita Rabo, Roy Krishna. Trainer: Juan Carlos Buzzetti (Uruguay).
TUV: Jay Timo, Mau Penisula, Lalesi Vaia, Papua Ulisese, Petio Semaia, Semese Alefaio (63.Mati Fusi), Paenui Fagota, Loisio Peni, Imo Fiamalua, Hetoa Kaio (30.Jelly Selau), Vilamu Sekifu. Trainer:

278

Toakai Puapua.
Goals: 1-0 Roy Krishna (6), 2-0 Pita Rabo (11), 3-0 Roy Krishna (14), 4-0 Pita Baleitoga (17), 5-0 Roy Krishna (22), 6-0 Malakai Tiwa (28), 7-0 Malakai Tiwa (30), 8-0 Pita Rabo (34), 9-0 Osea Vakatalesau (42), 10-0 Pita Rabo (45), 11-0 Osea Vakatalesau (46), 12-0 Osea Vakatalesau (65), 13-0 Peni Finau (68 penalty), 14-0 Osea Vakatalesau (73), 15-0 Osea Vakatalesau (82), 16-0 Osea Vakatalesau (89).
Cautions: Imo Fiamalua, Papua Ulisese.

27.08.2007, Toleafoa „Joseph S. Blatter" Complex, Apia (Samoa); Attendance: 250
Referee: Nelson Sogo (Solomon Islands)
TUVALU - NEW CALEDONIA   **0-1(0-0)**
TUV: Jay Timo, Mau Penisula, Paitela Kelemene, Papua Ulisese (87.Mati Fusi), Paenui Fagota, Loisio Peni, Fulisagafou Hauma (83.Hetoa Kaio), Peniuna Kaitu (65.Lolesi Vaia), Jelly Selau, Imo Fiamalua. Trainer: Toakai Puapua.
NCL: Adolphe Boaoutho, Andre Naxue, André Sinedo, George Wadenges, Yohann Mercier, Luther Wahnyamalla, Jean Louis Toto (32.Jean Chrys Xenie), Patrick Diaike (77.Jean-Patrick Wakanumuné), Iamel Kabeu, Patrick Drawilo (46.Pierre Wajoka), Jean Yann Dounezek. Trainer: Didier Chambaron (France).
Goal: 0-1 Iamel Kabeu (52).
Cautions: Jean Chrys Xenie.
Sent off: André Sinedo (72).

27.08.2007, Toleafoa „Joseph S. Blatter" Complex, Apia (Samoa); Attendance: 400
Referee: Lencie Fred (Vanuatu)
FIJI – COOK ISLANDS   **4-0(2-0)**
FIJ: Simione Tamanisau, Samuela Vula, Pita Baleitoga (59.Ronil Kumar), Joasaia Bukalidi, Peni Finau (68.Viliame Toma), Taniela Waqa, Salesh Kumar, Malakai Tiwa, Malakai Kainihewe, Osea Vakatalesau, Roy Krishna (65.Pita Rabo). Trainer: Juan Carlos Buzzetti (Uruguay).
COK: Tony Jamieson, Paul Luiz Van Eijk (69.Edward Drollet), Miitamariki Joseph (74.Edward Brogan), Steven Willis, Adrian Shepherd, Thomas Le Mouton, Eugenie Tatuava, Anonga Tisam (80.John Pareanga), Paavo Mustonen, Daniel Shepherd, Augusty Bartillard. Trainer: Tim Jerks (Australia).
Goals: 1-0 Osea Vakatalesau (19 penalty), 2-0 Taniela Waqa (40), 3-0 Joasaia Bukalidi (63), 4-0 Malakai Kainihewe (82).
Cautions: Daniel Shepherd, Thomas Le Mouton.
Sent off: Daniel Shepherd (39).

29.08.2007, Toleafoa „Joseph S. Blatter" Complex, Apia (Samoa); Attendance: 100
Referee: Christopher Lengeta (Solomon Islands)
TUVALU - TAHITI   **1-1(0-1)**
TUV: Jay Timo, Mau Penisula, Lolesi Vaia, Paitela Kelemene, Papua Ulisese (67.Peniuna Kaitu), Petio Semaia (Cap), Mati Fusi (74.Viliamu Sekifu), Paeniu Fagota, Fulisagafou Hauma (83.Semese Alefaio), Jelly Selau, Imo Fiamalua. Trainer: Toakai Puapua.
TAH: Daniel Tapeta, Teraimaru Mervin, Freddy Taumara, Samuel Garcia (46.Raimoana Bennett), Jerome Tetavahi, Raimana Lee Fung Kuee (38.Neuffer Taufa), Hiro Pororiae, Temarii Tinorua, Farahia Teuira, Axel Williams (74.Auguste Washetine), Teva Zaveroni (Cap). Trainer: Gerard Kautai.
Goals: 0-1 Axel Williams (45+1), 1-1 Viliamu Sekifu (87).
Cautions: Fulisagafou Hauma, Peniuna Kaitu, Petio Semaia.

29.08.2007, Toleafoa „Joseph S. Blatter" Complex, Apia (Samoa); Attendance: 200
Referee: Neil Fox (New Zealand)
NEW CALEDONIA – COOK ISLANDS   **3-0(1-0)**
NCL: Marc Ounemoa, Wilson Forest, Georges Wadenges, Yohann Mercier (87.Jean Chrys Xenie), Pierre Wajoka (Cap), Luther Wahnyamalla (76.Jean-Louis Toto), Jose Hmaé, Jean-Patrick Wakanumuné, Adolphe Boaoutho (83.Patrick Drawilo), Iamel Kabeu, Poulidor Toto. Trainer: Didier

Chambaron (France).

COK: Tony Jamieson, Pula Luiz Van Eijk, John Pareanga (82.Nathan Tisam), Miitamariki Joseph, Steven Willis, Adrian Shepherd (55.Edward Brogan), Thomas Le Mouton, Eugenie Tatuava, Anonga Tisam, Paavo Mustonen (70.John Michael Quijano), Augusty Bartillard. Trainer: Tim Jerks (Australia).
Goals: 1-0 Iamel Kabeu (35), 2-0 Iamel Kabeu (51 penalty), 3-0 Iamel Kabeu (85).
Cautions: Jean-Patrick Wakanumuné / Miitamariki Joseph, Adrian Shepherd.

01.09.2007, Toleafoa „Joseph S. Blatter" Complex, Apia (Samoa); Attendance: 200
Referee: Michael Hester (New Zealand)
COOK ISLANDS - TUVALU 4-1(1-0)
COK: Tony Jamieson, Paul Luiz Van Eijk, Miitamariki Joseph, Steven Willis, Adrian Shepherd (62.John Pareanga; 78.Edward Brogan), Thomas Le Mouton, Eugenie Tatuava, Teariki Mateariki, John Michael Quijano (53.Kunda Tom), Paavo Mustonen, Augusty Bartillard. Trainer: Tim Jerks (Australia).
TUV: Jay Timo, Mau Penisula, Lolesi Vaia (75.Papua Ulisese), Paitela Kelemene, Petio Semaia (Cap), Mati Fusi (69.Viliamu Sekifu), Fulisagafou Hauma (81.Semese Alefaio), Peniuna Kaitu, Jelly Selau, Imo Fiamalua, Tapeni Letueti. Trainer: Toakai Puapua.
Goals: 1-0 Teariki Mateariki (28), 2-0 Teariki Mateariki (69), 2-1 Steven Willis (83 own goal), 3-1 Thomas Le Mouton (88), 4-1 Kunda Tom (90+3).
Cautions: Steven Willis / Peniuna Kaitu.

01.09.2007, Toleafoa „Joseph S. Blatter" Complex, Apia (Samoa); Attendance: 200
Referee: Neil Fox (New Zealand)
TAHITI - FIJI 0-4(0-2)
TAH: Xavier Samin, Jean-Yves Li Wa Ut, Stéphane Gelima, Billy Mataitai, Raimoana Bennett (70.Temarii Tinorua), Auguste Washetine, Hiro Poroiae, Taufa Neuffer (63.Jerome Tetavahi), Axel Williams, Teva Zaveroni (Cap), Angelo Tchen. Trainer: Gerard Kautai.
FIJ: Simione Tamanisau, Samuela Vula (67.Waisake Sabutu), Ronil Kumar, Pita Baleitoga, Peni Finau, Taniela Waqa (53.Ratu Iniosi Vatucicila), Salesh Kumar (46.Thomas Vulivuli), Malakai Tiwa, Malakai Kainihewe, Osea Vakatalesau, Pita Rabo. Trainer: Juan Carlos Buzzetti (Uruguay).
Goals: 0-1 Taniela Waqa (17), 0-2 Pita Baleitoga (38), 0-3 Osea Vakatalesau (49), 0-4 Osea Vakatalesau (73).
Cautions: Stéphane Gelima, Taufa Neuffer, Axel Williams, Teva Zaveroni, Auguste Washetine / Taniela Waqa, Salesh Kumar, Pita Baleitoga, Samuela Vula, Peni Finau.
Sent off: Stéphane Gelima (31).

03.09.2007, Toleafoa „Joseph S. Blatter" Complex, Apia (Samoa); Attendance: 1,000
Referee: Lencie Fred (Vanuatu)
NEW CALEDONIA - FIJI 1-1(1-0)
NCL: Marc Ounemoa, Wilson Forest, Robert Wayaridi, George Wadenges (75.Jean-Patrick Wakanumuné), Yohann Mercier (46.Jean Chrys Xenie), Marys Mapou, Pierre Wajoka (Cap), Luther Wahnyamalla, Jose Hmaé, Adolphe Boaoutho, Poulidor Toto (82.Jean-Louis Toto). Trainer: Didier Chambaron (France).
FIJ: Simione Tamanisau, Ronil Kumar, Lorima Dau, Thomas Vulivuli, Viliame Toma, Malakai Tiwa, Malakai Kainihewe, Pita Rabo (Cap), Roy Krishna, Osea Vakatalesau, Ratu Inosi Vatucicila. Trainer: Juan Carlos Buzzetti (Uruguay).
Goals: 1-0 Pierre Wajoka (44), 1-1 Malakai Kainihewe (56).
Cautions: George Wadenges / Malakai Tiwa.

03.09.2007, Toleafoa „Joseph S. Blatter" Complex, Apia (Samoa); Attendance: 100
Referee: Fiti Aimaasu (Samoa)
COOK ISLANDS - TAHITI 0-1(0-0)
COK: Tony Jamieson, Paul Luiz Van Eijk (66.Edward Brogan), Miitamariki Joseph, Steven Willis, Adrian Shepherd, Thomas Le Mouton, Eugenie Tatuava, Anonga Tisam (38.Daniel Shepherd), Teariki

Mateariki (79.Nathan Tisam), Paavo Mustonen, Augusty Bartillard. Trainer: Tim Jerks (Australia).
TAH: Jonathan Torohia, Jean-Yves Li Wa Ut, Freddy Tauimara, Billy Mataitai, Jerome Tetavahi, Raimoana Bennett, Hiro Poroiae (79.Teraimaru Mervin), Temarii Tinorua (71.Auguste Washetine), Axel Williams, Teva Zaveroni, Angelo Tchen. Trainer: Gerard Kautai.
Goal: 0-1 Temarii Tinorua (64).
Cautions: Eugenie Tatuava, Tony Jamieson / Hiro Poroiae, Billy Mataitai, Axel Williams, Angelo Tchen.
Sent off: Raimoana Bennett (54), Miitamariki Joseph (65), Thomas Le Mouton (69).

GROUP B

25.08.2007	Apia	Solomon Islands – American Samoa	12-1(5-0)
25.08.2007	Apia	Vanuatu - Samoa	4-0(2-0)
27.08.2007	Apia	Solomon Islands - Tonga	4-0(2-0)
27.08.2007	Apia	American Samoa - Samoa	0-7(0-3)
29.08.2007	Apia	American Samoa - Vanuatu	0-15(0-5)
29.08.2007	Apia	Samoa - Tonga	2-1(1-0)
01.09.2007	Apia	Tonga – American Samoa	4-0(1-0)
01.09.2007	Apia	Vanuatu - Solomon Islands	0-2(0-0)
03.09.2007	Apia	Samoa - Solomon Islands	0-3(0-2)
03.09.2007	Apia	Tonga - Vanuatu	1-4(0-3)

FINAL STANDINGS

1.	**Solomon Islands**	4	4	0	0	21	-	1	12
2.	**Vanuatu**	4	3	0	1	23	-	3	9
3.	Samoa	4	2	0	2	9	-	8	6
4.	Tonga	4	1	0	3	6	-	10	3
5.	American Samoa	4	0	0	4	1	-	38	0

25.08.2007, Toleafoa „Joseph S. Blatter" Complex, Apia (Samoa); Attendance: 300
Referee: Salaiau Sosongan (Papua New Guinea)
SOLOMON ISLANDS – AMERICAN SAMOA   **12-1(5-0)**
SOL: Fred Hale, David Taro, Samson Takayama, George Suri, Alick Maemae (Stanley Waita 46), Judd Molea, Commins Menapi, George Lui, Benjamin Totori (Godwin Beubeu 46), Gideon Omokirio, Henry Fa'arodo (James Naka 46). Trainer: Ayrton Andrioli (Brazil).
ASA: Jordan Penitusi, Terence Sinapati, Pita Sinapati (67.Tuaoloina Solofa), Pesamino Victor, Alexander Victor (61.Thomas Leota), Natia Natia, Maika Molesi, Hansel Maiava, Tafuna Toilolo, Uasilaa Heleta, Ramin Ott (84.Sue Tonise). Trainer: David Brand (England).
Goals: 1-0 Benjamin Totori (12), 2-0 Benjamin Totori (15), 3-0 Commins Menapi (20 penalty), 4-0 Commins Menapi (41), 5-0 Henry Fa'arodo (43), 5-1 Ramin Ott (55 penalty), 6-1 Stanley Waita (58), 7-1 Godwin Beubeu (69), 8-1 Commins Menapi (75), 9-1 Judd Molea (77), 10-1 Commins Menapi (82), 11-1 Stanley Waita (85), 12-1 Samson Takayama (90+2).
Cautions: Pita Sinapati.

25.08.2007, Toleafoa „Joseph S. Blatter" Complex, Apia (Samoa); Attendance: 300
Referee: Averii Jacques (Tahiti)
VANUATU - SAMOA   **4-0(2-0)**
VAN: Chiku Mansale, Ken Masauvakalo, Fedy Vava, Moise Poida (89.Tom Philip Tomake), Jean Nako Naprapol (75.Seule Soromon), Fenedy Masauvakalo, Pita David Maki, Richard Iwai, Geoffrey Lego Gete, Jacques Mafil Nawan (70.Samson Obed), Maki Haitong. Trainer: Robert Calvo.
SAM: Pasi Schwalger, Damien Fonoti, Chris Cahill, Fauivi Ugapo, Desmond Faaiuaso, Junior Michael (77.Joseph Hoeflich), Filipo Bureta, Lionel Taylor, Bevan Kapisi (58.Fereti Gosche), Penitito Tumua, Sakaria Fuimaono. Trainer: Falevi Umutaua.
Goals: 1-0 Richard Iwai (21), 2-0 Jean Nako Naprapol (43), 3-0 Moise Poida (66), 4-0 Seule Soromon

(90+2).
Cautions: Pita David Maki / Chris Cahill, Junior Michael, Joseph Hoeflich.

27.08.2007, Toleafoa „Joseph S. Blatter" Complex, Apia (Samoa); Attendance: 350
Referee: Fiti Aimaasu (Samoa)
SOLOMON ISLANDS - TONGA   **4-0(2-0)**
SOL: Fred Hale, David Taro, Marlon Houkarawa, Samson Takayama, George Suri, Alick Maemae, Godwin Bebeu (69.James Naka), Commins Menapi, George Lui (46.Judd Molea), Henry Faarodo, George Aba (46.Stanley Waita). Trainer: Ayrton Andrioli (Brazil).
TGA: Kavakava Manumua, Sione Ongol Uhatahi, Kava Huihauhau, Folio Moeaki, Pio Palu, Sione Vea Tahitua, Kamaliele Papani, Ilalio Leakona (46.Tevita Takai), Unaloto-Ki-Atenoa Feao, Malakai Savieti (53.Lafaele Moala), Semisi Tuifangaloka. Trainer: Kilife Uele.
Goals: 1-0 Commins Menapi (5), 2-0 Commins Menapi (12), 3-0 Henry Faarodo (51), 4-0 Alick Maemae (66).
Cautions: George Lui, Marlon Houkarawa / Unaloto-Ki-Atenoa Feao, Kamaliele Papani, Pio Palu, Tevita Takai.

27.08.2007, Toleafoa „Joseph S. Blatter" Complex, Apia (Samoa); Attendance: 2,800
Referee: Job Ponis Minan (Papua New Guinea)
AMERICAN SAMOA - SAMOA   **0-7(0-3)**
ASA: Jordan Penitusi, Terence Sinapati, Pita Sinapati (78.Frankie Silao), Pesamino Victor, Alexander Victor (60.Thomas Leota), Natia Natia (75.Johnny Saelua), Maika Molesi, Hansel Maiava, Tafuna Toilolo, Uasilaa Heleta, Ramin Ott. Trainer: David Brand (England).
SAM: Pasi Schwalger (Filipo Uli 77), Damien Fonoti, Chris Cahill, Fauivi Ugapo, Desmond Faaiuaso, Junior Michael, Filipo Bureta, Lionel Taylor (Edwin Tyrell 73), Bevan Kapisi, Penitito Tumua, Sakaria Fuimaono (Horst Petana 80). Trainer: Falevi Umutaua.
Goals: 0-1 Penitito Tumua (24), 0-2 Desmond Faaiuaso (29), 0-3 Chris Cahill (43 penalty), 0-4 Penitito Tumua (51), 0-5 Damien Fonoti (61), 0-6 Chris Cahill (67), 0-7 Junior Michael (76).
Cautions: Terence Sinapati, Pesamino Victor / , Sakaria Fuimaono, Desmond Faaiuaso.

29.08.2007, Toleafoa „Joseph S. Blatter" Complex, Apia (Samoa); Attendance: 200
Referee: Michael Hester (New Zealand)
AMERICAN SAMOA - VANUATU   **0-15(0-5)**
ASA: Jordan Penitusi, Terence Sinapati (Cap), Pita Sinapati (58.Sue Tonise), Pesamino Victor (17.Johnny Saelua), Alexander Victor, Tuaoloina Solofa (70.Ieti Taulealo), Thomas Leota, Maika Molesi, Tafuna Toilolo, Uasilaa Heleta, Ramin Ott. Trainer: David Brand (England).
VAN: David Chilia, Ken Masauvakalo, Rexley Tarivuti, Andrew Chichirua, Fedy Vava, Moise Poida (Cap) (56.Derek Malas), Tom Philip Tomake, Etienne Mermer, Fenedy Masauvakalo (66.Samson Obed), François Sakama, Richard Iwai (46.Seule Soromon). Trainer: Alwyn Job.
Goals: 0-1 Moise Poida (19), 0-2 Etienne Mermer (24), 0-3 Etienne Mermer (45), 0-4 Etienne Mermer (45+1), 0-5 François Sakama (43), 0-6 Andrew Chichirua (56), 0-7 Richard Iwai (62), 0-8 Etienne Mermer (68), 0-9 Tom Phillip Tomake (72), 0-10 François Sakama (79), 0-11 Suele Soromon (81), 0-12 Suele Soromon (84), 0-13 Suele Soromon (86), 0-14 François Sakama (90+1), 0-15 Suele Soromon (90+2).
Cautions: Terence Sinapati.

29.08.2007, Toleafoa „Joseph S. Blatter" Complex, Apia (Samoa); Attendance: 1,850
Referee: Salaiau Sosongan (Papua New Guinea)
SAMOA - TONGA   **2-1(1-0)**
SAM: Pasi Schwalger, Damien Fonoti, Chris Cahill (Cap) (85.Voa Sauaga), Fauivi Ugapo, Desmond Faaiuaso, Junior Michael, Filipo Bureta, Lionel Taylor, Bevan Kapisi, Penitito Tumua, Sakaria Fuimaono. Trainer: Falevi Umutaua.
TGA: Kavakava Manumua, Sione Ongoi Uhatahi (9.Kaisani Uhatahi), Kava Huihahau, Folio Moeaki, Pio Palu, Sione Vea Tahitua, Kamaliele Papani, Unaloto-Ki-Atenoa Feao (Cap), Malakai Savieti

(86.Lafaele Moala), Sione Tovo, Semisi Tuifangaloka. Trainer: Kilifi Uele.
Goals: 1-0 Desmond Faaiuaso (45+1), 1-1 Unaloto-Ki-Atenoa Feao (54), 2-1 Lionel Taylor (83).
Cautions: Junior Michael, Chris Cahill, Lionel Taylor / Sione Vea Tahitua, Kamaliele Papani, Kaisani Uhatahi.

01.09.2007, Toleafoa „Joseph S. Blatter" Complex, Apia (Samoa); Attendance: 200
Referee: Job Ponis Minan (Papua New Guinea)
TONGA – AMERICAN SAMOA   **4-0(1-0)**
TGA: Kavakava Manumua, Folio Moeaki, Pio Palu, Sione Vea Tahitua, Unaloto Feao (76.Malakai Savieti), Lafaele Moala, Mark Uhatahi (82.Lisaniasi Kainga), Kaisani Uhatahi, Sione Tovo, Semisi Tuifangaloka, Kaliopasi Uele (46.Matana Paongo). Trainer: Kilifi Uele.
ASA: Jordan Penitusi, Pita Sinipati (88.Sue Tonise), Pesamino Victor, Thomas Leota (81.Johnny Saelua), Natia Natia, Maika Molesi, Hansel Maiava, Tafuna Toilolo, Uasilaa Heleta, Ramin Ott, Alexander Victor (74.Frankie Silao). Trainer: David Brand (England).
Goals: 1-0 Lafaele Moala (38), 2-0 Pio Palu (56), 3-0 Pio Palu (63), 4-0 Kaisani Uhatahi (86).
Cautions: Ramin Ott.

01.09.2007, Toleafoa „Joseph S. Blatter" Complex, Apia (Samoa); Attendance: 1,000
Referee: Averii Jacques (Tahiti)
VANUATU - SOLOMON ISLANDS   **0-2(0-0)**
VAN: Chikau Mansale, Ken Masauvakalo, Fedy Vava, Moise Poida (Cap), Jean Nako Naprapol, Seule Soromon (56.Tom Philip Tomake), Fenedy Masauvakalo, Pita David Maki (67.François Sakama), Richard Iwai (46.Etienne Mermer), Geoffrey Lego Gete, Jacques Mafil Nawan. Trainer: Alwyn Job.
SOL: Fred Hale, David Taro, Samson Takayama, George Suri, Alick Maemae, Godwin Bebeu (76.Benjamin Totori), Judd Molea, Commins Menapi (Cap), George Lui (52.Stanley Waita), Gideon Omokorio, Henry Faarodo. Trainer: Ayrton Andrioli (Brazil).
Goals: 0-1 Godwin Bebeu (60), 0-2 Henry Faarodo (64).
Cautions: Tom Philip Tomake / Gideon Omokorio, George Lui.

03.09.2007, Toleafoa „Joseph S. Blatter" Complex, Apia (Samoa); Attendance: 200
Referee: Michael Hester (New Zealand)
SAMOA - SOLOMON ISLANDS   **0-3(0-2)**
SAM: Pasi Schwalger, Damien Fonoti (53.Fereti Gosche), Jerrell Sale (61.Max Tom Hoeflich), Fauivi Ugapo, Desmond Faaiuaso, Filipo Bureta, Lionel Taylor, Bevan Kapisi (64.Voa Sauaga), Penitito Tumua, Horst Petana, Sakaria Fuimaono. Trainer: Falevi Umutaua.
SOL: Fred Hale, David Taro (65.Tome Faisi), Samson Takayama, George Suri, Godwin Bebeu (66.Commins Menapi), Judd Molea, James Naka, Benjamin Totori (66.Alick Maemae), Mostyn Beui, Stanley Waita, George Aba. Trainer: Ayrton Andrioli (Brazil).
Goals: 0-1 Benjamin Totori (1), 0-2 Benjamin Totori (37), 0-3 Alick Maemae (69).
Cautions: Bevan Kapisi, Lionel Taylor, Sakaria Fuimaono, Filipo Bureta / Mostyn Beui, Stanley Waita.

03.09.2007, Toleafoa „Joseph S. Blatter" Complex, Apia (Samoa); Attendance:
Referee: Job Ponis Minan (Papua New Guinea)
TONGA - VANUATU   **1-4(0-3)**
TGA: Kavakava Manumea (90+2.Kinikini Kau), Folio Moeaki, Matana Paongo (36.Lisaniasi Kainga), Pio Palu, Sione Vea Tahitua (65.Sione Tovo), Kamaliele Papani, Ilalio Leakona, Malakai Savieti, Lafaele Moala, Kaisani Uhatahi, Semisi Tuifangaloka. Trainer: Kilifi Uele.
VAN: Chikau Mansale, Ken Masauvakalo, Rexley Tarivuti, Andrew Chichirua, Fedy Vava, Moise Poida, Tom Philip Tomake (46.Derek Malas), Seule Soromon (75.Victor Maleb), Fenedy Masauvakalo, François Sakama, Maki Haitong (62.Richard Iwai). Trainer: Robert Calvo.
Goals: 0-1 Seule Soromon (24), 0-2 Seule Soromon (34), 0-3 Seule Soromon (41), 1-3 Malakai Savieti (50), 1-4 Victor Maleb (76).
Cautions: Kamaliele Papani.

SEMI-FINALS

05.09.2007, Toleafoa „Joseph S. Blatter" Complex, Apia (Samoa); Attendance: 1,500
Referee: Job Ponis Minan (Papua New Guinea)
SOLOMON ISLANDS – NEW CALEDONIA   **2-3(1-1)**
SOL: Fred Hale, David Taro, Samson Takayama, George Suri, Alick Maemae, Judd Molea, Commins Menapi (Cap) (89.Marlon Houkarawa), George Lui (66.Stanley Waita), Benjamin Totori, Gideon Omokirio, Henry Faarodo. Trainer: Ayrton Andrioli (Brazil).
NCL: Marc Ounemoa, André Naxue (46.Wilson Forest), Robert Wayaridi, George Wadenges, Yohann Mercier, Marius Mapou, Pierre Wajoka (Cap), Jose Hmaé (90+1.Luther Wahnyamalla), Adolphe Boaoutho, Iamel Kabeu, Poulidor Toto. Trainer: Didier Chambaron (France).
Goals: 0-1 Iamel Kabeu (37), 1-1 Henry Faarodo (40), 2-1 Commins Menapi (47), 2-2 Poulidor Toto (54), 2-3 Yohann Mercier (90+4).
Cautions: Alick Maemae, Benjamin Totori, George Suri, Gideon Omokirio / Pierre Wajoka.
Sent off: Alick Maemae (68), Gideon Omokirio (84).

05.09.2007, Toleafoa „Joseph S. Blatter" Complex, Apia (Samoa); Attendance: 600
Referee: Michael Hester (New Zealand)
FIJI - VANUATU   **3-0(1-0)**
FIJ: Simione Tamanisau, Samuela Vula, Ronil Kumar, Pita Baleitoga (62.Roy Krishna), Peni Finau (Cap), Taniela Waqa (70.Thomas Vulivuli), Salesh Kumar, Malakai Tiwa (77.Alvin Avinesh), Malakai Kainihewe, Osea Vakatalesau, Pita Rabo. Trainer: Juan Carlos Buzzetti (Uruguay).
VAN: Chikau Mansale, Samson Obed, Ken Masauvakalo, Fedy Vava, Moise Poida (Cap) (54.François Sakama), Tom Philip Tomake, Jean Nako Naprapol, Seule Soromon (79.Etienne Mermer), Fenedy Masauvakalo, Geoffrey Lego Gete, Jacques Mafil Nawan (75.Derek Malas). Trainer: Robert Calvo.
Goals: 1-0 Pita Baleitoga (44), 2-0 Osea Vakatalesau (69 penalty), 3-0 Roy Krishna (70).
Cautions: Geoffrey Lego Gete, Samson Obed, François Sakama, Tom Philip Tomake.

THIRD PLACE PLAY-OFF

07.09.2007, Toleafoa „Joseph S. Blatter" Complex, Apia (Samoa); Attendance: 200
Referee: Averii Jacques (Tahiti)
SOLOMON ISLANDS - VANUATU   **0-2(0-1)**
SOL: Fred Hale, David Taro, Marlon Houkarawa (71.George Aba), Samson Takayama, George Suri, Judd Molea, Commins Menapi (Cap), George Lui (46.Godwin Bebeu), Benjamin Totori, Stanley Waita (83.Mostyn Beui), Henry Faarodo. Trainer: Ayrton Andrioli (Brazil).
VAN: Chikau Mansale, Samson Obed, Ken Masauvakalo (Cap), Fedy Vava, Tom Philip Tomake (88.Moise Poida), Jean Nako Naprapol (69.Etienne Mermer), Seule Soromon, Fenedy Masauvakalo (69.Derek Malas), François Sakama, Geoffrey Lego Gete, Jacques Mafil Nawan. Trainer: Robert Calvo.
Goals: 0-1 Seule Soromon (45+3), 0-2 François Sakama (51).
Cautions: Benjamin Totori, George Suri, Stanley Waita, Mostyn Beui / François Sakama, Jacques Mafil Nawan, Tom Philip Tomake.

FINAL

07.09.2007, Toleafoa „Joseph S. Blatter" Complex, Apia (Samoa); Attendance: 400
Referee: Michael Hester (New Zealand)
NEW CALEDONIA - FIJI   **1-0(0-0)**
NCL: Marc Ounemoa, Wilson Forest, Robert Wayaridi, George Wadenges, Yohann Mercier, Marius Mapou, Pierre Wajoka (Cap), José Hmaé, Adolphe Boaoutho, Iamel Kabeu (69.Luther Wahnyamalla), Poulidor Toto. Trainer: Didier Chambaron (France).
FIJ: Simione Tamanisau, Samuela Vula, Ronil Kumar (65.Thomas Vulivuli), Pita Baleitoga (51.Roy

Krishna), Peni Finau (Cap), Taniela Waqa, Salesh Kumar, Malakai Tiwa, Malakai Kainihewe, Osea Vakatalesau, Pita Rabo. Trainer: Juan Carlos Buzzetti (Uruguay).
Goal: 1-0 José Hmaé (61).
Cautions: Pierre Wajoka, Poulidor Toto, Wilson Forest / Peni Finau, Taniela Waqa, Thomas Vulivuli, Osea Vakatalesau, Roy Krishna, Malakai Tiwa.

SECOND PHASE
(2008 OFC Nations Cup)

17.10.2007	Lautoka	Fiji – New Zealand	0-2(0-1)
17.11.2007	Port Vila	Vanuatu – New Zealand	1-2(1-0)
17.11.2007	Ba	Fiji – New Caledonia	3-3(2-0)
21.11.2007	Wellington	New Zealand - Vanuatu	4-1(3-0)
21.11.2007	Noumea	New Caledonia - Fiji	4-0(2-0)
14.06.2008	Port Vila	Vanuatu - New Caledonia	1-1(0-0)
21.06.2008	Noumea	New Caledonia - Vanuatu	3-0(1-0)
06.09.2008	Ba	Fiji - Vanuatu	2-0(1-0)
06.09.2008	Noumea	New Caledonia – New Zealand	1-3(0-1)
10.09.2008	Port Vila	Vanuatu - Fiji	2-1(0-0)
10.09.2008	Auckland	New Zealand - New Caledonia	3-0(0-0)
19.11.2008	Lautoka (Fiji)	New Zealand - Fiji	0-2(0-0)

FINAL STANDINGS

1.	**New Zealand**	6	5	0	1	14	-	5	15
2.	New Caledonia	6	2	2	2	12	-	10	8
3.	Fiji	6	2	1	3	8	-	11	7
4.	Vanuatu	6	1	1	4	5	-	13	4

17.10.2007, Churchill Park, Lautoka; Attendance: 6,000
Referee: Jair Marrufo (United States)
FIJI – NEW ZEALAND   **0-2(0-1)**
FIJ: Simione Tamanisau, Peni Finau, Malakai Kainihewe, Samuela Vula, Taniela Waga, Ronil Kumar (59.Pita Baleitoga), Salesh Kumar, Malakai Tiwa (71.Alvin Avinesh), Roy Krishna, Pita Rabo (Cap) (78.Maciu Samaidrawa Dunadamu), Osea Vakatalesau. Trainer: Juan Carlos Buzzetti (Uruguay).
NZL: Mark Nelson Paston, Ivan Robert Vicelich, Andrew Victor Boyens (64.Benjamin Robert Sigmund), Tony James Lochhead, David James Mulligan (58.Jeffrey Campbell), Timothy Brown (Cap), Jeremy John Christie, Duncan Edward Oughton, Leonida Christos Bertos, Shane Edward Smeltz, Christopher John Killen (88.Jarrod Brian Stockley Smith). Trainer: Richard Lloyd Herbert.
Goals: 0-1 Ivan Robert Vicelich (33), Shane Edward Smeltz (87).
Cautions: Alvin Avinesh / Christopher John Killen, Jeffrey Campbell.

17.11.2007, Korman Stadium, Port Vila; Attendance: 8,000
Referee: Job Ponis Minan (Papua New Guinea)
VANUATU – NEW ZEALAND   **1-2(1-0)**
VAN: Chikau Mansale (82.David Chilia), Geoffrey Gete, Pita David Maki (68.Moise Poida), Ken Masauvakalo, Jacques Mafil Nawan, Hubert Nake (50.Andrew Chichirua), Alphonse Qorig, Fedy Vava, Fenedy Masauvakalo, Jean Nako Naprapol, Seule Soromon. Trainer: Robert Calvo.
NZL: Mark Nelson Paston, Andrew Victor Boyens, Duncan Edward Oughton, James Keith Pritchett, Benjamin Robert Sigmund, Tony James Lochhead, Ivan Robert Vicelich (71.David James Mulligan), Timothy Brown, Christopher Paul James (68.Jarrod Brian Stockley Smith), Leonida Christos Bertos, Shane Edward Smeltz (84.Daniel Ellensohn). Trainer: Richard Lloyd Herbert.
Goals: 1-0 Jean Nako Naprapol (32), 1-1 Shane Edward Smeltz (53), 1-2 David James Mulligan (90+3).

Cautions: Geoffrey Gete / Timothy Brown.

17.11.2007, Govind Park, Ba; Attendance: 1,500
Referee: Peter O'Leary (New Zealand)
FIJI – NEW CALEDONIA   **3-3(2-0)**
FIJ: Shamal Kumar, Peni Finau, Malakai Kainihewe, Esava Maqeleea, Apisalome Tuvura, Taniela Waga, Pita Baleitoga (75.Ronil Kumar), Roy Krishna, Valerio Nawatu, Pita Rabo (Cap), Osea Vakatalesau. Trainer: Juan Carlos Buzzetti (Uruguay).
NCL: Marc Ounemoa, Adolphe Boaoutho, André Sinedo, Georges Wadenges, Benjamin Longue, Marius Mapou, Yohann Mercier, Fabien Saridjan (80.Jean Wenessia), Jean-Patrick Wakanumuné (39.Patrick Diaike), Ramon Djamali (70.Noel Kaudre), Michel Hmaé. Trainer: Didier Chambaron (France).
Goals: 1-0 Valerio Nawatu (2), 2-0 Osea Vakatalesau (27), 2-1 Ramon Djamali (66), 2-2 Noel Kaudre (83), 3-2 Osea Vakatalesau (86), 3-3 Michel Hmaé (87).
Cautions: Peni Finau / Marius Mapou.

21.11.2007, Westpac Stadium, Wellington; Attendance: 2,500
Referee: Averii Jacques (Tahiti)
NEW ZEALAND - VANUATU   **4-1(3-0)**
NZL: Mark Nelson Paston, Andrew Victor Boyens, Duncan Edward Oughton, Benjamin Robert Sigmund, Jeremy John Christie (76.James Keith Pritchett), Tony James Lochhead, David James Mulligan (87.Jeffrey Campbell), Ivan Robert Vicelich, Timothy Brown, Leonida Christos Bertos, Shane Edward Smeltz (73.Jarrod Brian Stockley Smith). Trainer: Richard Lloyd Herbert.
VAN: Chikau Mansale, Ephraim Kalorib (42.Rexley Tarivuti), Ken Masauvakalo, Tom Philip Tomake (90+1.Derek Malas), Moise Poida, François Sakama, Fedy Vava, Fenedy Masauvakalo (46.Seule Soromon), Jean Nako Naprapol, Jacques Mafil Nawan, Jean Robert Yelou. Trainer: Robert Calvo.
Goals: 1-0 David James Mulligan (17), 2-0 Shane Edward Smeltz (29 penalty), 3-0 Shane Edward Smeltz (34), 3-1 François Sakama (50), 4-1 David James Mulligan (81).
Cautions: David James Mulligan, Timothy Brown / Tom Philip Tomake, Jacques Mafil Nawan.
Sent off: Timothy Brown (90+4).

21.11.2007, Stade Numa-Daly Magenta, Noumea; Attendance: 1,000
Referee: Matthew Christopher Breeze (Australia)
NEW CALEDONIA - FIJI   **4-0(2-0)**
NCL: Marc Ounemoa, Adolphe Boaoutho (71.Marius Bako), André Sinedo, Georges Wadenges, Benjamin Longue, Marius Mapou, Yohann Mercier, Fabien Saridjan, Pierre Wajoka, Ramon Djamali (56.Patrick Diaike), Michel Hmaé (84.Noel Kaudre). Trainer: Didier Chambaron (France).
FIJ: Benaminio Mateinaaqara, Malakai Kainihewe (46.Apisalome Tuvura), Esava Maqeleea (65.Maciu Samaidrawa Dunadamu), Samuela Vula, Pita Baleitoga, Samuela Ibo Kautoga, Ronil Kumar, Jone Vesikula, Valerio Nawatu (46.Roy Krishna), Pita Rabo (Cap), Osea Vakatalesau. Trainer: Juan Carlos Buzzetti (Uruguay).
Goals: 1-0 Pierre Wajoka (29 penalty), 2-0 Michel Hmaé (32), 3-0 Michel Hmaé (61), 4-0 Marius Mapou (64).
Cautions: Benjamin Longue, Marius Mapou / Valerio Nawatu, Pita Rabo, Apisalome Tuvura.

14.06.2008, Korman Stadium, Port Vila; Attendance: 4,000
Referee: Rakesh Varman (Fiji)
VANUATU - NEW CALEDONIA   **1-1(0-0)**
VAN: John Presley Garae, Geoffrey Gete, Ken Masauvakalo, Samson Obed, Michael Kaltack (53.Jeffry Nimanian), Hubert Nake, Moise Poida (81.Jean Robert Yelou), Alphonse Qorig, François Sakama, Jean Nako Naprapol (73.Etienne Mermer), Robert Tom. Trainer: Robert Calvo.
NCL: Michel Hné, Wilson Forest, Georges Wadenges, Benjamin Longue, Bertrand Kai (19.Patrick Diaike), Marius Mapou, Pierre Wajoka, Jean-Patrick Wakanumuné, Luther Wahnyamalla (58.Noel Kaudre), Ramon Djamali, Michel Hmaé (67.Kalase Gnipate). Trainer: Didier Chambaron (France).

Goals: 0-1 Ramon Djamali (73), 1-1 Etienne Mermer (77).
Cautions: Alphonse Qorig, Samson Obed / Ramon Djamali.

21.06.2008, Stade Numa-Daly Magenta, Noumea; Attendance: 2,700
Referee: Michael Hester (New Zealand)
NEW CALEDONIA - VANUATU   **3-0(1-0)**
NCL: Michel Hné, Wilson Forest (88.Jaerson Haeweng), Georges Wadenges, Benjamin Longue, Bertrand Kai, Marius Mapou, Pierre Wajoka, Jean-Patrick Wakanumuné, Luther Wahnyamalla (19.Patrick Diaike), Ramon Djamali, Michel Hmaé (72.Jean-Christophe Xenie). Trainer: Didier Chambaron (France).
VAN: Chikau Mansale, Geoffrey Gete, Ken Masauvakalo, Jacques Mafil Nawan (36.Jeffry Nimanian), Hubert Nake, Moise Poida, Alphonse Qorig (52.Peter Toa), François Sakama, Fedy Vava, Etienne Mermer (66.Michael Kaltack), Jean Nako Naprapol. Trainer: Robert Calvo.
Goals: 1-0 Pierre Wajoka (36), 2-0 Michel Hmaé (60), 3-0 Patrick Diaike (87).
Cautions: Jean-Christophe Xenie, Wilson Forest / Chikau Mansale, Moise Poida.
Sent off: Ken Masauvakalo (12).

06.09.2008, Govind Park, Ba; Attendance: 3,000
Referee: Job Ponis Minan (Papua New Guinea)
FIJI - VANUATU   **2-0(1-0)**
FIJ: Benaminio Mateinaaqara, Malakai Kainihewe, Esava Maqeleea, Taniela Waga, Pita Baleitoga (80.Alvin Singh), Salesh Kumar, Ronil Kumar (64.Lagi Dyer), Rajnil Ritesh Chand, Malakai Tiwa (Cap), Roy Krishna, Tuimasi Manuca (61.Maciu Samaidrawa Dunadamu). Trainer: Juan Carlos Buzzetti (Uruguay).
VAN: Chikau Mansale (43.John Presley Garae), Geoffrey Gete, Pita David Maki, Joseph Namariau (77.Jeffry Nimanian), Samson Obed, Seimata Chilia, François Sakama (70.Michael Kaltack), Fedy Vava, Jean Nako Naprapol, Robert Tom, Jean Robert Yelou. Trainer: William Malas.
Goals: 1-0 Salesh Kumar (7), 2-0 Maciu Samaidrawa Dunadamu (87).
Cautions: Pita Baleitoga / Fedy Vava, Jean Robert Yelou.

06.09.2008, Stade Numa-Daly Magenta, Noumea; Attendance: 2,589
Referee: Rakesh Varman (Fiji)
NEW CALEDONIA – NEW ZEALAND   **1-3(0-1)**
NCL: Marc Ounemoa, Jonathan Kakou (73.Allan Hnautra), Georges Wadenges, Patrick Diaike, Bertrand Kai (23.Noel Kaudre), Marius Mapou, Pierre Wajoka, Jean-Patrick Wakanumuné, Luther Wahnyamalla, Ramon Djamali (68.Poulidor Toto), Michel Hmaé. Trainer: Didier Chambaron (France).
NZL: Glen Moss, Ryan William Nelsen, Duncan Edward Oughton, Benjamin Robert Sigmund, Tony James Lochhead, David James Mulligan, Simon John Elliott, Allan David Pearce (55.Jeremy John Christie), Jeremy Russell Brockie, Shane Edward Smeltz, Jarrod Brian Stockley Smith (90+1.Christopher Paul James). Trainer: Richard Lloyd Herbert.
Goals: 0-1 Benjamin Robert Sigmund (16), 1-1 Michel Hmaé (55), 1-2 Shane Edward Smeltz (65), 1-3 Shane Edward Smeltz (75).
Cautions: Poulidor Toto / Jeremy John Christie.

10.09.2008, Korman Stadium, Port Vila; Attendance: 1,200
Referee: Peter O'Leary (New Zealand)
VANUATU - FIJI   **2-1(0-0)**
VAN: John Presley Garae, Geoffrey Gete, Roger Joe, Pita David Maki (80.Derek Malas), Ken Masauvakalo, Joseph Namariau, Seimata Chilia, Hubert Nake (71.Michael Kaltack), Moise Poida (61.Rexley Tarivuti), François Sakama, Robert Tom. Trainer: William Malas.
FIJ: Benaminio Mateinaaqara, Malakai Kainihewe (46.Alvin Singh), Manueli Kalaou (39.Samuela Vula), Esava Maqeleea, Taniela Waga, Ronil Kumar (67.Rajnil Ritesh Chand), Malakai Tiwa, Maciu Samaidrawa Dunadamu, Lagi Dyer, Roy Krishna, Tuimasi Manuca. Trainer: Juan Carlos Buzzetti (Uruguay).

Goals: 1-0 François Sakama (59), 2-0 Derek Malas (90+2), 2-1 Maciu Samaidrawa Dunadamu (90+3).
Cautions: Pita David Maki, Geoffrey Gete, Robert Tom / Rajnil Ritesh Chand.
Sent off: Geoffrey Gete (52).

10.09.2008, North Harbour Stadium, Auckland; Attendance: 8,000
Referee: Norbert Hauata (Tahiti)
NEW ZEALAND - NEW CALEDONIA   **3-0(0-0)**
NZL: Mark Nelson Paston, Ryan William Nelsen (63.Andrew Victor Boyens), Duncan Edward Oughton (66.Jeremy John Christie), Benjamin Robert Sigmund, Tony James Lochhead, David James Mulligan, Timothy Brown, Simon John Elliott, Christopher Paul James, Shane Edward Smeltz (84.Steven David Old), Jarrod Brian Stockley Smith. Trainer: Richard Lloyd Herbert.
NCL: Michel Hné, Allan Hnautra (63.Patrick Diaike), Jonathan Kakou, André Sinedo, Georges Wadenges, Roy Kayara (46.Luther Wahnyamalla), Marius Mapou, Pierre Wajoka, Jean-Patrick Wakanumuné (84.Cédric Nonmeu), Ramon Djamali, Michel Hmaé. Trainer: Didier Chambaron (France).
Goals: 1-0 Shane Edward Smeltz (49), 2-0 Jeremy John Christie (69), 3-0 Shane Edward Smeltz (76).
Cautions: Timothy Brown.

19.11.2008, Churchill Park, Lautoka (Fiji)*; Attendance: 4,500
Referee: Lencie Fred (Vanuatu)
NEW ZEALAND - FIJI   **0-2(0-0)**
NZL: Glen Moss, Steven David Old, James Keith Pritchett, Benjamin Robert Sigmund, Jeremy John Christie, David James Mulligan, Cole Robert Peverley, Leonida Christos Bertos, Kosta Barbarouses (69.Kris Bright), Jeremy Russell Brockie, Gregory Alexander Draper (60.Jacob Spoonley). Trainer: Richard Lloyd Herbert.
FIJ: Simione Tamanisau, Peni Finau, Malakai Kainihewe (46.Jone Vonu), Esava Maqeleea, Laita Tuilau, Pita Baleitoga, Salesh Kumar, Malakai Tiwa, Roy Krishna, Alvin Singh, Osea Vakatalesau (78.Tuimasi Manuca). Trainer: Juan Carlos Buzzetti (Uruguay).
Goals: 0-1 Roy Krishna (63), 0-2 Roy Krishna (90).
Cautions: Salesh Kumar, Peni Finau.
Sent off: Glen Moss (60).
This game was originally scheduled for 13 October 2007, but was postponed by FIFA after Fijian goalkeeper Simione Tamanisau was denied a visa by the New Zealand immigration authorities. The match was first rescheduled to be played in the neutral country of Samoa, later moved to Fiji.

INTERCONTINENTAL PLAY-OFFS

10.10.2009, National Stadium, Manama; Attendance: 37,000
Referee: Viktor Kassai (Hungary)
BAHRAIN – NEW ZEALAND   **0-0**
BHR: Sayed Mohammed Jaffer Sabet, Sayed Mohamed Adnan, Hussain Ali Baba Mohamed, Mohamed Ahmed Hubail, Abdullah Omar Ismail, Mohamed Ahmed Yusuf Salmeen (Cap), Sayed Mahmood Jalal Al Wadaei, Faouzi Mubarak Aaish, Salman Issa Ghuloom (79.Mahmood Abdulrahman Mohammed Noor), Jaycee John Akwani Okwunwanne (86.A'ala Ahmed Hubail), Husain Ali Ahmed Ahmed Abdulla (86.Ismaeel Abdullatif Hasan). Trainer: Milan Máčala (Czech Republic).
NZL: Mark Nelson Paston, Ryan William Nelsen (Cap), Benjamin Robert Sigmund, Ivan Robert Vicelich, Leonida Christos Bertos, Tony James Lochhead, Timothy Brown (68.Michael Ryan McGlinchey), Simon John Elliott, Shane Edward Smeltz, Rory Michael Fallon (66.Christopher Grant Wood), Christopher John Killen. Trainer: Richard Lloyd Herbert.
Cautions: Mark Nelson Paston, Ryan William Nelsen

14.11.2009, Westpac Stadium, Wellington; Attendance: 36,500
Referee: Jorge Luis Larrionda Pietrafesa (Uruguay)
NEW ZEALAND - BAHRAIN   **1-0(1-0)**
NZL: Mark Nelson Paston, Ryan William Nelsen (Cap), Benjamin Robert Sigmund, Ivan Robert Vicelich, Leonida Christos Bertos, Tony James Lochhead, Timothy Brown (90.Andrew Victor Boyens), Michael Ryan McGlinchey (64.Andrew Barron), Shane Edward Smeltz, Rory Michael Fallon, Christopher John Killen (82.Christopher Grant Wood). Trainer: Richard Lloyd Herbert.
BHR: Sayed Mohammed Jaffer Sabet, Mohamed Ahmed Hubail (85.Ahmed Hassan Taleb), Babatunde Fatai-Baba Fatadi, Sayed Mohamed Adnan, Salman Issa Ghuloom, Hussain Ali Baba Mohamed, Mohamed Ahmed Yusuf Salmeen (Cap), Sayed Mahmood Jalal Al Wadaei (79.Mahmood Abdulrahman Mohammed Noor), Faouzi Mubarak Aaish (73.Ismaeel Abdullatif Hasan), Abdulla Abdi Omar Yasser, Jaycee John Akwani Okwunwanne. Trainer: Milan Máčala (Czech Republic).
Goal: 1-0 Rory Michael Fallon (45).
Cautions: Benjamin Robert Sigmund / Faouzi Mubarak Aaish, Jaycee John Akwani Okwunwanne.
NEW ZEALAND qualified for the Final Tournament.

15.11.2009, Estadio „Ricardo Saprissa", San José; Attendance: 19,500
Referee: Alberto Undiano Mallenco (Spain)
COSTA RICA - URUGUAY   **0-1(0-1)**
CRC: Keylor Antonio Navas Gamboa, Luis Antonio Marín Murillo (63.Rolando Fonseca Jiménez), Gilberto Martínez Vidal (23.Míchael Umaña Corrales), Roy Miller Hernández (77.Darío Alejandro Delgado Mora), Ángel Esteban Sirias Áviles, Cristian Bolaños Navarro, Wálter Centeno Corea (Cap), Randall Azofeifa Corrales, Celso Borges Mora, Bryan Ruiz González, Álvaro Alberto Saborío Chacón. Trainer: René Rodrigues Simões (Brazil).
URU: Néstor Fernando Muslera Micol, Mauricio Bernardo Victorino Dansilio, Diego Alfredo Moreno Lugano (Cap), Diego Roberto Godín Leal, Álvaro Rafael González Luengo, Álvaro Fernández Gay, Sebastián Eguren Ledesma, Álvaro Daniel Pereira Barragán, Marcelo Nicolás Lodeiro Benítez (61.Jorge Rodríguez), Luis Alberto Suárez Díaz (81.Sebastián Bruno Fernández Miglierina), Diego Martín Forlán Corazo. Trainer: Óscar Wáshington Tabárez Silva.
Goal: 0-1 Diego Alfredo Lugano Moreno (21).
Cautions: Randall Azofeifa Corrales, Wálter Centeno Corea / Mauricio Bernardo Victorino Dansilio, Álvaro Fernández Gay, Diego Roberto Godín Leal, Luis Alberto Suárez Díaz.
Sent off: Randall Azofeifa Corrales (52).

19.11.2009, Estadio Centenario, Montevideo; Attendance: 62,150
Referee: Massimo Busacca (Switzerland)
URUGUAY – COSTA RICA   **1-1(0-0)**
URU: Néstor Fernando Muslera Micol, Diego Roberto Godín Leal, Diego Alfredo Lugano Moreno (Cap), Victorio Maximiliano Pereira Páez, Álvaro Daniel Pereira Barragán, Andrés Scotti Ponce de León (72.Mauricio Bernardo Victorino Dansilio), Sebastián Eguren Ledesma, Diego Fernando Pérez Aguado, Marcelo Nicolás Lodeiro Benítez (84.Álvaro Fernández), Diego Martín Forlán Corazo, Luis Alberto Suárez Díaz (65.Washington Sebastián Abreu Gallo). Trainer: Óscar Wáshington Tabárez Silva.
CRC: Keylor Antonio Navas Gamboa, Pablo Herrera Barrantes, Luis Antonio Marín Murillo (69.Álvaro Alberto Saborío Chacón), Roy Miller Hernández, Míchael Umaña Corrales, Júnior Enrique Díaz Campbell, Cristian Bolaños Navarro, Wálter Centeno Corea (Cap), Celso Borges Mora (53.Michael Barrantes Rojas), Bryan Ruiz González, Víctor Nuñez Rodríguez (64.Rolando Fonseca Jiménez). Trainer: René Rodrigues Simões (Brazil).
Goals: 1-0 Washington Sebastián Abreu Gallo (70), 1-1 Wálter Centeno Corea (74).
Cautions: Diego Fernando Pérez Aguado / Cristian Bolaños Navarro, Roy Miller Hernández.
URUGUAY qualified for the Final Tournament.

WORLD CUP
THE FINAL TOURNAMENT

The 19th World Cup Final Tournament was for the first time hosted by an African country and took place between 11 June and 11 July 2010 in South Africa. The World Cup Final Tournament group draw was staged in Cape Town (South Africa), on 4 December 2009 at the Cape Town International Convention Centre. The seeding was based on the October 2009 FIFA World Ranking and seven teams joined hosts South Africa as seeded teams for the final draw. No two teams from the same confederation were to be drawn in the same group, except allowing a maximum of two European teams in a group.

Pot 1 (Seeds: host & top 7):
South Africa, Brazil, Spain, Netherlands, Italy, Germany, Argentina, England.
Pot 2 (Asia, North/Central America and Caribbean & Oceania):
Australia, Japan, Korea DPR, Korea Republic, Honduras, Mexico, United States, New Zealand.
Pot 3 (Africa & South America):
Algeria, Cameroon, Ivory Coast, Ghana, Nigeria, Chile, Paraguay, Uruguay.
Pot 4 (Europe):
Denmark, France, Greece, Portugal, Serbia, Slovakia, Slovenia, Switzerland.
The 32 teams were drawn in following groups:

GROUP A	GROUP B
South Africa	Argentina
Mexico	Nigeria
Uruguay	South Korea
France	Greece

GROUP C	GROUP D
England	Germany
United States	Australia
Algeria	Serbia
Slovenia	Ghana

GROUP E	GROUP F
Holland	Italy
Denmark	Paraguay
Japan	New Zealand
Cameroon	Slovakia

GROUP G	GROUP H
Brazil	Spain
North Korea	Switzerland
Ivory Coast	Honduras
Portugal	Chile

The teams finishing first and second in each group qualified for the Round of 16.

The venues were played in following cities: Bloemfontain (Free State Stadium – Capacity 48,000); Cape Town (Cape Town Stadium – 69,070); Durban („Moses Mabhida" Stadium – 70,000); Johannesburg (Ellis Park Stadium – 62,567, Soccer Stadium – 91,141); Nelspruit (Mbombela Stadium – 43,500); Polokwane („Peter Mokaba" Stadium – 46,000); Port Elizabeth („Nelson Mandela" Bay Stadium – 48,459); Pretoria (Loftus Versfeld Stadium – 51,762); Rustenburg (Royal Bafokeng Stadium – 42,000);

GROUP A

11.06.2010	Johannesburg	South Africa - Mexico	1-1(0-0)
11.06.2010	Cape Town	Uruguay - France	0-0
16.06.2010	Pretoria	South Africa - Uruguay	0-3(0-1)
17.06.2010	Polokwane	France - Mexico	0-2(0-0)
22.06.2010	Rustenburg	Mexico - Uruguay	0-1(0-1)
22.06.2010	Bloemfontein	France – South Africa	1-2(0-2)

FINAL STANDINGS

1.	**Uruguay**	3	2	1	0	4	-	0	7
2.	**Mexico**	3	1	1	1	3	-	2	4
3.	South Africa	3	1	1	1	3	-	5	4
4.	France	3	0	1	2	1	-	4	1

11.06.2010, Soccer City, Johannesburg; Attendance: 84,490
Referee: Ravshan Irmatov (Uzbekistan)
SOUTH AFRICA - MEXICO **1-1(0-0)**
RSA: Itumeleng Isaack Khune, Siboniso Pa Gaxa, Aaron Tebomo Mokoena (Cap), Bongani Khumalo, Lucas Bongane Thwala (46.Peter Tsepo Masilela), Lawrence Siphiwe Tshabalala, Kagiso Evidence Dikgacoi, Reneilwe Letsholonanye, Teko Tsholofelo Modise, Steven Jerome Pienaar (83.Bernard Melvin Parker), Katlego Abel Mphela. Trainer: Carlos Alberto Gomes Parreira (Brazil).
MEX: Óscar Pérez Rojas, Paul Nicolás Aguilar Rojas (55.José Andrés Guardado Hernández), Ricardo Osorio Mendoza, Francisco Javier Rodríguez Pinedo, Carlos Arnoldo Salcido Flores, Rafael Márquez Álvarez, Efraín Juárez Valdéz, Gerardo Torrado Díez de Bonilla (Cap), Giovani dos Santos Ramírez, Carlos Alberto Vela Garrido (69.Cuauhtémoc Blanco Bravo), Guillermo Luis Franco Farquarson (73.Javier Hernández Balcázar). Trainer: Javier Aguirre Onaindía.
Goals: 1-0 Lawrence Siphiwe Tshabalala (55), 1-1 Rafael Márquez Álvarez (79).
Cautions: Kagiso Evidence Dikgacoi, Peter Tsepo Masilela / Efraín Juárez Valdéz, Gerardo Torrado Díez de Bonilla.

11.06.2010, Cape Town Stadium, Cape Town; Attendance: 64,100
Referee: Yuichi Nishimura (Japan)
URUGUAY - FRANCE **0-0**
URU: Néstor Fernando Muslera Micol, Victorio Maximiliano Pereira Páez, Mauricio Bernardo Victorino Dansilio, Diego Alfredo Moreno Lugano (Cap), Diego Roberto Godín Leal, Álvaro Daniel Pereira Barragán, Diego Fernando Pérez Aguado (87.Sebastián Eguren Ledesma), Egidio Raúl Arévalo Ríos, Ignacio María González Gatti (63.Marcelo Nicolás Lodeiro Benítez), Luis Alberto Suárez Díaz (74.Washington Sebastián Abreu Gallo), Diego Martín Forlán Corazo. Trainer: Óscar Wáshington Tabárez Silva.
FRA: Hugo Lloris, Bakary Sagna, William Éric Gallas, Éric Abidal, Patrice Evra (Cap), Jérémy Toulalan, Yoann Miguel Gourcuff (75.Florent Malouda), Vassiriky Abou Diaby, Sidney Govou (85.André-Pierre Gignac), Franck Ribéry, Nicolas Sébastien Anelka (72.Thierry Henry). Trainer: Raymond Domenech.
Cautions: Mauricio Bernardo Victorino Dansilio, Marcelo Nicolás Lodeiro Benítez, Diego Alfredo Moreno Lugano / Patrice Evra, Franck Ribéry, Jérémy Toulalan.
Sent off: Marcelo Nicolás Lodeiro Benítez (81).

16.06.2010, Loftus Versfeld Stadium, Pretoria; Attendance: 42,658
Referee: Massimo Busacca (Switzerland)
SOUTH AFRICA - URUGUAY   **0-3(0-1)**
RSA: Itumeleng Isaack Khune, Siboniso Pa Gaxa, Aaron Tebomo Mokoena (Cap), Bongani Khumalo, Peter Tsepo Masilela, Lawrence Siphiwe Tshabalala, Kagiso Evidence Dikgacoi, Reneilwe Letsholonanye (57.Surprise Mohlomolleng Moriri), Teko Tsholofelo Modise, Steven Jerome Pienaar (79.Moeneeb Josephs), Katlego Abel Mphela. Trainer: Carlos Alberto Gomes Parreira (Brazil).
URU: Néstor Fernando Muslera Micol, Victorio Maximiliano Pereira Páez, Diego Alfredo Moreno Lugano (Cap), Diego Roberto Godín Leal, Jorge Ciro Fucile Perdomo (71.Álvaro Fernández Gay), Egidio Raúl Arévalo Ríos, Diego Fernando Pérez Aguado (90.Wálter Alejandro Gargano Guevara), Álvaro Daniel Pereira Barragán, Diego Martín Forlán Corazo, Luis Alberto Suárez Díaz, Edinson Roberto Cavani Gómez (89.Sebastián Fernández). Trainer: Óscar Wáshington Tabárez Silva.
Goals: 0-1 Diego Martín Forlán Corazo (24), 0-2 Diego Martín Forlán Corazo (80 penalty), 0-3 Álvaro Daniel Pereira Barragán (90).
Cautions: Steven Jerome Pienaar, Kagiso Evidence Dikgacoi.
Sent off: Itumeleng Isaack Khune (76).

17.06.2010, „Peter Mokaba" Stadium, Polokwane; Attendance: 35,370
Referee: Khalil Ibrahim Al Ghamdi (Saudi Arabia)
FRANCE - MEXICO   **0-2(0-0)**
FRA: Hugo Lloris, Bakary Sagna, William Éric Gallas, Éric Abidal, Patrice Evra (Cap), Jérémy Toulalan, Vassiriky Abou Diaby, Sidney Govou (69.Mathieu Valbuena), Franck Ribéry, Florent Malouda, Nicolas Sébastien Anelka (46.André-Pierre Gignac). Trainer: Raymond Domenech.
MEX: Óscar Pérez Rojas, Ricardo Osorio Mendoza, Héctor Alfredo Moreno Herrera, Francisco Javier Rodríguez Pinedo, Carlos Arnoldo Salcido Flores, Rafael Márquez Álvarez (Cap), Efraín Juárez Valdéz (55.Javier Hernández Balcázar), Gerardo Torrado Díez de Bonilla, Giovani dos Santos Ramírez, Carlos Alberto Vela Garrido (31.Pablo Edson Barrera Acosta), Guillermo Luis Franco Farquarson (62.Cuauhtémoc Blanco Bravo). Trainer: Javier Aguirre Onaindía.
Goals: 0-1 Javier Hernández Balcázar (64), 0-2 Cuauhtémoc Blanco Bravo (79 penalty).
Cautions: Jérémy Toulalan, Éric Abidal / Guillermo Luis Franco Farquarson, Efraín Juárez Valdéz, Héctor Alfredo Moreno Herrera, Francisco Javier Rodríguez Pinedo.

22.06.2010, Royal Bafokeng Stadium, Rustenburg; Attendance: 33,425
Referee: Viktor Kassai (Hungary)
MEXICO - URUGUAY   **0-1(0-1)**
MEX: Óscar Pérez Rojas, Ricardo Osorio Mendoza, Francisco Javier Rodríguez Pinedo, Héctor Alfredo Moreno Herrera (57.Israel Castro Macías), Carlos Arnoldo Salcido Flores, Gerardo Torrado Díez de Bonilla, Rafael Márquez Álvarez, José Andrés Guardado Hernández (46.Pablo Edson Barrera Acosta), Giovani dos Santos Ramírez, Cuauhtémoc Blanco Bravo (63.Javier Hernández Balcázar), Guillermo Luis Franco Farquarson. Trainer: Javier Aguirre Onaindía.
URU: Néstor Fernando Muslera Micol, Victorio Maximiliano Pereira Páez, Diego Alfredo Moreno Lugano (Cap), Mauricio Bernardo Victorino Dansilio, Jorge Ciro Fucile Perdomo, Egidio Raúl Arévalo Ríos, Diego Fernando Pérez Aguado, Álvaro Daniel Pereira Barragán (77.Andrés Scotti Ponce de León), Diego Martín Forlán Corazo, Luis Alberto Suárez Díaz (85.Álvaro Fernández Gay), Edinson Roberto Cavani Gómez. Trainer: Óscar Wáshington Tabárez Silva.
Goal: 0-1 Luis Alberto Suárez Díaz (43).
Cautions: Javier Hernández Balcázar, Israel Castro Macías / Jorge Ciro Fucile Perdomo.

22.06.2010, Free State Stadium, Bloemfontein; Attendance: 39,415
Referee: Óscar Julián Ruiz Acosta (Colombia)
FRANCE - SOUTH AFRICA **1-2(0-2)**
FRA: Hugo Lloris, Bakary Sagna, William Éric Gallas, Sébastien Squillaci, Gaël Clichy, Alou Diarra
(Cap) (82.Sidney Govou), Vassiriky Abou Diaby, André-Pierre Gignac (46.Florent Malouda), Yoann
Miguel Gourcuff, Franck Ribéry, Djibril Cissé (55.Thierry Henry). Trainer: Raymond Domenech
RSA: Moeneeb Josephs, Calvin Anele Ngcongca (55.Siboniso Pa Gaxa), Aaron Tebomo Mokoena
(Cap), Bongani Khumalo, Peter Tsepo Masilela, Ntuthuko MacBeth-Mao Sibaya, Thanduyise Khuboni
(78.Teko Tsholofelo Modise), Steven Jerome Pienaar, Lawrence Siphiwe Tshabalala, Katlego Abel
Mphela, Bernard Melvin Parker (68.Siyabonga Nomvethe). Trainer: Carlos Alberto Gomes Parreira
(Brazil).
Goals: 0-1 Bongani Khumalo (20), 0-2 Katlego Abel Mphela (37), 1-2 Florent Malouda (70).
Cautions: Vassiriky Abou Diaby.
Sent off: Yoann Miguel Gourcuff (25).

GROUP B

12.06.2010	Port Elizabeth	Korea Republic - Greece	2-0(1-0)
12.06.2010	Johannesburg	Argentina - Nigeria	1-0(1-0)
17.06.2010	Johannesburg	Argentina – Korea Republic	4-1(2-1)
17.06.2010	Bloemfontein	Greece - Nigeria	2-1(1-1)
22.06.2010	Durban	Nigeria – Korea Republic	2-2(1-1)
22.06.2010	Polokwane	Greece - Argentina	0-2(0-0)

FINAL STANDINGS

1.	**Argentina**	3	3	0	0	7	-	1	9
2.	**Korea Republic**	3	1	1	1	5	-	6	4
3.	Greece	3	1	0	2	2	-	5	3
4.	Nigeria	3	0	1	2	3	-	5	1

12.06.2010, „Nelson Mandela" Bay Stadium, Port Elizabeth; Attendance: 31,513
Referee: Michael Hester (New Zealand)
KOREA REPUBLIC - GREECE **2-0(1-0)**
KOR: Jung Sung-Ryong, Cha Du-Ri, Cho Yong-Hyung, Lee Jung-Soo, Lee Young-Pyo, Lee Chung-
Yong (90+1.Kim Jae-Sung), Ki Sung-Yueng (74.Kim Nam-Il), Kim Jung-Woo, Park Ji-Sung (Cap),
Yeom Ki-Hun, Park Chu-Young (87.Lee Seung-Yeol). Trainer: Huh Jung-Moo.
GRE: Alexandros Tzórvas, Giórgos Seitarídis, Vasílis Torosídis, Avraam Papadópoulos, Loukás
Víntra, Alexandros Tziólis, Konstantinos Katsouránis, Giórgos Karagoúnis (Cap) (46.Hrístos
Patsatzoglou), Angelos Haristéas (61.Pantelis Kapetános), Giórgos Samarás (59.Dimítris Salpingídis),
Theofánis Gékas. Trainer: Otto Rehhagel (Germany).
Goals: 1-0 Lee Jung-Soo (7), 2-0 Park Ji-Sung (52).
Cautions: Vasílis Torosídis.

12.06.2010, Ellis Park Stadium, Johannesburg; Attendance: 55,686
Referee: Wolfgang Stark (Germany)
ARGENTINA - NIGERIA **1-0(1-0)**
ARG: Sergio Germán Romero, Jonás Manuel Gutiérrez, Martín Gastón Demichelis, Walter Adrián
Samuel, Gabriel Iván Heinze, Javier Alejandro Mascherano (Cap), Juan Sebastián Verón
(74.Maximiliano Rubén Rodríguez), Ángel Fabián di María (85.Nicolás Andrés Burdisso), Lionel
Andrés Messi, Carlos Alberto Tévez, Gonzalo Gerardo Higuaín (79.Diego Alberto Milito). Trainer:

Diego Armando Maradona.
NGA: Vincent Enyeama, Chukwudi Odiah, Joseph Ikpo Yobo (Cap), Daniel Olusola Shittu, Taye Ismaila Taïwo (75.Kalu Uche), Sani Haruna Kaita, Dickson Paul Etuhu, Lukman Haruna, Chinedu Ogbuke Obasi (60.Osaze Peter Odemwingie), Abdulrasaq Yakubu Aiyegbeni, Victor Nsofor Obinna (52.Obafemi Akinwunmi Martins). Trainer: Lars Lagerbäck (Sweden).
Goal: 1-0 Gabriel Iván Heinze (6).
Cautions: Jonás Manuel Gutiérrez / Lukman Haruna.

17.06.2010, Soccer City Stadium, Johannesburg; Attendance: 82,174
Referee: Frank De Bleeckere (Belgium)
ARGENTINA - KOREA REPUBLIC   **4-1(2-1)**
ARG: Sergio Germán Romero, Jonás Manuel Gutiérrez, Martín Gastón Demichelis, Walter Adrián Samuel (23.Nicolás Andrés Burdisso), Gabriel Iván Heinze, Javier Alejandro Mascherano (Cap), Maximiliano Rubén Rodríguez, Ángel Fabián di María, Lionel Andrés Messi, Gonzalo Gerardo Higuaín (82.Mario Ariel Bolatti), Carlos Alberto Tévez (75.Sergio Leonel Agüero del Castillo). Trainer: Diego Armando Maradona.
KOR: Jung Sung-Ryong, Oh Beom-Seok, Cho Yong-Hyung, Lee Jung-Soo, Lee Young-Pyo, Ki Sung-Yueng (46.Kim Nam-Il), Kim Jung-Woo, Lee Chung-Yong, Park Ji-Sung (Cap), Yeom Ki-Hun, Park Chu-Young (81.Lee Dong-Gook). Trainer: Huh Jung-Moo.
Goals: 1-0 Park Chu-Young (17 own goal), 2-0 Gonzalo Gerardo Higuaín (33), 2-1 Lee Chung-Yong (45+1), 3-1 Gonzalo Gerardo Higuaín (76), 4-1 Gonzalo Gerardo Higuaín (80).
Cautions: Jonás Manuel Gutiérrez, Javier Alejandro Mascherano, Gabriel Iván Heinze / Yeom Ki-Hun, Lee Chung-Yong.

17.06.2010, Free State Stadium, Bloemfontein; Attendance: 31,593
Referee: Óscar Julián Ruiz Acosta (Colombia)
GREECE - NIGERIA   **2-1(1-1)**
GRE: Alexandros Tzórvas, Sotírios Kyrgiakos, Loukás Víntra, Avraam Papadópoulos, Vasílis Torosídis, Sokratís Papastathópoulos (37.Giórgos Samarás), Alexandros Tziólis, Konstantinos Katsouránis, Giórgos Karagoúnis (Cap), Dimítris Salpingídis, Theofánis Gékas (79.Sotírios Nínis). Trainer: Otto Rehhagel (Germany).
NGA: Vincent Enyeama, Chukwudi Odiah, Joseph Ikpo Yobo (Cap), Daniel Olusola Shittu, Taye Ismaila Taïwo (55.Uwa Elderson Echiéjilé; 77.Rabiu Afolabi), Sani Haruna Kaita, Dickson Paul Etuhu, Lukman Haruna, Kalu Uche, Osaze Peter Odemwingie (46.Chinedu Ogbuke Obasi), Abdulrasaq Yakubu Aiyegbeni. Trainer: Lars Lagerbäck (Sweden).
Goals: 0-1 Kalu Uche (16), 1-1 Dimítris Salpingídis (44), 2-1 Vasílis Torosídis (71).
Cautions: Sokratís Papastathópoulos, Alexandros Tziólis, Giórgos Samarás / Chinedu Ogbuke Obasi.
Sent off: Sani Haruna Kaita (33).

22.06.2010, Durban Stadium, Durban; Attendance: 61,874
Referee: Olegário Manuel Bartolo Faustino Benquerença (Portugal)
NIGERIA - KOREA REPUBLIC   **2-2(1-1)**
NGA: Vincent Enyeama, Chukwudi Odiah, Joseph Ikpo Yobo (46.Uwa Elderson Echiéjilé), Daniel Olusola Shittu, Rabiu Afolabi, Yusuf Ayila Atanda, Dickson Paul Etuhu, Chinedu Ogbuke Obasi, Kalu Uche, Nwankwo Christian Nwosu (Cap) (57.Obafemi Akinwunmi Martins), Abdulrasaq Yakubu Aiyegbeni (70.Victor Nsofor Obinna). Trainer: Lars Lagerbäck (Sweden).
KOR: Jung Sung-Ryong, Cha Du-Ri, Cho Yong-Hyung, Lee Jung-Soo, Lee Young-Pyo, Lee Chung-Yong, Ki Sung-Yueng (87.Kim Jae-Sung), Kim Jung-Woo, Park Ji-Sung (Cap), Yeom Ki-Hun (64.Kim Nam-Il), Park Chu-Young (90+3.Kim Dong-Jin). Trainer: Huh Jung-Moo.
Goals: 1-0 Kalu Uche (12), 1-1 (38), 1-2 (49), 2-2 Abdulrasaq Yakubu Aiyegbeni (69 penalty).
Cautions: Vincent Enyeama, Chinedu Ogbuke Obasi, Chinedu Ogbuke Obasi / Kim Nam-Il.

22.06.2010, „Peter Mokaba" Stadium, Polokwane; Attendance: 38,891
Referee: Ravshan Irmatov (Uzbekistan)
GREECE - ARGENTINA   **0-2(0-0)**
GRE: Alexandros Tzórvas, Sotírios Kyrgiakos, Loukás Víntra, Avraam Papadópoulos, Vasílis Torosídis (55.Hrístos Patsatzoglou), Evangélios Móras, Sokratís Papastathópoulos, Giórgos Karagoúnis (Cap) (46.Nikolaos Leonidas Spiropoulos), Alexandros Tziólis, Konstantinos Katsouránis (54.Sotírios Nínis), Giórgos Samarás. Trainer: Otto Rehhagel (Germany).
ARG: Sergio Germán Romero, Nicolás Andrés Burdisso, Martín Gastón Demichelis, Nicolás Hernán Otamendi, Clemente Juan Rodríguez, Juan Sebastián Verón, Mario Ariel Bolatti, Maximiliano Rubén Rodríguez (63.Ángel Fabián di María), Lionel Andrés Messi (Cap), Sergio Leonel Agüero del Castillo (77.Javier Matías Pastore), Diego Alberto Milito (80.Martín Palermo). Trainer: Diego Armando Maradona.
Goals: 0-1 Martín Gastón Demichelis (77), 0-2 Martín Palermo (89).
Cautions: Konstantinos Katsouránis / Mario Ariel Bolatti.

GROUP C

12.06.2010	Rustenburg	England – United States	1-1(1-1)
12.06.2010	Polokwane	Algeria - Slovenia	0-1(0-0)
17.06.2010	Johannesburg	Slovenia – United States	2-2(2-0)
17.06.2010	Cape Town	England - Algeria	0-0
22.06.2010	Port Elizabeth	Slovenia - England	0-1(0-1)
22.06.2010	Pretoria	United States - Algeria	1-0(0-0)

FINAL STANDINGS

1.	**United States**	3	1	2	0	4 - 3	5
2.	**England**	3	1	2	0	2 - 1	5
3.	Slovenia	3	1	1	1	3 - 3	4
4.	Algeria	3	0	1	2	0 - 2	1

12.06.2010, Royal Bafokeng Stadium, Rustenburg; Attendance: 38,646
Referee: Carlos Eugênio Simon (Brazil)
ENGLAND – UNITED STATES   **1-1(1-1)**
ENG: Robert Paul Green, Glen McLeod Johnson, John George Terry, Ledley Brenton King (46.James Lee Duncan Carragher), Ashley Cole, Aaron Justin Lennon, Frank James Lampard, Steven George Gerrard (Cap), James Philip Milner (30.Shaun Cameron Wright-Phillips), Wayne Mark Rooney, Emile William Ivanhoe Heskey (79.Peter James Crouch). Manager: Fabio Capello (Italy).
USA: Tim Howard, Steven Cherundolo, Jay Michael DeMerit, Oguchialu Chijioke Onyewu, Carlos Manuel Bocanegra (Cap), Clinton Drew Dempsey, Michael Sheehan Bradley, Ricardo Anthony Clark, Landon Timothy Donovan, Josmer Volmy Altidore (86.Stuart Holden), Robert Findley (77.Edson Michael Buddle). Trainer: Robert Bradley.
Goals: 1-0 Steven George Gerrard (4), 1-1 Clinton Drew Dempsey (40).
Cautions: James Philip Milner, James Lee Duncan Carragher, Steven George Gerrard / Steven Cherundolo, Jay Michael DeMerit, Robert Findley.

12.06.2010, „Peter Mokaba" Stadium, Polokwane; Attendance: 30,325
Referee: Carlos Alberto Batres González (Guatemala)
ALGERIA - SLOVENIA   **0-1(0-0)**
ALG: Faouzi Chaouchi, Anthar Yahia (Cap), Madjid Bougherra, Rafik Halliche, Nadir Belhadj, Mehdi Lacen, Karim Ziani, Hassan Yebda, Foued Kadir (82.Adlène Guedioura), Karim Matmour (81.Rafik

Saïfi), Rafik Djebbour (58.Abdelkader Ghezzal). Trainer: Rabah Saâdane.
SVN: Samir Handanovič, Mišo Brečko, Marko Šuler, Boštjan Cesar, Bojan Jokić, Andraž Kirm, Robert Koren (Cap), Aleksander Radosavljevič (87.Andrej Komac), Valter Birsa (84.Nejc Pečnik), Zlatko Dedič (53.Zlatan Ljubijankič), Milivoje Novakovič. Trainer: Matjaž Kek.
Goals: 0-1 Robert Koren (79).
Cautions: Abdelkader Ghezzal, Hassan Yebda / Aleksander Radosavljevič, Andrej Komac.
Sent off: Abdelkader Ghezzal (73).

17.06.2010, Ellis Park Stadium, Johannesburg; Attendance: 45,573
Referee: Koman Coulibaly (Mali)
SLOVENIA - UNITED STATES   **2-2(2-0)**
SVN: Samir Handanovič, Mišo Brečko, Marko Šuler, Boštjan Cesar, Bojan Jokić, Robert Koren (Cap), Aleksander Radosavljevič, Valter Birsa (87.Zlatko Dedič), Andraž Kirm, Zlatan Ljubijankč (74.Nejc Pečnik; 90+4.Andrej Komac), Milivoje Novakovič. Trainer: Matjaž Kek.
USA: Tim Howard, Steven Cherundolo, Jay Michael DeMerit, Oguchialu Chijioke Onyewu (80.Herculez Gomez), Carlos Manuel Bocanegra (Cap), Landon Timothy Donovan, José Francisco Torres Mezzell (46.Benny Feilhaber), Michael Sheehan Bradley, Clinton Drew Dempsey, Josmer Volmy Altidore, Robert Findley (46.Maurice Edu). Trainer: Robert Bradley.
Goals: 1-0 Valter Birsa (13), 2-0 Zlatan Ljubijankč (42), 1-2 Landon Timothy Donovan (48), 2-2 Michael Sheehan Bradley (82).
Cautions: Boštjan Cesar, Marko Šuler, Andraž Kirm, Bojan Jokić / Robert Findley.

17.06.2010, Cape Town Stadium, Cape Town; Attendance: 64,100
Referee: Ravshan Irmatov (Uzbekistan)
ENGLAND - ALGERIA   **0-0**
ENG: David Benjamin James, Glen McLeod Johnson, James Lee Duncan Carragher, John George Terry, Ashley Cole, Aaron Justin Lennon (63.Shaun Cameron Wright-Phillips), Frank James Lampard, Gareth Robert Barry (84.Peter James Crouch), Steven George Gerrard (Cap), Wayne Mark Rooney, Emile William Ivanhoe Heskey (74.Jermain Colin Defoe). Manager: Fabio Capello (Italy).
ALG: Raïs M'Bolhi, Madjid Bougherra, Nadir Belhadj, Anthar Yahia (Cap), Foued Kadir, Hassan Yebda (88.Djamel Mesbah), Mehdi Lacen, Rafik Halliche, Ryad Boudebouz (74.Djamel Abdoun), Karim Ziani (81.Adlène Guedioura), Karim Matmour. Trainer: Rabah Saâdane.
Cautions: James Lee Duncan Carragher / Mehdi Lacen.

22.06.2010, "Nelson Mandela" Bay Stadium, Port Elizabeth; Attendance: 36,893
Referee: Wolfgang Stark (Germany)
SLOVENIA - ENGLAND   **0-1(0-1)**
SVN: Samir Handanovič, Mišo Brečko, Marko Šuler, Boštjan Cesar, Bojan Jokić, Robert Koren (Cap), Aleksandar Radosavljevič, Valter Birsa, Andraž Kirm (79.Tim Matavž), Zlatan Ljubijankič (62.Zlatko Dedič), Milivoje Novakovič. Trainer: Matjaž Kek.
ENG: David Benjamin James, Glen McLeod Johnson, John George Terry, Matthew James Upson, Ashley Cole, James Philip Milner, Gareth Robert Barry, Frank James Lampard, Steven George Gerrard (Cap), Jermain Colin Defoe (86.Emile William Ivanhoe Heskey), Wayne Mark Rooney (72.Joseph John Cole). Manager: Fabio Capello (Italy).
Goals: 0-1 Jermain Colin Defoe (23).
Cautions: Bojan Jokić, Valter Birsa, Zlatko Dedič / Glen McLeod Johnson.

22.06.2010, Loftus Versfeld Stadium, Pretoria; Attendance: 35,827
Referee: Frank De Bleeckere (Belgium)
UNITED STATES - ALGERIA   **1-0(0-0)**
USA: Tim Howard, Jonathan Bornstein (80.DaMarcus Lamont Beasley), Jay Michael DeMerit, Carlos Manuel Bocanegra (Cap), Steven Cherundolo, Michael Sheehan Bradley, Maurice Edu (64.Edson Michael Buddle), Clinton Drew Dempsey, Landon Timothy Donovan, Josmer Volmy Altidore, Herculez Gomez (46.Benny Feilhaber). Trainer: Robert Bradley.

ALG: Raïs M'Bolhi, Madjid Bougherra, Rafik Halliche, Anthar Yahia (Cap), Foued Kadir, Hassan Yebda, Mehdi Lacen, Karim Ziani (69.Adlène Guedioura), Nadir Belhadj, Rafik Djebbour (65.Abdelkader Ghezzal), Karim Matmour (84.Rafik Saïfi). Trainer: Rabah Saâdane.
Goal: 1-0 Landon Timothy Donovan (90+1).
Cautions: Josmer Volmy Altidore, DaMarcus Lamont Beasley / Hassan Yebda, Anthar Yahia, Mehdi Lacen.
Sent off: Anthar Yahia (90+3).

GROUP D

13.06.2010	Pretoria	Serbia - Ghana	0-1(0-0)
13.06.2010	Durban	Germany - Australia	4-0(2-0)
18.06.2010	Port Elizabeth	Germany - Serbia	0-1(0-1)
19.06.2010	Rustenburg	Ghana - Australia	1-1(1-1)
23.06.2010	Johannesburg	Ghana - Germany	0-1(0-0)
23.06.2010	Nelspruit	Australia - Serbia	2-1(0-0)

FINAL STANDINGS

1.	**Germany**	3	2	0	1	5	-	1	6
2.	**Ghana**	3	1	1	1	2	-	2	4
3.	Australia	3	1	1	1	3	-	6	4
4.	Serbia	3	1	0	2	2	-	3	3

13.06.2010, Loftus Versfeld Stadium, Pretoria; Attendance: 38,833
Referee: Héctor Walter Baldassi (Argentina)
SERBIA - GHANA   **0-1(0-0)**
SRB: Vladimir Stojković, Branislav Ivanović, Aleksandar Luković, Nemanja Vidić, Aleksandar Kolarov, Nenad Milijaš (62.Zdravko Kuzmanović), Dejan Stanković (Cap), Miloš Krasić, Milan Jovanović (76.Neven Subotić), Marko Pantelić, Nikola Žigić (69.Danko Lazović). Trainer: Radomir Antić.
GHA: Richard Paul Franck Kingson, John Paintsil, Isaac Vorsah, John Mensah (Cap), Hans Adu Sarpei, Anthony Annan, Kevin-Prince Boateng (90+1.Lee Addy), Prince Tagoe, Kojo „Kwadwo" Asamoah (73.Stephen Appiah), André Ayew, Asamoah Gyan (90+3.Quincy James Owusu-Abeyie). Trainer: Milan Rajevac (Serbia).
Goal: 0-1 Asamoah Gyan (85 penalty).
Cautions: Nikola Žigić, Aleksandar Luković, Zdravko Kuzmanović / Isaac Vorsah, Prince Tagoe.
Sent off: Aleksandar Luković (74).

13.06.2010, „Moses Mabhida" Stadium, Durban; Attendance: 62,660
Referee: Marco Antonio Rodríguez Moreno (Mexico)
GERMANY - AUSTRALIA   **4-0(2-0)**
GER: Manuel Neuer, Philipp Lahm, Per Mertesacker, Arne Friedrich, Holger Badstuber, Bastian Schweinsteiger, Sami Khedira, Thomas Müller, Mesut Özil (74.Mario Gómez), Lukas Podolski (81.Marko Marin), Miroslav Klose (68.Claudemir Jerónimo Barretto da Silva „Cacau"). Trainer: Joachim Löw.
AUS: Mark Schwarzer, Luke Wilkshire, Craig Andrew Moore, Lucas Edward Neill (Cap), Scott Kenneth Chipperfield, Carl Valeri, Vincenzo Grella (46.Brett Trevor Holman), Brett Michael Emerton (74.Michael John Jedinak), Richard Garcia (64.Nikita Rukavytsya), Jason Čulina, Timothy Joel Cahill. Trainer: Peter Tim Verbeek (Holland).
Goals: 1-0 Lukas Podolski (8), 2-0 Miroslav Klose (26), 3-0 Thomas Müller (68), 4-0 Claudemir Jerónimo Barretto da Silva „Cacau" (70).

Cautions: Mesut Özil, Claudemir Jerónimo Barretto da Silva „Cacau"/ Craig Andrew Moore, Lucas Edward Neill, Carl Valeri.
Sent off: Timothy Joel Cahill (56).

18.06.2010, „Nelson Mandela" Bay Stadium, Port Elizabeth; Attendance: 38,294
Referee: Alberto Undiano Mallenco (Spain)
GERMANY - SERBIA   **0-1(0-1)**
GER: Manuel Neuer, Philipp Lahm, Per Mertesacker, Arne Friedrich, Holger Badstuber (77.Mario Gómez), Bastian Schweinsteiger, Sami Khedira, Thomas Müller (70.Claudemir Jerónimo Barretto da Silva „Cacau"), Mesut Özil (70 Marko Marin), Lukas Podolski, Miroslav Klose. Trainer: Joachim Löw.
SRB: Vladimir Stojković, Branislav Ivanović, Neven Subotić, Nemanja Vidić, Aleksandar Kolarov, Zdravko Kuzmanović (75.Radosav Petrović), Miloš Ninković (70.Gojko Kačar), Dejan Stanković (Cap), Miloš Krasić, Milan Jovanović (79.Danko Lazović), Nikola Žigić. Trainer: Radomir Antić.
Goal: 0-1 Milan Jovanović (38).
Cautions: Miroslav Klose, Sami Khedira, Philipp Lahm, Bastian Schweinsteiger / Branislav Ivanović, Aleksandar Kolarov, Neven Subotić, Nemanja Vidić.
Sent off: Miroslav Klose (37).

19.06.2010, Royal Bafokeng Stadium, Rustenburg; Attendance: 34,812
Referee: Roberto Rosetti (Italy)
GHANA - AUSTRALIA   **1-1(1-1)**
GHA: Richard Paul Franck Kingson (Cap), John Paintsil, Jonathan Mensah, Lee Addy, Hans Adu Sarpei, Anthony Annan, Kevin-Prince Boateng (87.Matthew Amoah), Prince Tagoe (56.Quincy James Owusu-Abeyie), Kojo „Kwadwo" Asamoah (77.Sulleyman Ali Muntari), André Ayew, Asamoah Gyan. Trainer: Milan Rajevac (Serbia).
AUS: Mark Schwarzer, Luke Wilkshire (85.Nikita Rukavytsya), Lucas Edward Neill (Cap), Craig Andrew Moore, David Raymond Carney, Jason Čulina, Carl Valeri, Brett Michael Emerton, Brett Trevor Holman (68.Joshua Blake Kennedy), Mark Bresciano (66.Scott Kenneth Chipperfield), Harold Kewell. Trainer: Peter Tim Verbeek (Holland).
Goals: 0-1 Brett Trevor Holman (12), 1-1 Asamoah Gyan (25 penalty).
Cautions: Lee Addy, Anthony Annan, Jonathan Mensah / Craig Andrew Moore.
Sent off: Harold Kewell (24).

23.06.2010, Soccer City, Johannesburg; Attendance: 83,391
Referee: Carlos Eugênio Simon (Brazil)
GHANA - GERMANY   **0-1(0-0)**
GHA: Richard Paul Franck Kingson, John Paintsil, John Mensah (Cap), Jonathan Mensah, Hans Adu Sarpei, Anthony Annan, Kevin-Prince Boateng, Kojo „Kwadwo" Asamoah, Prince Tagoe (64.Sulleyman Ali Muntari), André Ayew (90+2.Dominic Adiyiah), Asamoah Gyan (82.Matthew Amoah). Trainer: Milan Rajevac (Serbia).
GER: Manuel Neuer, Philipp Lahm, Per Mertesacker, Arne Friedrich, Jérôme Agyenim Boateng (73.Marcell Jansen), Sami Khedira, Bastian Schweinsteiger (81.Toni Kroos), Thomas Müller (68.Piotr Trochowski), Mesut Özil, Lukas Podolski, Claudemir Jerónimo Barretto da Silva „Cacau". Trainer: Joachim Löw.
Goal: 0-1 Mesut Özil (60).
Cautions: André Ayew / Thomas Müller.

23.06.2010, Mbombela Stadium, Nelspruit; Attendance: 37,836
Referee: Jorge Luis Larrionda Pietrafesa (Uruguay)
AUSTRALIA - SERBIA   **2-1(0-0)**
AUS: Mark Schwarzer, Luke Wilkshire (82.Richard Garcia), Michael Francis Beauchamp, Lucas Edward Neill (Cap), David Raymond Carney, Jason Čulina, Carl Valeri (65.Brett Trevor Holman), Brett Michael Emerton, Timothy Joel Cahill, Mark Bresciano (66.Scott Kenneth Chipperfield), Joshua Blake Kennedy. Trainer: Peter Tim Verbeek (Holland).

SRB: Vladimir Stojković, Branislav Ivanović, Nemanja Vidić, Aleksandar Luković, Ivan Obradović, Zdravko Kuzmanović (77.Danko Lazović), Dejan Stanković (Cap), Miloš Ninković, Miloš Krasić (62.Zoran Tošić), Milan Jovanović, Nikola Ž igić (67.Marko Pantelić). Trainer: Radomir Antić.
Goals: 1-0 Timothy Joel Cahill (69), 2-1 Brett Trevor Holman (73), 2-1 (84).
Cautions: Michael Francis Beauchamp, Luke Wilkshire, Brett Michael Emerton / Aleksandar Luković, Miloš Ninković.

GROUP E

14.06.2010	Johannesburg	Holland - Denmark	2-0(0-0)
14.06.2010	Bloemfontein	Japan - Cameroon	1-0(1-0)
19.06.2010	Durban	Holland - Japan	1-0(1-0)
19.06.2010	Pretoria	Cameroon - Denmark	1-2(1-1)
24.06.2010	Rustenburg	Denmark - Japan	1-3(0-2)
24.06.2010	Cape Town	Cameroon - Holland	1-2(0-1)

FINAL STANDINGS

1.	Holland	3	3	0	0	5	-	1	9
2.	Japan	3	2	0	1	4	-	2	6
3.	Denmark	3	1	0	2	3	-	6	3
4.	Cameroon	3	0	0	3	2	-	5	0

14.06.2010, Soccer City, Johannesburg; Attendance: 83,465
Referee: Stéphane Lannoy (France)
HOLLAND - DENMARK   **2-0(0-0)**
NED: Maarten Stekelenburg, Gregory Kurtley van der Wiel, John Gijsbert Alan Heitinga, Joris Mathijsen, Giovanni Christiaan van Bronckhorst (Cap), Mark Peter Gertruda Andreas van Bommel, Nigel de Jong (88.Demy Patrick René de Zeeuw), Dirk Kuijt, Wesley Benjamin Sneijder, Rafael Ferdinand van der Vaart (67.Eljero George Rinaldo Elia), Robin van Persie (77.Ibrahim Afellay). Trainer: Lambertus van Marwijk.
DEN: Thomas Sørensen, Lars Christian Jacobsen, Daniel Agger, Simon Kjær, Simon Busk Poulsen, Thomas Enevoldsen (56.Jesper Grønkjær), Christian Bjørnshøj Poulsen, Thomas Kahlenberg (73.Christian Eriksen), Martin Jørgensen (Cap), Dennis Rommedahl, Nicklas Bendtner (62.Mikkel Beckmann). Trainer: Morten Olsen.
Goals: 1-0 Daniel Agger (46 own goal), 2-0 Dirk Kuijt (85).
Cautions: Nigel de Jong, Robin van Persie / Simon Kjær.

14.06.2010, Free State Stadium, Bloemfontein; Attendance: 30,620
Referee: Olegário Manuel Bartolo Faustino Benquerença (Portugal)
JAPAN - CAMEROON   **1-0(1-0)**
JPN: Eiji Kawashima, Yūichi Komano, Yuji Nakazawa, Marcus Tulio Tanaka, Yuto Nagatomo, Makoto Hasebe (Cap) (88.Junichi Inamoto), Yuki Abe, Yasuhito Endō, Daisuke Matsui (69.Shinji Okazaki), Yoshito Ōkubo (82.Kisho Yano), Keisuke Honda. Trainer: Takeshi Okada.
CMR: Souleymanou Hamidou, Stéphane Mbia Etoundi, Nicolas Alexis Julio N'Koulou N'Doubena, Sébastien Bassong Nguena, Benoît Pierre David Assou-Ekotto, Joël Job Matip (63.Achille Emana Edzimbi), Jean II Makoun (75.Geremi Sorele Njitap Fotso), Eyong Tarkang Enoh, Samuel Eto'o (Cap), Pierre Achille Webó Kouamo, Jean-Eric Maxim Choupo-Moting (75.Mohammadou Idrissou). Trainer: Paul Le Guen (France).
Goal: 1-0 Keisuke Honda (39).
Cautions: Yuki Abe / Nicolas Alexis Julio N'Koulou N'Doubena.

300

19.06.2010, „Moses Mabhida" Stadium, Durban; Attendance: 62,010
Referee: Héctor Walter Baldassi (Argentina)
HOLLAND - JAPAN   **1-0(0-0)**
NED: Maarten Stekelenburg, Gregory Kurtley van der Wiel, John Gijsbert Alan Heitinga, Joris Mathijsen, Giovanni Christiaan van Bronckhorst (Cap), Mark Peter Gertruda Andreas van Bommel, Nigel de Jong, Dirk Kuijt, Wesley Benjamin Sneijder (83.Ibrahim Afellay), Rafael Ferdinand van der Vaart (72.Eljero George Rinaldo Elia), Robin van Persie (88.Klaas-Jan Huntelaar). Trainer: Lambertus van Marwijk.
JPN: Eiji Kawashima, Yuto Nagatomo, Yuji Nakazawa, Marcus Tulio Tanaka, Yūichi Komano, Yuki Abe, Daisuke Matsui (64.Shunsuke Nakamura), Yasuhito Endō, Makoto Hasebe (Cap) (77.Shinji Okazaki), Yoshito Ōkubo (77.Keiji Tamada), Keisuke Honda. Trainer: Takeshi Okada.
Goal: 1-0 Wesley Benjamin Sneijder (53).
Cautions: Gregory Kurtley van der Wiel.

19.06.2010, Loftus Versfeld Stadium, Pretoria; Attendance: 38,074
Referee: Jorge Luis Larrionda Pietrafesa (Uruguay)
CAMEROON - DENMARK   **1-2(1-1)**
CMR: Souleymanou Hamidou, Stéphane Mbia Etoundi, Nicolas Alexis Julio N'Koulou N'Doubena, Sébastien Bassong Nguena (72.Mohammadou Idrissou), Benoît Pierre David Assou-Ekotto, Alexandre Dimitri Song Billong, Geremi Sorele Njitap Fotso, Eyong Tarkang Enoh (46.Jean II Makoun), Achille Emana Edzimbi, Pierre Achille Webó Kouamo (78.Vincent Aboubakar), Samuel Eto'o (Cap). Trainer: Paul Le Guen (France).
DEN: Thomas Sørensen, Lars Christian Jacobsen, Simon Kjær, Daniel Agger, Simon Busk Poulsen, Christian Bjørnshøj Poulsen, Martin Jørgensen (46.Daniel Jensen), Dennis Rommedahl, Jesper Grønkjær (67.Thomas Kahlenberg), Jon Dahl Tomasson (Cap) (86.Jakob Poulsen), Nicklas Bendtner. Trainer: Morten Olsen.
Goals: 1-0 Samuel Eto'o (10), 1-1 Nicklas Bendtner (33), 1-2 Dennis Rommedahl (61).
Cautions: Sébastien Bassong Nguena, Stéphane Mbia Etoundi / Thomas Sørensen, Simon Kjær.

24.06.2010, Royal Bafokeng Stadium, Rustenburg; Attendance: 27,967
Referee: Jerome Damon (South Africa)
DENMARK - JAPAN   **1-3(0-2)**
DEN: Thomas Sørensen, Lars Christian Jacobsen, Daniel Agger, Per Krøldrup (56.Søren Larsen), Simon Busk Poulsen, Christian Bjørnshøj Poulsen, Martin Jørgensen (34.Jakob Poulsen), Thomas Kahlenberg (63.Christian Eriksen), Jon Dahl Tomasson (Cap), Dennis Rommedahl, Nicklas Bendtner. Trainer: Morten Olsen.
JPN: Eiji Kawashima, Yūichi Komano, Yuji Nakazawa, Marcus Tulio Tanaka, Yuto Nagatomo, Yuki Abe, Daisuke Matsui (74.Shinji Okazaki), Yasuhito Endō (90+1.Junichi Inamoto), Makoto Hasebe (Cap), Yoshito Ōkubo (88.Yasuyuki Konno), Keisuke Honda. Trainer: Takeshi Okada.
Goals: 0-1 Keisuke Honda (17), 0-2 Yasuhito Endō (30), 1-2 Jon Dahl Tomasson (81), 1-3 Shinji Okazaki (87).
Cautions: Per Krøldrup, Christian Bjørnshøj Poulsen, Nicklas Bendtner / Yasuhito Endō, Yuto Nagatomo.

24.06.2010, Cape Town Stadium, Cape Town; Attendance: 63,093
Referee: Pablo Antonio Pozo Quinteros (Chile)
CAMEROON - HOLLAND   **1-2(0-1)**
CMR: Souleymanou Hamidou, Geremi Sorele Njitap Fotso, Stéphane Mbia Etoundi, Nicolas Alexis Julio N'Koulou N'Doubena (73.Rigobert Song Bahanag), Benoît Pierre David Assou-Ekotto, Aurélian Bayard Chedjou Fongang, Joël Landry Tsafack N'Guémo, Jean II Makoun, Gaëtan Bong Songo (56.Vincent Aboubakar), Samuel Eto'o (Cap), Jean-Eric Maxim Choupo-Moting (72.Mohammadou Idrissou). Trainer: Paul Le Guen (France).
NED: Maarten Stekelenburg, Khalid Boulahrouz, John Gijsbert Alan Heitinga, Joris Mathijsen, Giovanni Christiaan van Bronckhorst (Cap), Mark Peter Gertruda Andreas van Bommel, Nigel de Jong,

Dirk Kuijt (66 Eljero George Rinaldo Elia), Wesley Benjamin Sneijder, Rafael Ferdinand van der Vaart (73.Arjen Robben), Robin van Persie (59.Klaas-Jan Huntelaar). Trainer: Lambertus van Marwijk.
Goals: 0-1 Robin van Persie (36), 1-1 Samuel Eto'o (65 penalty), 1-2 Klaas-Jan Huntelaar (83).
Cautions: Nicolas Alexis Julio N'Koulou N'Doubena, Stéphane Mbia Etoundi / Dirk Kuijt, Rafael Ferdinand van der Vaart, Giovanni Christiaan van Bronckhorst.

GROUP F

14.06.2010	Cape Town	Italy - Paraguay	1-1(0-1)
15.06.2010	Rustenburg	New Zealand - Slovakia	1-1(0-0)
20.06.2010	Bloemfontein	Slovakia - Paraguay	0-2(0-1)
20.06.2010	Nelspruit	Italy – New Zealand	1-1(1-1)
24.06.2010	Johannesburg	Slovakia - Italy	3-2(1-0)
24.06.2010	Polokwane	Paraguay – New Zealand	0-0

FINAL STANDINGS

1.	**Paraguay**	3	1	2	0	3	-	1	5
2.	**Slovakia**	3	1	1	1	4	-	5	4
3.	New Zealand	3	0	3	0	2	-	2	3
4.	Italy	3	0	2	1	4	-	5	2

14.06.2010, Cape Town Stadium, Cape Town; Attendance: 62,869
Referee: Benito Armando Archundia Téllez (Mexico)
ITALY - PARAGUAY   **1-1(0-1)**
ITA: Gianluigi Buffon (46.Federico Marchetti), Gianluca Zambrotta, Fabio Cannavaro (Cap), Giorgio Chiellini, Domenico Criscito, Daniele De Rossi, Riccardo Montolivo, Simone Pepe, Claudio Marchisio (59.Mauro Camoranesi), Vincenzo Iaquinta, Alberto Gilardino (73.Antonio Di Natale). Trainer: Marcello Lippi.
PAR: Justo Wilmar Villar Viveros (Cap), Carlos Bonet Cáceres, Antolín Alcaraz Viveros, Paulo César da Silva Barrios, Claudio Marcelo Morel Rodríguez, Víctor Javier Cáceres Centurión, Enrique Daniel Vera Torres, Cristian Miguel Riveros Núñez, Aureliano Torres Román (60.Jonathan Santana Ghere), Nelson Antonio Haedo Valdéz (68.Roque Luis Santa Cruz Cantero), Lucas Ramón Barrios Cáceres (76.Óscar René Cardozo Marín). Trainer: Gerardo Daniel Martino (Argentina).
Goals: 0-1 Antolín Alcaraz Viveros (39), 1-1 Daniele De Rossi (63).
Cautions: Mauro Camoranesi / Víctor Javier Cáceres Centurión.

15.06.2010, Royal Bafokeng Stadium, Rustenburg; Attendance: 23,871
Referee: Jerome Damon (South Africa)
NEW ZEALAND - SLOVAKIA   **1-1(0-0)**
NZL: Mark Nelson Paston, Winston Wiremu Reid, Ryan William Nelsen (Cap), Ivan Robert Vicelich (78.Jeremy John Christie), Thomas Jefferson Smith, Leonida Christos Bertos, Simon John Elliott, Tony James Lochhead, Rory Michael Fallon, Christopher John Killen (72.Christopher Grant Wood), Shane Edward Smeltz. Trainer: Richard Lloyd Herbert.
SVK: Ján Mucha, Radoslav Zabavník, Ján Ďurica, Martin Škrteľ, Marek Čech, Zdeno Štrba, Vladimír Weiss (90+1. Juraj Kucka), Stanislav Šesták (81.Filip Hološko), Marek Hamšík (Cap), Róbert Vittek (84.Miroslav Stoch), Erik Jendrišek. Trainer: Vladimír Weiss.
Goals: 0-1 Róbert Vittek (50), 1-1 Winston Wiremu Reid (90+3).
Cautions: Tony James Lochhead, Winston Wiremu Reid / Zdeno Štrba.

20.06.2010, Free State Stadium, Bloemfontein; Attendance: 26,643
Referee: Eddy Allen Maillet Guyto (Seychelles)
SLOVAKIA - PARAGUAY 0-2(0-1)
SVK: Ján Mucha, Peter Pekarík, Martin Škrteľ, Kornel Saláta (83.Miroslav Stoch), Ján Ďurica, Zdeno Štrba, Marek Hamšík (Cap), Stanislav Šesták (70.Filip Hološko), Vladimír Weiss, Ján Kozák, Róbert Vittek. Trainer: Vladimír Weiss.
PAR: Justo Wilmar Villar Viveros (Cap), Carlos Bonet Cáceres, Paulo César da Silva Barrios, Antolín Alcaraz Viveros, Claudio Marcelo Morel Rodríguez, Víctor Javier Cáceres Centurión, Enrique Daniel Vera Torres (88.Édgar Osvaldo Barreto Cáceres), Cristian Miguel Riveros Núñez, Nelson Antonio Haedo Valdéz (68.Aureliano Torres Román), Roque Luis Santa Cruz Cantero, Lucas Ramón Barrios Cáceres (82.Óscar René Cardozo Marín). Trainer: Gerardo Daniel Martino (Argentina).
Goals: 0-1 Enrique Daniel Vera Torres (27), 0-2 Cristian Miguel Riveros Núñez (86).
Cautions: Ján Ďurica, Stanislav Šesták, Vladimír Weiss / Enrique Daniel Vera Torres.

20.06.2010, Mbombela Stadium, Nelspruit; Attendance: 38,229
Referee: Carlos Alberto Batres González (Guatemala)
ITALY - NEW ZEALAND 1-1(1-1)
ITA: Federico Marchetti, Gianluca Zambrotta, Fabio Cannavaro (Cap), Giorgio Chiellini, Domenico Criscito, Simone Pepe (46.Mauro Camoranesi), Daniele De Rossi, Riccardo Montolivo, Claudio Marchisio (61.Giampaolo Pazzini), Alberto Gilardino (46.Antonio Di Natale), Vincenzo Iaquinta. Trainer: Marcello Lippi.
NZL: Mark Nelson Paston, Winston Wiremu Reid, Ryan William Nelsen (Cap), Ivan Robert Vicelich (81.Jeremy John Christie), Thomas Jefferson Smith, Leonida Christos Bertos, Simon John Elliott, Tony James Lochhead, Rory Michael Fallon (63.Christopher Grant Wood), Christopher John Killen (90+3.Andrew Barron), Shane Edward Smeltz. Trainer: Richard Lloyd Herbert.
Goals: 0-1 Shane Edward Smeltz (7), 1-1 Vincenzo Iaquinta (29 penalty).
Cautions: Rory Michael Fallon, Thomas Jefferson Smith, Ryan William Nelsen, Christopher John Killen.

24.06.2010, Ellis Park Stadium, Johannesburg; Attendance: 53,412
Referee: Howard Melton Webb (England)
SLOVAKIA - ITALY 3-2(1-0)
SVK: Ján Mucha, Peter Pekarík, Martin Škrteľ, Ján Ďurica, Radoslav Zabavník, Zdeno Štrba (87.Kamil Kopúnek), Juraj Kucka, Marek Hamšík (Cap), Miroslav Stoch, Róbert Vittek (90+2.Stanislav Šesták), Erik Jendrišek (90+4.Martin Petráš). Trainer: Vladimír Weiss.
ITA: Federico Marchetti, Gianluca Zambrotta, Fabio Cannavaro (Cap), Giorgio Chiellini, Domenico Criscito (46.Christian Maggio), Riccardo Montolivo (56.Andrea Pirlo), Daniele De Rossi, Gennaro Gattuso (46.Fabio Quagliarella), Simone Pepe, Vincenzo Iaquinta, Antonio Di Natale. Trainer: Marcello Lippi.
Goals: 1-0 Róbert Vittek (25), 2-0 Róbert Vittek (73), 2-1 Antonio Di Natale (81), 3-1 Kamil Kopúnek (89), 3-2 Fabio Quagliarella (90+2).
Cautions: Zdeno Štrba, Róbert Vittek, Peter Pekarík, Ján Mucha / Fabio Cannavaro, Giorgio Chiellini, Simone Pepe, Fabio Quagliarella.

24.06.2010, „Peter Mokaba" Stadium, Polokwane; Attendance: 34,450
Referee: Yuichi Nishimura (Japan)
PARAGUAY - NEW ZEALAND 0-0
PAR: Justo Wilmar Villar Viveros, Denis Ramón Caniza Acuña (Cap), Julio César Cáceres López, Paulo César da Silva Barrios, Claudio Marcelo Morel Rodríguez, Víctor Javier Cáceres Centurión, Cristian Miguel Riveros Núñez, Enrique Daniel Vera Torres, Roque Luis Santa Cruz Cantero, Nelson Antonio Haedo Valdéz (67.Edgar Benítez Santander), Óscar René Cardozo Marín (66.Lucas Ramón Barrios Cáceres). Trainer: Gerardo Daniel Martino (Argentina).
NZL: Mark Nelson Paston, Winston Wiremu Reid, Ryan William Nelsen (Cap), Thomas Jefferson

Smith, Simon John Elliott, Ivan Robert Vicelich, Leonida Christos Bertos, Tony James Lochhead, Christopher John Killen (79.Jeremy Russell Brockie), Shane Edward Smeltz, Rory Michael Fallon (69.Christopher Grant Wood). Trainer: Richard Lloyd Herbert.
Cautions: Víctor Javier Cáceres Centurión, Roque Luis Santa Cruz Cantero / Ryan William Nelsen.

GROUP G

15.06.2010	Port Elizabeth	Ivory Coast - Portugal	0-0
15.06.2010	Johannesburg	Brazil – Korea D.P.R.	2-1(0-0)
20.06.2010	Johannesburg	Brazil – Ivory Coast	3-1(1-0)
21.06.2010	Cape Town	Portugal – Korea D.P.R.	7-0(1-0)
25.06.2010	Durban	Portugal - Brazil	0-0
25.06.2010	Nelspruit	Korea D.P.R. – Ivory Coast	0-3(0-2)

FINAL STANDINGS

1.	**Brazil**	3	2	1	0	5	-	2	7
2.	**Portugal**	3	1	2	0	7	-	0	5
3.	Ivory Coast	3	1	1	1	4	-	3	4
4.	Korea D.P.R.	3	0	0	3	1	-	12	0

15.06.2010, „Nelson Mandela" Bay Stadium, Port Elizabeth; Attendance: 37,034
Referee: Jorge Luis Larrionda Pietrafesa (Uruguay)
IVORY COAST - PORTUGAL   **0-0**
CIV: Boubacar Barry, Guy Roland Demel, Kolo Habib Touré (Cap), Alain Didier Zokora Deguy, Siaka Tiéné, Gnegneri Yaya Touré, Emmanuel Eboué (89.Christian Koffi Ndri „Romaric"), Cheik Ismael Tioté, Gervais Yao Kouassi „Gervinho" (82.Abdul Kader Keïta), Salomon Kalou (66.Didier Yves Drogba Tébily), Aruna Dindane. Trainer: Sven-Göran Eriksson (Sweden).
POR: Eduardo dos Reis Carvalho, Paulo Renato Rebocho Ferreira, Bruno Eduardo Regufe Alves, Ricardo Alberto Silveira de Carvalho, Fábio Alexandre da Silva Coentrão, Pedro Miguel da Silva Mendes, Anderson Luís de Souza „Deco" (62.Tiago Cardoso Mendes), Raúl José Trindade Meireles „Raul Meireles" (85.Ruben Filipe Marques Amorim), Cristiano Ronaldo dos Santos Aveiro (Cap), Daniel Miguel Alves Gomes „Danny" (55.Simão Pedro Fonseca Sabrosa), Liédson da Silva Muniz. Trainer: Carlos Manuel Brito Leal Queiroz.
Cautions: Alain Didier Zokora Deguy, Guy Roland Demel / Cristiano Ronaldo dos Santos Aveiro.

15.06.2010, Ellis Park Stadium, Johannesburg; Attendance: 54,331
Referee: Viktor Kassai (Hungary)
BRAZIL – KOREA D.P.R.   **2-1(1-0)**
BRA: Júlio César Soares de Espíndola, Maicon Douglas Sisenando, Lucimar Ferreira da Silva „Lúcio" (Cap), Juan Silveira dos Santos, Michel Fernandes Bastos, Gilberto Aparecido da Silva, Elano Ralph Blumer (73.Daniel Alves da Silva „Dani Alves"), Felipe Melo de Carvalho (84.Ramires Santos do Nascimento), Ricardo Izecson dos Santos Leite „Kaká" (78.Nilmar Honorato da Silva), Róbson de Souza „Robinho", Luís Fabiano Clemente. Trainer: Carlos Caetano Bledorn Verri „Dunga".
PRK: Ri Myong-Guk, Cha Jong-Hyok, Pak Chol-Jin, Pak Nam-Chol I, Ri Kwang-Chon, Ri Jun-Il, Mun In-Guk (80.Kim Kum-Il), Ji Yun-Nam, Hong Yong-Jo (Cap), An Yong-Hak, Jong Tae-Se. Trainer: Kim Jong-Hun.
Goals: 1-0 Maicon Douglas Sisenando (55), 2-0 Elano Ralph Blumer (72), 2-1 Ji Yun-Nam (88).
Cautions: Ramires Santos do Nascimento.

20.06.2010, Soccer City, Johannesburg; Attendance: 84,455
Referee: Stéphane Lannoy (France)
BRAZIL – IVORY COAST   **3-1(1-0)**
BRA: Júlio César Soares de Espíndola, Maicon Douglas Sisenando, Lucimar Ferreira da Silva „Lúcio"
(Cap), Juan Silveira dos Santos, Michel Fernandes Bastos, Gilberto Aparecido da Silva, Elano Ralph
Blumer (67.Daniel Alves da Silva „Dani Alves"), Felipe Melo de Carvalho, Ricardo Izecson dos Santos
Leite „Kaká", Róbson de Souza „Robinho" (90+3.Ramires Santos do Nascimento), Luís Fabiano
Clemente. Trainer: Carlos Caetano Bledorn Verri „Dunga".
CIV: Boubacar Barry, Guy Roland Demel, Kolo Habib Touré, Alain Didier Zokora Deguy, Siaka
Tiéné, Gnegneri Yaya Touré, Emmanuel Eboué (72.Christian Koffi Ndri „Romaric"), Cheik Ismael
Tioté, Aruna Dindane (54.Gervais Yao Kouassi „Gervinho"), Salomon Kalou (68.Abdul Kader Keïta),
Didier Yves Drogba Tébily (Cap). Trainer: Sven-Göran Eriksson (Sweden).
Goals: 1-0 Luís Fabiano Clemente (25), 2-0 Luís Fabiano Clemente (50), 3-0 Elano Ralph Blumer (62),
3-1 Didier Yves Drogba Tébily (79).
Cautions: Ricardo Izecson dos Santos Leite „Kaká" / Siaka Tiéné, Abdul Kader Keïta, Cheik Ismael
Tioté.
Sent off: Ricardo Izecson dos Santos Leite „Kaká" (88).

21.06.2010, Cape Town Stadium, Cape Town; Attendance: 63,644
Referee: Pablo Antonio Pozo Quinteros (Chile)
PORTUGAL - KOREA D.P.R.   **7-0(1-0)**
POR: Eduardo dos Reis Carvalho, Luís Miguel Brito Garcia Monteiro, Ricardo Alberto Silveira de
Carvalho, Bruno Eduardo Regufe Alves, Fábio Alexandre da Silva Coentrão, Pedro Miguel da Silva
Mendes, Raúl José Trindade Meireles „Raul Meireles" (70.Miguel Luís Pinto Veloso), Tiago Cardoso
Mendes, Cristiano Ronaldo dos Santos Aveiro (Cap), Simão Pedro Fonseca Sabrosa (74.Sérgio Paulo
Barbosa Valente „Duda"), Hugo Miguel Pereira de Almeida (77.Liédson da Silva Muniz). Trainer:
Carlos Manuel Brito Leal Queiroz.
PRK: Ri Myong-Guk, Cha Jong-Hyok (75.Nam Song-Chol), Pak Chol-Jin, Ri Jun-Il, Ji Yun-Nam, Ri
Kwang-Chon, An Yong-Hak, Mun In-Guk (58.Kim Yong-Jun), Pak Nam-Chol II (58.Kim Kum-Il),
Hong Yong-Jo (Cap), Jong Tae-Se. Trainer: Kim Jong-Hun.
Goals: 1-0 Raúl José Trindade Meireles „Raul Meireles" (29), 2-0 Simão Pedro Fonseca Sabrosa (53),
3-0 Hugo Miguel Pereira de Almeida (56), 4-0 Tiago Cardoso Mendes (60), 5-0 Liédson da Silva
Muniz (81), 6-0 Cristiano Ronaldo dos Santos Aveiro (87), 7-0 Tiago Cardoso Mendes (89).
Cautions: Pedro Miguel da Silva Mendes, Hugo Miguel Pereira de Almeida / Pak Chol-Jin, Hong
Yong-Jo.

25.06.2010, „Moses Mabhida" Stadium, Durban; Attendance: 62,712
Referee: Benito Armando Archundia Téllez (Mexico)
PORTUGAL - BRAZIL   **0-0**
BRA: Júlio César Soares de Espíndola, Maicon Douglas Sisenando, Lucimar Ferreira da Silva „Lúcio"
(Cap), Juan Silveira dos Santos, Michel Fernandes Bastos, Gilberto Aparecido da Silva, Daniel Alves
da Silva „Dani Alves", Felipe Melo de Carvalho (44.Josué Anunciado de Oliveira), Nilmar Honorato
da Silva, Júlio César Baptista (82.Ramires Santos do Nascimento), Luís Fabiano Clemente
(85.Edinaldo Batista Libânio „Grafite"). Trainer: Carlos Caetano Bledorn Verri „Dunga".
POR: Eduardo dos Reis Carvalho, Ricardo Miguel Moreira da Costa, Ricardo Alberto Silveira de
Carvalho, Képler Laveran Lima Ferreira „Pepe" (64.Pedro Miguel da Silva Mendes), Bruno Eduardo
Regufe Alves, Fábio Alexandre da Silva Coentrão, Sérgio Paulo Barbosa Valente „Duda" (54.Simão
Pedro Fonseca Sabrosa), Tiago Cardoso Mendes, Raúl José Trindade Meireles „Raul Meireles"
(84.Miguel Luís Pinto Veloso), Daniel Miguel Alves Gomes „Danny", Cristiano Ronaldo dos Santos
Aveiro (Cap). Trainer: Carlos Manuel Brito Leal Queiroz.
Cautions: Sérgio Paulo Barbosa Valente „Duda", Tiago Cardoso Mendes, Képler Laveran Lima
Ferreira „Pepe", Fábio Alexandre da Silva Coentrão / Luís Fabiano Clemente, Juan Silveira dos Santos,
Felipe Melo de Carvalho.

25.06.2010, Mbombela Stadium, Nelspruit; Attendance: 34,763
Referee: Alberto Undiano Mallenco (Spain)
KOREA D.P.R. – IVORY COAST   **0-3(0-2)**
PRK: Ri Myong-Guk, Ri Jun-Il, Cha Jong-Hyok, Pak Chol-Jin, Ji Yun-Nam, Ri Kwang-Chon, Hong Yong-Jo (Cap), An Yong-Hak, Pak Nam-Chol II, Mun In-Guk (67.Choe Kum-Chol), Jong Tae-Se. Trainer: Kim Jong-Hun.
CIV: Boubacar Barry, Emmanuel Eboué, Kolo Habib Touré, Alain Didier Zokora Deguy, Arthur Etienne Boka, Gnegneri Yaya Touré, Christian Koffi Ndri „Romaric" (79.Seydou Doumbia), Cheik Ismael Tioté, Abdul Kader Keïta (64.Aruna Dindane), Gervais Yao Kouassi „Gervinho" (64.Salomon Kalou), Didier Yves Drogba Tébily (Cap). Trainer: Sven-Göran Eriksson (Sweden).
Goals: 0-1 Gnegneri Yaya Touré (14), 0-2 Christian Koffi Ndri „Romaric" (20), 0-3 Salomon Kalou (82).

GROUP H

16.06.2010	Nelspruit	Honduras - Chile	0-1(0-1)
16.06.2010	Durban	Spain - Switzerland	0-1(0-0)
21.06.2010	Port Elizabeth	Chile - Switzerland	1-0(0-0)
21.06.2010	Johannesburg	Spain - Honduras	2-0(1-0)
25.06.2010	Pretoria	Chile - Spain	1-2(0-2)
25.06.2010	Bloemfontein	Switzerland - Honduras	0-0

FINAL STANDINGS

1.	**Spain**	3	2	0	1	4 - 2	6
2.	**Chile**	3	2	0	1	3 - 2	6
3.	Switzerland	3	1	1	1	1 - 1	4
4.	Honduras	3	0	1	2	0 - 3	1

16.06.2010, Mbombela Stadium, Nelspruit; Attendance: 32,664
Referee: Eddy Allen Maillet Guyto (Seychelles)
HONDURAS - CHILE   **0-1(0-1)**
Noel Eduardo Valladares Bonilla, Sergio Giovany Mendoza Escobar, Osman Danilo Chávez Guity, Maynor Alexis Figueroa Róchez, Emilio Arturo Izaguirre Girón, Wilson Roberto Palacios Suazo, Amado Guevara (Cap) (66.Hendry Thomas), Edgard Anthony Álvarez Reyes, Ramón Fernando Núñez Reyes (78.Walter Julián Martínez Ramos), Roger Espinoza Ramírez, Carlos Alberto Pavón Plummer (60.Georgie Wilson Welcome Collins). Trainer: Alexis Antonio Mendoza Barrina (Colombia)*.
CHI: Claudio Andrés Bravo Muñoz (Cap), Mauricio Aníbal Isla Isla, Gary Alexis Medel Soto, Waldo Alonso Ponce Carrizo, Arturo Erasmo Vidal Pardo (81.Pablo Andrés Contreras Fica), Rodrigo Javier Millar Carvajal (52.Gonzalo Alejandro Jara Reyes), Carlos Emilio Carmona Tello, Matías Ariel Fernández Fernández, Jorge Luis Valdivia Toro (87.Mark Dennis González Hoffman), Alexis Alejandro Sánchez Sánchez, Jean André Emanuel Beausejour Coliqueo. Trainer: Marcelo Alberto Bielsa Caldera (Argentina).
Goal: 0-1 Jean André Emanuel Beausejour Coliqueo (34).
Cautions: Wilson Roberto Palacios Suazo / Carlos Emilio Carmona Tello, Matías Ariel Fernández Fernández.
* *Assistant coach Alexis Mendoza took the place of head coach Reinaldo Rueda Rivera due to a one-match suspension.*

306

16.06.2010, „Moses Mabhida" Stadium, Durban; Attendance: 62,453
Referee: Howard Melton Webb (England)
SPAIN - SWITZERLAND   **0-1(0-0)**
ESP: Iker Casillas Fernández (Cap), Sergio Ramos García, Carles Puyol Saforcada, Gerard Piqué Bernabeu, Joan Capdevila Méndez, Sergio Busquets Burgos (61.Fernando José Torres Sanz), Xabier „Xabi" Alonso Olano, Xavier Hernández Creus „Xavi", David Josué Jiménez Silva (62.Jesús Navas González), Andrés Iniesta Luján (77.Pedro Eliezer Rodríguez Ledesma), David Villa Sánchez. Trainer: Vicente Del Bosque González.
SUI: Diego Benaglio, Stephan Lichtsteiner, Philippe Senderos (36.Steve von Bergen), Stéphane Grichting, Reto Ziegler, Tranquillo Barnetta (90+2.Mario Eggimann), Gökhan Inler (Cap), Benjamin Huggel, Gelson Tavares Fernandes, Eren Derdiyok (79.Hakan Yakin), Blaise Nkufo. Trainer: Ottmar Hitzfeld (Germany).
Goal: 0-1 Gelson Tavares Fernandes (52).
Cautions: Stéphane Grichting, Reto Ziegler, Diego Benaglio, Hakan Yakin.

21.06.2010, „Nelson Mandela" Bay Stadium, Port Elizabeth; Attendance: 34,872
Referee: Khalil Ibrahim Al Ghamdi (Saudi Arabia)
CHILE - SWITZERLAND   **1-0(0-0)**
CHI: Claudio Andrés Bravo Muñoz (Cap), Mauricio Aníbal Isla Isla, Gary Alexis Medel Soto, Waldo Alonso Ponce Carrizo, Gonzalo Alejandro Jara Reyes, Arturo Erasmo Vidal Pardo (46.Jorge Luis Valdivia Toro), Carlos Emilio Carmona Tello, Matías Ariel Fernández Fernández (65.Esteban Efraín Paredes Quintanilla), Alexis Alejandro Sánchez Sánchez, Humberto Andrés Suazo Pontivo (46.Mark Dennis González Hoffman), Jean André Emanuel Beausejour Coliqueo. Trainer: Marcelo Alberto Bielsa Caldera (Argentina).
SUI: Diego Benaglio, Stephan Lichtsteiner, ,Steve von Bergen Stéphane Grichting, Reto Ziegler, Valon Behrami, Gökhan Inler (Cap), Benjamin Huggel, Gelson Tavares Fernandes (77.Albert Bunjaku), Alexander Frei (42.Tranquillo Barnetta), Blaise Nkufo (68.Eren Derdiyok). Trainer: Ottmar Hitzfeld (Germany).
Goal: 1-0 Mark Dennis González Hoffman (75).
Cautions: X Humberto Andrés Suazo Pontivo, Carlos Emilio Carmona Tello, Waldo Alonso Ponce Carrizo, Matías Ariel Fernández Fernández, Gary Alexis Medel Soto, Jorge Luis Valdivia Toro / Blaise Nkufo, Tranquillo Barnetta, Gökhan Inler.
Sent off: Valon Behrami (31).

21.06.2010, Ellis Park Stadium, Johannesburg; Attendance: 54,386
Referee: Yuichi Nishimura (Japan)
SPAIN - HONDURAS   **2-0(1-0)**
ESP: Iker Casillas Fernández (Cap), Sergio Ramos García (77.Álvaro Arbeloa Coca), Carles Puyol Saforcada, Gerard Piqué Bernabeu, Joan Capdevila Méndez, Sergio Busquets Burgos, Jesús Navas González, Xabier „Xabi" Alonso Olano, Xavier Hernández Creus „Xavi" (66.Francesc „Cesc" Fàbregas Soler), Fernando José Torres Sanz (70.Juan Manuel Mata García), David Villa Sánchez. Trainer: Vicente Del Bosque González.
Noel Eduardo Valladares Bonilla, Sergio Giovany Mendoza Escobar, Osman Danilo Chávez Guity, Maynor Alexis Figueroa Róchez, Emilio Arturo Izaguirre Girón, Wilson Roberto Palacios Suazo, Amado Guevara (Cap), Danilo Elvis Turcios Funes (63.Ramón Fernando Núñez Reyes), Walter Julián Martínez Ramos, Roger Espinoza Ramírez (46.Georgie Wilson Welcome Collins), Óscar David Suazo Velázquez (84.Jerry Nelson Palacios Suazo). Trainer: Reinaldo Rueda Rivera (Colombia).
Goals: 1-0 David Villa Sánchez (17), 2-0 David Villa Sánchez (51).
Cautions: Danilo Elvis Turcios Funes, Emilio Arturo Izaguirre Girón.

25.06.2010, Loftus Versfeld Stadium, Pretoria; Attendance: 41,958
Referee: Marco Antonio Rodríguez Moreno (Mexico)
CHILE - SPAIN **1-2(0-2)**
CHI: Claudio Andrés Bravo Muñoz (Cap), Mauricio Aníbal Isla Isla, Gary Alexis Medel Soto, Waldo Alonso Ponce Carrizo, Gonzalo Alejandro Jara Reyes, Arturo Erasmo Vidal Pardo, Marco Andrés Estrada Quinteros, Mark Dennis González Hoffman (46.Rodrigo Javier Millar Carvajal), Jorge Luis Valdivia Toro (46.Esteban Efraín Paredes Quintanilla), Alexis Alejandro Sánchez Sánchez (65.Fabián Ariel Orellana Valenzuela). Trainer: Marcelo Alberto Bielsa Caldera (Argentina).

ESP: Iker Casillas Fernández (Cap), Sergio Ramos García, Gerard Piqué Bernabeu, Carles Puyol Saforcada, Joan Capdevila Méndez, Sergio Busquets Burgos, Xavier Hernández Creus „Xavi", Xabier „Xabi" Alonso Olano (73.Javier „Javi" Martínez Aguinaga), Andrés Iniesta Luján, David Villa Sánchez, Fernando José Torres Sanz (55.Francesc „Cesc" Fàbregas Soler). Trainer: Vicente Del Bosque González.

Goals: 0-1 David Villa Sánchez (24), 0-2 Andrés Iniesta Luján (37), 1-2 Rodrigo Javier Millar Carvajal (47).

Cautions: Gary Alexis Medel Soto, Waldo Alonso Ponce Carrizo, Marco Andrés Estrada Quinteros.
Sent off: Marco Andrés Estrada Quinteros (37).

25.06.2010, Free State Stadium, Bloemfontein; Attendance: 28,042
Referee: Héctor Walter Baldassi (Argentina)
SWITZERLAND - HONDURAS **0-0**
SUI: Diego Benaglio, Stephan Lichtsteiner, Steve von Bergen, Stéphane Grichting, Reto Ziegler, Tranquillo Barnetta, Benjamin Huggel (78.Xherdan Shaqiri), Gökhan Inler (Cap), Gelson Tavares Fernandes (46.Hakan Yakin), Eren Derdiyok, Blaise Nkufo (69.Alexander Frei). Trainer: Ottmar Hitzfeld (Germany).

Noel Eduardo Valladares Bonilla (Cap), Mauricio Alberto Sabillón Peña, Osman Danilo Chávez Guity, Víctor Salvador Bernárdez Blanco, Maynor Alexis Figueroa Róchez, Wilson Roberto Palacios Suazo, Hendry Thomas, Edgard Anthony Álvarez Reyes, Ramón Fernando Núñez Reyes (67.Walter Julián Martínez Ramos), Jerry Nelson Palacios Suazo (78.Georgie Wilson Welcome Collins), Óscar David Suazo Velázquez (87.Danilo Elvis Turcios Funes). Trainer: Reinaldo Rueda Rivera (Colombia).

Cautions: Gelson Tavares Fernandes / Hendry Thomas, Óscar David Suazo Velázquez, Osman Danilo Chávez Guity, Wilson Roberto Palacios Suazo.

ROUND OF 16

26.06.2010	Port Elizabeth	Uruguay – Korea Republic	2-1(1-0)
26.06.2010	Rustenburg	United States - Ghana	1-2(0-1,1-1)
27.06.2010	Bloemfontein	Germany - England	4-1(2-1)
27.06.2010	Johannesburg	Argentina - Mexico	3-1(2-0)
28.06.2010	Durban	Holland - Slovakia	2-1(1-0)
28.06.2010	Johannesburg	Brazil - Chile	3-0(1-0)
29.06.2010	Pretoria	Paraguay - Japan	0-0
			5-3 penalties
29.06.2010	Cape Town	Spain - Portugal	1-0(0-0)

26.06.2010, „Nelson Mandela" Bay Stadium, Port Elizabeth; Attendance: 30,597
Referee: Wolfgang Stark (Germany)
URUGUAY – KOREA REPUBLIC   **2-1(1-0)**
URU: Néstor Fernando Muslera Micol, Victorio Maximiliano Pereira Páez, Diego Alfredo Moreno Lugano (Cap), Diego Roberto Godín Leal (46.Mauricio Bernardo Victorino Dansilio), Jorge Ciro Fucile Perdomo, Egidio Raúl Arévalo Ríos, Diego Fernando Pérez Aguado, Álvaro Daniel Pereira Barragán (74.Marcelo Nicolás Lodeiro Benítez), Diego Martín Forlán Corazo, Luis Alberto Suárez Díaz (84.Álvaro Fernández Gay), Edinson Roberto Cavani Gómez. Trainer: Óscar Wáshington Tabárez Silva.
KOR: Jung Sung-Ryong, Cha Du-Ri, Cho Yong-Hyung, Lee Jung-Soo, Lee Young-Pyo, Ki Sung-Yueng (85.Yeom Ki-Hun), Kim Jung-Woo, Kim Jae-Sung (61.Lee Dong-Gook), Park Ji-Sung (Cap), Lee Chung-Yong, Park Chu-Young. Trainer: Huh Jung-Moo.
Goals: -0 Luis Alberto Suárez Díaz (8), 1-1 Lee Chung-Yong (68), 2-1 Luis Alberto Suárez Díaz (80).
Cautions: Kim Jung-Woo, Cha Du-Ri, Cho Yong-Hyung.

26.06.2010, Royal Bafokeng Stadium, Rustenburg; Attendance: 34,976
Referee: Viktor Kassai (Hungary)
UNITED STATES - GHANA   **1-2(0-1,1-1)**
Tim Howard, Steven Cherundolo, Jay Michael DeMerit, Carlos Manuel Bocanegra (Cap), Jonathan Bornstein, Michael Sheehan Bradley, Ricardo Anthony Clark (31.Maurice Edu), Clinton Drew Dempsey, Landon Timothy Donovan, Josmer Volmy Altidore (91.Herculez Gomez), Robert Findley (46.Benny Feilhaber). Trainer: Robert Bradley.
GHA: Richard Paul Franck Kingson, Samuel Inkoom (113.Sulleyman Ali Muntari), John Paintsil, John Mensah (Cap), Jonathan Mensah, Hans Adu Sarpei (73.Lee Addy), Anthony Annan, Kevin-Prince Boateng (78.Stephen Appiah), Kojo „Kwadwo" Asamoah, André Ayew, Asamoah Gyan. Trainer: Milan Rajevac (Serbia).
Goals: 0-1 Kevin-Prince Boateng (5), 1-1 Landon Timothy Donovan (62 penalty), 1-2 Asamoah Gyan (93).
Cautions: Ricardo Anthony Clark, Steven Cherundolo, Carlos Manuel Bocanegra / Jonathan Mensah, André Ayew.

27.06.2010, Free State Stadium, Bloemfontein; Attendance: 40,510
Referee: Jorge Luis Larrionda Pietrafesa (Uruguay)
GERMANY - ENGLAND **4-1(2-1)**
GER: Manuel Neuer, Philipp Lahm, Per Mertesacker, Arne Friedrich, Jérôme Agyenim Boateng, Bastian Schweinsteiger, Sami Khedira, Thomas Müller (72.Piotr Trochowski), Mesut Özil (83.Stefan Kießling), Lukas Podolski, Miroslav Klose (72.Mario Gómez). Trainer: Joachim Löw.
ENG: David Benjamin James, Glen McLeod Johnson (87.Shaun Cameron Wright-Phillips), John George Terry, Matthew James Upson, Ashley Cole, James Philip Milner (64.Joseph John Cole), Frank James Lampard, Gareth Robert Barry, Steven George Gerrard (Cap), Wayne Mark Rooney, Jermain Colin Defoe (71.Emile William Ivanhoe Heskey). Manager: Fabio Capello (Italy).
Goals: 1-0 Miroslav Klose (20), 2-0 Lukas Podolski (32), 2-1 Matthew James Upson (37), 3-1 Thomas Müller (67), 4-1 Thomas Müller (70).
Cautions: Arne Friedrich / Glen McLeod Johnson.

27.06.2010, Soccer City, Johannesburg; Attendance: 84,377
Referee: Roberto Rosetti (Italy)
ARGENTINA - MEXICO **3-1(1-0)**
ARG: Sergio Germán Romero, Nicolás Hernán Otamendi, Martín Gastón Demichelis, Nicolás Andrés Burdisso, Gabriel Iván Heinze, Javier Alejandro Mascherano (Cap), Maximiliano Rubén Rodríguez (87.Javier Matías Pastore), Ángel Fabián di María (79.Jonás Manuel Gutiérrez), Lionel Andrés Messi, Carlos Alberto Tévez (69.Juan Sebastián Verón), Gonzalo Gerardo Higuaín. Trainer: Diego Armando Maradona.
MEX: Óscar Pérez Rojas, Ricardo Osorio Mendoza, Francisco Javier Rodríguez Pinedo, Rafael Márquez Álvarez (Cap), Carlos Arnoldo Salcido Flores, Efraín Juárez Valdéz, Gerardo Torrado Díez de Bonilla, José Andrés Guardado Hernández (61.Guillermo Luis Franco Farquarson), Giovani dos Santos Ramírez, Adolfo Bautista (46.Pablo Edson Barrera Acosta), Javier Hernández Balcázar. Trainer: Javier Aguirre Onaindía.
Goals: 1-0 Carlos Alberto Tévez (26), 2-0 Gonzalo Gerardo Higuaín (33), 3-0 Carlos Alberto Tévez (52), 3-1 Javier Hernández Balcázar (71).
Cautions: Rafael Márquez Álvarez.

28.06.2010, „Moses Mabhida Stadium", Durban; Attendance: 61,962
Referee: Alberto Undiano Mallenco (Spain)
HOLLAND - SLOVAKIA **2-1(1-0)**
NED: Maarten Stekelenburg, Gregory Kurtley van der Wiel, John Gijsbert Alan Heitinga, Joris Mathijsen, Giovanni Christiaan van Bronckhorst (Cap), Mark Peter Gertruda Andreas van Bommel, Nigel de Jong, Dirk Kuijt, Wesley Benjamin Sneijder (90+2.Ibrahim Afellay), Arjen Robben (71.Eljero George Rinaldo Elia), Robin van Persie (80.Klaas-Jan Huntelaar). Trainer: Lambertus van Marwijk.
SVK: Ján Mucha, Peter Pekarík, Martin Škrteľ, Ján Ďurica, Radoslav Zabavník (88.Martin Jakubko), Juraj Kucka, Vladimír Weiss, Miroslav Stoch, Marek Hamšík (Cap) (87. Marek Sapara), Erik Jendrišek (71.Kamil Kopúnek), Róbert Vittek. Trainer: Vladimír Weiss.
Goals: 1-0 Arjen Robben (18), 2-0 Wesley Benjamin Sneijder (84), 2-1 Róbert Vittek (90+4).
Cautions: Arjen Robben, Maarten Stekelenburg / Juraj Kucka, Kamil Kopúnek, Martin Škrteľ.

28.06.2010, Ellis Park Stadium, Johannesburg; Attendance: 54,096
Referee: Howard Melton Webb (England)
BRAZIL - CHILE **3-0(2-0)**
BRA: Júlio César Soares de Espíndola, Maicon Douglas Sisenando, Lucimar Ferreira da Silva „Lúcio" (Cap), Juan Silveira dos Santos, Michel Fernandes Bastos, Gilberto Aparecido da Silva, Daniel Alves da Silva „Dani Alves", Ramires Santos do Nascimento, Ricardo Izecson dos Santos Leite „Kaká" (81.José Kléberson Pereira), Róbson de Souza „Robinho" (85.Gilberto da Silva Melo), Luís Fabiano Clemente (76.Nilmar Honorato da Silva). Trainer: Carlos Caetano Bledorn Verri „Dunga".
CHI: Claudio Andrés Bravo Muñoz (Cap), Mauricio Aníbal Isla Isla (62.Rodrigo Javier Millar

Carvajal), Pablo Andrés Contreras Fica (46.Jorge Luis Valdivia Toro), Gonzalo Alejandro Jara Reyes, Ismael Ignacio Fuentes Castro, Arturo Erasmo Vidal Pardo, Carlos Emilio Carmona Tello, Jean André Emanuel Beausejour Coliqueo, Alexis Alejandro Sánchez Sánchez, Humberto Andrés Suazo Pontivo, Mark Dennis González Hoffman (46.Rodrigo Álvaro Tello Valenzuela). Trainer: Marcelo Alberto Bielsa Caldera (Argentina).

Goals: 1-0 Juan Silveira dos Santos (35), 2-0 Luís Fabiano Clemente (38), 3-0 Róbson de Souza „Robinho" (59).

Cautions: Ricardo Izecson dos Santos Leite „Kaká", Ramires Santos do Nascimento / Arturo Erasmo Vidal Pardo, Ismael Fuentes, Rodrigo Javier Millar Carvajal.

29.06.2010, Loftus Versfeld Stadium, Pretoria; Attendance: 36,742
Referee: Frank De Bleeckere (Belgium)
PARAGUAY - JAPAN   **0-0; 5-3 on penalties**
PAR: Justo Wilmar Villar Viveros (Cap), Carlos Bonet Cáceres, Paulo César da Silva Barrios, Antolín Alcaraz Viveros, Claudio Marcelo Morel Rodríguez, Néstor Ortigoza (75.Édgar Osvaldo Barreto Cáceres), Enrique Daniel Vera Torres, Cristian Miguel Riveros Núñez, Roque Luis Santa Cruz Cantero (94.Óscar René Cardozo Marín), Edgar Benítez Santander (60.Nelson Antonio Haedo Valdéz), Lucas Ramón Barrios Cáceres. Trainer: Gerardo Daniel Martino (Argentina).
JPN: Eiji Kawashima, Yūichi Komano, Yuji Nakazawa, Marcus Tulio Tanaka, Yuto Nagatomo, Yuki Abe (81.Kengo Nakamura), Daisuke Matsui (65.Shinji Okazaki), Yasuhito Endō, Makoto Hasebe (Cap), Yoshito Ōkubo (106.Keiji Tamada), Keisuke Honda. Trainer: Takeshi Okada.
Penalties: Édgar Osvaldo Barreto Cáceres 1-0, Yasuhito Endō 1-1, Lucas Ramón Barrios Cáceres 2-1, Makoto Hasebe 2-2, Cristian Miguel Riveros Núñez 3-2, Yūichi Komano (missed), Nelson Antonio Haedo Valdéz 4-2, Keisuke Honda 4-3, Óscar René Cardozo Marín 5-3.
Cautions: Cristian Miguel Riveros Núñez / Daisuke Matsui, Yuto Nagatomo, Keisuke Honda, Yasuhito Endō.

29.06.2010, Cape Town Stadium, Cape Town; Attendance: 62,955
Referee: Héctor Walter Baldassi (Argentina)
SPAIN - PORTUGAL   **1-0(0-0)**
ESP: Iker Casillas Fernández (Cap), Sergio Ramos García, Gerard Piqué Bernabeu, Carles Puyol Saforcada, Joan Capdevila Méndez, Sergio Busquets Burgos, Xabier „Xabi" Alonso Olano (90+3.Carlos Marchena López), Xavier Hernández Creus „Xavi", Andrés Iniesta Luján, David Villa Sánchez (88.Pedro Eliezer Rodríguez Ledesma), Fernando José Torres Sanz (58.Fernando Llorente Torres). Trainer: Vicente Del Bosque González.
POR: Eduardo dos Reis Carvalho, Ricardo Miguel Moreira da Costa, Ricardo Alberto Silveira de Carvalho, Bruno Eduardo Regufe Alves, Fábio Alexandre da Silva Coentrão, Képler Laveran Lima Ferreira „Pepe" (72.Pedro Miguel da Silva Mendes), Tiago Cardoso Mendes, Raúl José Trindade Meireles „Raul Meireles", Simão Pedro Fonseca Sabrosa (72.Liédson da Silva Muniz), Cristiano Ronaldo dos Santos Aveiro (Cap), Hugo Miguel Pereira de Almeida (58.Daniel Miguel Alves Gomes „Danny"). Trainer: Carlos Manuel Brito Leal Queiroz.
Goal: 1-0 David Villa Sánchez (63).
Cautions: Xabier „Xabi" Alonso Olano / Tiago Cardoso Mendes.
Sent off: Ricardo Miguel Moreira da Costa (89).

QUARTER-FINALS

02.07.2010	Port Elizabeth	Holland - Brazil	2-1(0-1)
02.07.2010	Johannesburg	Uruguay - Ghana	1-1(0-1,1-1)
			4-2 penalties
03.07.2010	Cape Town	Argentina - Germany	0-4(0-1)
03.07.2010	Johannesburg	Paraguay - Spain	0-1(0-0)

02.07.2010, „Nelson Mandela" Bay Stadium, Port Elizabeth; Attendance: 40,186
Referee: Yuichi Nishimura (Japan)

HOLLAND - BRAZIL   **2-1(0-1)**

NED: Maarten Stekelenburg, Gregory Kurtley van der Wiel, John Gijsbert Alan Heitinga, André Antonius Maria Ooijer, Giovanni Christiaan van Bronckhorst (Cap), Mark Peter Gertruda Andreas van Bommel, Nigel de Jong, Arjen Robben, Wesley Benjamin Sneijder, Dirk Kuijt, Robin van Persie (85.Klaas-Jan Huntelaar). Trainer: Lambertus van Marwijk.

BRA: Júlio César Soares de Espíndola, Maicon Douglas Sisenando, Lucimar Ferreira da Silva „Lúcio" (Cap), Juan Silveira dos Santos, Michel Fernandes Bastos (62.Gilberto da Silva Melo), Felipe Melo de Carvalho, Daniel Alves da Silva „Dani Alves", Gilberto Aparecido da Silva, Ricardo Izecson dos Santos Leite „Kaká", Róbson de Souza „Robinho", Luís Fabiano Clemente (77.Nilmar Honorato da Silva). Trainer: Carlos Caetano Bledorn Verri „Dunga".

Goals: 0-1 Róbson de Souza „Robinho" (10), 1-1 Wesley Benjamin Sneijder (53), 2-1 Wesley Benjamin Sneijder (68).

Cautions: John Gijsbert Alan Heitinga, Gregory Kurtley van der Wiel, Nigel de Jong, André Antonius Maria Ooijer / Michel Fernandes Bastos.

Sent off: Felipe Melo de Carvalho (73).

02.07.2010, Soccer City, Johannesburg; Attendance: 84,017
Referee: Olegário Manuel Bartolo Faustino Benquerença (Portugal)

URUGUAY - GHANA   **1-1(0-1,1-1,1-1)**
                                                          4-2 on penalties

URU: Néstor Fernando Muslera Micol, Victorio Maximiliano Pereira Páez, Diego Alfredo Moreno Lugano (Cap) (38.Andrés Scotti Ponce de León), Mauricio Bernardo Victorino Dansilio, Jorge Ciro Fucile Perdomo, Álvaro Fernández Gay (46.Marcelo Nicolás Lodeiro Benítez), Diego Fernando Pérez Aguado, Egidio Raúl Arévalo Ríos, Edinson Roberto Cavani Gómez (76.Washington Sebastián Abreu Gallo), Luis Alberto Suárez Díaz, Diego Martín Forlán Corazo. Trainer: Óscar Wáshington Tábárez Silva.

GHA: Richard Paul Franck Kingson, John Paintsil, Isaac Vorsah, John Mensah (Cap), Hans Adu Sarpei, Anthony Annan, Samuel Diadie Inkoom (74.Stephen Appiah), Kojo „Kwadwo" Asamoah, Kevin-Prince Boateng, Sulleyman Ali Muntari (88.Dominic Adiyiah), Asamoah Gyan. Trainer: Milan Rajevac (Serbia).

Goals: 0-1 Sulleyman Ali Muntari (45+2), 1-1 (55).

Penalties: Diego Martín Forlán Corazo 1-0, Asamoah Gyan 1-1, Mauricio Bernardo Victorino Dansilio 2-1, Stephen Appiah 2-2, Andrés Scotti Ponce de León 3-2, John Mensah (missed), Washington Sebastián Abreu Gallo 4-2, Dominic Adiyiah (missed).

Cautions: Jorge Ciro Fucile Perdomo, Egidio Raúl Arévalo Ríos, Diego Fernando Pérez Aguado / John Paintsil, Hans Adu Sarpei, John Mensah.

Sent off: Luis Alberto Suárez Díaz (120+1).

03.07.2010, Cape Town Stadium, Cape Town; Attendance: 64,100
Referee: Ravshan Irmatov (Uzbekistan)
ARGENTINA - GERMANY   **0-4(0-1)**
ARG: Sergio Germán Romero, Nicolás Hernán Otamendi (70.Javier Matías Pastore), Martín Gastón Demichelis, Nicolás Andrés Burdisso, Gabriel Iván Heinze, Maximiliano Rubén Rodríguez, Javier Alejandro Mascherano (Cap), Ángel Fabián di María (75.Sergio Leonel Agüero del Castillo), Lionel Andrés Messi, Carlos Alberto Tévez, Gonzalo Gerardo Higuaín. Trainer: Diego Armando Maradona.
GER: Manuel Neuer, Philipp Lahm, Per Mertesacker, Arne Friedrich, Jérôme Agyenim Boateng (72.Marcell Jansen), Sami Khedira (77.Toni Kroos), Bastian Schweinsteiger, Thomas Müller (84.Piotr Trochowski), Mesut Özil, Lukas Podolski, Miroslav Klose. Trainer: Joachim Löw.
Goals: 0-1 Thomas Müller (3), 0-2 Miroslav Klose (68), 0-3 Arne Friedrich (74), 0-4 Miroslav Klose (89).
Cautions: Nicolás Hernán Otamendi, Javier Alejandro Mascherano / Thomas Müller.

03.07.2010, Ellis Park Stadium, Johannesburg; Attendance: 55,359
Referee: Carlos Alberto Batres González (Guatemala)
PARAGUAY - SPAIN   **0-1(0-0)**
PAR: Justo Wilmar Villar Viveros (Cap), Darío Anastacio Verón Maldonado, Paulo César da Silva Barrios, Antolín Alcaraz Viveros, Claudio Marcelo Morel Rodríguez, Víctor Javier Cáceres Centurión (84.Lucas Ramón Barrios Cáceres), Jonathan Santana Ghere, Édgar Osvaldo Barreto Cáceres (64.Enrique Daniel Vera Torres), Cristian Miguel Riveros Núñez, Nelson Antonio Haedo Valdéz (72.Roque Luis Santa Cruz Cantero), Óscar René Cardozo Marín. Trainer: Gerardo Daniel Martino (Argentina).
ESP: Iker Casillas Fernández (Cap), Sergio Ramos García, Gerard Piqué Bernabeu, Carles Puyol Saforcada (84.Carlos Marchena López), Joan Capdevila Méndez, Sergio Busquets Burgos, Andrés Iniesta Luján, Xavier Hernández Creus „Xavi", Xabier „Xabi" Alonso Olano (75.Pedro Eliezer Rodríguez Ledesma), David Villa Sánchez, Fernando José Torres Sanz (56.Francesc „Cesc" Fàbregas Soler). Trainer: Vicente Del Bosque González.
Goal: 0-1 David Villa Sánchez (83).
Cautions: Antolín Alcaraz Viveros, Víctor Javier Cáceres Centurión, Claudio Marcelo Morel Rodríguez, Jonathan Santana Ghere / Gerard Piqué Bernabeu, Sergio Busquets Burgos.

SEMI-FINALS

06.07.2010	Cape Town	Uruguay - Holland	2-3(1-1)
07.07.2010	Durban	Germany - Spain	0-1(0-0)

06.07.2010, Cape Town Stadium, Cape Town; Attendance: 62,479
Referee: Ravshan Irmatov (Uzbekistan)
URUGUAY - HOLLAND **2-3(1-1)**
URU: Néstor Fernando Muslera Micol, Victorio Maximiliano Pereira Páez, Mauricio Bernardo Victorino Dansilio, Diego Roberto Godín Leal, José Martín Cáceres Silva, Diego Fernando Pérez Aguado, Wálter Alejandro Gargano Guevara, Egidio Raúl Arévalo Ríos, Álvaro Daniel Pereira Barragán (78.Washington Sebastián Abreu Gallo), Edinson Roberto Cavani Gómez, Diego Martín Forlán Corazo (Cap) (84.Sebastián Bruno Fernández Miglierina). Trainer: Óscar Wáshington Tabárez Silva.
NED: Maarten Stekelenburg, Khalid Boulahrouz, John Gijsbert Alan Heitinga, Joris Mathijsen, Giovanni Christiaan van Bronckhorst (Cap), Mark Peter Gertruda Andreas van Bommel, Demy Patrick René de Zeeuw (46.Rafael Ferdinand van der Vaart), Arjen Robben (89.Eljero George Rinaldo Elia), Wesley Benjamin Sneijder, Dirk Kuijt, Robin van Persie. Trainer: Lambertus van Marwijk.
Goals: 0-1 Giovanni Christiaan van Bronckhorst (18), 1-1 Diego Martín Forlán Corazo (41), 1-2 Wesley Benjamin Sneijder (70), 1-3 Arjen Robben (73), 2-3 Victorio Maximiliano Pereira Páez (90+2).
Cautions: Victorio Maximiliano Pereira Páez, José Martín Cáceres Silva / Wesley Benjamin Sneijder, Khalid Boulahrouz, Mark Peter Gertruda Andreas van Bommel.

07.07.2010, „Moses Mabhida" Stadium, Durban; Attendance: 60,960
Referee: Viktor Kassai (Hungary)
GERMANY - SPAIN **0-1(0-0)**
GER: Manuel Neuer, Philipp Lahm, Per Mertesacker, Arne Friedrich, Jérôme Agyenim Boateng (52.Marcell Jansen), Bastian Schweinsteiger, Sami Khedira (81.Mario Gómez), Piotr Trochowski (62.Toni Kroos), Mesut Özil, Lukas Podolski, Miroslav Klose. Trainer: Joachim Löw.
ESP: Iker Casillas Fernández (Cap), Sergio Ramos García, Gerard Piqué Bernabeu, Carles Puyol Saforcada, Joan Capdevila Méndez, Sergio Busquets Burgos, Xabier „Xabi" Alonso Olano (90+3.Carlos Marchena López), Andrés Iniesta Luján, Xavier Hernández Creus „Xavi", Pedro Eliezer Rodríguez Ledesma (86.David Josué Jiménez Silva), David Villa Sánchez (81.Fernando José Torres Sanz). Trainer: Vicente Del Bosque González.
Goal: 0-1 Carles Puyol Saforcada (73).

3rd PLACE PLAY-OFF

10.07.2010, „Nelson Mandela" Bay Stadium, Port Elizabeth; Attendance: 36,254
Referee: Benito Armando Archundia Téllez (Mexico)
URUGUAY - GERMANY   **2-3(1-1)**
URU: Néstor Fernando Muslera Micol, Jorge Ciro Fucile Perdomo, Diego Alfredo Moreno Lugano (Cap), Diego Roberto Godín Leal, José Martín Cáceres Silva, Victorio Maximiliano Pereira Páez, Diego Fernando Pérez Aguado (77.Wálter Alejandro Gargano Guevara), Egidio Raúl Arévalo Ríos, Edinson Roberto Cavani Gómez (88.Washington Sebastián Abreu Gallo), Luis Alberto Suárez Díaz, Diego Martín Forlán Corazo. Trainer: Óscar Wáshington Tabárez Silva.
GER: Hans-Jörg Butt, Jérôme Agyenim Boateng, Per Mertesacker, Arne Friedrich, Dennis Aogo, Sami Khedira, Bastian Schweinsteiger, Thomas Müller, Mesut Özil (90.Serdar Tasci), Marcell Jansen (81.Toni Kroos), Claudemir Jerónimo Barretto da Silva „Cacau" (73.Stefan Kießling). Trainer: Joachim Löw.
Goals: 0-1 Thomas Müller (19), 1-1 Edinson Roberto Cavani Gómez (28), 2-1 Diego Martín Forlán Corazo (51), 2-2 Marcell Jansen (56), 3-2 Sami Khedira (82).
Cautions: Diego Fernando Pérez Aguado / Dennis Aogo, Claudemir Jerónimo Barretto da Silva „Cacau", Arne Friedrich.

FINAL

11.07.2010, Soccer City, Johannesburg; Attendance: 84,490
Referee: Howard Melton Webb (England)
HOLLAND - SPAIN   **0-1(0-0,0-0)**
NED: Maarten Stekelenburg, Gregory Kurtley van der Wiel, John Gijsbert Alan Heitinga, Joris Mathijsen, Giovanni Christiaan van Bronckhorst (Cap) (105.Edson René Braafheid), Mark Peter Gertruda Andreas van Bommel, Nigel de Jong (99.Rafael Ferdinand van der Vaart), Arjen Robben, Wesley Benjamin Sneijder, Dirk Kuijt (71.Eljero George Rinaldo Elia), Robin van Persie. Trainer: Lambertus van Marwijk.
ESP: Iker Casillas Fernández (Cap), Sergio Ramos García, Gerard Piqué Bernabeu, Carles Puyol Saforcada, Joan Capdevila Méndez, Sergio Busquets Burgos, Xabier „Xabi" Alonso Olano (87.Francesc „Cesc" Fàbregas Soler), Andrés Iniesta Luján, Xavier Hernández Creus „Xavi", Pedro Eliezer Rodríguez Ledesma (60.Jesús Navas González), David Villa Sánchez (106.Fernando José Torres Sanz). Trainer: Vicente Del Bosque González.
Goal: 0-1 Andrés Iniesta Luján (116).
Cautions: Robin van Persie, Mark Peter Gertruda Andreas van Bommel, Nigel de Jong, Giovanni Christiaan van Bronckhorst, John Gijsbert Alan Heitinga, Arjen Robben, Gregory Kurtley van der Wiel / Carles Puyol Saforcada, Sergio Ramos García, Joan Capdevila Méndez, Andrés Iniesta Luján, Xavier Hernández Creus „Xavi".
Sent off: John Gijsbert Alan Heitinga (109).

WORLD CUP 2010 FINAL RANKING

1.	**Spain**	7	6	0	1	8	-	2	18
2.	Holland	7	6	0	1	12	-	6	18
3.	Germany	7	5	0	2	16	-	5	15
4.	Uruguay	7	3	2	2	11	-	8	11
5.	Argentina	5	4	0	1	10	-	6	12
6.	Brazil	5	3	1	1	9	-	4	10
7.	Ghana	5	2	2	1	5	-	4	8
8.	Paraguay	5	1	3	1	3	-	2	6
9.	Japan	4	2	1	1	4	-	2	7
10.	Chile	4	2	0	2	3	-	5	6
11.	Portugal	4	1	2	1	7	-	1	5
12.	United States	4	1	2	1	5	-	5	5
13.	England	4	1	2	1	3	-	5	5
14.	Mexico	4	1	1	2	4	-	5	4
15.	Korea Republic	4	1	1	2	6	-	8	4
16.	Slovakia	4	1	1	2	5	-	7	4
17.	Ivory Coast	3	1	1	1	4	-	3	4
18.	Slovenia	3	1	1	1	3	-	3	4
19.	Switzerland	3	1	1	1	1	-	1	4
20.	South Africa	3	1	1	1	3	-	5	4
21.	Australia	3	1	1	1	3	-	6	4
22.	New Zealand	3	0	3	0	2	-	2	3
23.	Serbia	3	1	0	2	2	-	3	3
24.	Denmark	3	1	0	2	3	-	6	3
25.	Greece	3	1	0	2	2	-	5	3
26.	Italy	3	0	2	1	4	-	5	2
27.	Nigeria	3	0	1	2	3	-	5	1
28.	Algeria	3	0	1	2	0	-	2	1
29.	France	3	0	1	2	1	-	4	1
30.	Honduras	3	0	1	2	0	-	3	1
31.	Cameroon	3	0	0	3	2	-	5	0
32.	Korea D.P.R.	3	0	0	3	1	-	12	0

WORLD CUP AWARDS

GOLDEN BALL (best player of the World Cup final tournament)

DIEGO MARTÍN FORLÁN CORAZO (Uruguay)

GOLDEN BOOT (best goalscorer)

THOMAS MÜLLER (Germany)

GOLDEN GLOVE (best goalkeeper of the tournament)

IKER CASILLAS FERNÁNDEZ (Spain)

BEST YOUNG PLAYER

THOMAS MÜLLER (Germany)

FIFA FAIR-PLAY TROPHY

SPAIN

GOALSCORERS

5 goals: **Thomas Müller (Germany)***
Wesley Benjamin Sneijder (Holland)
David Villa Sánchez (Spain)
Diego Martín Forlán Corazo (Uruguay)

4 goals: Gonzalo Gerardo Higuaín (Argentina)
Miroslav Klose (Germany)
Róbert Vittek (Slovakia)

3 goals: Luís Fabiano Clemente (Brazil)
Asamoah Gyan (Ghana)
Landon Timothy Donovan (United States)
Luis Alberto Suárez Díaz (Uruguay)

2 goals: Carlos Alberto Tévez (Argentina)
Brett Trevor Holman (Australia)
Elano Ralph Blumer, Róbson de Souza „Robinho" (Brazil)
Samuel Eto'o Fils (Cameroon)
Lukas Podolski (Germany)
Arjen Robben (Holland)
Keisuke Honda (Japan)
Lee Jung-Soo, Lee Chung-Yong (Korea Republic)
Javier Hernández Balcázar (Mesico)
Kalu Uche (Nigeria)
Tiago Cardoso Mendes (Portugal)
Andrés Iniesta Luján (Spain)

1 goal: Martín Gastón Demichelis, Gabriel Iván Heinze, Martín Palermo (Argentina)
Timothy Joel „Tim" Cahill (Australia)
Maicon Douglas Sisenando, Juan Silveira dos Santos (Brazil)
Rodrigo Javier Millar Carvajal, Mark Dennis González Hoffman, Jean André Emanuel Beausejour Coliqueo (Chile)
Jon Dahl Tomasson, Nicklas Bendtner, Dennis Rommedahl (Denmark)
Matthew James Upson, Steven George Gerrard, Jermain Colin Defoe (England)
Florent Malouda (France)
Marcell Jansen, Arne Friedrich, Sami Khedira, Mesut Özil, Claudemir Jerónimo Barretto da Silva „Cacau" (Germany)
Sulleyman Ali Muntari, Kevin-Prince Boateng (Ghana)
Vasílis Torosídis, Dimítris Salpingídis (Greece)
Giovanni Christiaan van Bronckhorst, Dirk Kuijt, Robin van Persie, Klaas-Jan Huntelaar (Holland)
Daniele De Rossi, Vincenzo Iaquinta, Antonio Di Natale, Fabio Quagliarella (Italy)
Christian Koffi Ndri „Romaric", Gnegneri Yaya Touré, Salomon Kalou, Didier Yves Drogba Tébily (Ivory Coast)
Yasuhito Endō, Shinji Okazaki (Japan)
Ji Yun-Nam (Korea D.P.R.)
Park Ji-Sung, Park Chu-Young (Korea Republic)
Rafael Márquez Álvarez, Cuauhtémoc Blanco Bravo (Mexico)
Winston Wiremu Reid, Shane Edward Smeltz (New Zealand)
Abdulrasaq Yakubu Aiyegbeni (Nigeria)
Antolín Alcaraz Viveros, Enrique Daniel Vera Torres, Cristian Miguel Riveros Núñez (Paraguay)
Raúl José Trindade Meireles „Raul Meireles", Cristiano Ronaldo dos Santos Aveiro, Liédson da Silva Muniz, Simão Pedro Fonseca Sabrosa, Hugo Miguel Pereira de Almeida (Portugal)

Milan Jovanović, Marko Pantelić (Serbia)
Kamil Kopúnek (Slovakia)
Robert Koren, Valter Birsa, Zlatan Ljubijankič (Slovenia)
Bongani Sandile Khumalo, Lawrence Siphiwe Tshabalala, Katlego Abel Mphela (South Africa)
Carles Puyol Saforcada (Spain)
Gelson Tavares Fernandes (Switzerland)
Michael Sheehan Bradley, Clinton „Clint" Drew Dempsey (United States)
Victorio Maximiliano Pereira Páez, Álvaro Daniel Pereira Barragán, Edinson Roberto Cavani Gómez (Uruguay)
*Thomas Müller won due to the fact that he had the most assists of all players scoring 5 goals.

Own goals:
2   Daniel Munthe Agger (Denmark), against Holland
Park Chu-Young (Korea Republic), against Argentina

Total number og goals scored: **145**
Average goals per match: **2.27**
Total number of penalty kicks awarded: **15**
Total number of penalty kicks scored: **9**

LIST OF REFEREES

Name	DOB	Country	M
Ravshan Irmatov	09.08.1977	Uzbekistan	5
Héctor Walter Baldassi	05.01.1966	Argentina	4
Howard Melton Webb	14.07.1971	England	4
Viktor Kassai	10.09.1975	Hungary	4
Yuichi Nishimura	17.04.1972	Japan	4
Jorge Luis Larrionda Pietrafesa	09.03.1968	Uruguay	4
Frank De Bleeckere	01.07.1966	Belgium	3
Wolfgang Stark	20.11.1969	Germany	3
Carlos Alberto Batres González	02.04.1968	Guatemala	3
Benito Armando Archundia Téllez	21.03.1966	Mexico	3
Olegário Manuel Bartolo Faustino Benquerença	18.10.1969	Portugal	3
Alberto Undiano Mallenco	08.10.1973	Spain	3
Carlos Eugênio Simon	03.09.1965	Brazil	2
Pablo Antonio Pozo Quinteros	27.03.1973	Chile	2
Óscar Julián Ruiz Acosta	01.11.1969	Colombia	2
Stéphane Lannoy	18.09.1969	France	2
Roberto Rosetti	18.09.1967	Italy	2
Marco Antonio Rodríguez Moreno	10.11.1973	Mexico	2
Khalil Ibrahim Al Ghamdi	02.09.1970	Saudi Arabia	2
Eddy Allen Maillet Guyto	19.10.1967	Seychelles	2
Jerome Damon	04.04.1972	South Africa	2
Koman Coulibaly	04.07.1970	Mali	1
Michael Hester	02.05.1972	New Zealand	1
Massimo Busacca	06.02.1969	Switzerland	1

WORLD CUP SQUADS

ALGERIA

	Name	DOB	Club	M	G
		Goalkeepers			
1	Lounès GAOUAOUI	28.09.1977	ASO Chlef	0	0
16	Faouzi CHAOUCHI	05.12.1984	ES Sétif	1	0
23	Raïs M'BOLHI	25.04.1986	PFC Slavia Sofia (BUL)	2	0
		Defenders			
2	Madjid BOUGHERRA	07.10.1982	Glasgow Rangers FC (SCO)	3	0
3	Nadir BELHADJ	18.06.1982	Portsmouth FC (ENG)	3	0
4	Anthar YAHIA	21.03.1982	VfL Bochum (GER)	3	0
5	Rafik HALLICHE	02.09.1986	Sport Lisboa e Benfica (POR)	2	0
12	Habib BELLAID	28.03.1986	SG Eintracht Frankfurt (GER)	0	0
14	Abdelkader LAIFAOUI	29.07.1981	ES Sétif	0	0
18	Carl MEDJANI	15.05.1985	AC Ajaccio (FRA)	0	0
20	Djamel MESBAH	09.10.1984	US Lecce (ITA)	1	0
		Midfielders			
6	Yazid MANSOURI	25.02.1978	FC Lorient-Bretagne Sud (FRA)	0	0
7	Ryad BOUDEBOUZ	19.02.1990	FC Sochaux-Montbéliard (FRA)	1	0
8	Mehdi LACEN	15.05.1984	Racing Club Santander (ESP)	3	0
13	Karim MATMOUR	25.06.1985	VfL Borussia M'gladbach (GER)	3	0
15	Karim ZIANI	17.08.1982	VfL Wolfsburg (GER)	3	0
17	ADLÈNE GUEDIOURA	12.11.1985	Wolverhampton Wanderers FC (ENG)	3	0
19	Hassan YEBDA	14.04.1984	Portsmouth FC (ENG)	3	0
21	Foued KADIR	05.12.1983	Valenciennes FC (FRA)	3	0
22	Djamal ABDOUN	14.02.1986	FC Nantes (FRA)	0	0
		Forwards			
9	Abdelkader GHEZZAL	05.12.1984	AC Siena (ITA)	2	0
10	Rafik SAÏFI	07.02.1975	Al-Khor Sports Club (QAT)	2	0
11	Rafik DJEBBOUR	08.03.1984	AEK Athína (GRE)	2	0
		Trainer			
	Rabah SAÂDANE	03.05.1946			

ARGENTINA

	Name	DOB	Club	M	G
	Goalkeepers				
1	Diego Raúl POZO	16.02.1978	CA Colón de Santa Fé	0	0
21	Mariano Gonzalo ANDÚJAR	30.07.1983	Calcio Catania (ITA)	0	0
22	Sergio Germán ROMERO	22.02.1987	AZ'67 Alkmaar (NED)	5	0
	Defenders				
2	Martín Gastón DEMICHELIS	20.12.1980	FC Bayern München (GER)	5	1
3	Clemente Juan RODRÍGUEZ	31.07.1981	Club Estudiantes de La Plata	1	0
4	Nicolás Andrés BURDISSO	12.04.1981	AS Roma	5	0
6	Gabriel Iván HEINZE	19.04.1978	Olympique de Marseille (FRA)	4	1
12	Ariel Hernán GARCÉ	14.07.1979	CA Colón de Santa Fé	0	0
13	Wálter Adrián SAMUEL	23.05.1978	Internazionale FC Milano (ITA)	2	0
15	Nicolás Hernán OTAMENDI	12.02.1988	CA Vélez Sársfield Buenos Aires	3	0
	Midfielders				
5	Mario Ariel BOLATTI	17.02.1985	AC Fiorentina Firenze (ITA)	2	0
7	Ángel Fabián DI MARÍA	14.02.1988	Sport Lisboa e Benfica (POR)	5	0
8	Juan Sebastián VERÓN	09.03.1975	Club Estudiantes de La Plata	3	0
14	Javier Alejandro MASCHERANO	08.06.1984	Liverpool FC (ENG)	4	0
17	Jonás Manuel GUTIÉRREZ	05.07.1983	Newcastle United FC (ENG)	3	0
20	Maximiliano Rubén RODRÍGUEZ	02.01.1981	Club Atlético de Madrid (ESP)	5	0
23	Javier Matías PASTORE	20.06.1989	US Città di Palermo (ITA)	3	0
	Forwards				
9	Gonzalo Gerardo HIGUAÍN	10.12.1987	Real Madrid CF (ESP)	4	4
10	Lionel Andrés MESSI	24.06.1987	FC Barcelona (ESP)	5	0
11	Carlos Alberto TÉVEZ	05.02.1984	Manchester City FC (ENG)	4	2
16	Sergio Leonel AGÜERO del Castillo	02.06.1988	Club Atlético de Madrid (ESP)	3	0
18	Martín PALERMO	07.11.1973	CA Boca Juniors Buenos Aires	1	1
19	Diego Alberto MILITO	12.06.1979	Internazionale FC Milano (ITA)	2	0
	Trainer				
	Diego Armando MARADONA	30.10.1960			

AUSTRALIA

FOOTBALL
FEDERATION
AUSTRALIA

	Name	DOB	Club	M	G
		Goalkeepers			
1	Mark SCHWARZER	06.10.1972	Fulham FC London (ENG)	3	0
12	Adam Jay FEDERICI	31.01.1985	Reading FC London (ENG)	0	0
18	Eugen-Josip GALEKOVIĆ	12.01.1981	Adelaide United FC	0	0
		Defenders			
2	Lucas Edward NEILL	09.03.1978	Galatasaray SK Istanbul (TUR)	3	0
3	Craig Andrew MOORE	12.12.1975	*Unattached*	2	0
6	Michael Francis BEAUCHAMP	08.03.1981	Al Jazira SC Abu Dhabi (UAE)	1	0
8	Luke WILKSHIRE	02.10.1981	FK Dinamo Moskva (RUS)	3	0
11	Scott Kenneth CHIPPERFIELD	30.12.1975	FC Basel (SUI)	3	0
20	Mark Daniel MILLIGAN	04.08.1985	JEF United Ichihara Chiba (JPN)	0	0
21	David Raymond CARNEY	30.11.1983	FC Twente Enschede (NED)	2	0
		Midfielders			
5	Jason ČULINA	05.08.1980	Gold Coast United FC	3	0
7	Brett Michael EMERTON	22.02.1979	Blackburn Rovers FC (ENG)	3	0
13	Vincenzo „Vince" GRELLA	05.10.1979	Blackburn Rovers FC (ENG)	1	0
15	Michael John „Mile" JEDINAK	03.08.1984	Antalyaspor Kulübü (TUR)	1	0
16	Carl VALERI	14.08.1984	US Sassuolo Calcio (ITA)	3	0
22	Dario VIDOŠIĆ	08.04.1987	MSV Duisburg (GER)	3	0
		Forwards			
4	Timothy Joel „Tim" CAHILL	06.12.1979	Everton FC Liverpool (ENG)	2	1
9	Joshua Blake KENNEDY	20.08.1982	Nagoya Grampus Eight (JPN)	2	0
10	Harold „Harry" KEWELL	22.09.1978	Galatasaray SK Istanbul (TUR)	1	0
14	Brett Trevor HOLMAN	27.03.1984	AZ'67 Alkmaar (NED)	3	2
17	Nikita RUKAVYTSYA	22.06.1987	FC Twente Enschede (NED)	2	0
19	Richard GARCIA	04.09.1981	Hull City AFC (ENG)	2	0
23	Mark BRESCIANO	11.02.1980	US Città di Palermo (ITA)	2	0
		Trainer			
	Peter Tim „Pim" VERBEEK	12.03.1956	(Holland)		

BRAZIL

BRASIL

	Name	DOB	Club	M	G
	Goalkeepers				
1	JÚLIO CÉSAR Soares de Espíndola	03.09.1979	Internazionale FC Milano (ITA)	5	0
12	Heurelho da Silva GOMES	15.02.1981	Tottenham Hotspur FC London (ENG)	0	0
22	Doniéber Alexander Marangon „DONI"	22.10.1979	AS Roma (ITA)	0	0
	Defenders				
2	MAICON Douglas Sisenando	26.07.1981	Internazionale FC Milano (ITA)	5	1
3	Lucimar Ferreira da Silva „LÚCIO"	08.05.1978	Internazionale FC Milano (ITA)	5	0
4	JUAN Silveira dos Santos	01.02.1979	AS Roma (ITA)	5	1
6	MICHEL Fernandes BASTOS	02.08.1983	Olympique Lyonnais (FRA)	5	0
13	Daniel Alves da Silva „DANI ALVES"	06.05.1983	FC Barcelona (ESP)	5	0
14	Ânderson Luís da Silva „LUISÃO"	13.02.1981	Sport Lisboa e Benfica (POR)	0	0
15	THIAGO Emiliano da SILVA	22.09.1984	Milan AC (ITA)	0	0
16	GILBERTO da Silva Melo	25.04.1976	Cruzeiro EC Belo Horizonte (BRA)	2	0
	Midfielders				
5	FELIPE MELO de Carvalho	26.06.1983	FC Juventus Torino (ITA)	4	0
7	ELANO Ralph Blumer	14.06.1981	Galatasaray SK Istanbul (TUR)	2	2
8	GILBERTO Aparecido da SILVA	07.10.1976	PAE Panathinaïkos Athína (GRE)	5	0
10	Ricardo Izecson dos Santos Leite „KAKÁ"	22.04.1982	Real Madrid CF (ESP)	4	0
17	JOSUÉ Anunciado de Oliveira	19.07.1979	VfL Wolfsburg (GER)	1	0
18	RAMIRES Santos do Nascimento	24.03.1987	Sport Lisboa e Benfica (POR)	4	0
19	JÚLIO César BAPTISTA	01.10.1981	AS Roma (ITA)	1	0
20	José KLÉBERSON Pereira	19.06.1979	CR Flamengo Rio de Janeiro	1	0
	Forwards				
9	LUÍS FABIANO Clemente	08.11.1980	Sevilla CF (ESP)	5	3
11	Róbson de Souza „ROBINHO"	25.01.1984	Santos FC	4	2
21	NILMAR Honorato da Silva	14.07.1984	Villarreal CF (ESP)	4	0
23	Edinaldo Batista Libânio „GRAFITE"	02.04.1979	VfL Wolfsburg (GER)	1	0
	Trainer				
	Carlos Caetano Bledorn Verri „DUNGA"	31.10.1963			

CAMEROON

	Name	DOB	Club	M	G
	Goalkeepers				
1	Idriss Carlos KAMENI	18.02.1984	RCD Espanyol Barcelona (ESP)	0	0
16	SOULEYMANOU Hamidou	22.11.1973	Kayserispor (TUR)	3	0
22	Guy Roland N'DY ASSEMBÉ	28.02.1986	FC Nantes (FRA)	0	0
	Defenders				
2	Benoît Pierre David ASSOU-EKOTTO	24.03.1984	Tottenham Hotspur FC London (ENG)	3	0
3	Nicolas Alexis Julio N'KOULOU N'Doubena	27.03.1990	AS Monaco (FRA)	3	0
4	Rigobert SONG Bahanag	01.07.1976	Trabzonspor Kulübü (TUR)	1	0
5	Sébastien BASSONG Nguena	09.07.1986	Tottenham Hotspur FC London (ENG)	2	0
8	GEREMI Sorele Njitap Fotso	20.12.1978	MKE Ankaragücü (TUR)	3	0
12	Gaëtan BONG Songo	25.04.1988	Valenciennes FC (FRA)	1	0
14	Aurélian Bayard CHEDJOU Fongang	20.06.1985	Lille OSC (FRA)	1	0
19	Stéphane MBIA Etoundi	20.05.1986	Olympique de Marseille (FRA)	3	0
	Midfielders				
6	Alexandre Dimitri SONG Billong	09.09.1987	Arsenal FC London (ENG)	1	0
7	Joël Landry Tsafack N'GUÉMO	28.11.1985	Celtic Glasgow FC (SCO)	1	0
11	Jean II MAKOUN	29.05.1983	Olympique Lyonnais (FRA)	3	0
18	Eyong Tarkang ENOH	23.03.1986	AFC Ajax Amsterdam (NED)	2	0
20	Georges Constant MANDJECK	09.12.1988	VfB Stuttgart (GER)	0	0
21	Joël Job MATIP	08.08.1991	FC Schalke 04 Gelsenkirchen (GER)	1	0
	Forwards				
9	Samuel ETO'O Fils	10.03.1981	Internazionale FC Milano (ITA)	3	2
10	Achille EMANA Edzimbi	05.06.1982	Real Betis Balompié Sevilla (ESP)	2	0
13	Jean-Eric Maxim CHOUPO-MOTING	23.01.1989	1.FC Nürnberg (GER)	2	0
15	Pierre Achille WEBÓ Kouamo	20.01.1982	Real CD Mallorca (ESP)	2	0
17	Mohammadou IDRISSOU	08.03.1980	SC Freiburg (GER)	3	0
23	Vincent ABOUBAKAR	22.01.1992	Valenciennes FC (FRA)	2	0
	Trainer				
	Paul LE GUEN	01.03.1964	(France)		

CHILE

	Name	DOB	Club	M	G
	Goalkeepers				
1	Claudio Andrés BRAVO Muñoz	13.04.1983	Real Sociedad de Fútbol San Sebastián (ESP)	4	0
12	Miguel Ángel PINTO Jerez	04.07.1983	CFP de la Universidad de Chile Santiago	0	0
23	Luis MARÍN Baharona	18.05.1983	Unión Española Santiago	0	0
	Defenders				
2	Ismael Ignacio FUENTES Castro	04.08.1981	CD Universidad Católica Santiago	1	0
3	Waldo Alonso PONCE Carrizo	04.12.1982	CD Universidad Católica Santiago	3	0
4	Mauricio Aníbal ISLA Isla	12.06.1988	Udinese Calcio (ITA)	4	0
5	Pablo Andrés CONTRERAS Fica	11.09.1978	PAOK Thessaloníki (GRE)	2	0
17	Gary Alexis MEDEL Soto	03.08.1987	CA Boca Juniors Buenos Aires (ARG)	3	0
18	Gonzalo Alejandro JARA Reyes	29.08.1985	West Bromwich Albion FC (ENG)	4	0
	Midfielders				
6	Carlos Emilio CARMONA Tello	21.02.1987	Reggina Calcio Reggio Emilia (ITA)	3	0
8	Arturo Erasmo VIDAL Pardo	22.05.1987	TSV Bayer 04 Leverkusen (GER)	4	0
10	Jorge Luis VALDIVIA Toro	19.10.1983	Al-Ain Sports Club (UAE)	4	0
13	Marco Andrés ESTRADA Quinteros	28.05.1983	CFP de la Universidad de Chile Santiago	1	0
14	Matías Ariel FERNÁNDEZ Fernández	15.05.1986	Sporting Clube de Portugal Lisboa (POR)	2	0
19	Gonzalo Antonio FIERRO Caniullán	21.03.1983	CR do Flamengo Rio de Janeiro (BRA)	0	0
20	Rodrigo Javier MILLAR Carvajal	03.11.1981	CSD Colo-Colo Santiago	3	1
21	Rodrigo Álvaro TELLO Valenzuela	14.10.1979	Beşiktaş JK Istanbul (TUR)	1	0
	Forwards				
7	Alexis Alejandro SÁNCHEZ Sánchez	19.12.1988	Udinese Calcio (ITA)	4	0
9	Humberto Andrés SUAZO Pontivo	10.05.1981	Club de Futbol Monterrey (MEX)	2	0
11	Mark Dennis GONZÁLEZ Hoffman	10.07.1984	FK CSKA Moskva (RUS)	4	1
15	Jean André Emanuel BEAUSEJOUR Coliqueo	01.06.1984	Club América Ciudad de México (MEX)	4	1
16	Fabián Ariel ORELLANA Valenzuela	27.01.1986	CD Xerez (ESP)	1	0
22	Esteban Efraín PAREDES Quintanilla	01.08.1980	CSD Colo-Colo Santiago	2	0
	Trainer				
	Marcelo Alberto BIELSA Caldera	21.07.1955	(Argentina)		

DENMARK

	Name	DOB	Club	M	G
	Goalkeepers				
1	Thomas Løvendahl SØRENSEN	12.06.1976	Stoke City FC (ENG)	3	0
16	Stephan Maigaard ANDERSEN	26.11.1981	Brøndby IF København	0	0
22	Jesper Ringsborg CHRISTIANSEN	24.04.1978	FC København	0	0
	Defenders				
3	Simon KJÆR	26.03.1989	US Città di Palermo (ITA)	2	0
4	Daniel Munthe AGGER	12.12.1984	Liverpool FC (ENG)	3	0
6	Lars Christian JACOBSEN	20.09.1979	Blackburn Rovers FC (ENG)	3	0
13	Per Billeskov KRØLDRUP	31.07.1979	AC Fiorentina (ITA)	1	0
15	Simon Busk POULSEN	07.10.1984	AZ'67 Alkmaar (NED)	3	0
23	Patrick Jan MTILIGA	28.01.1981	Málaga CF (ESP)	0	0
	Midfielders				
2	Christian Bjørnshøj POULSEN	28.02.1980	FC Juventus Torino (ITA)	3	0
5	William Kvist JØRGENSEN	24.02.1985	FC København	0	0
7	Daniel Monberg JENSEN	25.06.1979	SV Werder Bremen (GER)	1	0
10	Lars Martin JØRGENSEN	06.10.1975	AGF Aarhus	3	0
12	Thomas KAHLENBERG	20.03.1983	VfL Wolfsburg (GER)	3	0
14	Jakob POULSEN	07.07.1983	AGF Aarhus	2	0
20	Thomas ENEVOLDSEN	27.07.1987	FC Groningen (NED)	1	0
21	Christian Dannemann ERIKSEN	14.02.1992	AFC Ajax Amsterdam (NED)	2	0
	Forwards				
8	Jesper GRØNKJÆR	12.08.1977	FC København	2	0
9	Jon Dahl TOMASSON	29.08.1976	Feyenoord Rotterdam (NED)	2	1
11	Nicklas BENDTNER	16.01.1988	Arsenal FC London (ENG)	3	1
17	Mikkel BECKMANN	24.10.1983	Randers FC	1	0
18	Søren LARSEN	06.09.1981	Toulouse FC (FRA)	1	0
19	Dennis ROMMEDAHL	22.07.1978	AFC Ajax Amsterdam (NED)	3	1
	Trainer				
	Morten Per OLSEN	14.08.1949			

ENGLAND

	Name	DOB	Club	M	G
	Goalkeepers				
1	David Benjamin JAMES	01.08.1970	Portsmouth FC	3	0
12	Robert Paul GREEN	18.01.1980	West Ham United FC London	1	0
23	Charles Joseph John HART	19.04.1987	Birmingham City FC	0	0
	Defenders				
2	Glen McLeod JOHNSON	23.08.1984	Liverpool FC	4	0
3	Ashley COLE	20.12.1980	Chelsea FC London	4	0
5	Michael Richard DAWSON	18.11.1983	Tottenham Hotspur FC London	0	0
6	John George TERRY	07.12.1980	Chelsea FC London	4	0
13	Stephen David WARNOCK	12.12.1981	Aston Villa FC Birmingham	0	0
15	Matthew James UPSON	18.04.1979	West Ham United FC London	2	1
18	James Lee Duncan CARRAGHER	28.01.1978	Liverpool FC	2	0
20	Ledley Brenton KING	12.10.1980	Tottenham Hotspur FC London	1	0
	Midfielders				
4	Steven George GERRARD	30.05.1980	Liverpool FC	4	1
7	Aaron Justin LENNON	16.04.1987	Tottenham Hotspur FC London	2	0
8	Frank James LAMPARD	20.06.1978	Chelsea FC London	4	0
11	Joseph John COLE	08.11.1981	Chelsea FC London	2	0
14	Gareth Robert BARRY	23.02.1981	Manchester City FC	3	0
16	James Philip MILNER	04.01.1986	Aston Villa FC Birmingham	3	0
17	Shaun Cameron WRIGHT-PHILLIPS	25.10.1981	Manchester City FC	3	0
22	Michael CARRICK	28.07.1981	Manchester United FC	0	0
	Forwards				
9	Peter James CROUCH	30.01.1981	Tottenham Hotspur FC London	2	0
10	Wayne Mark ROONEY	24.10.1985	Manchester United FC	4	0
19	Jermain Colin DEFOE	07.10.1982	Tottenham Hotspur FC London	3	1
21	Emile William Ivanhoe HESKEY	11.01.1978	Aston Villa FC Birmingham	4	0
	Trainer				
	Fabio CAPELLO	18.06.1946	(Italy)		

FRANCE

	Name	DOB	Club	M	G
	Goalkeepers				
1	Hugo LLORIS	26.12.1986	Olympique Lyonnais	3	0
16	Stève MANDANDA	28.03.1985	Olympique de Marseille	0	0
23	Cédric CARRASSO	30.12.1981	Girondins de Bordeaux	0	0
	Defenders				
2	Bakary SAGNA	14.02.1983	Arsenal FC London (ENG)	3	0
3	Éric ABIDAL	11.09.1979	FC Barcelona (ESP)	2	0
4	Anthony REVEILLÈRE	10.11.1979	Olympique Lyonnais	0	0
5	William Éric GALLAS	17.08.1977	Arsenal FC London (ENG)	3	0
6	Marc PLANUS	07.03.1982	Girondins de Bordeaux	0	0
13	Patrice EVRA	15.05.1981	Manchester United FC (ENG)	2	0
17	Sébastien SQUILLACI	11.08.1980	Sevilla CF (ESP)	1	0
22	Gaël CLICHY	26.07.1985	Arsenal FC London (ENG)	1	0
	Midfielders				
8	Yoann Miguel GOURCUFF	11.07.1986	Girondins de Bordeaux	2	0
14	Jérémy TOULALAN	10.09.1983	Olympique Lyonnais	2	0
15	Florent MALOUDA	13.06.1980	Chelsea FC London (ENG)	3	1
18	Alou DIARRA	15.07.1981	Girondins de Bordeaux	1	0
19	Vassiriky Abou DIABY	11.05.1986	Arsenal FC London (ENG)	3	0
20	Mathieu VALBUENA	28.09.1984	Olympique de Marseille	1	0
	Forwards				
7	Franck RIBÉRY	07.04.1983	FC Bayern München (GER)	3	0
9	Djibril CISSÉ	12.08.1981	PAE Panathinaïkos Athína	1	0
10	Sidney GOVOU	27.07.1979	Olympique Lyonnais	3	0
11	André-Pierre GIGNAC	05.12.1985	Toulouse FC	3	0
12	Thierry HENRY	17.08.1977	FC Barcelona (ESP)	2	0
21	Nicolas Sébastien ANELKA	14.03.1979	Chelsea FC London (ENG)	2	0
	Trainer				
	Raymond DOMENECH	24.01.1952			

GERMANY

	Name	DOB	Club	M	G
	Goalkeepers				
1	Manuel NEUER	27.03.1986	FC Schalke 04 Gelsenkirchen	6	0
12	Tim WIESE	17.12.1981	SV Werder Bremen	0	0
22	Hans-Jörg BUTT	28.05.1974	FC Bayern München	1	0
	Defenders				
2	Marcell JANSEN	04.11.1985	Hamburger SV	4	1
3	Arne FRIEDRICH	29.05.1979	Hertha BSC Berlin	7	1
4	Dennis AOGO	14.01.1987	Hamburger SV	1	0
5	Serdar TASCI	24.04.1987	VfB Stuttgart	1	0
14	Holger BADSTUBER	13.03.1989	FC Bayern München	2	0
16	Philipp LAHM	11.11.1983	FC Bayern München	6	0
17	Per MERTESACKER	29.09.1984	SV Werder Bremen	7	0
20	Jérôme Agyenim BOATENG	03.09.1988	Hamburger SV	5	0
	Midfielders				
6	Sami KHEDIRA	04.04.1987	VfB Stuttgart	7	1
7	Bastian SCHWEINSTEIGER	01.08.1984	FC Bayern München	7	0
8	Mesut ÖZIL	15.10.1988	SV Werder Bremen	7	1
13	Thomas MÜLLER	13.09.1989	FC Bayern München	6	5
15	Piotr TROCHOWSKI	22.03.1984	Hamburger SV	4	0
18	Toni KROOS	04.01.1990	TSV Bayer 04 Leverkusen	4	0
21	Marko MARIN	13.03.1989	SV Werder Bremen	2	0
	Forwards				
9	Stefan KIEßLING	25.01.1984	TSV Bayer 04 Leverkusen	2	0
10	Lukas PODOLSKI	04.06.1985	1.FC Köln	6	2
11	Miroslav KLOSE	09.06.1978	FC Bayern München	5	4
19	Claudemir Jerónimo Barretto da Silva „CACAU"	27.03.1981	VfB Stuttgart	4	1
23	Mario GÓMEZ	10.07.1985	FC Bayern München	4	0
	Trainer				
	Joachim LÖW	03.02.1960			

GHANA

	Name	DOB	Club	M	G
	Goalkeepers				
1	Daniel Yaw ADJEI	10.11.1989	Liberty Professionals FC Accra	0	0
16	Stephen AHORLU	05.09.1988	Heart of Lions FC Kpandu	5	0
22	Richard Paul Franck KINGSON	13.06.1978	Wigan Athletic FC (ENG)	0	0
	Defenders				
2	Hans Adu SARPEI	28.06.1976	TSV Bayer 04 Leverkusen (GER)	5	0
4	John PAINTSIL	15.06.1981	Fulham FC London (ENG)	5	0
5	John MENSAH	29.11.1982	Olympique Lyonnais (FRA)	4	0
7	Samuel Diadie INKOOM	22.08.1989	FC Basel (SUI)	1	0
8	Jonathan MENSAH	13.07.1990	Free State Stars FC Bethlehen (RSA)	2	0
15	Isaac VORSAH	21.06.1988	TSG Hoffenheim 1899 (GER)	2	0
17	Abdul Ibrahim AYEW	16.04.1988	Zamalek SC Cairo (EGY)	0	0
19	Lee ADDY	26.09.1985	Bechem Chelsea FC	3	0
	Midfielders				
6	Anthony ANNAN	21.07.1986	Rosenborg BK Trondheim (NOR)	5	0
9	Derek Owusu BOATENG	02.05.1983	Getafe CF (ESP)	0	0
10	Stephen APPIAH	24.12.1980	Bologna FC (ITA)	3	0
11	Sulleyman Ali MUNTARI	27.08.1984	Internazionale FC Milano (ITA)	4	1
13	André „Dede" AYEW	17.12.1989	AC Arles-Avignon (FRA)	4	0
21	Kojo „Kwadwo" ASAMOAH	09.09.1988	Udinese Calcio (ITA)	5	0
23	Kevin-Prince BOATENG	06.03.1987	Portsmouth FC (ENG)	5	1
	Forwards				
3	Asamoah GYAN	22.11.1985	Stade Rennais FC (FRA)	5	3
12	Prince TAGOE	09.11.1986	TSG Hoffenheim 1899 (GER)	3	0
14	Matthew AMOAH	24.10.1980	NAC Breda (NED)	2	0
18	Dominic ADIYIAH	10.07.1989	Milan AC (ITA)	2	0
20	Quincy James OWUSU-ABEYIE	15.04.1986	Al Sadd SC Doha (QAT)	2	0
	Trainer				
	Milovan RAJEVAC	02.01.1954	(Serbia)		

GREECE

	Name	DOB	Club	M	G
	Goalkeepers				
1	Konstantinos HALKIÁS	30.05.1974	PAOK Thessaloníki	0	0
12	Alexandros TZÓRVAS	12.08.1982	Panathinaïkos AO Athína	3	0
13	Mihális SIFÁKIS	09.09.1984	PAE Aris Thessaloníki	0	0
	Defenders				
2	Giórgos SEITARÍDIS	04.06.1981	Panathinaïkos AO Athína	1	0
3	Hrístos PATSATZOGLOU	19.03.1979	AC Omonia Nicosia (CYP)	2	0
4	Nikolaos Leonidas SPIROPOULOS	10.10.1983	Panathinaïkos AO Athína	1	0
5	Evangélios MÓRAS	26.08.1981	Bologna FC (ITA)	1	0
8	Avraam PAPADÓPOULOS	03.12.1984	PAE Olympiakos Peiraiás	3	0
11	Loukás VÍNTRA	05.02.1981	Panathinaïkos AO Athína	3	0
15	Vasílis TOROSÍDIS	10.06.1985	PAE Olympiakos Peiraiás	3	1
16	Sotírios KYRGIAKOS	23.07.1979	Liverpool FC (ENG)	2	0
19	Sokratís PAPASTATHÓPOULOS	09.06.1988	Genoa CFC (ITA)	2	0
22	Stélios MALEZÁS	11.03.1985	PAOK Thessaloníki	0	0
	Midfielders				
6	Alexandros TZIÓLIS	13.02.1985	AC Siena (ITA)	3	0
10	Giórgos KARAGOÚNIS	06.03.1977	Panathinaïkos AO Athína	3	0
18	Sotírios NÍNIS	03.04.1990	Panathinaïkos AO Athína	2	0
21	Konstantinos KATSOURÁNIS	21.06.1979	Panathinaïkos AO Athína	3	0
23	Athanásios PRITTAS	09.01.1979	PAE Aris Thessaloníki	0	0
	Forwards				
7	Giórgos SAMARÁS	21.02.1985	Celtic FC Glasgow (SCO)	3	0
9	Angelos HARISTÉAS	09.02.1980	1. FC Nürnberg (GER)	1	0
14	Dimítris SALPINGÍDIS	18.08.1981	Panathinaïkos AO Athína	2	1
17	Theofánis GÉKAS	23.05.1980	SG Eintracht Frankfurt (GER)	2	0
20	Pantelis KAPETÁNOS	08.06.1983	FC Steaua Bucureşti (ROU)	1	0
	Trainer				
	Otto REHHAGEL	09.08.1938	(Germany)		

HOLLAND

	Name	DOB	Club	M	G
	Goalkeepers				
1	Maarten STEKELENBURG	22.09.1982	AFC Ajax Amsterdam	7	0
16	Michel VORM	20.10.1983	FC Utrecht	0	0
22	Sander Bernard Jozef BOSCHKER	20.10.1983	FC Twente Enschede	0	0
	Defenders				
2	Gregory Kurtley VAN DER WIEL	03.02.1988	AFC Ajax Amsterdam	5	0
3	John Gijsbert Alan HEITINGA	15.11.1983	Everton FC Liverpool (ENG)	7	0
4	Joris MATHIJSEN	05.04.1980	Hamburger SV	6	0
5	Giovanni Christiaan VAN BRONCKHORST	05.02.1975	Feyenoord Rotterdam	7	1
12	Khalid BOULAHROUZ	28.12.1981	VfB Stuttgart (GER)	2	0
13	André Antonius Maria OOIJER	11.07.1974	PSV Eindhoven	1	0
15	Edson René BRAAFHEID	08.04.1983	Celtic Glasgow FC (SCO)	1	0
	Midfielders				
6	Mark Peter Gertruda Andreas VAN BOMMEL	22.04.1977	FC Bayern München (GER)	7	0
8	Nigel DE JONG	30.11.1984	Manchester City FC	6	0
10	Wesley Benjamin SNEIJDER	09.06.1984	Internazionale FC Milano	7	5
14	Demy Patrick René DE ZEEUW	26.05.1983	AFC Ajax Amsterdam	2	0
18	Stefanus Johannes „Stijn" SCHAARS	11.01.1984	AZ'67 Alkmaar	0	0
20	Ibrahim AFELLAY	02.04.1986	PSV Eindhoven	3	0
23	Rafael Ferdinand VAN DER VAART	11.02.1983	Real Madrid CF (ESP)	5	0
	Forwards				
7	Dirk KUIJT	22.07.1980	Liverpool FC (ENG)	7	1
9	Robin VAN PERSIE	06.08.1983	Arsenal FC London (ENG)	7	1
11	Arjen ROBBEN	23.01.1984	FC Bayern München (GER)	5	2
17	Eljero George Rinaldo ELIA	13.02.1987	Hamburger SV (GER)	6	0
19	Ryan Guno BABEL	19.12.1986	Liverpool FC (ENG)	0	0
21	Klaas-Jan HUNTELAAR	12.08.1983	Milan AC (ITA)	4	1
	Trainer				
Lambertus „Bert" VAN MARWIJK		19.05.1952			

HONDURAS

	Name	DOB	Club	M	G
	Goalkeepers				
1	Ricardo Gabriel CANALES Lanza	30.05.1982	CD Motagua Tegucigalpa	0	0
18	Noel Eduardo VALLADARES Bonilla	03.05.1977	CD Olimpia Tegucigalpa	3	0
22	Donis Salatiel ESCOBER Izaguirre	03.02.1980	CD Olimpia Tegucigalpa	0	0
	Defenders				
2	Osman Danilo CHÁVEZ Guity	29.07.1984	CD Platense Puerto Cortés	3	0
3	Maynor Alexis FIGUEROA Róchez	02.05.1983	Wigan Athletic FC (ENG)	3	0
4	Johnny Eulogio PALACIOS Cacho	20.12.1986	CD Olimpia Tegucigalpa	0	0
5	Víctor Salvador BERNÁRDEZ Blanco	24.05.1982	RSC Anderlecht Bruxelles (BEL)	1	0
14	Oscar Boniek GARCÍA Ramírez	04.09.1984	CD Olimpia Tegucigalpa	0	0
16	Mauricio Alberto SABILLÓN Peña	11.11.1978	Hangzhou Nabel Greentown (CHN)	1	0
21	Emilio Arturo IZAGUIRRE Girón	10.05.1986	CD Motagua Tegucigalpa	2	0
23	Sergio Giovany MENDOZA Escobar	23.05.1981	CD Motagua Tegucigalpa	2	0
	Midfielders				
6	Hendry THOMAS	23.02.1985	Wigan Athletic FC (ENG)	2	0
7	Ramón Fernando NÚÑEZ Reyes	14.11.1984	CD Olimpia Tegucigalpa	3	0
8	Wilson Roberto PALACIOS Suazo	29.07.1984	Tottenham Hotspur FC London (ENG)	3	0
10	Jerry Nelson PALACIOS Suazo	01.11.1981	Hangzhou Nabel Greentown (CHN)	2	0
17	Edgard Anthony ÁLVAREZ Reyes	09.01.1980	AS Bari (ITA)	2	0
19	Danilo Elvis TURCIOS Funes	08.05.1978	CD Olimpia Tegucigalpa	2	0
20	Amado GUEVARA	02.05.1976	CD Motagua Tegucigalpa	2	0
	Forwards				
9	Carlos Alberto PAVÓN Plummer	19.10.1973	Real CD España San Pedro Sula	1	0
11	Óscar David SUAZO Velázquez	05.11.1979	Genoa CFC (ITA)	2	0
12	Georgie Wilson WELCOME Collins	09.03.1985	CD Motagua Tegucigalpa	3	0
13	Roger ESPINOZA Ramírez	25.10.1986	Kansas City Wizards (USA)	2	0
15	Walter Julián MARTÍNEZ Ramos	29.03.1982	CD Marathón San Pedro Sula	3	0
	Trainer				
	Reinaldo RUEDA Rivera	03.02.1957	(Colombia)		

ITALY

	Name	DOB	Club	M	G
	Goalkeepers				
1	Gianluigi BUFFON	28.01.1978	FC Juventus Torino	1	0
12	Federico MARCHETTI	07.02.1983	Cagliari Calcio	3	0
14	Morgan DE SANCTIS	26.03.1977	SSC Napoli	0	0
	Defenders				
2	Christian MAGGIO	11.02.1982	SSC Napoli	1	0
3	Domenico CRISCITO	30.12.1986	Genoa CFC	3	0
4	Giorgio CHIELLINI	14.08.1984	FC Juventus Torino	3	0
5	Fabio CANNAVARO	13.09.1973	FC Juventus Torino	3	0
13	Salvatore BOCCHETTI	30.11.1986	Genoa CFC	0	0
19	Gianluca ZAMBROTTA	19.02.1977	Milan AC	3	0
23	Leonardo BONUCCI	01.05.1987	AS Bari	0	0
	Midfielders				
6	Daniele DE ROSSI	24.07.1983	AS Roma	3	1
7	Simone PEPE	30.08.1983	Udinese Calcio	3	0
8	Gennaro GATTUSO	09.01.1978	Milan AC	1	0
15	Claudio MARCHISIO	19.01.1986	FC Juventus Torino	2	0
16	Mauro CAMORANESI	04.10.1976	FC Juventus Torino	2	0
17	Angelo PALOMBO	25.09.1981	UC Sampdoria Genova	0	0
21	Andrea PIRLO	19.05.1979	Milan AC	1	0
22	Riccardo MONTOLIVO	18.01.1985	AC Fiorentina	3	0
	Forwards				
9	Vincenzo IAQUINTA	21.11.1979	FC Juventus Torino	3	1
10	Antonio DI NATALE	13.10.1977	Udinese Calcio	3	1
11	Alberto GILARDINO	05.07.1982	AC Fiorentina	2	0
18	Fabio QUAGLIARELLA	31.01.1983	SSC Napoli	1	1
20	Giampaolo PAZZINI	02.08.1984	UC Sampdoria Genova	1	0
	Trainer				
	Marcello LIPPI	12.04.1948			

IVORY COAST

	Name	DOB	Club	M	G
	Goalkeepers				
1	Boubacar BARRY	30.12.1979	KSC Lokeren (BEL)	3	0
16	Aristide Benoît ZOGBO	30.12.1981	Maccabi Netanya FC (ISR)	0	0
23	Daniel YÉBOAH Tétchi	13.11.1984	ASEC Mimosas Abidjan	0	0
	Defenders				
2	Benjamin ANGOUA Brou	28.11.1986	Valenciennes FC (FRA)	0	0
3	Arthur Etienne BOKA	02.04.1983	VfB Stuttgart (GER)	1	0
4	Kolo Habib TOURÉ	19.03.1981	Manchester City FC (ENG)	3	0
5	Alain Didier ZOKORA Deguy	14.12.1980	Sevilla CF (ESP)	3	0
6	Steven Lohoré GOHOURI	08.02.1981	Wigan Athletic FC (ENG)	0	0
17	Siaka TIÉNÉ	22.02.1982	Valenciennes FC (FRA)	2	0
20	Guy Roland DEMEL	13.06.1981	Hamburger SV (GER)	2	0
22	Souleymane BAMBA	13.01.1985	Hibernian FC Edinburgh (SCO)	0	0
	Midfielders				
9	Cheik Ismael TIOTÉ	21.06.1986	FC Twente Enschede (NED)	3	0
12	Jean-Jacques GOSSO	03.03.1983	AS Monaco (FRA)	0	0
13	Christian Koffi Ndri „ROMARIC"	04.06.1983	Sevilla CF (ESP)	3	1
14	Emmanuel KONÉ	31.12.1986	FC CFR 1907 Cluj (ROU)	0	0
19	Gnegneri Yaya TOURÉ	13.03.1983	FC Barcelona (ESP)	3	1
21	Emmanuel EBOUÉ	04.06.1983	Arsenal FC London (ENG)	3	0
	Forwards				
7	Seydou DOUMBIA	31.12.1987	BSC Young Boys Bern (SUI)	1	0
8	Salomon KALOU	15.08.1985	Chelsea FC London (ENG)	3	1
10	Gervais Yao Kouassi „GERVINHO"	27.05.1987	Lille OSC (FRA)	3	0
11	Didier Yves DROGBA Tébily	11.03.1978	Chelsea FC London (ENG)	3	1
15	Aruna DINDANE	26.11.1980	Portsmouth FC (ENG)	3	0
18	Abdul Kader KEÏTA	06.08.1981	Galatasaray SK Istanbul (TUR)	3	0
	Trainer				
	Sven-Göran ERIKSSON	05.02.1948	(Sweden)		

JAPAN

	Name	DOB	Club	M	G
	Goalkeepers				
1	Seigo NARAZAKI	15.04.1976	Nagoya Grampus	0	0
21	Eiji KAWASHIMA	20.03.1983	Kawasaki Frontale	4	0
23	Yoshikatsu KAWAGUCHI	15.08.1975	Júbilo Iwata	0	0
	Defenders				
3	Yūichi KOMANO	25.07.1981	Júbilo Iwata	4	0
4	Marcus Tulio TANAKA	24.04.1981	Nagoya Grampus Eight	4	0
5	Yuto NAGATOMO	12.09.1986	Tokyo FC	4	0
6	Atsuto UCHIDA	27.03.1988	Kashima Antlers	0	0
13	Daiki IWAMASA	30.01.1982	Kashima Antlers	0	0
15	Yasuyuki KONNO	25.01.1983	Tokyo FC	1	0
22	Yuji NAKAZAWA	25.02.1978	Yokohama F. Marinos	4	0
	Midfielders				
2	Yuki ABE	06.09.1981	Urawa Red Diamonds	4	0
7	Yasuhito ENDŌ	28.01.1980	Gamba Osaka	4	1
8	Daisuke MATSUI	11.05.1981	Grenoble Foot 38 (FRA)	4	0
10	Shunsuke NAKAMURA	24.06.1978	Yokohama F. Marinos	1	0
14	Kengo NAKAMURA	31.10.1980	Kawasaki Frontale	1	0
17	Makoto HASEBE	18.01.1984	VfL Wolfsburg (GER)	4	0
18	Keisuke HONDA	13.06.1986	FK CSKA Moskva (RUS)	4	2
20	Junichi INAMOTO	18.09.1979	Kawasaki Frontale	2	0
	Forwards				
9	Shinji OKAZAKI	16.04.1986	Shimizu S-Pulse	4	1
11	Keiji TAMADA	11.04.1980	Nagoya Grampus	2	0
12	Kisho YANO	05.04.1984	Albirex Niigata	1	0
16	Yoshito ŌKUBO	09.06.1982	Vissel Kobe	4	0
19	Takayuki MORIMOTO	07.06.1988	Calcio Catania (ITA)	0	0
	Trainer				
	Takeshi OKADA	25.08.1956			

KOREA D.P.R.

	Name	DOB	Club	M	G
	Goalkeepers				
1	RI Myong-Guk	09.09.1986	P'yŏngyang City Sports Group	3	0
18	KIM Myong-Gil	16.10.1984	Amrokgang Sport Group	0	0
20	KIM Myong-Won*	15.07.1983	Amrokgang Sport Group	0	0
	Defenders				
2	CHA Jong-Hyok	25.09.1985	Amrokgang Sport Group	3	0
3	RI Jun-Il	24.08.1987	Sobaeksu Sports Group	3	0
5	RI Kwang-Chon	04.09.1985	4.25 Sports Group Namp'o	3	0
8	JI Yun-Nam	04.07.1985	4.25 Sports Group Namp'o	3	1
13	PAK Chol-Jin	05.09.1985	Amrokgang Sport Group	3	0
14	PAK Nam-Chol (I)	03.10.1988	Amrokgang Sport Group	0	0
16	NAM Song-Chol	07.05.1982	4.25 Sports Group Namp'o	1	0
21	RI Kwang-Hyok	17.08.1987	Kyonggongop Sports Group	0	0
	Midfielders				
4	PAK Nam-Chol (II)	02.07.1985	4.25 Sports Group Namp'o	3	0
6	KIM Kum-Il	10.10.1987	4.25 Sports Group Namp'o	2	0
11	MUN In-Guk	29.09.1978	4.25 Sports Group Namp'o	3	0
15	KIM Yong-Jun	19.07.1983	P'yŏngyang City Sports Group	1	0
17	AN Yong-Hak	25.10.1978	Omiya Ardija (JPN)	3	0
19	RI Chol-Myong	18.02.1988	P'yŏngyang City Sports Group	0	0
22	KIM Kyong-Il	11.12.1988	Rimyongsu Sports Group	0	0
23	PAK Sung-Hyok	30.05.1990	Sobaeksu Sports Group	0	0
	Forwards				
7	AN Chol-Hyok	27.06.1985	Rimyongsu Sports Group	0	0
9	JONG Tae-Se	02.03.1984	Kawasaki Frontale (JPN)	3	0
10	HONG Yong-Jo	22.05.1982	FK Rostov-na-Donu (RUS)	3	0
12	CHOE Kum-Chol	09.02.1987	4.25 Sports Group Namp'o	1	0
	Trainer				
	KIM Jong-Hun	01.09.1956			

Forward nominated as a goalkeeper!

KOREA REPUBLIC

	Name	DOB	Club	M	G
	Goalkeepers				
1	LEE Woon-Jae	26.04.1973	Suwon Samsung Bluewings FC	0	0
18	JUNG Sung-Ryong	04.01.1985	Seongnam Ilhwa Chunma	4	0
21	KIM Young-Kwang	28.06.1983	Ulsan Hyundai Horang-i	0	0
	Defenders				
2	OH Beom-Seok	29.07.1984	Ulsan Hyundai Horang-i	1	0
3	KIM Hyung-Il	27.04.1984	Pohang Steelers FC	0	0
4	CHO Yong-Hyung	03.11.1983	Jeju United FC	4	0
12	LEE Young-Pyo	23.04.1977	Al Hilal SC Riyadh (KSA)	4	0
14	LEE Jung-Soo	08.01.1980	Kashima Antlers (JPN)	4	2
15	KIM Dong-Jin	09.01.1982	Ulsan Hyundai Horang-i	1	0
22	CHA Du-Ri	25.07.1980	SC Freiburg (GER)	3	0
23	KANG Min-Soo	14.02.1986	Suwon Samsung Bluewings FC	0	0
	Midfielders				
5	KIM Nam-Il	14.03.1977	FK Tom Tomsk (RUS)	3	0
6	KIM Bo-Kyung	06.10.1989	Oita Trinita (JPN)	0	0
7	PARK Ji-Sung	25.02.1981	Manchester United FC (ENG)	4	1
8	KIM Jung-Woo	09.05.1982	Gwangju Sangmu FC	4	0
13	KIM Jae-Sung	03.10.1983	Pohang Steelers FC	3	0
16	KI Sung-Yueng	24.01.1989	Celtic Glasgow FC (SCO)	4	0
17	LEE Chung-Yong	02.07.1988	Bolton Wanderers FC (ENG)	4	2
19	YEOM Ki-Hun	30.03.1983	Suwon Samsung Bluewings FC	4	0
	Forwards				
9	AHN Jung-Hwan	27.01.1976	Dalia Shide FC (CHN)	0	0
10	PARK Chu-Young	10.07.1985	AS Monaco (FRA)	4	1
11	LEE Seung-Yeol	06.03.1989	FC Seoul	1	0
20	LEE Dong-Gook	29.04.1979	Jeonbuk Hyundai Motors FC	2	0
	Trainer				
	HUH Jung-Moo	13.01.1955			

MEXICO

	Name	DOB	Club	M	G
	Goalkeepers				
1	Óscar PÉREZ Rojas	01.02.1973	Jaguares de Chiapas FC	4	0
13	Francisco Guillermo OCHOA Magaña	13.07.1985	Club América Ciudad de México	0	0
23	Luis Ernesto MICHEL Vergara	21.07.1979	CD Guadalajara	0	0
	Defenders				
2	Francisco Javier RODRÍGUEZ Pinedo	20.10.1981	PSV Eindhoven (NED)	4	0
3	Carlos Arnoldo SALCIDO Flores	02.04.1980	PSV Eindhoven (NED)	4	0
4	Rafael MÁRQUEZ Álvarez	13.02.1979	FC Barcelona (ESP)	4	1
5	Ricardo OSORIO Mendoza	30.03.1980	VfB Stuttgart (GER)	4	0
12	Paul Nicolás AGUILAR Rojas	06.03.1986	CF Pachuca	1	0
15	Héctor Alfredo MORENO Herrera	17.01.1988	AZ'67 Alkmaar (NED)	2	0
16	Efraín JUÁREZ Valdéz	22.02.1988	Club UNAM Ciudad de México	3	0
19	José Jonny MAGALLÓN Oliva	21.11.1981	CD Guadalajara	0	0
	Midfielders				
6	Gerardo TORRADO Díez de Bonilla	30.04.1979	CDSC Cruz Azul Ciudad de México	4	0
8	Israel CASTRO Macías	20.12.1980	Club UNAM Ciudad de México	1	0
18	José Andrés GUARDADO Hernández	28.09.1986	RC Deportivo La Coruña (ESP)	3	0
20	Jorge Emmanuel TORRES Nilo	16.01.1988	CSD Atlas Guadalajara	0	0
	Forwards				
7	Pablo Edson BARRERA Acosta	21.06.1987	Club UNAM Ciudad de México	3	0
9	Guillermo Luis FRANCO Farquarson	03.11.1976	West Ham United FC London (ENG)	4	0
10	Cuauhtémoc BLANCO Bravo	17.01.1973	Tiburones Rojos de Veracruz	3	1
11	Carlos Alberto VELA Garrido	01.03.1989	Arsenal FC London (ENG)	2	0
14	Javier HERNÁNDEZ Balcázar	01.06.1988	CD Guadalajara	4	2
17	Giovani DOS SANTOS Ramírez	11.05.1989	Galatasaray SK Istanbul (TUR)	4	0
21	Adolfo BAUTISTA Herrera	15.05.1979	CD Guadalajara	1	0
22	Alberto MEDINA Briseño	29.05.1983	CD Guadalajara	0	0
	Trainer				
	Javier AGUIRRE Onaindía	01.12.1958			

NEW ZEALAND

NEW ZEALAND FOOTBALL

	Name	DOB	Club	M	G
	Goalkeepers				
1	Mark Nelson PASTON	13.12.1976	Wellington Phoenix FC	3	0
12	Glen MOSS	19.01.1983	Melbourne Victory FC (AUS)	0	0
23	James BANNATYNE	30.06.1975	Team Wellington	0	0
	Defenders				
2	Benjamin Robert SIGMUND	03.02.1981	Wellington Phoenix FC	0	0
3	Tony James LOCHHEAD	12.01.1982	Wellington Phoenix FC	3	0
4	Winston Wiremu REID	03.07.1988	FC Midtjylland (DEN)	3	1
5	Ivan Robert VICELICH	03.09.1976	Auckland City FC	3	0
6	Ryan William NELSEN	18.10.1977	Blackburn Rovers FC (ENG)	3	0
18	Andrew Victor BOYENS	18.09.1983	New York Red Bulls (USA)	0	0
19	Thomas Jefferson „Tommy" SMITH	31.03.1990	Ipswich Town FC (ENG)	3	0
	Midfielders				
7	Simon John ELLIOTT	10.06.1974	*Unattached*	3	0
8	Timothy BROWN	06.03.1981	Wellington Phoenix FC	0	0
11	Leonida „Leo" Christos BERTOS	24.12.1980	Wellington Phoenix FC	3	0
13	Andrew BARRON	24.12.1980	Team Wellington	1	0
15	Michael Ryan McGLINCHEY	07.01.1987	Motherwell FC (SCO)	0	0
16	Aaron Daniel CLAPHAM	15.01.1987	Canterbury United FC Christchurch	0	0
17	David James MULLIGAN	24.03.1982	*Unattached*	0	0
21	Jeremy John CHRISTIE	22.05.1983	FC Tampa Bay (USA)	2	0
	Forwards				
9	Shane Edward SMELTZ	29.09.1981	Gold Coast United FC (AUS)	3	1
10	Christopher John KILLEN	08.10.1981	Middlesbrough FC (ENG)	3	0
14	Rory Michael FALLON	20.03.1982	Plymouth Argile FC (ENG)	3	0
20	Christopher Grant WOOD	07.12.1991	West Bromwich Albion FC (ENG)	3	0
22	Jeremy Russell BROCKIE	07.10.1987	Newcastle United Jets FC (AUS)	1	0
	Trainer				
	Richard „Ricki" Lloyd HERBERT	10.04.1961			

NIGERIA

	Name	DOB	Club	M	G
	Goalkeepers				
1	Vincent ENYEAMA	29.08.1982	Hapoel Tel Aviv FC (ISR)	3	0
16	Augustine Amamchukwu EJIDE	08.04.1984	Hapoel Petah Tikva FC (ISR)	0	0
23	Dele AIYENUGBA	20.11.1983	Bnei Yehuda FC (ISR)	0	0
	Defenders				
2	Joseph Ikpo YOBO	06.09.1980	Everton FC Liverpool (ENG)	3	0
3	Taye Ismaila TAÏWO	16.04.1985	Olympique de Marseille (FRA)	2	0
5	Rabiu AFOLABI	18.04.1980	FC Red Bull Salzburg (AUT)	2	0
6	Daniel Olusola SHITTU	02.09.1980	Bolton Wanderers FC (ENG)	3	0
17	Chukwudi „Chidi" ODIAH	17.12.1983	FK CSKA Moskva (RUS)	3	0
21	Uwa Elderson ECHIÉJILÉ	20.01.1988	Stade Rennais FC (FRA)	2	0
22	Ayodele „Dele" ADELEYE	25.12.1988	Sparta Rotterdam (NED)	0	0
	Midfielders				
4	Nwankwo Christian Nwosu KANU	01.08.1976	Portsmouth FC (ENG)	1	0
12	Kalu UCHE	15.11.1982	UD Almería (ESP)	3	2
13	Yusuf AYILA Atanda	04.11.1984	FK Dinamo Kyiv (UKR)	1	0
14	Sani Haruna KAITA	02.05.1986	FK Alania Vladikavkaz (RUS)	2	0
15	Lukman HARUNA	04.12.1990	AS Monaco (FRA)	2	0
20	Dickson Paul ETUHU	08.06.1982	Fulham FC London (ENG)	3	0
	Forwards				
7	John Chukwudi UTAKA	08.01.1982	Portsmouth FC (ENG)	0	0
8	Abdulrasaq Yakubu AIYEGBENI	22.11.1982	Everton FC Liverpool (ENG)	3	1
9	Obafemi Akinwunmi MARTINS	28.10.1984	VfL Wolfsburg (GER)	2	0
10	Brown IDEYE	10.10.1988	FC Sochaux-Montbéliard (FRA)	0	0
11	Osaze Peter ODEMWINGIE	15.07.1981	FK Lokomotiv Moskva (RUS)	2	0
18	Victor Nsofor OBINNA	25.03.1987	FC Internazionale Milano (ITA)	2	0
19	Chinedu OBASI Ogbuke	01.06.1986	TSG 1899 Hoffenheim (GER)	3	0
	Trainer				
	Lars LAGERBÄCK	16.07.48	(Sweden)		

PARAGUAY

	Name	DOB	Club	M	G
	Goalkeepers				
1	Justo Wilmar VILLAR Viveros	30.06.1977	Real Valladolid CF (ESP)	5	0
12	Diego Daniel BARRETO Cáceres	16.07.1981	Club Cerro Porteño Asunción	0	0
22	Aldo Antonio BOBADILLA Ávalos	20.04.1976	CD Independiente Medellín (COL)	0	0
	Defenders				
2	Darío Anastacio VERÓN Maldonado	26.06.1979	Club UNAM Ciudad de México (MEX)	1	0
3	Claudio Marcelo MOREL Rodríguez	02.02.1978	CA Boca Juniors Buenos Aires (ARG)	5	0
4	Denis Ramón CANIZA Acuña	29.08.1974	CSD León (MEX)	1	0
5	Julio César CÁCERES López	05.10.1979	Clube Atlético Mineiro Belo Horizonte (BRA)	1	0
14	Paulo César DA SILVA Barrios	01.02.1980	Sunderland AFC (ENG)	5	0
17	Aureliano TORRES Román	16.06.1982	CA San Lorenzo de Almagro (ARG)	2	0
21	Antolín ALCARAZ Viveros	30.07.1982	Club Brügge KV (BEL)	4	1
	Midfielders				
6	Carlos BONET Cáceres	02.10.1977	Club Olimpia Asunción	3	0
8	Édgar Osvaldo BARRETO Cáceres	15.07.1984	Atalanta Bergamasca Calcio (ITA)	3	0
11	Jonathan SANTANA Ghere	19.10.1981	VfL Wolfsburg (GER)	2	0
13	Enrique Daniel VERA Torres	10.03.1979	LDU de Quito (ECU)	5	1
15	Víctor Javier CÁCERES Centurión	25.03.1985	Club Libertad Asunción	4	0
16	Cristian Miguel RIVEROS Núñez	16.10.1982	CDSC Cruz Azul (MEX)	5	1
20	Néstor Ezequiel ORTIGOZA	07.10.1984	AA Argentinos Juniors Buenos Aires (ARG)	1	0
	Forwards				
7	Óscar René CARDOZO	20.05.1983	Sport Lisboa e Benfica (POR)	5	0
9	Roque Luis SANTA CRUZ Cantero	16.08.1981	Manchester City FC (ENG)	5	0
10	Edgar BENÍTEZ Santander	08.11.1987	Club de Fútbol Pachuca (MEX)	2	0
18	Nelson Antonio Haedo VALDÉZ	28.11.1983	BVB Borussia Dortmund (GER)	5	0
19	Lucas Ramón BARRIOS Cáceres	13.11.1984	BVB Borussia Dortmund (GER)	5	0
23	Rodolfo Vicente GAMARRA Varela	10.12.1988	Club Libertad Asunción	0	0
	Trainer				
	Gerardo Daniel MARTINO	20.11.1962	(Argentina)		

PORTUGAL

	Name	DOB	Club	M	G
	Goalkeepers				
1	EDUARDO dos Reis Carvalho	19.09.1982	Sporting Clube de Braga	4	0
12	António Alberto Bastos Pimparel „BETO"	01.05.1982	FC do Porto	0	0
22	DANIEL Márcio FERNANDES	25.09.1983	VfL Bochum (GER)	0	0
	Defenders				
2	BRUNO Eduardo Regufe ALVES	27.11.1981	FC do Porto	4	0
3	PAULO Renato Rebocho FERREIRA	18.01.1979	Chelsea FC London (ENG)	1	0
4	ROLANDO Jorge Pires da Fonseca	31.08.1985	FC do Porto	0	0
6	RICARDO Alberto Silveira de CARVALHO	18.05.1978	Chelsea FC London	4	0
13	Luís MIGUEL Brito Garcia Monteiro	04.01.1980	CF Valencia (ESP)	1	0
15	Képler Laveran Lima Ferreira „PEPE"	26.02.1983	Real Madrid CF (ESP)	2	0
21	RICARDO Miguel Moreira da COSTA	16.05.1981	Lille OSC (FRA)	2	0
23	FÁBIO Alexandre da Silva COENTRÃO	11.03.1988	Sport Lisboa e Benfica	4	0
	Midfielders				
5	Sérgio Paulo Barbosa Valente „DUDA"	27.06.1980	Málaga CF (ESP)	2	0
8	PEDRO Miguel da Silva MENDES	26.02.1979	Sporting Clube de Portugal	4	0
14	MIGUEL Luís Pinto VELOSO	11.05.1986	Sporting Clube de Portugal	2	0
16	Raúl José Trindade Meireles „RAUL MEIRELES"	17.03.1983	FC do Porto	4	1
17	RUBEN Filipe Marques AMORIM	27.01.1985	Sport Lisboa e Benfica	1	0
19	TIAGO Cardoso Mendes	02.05.1981	Club Atlético de Madrid (ESP)	4	2
20	Anderson Luís de Souza „DECO"	27.08.1977	Chelsea FC London (ENG)	1	0
	Forwards				
7	CRISTIANO RONALDO dos Santos Aveiro	05.02.1985	Real Madrid CF (ESP)	4	1
9	LIÉDSON da Silva Muniz	17.12.1977	Sporting Clube de Portugal	3	1
10	Daniel Miguel Alves Gomes „DANNY"	07.08.1983	FK Zenit St. Petersburg (RUS)	3	0
11	SIMÃO Pedro Fonseca SABROSA	31.10.1979	Club Atlético de Madrid (ESP)	4	1
18	HUGO Miguel Pereira de ALMEIDA	23.05.1984	SV Werder Bremen (GER)	2	1
	Trainer				
	Carlos Manuel Brito Leal QUEIROZ	01.03.1953			

SERBIA

	Name	DOB	Club	M	G
		Goalkeepers			
1	Vladimir STOJKOVIĆ	28.07.1983	Sporting Clube de Portugal (POR)	3	0
12	Bojan ISAILOVIĆ	25.03.1980	KGHM Zagłębie Lubin (POL)	0	0
23	Anđelko ĐURIČIĆ	21.11.1980	União Desportiva de Leiria (POR)	0	0
		Defenders			
2	Antonio RUKAVINA	26.01.1984	TSV München 1860 (GER)	0	0
3	Aleksandar KOLAROV	10.11.1985	SS Lazio Roma (ITA)	2	0
5	Nemanja VIDIĆ	21.10.1981	Manchester United FC (ENG)	3	0
6	Branislav IVANOVIĆ	22.02.1984	Chelsea FC London (ENG)	3	0
13	Aleksandar LUKOVIĆ	23.10.1982	Udinese Calcio (ITA)	2	0
16	Ivan OBRADOVIĆ	25.07.1988	Real Zaragoza (ESP)	1	0
20	Neven SUBOTIĆ	10.12.1988	BVB Borussia Dortmund (GER)	2	0
		Midfielders			
4	Gojko KAČAR	26.01.1987	Hertha BSC Berlin (GER)	1	0
7	Zoran TOŠIĆ	28.04.1987	1.FC Köln (GER)	1	0
10	Dejan STANKOVIĆ	11.09.1978	Internazionale FC Milano (ITA)	3	0
11	Nenad MILIJAŠ	30.04.1983	Wolverhampton Wanderers FC (ENG)	1	0
14	Milan JOVANOVIĆ	18.04.1981	R Standard Liège (BEL)	3	1
17	Miloš KRASIĆ	01.11.1984	FK CSKA Moskva (RUS)	3	0
18	Miloš NINKOVIĆ	25.12.1984	FK Dinamo Kyiv (UKR)	2	0
19	Radosav PETROVIĆ	08.03.1989	FK Partizan Beograd	1	0
22	Zdravko KUZMANOVIĆ	22.09.1987	VfB Stuttgart (GER)	3	0
		Forwards			
8	Danko LAZOVIĆ	17.05.1983	FK Zenit St. Petersburg (RUS)	3	0
9	Marko PANTELIĆ	15.09.1978	AFC Ajax Amsterdam (NED)	2	1
15	Nikola ŽIGIĆ	25.09.1980	Valencia CF (ENG)	3	0
21	Dragan MRĐA	23.01.1984	FK Vojvodina Novi Sad	0	0
		Trainer			
	Radomir ANTIĆ	22.11.1948			

SLOVAKIA

	Name	DOB	Club	M	G
	Goalkeepers				
1	Ján MUCHA	05.12.1982	KP Legia Warszawa (POL)	4	0
12	Dušan PERNIŠ	28.11.1984	Dundee United FC (SCO)	0	0
23	Dušan KUCIAK	21.05.1985	FC Vaslui (ROU)	0	0
	Defenders				
2	Peter PEKARÍK	30.10.1986	VfL Wolfsburg (GER)	3	0
3	Martin ŠKRTEL'	15.12.1984	Liverpool FC (ENG)	4	0
4	Marek ČECH	26.01.1983	West Bromwich Albion FC (ENG)	1	0
5	Radoslav ZABAVNÍK	16.09.1980	FSV Mainz 05 (GER)	3	0
16	Ján ĎURICA	10.12.1981	Hannover'96 (GER)	4	0
21	Kornel SALÁTA	24.01.1985	ŠK Slovan Bratislava	1	0
22	Martin PETRÁŠ	02.11.1979	AC Cesena (ITA)	1	0
	Midfielders				
6	Zdeno ŠTRBA	09.06.1976	PAE Skoda Xanthi AO (GRE)	3	0
7	Vladimír WEISS jr.	30.11.1989	Bolton Wanderers FC (ENG)	3	0
8	Ján KOZÁK	22.04.1980	FC Timişoara (ROU)	1	0
10	Marek SAPARA	31.07.1982	MKE Ankaragücü (TUR)	1	0
15	Miroslav STOCH	19.10.1989	FC Twente Enschede (NED)	4	0
17	Marek HAMŠÍK	27.07.1987	SSC Napoli (ITA)	4	0
19	Juraj KUCKA	26.02.1987	AC Sparta Praha (CZE)	3	0
20	Kamil KOPÚNEK	18.05.1984	FC Spartak Trnava	2	1
	Forwards				
9	Stanislav ŠESTÁK	16.12.1982	VfL Bochum (GER)	3	0
11	Róbert VITTEK	01.04.1982	MKE Ankaragücü (TUR)	4	4
13	Filip HOLOŠKO	17.01.1984	Beşiktaş JK Istanbul (TUR)	2	0
14	Martin JAKUBKO	26.02.1980	FK Saturn Moskva Oblast	1	0
18	Erik JENDRIŠEK	26.10.1986	1.FC Kaiserslautern (GER)	3	0
	Trainer				
	Vladimír WEISS	22.09.1964			

SLOVENIA

SLOVENIJA

	Name	DOB	Club	M	G
	Goalkeepers				
1	Samir HANDANOVIČ	14.07.1984	Udinese Calcio (ITA)	3	0
12	Jasmin HANDANOVIČ	28.01.1978	AC Mantova (ITA)	0	0
16	Aleksander ŠELIGA	01.02.1980	Sparta Rotterdam (NED)	0	0
	Defenders				
2	Mišo BREČKO	01.05.1984	1.FC Köln (GER)	3	0
3	Elvedin DŽINIČ	25.08.1985	NK Maribor	0	0
4	Marko ŠULER	09.03.1983	KAA Gent (BEL)	3	0
5	Boštjan CESAR	09.07.1982	Grenoble Foot 38 (FRA)	3	0
6	Branko ILIČ	06.02.1983	FK Moskva (RUS)	0	0
13	Bojan JOKIĆ	17.05.1986	AC Chievo Verona (ITA)	3	0
19	Suad FILEKOVIČ	16.09.1978	NK Maribor	0	0
22	Matej MAVRIČ	29.01.1979	TuS Koblenz (GER)	0	0
	Midfielders				
8	Robert KOREN	20.09.1980	West Bromwich Albion FC (ENG)	3	1
10	Valter BIRSA	07.08.1986	AJ Auxerre (FRA)	3	1
15	Rene KRHIN	21.05.1990	Internazionale FC Milano (ITA)	0	0
17	Andraž KIRM	06.09.1984	Wisł a Kraków (POL)	3	0
18	Aleksandar RADOSAVLJEVIČ	25.04.1979	AE Larissa (GRE)	3	0
20	Andrej KOMAC	04.12.1979	Maccabi Tel Aviv FC (ISR)	2	0
21	Dalibor STEVANOVIČ	27.09.1984	SBV Vitesse Arnhem (NED)	0	0
	Forwards				
7	Nejc PEČNIK	03.01.1986	CD Nacional Funchal (POR)	2	0
9	Zlatan LJUBIJANKIČ	15.12.1983	KAA Gent (BEL)	3	1
11	Milivoje NOVAKOVIČ	18.05.1979	1.FC Köln (GER)	3	0
14	Zlatko DEDIČ	10.05.1984	VfL Bochum (GER)	3	0
23	Tim MATAVŽ	13.01.1989	FC Groningen (NED)	1	0
	Trainer				
Matjaž KEK		09.09.1961			

SOUTH AFRICA

SOUTH AFRICAN
FOOTBALL ASSOCIATION

	Name	DOB	Club	M	G
	Goalkeepers				
1	Moeneeb JOSEPHS	19.05.1980	Orlando Pirates FC Johannesburg	2	0
16	Itumeleng Isaack KHUNE	20.06.1987	Kaizer Chiefs FC Johannesburg	2	0
22	Shu-Aib WALTERS	26.12.1981	Maritzburg United FC	0	0
	Defenders				
2	Siboniso Pa GAXA	06.04.1984	Mamelodi Sundowns FC	3	0
3	Peter Tsepo MASILELA	05.05.1985	Maccabi Haifa FC (ISR)	3	0
4	Aaron Tebomo MOKOENA	25.11.1980	Portsmouth FC (ENG)	3	0
5	Calvin Anele NGCONGCA	20.10.1987	KRC Genk (BEL)	1	0
14	Matthew Paul BOOTH	14.03.1977	Mamelodi Sundowns FC	0	0
15	Lucas Bongane THWALA	19.10.1981	Orlando Pirates FC Johannesburg	1	0
20	Bongani Sandile KHUMALO	06.01.1987	Supersport United FC Pretoria	3	1
21	Siyabonga SANGWENI	29.09.1981	Lamontville Golden Arrows FC	0	0
	Midfielders				
6	Ntuthuko MacBeth-Mao SIBAYA	25.11.1977	FK Rubin Kazan (RUS)	1	0
7	Lance DAVIDS	11.04.1985	Ajax Cape Town FC	0	0
8	Lawrence Siphiwe TSHABALALA	25.09.1984	Kaizer Chiefs FC Johannesburg	3	1
10	Steven Jerome PIENAAR	17.05.1982	Everton FC Liverpool (ENG)	3	0
11	Teko Tsholofelo MODISE	22.12.1982	Orlando Pirates FC Johannesburg	3	0
12	Reneilwe LETSHOLONYANE	24.12.1984	Kaizer Chiefs FC Johannesburg	2	0
13	Kagiso Evidence DIKGACOI	24.11.1984	Fulham FC London (ENG)	2	0
19	Surprise Mohlomolleng MORIRI	20.03.1980	Mamelodi Sundowns FC	1	0
23	Thanduyise KHUBONI	23.05.1986	Lamontville Golden Arrows FC	0	0
	Forwards				
9	Katlego Abel MPHELA	29.11.1984	Mamelodi Sundowns FC	3	1
17	Siyabonga NOMVETHE	02.12.1977	Moroka Swallows FC Johannesburg	1	0
18	Bernard Melvin PARKER	16.03.1986	FC Twente Enschede (NED)	2	0
	Trainer				
	Carlos Alberto Gomes PARREIRA	27.02.1943	(Brazil)		

SPAIN

	Name	DOB	Club	M	G
	Goalkeepers				
1	Iker CASILLAS Fernández	20.05.1981	Real Madrid CF	7	0
12	VÍCTOR VALDÉS Arribas	14.01.1982	FC Barcelona	0	0
23	José Manuel „Pepe" REINA Páez	31.08.1982	Liverpool FC (ENG)	0	0
	Defenders				
2	Raúl ALBIOL Tortajada	04.09.1985	Real Madrid CF	0	0
3	Gerard PIQUÉ Bernabeu	02.02.1987	FC Barcelona	7	0
4	Carlos MARCHENA López	31.07.1979	Valencia CF	3	0
5	Carles PUYOL Saforcada	13.04.1978	FC Barcelona	7	1
11	Joan CAPDEVILA Méndez	03.02.1978	Villarreal CF	7	0
15	SERGIO RAMOS García	30.03.1986	Real Madrid CF	7	0
17	Álvaro ARBELOA Coca	17.01.1983	Real Madrid CF	1	0
	Midfielders				
6	Andrés INIESTA Luján	11.05.1984	FC Barcelona	6	2
8	Xavier Hernández Creus „XAVI"	25.01.1980	FC Barcelona	7	0
10	Francesc „CESC" FÀBREGAS Soler	04.05.1987	Arsenal FC London (ENG)	4	0
14	Xabier „XABI" ALONSO Olano	25.11.1981	Real Madrid CF	7	0
16	Sergio BUSQUETS Burgos	16.07.1988	FC Barcelona	7	0
20	Javier "JAVI" MARTÍNEZ Aguinaga	02.09.1988	Athletic Club Bilbao	1	0
21	David Josué Jiménez SILVA	08.01.1986	Valencia CF	2	0
	Forwards				
7	DAVID VILLA Sánchez	03.12.1981	Valencia CF	7	5
9	FERNANDO José TORRES Sanz	20.03.1984	Liverpool FC (ENG)	7	0
13	Juan Manuel MATA García	28.04.1988	Valencia CF	1	0
18	PEDRO Eliezer Rodríguez Ledesma	28.07.1987	FC Barcelona	5	0
19	Fernando LLORENTE Torres	26.02.1985	Athletic Club Bilbao	1	0
22	JESÚS NAVAS González	21.11.1985	Sevilla CF	3	0
	Trainer				
	Vicente DEL BOSQUE González	23.12.1950			

SWITZERLAND

	Name	DOB	Club	M	G
	Goalkeepers				
1	Diego BENAGLIO	08.09.1983	VfL Wolfsburg (GER)	3	0
12	Marco WÖLFLI	22.08.1982	BSC Young Boys Bern	0	0
21	Johnny LEONI	30.06.1984	FC Zürich	0	0
	Defenders				
2	Stephan LICHTSTEINER	16.01.1984	SSC Napoli (ITA)	3	0
3	Ludovic MAGNIN	20.04.1979	FC Zürich	0	0
4	Philippe SENDEROS	14.02.1985	Everton Liverpool FC (ENG)	1	0
5	Steve VON BERGEN	10.06.1983	Hertha BSC Berlin (GER)	3	0
13	Stéphane GRICHTING	30.03.1979	AJ Auxerre (FRA)	3	0
17	Reto ZIEGLER	16.01.1986	UC Sampdoria Genova (ITA)	3	0
22	Mario EGGIMANN	24.01.1981	Hannover'96 (GER)	1	0
	Midfielders				
6	Benjamin HUGGEL	07.07.1977	FC Basel	3	0
7	Tranquillo BARNETTA	22.05.1985	TSV Bayer 04 Leverkusen (GER)	3	0
8	Gökhan INLER	27.06.1984	Udinese Calcio (ITA)	3	0
11	Valon BEHRAMI	19.04.1985	West Ham United FC London (ENG)	1	0
14	Marco PADALINO	08.12.1983	UC Sampdoria Genova (ITA)	0	0
15	Hakan YAKIN	22.02.1977	FC Luzern	2	0
16	Gelson Tavares FERNANDES	02.09.1986	AS St. Étienne (FRA)	3	1
20	Pirmin SCHWEGLER	09.03.1987	SG Eintracht Frankfurt (GER)	0	0
23	Xherdan SHAQIRI	10.10.1991	FC Basel	1	0
	Forwards				
9	Alexander FREI	15.07.1979	FC Basel	2	0
10	Blaise NKUFO	25.05.1975	FC Twente Enschede (NED)	3	0
18	Albert BUNJAKU	29.11.1983	1.FC Nürnberg (GER)	1	0
19	Eren DERDIYOK	12.06.1988	TSV Bayer 04 Leverkusen (GER)	3	0
	Trainer				
	Ottmar HITZFELD	12.01.1949	(Germany)		

UNITED STATES

	Name	DOB	Club	M	G
	Goalkeepers				
1	Tim HOWARD	06.03.1979	Everton FC Liverpool (ENG)	4	0
18	Bradley „Brad" Edwin GUZAN	09.09.1984	Aston Villa FC Birmingham (ENG)	0	0
23	Marcus Stephan HAHNEMANN	15.06.1972	Wolverhampton Wanderers FC (ENG)	0	0
	Defenders				
2	Jonathan Michael Paul SPECTOR	01.03.1986	West Ham United FC London (ENG)	0	0
3	Carlos Manuel BOCANEGRA	25.05.1979	Stade Rennais FC (FRA)	4	0
5	Oguchialu „Oguchi" Chijioke ONYEWU	13.05.1982	Milan AC (ITA)	2	0
6	Steven CHERUNDOLO	19.02.1979	Hannover'96 (GER)	4	0
12	Jonathan BORNSTEIN	07.11.1984	CD Chivas USA	2	0
15	Jay Michael DeMERIT	04.12.1979	Watford FC (ENG)	4	0
21	Clarence GOODSON	17.05.1982	IK Start Kristiansand (NOR)	0	0
	Midfielders				
4	Michael Sheehan BRADLEY	31.07.1987	Borussia VfL Mönchengladbach (GER)	4	1
7	DaMarcus Lamont BEASLEY	24.05.1982	Glasgow Rangers FC (SCO)	1	0
8	Clinton „Clint" Drew DEMPSEY	09.03.1983	Fulham FC London (ENG)	4	1
10	Landon Timothy DONOVAN	04.03.1982	Los Angeles Galaxy	4	3
11	Stuart HOLDEN	01.08.1985	Bolton Wanderers FC (ENG)	1	0
13	Ricardo Anthony CLARK	10.02.1983	SG Eintracht Frankfurt (GER)	2	0
16	José Francisco TORRES Mezzell	29.10.1987	CF Pachuca (MEX)	1	0
19	Maurice EDU	18.04.1986	Glasgow Rangers FC (SCO)	3	0
22	Benny FEILHABER	19.01.1985	AGF Aarhus (DEN)	3	0
	Forwards				
9	Herculez GOMEZ	06.04.1982	Puebla CF (MEX)	3	0
14	Edson Michael BUDDLE	21.05.1981	Los Angeles Galaxy	2	0
17	Josmer „Jozy" Volmy ALTIDORE	06.11.1989	Hull City FC (ENG)	4	0
20	Robert „Robbie" FINDLEY	04.08.1985	Real Salt Lake	3	0
	Trainer				
	Robert „Bob" BRADLEY	03.03.1958			

URUGUAY

★★★★

	Name	DOB	Club	M	G
	Goalkeepers				
1	Néstor Fernando MUSLERA Micol	16.06.1986	SS Lazio Roma (ITA)	7	0
12	Juan Guillermo CASTILLO Iriart	17.04.1978	Asociación Deportivo Cali (COL)	0	0
23	Martín Andrés SILVA Leites	25.03.1983	Defensor SC Montevideo	0	0
	Defenders				
2	Diego Alfredo LUGANO Moreno	02.11.1980	Fenerbahçe SK Istanbul (TUR)	6	0
3	Diego Roberto GODÍN Leal	16.02.1986	Villarreal CF (ESP)	5	0
4	Jorge Ciro FUCILE Perdomo	19.11.1984	FC do Porto (POR)	5	0
6	Mauricio Bernardo VICTORINO Dansilio	11.10.1982	CF Universidad de Chile Santiago (CHI)	5	0
16	Victorio Maximiliano PEREIRA Páez	08.06.1984	Sport Lisboa e Benfica (POR)	7	1
19	Andrés SCOTTI Ponce de León	14.12.1975	CSD Colo Colo Santiago (CHI)	2	0
22	José Martín CÁCERES Silva	07.04.1987	FC Juventus Torino (ITA)	2	0
	Midfielders				
5	Walter Alejandro GARGANO Guevara	27.07.1984	SSC Napoli (ITA)	3	0
8	Sebastián EGUREN Ledesma	08.01.1981	Villarreal CF (ESP)	1	0
11	Álvaro Daniel PEREIRA Barragán	28.01.1985	FC do Porto (POR)	5	1
14	Marcelo Nicolás LODEIRO Benítez	21.03.1989	AFC Ajax Amsterdam (NED)	3	0
15	Diego Fernando PÉREZ Aguado	18.05.1980	AS Monaco (FRA)	7	0
17	Egidio ARÉVALO Ríos	29.09.1982	CA Peñarol Montevideo	7	0
18	Ignacio María GONZÁLEZ Gatti	14.05.1982	APO Levadeon (GRE)	1	0
20	Álvaro FERNÁNDEZ Gay	11.10.1985	CF Universidad de Chile Santiago (CHI)	4	0
	Forwards				
7	Edinson Roberto CAVANI Gómez	14.02.1987	US Città di Palermo (ITA)	6	1
9	Luis Alberto SUÁREZ Díaz	24.01.1987	AFC Ajax Amsterdam (NED)	6	3
10	Diego Martín FORLÁN Corazo	19.05.1979	Club Atlético de Madrid (ESP)	7	5
13	Washington Sebastián ABREU Gallo	17.10.1976	Botafogo FR Rio de Janeiro (BRA)	4	0
21	Sebastián Bruno FERNÁNDEZ Miglierina	23.05.1985	CA Banfield (ARG)	2	0
	Trainer				
	Óscar Wáshington TABÁREZ Silva	03.03.1947			